Planning and Administering
Early Childhood Programs

Eighth Edition

Celia A. Decker
Northwestern State University

John R. Decker
Sabine Parish, Louisiana, School System

PEARSON

Merrill
Prentice Hall

Upper Saddle River, New Jersey
Columbus, Ohio

Library of Congress Cataloging-in-Publication Data

Decker, Celia Anita.
    Planning and administering early childhood programs/Celia A. Decker, John R.
Decker.—8th ed.
      p. cm.
    Includes bibliographical references and index.
    ISBN 0-13-112548-6
    1. Early childhood education—United States. 2. Educational planning—United States. 3. Day care centers—
United States—Administration. 4. Instructional systems—United States. I. Decker, John R. II. Title.

LB1139.25.D43 2005
372.21′0973—dc22

2003068865

Vice President and Executive Publisher: Jeffery W. Johnston
Publisher: Kevin M. Davis
Acquisitions Editor: Julie Peters
Editorial Assistant: Autumn Benson
Production Editor: Linda Hillis Bayma
Production Coordination: WordCrafters Editorial
    Services, Inc.
Design Coordinator: Diane C. Lorenzo

Photo Coordinator: Sandy Schaefer
Cover Designer: Jason Moore
Cover image: Getty Images
Production Manager: Laura Messerly
Director of Marketing: Ann Castel Davis
Marketing Manager: Autumn Purdy
Marketing Coordinator: Tyra Poole

This book was set in New Baskerville by Pine Tree Composition, Inc. It was printed and bound by R.R. Donnelley & Sons Company. The cover was printed by Phoenix Color Corp.

Photo Credits: pp. 1, 63, 96 by Scott Cunningham/Merrill; pp. 30, 142, 278, 349 by Anthony Magnacca/Merrill; p. 213 by Teri Stratford/PH College; p. 238 by Dan Floss/Merrill; p. 313 by Anne Vega/Merrill; p. 379 by Shirley Zeiberg/PH College.

Pearson Education Ltd.
Pearson Education Singapore Pte. Ltd.
Pearson Education Canada, Ltd.
Pearson Education—Japan

Pearson Education Australia Pty. Limited
Pearson Education North Asia Ltd.
Pearson Educación de Mexico, S.A. de C.V.
Pearson Education Malaysia Pte. Ltd.

PEARSON

Merrill
Prentice Hall

10 9 8 7 6 5 4 3 2
ISBN:0-13-112548-6

To Kelcey and Keith, our twin sons, and Kristiana, our daughter.

About the Authors

Celia A. Decker retired after 38 years of service in early childhood education. At the time of her retirement, she held the position of professor of early childhood education at Northwestern State University and served as the program coordinator of graduate studies in early childhood education. In addition to coauthoring this text, she is the author of *Children: The Early Years* and its supplements and coauthor of *Parents and Their Children,* both published by Goodheart-Willcox Publisher. She has presented papers at national, regional, and state annual meetings of professional associations such as the National Association for the Education of Young Children, the Southern Early Childhood Association, and the Association for Childhood Education International. She has served as a consultant for Head Start, Even Start, and local school systems.

During her years of teaching as a kindergarten teacher in an inner-city school system and as a college professor, she has received many honors. Dr. Decker has been named to the Who's Who in Child Development Professionals, Who's Who in Personalities of the South, Who's Who in American Women, and the World's Who's Who in Education. In 1994, she was selected as the Outstanding Professor at Northwestern State University.

John R. Decker retired after an elementary teaching and administrative career of 37 years. Before entering the field of education, he served as a district scout executive for Kaw Council, Boy Scouts of America, Kansas City, Kansas. His educational career included elementary teaching positions in inner-city schools, in an open education program, and in rural public schools. He also served as assistant professor of education and taught college courses in education and supervised preservice teachers in a federally supported college-based program. He has frequently given speeches and workshops for professional organizations. Recently, he was recognized for his 30-year membership in Phi Delta Kappa.

Preface

Planning and Administering Early Childhood Programs, Eighth Edition, is built on the conviction that thoughtful planning and administration are essential to the success of early childhood programs. We agree with G. Morgan (2000a), who stated, "Those of us who work with children's program organizations believe that the director is a key to quality" (p. 41). The more administrators know about factors influencing quality programs, the better equipped they will be to plan and administer programs. From our perspective, each child, family member, staff member, and sponsor deserves nothing less. Because we know how important planning is, we are committed to helping new and experienced administrators and students of administration make sense of what they are doing.

NEW CONTENT

The eighth edition has been extensively revised to reflect changes in the knowledge base. Similar to the previous edition, the text reflects a balanced concern for all types of early childhood programs with their varying purposes, sponsorships, and ages of children served. Early childhood is a broad field, and this text reflects that outlook both in early education and in child care.

This edition's perspective is that the lack of high-quality early childhood programs is today's overriding concern. Because all aspects of early childhood programs are linked, quality is related to each aspect. Thus, administrators hold the key to quality as local change agents and effective advocates of a professionally shared vision of quality.

New content reflects the latest thinking on these and other areas:

- Considering **ecological perspectives** in planning and implementing early childhood programs.
- Determining specific **competencies** of program directors and the pros and cons of mandatory certification for child care directors.
- Examining the director's need for a knowledge base of the local **community culture.**
- Using **mentoring** as an effective method of individual staff development.
- Considering how funding agencies contribute to lower-quality services through payments at market rate and how quality depends on financing a system of **coordinated services**.
- Relating factors contributing to the movement toward curriculum content standards, the risks and benefits of these **"early learning standards,"** and the new "standards on standards."
- Discussing infants' needs for **a "caring" curriculum** and young children's needs for **affective learnings** (e.g., developing emotional literacy, learning social competence, and coping with stress).
- Ascertaining the problems of high-stakes testing and the call for **"responsible assessment."**
- Reflecting on collaboratively shaped local programs and **linkages to the community.**

The extensive references and resources listed in this edition provide readers with more in-depth understandings of many topics. Suggested electronic resources can be used for staying even more up-to-date in this quickly changing field.

TEXT ORGANIZATION

Chapter 1, Overview of Early Childhood Programs, shows that, historically, early childhood programs have attempted to meet the needs of children and their families. Today, more than ever, high-quality programs are needed to provide for children's development and learning and to support families' economic and social needs. Although recent reports confirm the benefits of high-quality programs, several national studies show that quality is often lacking. Many complex changes are needed to achieve the vision for high quality.

Directors of early childhood programs must structure their thinking and be responsive to the need for high-quality programs as they make decisions about their local program and collaborate with others to promote the professional vision. To show how this can be done, we have divided the text into three parts.

Part One, Constructing the Early Childhood Program's Framework, comprises two chapters. Chapter 2 explains that planning begins with a needs assessment to help planners choose a program base in response to local needs and values. The chapter includes six major curriculum models and an outline on how a given base affects the operational and pedagogical components of a program. The chapter closes with general guidelines for implementing and evaluating the program. Chapter 3 examines the protective regulations moving from baseline (minimum) to the highest (most stringent) regulations. Legal or business regulations and fiscal regulations are also described. The chapter closes with a discussion of policies and procedures based on regulations and how they are designed and implemented to meet the needs of local programs.

Part Two, Operationalizing the Early Childhood Program, includes three chapters on administrative topics. Chapter 4 provides an overview of staffing trends and the roles and qualifications of various staff members. A discussion of needs assessment and staff recruitment follows. The chapter also addresses how effective directors develop and use knowledge of the local community and explains in depth the director's leadership, collaborative, and management roles. Chapter 5 explains how the physical facility must physically and psychologically enable the program to meet its care and educational goals while also supporting the adults involved in the program. Chapter 6 explains how meager funding weakens the quality of programs and discusses innovative funding ideas, sources of funds, the process of developing a budget, and proposals for financing a system.

Part Three, Implementing the Children's Program, discusses the administrator's role in planning and overseeing the program's services. Chapter 7 addresses the director's role in deciding curricular content and organization, implementing the program, and providing needed program supports. Chapter 8 concerns the administrator's roles in meeting nutritional requirements, controlling infectious diseases, and ensuring a safe environment while instilling lifelong nutrition, health, and safety habits. Chapter 9 examines the issues and gives practical suggestions concerning assessing, recording, and reporting children's development and learning. Chapter 10 summarizes the trend of professionals serving in a collaborative relationship with adult family members from diverse family contexts and working as advocates for families within the local community context. The chapter provides many specific suggestions for these professional roles. Chapter 11 encourages professionals to become *professionals* in the truest sense of the word.

PEDAGOGICAL FEATURES

Readers will find the three subdivisions of the book helpful because they parallel the administrator's planning processes—namely, deciding on the program's framework, placing the program into operation, and implementing the program. Tables and figures are used throughout the text to (a) summarize research or show conflicting points of view, (b) visually present the organization of a concept, and (c) give practical examples. The Trends and Issues and Summary sections of each chapter will also help readers focus on the main themes of the book.

We have raised issues to stimulate early childhood leaders to reexamine their beliefs and then take another look at their programs' rationales and practices. Thus, relevant studies are included throughout. Cookbook formulas are omitted and options are given because single solutions are not appropriate for everyone.

The text provides information needed by all early childhood programs. The field is diverse, but there is a great deal of overlap among the types of competencies needed in various programs. We have attempted to provide a balance among research and supported statements, applied ideas for implementation, and resources for further thought and consideration.

Like the seven editions before it, this edition will aid in the initial planning of early childhood programs and be a source of helpful information after programs are under way. The purpose of this book will be fulfilled when the reader makes wiser judgments about planning and administering early childhood programs.

ACKNOWLEDGMENTS

We thank the following reviewers of this edition for their helpful comments: Nancy Baptiste, New Mexico State University; James E. Johnson, The Pennsylvania State University; S. Jayne Ozier, Eastern Illinois University; Jyotsna Pattnaik, California State University, Long Beach; and Anne Ure, Brigham Young University.

Celia A. Decker
John R. Decker

Discover the Companion Website Accompanying This Book

**The Prentice Hall Companion Website:
A Virtual Learning Environment**

Technology is a constantly growing and changing aspect of our field that is creating a need for content and resources. To address this emerging need, Prentice Hall has developed an online learning environment for students and professors alike—Companion Websites—to support our textbooks.

In creating a Companion Website, our goal is to build on and enhance what the textbook already offers. For this reason, the content for each user-friendly website is organized by topic and provides the professor and student with a variety of meaningful resources. Common features of a Companion Website include:

For the Professor—

Every Companion Website integrates **Syllabus Manager**™, an online syllabus creation and management utility.

- **Syllabus Manager**™ provides you, the instructor, with an easy, step-by-step process to create and revise syllabi, with direct links into Companion Website and other online content without having to learn HTML.
- Students may log on to your syllabus during any study session. All they need to know is the web address for the Companion Website and the password you've assigned to your syllabus.
- After you have created a syllabus using **Syllabus Manager**™, students may enter the syllabus for their course section from any point in the Companion Website.
- Clicking on a date, the student is shown the list of activities for the assignment. The activities for each assignment are linked directly to actual content, saving time for students.
- Adding assignments consists of clicking on the desired due date, then filling in the details of the assignment—name of the assignment, instructions, and whether it is a one-time or repeating assignment.
- In addition, links to other activities can be created easily. If the activity is online, a URL can be entered in the space provided, and it will be linked automatically in the final syllabus.
- Your completed syllabus is hosted on our servers, allowing convenient updates from any computer on the Internet. Changes you make to your syllabus are immediately available to your students at their next logon.

For the Student—

- **Introduction**—General information about the topic and how it will be covered in the website.
- **Web Links**—A variety of websites related to topic areas.
- **Timely Articles**—Links to online articles that enable you to become more aware of important issues in early childhood.
- **Learn by Doing**—Put concepts into action, participate in activities, examine strategies, and more.

- **Visit a School**—Visit a school's website to see concepts, theories, and strategies in action.

- **For Teachers/Practitioners**—Access information you will need to know as an educator, including information on materials, activities, and lessons.

- **NEW! Observation Tools**—A collection of checklists and forms to print out and use when observing and assessing children's development.

- **Current Policies and Standards**—Find out the latest early childhood policies from the government and various organizations, and view state, federal, and curriculum standards.

- **Resources and Organizations**—Discover tools to help you plan your classroom or center and organizations to provide current information and standards for each topic.

- **Electronic Bluebook**—Paperless method of completing homework or essays assigned by a professor. Finished work can be sent to the professor via email.

- **Message Board**—Virtual bulletin board to post and respond to questions and comments from a national audience.

To take advantage of these and other resources, please visit the *Planning and Administering Early Childhood Programs,* Eighth Edition, Companion Website at

www.prenhall.com/decker

EDUCATOR LEARNING CENTER: AN INVALUABLE ONLINE RESOURCE

Merrill Education and the Association for Supervision and Curriculum Development (ASCD) invite you to take advantage of a new online resource, one that provides access to the top research and proven strategies associated with ASCD and Merrill—the Educator Learning Center. At **www.EducatorLearningCenter.com** you will find resources that will enhance your students' understanding of course topics and of current educational issues, in addition to being invaluable for further research.

How the Educator Learning Center will Help Your Students Become Better Teachers

With the combined resources of Merrill Education and ASCD, you and your students will find a wealth of tools and materials to better prepare them for the classroom.

Research

- More than 600 articles from the ASCD journal *Educational Leadership* discuss everyday issues faced by practicing teachers.
- A direct link on the site to Research Navigator™ gives students access to many of the leading education journals, as well as extensive content detailing the research process.
- Excerpts from Merrill Education texts give your students insights on important topics of instructional methods, diverse populations, assessment, classroom management, technology, and refining classroom practice.

Classroom Practice

- Hundreds of lesson plans and teaching strategies are categorized by content area and age range.
- Case studies and classroom video footage provide virtual field experience for student reflection.
- Computer simulations and other electronic tools keep your students abreast of today's classrooms and current technologies.

Look into the Value of Educator Learning Center Yourself

A four-month subscription to Educator Learning Center is $25 but is **FREE** when used in conjunction with this text. To obtain free passcodes for your students, simply contact your local Merrill/Prentice Hall sales representative, and your representative will give you a special ISBN to give your bookstore when ordering your textbooks. To preview the value of this website to you and your students, please go to **www.EducatorLearningCenter.com** and click on "Demo."

Brief Contents

Contents

PART ONE
Constructing the Early Childhood Program's Framework

Chapter 2
Planning, Implementing, and Evaluating the Program   30

Chapter 3
Considering Regulations and Establishing Policies   63

PART TWO
Operationalizing the Early Childhood Program

Chapter 4
Leading and Managing Personnel   96

Chapter 5
Planning the Physical Facility   142

Chapter 6
Financing and Budgeting   213

PART THREE
Implementing the Children's Program

Chapter 7
Planning the Children's Program   238

Chapter 10
Working Within the Family and Community Contexts   349

Chapter 11
Contributing to the Profession   379

NOTE: Every effort has been made to provide accurate and current Internet information in this book. However, the Internet and information posted on it are constantly changing, and it is inevitable that some of the Internet addresses listed in this textbook will change.

Overview of Early Childhood Programs

1

A new millennium and a new century have dawned. Over and over we heard President George W. Bush use the Children's Defense Fund (CDF) trademarked mission phrase, "Leave No Child Behind." On January 23, 2001, just days into his presidency, President Bush sent his "No Child Left Behind" plan to Congress. (The Act, a reform of the Elementary and Secondary Education Act, was signed into law on January 8, 2002.)

With hopeful eyes we focused on a White House Summit on Early Childhood Cognitive Development, "Ready to Read and Learn," on July 26–27, 2001. At the Summit the Bush administration officials announced a new federal task force on preschool programs. A few days later, on July 31, 2001, we listened to a hearing in the U.S. House of Representatives Subcommittee on Education Reform called "The Dawn of Learning: What's Working in Early Childhood Education."

As we were looking and listening, our world changed on September 11, 2001. We saw stress, poverty, racism and other hatreds, and violence at its worst. Out of the fire, smoke, and death, we also saw support, nurturing, and connectedness. This day, perhaps like no other, challenged any complacency we may have felt about the quality and accessibility of early childhood programs for all children. More than ever before, all children need support from wise and understanding adults to help them become adaptive thinkers and resilient individuals and live happy, caring, and productive lives in this world of flux, complexity, and turbulence.

The United States has a long history of interest in and support for early childhood care and education. Throughout the years, the reasons for programs have changed from supporting families and children during times of war and economic depression to meeting the needs of economically disadvantaged children during the War on Poverty in the 1960s. Today's public interest in early childhood programs seems to be due to the following needs, among others:

1. We need available and affordable child care for children whose mothers are in the workforce (Olson, 2002), including the 1 million additional children who are now enrolled in child care as a result of the Personal Responsibility Act (Growing Up in Poverty Project, 2002).

2. We need to minimize the effects of social and economic problems that lead to school failure (Council of Chief State School Officers, 1999; Kagan & Garcia, 1991).

3. We need a competitive workforce for the future to maintain our leadership in the world's marketplace (Carnegie Task Force on Meeting the Needs of Young Children, 1994; Committee for Economic Development, Research, and Policy, 1987, 1991, 1993).

4. We need to provide a support system for families as they try to meet their many demands (Henry, 2000; Lally, Lerner, & Lurie-Hurvitz, 2001).

As a result of society's need for high-quality early childhood programs, the profession has moved forward rapidly. Our knowledge base, confirming the benefits of high-quality programs for young children and support for families, is greatly expanding. For example, major reports have recently been published concerning early literacy (C. E. Snow, Burns, & Griffin, 1998), how people learn (Bransford, Brown, & Cocking, 1999), early childhood program content and pedagogy (National Research Council [NRC], 2001), integrated child development knowledge (Shonkoff & Phillips, 2000), and fostering children's mental health and positive relationships (Child Mental Health Foundations and Agencies Network, 2000).

Early childhood initiatives seem to be at an all-time high. Efforts include increasing state funding for early childhood programs, increasing program standards, enhancing teacher quality, assessing young children in more appropriate ways, compensating teachers for professional development, and promoting leadership.

Early childhood education is a big business. Hill-Scott (2000) compared early childhood education revenues with the revenues of other industries. She explained that federal contributions to early child efforts alone would place early childhood education at number 100 in the *Fortune* 500 list. Adding state and local revenues and parents' fees to the federal funds, the gross revenues of early childhood education would be similar to the gross revenues of the entertainment industry in 1997. Yet, the gross revenues of early childhood education do not pay the full costs of high-quality programs.

Despite the obvious need for high-quality early childhood programs, the empirically based rationale for providing such programs for all children, the initiatives, and the seeds of political and economic support, we do not have the infrastructure (e.g., laws, financing administration) to provide affordable and accessible high-quality programs for all children. Complex changes are needed. Support for quality is growing broadly, even beyond the professional base. To be responsive to the diversity of needs and accelerating social change, our current leadership must be willing to change—to become more dedicated to quality, not only in pedagogical services but also in the nonpedagogical aspects that are the framework of our early childhood programs.

NATURE AND EXTENT OF PROGRAMS

Effective planning and administration begin with some perspective on the nature and extent of early childhood programs. An overview of the influential factors and the status and types of programs for young children will provide a setting from which to view the nature of program planning and administration.

Factors Influencing Early Childhood Programs

Early childhood programs are the product of their exciting heritage and an expression of our society's determination to provide the best for its young. Several factors appear to influence the nature and extent of today's programs. First, literature reveals a growing conviction that a child's early years are highly important to the remainder of development. For example, new research on brain development builds support for early childhood care and education (Bruer, 1999; Newberger, 1997; Shore, 1997). Because of evidence that early life experiences, including those of the newborn, influence later development, the quality of early childhood experiences is believed to determine to a large extent the progress of later development (Shonkoff & Phillips, 2000). Consequently, programs designed to meet the needs of young children are receiving high priority.

Further, major changes have occurred in the ecology of childhood. The CDF (2001) reported that 17% of U.S. children live in poverty. The numbers are even higher for children who are born poor (20%) and those who will be poor at some point during childhood (33%). Of those who are born poor, 1 in 15 lives at less than half the poverty level. Minority children are more apt to be poor than majority children. About 1 million children are not only poor but also homeless (Nunez, 1996). Nunez found that the average age of a homeless person is 9, and that the average homeless family is composed of a single mother with two children under the age of 6. Poor and homeless children have poor health status, high rates of developmental delay, and emotional and behavioral problems, and they experience high rates of abuse, neglect, and academic failure (CDF, 2001; Nunez, 1996; Shane, 1996). Economic conditions are far more important to positive child outcomes in early childhood than they are in later childhood (Brooks-Gunn & Duncan, 1997).

In the 1960s, less than 10% of all children under age 18 lived with one parent; now 24% do, and 1 in 24 children lives with neither parent. This trend is primarily due to high divorce rates and births to unmarried mothers. Almost half of all children can expect to live an average of 5 years in a single-parent family. One third of all children are born to unmarried parents (CDF, 2001), and 1 child in 8 is born to a teenage mother (CDF, 2001). Zimiles (1986) called these changes in family lifestyles (e.g., more divorce, more single-parent families, fewer extended families, more teenage parents) the *diminishing mothers factor.*

Confirmed child abuse and neglect cases have decreased somewhat since peaking in 1993. Approximately 879,000 children were identified as victims in the almost 3 million reported cases of maltreatment in 2002 (U.S. Department of Health and Human Services [HHS], 2002). Of the children who were maltreated, 62% suffered neglect, 10% were sexually abused, and 8% were psychologically maltreated (HHS, 2002). Infants and toddlers had the highest rates of maltreatment and, of the child victims killed, 75% were under age 3 (National Center on Child Abuse and Neglect, 1997). Maltreatment is often devastating for a child's development (Cicchetti & Toth, 2000; R. Thompson & Wyatt, 1999). Maltreatment that occurs in the context of other adverse family circumstances results in worse consequences for the child (Rutter, 2000; Werner, 2000). Abuse is even occurring prenatally by women who engage in activities known to harm the unborn. *Developmental neurotoxins* (substances that are damaging) and their effects are well documented (Slikker & Chang, 1998).

Approximately 568,000 vulnerable children were in foster care in the United States in 1999; this number represented an increase of 48.3% over the previous decade. About 75% of foster children are clustered in one third of the states. Infants are the largest group of children entering foster care. About 60% of foster children are children of color (CDF, 2001).

Basic health care for many children is lacking. One in 6 children is born to a mother who did not receive prenatal care during the first 3 months of pregnancy, and 1 in 26 children is born to a mother who received late or no prenatal care. The lack of prenatal care increases the likelihood of low birth weight—now 1 in 13 births—and increases the risk of infant mortality, which is 7.2 per 1,000 for all races combined, but much higher for minority children (CDF, 2001).

Approximately 1 in 12 children has a disability (CDF, 2001). Children in special populations include children with physical and sensory impairments, motor disabilities, chronic health problems, serious neurological conditions, or behavioral disorders. Government statistics indicated that from 1988 to 1997 the number of preschool children with disabilities who were receiving interventions had increased 168% (U.S. Department of Education, 1999).

More and more children need high-quality care in productive group environments, a reflection of our concern over the high proportions of children doing poorly in school and the increased numbers of mothers in the workforce. About 51% of married mothers and 71.5% of single mothers work outside the home. Looking at the general population, 58% of mothers of children under age 1 are working or looking for work (Rusakoff, 2000); 64% of mothers of preschoolers and 78% of mothers of school-age children are currently employed (U.S. Bureau of Labor Statistics, 1999). This trend of maternal employment continues to increase. Among mothers with children at least a year old, nearly 75% were in the labor force in 2000 (Olson, 2002). As a result of the 1996 changes in the welfare law, more mothers in poverty are also working. Many of these women work a "nonday" work shift (i.e., the majority of hours outside the 8:00 A.M. to 4:00 P.M. time period), which affects about one half of all children under the age of 5 (Presser & Cox, 1997). Of the children whose mothers are employed, 60% are in the care of someone other than their parents (Olson, 2002).

Children of working mothers often enter child care at a young age. About 75% of children who enter child care during infancy enter prior to age 4 months (NICHD Early Child Care Research Network, 1997a). Besides the children of working mothers, about one third of preschoolers whose mothers are not in the labor force attend child care programs (National Center for Educational Statistics, 1996). By age 6, more than 80% of all children have had some child care experience (J. West, Wright, & Hausken, 1995).

Our nation is becoming more diverse. The racial and ethnic diversity of the U.S. population grows as a result of immigration and high birth rates among immigrants and their descendants. Today, the United States is made up of 100 ethnic and language groups (National Research Council & Institute of Medicine [NRC & IOM], 1998). As of the last U.S. Census, people were allowed to register their identification with more than one heritage group. Wardle (2001) reported that the number of multiracial babies born since the 1970s had increased more than 260% compared to a 15% increase of single-race babies. The CDF (2001) reported that 38% of children are minorities. For the foreseeable future, U.S. culture will continue to be reshaped by newly arrived groups (Washington & Andrews, 1998). By 2030, children in families of European origin will make up less than 50% of the population under age 5 (NRC & IOM, 1998). These changes in demographics represent both an opportunity and a challenge for early childhood programs.

Finally, against the background of today's social problems, early childhood programs are seen as support systems for families. In some ways, these programs have come full circle. They are seen today—just as they were seen under the leadership of visionaries such as Jean Oberlin, Friedrich Froebel, Elizabeth Peabody, Susan E. Blow, Kate Wiggin, Patty S. Hill, Maria Montessori, and Rachel and Margaret McMillan—as the best hope of reducing poverty of mind and body.

Even today's advantaged families often feel inadequate in trying to meet the demands of our rapidly changing society. Thus, universally available early childhood programs are now considered worthwhile to provide an essential service to families and an enriched, productive environment for young children.

Status of Early Childhood Programs

Early childhood programs come in all sizes and shapes and with differing perspectives that form the basis for their practices and, like most things, with various degrees of excellence. Young children and early childhood programs are big business from almost every standpoint. Early childhood programs, which came into their own in the 1960s with concern for the economically disadvantaged, are no longer the additional service of an affluent public school system, the special project of a philanthropic organization, an undertaking of a state welfare agency, or the result of a federal program. Currently, all states provide monies for universal public school kindergartens, and more than 40 states are engaged in various types of prekindergarten initiatives. More and more children from infancy to school age are in child care and education programs; the federal government funds such projects as Head Start, corporations operate early childhood programs, and child care resource and referral (CCR&R) agencies provide needed services.

With the expansion of early childhood programs, several trends are evident. On the one hand, universal education for all 5-year-olds is for all practical purposes a reality, with 98% of all children attending kindergarten (Zill, Collins, West, & Hausken, 1995). Yet, only 8 states and the District of Columbia require school districts to offer full-day kindergarten programs (Olson, 2002). Many other types of early childhood programs are relatively scarce. Although programs for low-income children are expanding, this expansion lags further and further behind the growing numbers of impoverished children in the United States. For example, Head Start serves only 60% of eligible children. Only 12% of children eligible for child care subsidies under the Child Care Development Fund (CCDF) actually receive them. The proportion of 4-year-olds served in state-financed prekindergarten programs ranges from 2% in one state to 50% in another state (Olson, 2002). Shortages of care are particularly common for infants and toddlers, sick children, children with disabilities, school-age children (Ewen & Goldstein, 1996), and children of mothers who work odd-hour shifts (U.S. Department of Labor, Women's Bureau, 1995).

In addition to providing programs for young children, many efforts are under way to improve the quality of early childhood programs (a topic discussed later in this chapter). In sum, no state has a comprehensive system of early care and education that makes high-quality services available to all families.

TYPES OF EARLY CHILDHOOD PROGRAMS

One of the first problems encountered when attempting to differentiate among the various types of early childhood programs is that the term *early childhood* lacks a precise definition. Educators, child psychologists, and others have used vague synonyms or different chronological ages or developmental milestones. The National Association for the Education of Young Children (NAEYC) has defined *early childhood* as birth through age 8 (NAEYC, 1991, p. 1).

One simple classification of early childhood programs is determined by the program's source of funding. Generally, early childhood programs are under the jurisdiction of one of the following:

- public schools (e.g., kindergartens)
- private control (e.g., nursery schools; parent cooperatives, business-operated programs; and programs for young children sponsored by churches, service organizations, and charities)
- federal programs (e.g., Head Start)

- national private agency programs (e.g., American Montessori schools)
- university laboratory programs (e.g., nursery, kindergarten, and primary-level schools)

Closely paralleling the sources of funding are the legal forms of organization: proprietorships, partnerships, corporations, and public agencies. (For details on these legal forms of organization, see chapter 3.)

Early childhood programs are also classified by their service delivery formats. Some programs are more child focused, whereas others are family focused. Other programs have both foci and thus use a combination of center-based and home-based services.

Finally, early childhood programs may also be described according to their origins. Their historical roots extend to various professional domains, such as health, social services, and education (Meisels & Shonkoff, 2000). As noted earlier in this chapter in the section "Factors Influencing Early Childhood Programs," early childhood programs are conceived in terms of the society in which children are reared. Thus, early childhood programs historically reflected the social concerns of the time (Garbarino & Ganzel, 2000; Sameroff & Fiese, 2000).

Colonial Education

Early childhood education has a history of more than 200 years. During Colonial America, *common schools*, which were designed to provide a classical education for boys through drill and memorization methods coupled with harsh discipline, constituted the major form of education. **Dame schools** were provided for some 4- to 7-year-old boys and girls and were patterned after the French *knitting schools* of Jean F. Oberlin. After the signing of the Constitution, dame schools began to emphasize women's education and eventually evolved into fashionable boarding schools.

Infant Schools

For the most part, early childhood programs in the United States began during the Industrial Revolution. The Industrial Revolution saw advances in machinery, but long hours, unsafe environmental work conditions, and the overreliance on women and on child labor took their toll on humans and family living. Social reformers began to express their concerns. Robert Owen, a mill owner and social reformer in Scotland, instituted changes in families' lives through reduced hours, better wages, and the establishment of child labor reforms.

To prepare people for a new society as he envisioned it, Owen established the Institute for the Formation of Character in New Lanark, Scotland, in 1816 (Reisner, 1930). The purpose of the school was to train children of workers, and even young adult employees, in his model mills. When Owen and his followers came to Indiana in 1825, they brought the *infant school* with them. Owen's school gained the attention of reformers, who saw it as a way to help poor children. Because of civic-minded women, working men, and journalists (Strickland, 1969), Owen's educational ideas flourished from New England through the Middle Atlantic states (May & Vinovskis, 1977).

Unlike the dame schools and the common schools, Owen's schools were to be "happy places" in which children learned by reason, not by coercion. The schools were designed to train children in "good practical habits." The curriculum for the first level was for children ages 3 to 6. It consisted of the three Rs, geography, history, sewing, dance, music, and moral principles. Unlike many other schools of the time, activity prevailed in Owen's schools. This was because of the influence of Pestalozzi (Spodek, 1973b), an influential German-born educator in Switzerland who advocated allowing children to learn through use of activities—instruction with objects, excursions into the fields and forests, games, and the like. Not all infant schools followed the child-centered approach, however (S. White & Buka, 1987).

The most famous infant school in the United States was founded by Bronson Alcott (McCuskey, 1940). Because of his belief in transcendentalism, Alcott began to study children's moral insights. His publication of *Conversations With Children on the Gospels* and the admission of a Black child caused his school to fail (O. Shepard, 1937). Because of the controversy over Alcott's practices, families removed their children from infant schools. The schools thus declined because they lost their sole financial support—parents' fees (Pence, 1986; O. Shepard, 1937).

Fireside Education

The collapse of the infant school movement and the development of print media led to *fireside education,* an antebellum parent education movement. Clergy and women were beginning to see the family as weakening. Because of this concern, the three themes that emerged were the home, the mother, and the child. The home, no longer the center of economic productivity, was seen as the upholder of morals in a materialistic society. Mothers' responsibilities were to nurture their children and provide moral education. Emphasis on cognitive development, especially intellectual precocity, was considered evil (Kuhn, 1947; Strickland, 1982).

Fireside education did not meet the needs of the poor. Poor mothers did not have the formal education needed to educate their children. Furthermore, mothers could not be full-time homemakers unless the family was financially comfortable. Thus, poor children did not receive a fireside education. In fact, the poor were seen as a threat to child-rearing practices in "proper" homes (Ryan, 1975). Well-to-do parents were concerned that their children would be negatively influenced through contact with children of the poor who did not receive "proper" education.

Kindergartens

Kindergartens are publicly or privately operated programs for 4- and 5-year-old children. More specifically, the term *kindergarten* is used to define the unit of school that enrolls 5-year-olds prior to entrance into the first grade.

Historically, the kindergarten ("children's garden") was an 1837 German institution that enrolled children 3 through 7 years of age and provided teaching suggestions to mothers of infants. As the founder of the kindergarten, Friedrich Froebel presented ideas that focused on romanticism and transcendentalism, as had his predecessors in the infant school movement (Snyder, 1972). Froebel's farsighted contributions included

- freedom of movement for the child;
- a planned sequence of activities centered on the "gifts" (small blocks for building, developing mathematical concepts, making designs), reinforced by the "occupations" (craft work) as well as other activities, and surrounded by a verbal "envelope" (poems, songs, storytelling, discussions);
- an emphasis on the relationship and order of ideas;
- the education of mothers, nurses (baby-sitters), and prospective kindergarten teachers; and
- the desire that the kindergarten become a state-supported institution.

Kindergartens came to the United States in 1855 via a German immigrant, Margarethe Meyer (Mrs. Carl) Schurz. Although many kindergartens became English-speaking institutions, following the endeavors of Elizabeth Peabody (an American-born educator who established the first English-speaking private kindergarten and the first nonpermanent public school kindergarten in the United States), they were philosophically a Froebelian transplant.

In the late 1800s, two influences undermined Froebel's kindergarten: the growth of public school kindergartens and the child study movement of G. Stanley Hall coupled with the progressive education movement of John Dewey (Woody, 1934). Although the first public school kindergartens were Froebelian, the trickle-down phenomenon from elementary education began with the expansion of kindergartens (Snyder, 1972). Less gifted teachers began to prescribe a rigid teaching sequence (Downs, 1978; S. White & Buka, 1987), and teachers modeled activities with the gifts rather than allowing children time to play (Troen, 1975).

When the child study movement began in the early 1900s under the direction of G. Stanley Hall, a divisive debate ensued between the Froebelian kindergarten leaders (under the direction of Susan E. Blow) and the progressive kindergarten leaders (headed by Patty S. Hill). Dewey thought the use of Froebel's gifts resulted in contrived experiences for children. He wanted children to learn from the real experiences of his day, such as carpentry and weaving. Constructive play and concepts integrated across curriculum areas were the cornerstones of Dewey's curriculum (Dewey, 1964). The role of the teacher was not only to plan the environment and guide the children but also to act as a researcher who gained insights through observations and recordings, a close tie to the ongoing child study movement (National Society for the Study of Education, 1929). Eventually, the progressives gained control of the kindergarten leadership and replaced the Froebelian curriculum.

The Depression was devastating to the growth of the public school kindergarten, which had begun to expand by the 1890s. Since the 1940s, however, enrollment in public school kindergartens has steadily increased. Today, every state subsidizes kindergartens in at least some districts or for a portion of the day. Several states do not require districts to offer kindergartens, and children in some states attend three times as many hours as children in other states (S. Robinson & Lyon, 1994).

Concerns about the kindergarten curriculum have been voiced since kindergartens became a part of public education. Kindergartens vary in the amount of emphasis on academic skills, but academic programs, which began in the 1960s, have seemingly increased despite the concerns of professional associations (see chapter 2).

Montessori Schools

Maria Montessori, the first woman to graduate from an Italian medical school, became interested in children with mental disabilities as a result of her medical practice at the psychiatric clinic at the University of Rome, where children with mental disabilities were institutionalized with insane children. Montessori studied the works of two French physicians—Jean Itard and his student Edouard Séguin—who worked to educate persons with disabilities. Montessori's lectures on persons with disabilities led to the creation of an orthophrenic school (i.e., a school for children with mental disabilities) in Italy, which she directed. Montessori actually taught the children enrolled in the school, and at night she analyzed the results and prepared new curriculum ideas, methodology, and materials. Almost from the beginning, Montessori believed that children with disabilities learn in the same way as children without disabilities. After 2 years of directing the school, she resigned and enrolled in philosophy and psychology courses.

In 1906, a building concern backed by the principal banks of Italy constructed some apartments in a slum area of Rome. Because the children damaged the property while their parents worked, the property owners decided that it was more economical to provide group care than to make repairs. Montessori was asked to oversee the program, which was housed in a room in the apartment complex. Thus, the *Casa dei Bambini*

(Children's House) was founded in Rome in 1907. Slum children between the ages of 2 1/2 and 7 years attended the all-day program. Montessori's contributions included the following ideas:

- Parents should be given training in child development and regulations for extending the principles taught to their children.
- Parents collectively owned the Children's House.
- Children have "sensitive periods" in which they are ready to "absorb" certain concepts.
- Children can teach themselves with minimal adult guidance, and this mode of learning carries over into adulthood when they are spontaneous learners and self-starters (Elkind, 1983).
- Children develop sensory perceptions that serve as a basis for all other learnings with Montessori-designed didactic materials; learn care of self and of environment through "work" with reality-oriented, practical-life experiences; and become language and math literate through the use of manipulative and self-correcting materials.
- Teachers learn through their interactions with children, prepare the environment, trust children to take the lead in their own learning, and do not force children to focus on more limited and adult-determined directions (Elkind, 1983).
- Children need a child-sized and orderly environment (Kramer, 1988).

Montessori's ideas were immediately popular, but their popularity suddenly declined in the 1920s because her ideas were dissonant with the psychology of the times (J. Hunt, 1968). Progressives did not like the backseat taken by Montessori teachers (Weber, 1969), and Americans did not want to rely on ideas from European educators (S. White & Buka, 1987). Montessori's ideas were revitalized in the 1960s for two reasons. First, new conceptions of psychological development formulated in the 1960s were more in step with Montessori's pedagogy (J. Hunt, 1968). For example, J. Hunt's (1961) and B. Bloom's (1964) works provided validation for the contributing role of the environment. Second, an Americanized version of Montessori practice was introduced with the 1958 opening of the Montessori school in Greenwich, Connecticut, and with the publication of Rambusch's *Learning How to Learn: An American Approach to Montessori* (1962). The Americanized Montessori approach included some of the content of other early childhood programs, such as creative art, dramatic play, science activities, and large-muscle play on playground equipment, as well as the traditional Montessori content. Much debate stemmed from these new practices, and the dispute later led to a division of thinking within the Montessori ranks. Those who hold to the traditional Montessori method are members of the Association Montessori Internationale (AMI), and those who support innovations join the American Montessori Society (AMS; see appendix 5). As interest in the curriculum models diminished in the late 1970s and 1980s, so did interest in Montessori education. Recently, however, Montessori education has become popular in public school magnet programs (Chattin-McNichols, 1992).

Nursery Schools

The term *nursery school* is difficult to define because these programs are a loose array of individual facilities. The term is often applied to programs for 3- and 4-year-old children, although some nursery schools serve younger children.

Nursery schools developed in the 20th century. Rachel and Margaret McMillan opened a medical clinic in London to serve children who had repeated illnesses because of their impoverished environment. To protect the children's health, the McMillan sisters opened an early childhood program in 1911. These nursery schools, as they were named, made such an impression on the British government that it passed the Education Act of 1918. This act provided tax money for services to 2- to 5-year-old children.

The McMillan nursery schools were designed to meet the needs of poor children and to establish cooperation between home and school (Bradburn, 1989). Like Montessori, the McMillan sisters believed in providing children with sensory experiences, but unlike Montessori, they preferred real experiences—the atrium garden and everyday experiences—rather than apparatuses. The curriculum consisted of physical care of the child, perceptual-motor activities, self-expressive activities (e.g., art, block building, dramatic play), and language activities (e.g., stories, songs, discussions). The teacher's role was that of both teacher and nurse (Steedman, 1990).

With the advent of nursery schools came the beginning of scientific child study. Those involved in scientific child study thought that parents at all socioeconomic levels failed to provide the "best" for their children. In contrast with the English nursery schools, nursery schools in the United States were middle- and upper-class institutions. In 1923, the child study movement and nursery education received the Lucy Spelman Rockefeller memorial funds. The trustees of these funds decided to use the monies for three purposes. The first purpose was to model exemplary educational practices. Common philosophies of these nursery schools were that

- young children have a developmental need for group association with peers;
- play is beneficial for investigating the environment and for alleviating emotional stress;
- children should begin the process of social weaning, that is, becoming detached from parents;
- the routine bodily functions of sleeping, eating, and eliminating should be managed; and
- teachers should provide guidance and guard against emotional stress (Forest, 1927).

The second purpose was to provide resources for child study research. Parent education and participation, often an admission requirement, emphasized child development and observation in home and school (Davis, 1932). Because the scientific child study movement attracted people from many different disciplines, nursery schools established in various institutions had somewhat different objectives. The third purpose was to educate parents about the implications of research. Parent education was perhaps the nursery school's strongest selling point because many parents were hesitant about early education outside the home (Eliot, 1978).

Day Nurseries and Child Care

The term **child care** generally refers to programs that operate for extended hours (often 12 hours) and offer services for children from birth through school age. Most programs for young children are of the child care type because they involve the care and education of children separated from their parents for all or part of the day. Child care programs may also involve night care.

The forerunners of child care centers in the United States were the **day nurseries.** Day nurseries came into existence about the same time as infant schools were flourishing. Medical discoveries of the mid-1800s aroused greater concern for children's sanitation and health. In 1854, a Nursery School for Children of Poor Women was established in cooperation with the Child's Hospital of New York City. It was patterned after the 1844 French *crèche,* which was designed as child care for working French women and as a method of reducing infant mortality rates. Concern for physical well-being soon broadened to include concern for habits, manners, and vocational skills (Forest, 1927).

As immigrants settled in urban areas, settlement-house day nurseries opened (e.g., Hull House nursery in 1898; E. Kahn, 1989). These day nurseries were considered necessary to counter many social evils (e.g., the exploitation of women and children in the labor force) and to help alleviate immigrants' cultural assimilation problems. Education was deemed essential for true social reform. Thus, some day nurseries added kindergartens, and some were sponsored by boards of education and opened in public schools (e.g., Los Angeles). Parent education became a component of the day nursery's educational program. Parents were taught various household skills and about the management and care of children (Wipple, 1929).

In time, some social reformers began to believe that day nurseries might supplant the role of the family in child rearing. Consequently, emphasis was placed on the importance of mothering (nurturing), and mothers were encouraged to remain in the home. To help mothers afford to stay in the home, the Mother's Pension Act was enacted in 1911, a forerunner of Aid to Families With Dependent Children. Thus, the stigma of child care began. (It was thought essential for mothers to care for their own children. When the Pension Act provided financial help to stay-at-home mothers, mothers who still elected to put their children in child care were considered mothers who were not fulfilling their most important role.) Enthusiasm for day nurseries further declined when the National Federation of Day Nurseries drew attention to the poor quality of some programs. Concern over the appropriateness of day nurseries stimulated the development of nursery schools in the 1920s (Forest, 1927).

Day nurseries regained their status during the Depression, when the government for the first time subsidized all-day programs to aid children and unemployed schoolteachers. Although they were called Works Progress Administration (WPA) nursery schools, they are included here because of their all-day schedule. Early childhood nursery school educators associated with the National Association of Nursery Education, the Association for Childhood Education International (ACEI), and the National Council on Parent Aid formed an advisory committee to assist in supervising and training teachers for WPA nursery schools and in developing guides and records (Davis, 1964). The positive effect was a nursery school philosophy that included all children (J. Anderson, 1947); however, nursery school teacher training standards were undermined (Frank, 1937). The major focus of the WPA nurseries was habit training, although health and nutrition services were also provided. Federal funds were withdrawn at the end of the Depression.

Federal funds for all-day child care were again provided in 1942 by Public Law (P.L.) 137 (the Lanham, or Community Facilities, Act). The stigma of enrolling in public nurseries was replaced by the spirit of patriotism because parents were now working for the war effort. The purpose of the funds was to provide for the child's physical needs, and nursery school educators again assisted. Although some centers had inadequately trained staff, outstanding examples of such centers were the two Child Service Centers established by Kaiser Shipbuilding Corporation in Portland, Oregon, and directed by Lois Meek Stolz and James L. Hymes, Jr. (Hymes, 1944). To ease the burden of working parents, these centers also provided such support services as precooked meals for parents and children, on-site grocery stores, and clothes repair. The theories of the child study movement had replaced habit training. The philosophy was based on the work of Isaacs (1930, 1933) and Baruch (1939). Play was considered important as mental health therapy (Hartley, Frank, & Goldenson, 1957).

Support for the centers ended with the termination of the Lanham Act in 1946. During the Korean War, appropriation of funds under the Defense Housing and Community Facilities and Services Act (1951) was negligible (Kerr, 1973).

In the 1960s, the Economic Opportunity Act (1964) funded Head Start, child care services for migrant workers, and child care for children whose parents were involved in the various manpower projects (e.g., Job Corps, Foster Grandparents). The Housing and Urban Development Act, Title VII (1965), the Model Cities Act (1966), and the Parent and Child Centers (funded with Head Start monies) also assisted the child care efforts.

In the 1980s, federal funds for various types of child care programs decreased. Today, governmental support for child care is seen in the Child Care and Dependent Care Tax Credit, begun in 1975–1976 and expanded in 1982–1983, and in the Child Care and Development Block Grant (CC&DBG) Act of 1990, which provides funds to states to cover child care services. Thus child care has shifted back to state and local control for the most part.

Basic Types of Child Care.   The two basic types of child care are center care and family child care. A **child care center** is defined as an out-of-home program and facility serving children who need care for a greater portion of the day. Usually, the schedule fits the working hours of families who use the center. Drop-in centers also provide occasional and part-time care. Child care centers are regulated by state licensing requirements and other standards and may be licensed to serve children from infancy through school age. For-profit centers are usually owned and operated by individuals or family corporations, and some are operated as large chains or franchises. Not-for-profit centers are sponsored by state and local governments, religious groups, women's organizations, and parent cooperatives.

Family child care is defined as nonresidential care provided in a private home other than the child's own. Family child care may have its origins in the slave nurses of ancient Rome. For centuries, members of the European aristocracy employed wet nurses, nannies, and tutors to care for children. In the United States in the antebellum South, slave women raised their masters' children. When immigrant working-class women began to hire older women in the community for child care purposes, a status congruity between parents and providers began (Kessler-Harris, 1982) which has continued (Nelson, 1990). In family child care, the group of children is small—approximately 6 children, including the caregiver's own children. About half the states also define private homes in which 7 to 12 children are cared for and additional staff are hired to meet adult–child ratios as **large family child care homes, group child care homes**, or **group day homes.**

Family child care may be operated as an independent business or may be part of a **system** (i.e., have a sponsoring organization that has been authorized by the state or territory to approve and monitor its services). System staff members refer families to homes in the system and provide administrative functions for these homes. Besides systems that work on behalf of providers, professional associations, such as the National Association for Family Child Care (NAFCC), work on behalf of providers.

Trends in Child Care.   Child care programs are a major part of the field of early child care and education. Before entering school, many children will spend more than 2,000 hours per year in child care, in contrast to just over half that amount of time for a 7-hour daily public school program. Because of school-age child care, the time children spend in child care may equal the time spent in school from kindergarten until graduation.

Increased Demands.   A rather large number of parents take care of their own children, especially those in two-parent families and those with children under age 3. Many do so through part-time employment. Fathers provide about 25% of this care (NICHD Early Child Care Research Network, 1997a). Over the past decade, care of children outside the home has increased substantially. Only 38% of children from birth to age 5, and less than 25% of 3- to 5-year-olds receive care only from their parents (Yarosz & Barnett, 2001).

Demand for child care has increased because of maternal employment and the child care desires of mothers who are not employed outside the home. One study found that four out of five

children had some child care experience before age 6 (J. West, Wright, & Hausken, 1995), a 5% increase over the previous 5 years (J. West, Hausken, Chandler, & Collins, 1991). However, even with government subsidies, high-quality child care is out of reach for many families (Olson, 2002). Access to child care programs is not equal across the nation (Cadden, 1994).

About 27% of infants and toddlers are cared for by relatives; however, this figure declines to 17% for preschoolers (Capizzano, Adams, & Sonenstein, 2000). Relative care serves about 15% and nonrelative family child care serves about 11% of all children from birth to age 5 (Yarosz & Barnett, 2001). These statistics are supported by K. Smith (2000), who reported that approximately one fourth of all children are enrolled in family child care.

Reliance on center-based care is growing as the use of family child care is declining. Capizzano, Adams, and Sonenstein (2000) reported that 22% of infants and toddlers and 45% of preschoolers attend center-based child care. The shift away from family child care to center care is the result of the decrease in care by relatives (Perreault, 1991).

Different kinds of families use different kinds of care. Family child care is preferred by parents who see it as more homelike (Foote, 1990). Because "expert" advice has often been that mothers should stay at home with young children, mothers often seek care that replicates the experiences they would provide if they could stay at home (Young, 1990). Children are more like siblings in a home (i.e., of mixed ages). Parents can also choose the place and the provider, unlike center care in which they can choose only the place. Family child care offers more flexible hours than centers offer. Family child care programs are more apt than centers to accept infants and toddlers, children needing full-time care or evening care (but *not* weekend care), school-age children, and children who are ill (Hofferth, Brayfield, Deich, & Holcomb, 1991; D. Phillips, 1991). Family child care serves more children with disabilities than any other child care arrangement (Fewell, 1986). For these reasons, family child care is increasingly seen as a viable option in the child care field. Various groups are promoting the growth of family child care. These groups include the military, in which all branches have family child care; corporations such as Bank of America, Dayton Hudson, and American Express (Hayes, Palmer, & Zaslow, 1990); and professional groups such as the NAFCC, National Black Child Development Institute (NBCDI), and NAEYC.

Center care is preferred by some parents. Families with preschoolers rather than infants and toddlers use center care more than do families with very young children (Capizzano, Adams, & Sonenstein, 2000). African American mothers are more likely than Anglo American or Hispanic mothers to enroll their children, including infants and toddlers, in centers. Mothers with more formal education and who work in management or the professions use centers more than less educated and service-employed mothers. Mothers who work full time use centers more often than mothers who work part time (Hayes, Palmer, & Zaslow, 1990).

Figure 1–1 shows settings for center-based early childhood care and education. In reviewing statistics, it is important to keep in mind that many families use more than one type of care, especially if they have children of different ages and if they need supplemental care in addition to their regular arrangements. As children go through the elementary grades, families often add more child care arrangements (Laird, Pettit, Dodge, & Bates, 1998).

Groups of Children Served.   As already noted, most 5-year-olds are now in kindergarten programs, but 3- and 4-year-olds form the bulk of the enrollment for all programs combined. The trend, however, is increasingly toward extending the age range of the children served (infants and toddlers and school-age) as well as including children who are mildly ill.

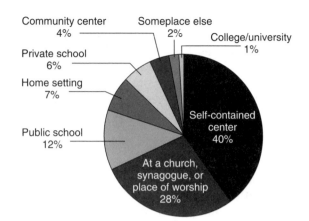

Figure 1–1   **Settings for Early Childhood Care and Education in Center-Based Programs**
Note: From *Early Care and Education Program Participation: 1991–1999,* by D. J. Yaroz and W. S. Barnett, 2001, New Brunswick, NJ: Rutgers University, Center for Early Education Research. Reprinted with permission.

Infant and toddler child care usually refers to care given to children from birth to age 3. Although the number of infant and toddler programs is increasing, such programs still constitute one of the most difficult forms of child care to find. Neugebauer (1993a) reported that center care for infants and toddlers is the number one demand from employers. This is expected, given the fact that more than half of mothers return to work during their child's first year (Rusakoff, 2000). Some concerns have been expressed about infant programs. For example, one study found few differences between infants attending group child care and infants who stayed home with their mothers (NICHD Early Child Care Research Network, 1998b), although some infants in long hours of group care seemed to experience less sensitive mothering. On the other hand, in another study all infants enrolled in higher quality programs appeared to experience maternal sensitivity (NICHD Early Child Care Research Network, 1999). Higher quality infant and toddler programs have also been found to be associated with positive cognitive and linguistic outcomes (Peisner-Feinburg & Burchinal, 1997). Thus, characteristics of the infant and toddler programs have been strongly implicated in the outcomes for infants and toddlers (Howes & Hamilton, 1993). (See appendix 1 for resources for program planning.)

A second trend is referred to as **school-age child care (SACC)** programs. SACC is a more encompassing term, defined as nonparental care of 5- to 16-year-olds during periods when school is not in session—before and after school, on holidays or vacations during the school term, and during the summer. The term *out-of-schooltime programs* may be more appropriate than *school-age child care* because not all programs are necessarily "care" programs. School-age children make up the bulk of children (5 to 7 million; Seligson, 2001) referred to as *latchkey children,* or *children in self-care,* an alternative label many think is a linguistic cop-out for such a serious problem. More than 35% of parents use self-care at least occasionally. Children most often in self-care are older school-age children, boys, and children seen as capable by their parents (Vandell & Su, 1999). Probably as a result of the perceived safety of their homes and neighborhoods, self-care is most often chosen by families with higher incomes, mothers who are better educated, and non-Hispanic White families (Belle, 1997). Sibling care, a form of self-care, is the most common arrangement used by employed single mothers with low incomes (B. Miller, O'Connor, & Sirignono, 1995).

Being unsupervised after school is believed to contribute to childhood fear, depression, loneliness, depressed school achievement, crime, and increased sexual activity (Todd, Albrecht, & Coleman, 1990). One study revealed that children evidenced more social and academic problems when self-care occurred in the early school years, when they had behavioral problems, and when the form of self-care was "hanging out" with peers (Pettit, Laird, Bates, & Dodge, 1997).

As we have discussed, more than three out of four mothers of school-age children are em-

ployed outside the home (U.S. Bureau of Labor Statistics, 1999) and in need of SACC programs for their children. However, SACC programs will meet as little as 25% of the demand in some areas (Seligson, 2001).

The number of SACC programs is growing. A majority of programs are affiliated with schools, child care centers, and youth-serving agencies. In the majority of schools, space is provided to other sponsors of SACC, such as the YMCA, to operate these programs. In addition to youth organizations, other groups that operate SACC programs are churches, park and recreation facilities, housing authorities, military bases, family child care programs, and companies (e.g., in Houston a consortium of employers helps the public schools provide needed after-school services). High-quality programs are often collaborative in nature because several programs can provide more diverse activities as well as share expenses. Gannett (1990) profiled six models of city collaboration projects. Regardless of sponsorship, the basic goals of school-age programs are (a) supervision (protection, shelter, food, guidance), (b) recreation (supervised play to specific skill development), (c) diversion (e.g., crafts, drama, field trips), and (d) stimulation (formal lessons or practices). SACC programs can foster self-esteem and cultural identities, too (Hellison & Cutforth, 1997). A new type of SACC activity is called "clubs," in which parents choose from a "menu" for their children (Howells, 1993). Many resources are now available for activities (see appendix 1).

SACC is not without problems. A survey conducted by the National School-Age Care Alliance (NSACA; Neugebauer, 1993c) found that the main challenges as seen by providers were (a) providing appropriate activities for older children, (b) finding staff who can work split shifts, (c) providing quality programs that parents can afford and that pay adequate wages to staff, and (d) having to share space with public schools. The concerns expressed over schools entering the child care business center on the extent of school liability, charges for building use and maintenance, and the financial burden of providing programs on an already tight budget (Seligson, 1986). Because SACC has so many models and sponsors, checks on quality (as discussed in chapter 3) are a problem.

Another trend is the growing need to find **special alternative care** for children who attend child care centers and other programs but are either too ill to attend their regular program or are prohibited from attending by policy. According to the National Association for Sick Child Daycare (NASCD, 2000), working mothers are absent from their jobs from a week to more than a month each year, which is highly expensive to employers. At least three types of alternative care are being used: (a) centers specializing in the care of sick children; (b) infirmary care in pediatric wards of hospitals; and (c) trained workers who care for ill children in the child's home.

Child Care and the Employer.   Business has become an important player in early childhood care and education. Prior to World War II, business and labor involvement in child care was primarily limited to the health professions and a few industries. With mothers entering the workforce during World War II, public child care in defense plants (e.g., Kaiser Shipbuilding Corporation) served thousands of children. After the war, however, industry-sponsored child care declined sharply. In 1987, the U.S. Department of Labor released a report called *Workforce 2000* (W. Johnston & Packer, 1987), which provided businesses with the rationale for addressing work and family concerns. This study was followed by the Families and Work Institute study (Galinsky, Bond, & Friedman, 1993), which again showed that family issues were far from a marginal concern for businesses. One study showed that 25% of employed parents with children under age 13 had experienced a breakdown in their child care arrangements in the past 3 months (Neugebauer, 1993a). As we have discussed, businesses also see child

care as an important investment in 21st-century productivity.

More businesses are now offering **employer-supported child care.** Employer interest in child care varies by type of business. Government agencies and service industries offer more child care benefits than goods-producing industries. The military has the largest employer-sponsored early childhood program in the country. College campuses often have child care programs as well. Other major sponsors of child care are employers who (a) have a local labor shortage, (b) have a local culture of community involvement, (c) are located in areas where high-quality care is unavailable, (d) hire many women, (e) are in good financial health or are not in good financial health and want to recruit employees, and (f) employ one or more individuals who have taken up child care issues.

Employer-supported child care may take a variety of forms (Galinsky, 1989). Only 3% of all centers are employer supported (Hill-Scott, 2000). In some cases these are **single-business centers** in which a corporation owns and operates an on-site facility. Small businesses in an area may join together to form a **multibusiness center** or **consortium.** Corporations may manage their own centers or turn to outside contractors. More often, support for child care is more indirect. Employers may reserve spaces and subsidize fees in local child care agencies, which are called **corporate reserve slots.** Employers may assist employees in establishing **family satellite programs.** Corporations also use **voucher systems** in which subsidies are portable (i.e., used for any child care service the parent chooses). Employers frequently provide child care assistance through a **tax savings plan** under the firm's flexible benefit package, whereby salary reductions (and thus tax savings) are used to fund child care. Employers often offer personnel resource and referral services such as seminars or one-on-one assistance in locating child care services.

Work schedules are sometimes adjusted for employees with children. These work schedule adjustments include **flextime** (employees have core work hours with flexible starting and stopping times); **compressed time** (employees work more hours per day but fewer days); **task contracting** (employees must complete assigned tasks within a given time frame but need not specify time worked); **flexiplace** (location of the place where work performed is flexible, such as in one's home); and **job sharing** (two or more employees share one job and the salary or profits).

Head Start

In 1964, the federal government asked a panel of child development experts to develop program guidelines to help communities overcome the disadvantages borne by preschool children from low-income families. The report became the blueprint for Project Head Start, launched as an 8-week summer program that soon became a full-year program (Greenberg, 1990). In 1965, Head Start was administered by the Office of Economic Opportunity (OEO), but it is now administered by the Administration for Children and Families (ACF) in HHS.

Head Start is administered locally through community action agencies and single-purpose, not-for-profit agencies such as school districts and YMCAs. Grants are awarded by the HHS Regional Offices (10 regional offices, American Indian Program branch, and Migrant Program branch). Head Start legislation states that the federal grant to operate a local Head Start program shall not exceed 80% of the approved costs of the program, with 20% to be contributed by the community in either cash or services. Head Start experience has shown that the needs of children vary considerably among communities and that programs should be individualized to serve local needs most effectively. Therefore, Head Start permits and encourages local sponsors to develop and implement various options (see appendix 7).

Head Start provides comprehensive developmental services for America's preschool children from low-income families. It also provides parents with education so they can better provide for their children. The Head Start Act Amendments of 1994 established the Early Head Start program, which expands the benefits of early childhood development to low-income families with children under the age of 3 and to pregnant women. Table 1–1 lists the goals of Head Start and Early Head Start. R. Collins (1993), in defining Head Start as a two-generational program, stated, "A two-generational program is one that promotes children's development within a family context. Major

Table 1–1   Goals of Head Start and Early Head Start

Goals of Head Start

- **Education**—Head Start's educational program is designed to meet the needs of each child, the community served, and its ethnic and cultural characteristics.

- **Health**—Head Start emphasizes the importance of the early identification of health problems. The health program includes immunizations and medical, dental, mental health, and nutritional services.

- **Parental Involvement**—An essential part of Head Start is the involvement of parents in parent education, program planning, and operating activities.

- **Social Services**—Specific services, such as community outreach, referrals, and crisis intervention, are geared to each family after its needs are determined.

Goals of Early Head Start

- Enhance children's total development
- Enable parents to be better caregivers of and teachers to their children
- Help parents meet their own goals including that of economic independence

Note: From *Fact Sheet* (January 25, 2001), by Administration for Children and Families, Washington, DC: U.S. Department of Health and Human Services. Retrieved July 27, 2002, from http://www.acf.dhhs.gov/programs/opa/facts/headst.html

program goals target children together with parents and other family members" (p. 27).

According to N. Mallory and Goldsmith (1990), Head Start has been successful because it (a) has provided comprehensive services to children and their families; (b) has involved parents in parent education classes, in policy-making bodies, and as program volunteers and paid staff; (c) is designed to meet local community needs and to use the most feasible delivery system; (d) is supported by training and technical assistance; and (e) has used a collaborative approach with other organizations at the national and local levels. To ensure that local programs meet their goals, performance standards were adopted beginning in 1975. Chapter 2 gives additional information on research results.

Since Head Start's inception 3 decades ago, the face of poverty and thus the needs of children and their families have changed. Many new initiatives are being tried to meet today's needs. Some examples include

- the Early Childhood Initiative, which includes a new accountability system to ensure that every Head Start center assesses standards;

- the Early Literacy Initiative, which provides Head Start programs with assistance in preparing children to be ready for school;

- the Early Head Start Initiative, which expands the benefits and assesses family and child outcomes;

- the Fatherhood Initiative, which explores new approaches to sustaining fathers' involvement in their children's lives;

- the Improving Quality Initiative, which aids Head Start programs in their pursuit of quality;

- the Research Initiative, which is designed to evaluate Head Start program performance and to seek improvment; and

- the National Head Start Impact Study Initiative, which is designed to provide a national

analysis of the impact of Head Start on the development and school readiness of children from low-income families.

Primary Schools

Primary schools grew out of the common schools. The original purpose of primary schools in the United States was to instruct children in the three Rs, especially in reading, as expounded in the Preamble to the Puritan School Law of 1647 (commonly referred to as the "Old Deluder Satan Law"). The methodology was rote memorization and recitation. During the 18th century, the schools were seen as a unifying force for the emerging nation. State support of education and the concept of free, universal education were born during this century. Curriculum and methodology changed in the primary schools of the 19th century as they began to add aesthetic education, nature study, geography, and physical education to the three Rs curriculum. The Pestallozzian system of an activity-oriented methodology was accepted, and the still frequently used unit system of teaching evolved from the 19th-century Herbartian method. *Normal schools* began teacher training programs as the need for trained teachers emerged. Although primary schools have continued to change with the demands of the times, many people still consider them the level at which the skill subjects of reading, writing, and arithmetic must be mastered and the content subjects (e.g., science, social studies) are introduced in a more structured atmosphere than is found in most preprimary programs.

State-Financed Prekindergarten Programs

Although state-financed prekindergarten (also called *preschool*) programs have had more than a 2-decade history, these programs have recently expanded. In 1980, only 10 states financed any prekindergarten programs (Olson, 2002). Today,

39 states and the District of Columbia offer state-financed prekindergartens for some preschoolers. Most states are implementing preschool policies for 4-year-olds and some for 3-year-olds, but younger children have received little attention (Jacobson, 2002). Besides funding programs for children with special needs, state-financed programs are for financially needy preschoolers and those with other risk factors (Olson, 2002). Only Georgia, New York, Oklahoma, and the District of Columbia are moving toward universal prekindergarten programs for 4-year-olds. Most states see universal programs as too costly.

Many professionals are debating who should be responsible for prekindergarten services. Some states fund preschool programs in public schools, whereas others provide financial support for community groups to expand early childhood care and education services, such as Head Start (Blank & Adams, 1997; Knitzer & Page, 1998). Some early childhood professionals advocate shifting all prekindergarten funding to local school systems, thereby pooling all funding for a more coordinated and comprehensive system. These professionals point out that school systems already receive federal funding for children with disabilities and their families and funds for Title 1 of the Elementary and Secondary Education Act. Some local school systems are Head Start grantees or delegate agencies. Other reasons are also given for public school funding. Public schools set high standards and compensate teachers at a higher rate than most private programs. Public school prekindergarten programs are often staffed by state-certified teachers who earn the same benefits as other teachers in the school district. Lubeck (1989) stated that she favors universal public education because she believes that serving only "at-risk" children fosters racial and income segregation.

Conversely, many early childhood leaders have voiced concern about public school prekindergarten programs. Some leaders point out that the hours of operation and the calendar of public schools do not meet the needs of working parents. Surbeck (1998) stated that teachers in public school classrooms cannot meet the diverse needs of young children and their families. Most concerns focus on the possible curriculum of public school prekindergarten programs. The concerned leaders have said that the public schools do not appropriately serve 5- to 8-year-old children and have expressed fears that prekindergartens would have inappropriate curricular content and teaching strategies and that public programs would also harm the enrollments of privately sponsored programs (G. Morgan, 1985). The Public School Early Childhood Study (Marx & Seligson, 1988), which compared public school–operated programs and community-based programs, found that (a) the range of practices in both went from very appropriate to not appropriate; (b) although public school programs were well equipped, equipment often was not used well; (c) public school programs neglected large-muscle play; and (d) public school programs were good if the program administrators were well grounded in early childhood education and child development and had influence with the district superintendent.

Child Care Resource and Referral (CCR&R) Agencies

CCR&Rs are counseling and research services designed to help parents meet their child care services needs. The pioneers of CCR&Rs were parents who wanted change in their communities. The earliest CCR&Rs began in the 1960s and were called *information and referral services* (I&Rs). The early leaders realized that sharing information with parents did not resolve all the problems such as costs, quality, and availability. Thus, leaders realized that they needed to work on behalf of parents. In the 1980s, I&Rs became CCR&Rs. The National Association of Child Care Resource and Referral Agencies (NACCR&RA) was conceived in 1984, incorporated in 1987, and opened its national office in Washington, DC, in 1993 (see appendix 5).

Most CCR&Rs are community funded, and some are state funded. National referral services (e.g., Work/Family Directions, created by IBM) also exist (Galinsky & Friedman, 1993). All CCR&Rs serve in the following four ways:

1. They support families by helping them manage their responsibilities.
2. They compile, analyze, and share information on community needs and the supply and availability of child care.
3. They support family and center child care programs, including recruitment of new providers.
4. They collaborate with various community groups to provide high-quality care.

SERVICES AND PROGRAMS ADDRESSING POPULATIONS WITH SPECIAL NEEDS

Vulnerability has always been a reality for children with special needs—children who are at or near the poverty level, children with disabilities, and children who are part of our linguistically and culturally diverse population. All of these children have special needs in today's early childhood care and education programs.

Children Who Are at Risk

As we have discussed, early childhood programs have always been partners in social initiatives for the poor throughout history. During the 1960s and 1970s, several hundred intervention programs were funded. A descriptive compilation of many of these programs and the research results is available (M. Day & Parker, 1977; Fallon, 1973; Haith, 1972; Maccoby & Zellner, 1970; Weber, 1970).

Some of the early childhood intervention programs were for infants and toddlers as part of family services, but most of these programs were for 3- and 4-year-old children. All of the model programs designed for disadvantaged preschoolers were effective in attaining some program goals because they were well conceptualized and coherent versions of a particular knowledge base. Today, Head Start programs and public school prekindergartens are serving many at-risk preschoolers. Spodek and Brown (1993) stated that the most consistently popular curriculum approach from the initiatives of the 1960s is the High/Scope model. They think this may be because of the availability of written materials and of teacher training programs.

Special kindergarten programs are being provided for at-risk 5-year-olds. Karweit (1993), after reviewing the research on effective kindergarten programs, concluded that the "systematic aspects" of the program were more important than the "philosophical approach." Similar to effective preschool programs, effective kindergarten approaches had teachers who followed a systematic plan and incorporated specific materials, activities, and management techniques that fit the context of the program.

Many programs for at-risk children are not well planned. Others that attempt to follow a model do not have the funds to keep an optimal child–staff ratio, hire well-qualified staff, and so on. Research is needed on how far a program may deviate from its model and still be effective.

Children with Disabilities

The history of serving children with disabilities in early childhood care and education programs has two roots: school programs serving school-age children with disabilities and early childhood programs serving disadvantaged (at-risk) children. Parents of children with disabilities started preschools and also advocated for governmental funding. P.L. 90-538, the Handicapped Children's Education Assistance Act, was passed in 1968. Head Start began the inclusion of children with disabilities in 1972. Thus, an early intervention focus was beginning.

Programs for children with special needs solidified with the passage of P.L. 94-142, the Education for All Handicapped Children Act of 1975 (renamed the Individuals With Disabilities Education Act, P.L. 101-476, in 1990). From the mid-1970s until the mid-1990s, experimentation in curriculum content, methodology, and program delivery occurred.

Early childhood care and education and special education became inseparable partners with the passage of P.L. 99-457, now reauthorized as P.L. 102-119, which extended the ideas of P.L. 101-476 to children from birth to age 3 and emphasized the family as the most viable supportive partner. With the passage of P.L. 102-119, a new field, early childhood special education (ECSE), was born and is rapidly growing.

Because intervention includes both young children and their families, many programs for young children with special needs use home visits as the delivery system (see "Family Services" in this chapter). The Portage Project (Shearer & Shearer, 1972; Sturmey & Crisp, 1986), which began in 1969, has been a longtime successful model for home-visiting programs serving children with special needs and their families. The other basic delivery system, the inclusion of children in early childhood programs to fulfill the "least restrictive environment" mandate of P.L. 101-476, has moved from mainstreaming (in which children were placed in general education programs for short, daily time periods but without constant supports from ECSE personnel), to integration (in which children with special needs were helped by ECSE professionals to adjust to the general education program), and now to inclusion (in which early childhood programs are designed to meet the needs of all children). The Jowonio School, created in 1969, is an early model of inclusion (Donovan, 1987).

In addition to the Portage Project and the Jowonio School, many other model programs for children with special needs have been attempted (W. Brown, Horn, Heiser, & Odom, 1996; Chandler, 1994; Udel, Peters, & Templemann, 1998.)

Similar to the findings regarding programs for at-risk children, research on intervention programs (e.g., Buysee, Wesley, & Keyes, 1998; Odom & Diamond, 1998; Odom & McEvoy, 1988) has resulted in findings that inclusion is not enough in itself; program quality is the critical factor.

Children from Linguistically and Culturally Diverse Backgrounds

The United States has always been a land of many peoples, and our population has become increasingly diverse. By 2020, almost half of the nation's school children will be children of color (Pallas, Natriello, & McDill, 1989). Our society has moved away from the early 1900s idea of the great melting pot to the idea that we are a diverse nation in which all children should have equal educational opportunities and should develop positive attitudes and behaviors toward all others. Spodek and Brown (1993) classified early childhood models concerned with diversity as programs designed to serve specific populations and as programs for all children that foster positive attitudes and behaviors concerning diversity.

Programs designed to serve linguistically and culturally different populations were included in the program models created for at-risk children. Some of these programs were bilingual efforts (Saracho & Spodek, 1983), and others were models that incorporated the child's culture (Arizona Center for Educational Research and Development, 1983; Yawkey, 1987).

The multicultural approach designed to aid all children in developing positive attitudes and behaviors toward others grew out of the intergroup movement of the 1950s and the ethnic studies movement of the 1970s. Today, the trend is to integrate learning about diversity into the ongoing early childhood program. For example, Derman-Sparks and the A.B.C. Task Force (1989) developed the *Anti-Bias Curriculum.* Multicultural approaches are value laden and thus subject to much criticism (Derman-Sparks & the A.B.C. Task Force, 1989; C. Grant & Sleeter, 1989), although the need for such programs is not debated (Derman-Sparks & Ramsey, 1992).

FAMILY SERVICES

The field of early childhood care and education has had a long history of interest in the family as evidenced by the work of the day nursery, nursery schools, Montessori schools, kindergartens, and Head Start programs. Because research has confirmed the importance of the role of families in their children's development, programs designed for families, especially low-income families, have become increasingly popular.

Today's programs have their roots in the parent–infant classes begun in the late 1960s, such as Caldwell-Lally Children's Center (B. Caldwell, 1968), the Florida Intervention Program (I. Gordon, 1969), the Gray and Klaus project (Gray & Klaus, 1970), and the Levenstein Toy Demonstration project (Levenstein, 1970). Other projects based on the encouraging results of these pioneering programs were soon initiated. Head Start, too, had launched 36 Parent and Child Centers (PCCs) in 1967 (Head Start Bureau, 1991); however, the longitudinal research project on the PCCs was never completed (Dokecki, Hargrove, & Sandler, 1983).

By the mid- to late 1970s, policy makers were disenchanted with the idea of remediating family weaknesses. Now early childhood programs and families are seen as having distinct, but related, roles.

The Family Resource Coalition (FRC) was founded in 1981. Leaders of the family resource and support projects were interested in developing services that would serve as partners with families. They recognized the value of early childhood programs in promoting services that respond to ongoing changes that affect families and enrich family life. More specifically, the FRC assumes that (a) families have the responsibility for their children's development, (b) children must be viewed as part of families, and (c) families must be seen as part of their communities (Family Resource Coalition, 1993).

Because family resource and support programs focus on the services most needed in a community or neighborhood at a given time (Kagan, 1994a; National Task Force on School Readiness, 1991), they differ significantly. Some of these programs are federal initiatives, such as Even Start Family Literacy programs launched in 1988. Other programs are state and local initiatives. Typical programs include life skills training (e.g., literacy education, vocational training), parent information, family activities (i.e., social events for the entire family), information and referral services, and crisis intervention and counseling.

Family service projects may be center based or home based. **Home-visiting programs,** as home-based programs are often called, are strategies for supporting the development of young children through professional home visits. Home-visiting programs vary in their approach. D. Powell (1990) discussed three ways in which they may differ:

1. *The content of the visit may focus on the child only* (Levenstein, 1987) *or on the child and the family* (Kagan, Powell, Weissbourd, & Zigler, 1987). It is argued that unless the family's needs are met, the child's needs will be unfulfilled. Conversely, the child's needs may go unmet if the family needs are too pressing, or the general quality of services may diminish when home visitors attempt to provide a broad range of services.

2. *The relations between parent and home visitor differ from program to program.* Because the home visitor is on the "parents' turf," the visitor is the one who adapts. In some programs, parents are very actively involved, but in other programs, parents assume a spectator role. Programs also differ in the ways in which they attempt to get parents involved. In some programs, the professionals develop and model the activities for the parent,

whereas in other programs, parents gradually assume the planning and executing roles.

3. *Individualization of the home visit differs from program to program.* Some professionals individualize program services as they feel the need. Others individualize the content of the curriculum, sequencing activities in the order that seems most appropriate for a parent or child, selecting activities from a predetermined range of options, or encouraging parents to adopt the activities. (Families in early childhood programs are discussed further in chapter 10.)

QUALITY: THE OVERRIDING CONCERN

Although quality has been a long-discussed problem, attention has once again focused on the quality of early childhood programs, especially child care. National attention resulted from the release of data from these three studies:

1. The Cost, Quality, and Outcomes study (Helburn, 1995) found that of those centers studied, 12% were of poor quality, 15% were of high quality, and 73% were somewhere in between. The data may be skewed toward the high end because almost half of the chosen centers refused to participate (Vandell & Wolfe, 2000).

2. The Quality in Family Child Care and Relative Care study (Kontos, Howes, Shinn, & Galinsky, 1995) found quality to be lower than was noted by the Cost, Quality, and Outcomes study. Data revealed that 34% of home care programs were of poor quality, 58% were of adequate quality, and 8% were of good quality.

3. The National Institute for Child Health and Development's Study of Early Child Care (Friedman & Haywood, 1994) looked at quality in all types of settings. After the results were weighted to reflect the chosen options, researchers found that 8% of child care options provided poor care, 53% provided fair care, 30%

offered good care, and 9% offered high-quality care.

Furthermore, the studies showed that poor quality affects all age groups, including infants (NICHD Early Child Care Research Network, 1996). Higher quality programs are inequitably distributed. Children from lower income families attend poor-quality programs more often than other children unless they are poor enough to receive subsidized care (NICHD Early Child Care Research Network, 1997b). Besides the poor, most families who have children with disabilities are faced with many challenges in finding high-quality and affordable providers who will enroll their children (Booth & Kelly, 1999; J. Kelly & Booth, 1999; Warfield & Hauser-Cram, 1996).

Importance of Quality

The importance of quality has been confirmed by two reports. *Eager to Learn: Educating Our Preschoolers* (NRC, 2001) stressed that care and education are intertwined. *From Neurons to Neighborhoods: The Science of Early Childhood Development* (Shonkoff & Phillips, 2000) concluded that "the effects of child care derive not from its use or non-use but from the quality of experiences it provides to young children" (p. 307).

High-quality early childhood programs have a positive effect on learning, language, cognitive development, and school achievement (Barnett, 1995; Burchinal, Robert, Nabors, & Bryant, 1996; Ramey & Ramey, 1998). The results are often stronger for children from lower income families (C. Campbell & Ramey, 1994; Peisner-Feinberg & Burchinal, 1997). High-quality intervention should begin in the child's second year of life for maximum impact on cognitive development (NICHD Early Child Care Research Network, 2000). High-quality early childhood programs are also associated with positive social and emotional outcomes (Howes, 2000; NICHD Early Child Care Research Network, 1998a). Research from other nations supports these findings (Boocock, Barnett, & Frede, 2001).

Barriers to Program Quality

Many barriers keep early childhood programs at poor quality levels. The NAEYC (1995a) reaffirmed that the provision of high-quality early childhood programs depends on high-quality programming for children, equitable compensation for staff, and affordable services for families. Kagan, Brandon, Ripple, Maher, and Joesch (2002) stated that high-quality programs require compensation and infrastructure (regulation, professional development, and governance). The Carnegie Corporation of New York (1996) stated that the two major barriers to program quality are a lack of comprehensive community services and an insufficient integration of exiting ones.

Vision and monies are needed to achieve quality in early childhood programs. Various initiatives to enhance quality are being financed through both federal and state monies. (See chapter 6 for more details.)

Several programs are exemplars of quality. Quality in the military child development program was made possible through the Military Child Care Act of 1989, Title XV. The complete story of the military's achievement of high-quality early childhood programs is worthwhile reading (N. Campbell, Applebaum, Martinson, & Martin, 2000). Head Start also provides lessons for quality in early childhood programs. Employer-supported child care centers are often rated as excellent programs, too.

Aspects of High-Quality Programs

All aspects of early childhood programs are linked, and quality is related to each aspect. Thus, Katz (1999) called for five perspectives in judging the quality of programs for young children: "top-down" (Does the program meet licensing or other standards of quality?); "bottom-up" (What is the quality of life experienced by children on a day-by-day basis?); "outside-inside" (How do parents see their relationships with teachers?); "inside" (Are the relationships staff have with colleagues, parents, and members of the sponsoring agency cooperative and supportive?); and "outside" (How do citizens and sponsors view the program?). The need for quality and recommendations for improvement will be discussed in detail in later chapters.

Parent Choice and Quality

Families may not consider quality differences in choosing programs. In fact, discrepancies often exist between parent and expert ratings (Helburn & Culkin, 1995a, 1995b). These reasons may explain the discrepancies:

1. Parents may not have good consumer information on choosing child care. Some parents choose programs without any expert advice. Other parents may have information, but they may not read or understand it. Many parents have never seen good programs for comparison purposes. CCR&Rs are moving toward providing parents with more specific information on programs, such as the staff's education or training given as percentages, the director's qualifications, the adult–child ratio, and regulatory compliance. Some states are rating centers, which is the easiest way to make parents good consumers.

2. Parents may not monitor the services of a program before choosing and during their child's enrollment.

3. Parents may have few choices in some geographical areas.

4. The values parents place on a specific aspect of a program may overshadow quality aspects. Parents may be looking at costs, hours of services, and convenience of location. Research findings suggest that parents also seem to look for a shared value system with providers. Even

model programs have experienced low atten- dance rates (Weikart & Schweinhart, 1992). Several studies indicate that experts need to reevaluate the 'fit' between program goals and what families perceive as their needs. For exam- ple, Zinzeleta and Little (1997) found that parents were seeking programs with a heavy academic emphasis and shared religious values. A. Mitchell, Cooperstein, and Larner (1992) found that parents often choose child care in an attempt to protect their children from certain values. Thus, family members must be involved in designing and implementing high-quality ser- vices for children.

Some parents will continue to choose pro- grams of lesser quality until all programs reach an acceptable level of quality and are affordable. Until that day, quality will continue to be an over- riding concern.

TRENDS AND ISSUES

Throughout their history, early childhood pro- grams have been embedded in several profes- sions, such as psychology; education, including special education; family and consumer sciences (previously home economics); social work; and health. Programs exist in diverse settings, such as child care centers, family child care, public schools, hospitals, community centers, and social service agencies. These programs have operated under different auspices, mainly government, commercial, and not-for-profit. Most important, early childhood programs have been designed to meet various societal goals. Grubb (1991) traced the following four goals: (a) to extend the functions of the home by serving as a mother surrogate and by aiding children's learning and socialization; (b) to provide custodial care for children while parents learn job skills or work so as to avoid public assistance (e.g., the provision of child care under the Family Support Act of 1988 as part of the Job Opportunities and Basic

Skills Program); (c) to provide child care and ed- ucation while parents work; and (d) to provide compensatory education for children from low- income families and for children with special needs.

Thus, social needs have resulted in early childhood programs that have changed direc- tions frequently to reflect diverse goals. Although many needs have been met, the historical diver- sity of early childhood programs has led to new is- sues and new thinking.

From Different Historical Perspectives to a Kaleidoscope of Program Practices

The different historical perspectives have led to a kaleidoscope of practices in the implementation of children's programs. These contrasting orien- tations come from program planners', administ- rators', and teachers' beliefs about what is right for children. Programs designed by researchers often have a consistent adherence to one theo- retical and philosophical view about how chil- dren learn and about what is important for chil- dren to learn. Many programs, however, use eclectic approaches that combine differing theo- ries and philosophies. Sometimes these differing approaches are at opposite ends of a continuum from a narrow learning emphasis to a holistic de- velopment emphasis, and yet the staff members do not see the practices as possibly contradictory. For example, in some early childhood programs, teachers use drill and structured materials to teach the three Rs but allow independent explo- ration of science materials, blocks, and puppets. As another example, in some programs, children engage in projects with adults helping each child reflect on his or her learnings, and yet class man- agement centers on teacher-prescribed rules re- inforced through the use of objects, food treats, or stickers. Often, the staff of early childhood programs cannot articulate what they do in terms of theory and philosophy. Rather, they say, "It works for us," "The parents like our program," "I've always done it this way," "Today's children need . . .," and "It's required" (e.g., in terms of state curriculum guidelines).

In chapter 2, we will discuss early childhood programs designed by researchers as well as programmatic research. We will also examine in more detail the lack of consensus in program goals.

From a Focus on the Child to a Family-Centered Vision

The historical roots of early childhood programs focused on the child. Parent education programs, however, also have a rich heritage. Until recently, parents were primarily passive recipients of what early childhood educators thought was in the parents' best interests.

A shift toward a family-centered approach has begun. The trend was stimulated by the research that looked at the child's development within the context of the family (Bronfenbrenner, 1979) and by the research on model early childhood programs that found programs to be more effective when the focus was on the parent rather than only on the child (Lally, Mangione, & Honig, 1987). In addition to the research, the family support movement, begun in the 1970s and 1980s, took the ecological perspective that the child was not separate from the family and that the family was not distinct from the local community and even the larger society. This new thinking led to the family-centered approach, a "community center in which parents and teachers learn from one another and in which parents' adult needs are met" (Galinsky & Weissbourd, 1992, p. 47).

From Working in Isolation to New Community Partnerships

Family cultural values create a challenge to the delivery of child care and education in a pluralistic society (Garcia Coll & Magnuson, 2000; Lewis, 2000). As previously discussed, incorporating

more "parent culture" is important in getting parents to choose high-quality programs (Andreasen, 1995).

In the past, the early childhood community has reflected its European roots. The body of literature focusing on the need for culturally relevant programs is represented in the following documents:

1. *The Antibias Curriculum: Tools for Empowering Young Children* (Derman-Sparks & A.B.C. Task Force, 1989), which spotlighted the need for antibias education.
2. The NAEYC (1995b) position statement on linguistic and cultural diversity, which stated that early childhood programs should be responsive to children's families; communities; and "racial, ethnic, and cultural backgrounds."
3. The NAEYC's revised statement on developmentally appropriate practice (Bredekamp & Copple, 1997), which stated that decision making should be based on three areas of knowledge—what is developmentally appropriate, what is individually appropriate, and what is culturally appropriate.
4. The NAEYC's code of ethics (Feeney & Freeman, 1999), which calls for creating bridges between families' cultures, values, and child-rearing practices and those of educators.

Diversity is a hallmark of early childhood programs. Child care and education programs are always local. Thus, to be successful, programs must incorporate community culture and address constantly changing local conditions. (Program diversity will be addressed throughout the remaining chapters.)

From a Diversity of Services to Program Linkages and New Systems

The diversity of early childhood programs has led to many services, such as child care referral, child care, education, family education, employment, advocacy, and research. B. Caldwell (1991) described the situation as the "diversity of settings in which early childhood programs operate and the cacophony of labels applied to them" (p. 72). The lack of coordination among services has led to the formation of many programs, causing many services to be "stacked" in high-need areas and not available in other areas. These diverse services are provided under at least two regulatory systems (see appendix 2), and at the federal level, early childhood programs are administered by many agencies and offices (see appendix 7). Programs are pitted against each other for staff, space, and children. Many other problems are discussed throughout this book (Goodman & Brady, 1988; Kagan, 1991a).

At the 1993 National Institute for Early Childhood Professional Development, eight critical components for systemic reform were identified. One of these components was linkages across all programs serving families and children. The panel recommended that instead of providing services in isolation, professionals go beyond collaboration and "create new systems" (Galinsky, Shubilla, Willer, Levine, & Daniel, 1994, p. 54). The question becomes: Who is going to be responsible for financing, delivering, and governing services?

From Care versus Education to Comprehensive Services

The diversity of early childhood programs has led many to see care and education as two different entities. This misunderstanding perhaps emanates from the fact that kindergartens and nursery schools developed separately from child care programs. Some writers have indicated that in the 1930s child care was an essential part of child welfare programs. Efforts were made to differentiate between child care as a philanthropic activity and nursery school as an educational activity, as noted in the following statement: "This purpose (care and protection), the reasons for which a family and child may need it, and the responsibilities shared with parents distinguish a child care service from educational programs" (Child Welfare League of America [CWLA], 1960). Conversely, others believe that nursery school thinking was assimilated by workers prior to World War II in that child care programs, in keeping with the nursery school philosophy, see the teacher as assisting the child in each developmental stage, use play as the core of their curriculum, and seem to rank language and intellectual development slightly behind children's physical and affective well-being (Read, 1976).

Looking at the issue from the perspective of care, B. Caldwell (1990) believed that through these artificial distinctions between care and education and our devotion to labels, we exclude rather than include. Similarly, Kagan (1988) stated that such a differentiation leads to "undervaluing our profession" and to inappropriate practices by those who are trying to prove they teach. Seeing the issue from the perspective of education, Lombardi (1999) saw the term *education* as too limiting in terms of the traditional purposes of education. Kagan (1989) pointed out that three forces have mandated an interdependence between care and education: (a) the mandates of equal educational opportunities (e.g., *Brown v. Board of Education* decisions [1954, 1955], Title I of the Elementary and Secondary Education Act of 1965, P.L. 94–142); (b) research that underscores the interdependence of parent, child, and community; and (c) policy makers' concern about the state of our children and the ineffectiveness of delivering public services in uncoordinated ways. Early childhood professionals understand that, in fact, the field combines both education and caring. As a whole, society values education more than caring. However, a new social movement sees the necessity of providing caring supports to families (D. Stone, 2000). Noddings (1992) proposed that education be organized around centers of care.

This new thinking of early childhood programs as part of the family, the school, and the community naturally leads to a holistic approach to meeting the needs of the child within an ecological context. Comprehensive services are needed to meet these needs. With growing consensus that programs should provide for both care and education, B. Caldwell (1990) proposed the term *educare* as a way to enhance the field conceptually to embrace the many services provided. Kagan (2000c) stated that a common name would "signal our unity and force" (p. 4).

SUMMARY

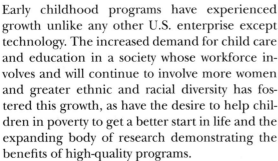

Early childhood programs have experienced growth unlike any other U.S. enterprise except technology. The increased demand for child care and education in a society whose workforce involves and will continue to involve more women and greater ethnic and racial diversity has fostered this growth, as have the desire to help children in poverty to get a better start in life and the expanding body of research demonstrating the benefits of high-quality programs.

Early childhood programs, taken collectively, constitute a diverse, rather uncoordinated system supported by various individuals and by public and private organizations with differing historical roots. The quality of early childhood programs has become an overriding concern following the release of data from three national studies of child care. Besides the concern over quality, other trends and issues include (a) very diverse program practices; (b) more emphasis on the child within the family setting and meeting the family's needs; (c) a belief in the need to build community partnerships that consider local needs and cultural values; (d) an emphasis on collaboration and linkages across various auspices funding early childhood programs; and (e) a comprehensive view (i.e., care and education) of high-quality programs for *all* children.

FOR FURTHER READING

Baum, S. J., & Edwards, E. P. (1972). *History and theory of early childhood education.* Belmont, CA: Wadsworth.

Bradburn, E. (1989). *Margaret McMillan: Portrait of a pioneer.* London: Routledge.

Elkind, D. (1983). Montessori education: Abiding contributions and contemporary challenges. *Young Children, 38*(2), 3–10.

Hansen, K. A., Kaufmann, R. K., & Saifer, S. (1996). *Education and the culture of democracy: Early childhood practice.* Washington, DC: Children's Resources International.

Hernandez, D. J. (1993). *America's children: Resources from family, government, and the economy.* New York: Sage.

Hymes, J. L., Jr. (1991). *Twenty years in review: A look at 1971–1990.* Washington, DC: National Association for the Education of Young Children.

Kagan, S. L., Goffin, S., Golub, S., & Pritchard, E. (1995). *Toward systemic reform: Service integration for young children and their families.* Falls Church, VA: National Center for Service Integration.

Weber, E. (1969). *The kindergarten: Its encounter with educational thought in America.* New York: Teachers College Press.

Zigler, E., & Muenchow, S. (1992). *Head Start: The inside story of America's most successful education experiment.* New York: Basic Books.

TO REFLECT

1. More than 150 years ago, Froebel reacted to the schools of his day by saying he did not want young children to be "schooled." He saw the kindergarten as a "children's garden" and the teacher as a gardener who nurtured the "plants" (children). What images do you see as you think of a garden and a gardener whose plants are human? If you were writing about the kindergarten of today for readers in 2150, how would you describe it? How far have we strayed from our Froebelian roots? Are the Froebelian concepts appropriate for a child in the 21st century?

2. A director of a Head Start program is writing a grant for a local program. What local needs and cultural values should be considered?

3. An early childhood director/supervisor has been asked to address a school board meeting about the need for both a care and an education focus in the new systemwide preschool program. What arguments for care would be effective in a group whose members are more likely to be concerned about educational benefits in a rather narrow sense—that is, achievement in basic academic skills?

Planning, Implementing, and Evaluating the Program

2

Directing program planning, implementation, and evaluation is the major task of the early childhood *administrator* or *director* (the terms are used interchangeably). Every aspect of a program must be designed to contribute to children's development and family needs. Directing or administering successfully requires developing a vision for a high-quality program in the planning stage, carefully implementing the program to achieve desired outcomes, and evaluating the program to determine progress toward those outcomes. In a continuous cycle of administrative tasks, program outcomes become the starting point for future planning.

PLANNING THE PROGRAM BASE

All high-quality early childhood programs have some common characteristics. All meet certain regulations or standards. For example, all have housing and equipment that are more or less designed with children in mind, and all provide activities for children.

Beyond these basic features, high-quality programs vary enormously. There is no consensus as to what goals are the best for children, how educators should achieve these goals, where to conduct the program, how to time the experiences, or how to evaluate the results. Implicit or explicit individual perspectives form the basis for each program's practice. Such a viewpoint that is well constructed may be referred to as a *program base*. Simply defined, a **program base** is a statement about the experiences of learning and teaching and the choices that educators make to control these experiences.

Either the board of directors or the administrator must determine or select a program base and use this base to develop the program rationale. In small, privately owned programs, the director (who is often the owner as well) usually makes the decision about program goals and implements the program. In larger programs, the director may present his or her views to the board of directors for approval, or the director may

work with a board of advisors in planning goals; in either case, the director implements the program. Boards of large corporations that provide services either to a large center or to centers at several sites or that provide management services only (e.g., Bright Horizons) hire program managers who make all major program decisions. The local directors are then answerable to their boards for implementation. Because all site directors are responsible for making implementation decisions consistent with the rationale, as well as for assessing program outcomes, they need to be completely familiar with and accepting of the program base.

STEPS IN PLANNING

The board's or the administrator's responsibility for planning begins with a needs assessment. (A **needs assessment** is a determination of the types of services desired and the number of children or families who could use each service.) Thus, the determination of legitimate goals for children and families who will be served by the local program is the first step in planning. Early childhood administrators need to target their efforts in response to local needs and values. Being able to address local conditions effectively is often referred to as being **culturally competent** or **sensitive** (see Table 2–1).

Once these goals are chosen, all other decisions should be consistent with the chosen view. To achieve consistency, the director must articulate these goals clearly to all those involved in the planning and implementation process. Administrators must then determine the process by which these goals will be met, operationalize the means for their achievement, and provide feedback and evaluation. In addition, directors have responsibilities for meeting regulation requirements.

Except for choosing the program base or goals, there is no linear progression in planning an early childhood program. In fact, all other aspects of planning should be considered simultaneously because all facets influence each other.

Table 2–1   Assessing Local Needs Through Culturally Sensitive Questions

What are the needs of local families? What services are valid for the group to be served?

What are the local values (e.g., tradition versus change; competition versus cooperation; perceived value of early childhood programs)? How diverse is the local population, and how does this diversity affect generalizations concerning local values?

What communication skills are needed?

What services are now available? Are there children or families who do not get needed, but locally available, services? Are there any cultural barriers preventing these children or families from being served?

What human resources are available in the local community? How can the community be involved in the planning and delivery of these services? How should we organize to get these services? What type of leadership style is preferred in the local community?

What material resources (e.g., parks, health care, social agencies) are available in the community? How are these resources perceived by the local population? Is there a single institution serving as the center of a service network?

Figure 2–1 depicts the administrator's role in planning, implementing, and evaluating the program.

FACTORS DETERMINING THE PROGRAM BASE

Few early childhood educators have a systematic program base from which they determine practice. Without such a base, problems and confusions arise. And all too often, the reverse happens—namely, theories and value statements are used to justify current practices.

Proper Sources

The two most relevant sources for determining program base are theoretical and philosophical positions. The theoretical position comes from

(a) psychological theories that help in answering questions about what children can learn and (b) the ecological perspective of the child (the sociocultural context) that examines the impact of the socialization processes on the child's development. The philosophical position comes from values for children individually and collectively, both now and in the future, and thus is concerned with what children ought to know.

Psychological Theories.   Three major psychological theories have influenced early childhood education. The first school of thought, which permeated the literature from the 1930s through the 1950s, is the **maturational view,** in which development is seen as the result of the maturation of structures within the individual (Gesell, 1931). According to this view, the dominant aspect of development is genetic construction.

Genetic influences are substantial (Plomin, 1997). The maturational view holds that teachers should provide educative experiences when the child shows interest. Today's maturationists believe that the genes guide the process of maturation, and teaching or nurturing determines the specific content of what an individual learns (e.g., naming colors) and influences to some degree the rate and extent of learning. Through the use of norms, the maturationists have developed "expectations" for children at different ages that prevent a child from being hurried by poorly timed experiences. In the 1950s, the integration of assumptions from the psychoanalytic theories with the maturational theory brought about the child development approach (Jersild, 1946).

The second school of thought is the **behavioral-environmental view** (Skinner, 1938). In this view, the environment, rather than genetic construction, has the dominant role in learning. Learning is viewed as environmental inputs and behavioral outputs. The focus is not on mental processes but on eliciting and reinforcing verbal, perceptual, and motor behaviors. Behaviorism provides the theoretical rationale for the traditional view of teaching as direct instruction with

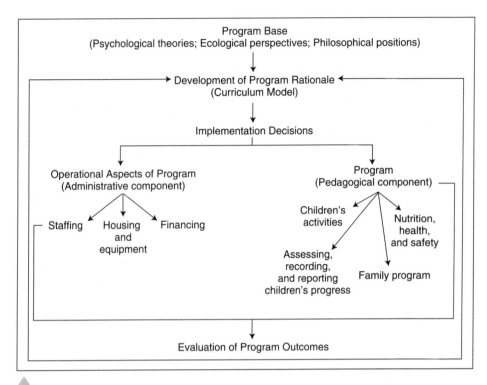

Figure 2–1   Framework for Program Planning, Implementation, and Evaluation

sequenced goals and objectives and corresponding materials. The teacher verbally communicates the desired behavior or physically models the behavior and reinforces the child for making the appropriate response following the cue. Some psychologists see this approach as having these two serious limitations: (a) learnings are limited to the acquisition of specific items of information and (b) the child's motivation for learning may be different from what the teacher intended (e.g., the child was motivated by individual attention from the teacher rather than by his or her own success).

The third school of thought is the **constructivist view.** Constructivism, as formulated by Jean Piaget in the 1920s, saw children as interacting with their environment and constructing their own intellect. Constructivists, who directly challenge the behaviorists, see genetic makeup and

environment (nature and nurture) as more or less equal in shaping development. Unlike the behaviorists, both the maturationists and the constructivists describe the child as moving from one stage to another. Unlike the maturationists, who see the progression of development at more or less predictable ages, constructivists see development as the result of experience with objects and consultation with people coupled with the way in which the individual interprets, recognizes, or modifies experience.

Lev Vygotsky was a contemporary of Piaget. His theory (Vygotsky, 1978) complements Piaget's by emphasizing socially constructed knowledge. Although Vygotsky agreed with Piaget concerning the role of personal experiences, he also felt that knowledge was constructed as a result of social experiences with peers and adults. To Vygotsky, initial learning begins on the social plane—that is, learners are guided by the instruction of others. Cognitive strategies are eventually transferred to the psychological plane (i.e., humans learn of their own volition), but these learnings are permanently imbued with their social origins. Because he theorized that cognitive development occurs in a social–cultural context, his theory can be classified as **social constructivism.** Along with the ideas of Vygotsky, post-Piagetian theorists speak of more than one type of intelligence (Gardner, 1983).

Ecological Perspectives. Ecological perspectives are concerned with how learning and development are influenced by the uniqueness of a person's environments. Bronfenbrenner (1979, 1989) suggested that an ecological perspective be applied to all behaviors. Bronfenbrenner (1986) suggested that people live in multiple environments simultaneously. He described the ecological context that a child experiences and that affects development as four different but overlapping systems:

- The microsystem, the immediate and powerful socializer of children, comprises the family, child care or school, peers, media, and community.

- The mesosystem consists of overlapping microsystems, such as parent–teacher interaction or employer-supported child care.

- The exosystem consists of parents' jobs, city government, the school board, community services, and the federal government. A child may be influenced indirectly by the exosystem. For example, parents whose employment requires conformity are likely to adopt an autocratic or authoritarian parenting style.

- The macrosystem or culture consists of socioeconomic, racial or ethnic, geographic and American ideological, religious, and political cultures. Because culture has a profound effect, Cole (1998) embedded environments within a cultural context.

Two theories with ecological perspectives are of interest to early childhood educators. Erik Erikson's (1950) *psychosocial theory* describes how children develop the foundation for personality and mental health. Erikson noted that the environment shapes personality through both limitations and freedoms (i.e., provides the range of behaviors and learning circumscribed by society as directed through significant relations, such as parents, and provides freedom of choice for the individual throughout his life). He stated that his eight developmental crises (e.g., sense of trust versus mistrust) are universal, but that the central problem (e.g., weaning) faced in a given crisis period is culturally determined.

As previously mentioned, Vygotsky's theory, which he aptly described as "mind in society" (Vygotsky, 1978), has a decided ecological perspective. According to Vygotsky, the learner engages in problem-solving activities in which an adult or more capable peer guides and models (called *scaffolding* by D. Wood, Bruner, and Ross, 1976) ways to solve the task that are between each child's independent problem-solving capability and what he or she can do with assistance, called the **zone of proximal development (ZPD).** Through participation in authentic cultural activities with social interactions, children learn cultural "tools of the mind" (i.e., symbol systems, such as language) and eventually use these tools to engage in internal cognitive activity. Thus, the child's social environment provides the needed support system that allows the child to develop new competencies; that is, learning in a social context leads to development.

Philosophical Positions. Schools are designed to meet social purposes. This fact has been recognized since the time of Plato, who described education in *The Republic* as preparation of children to do the state's bidding. Like Plato, Dewey believed that education is the fundamental lever of social progress (Dewey, 1897). Conversely, during the 1960s the emphasis on psychological theories almost overshadowed philosophical positions.

Some early childhood professionals expressed the opinion that psychological theory alone cannot be the sole basis for determining program design (Egan, 1983; J. Hunt, 1961).

Several program designers suggested that a blend of the psychological and philosophical views was needed. Kohlberg and Mayer (1972) stated that philosophically desirable ends must be rooted in the "facts of development." "Philosophical principles cannot be stated as ends of education until they can be stated psychologically" (p. 485). They also saw psychological theories as having either implicit or explicit values and stated that when theories are used as the basis for program design they become ideologies.

B. Caldwell (1977) pointed out that the current generation seems afraid to specify what it wants for its children. According to Caldwell, Americans say they want their children to become "what they are capable of becoming"; however, we know that what they are capable of becoming depends to a great extent on experiences chosen for them by adults. Similarly, Americans say the school's purpose is "to let children find out who they are," and it is unfashionable "to say we teach them anything." Caldwell believes that this lack of specific educational goals is a result of a vague national ideology or a voiced national ideology inconsistent with what is observed (e.g., a lack of ethics in high places). She concludes that U.S. schools must be based on articulated values—values considered good for society.

The need for a philosophical position as a base for program design seems clear. Whether the lack of a philosophical basis is the result of a vague ideology, dominance of psychological theories, or other causes, the dilemma posed by this gap in value base was pinpointed by Sommerville (1982), who stated, "Children are going to school for an ever-longer period, but we seem less and less sure about what they should be getting from it" (p. 16). Thus, the critical question is, What kind of U.S. citizen do we need to meet the challenges and opportunities of the 21st century? Like Dewey (1916), we must emphasize the im-

portance of communicating with each other the values we will share in our programs and schools.

Several ideas for values have been suggested, including the Golden Rule, which is seen as a common value taught in most major religions. Other values often suggested are "honesty, caring, fairness, respect, and perseverance" (B. Smith, 1997, p. 233). The NAEYC and the National Association of Early Childhood Specialists in State Departments of Education (1991) have suggested that a free society "should reflect the ideals of a participatory democracy, such as personal autonomy, decision making, equality, and social justice" (p. 28).

Synthesis of Proper Sources. When the NAEYC first issued its position statements on developmentally appropriate practice (DAP; Bredekamp, 1987), the statements seemed to lean heavily on psychological theories for age-appropriate and individually appropriate curricula. Some asserted that DAP did not address (or obscured) other aspects of program planning (Kostelnik, 1992; Spodek, 1991a, B. Swadener & Kessler, 1991b). In an attempt to address these concerns, the NAEYC (1997a) issued a revised statement acknowledging that curricular decisions must be based on a knowledge of child development and learning, individual children's characteristics and strengths, and the social and cultural contexts in which children live.

Spodek's (1991a) dimensions for program planning and evaluation seem to be a synthesis of psychological theories, ecological perspectives, and philosophical positions. Spodek called for the use of these three dimensions for judging educational programs: (a) developmental (considers what children can learn and the methodology employed in teaching), (b) cultural (acknowledges society's values—that is, what we want children to be and become), and (c) knowledge (addresses what children need to know today and in the future to function successfully). Katz (1991a) said that three interrelated a priori questions must be asked to identify appropriate program development: (a) What should be learned? (this deals with goals), (b) When should it be learned? (this deals with child development), and (c) How is it best learned? (this considers program implementation of goals).

Improper Sources

Several improper sources have been used for program design. Later school content and narrow definitions of readiness, assessment practices, and policies of funding agencies are the most common improper sources.

Later School Content and Narrow Definitions of Readiness. On the one hand, goals of the present program should be consistent with those of the programs that children will be involved in later. Without continuity, the child may experience a loss of gains. Participation in one type of preschool program may interfere with learning in a later program if the programs are greatly disparate in approach. The concern for continuity in early childhood programs in all areas, such as curriculum and assessment, environment, management, and links to parents and the community, is a major concern today (Barbour & Seefeldt, 1993; Love, Logue, Trudeau, & Thayer, 1992).

On the other hand, the goals of any program should center on the child's present benefit and not merely on preparation for the future. A great deal of concern has been expressed over the accelerating downward shift of what were next-grade expectations into lower grades (L. Shepard & Smith, 1988, p. 136), a top-down curricular perspective.

Closely related to a top-down curriculum is the narrow definition of readiness. For many years, the term *readiness* has been applied to many activities of the early childhood program (e.g., reading readiness, mathematics readiness) and even to the names of some of the assessment devices used with young children. These readiness skills were considered necessary to prepare children for later schooling. Recently, concerns

have surfaced over using an academically narrow definition of readiness to learn (Goal 1 Technical Planning Group, 1993; R. Hitz & Richter, 1993; S. Robinson, 1993/94). Although some readiness skills may be worth learning and continuity between present and future programs is valuable, planning a program solely on the basis of future content is faulty because (a) readiness skills are not goals in themselves but rather are means to goals, (b) the advantages gained in "crash" preparation may be lost, (c) formal readiness training may be detrimental in itself (Burts, Hart, Charlesworth, Fleege, Mosley, & Thomasson, 1992; Charlesworth, Hart, Burts, & DeWolf, 1993; Hart, Burts, Durland, Charlesworth, DeWolf, & Fleege, 1998; Marcon, 1992, 1994a), and (d) the use of later school content as a source for early childhood program design reflects circular reasoning that avoids assessing value.

Assessment Practices. Assessment of children's progress in a program is essential. If the content of the assessment instruments and the techniques used in the assessment process relate closely to a program's objectives, assessment results may be used to add to or revise content or methodology to help meet stated objectives. However, one must avoid the pitfall of using assessment instruments that do not match a program's goals and of letting those instruments determine content or methodology.

Policies of Funding Agencies. Funding agencies have a great deal of control over programs. Examples of this control may be seen in the established goals of federal programs (e.g., Head Start Performance Objectives), legislation and master plans developed by state task forces for public school curricula, local boards' (school boards or boards of directors or advisors) decisions on curricular practices, and curriculum guides published by the funding agencies. Program design must be in the hands of professionals. Funding agencies alone determining program design is similar to test items being used for program design (the "tail wagging the dog").

OVERVIEW OF CURRICULUM MODELS

A **curriculum model** is based on the program base and contains the administrative and pedagogical components of an educational plan. Curriculum models are associated with the intervention programs of the 1960s. Following J. Hunt's (1961) and P. Bloom's (1964) work, which showed intellectual plasticity, psychologists wanted to learn whether the early years were critical and whether early childhood programs could compensate for children's disadvantaged environments (Clarke-Stewart, 1988). Their research extended to curriculum development. The curriculum model was presumed valid for achieving certain outcomes (Spodek, 1973a).

Models Based on Psychological Theories

Fein and Schwartz (1982) contrasted theories of development with theories in practice. A **theory of development** offers general statements about factors affecting children's behaviors. Such theories do not offer principles for modifying or generating those factors. In contrast, a **theory in practice** describes what a practitioner must do to encourage particular behaviors. This section discusses six theories of practice.

Child Development Model.   Until the 1960s, most early childhood programs serving middle-class populations were based on concepts stemming from the maturational theory and were called the **child development model.** Many authors now refer to it as the traditional nursery school model (Goffin & Wilson, 2001). Although initial Head Start programs followed this model rather closely, many psychologists believed that the model, developed for middle-class children, would not be effective for children from low-income families who were not developing certain academic competencies in their homes (Powell, 1987a). Although the model is seldom used in research today, Table 2–2 presents a synopsis of its components.

Direct-Instruction Models.   Direct instruction (D-I) models follow the *behavioral-environmental theory* which is now called *educational learning theory* (Bereiter, 1990). Educational learning theory is not based on a theory of child development; rather, it is based on certain principles of learning not related to age or development.

The first D-I model was called the **Bereiter-Englemann model (B-E),** a preschool model. The B-E was replaced with the **Englemann-Becker Direct Instruction model** and was later called the D-I model. D-I models are designed to make the curriculum more effective in reaching the academic goals of the school. The teachers aim to teach facts and skills that the program designers consider necessary for functioning in the mainstream culture which are lacking in the children served. Thus, carefully structured academic content (i.e., sequences from simple to complex) is taught in direct ways (i.e., instruction begins with showing students each step in the problem-solving process with a heavy emphasis on language), and reinforcers are applied.

With the D-I programs came tensions between developmental and academic orientations. Because D-I approaches are so aligned with the practices of the schools and are seen as a "quick fix" for high-risk children, these models, with some modifications, are still popular. For example, D-I is used in the "Success for All" model (Fashola & Slavin, 1998; Slavin & Madden, 2001; Slavin, Madden, Dolan, & Wasik, 1996).

Table 2–3 presents a synopsis of three components of the D-I models.

Specific programs differ and are discussed in the section "Differences Within a Theory." Additional information on specific programs is located in appendix 1.

Piagetian-Based Models.   Piaget's theory of the development of rational thinking became accepted in the 1960s at the beginning of the focus on science and technology in the United States (Silin, 1995). Originally, several program designers used specific Piagetian experimental tasks, such as those outlined in the Cognitively Ori-

Table 2–2   Child Development Model

Program Base

Based on the theories of Gesell, Freud, and Erikson.

Considers children to be born with a genetic blueprint for certain patterns of behavior. Sees behavioral changes occurring as a result of physiological maturation (readiness) and environmental situations that encourage certain behaviors (developmental tasks).

Administrative Component

Housing	Roomy environment is calculated to give maximum mobility. Learning centers are only somewhat defined.
Equipment	Rich assortment of multidimensional materials that serve many modes of expression (e.g., language, mathematics, motor, aesthetic) are chosen.
	Developmental levels of children served are considered.
Staff	Provide a warm, supportive environment. Do few, if any, prescribed learning activities, but "enrich" ongoing activities when children need to expand their understandings/skills.
	Set limits and redirect unacceptable social behaviors.

Pedagogical Component

Activities	Units and broad themes based on studies of children's interests are introduced; children are free to "sample" activities as they wish.
	Activities based on the theme are carried out by play with materials located in the learning centers and by field trips.
	Activities are almost completely child selected, rather than adult prescribed.
Motivational strategy	Verbal extrinsic motivation (e.g., praise).
Grouping	Heterogeneous grouping (family grouping) is most common. Occasional, loosely defined homogeneous groups are based on age/stage.
Scheduling	Flexible schedules are designed to fit children's needs and interests.
	Large blocks of time in which a child may work on a single activity or change activities are typical.
Assessment of children	Attempts are made to observe the whole child (physical, cognitive, and affective), primarily using naturalistic observations.

Program Evaluation

A program is seen as successful if children progress according to physical, cognitive, and affective norms.

Allowances are made when children are seen as having hereditary or environmental constraints placed on their development.

Table 2–3   Direct-Instruction Models

Program Base

Based on theories of Skinner, Baer, Bijou, and Bandura.

Considers children to be born with a "blank slate"; passive children's behaviors are shaped by the environment.

Sees behavioral changes occurring as a result of reinforcing planned or unplanned events.

Administrative Component

Housing	Less roomy environment is calculated to focus children's attention and to avoid distractions. Areas within the room are clearly defined—often with high dividers.
Equipment	More narrowly focused and unidimensional materials are used that meet program-selected objectives and serve one mode of expression (e.g., language).
Staff	Plan and control the environment. Almost all activities are adult prescribed. Do much direct (expository) teaching of small units of materials that have been broken down from larger tasks and sequenced.
	Use principles of behavior modification to prevent and control deviant behavior.

Pedagogical Component

Activities	Goal-oriented activities designed to achieve specific cultural learnings, usually academic in nature, are provided; the same learnings are often expected of all children.
	Activities are conducted by direct teaching, often in a drill format.
	Activities are adult prescribed, rather than child selected.
Motivational strategy	Incentive systems with extensive sources of motivation-token-economy systems.
Grouping	Homogeneous grouping dominates.
Scheduling	Brisk-paced program is presented on a tight (clock-bound) schedule.
	Blocks of time are short, with all children in a group staying on task throughout the lesson.
Assessment of children	Instructional levels are sequenced. Initial instructional levels are diagnosed by formal evaluation. As children meet the objectives at a given level, they progress to the next "rung on the instructional ladder."

Program Evaluation

A program is seen as successful if children have achieved specific learnings, which are often academic (a preparation for later school learnings).

ented Curriculum, now revised and called High/Scope (Weikart, Rogers, Adcock, & McClelland, 1971) and in the curriculum developed by Lavatelli (1970).

Further studies of the educational implications of Piaget's theory led most researchers to be concerned with Piaget's general theory of cognitive development, referred to as *constructivism,* and with the stages that emerged from his clinical studies of children, called *structuralism.* Today, some researchers emphasize constructivism, whereas others focus on structuralism.

High/Scope, which now has programs designed for infants and toddlers, preschoolers, and children in kindergarten through the primary grades, is perhaps the most popular Piagetian-based program in early childhood. High/Scope is based on the Piagetian principle that through active learning children construct knowledge that is critical for academic success. Preschoolers are involved in a child-initiated "plan–do–review" sequence in which they establish goals, carry them out, and recall the activities. Other activities are teacher-initiated small-group projects, large-group activities, and outdoor play. Four dispositions associated with this active learning process are (a) initiative (as the child acts on objects), (b) reflections on actions, (c) intrinsic motivation, and (d) problem solving of real-life problems by acting on objects and interacting with others. Besides active learning, the curriculum focuses on social and communication skills and representations. Key experiences, based on the works of theorists, serve as teachers' guideposts for the content knowledge and cognitive processes inherent in all activities and are used in planning activities, encouraging children's active learning, and interpreting their actions (M. Hohmann & Weikart, 1995).

Table 2–4 presents a synopsis of the three components of the constructivist mode. Additional information on specific programs is located in appendix 1.

Developmental-Interaction Model. The developmental-interaction model was formerly called the Bank Street approach. The approach has its roots in the experimental nursery school and is linked to the progressive education movement. The developmental-interaction approach is part of psychodynamic theory, in which development is seen as dynamic and individual. Thus, these researchers see the educational process as a dynamic exchange between the child and the environment.

For many years, the approach was an experimental practice. The theoretical framework was eventually shaped by Biber so the program could be used for comparative studies. Once written, practice began to be related to the curriculum, and curriculum guidelines have now been published. The approach has changed over the years because supporters see research and practice constantly informing each other (Biber, 1984; Shapiro & Biber, 1972). Shapiro and Nager (2000) are now looking at the future prospects for the approach.

Table 2–5 presents a synopsis of the components of the developmental-interaction model. Additional information is located in appendix 1.

Montessori Model. Montessori did not rely on one or more of the theorists; her roots were in special education. Beyond this experience, Montessori was singly responsible for the design and dissemination of her ideas. Her programs are often referred to as the *structured environment* or *prepared environment* approach.

After the late 1970s decline in interest in models, the Montessori method was used primarily in private schools. More recently, however, the Montessori method is being used in public schools and publicly funded charter school programs (Schapiro & Hellen, 1998). There are many questions about models that, like the Montessori approach, remain static (Simons & Simons, 1986). Table 2–6 presents a synopsis of the components of Montessori's program. Additional information on the approach is found in appendix 1.

Ecologically Based Models. Vygotsky saw social interactions and assisted discovery as critical to higher mental functions. Through interactions, children learn to use cultural "tools of the mind" (i.e., culturally embedded forms of representation, such as language, art, and maps). These tools serve as a bridge between the sociocultural world and individual mental functionings. Thus, the social environment constitutes the support system for internalized psychological development. Because mental activity is derived from the cultural context, wide variations in cognitive capacities occur.

Table 2–4   Piagetian-Based Models

Program Base
Based primarily on the theories of Piaget and Vygotsky.
Considers children a product of heredity and environment.
Describes development as occurring when a person's self-organization (denoted by a stage that is qualitatively different from other stages) is challenged to an optimal degree by experiential events.

Administrative Component	
Housing	Roomy environment is designed to give children opportunities to be actively involved. Learning centers are more defined than in the maturational model, but children's interaction among learning centers is encouraged.
Equipment	Multidimensional materials encourage exploration and problem solving and are arranged in a way to convey the idea of a conceptual order.
	Children's needs for concrete and representational materials are considered.
Staff	Arrange activities that challenge the current level of development. At times, the adult is active (giving new challenges); at other times, the adult is passive (waiting for the child's new learnings to be stabilized). Adults often emphasize language that accompanies children's developing concepts.
	Plan and guide children toward self-discipline.

Pedagogical Component	
Activities	Emphasis is placed on the heuristics of learning (e.g., problem-solving strategies, elaboration skills, questioning techniques); academic content, often presented in units or themes, is seen as a means to an end, not an end in itself.
	Planned activities are provided, and children are encouraged to be actively involved. Adults interact in ways to help structure children's activities (e.g., ask open-ended questions).
	Activities are adult arranged for their potential to engage and challenge; children select among the activities.
Motivational strategy	Intrinsic motivation (e.g., epistemic curiosity).
Grouping	Heterogeneous grouping dominates; much individual work.
Scheduling	Sequenced activities are thought to aid children's temporal concepts; however, there is built-in flexibility.
	Large blocks of time are provided so that children may explore.
Assessment of children	Progress is noted if thinking skills change (if a child moves to a more advanced stage of development).

Program Evaluation
A program is seen as successful if children progress to higher stages of development in terms of Piaget's theory (e.g., physical knowledge, logico-mathematical knowledge, spatiotemporal knowledge, social knowledge, representation).

Table 2–5   Developmental-Interaction Model

Program Base

Based primarily on the theories of Wertheimer, Lewin, Erikson, Werner, and Piaget and the educational researchers and practitioners of Dewey, Issacs, Johnson, Mitchell, and Pratt.

The name refers to the emphasis on identifiable patterns of growth and ways of perceiving (developmental) and to the child's interactions with the environment and to the interactions between the cognitive and affective spheres (interaction).

Administrative Component

Housing	Roomy environment is designed to give children opportunities to be involved. Learning centers are marked.
Equipment	Materials for painting, water play, block building, dramatic play; books placed on open shelves. These materials are often mass produced and homemade. Some structured materials are available to aid perceptual discrimination and manipulative problem solving (e.g., peg form boards and puzzles).
Staff	Establish mutually trusting relationship. Teacher is the mediator of children's learning experiences, a reflective surface for the evolving self-concept, and the model for human interchange. Considered the most important figure in creating the classroom climate.

Pedagogical Component

Activities	Explore the physical world to develop powers of observation and discrimination, extend modes of symbolic expression (dramatic play and the arts), develop language facility and stimulate verbal-conceptual organization, learn about the social environment, learn impulse control and how to cope with conflicts, and develop a self-concept. Social studies is the core of the integrated curriculum.
Motivational strategy	Emphasize intrinsic motivation toward competence and satisfaction of meaningful learning; consider motivation as an aid to becoming an autonomous individual.
Grouping	Heterogeneous grouping.
Scheduling	Sequenced activities are scheduled so that children know what to expect and can develop a sense of temporal order.
Assessment of children	Goals are not endpoints but informants that support the developmental processes in children.

Program Evaluation

The program is based not on understanding children but on informing practice. The overall value is based on humanistic views of optimal human functioning linked to John Dewey's philosophy of democratic living.

Table 2–6   Montessori Model

Program Base

Based solely on Montessori's own theory.

Considers children as psychological, spiritual, and biological "creatures" endowed with a plan of organic development.

Development is expressed through spontaneous activity.

Administrative Component

Housing	Roomy environment that consists of several rooms (e.g., principal room has space for intellectual work—didactic materials; sitting room or parlor for children's casual interactions; dining room with accessible cupboards, etc.; and direct access to a real garden) or one room with low shelves and materials arranged by type and sequenced by difficulty level.
Equipment	Didactic materials were designed to exercise the senses and bring order to the perceptions. Writing and reading are taught with specialized didactic materials.
	Practical life activities were designed to facilitate independence in care of self and the environment.
Staff	Teachers structure the alignment between the child and the auto-educational activities. Because teachers do not teach but ensure the child–material match, teachers are called "directors" and "directresses."

Pedagogical Component

Activities	Emphasis is placed on a carefully planned and orderly environment; sensory, language, mathematics, motor, and practical-life activities are designed to be used in a self-pacing way.
Motivational strategy	Intrinsic motivation.
Grouping	Heterogeneous grouping.
Scheduling	Most types of activities are conducted in 1-hour intervals (see Goffin & Wilson, 2001, p. 57).
Assessment of children	Progress is noted through the naturalistic observation of children. Most materials have a self-correcting component that provides feedback to the child.

Program Evaluation

The program is seen as successful if children have sequential mastery of the materials.

Vygotsky's sociocultural theory is used primarily in the Reggio Emilia schools in Italy. As a result of early childhood educators' interest in the preschools of Reggio Emilia in the 1980s, Vygotsky's theory and the Reggio Emilia approach have received much attention. Although Loris Malguizzi conceived the Reggio Emilia approach in 1945, the preprimary schools for 3- to 6-year-old children began in 1968, and the infant schools for 4-month to 3-year-old children began in 1971. The preschools' curriculum is designed as long-term projects with many facets to develop all the "languages" of children, such as the expressive, cognitive, and logical (Gardner, 1998). Emphasis is placed on the use of cultural symbol systems. The themes, determined through joint teacher and child decision making, often focus on the community and its activities. The school is seen as a community of learners—a sociocultural system whose central focus is the social construction of knowledge. Children are supported in their learnings through adult and peer scaffolding; teachers are supported by other professionals and parents in their reflective practice; and the school is supported through its visibility and linkages with the community at large.

Table 2–7 presents information on programs based on Vygotsky's theory. Additional information is found in appendix 1.

Table 2–7   Ecologically Based Model (Reggio Emilia)

Program Base

Based on the theories of Vygotsky, Dewey, Piaget, Bronfenbrenner, J. Bruner, D. Hawkins, and J. Gardner.
Considers the school a culture of learning for adults and children.
Relies on "different wisdoms" of families (Spaggiari, 1998).

Administrative Component

Housing	Aesthetically attractive environment.
	Large spaces for work areas and for sharing ideas with all involved.
	Adult space is considered important.
	Classroom space is considered an educational component (Gandini, 1998).
Equipment	Many diverse materials to carry out projects.
Staff	Construct the curriculum through collaboration with the entire community.
	Provide direct assistance to children by scaffolding.
	Observe and document children's work.
	Use collaboration and reflection to guide teaching.
	Raise the community's understanding of the program's benefits.

Pedagogical Component

Activities	In-depth project work that emerges from the interests of children and teachers.
Motivational strategy	Interests in projects and interactions with others (Gandini, 1993; Malaguzzl, 1993).
Grouping	Heterogeneous grouping through mixed ages.
Scheduling	Large blocks of time for work on projects.
Assessment of children	Observation and documentation helps teachers reflect (C. Edwards, 1998), aids children's recall of their work (G. Forman & Fyfe, 1998), and serves as the basis for communication with families and the community (Rabitti, 1994).

Program Evaluation

A program is seen as successful when documentation is presented to families and the community showing children's and teachers' learnings.

Differences Within a Theory. Models that derive their program rationale from the same theoretical base often differ in many essential ways because some elements of theory get discarded and others are added. For example, G. Forman and Fosnot (1982) analyzed six Piagetian programs in relationship to four propositions that undergird Piagetian theory. Each of these programs' pedagogical designs focused on the propositions in a different way. Another example is the differences seen by Kamii and DeVries, who are Piagetian researchers. Although neither researcher is presently involved in programmatic research, at one time Kamii focused on the process by which cognitive development occurred (constructivism). Conversely, DeVries collaborated with Kohlberg in establishing curriculum goals using Piaget's stages as a frame of reference (structuralism); they saw development (i.e., sequence through the stages) as the aim of education. (For a more complete discussion, see Goffin and Wilson, 2001, pp. 132–150.) As an example of within-theory differences under the D-I theoretical umbrella, the Behavioral Analysis Program of Project Follow Through focused on a set of narrow goals (Bushell, 1973), in comparison with the goals set forth by Bijou (1976).

Within-theory differences also occur in model programs because of the ages of the children served. On the one hand, Honig and Brill (1970) used the sensorimotor stage theory of Piaget to enhance the development of infants during their first year of life. On the other hand, the Early Childhood Education Project (Sigel, Secrist, & Forman, 1973) in Buffalo, New York, used the Piagetian theory of representational knowledge (noting that real "things" can be represented in two- and three-dimensional forms) as the pedagogical component for 2- and 3-year-old children.

When more than one theoretical base is combined in a model program, the pedagogical design differs from single-base programs. For example, Biber's (M. Day, 1977) initial foundation for the Bank Street program was the educational philosophy of John Dewey. Later, Piaget's and Erikson's psychological theories were used to give a firmer foundation for the Bank Street program's pedagogical component. Both High/Scope and the Reggio Emilia schools also rely on more than one theory as the foundation for practice. Biber (1984) supported the concept of a broader theoretical base achieved by combinations of theories that have a common ideological base but differ in substantive ways.

Finally, a curriculum model is an on-paper representation of a program. For research purposes, curriculum models stress uniform ways of teaching and learning. However, once implemented, a program will only approach the model. For example, even in a study of the highly articulated High/Scope curriculum model, O'Brien (1993) found that children's learning environments varied with what teachers thought was important for children's development and learning. Perhaps even greater variation would occur in programs based on less articulated models.

Current Thinking. Development of program models slowed by the 1980s because of cutbacks in federal funds. Program designers continued to make program modifications based on their research. A few new program initiatives occurred in the 1980s that were concerned with specific populations in our diverse society (Carlsson-Paige and Levin, 1985; Derman-Sparks & the A.B.C. Task Force, 1989; Hale-Benson, 1982, 1986).

In the 1990s there was a resurgence of interest in the models due to the first goal of Goals 2000 (U.S. Department of Education, 1991), heightened concern about the low academic achievement of children from low-income families and the demands for accountability (Carnegie Corporation of New York, 1996; Kagan & Cohen, 1997), findings from neuroscience on early brain development (Bruer, 1999), and studies showing the low quality of U.S. child care programs as discussed in chapter 1. Many believed that the adoption of models was the best way to bolster program quality (Pogrow, 1996) and to provide a cost-beneficial program with proven outcomes that ensured children's readiness to enter school (Weikart, 1995). Interest also moved beyond models to specific subject matter, especially literacy (NRC, 1999c).

Summary of Programmatic Research

Three waves of programmatic research have occurred. The first wave of research was conducted on compensatory programs that began in the 1960s and early 1970s. In the 1960s, many early childhood programs were designed to break the cycle of poverty. The assumption was that family poverty led to scholastic failure and to subsequent poverty as an adult. Many types of models were tried and compared. Some of these early programs were thought to develop the whole child, but most were designed to correct perceived language, perceptual, and conceptual deficits. Proponents of academically oriented programs argued that their programs were most important in enhancing intellectual and school achievement. Discovery, or informal, method supporters saw social skills and autonomy as areas of major importance to young children. Taking a middle view were those who looked to Piagetian theory as a basis of curriculum design. These programs tried to influence children's thinking and processing skills. Programs were also extended upward (e.g., Follow Through) and downward (e.g., infant and toddler programs). Researchers sought the link between short-, mid-, and long-term effects. The model for linking the effects is as follows:

1. Children from impoverished families who attend a high-quality preschool program are better prepared for school cognitively and affectively.
2. This preparedness results in greater school success (i.e., fewer grade retentions and less need for special education placements).

3. This greater success in school leads to greater life success (i.e., lower rates of delinquency, teenage pregnancy, and welfare usage and higher rates of school completion). Table 2–8 presents a summary of the research on the compensatory education models of the 1960s and 1970s.

The second wave of programmatic research was conducted primarily on state-launched prekindergarten programs serving young children such as Head Start, public school prekindergartens, and child care programs in the late 1970s and throughout the 1980s. Table 2–9 presents a synopsis of findings.

The third wave of programmatic research, begun in the 1980s and early 1990s, was conducted on family-focused programs. Some of these programs were family support programs that served families with children under age 3 and involved parents in acquiring child development knowledge and parenting skills. Other programs were two-generational programs that linked programs for children and parenting support with adult-oriented services (e.g., adult education, job training). Table 2–10 presents a synopsis of the preliminary research findings for these programs.

The two themes dominating early childhood special education studies prior to the mid-1980s were the efficacy of early intervention and full-inclusion programs. With the passage of P.L. 99–457 in 1986, the social context, especially the family, was included in the studies of early intervention. Table 2–11 presents a summary of the findings from major studies on early childhood special education.

Although early studies of curriculum models seemed to produce program outcomes consistent with program goals, for many years professionals considered the comparative outcomes of different program bases negligible. In recent years, however, a resurgence of interest in the models has occurred. Researchers are again examining the effectiveness of various models by doing

Table 2–8   Summary of Research on Compensatory Education: Models of the 1960s and Early 1970s

Single-Project Research Results

Cognitive functioning (as measured by IQ tests) for participants was immediately sizable but diminished throughout the elementary years (Berrueta-Clement, 1984; Gray, Ramsey, & Klaus, 1982; Irvine, 1982; McKey et al., 1985; Westinghouse Learning Corporation, 1969).

Participants had fewer grade repetitions, fewer special education placements, and more high school completions (Berrueta-Clement et al., 1984; Gray, Ramsey, & Klaus, 1982; Irvine, 1982; McKey et al., 1985).

Participants were more likely to be employed as adults (Berrueta-Clement et al., 1984).

Participants had fewer arrests (Berrueta-Clement et al., 1984).

Achievement differences for participants were minimal and tended to fade out (Berrueta-Clement et al., 1984; Gray, Ramsey, & Klaus, 1982; Westinghouse Learning Corporation, 1969).

When Gray, Ramsey, and Klaus's (1982) data were analyzed by gender, the program was shown to benefit girls more than boys.

Curriculum Comparison Studies

Head Start Planned Variation Study (M. Smith, 1975)

All children who participated scored higher on IQ tests and other cognitive measures than nonparticipants.

Children in constructivist models scored better on IQ tests than children in other models.

Children in behaviorist models scored better on recognition of letters and numbers than children in other models.

Children who were called "less ready" did better in directive models, whereas "more competent" children did better in less directive models.

Louisville Experiment (L. Miller & Dyer, 1975)

Immediate effects on cognitive functioning were greater for the more didactic programs, but stable effects (more than 4 years) were greater in noncognitive areas.

Different effects were found on the different preschool models for boys (e.g., boys in the Montessori program did better on achievement tests later in the elementary school).

Curriculum Demonstration Project (Karnes, Shwedel, & Williams, 1983)

No one preschool model was superior in effects.

Positive effects of all models faded.

Three Preschool Curriculum Models (Schweinhart & Weikart, 1997b)

The three models compared were a child-centered approach, a direct-instruction approach, and High/Scope (a Piagetian-based approach). The three curricula did not differ in terms of variables associated with academics (e.g., graduation rates, post-high-school education, employment rates, and earnings).

The comparison of High/Scope and the direct-instruction groups showed differences in socioemotional variables, with High/Scope participants showing the more positive affective behaviors (e.g., marrying and living with spouses, doing volunteer work) and the direct-instruction group showing the more negative affective behaviors (e.g., placements in special education for emotional disturbances, suspension from work, felony arrests for property crimes and assaults).

Table 2–9   Summary of Research on Early Childhood Programs of the Late 1970s and 1980s

Early childhood care and education can greatly affect IQ during the early childhood years, but for the most part, the effects on IQ seem to fade after the child leaves the program (Barnett, 1995).

Unlike IQ gains, effects on achievement, grade retention, special education placements, high school graduation, and positive socioemotional behaviors seem to persist (Barnett, 1995).

The effects of early childhood care and education are related to socioeconomic class. Quality programs had positive effects on reading and mathematics achievement for low socioeconomic children but negative effects for children in the highest-income families. This finding was probably the result of differences in the quality and amount of cognitive and social support disadvantaged and advantaged children received from their homes (Caughy, DiPietro, & Strobino, 1994). Karoly and her associates (1998) found that the benefits exceed the costs for higher-risk children and their families (e.g., those enrolled in the Perry Preschool), but savings to the government are unlikely to exceed costs for lower risk participants (e.g., those enrolled in the Elmira Prenatal/Early Infancy Project).

Higher quality care is associated with better overall development while children are in early childhood programs and during the first few years of school (Helburn & Culkin, 1995a; Zaslow, 1991). For example, model programs can produce greater and more long-term benefits than large-scale programs (e. g., public school prekindergarten programs); Head Start has been less effective than better funded public prekindergarten programs (Barnett, 1995). Poor-quality programs have negative effects on children's play and relationships with teachers (Helburn, 1995).

Table 2–10   Summary of Research on Family Support Programs of the 1980s and Early 1990s

Studies of family support programs show some effects on parents but weak effects on children except when the parent services are linked to full-day developmental child care (Ramey, Ramey, Gaines, & Blair, 1995). The intensity of the program's involvement with children is directly related to cognitive gains (Ramey, Bryant, & Suarez, 1985). For example, home visiting programs are less effective in producing cognitive gains than programs that work directly with children (D.Olds & Kitzman, 1993). Parent involvement may be a contributor to the success of a program but not sufficient in itself to produce long-term benefits for children (Weiss, 1993).

Family support and two-generational programs have had only modest effects on parents. The intensity of support may not be realistic in overcoming the challenges of poverty (Ramey, Ramey, Gaines, & Blair, 1995; S. Smith, 1995). Changing patterns of behavior is difficult, and positive benefits may take time to emerge (Halpern, 1992).

1. Intervention beyond the preschool years is critical to maintaining the academic achievement of children enrolled in D-I models (L. Miller & Bizzell, 1983; Reynolds, 1994).

2. Positive social and emotional factors are associated with nondidactic programs, and this impact becomes more evident when the child participants reach adulthood (DeVries, Haney, & Zan, 1991; Schweinhart & Weikart, 1997a, 1997b).

3. The way those involved in a program react to the specific approach affects program outcomes. This seemed to hold true for children (L. Miller, Bugbee, & Hyberton, 1985; Ramey & Ramey, 1998), teachers (Walsh, Smith, Alexander, & Ellwein, 1993), and families (Inoway-Ronnie, 1998). The desire to match the program approach with those involved is stimulating more interest in ecological per-

further analyses of earlier data on the approaches and by continuing longitudinal studies of those who were enrolled in the programs decades earlier. Recent studies seem to support the complexity of outcomes. Some examples of recent conclusions are as follows:

Table 2–11 Summary of Research on Early Childhood Special Education

Efficacy of Early Intervention

Intervention is powerful during the first 3 years of life (Guralnick, 1989).

Secondary handicaps may not occur if early intervention remediates a primary handicap (Hanson, Hanson & Lynch, 1989).

Intervention services improve the developmental status of the child (Meisels, 1985; Schweinhart & Weikart, 1985).

Early intervention reduces the need for special education programs later (Barnett & Escobar, 1990).

Benefits of Inclusion

Social interaction between children with disabilities and children who are developing normally requires teacher planning and teaching interaction to be effective (Guralnick, 1990).

Social interactions benefit children with disabilities (Jenkins, Speltz, & Odom, 1985) and "typical" children (Strain, Hoyson, & Jamieson, 1985).

Full inclusion may not be in the best interests of all children (Fuchs & Fuchs, 1994) and can create problems in the "regular" classroom (Sapon-Shevin, 1996).

Family Involvement

Studies of intervention directed to infants and toddlers alone have not yielded clear results (Simeonsson & Bailey, 1990).

Intervention with infants and toddlers is much more likely when a family's needs are met and family members take an active role in the intervention process (Guralnick, 1989).

spectives on program design and implementation (Schorr, 1997).

4. Research on family-focused programs is just beginning. Early efficacy studies on family intervention seem promising. Full-inclusion programs for children with disabilities are

successful when the articulated program base emphasizes the importance of accepting diversity (Peck, Furman, & Helmstetter, 1993).

OBSTACLES IN DEVELOPING PROGRAM GOALS

As we can see from the discussion of theories of practice, early childhood programs are both diverse and constantly evolving. Programmatic research confirms the consistency between program goals (including the reception of these goals by children, teachers, and families) and program outcomes. Thus, the selection of program goals is critical in achieving what we desire for children and their families.

History of Goals for Early Childhood Programs

Before the intervention programs of the 1960s, most early childhood programs were child centered. Although there were programmatic differences, the main goal was children's life adjustment (Kliebard, 1986). Early childhood programs were out of the spotlight and therefore insulated from outside pressures. Most people thought of the primary grades as the beginning of education.

Trend Toward Academic Programs. New thinking took hold in the 1960s. Elkind (1986) described political, social, and economic pressures as responsible for this trend. At this time, three pressures converged, putting early childhood programs in the center arena. First, achievement test results had raised concerns as early as World War II and especially following the Soviet Union's launching of *Sputnik I* in the late 1950s. Progressives became the scapegoat for all educational concerns (Goodlad, Klein, & Novotney, 1973).

Second, according to Elkind, the civil rights of ethnically and linguistically diverse populations had become an issue. Many children from diverse backgrounds were experiencing school failure. Hence, Head Start and other early childhood programs were funded with the idea of helping this group of young children to "catch up" with their middle-class cohorts. Many of the program initiatives of the 1960s were based on the *deficit model*, designed for quick cognitive success in the three Rs (a behaviorist view), although some programs had a constructivist orientation.

Third, the concept of the competent child was fostered by the emotions of these political and social movements. According to Elkind, no new data surfaced that suggested changes in the competence of children. However, the competent child idea was promoted through (a) the "selection and interpretation" of certain theories (B. Bloom, 1964; J. Hunt, 1961); (b) the changing life-styles of families, especially working mothers, who desired an academic education for their children; and (c) those who associated the growth of competence with the influence of high technology.

Leading psychologists and educators were encouraged to apply conceptual curriculum alternatives in programs for young children. Program approaches were to a great extent reduced to two major orientations: (a) to nurture the total development of the whole child (basically all of the models except the D-I model) and (b) to help the child master school literacy demands (primarily the D-I model).

These two approaches are radically different in terms of their perceived aims of education and in the curriculum content and methodology deemed necessary to achieve these aims. On the one hand, those who advocate the holistic or developmental approach believe that the primary goal of education is to develop individuals who are "creative, inventive, and discoverers" and that the secondary goal of education is to develop critical minds that question rather than merely accept information (Ripple & Rockcastle, 1964). To help children "want to know" (Elkind, 1989), teachers choose curriculum materials matched to developmental levels that are real and relevant for the children's present life and with general future needs in mind, as opposed to specific future school content.

Those who advocate the D-I approach, on the other hand, believe that the primary aim of education is to help children achieve the facts and skills possessed by literate adults. (Other aspects of development are at least secondary to mental development and may be totally ignored.) This "derived" type of knowledge (Elkind, 1989) is then analyzed to determine the level of mental ability required for its mastery. Children are then ability-matched to the curriculum. Learning consists of the acquisition of a set of isolated skills (often the three Rs) accomplished primarily by direct teaching and reinforcement. With this approach, according to Elkind (1989), children come to "know what we want" (p. 116).

In the 1980s two major publications outlined new demands and reforms for education: the National Commission on Excellence in Education's *A Nation at Risk* (1983, 1984) and the Carnegie Forum on Education and the Economy's *A Nation Prepared* (1986). Demands such as these were translated by state legislative bodies into legislation for policy statements that dictate when children may be legally enrolled in public school programs, what they should learn, and how they should be taught and assessed.

Exacerbation of the Academic Trend. As early childhood programs became more academic in orientation and D-I approaches were used, the kindergarten curriculum was seen as becoming too difficult for young children. Solutions were sought, such as (a) raising the entrance age for kindergarten; (b) placing kindergarten-age children in developmental programs for 1 year before enrolling them in kindergarten; (c) retaining kindergarten children by having them repeat kindergarten or by enrolling them in a 1-year transition program prior to first grade; and (d) lengthening the kindergarten to a full-day session. Although these methods exacerbated the problem and led to other negative consequences, they are still practiced today (Hills, 1987; Meisels, 1992; Spitzer, Cupp, & Parke, 1992). (For a more comprehensive discussion, see Decker and Decker, 2001, pp. 49–51.)

Parents, administrators, and teachers all have exacerbated the problem (Seefeldt & Barbour, 1988). Today's parents are influenced by toys that promise early achievement, publications about raising smarter children, and other parents' claims of their children's achievements (Simmons & Brewer, 1985). Parents may even be misled by their own child's knowledge of "bits and pieces" (e.g., ability to sing the alphabet song at an early age). Research studies show that middle-class parents no longer prefer child-centered programs (D. Powell, 1994), and lower-income and ethnically diverse parents also prefer didactic academic programs (Carlson & Stenmalm-Sjoblom, 1989; Elkind, 1986). Thus, parents insist that their children be taught more—especially expecting their children to learn to read before first grade. Parents overestimate children's academic performance in basic skill areas (Hiebert & Adams, 1987). And in their focus on cursory academic skills, they rank academic learning higher than do children's preschool and kindergarten teachers (Olmstead & Lockhart, 1995; Rescorla, 1991). They fail to see how other aspects of the curriculum (e.g., the arts, block building, dramatic play) contribute to the overall learning experience (Hills, 1987; Simmons & Brewer, 1985) and also rank children's independence lower than do teachers (Knudsen-Lindauer & Harris, 1989).

Administrators are also pressuring early childhood teachers. In some cases, this attitude is a result of their lack of knowledge about young children (Schweinhart, Koshel, & Bridgmann, 1987). In addition, administrators are influenced from the outside by public demand for more stringent educational standards. These are evidenced in mandated objectives, curriculum guides, and report cards (Goffin, 1989; Walsh, 1989); through the measurement of children's achievement on standardized tests (Charlesworth, Hart, Burts, Thomasson, Mosley, & Fleege, 1993; Kamii, 1990); and from the inside by pressures from primary teachers who in turn are feeling pressures because of escalating elementary school standards (Hatch & Freeman, 1988a).

Early childhood teachers themselves are also unwittingly responsible for the academic trend. Teachers are reporting philosophy–reality conflicts—that is, discrepancies between their beliefs and required instructional practices (Hatch & Freeman, 1988a). They report that they have "little control over what they are being asked to do," and this reality conflicts with "their views of what is best for children" (Hills, 1987, p. 266). However, although teachers often say that young children learn best through direct encounters with materials and events, in practice they eschew the dramatic play, music, and art materials in favor of workbooks and worksheets. Durkin (1987) reported that most teachers said reading should not be taught in kindergarten, but they considered the drill work in phonics to be "readiness," not "reading." As noted, teachers have been in favor of raising the entrance age, screening for placement, retention, and full-day kindergarten for academic purposes because they wanted to relieve the stress placed on children at risk for failure and to free themselves from accountability for children's academic achievement as measured by their groups' assessment scores.

Professional Reactions and the Conception of Developmentally Appropriate Practices

Professional associations began to see the need to take a stand on the issues of innappropriate practices. Thus, position statements were issued on behalf of young children. The Early Childhood and Literacy Development Committee of the International Reading Association (1986) issued one of the first statements. The NAEYC also developed a position statement on developmentally appropriate education (DAP) for young children. The statement was first published in 1986 and was expanded a year later (Bredekamp, 1987). The statement was widely read, and soon the term *DAP* appeared everywhere in speeches and written materials. The following professional associations have issued position statements supporting DAP: the Association for Childhood Education International (ACEI; 1986), the Association for Supervision and Curriculum Development (1988), the National Association of Early Childhood Specialists in State Departments of Education (1987), the National Association of Elementary School Principals (1990), the National Association of State Boards of Education (1988), the National Black Child Development Institute (1987), and the National Council of Teachers of Mathematics (1991). Numerous state organizations have issued position statements too.

Position statements are not concerned only with curriculum content and pedagogy. Readiness as gatekeeping (used for placement and retention decisions) is also of major concern (R. Hitz & Richter, 1993; Kagan, 1992; Katz, 1991a; Willer & Bredekamp, 1990). Concern about readiness as gatekeeping prompted a position statement on this aspect of DAP (NAEYC, 1990). Other position statements have been published regarding assessment, as discussed in chapter 9.

Lack of Consensus About DAP. Although DAP has been discussed for almost 2 decades, a lack of professional consensus remains. One source of the problem in consensus is the fact that behavioral approaches to early childhood education have been in use since the 1960s. Elkind (1988) stated that behaviorist ideas are even more entrenched in elementary and secondary education. Also, as discussed earlier, a top-down perspective and standardized tests have influenced early childhood practice. Furthermore, many public school early childhood teachers had their elementary teaching certificates endorsed for early childhood programs and thus carry their elementary practices into teaching younger children. Some early childhood teachers were trained in college programs using the more aca-

demic approaches and are thus finding a change to DAP difficult (Ayers, 1992). Similarly, public school administrators, who often do not have teaching experience in early childhood programs, are not familiar with DAP or may find it "foreign" to their training (Rusher, McGrevin, & Lambiotte, 1992).

A growing voice against DAP has been a group of early childhood educators who call themselves the *reconceptualists.* In 1989, this group began to take issue with DAP. Two decades earlier, they had begun to move away from traditional behavioral objectives, planning, and evaluation to an emphasis on politics, culture, gender, and other social issues. The reconceptualists criticize child development as a conceptual basis for early childhood care and education and, more particularly, DAP as the guiding construct for the program base for early childhood. They refer to DAP as a "well-intentioned white liberal or progressive education" trend (B. Swadener & Kessler, 1991a, p. 88). Table 2–12 contrasts the views of the reconceptualists and those of the proponents of DAP.

Efforts to Resolve the Issue.   Professionals have considered some of the misunderstandings and criticisms of DAP. Soon after the controversy over DAP arose, some professionals indicated that the issue could be resolved if the framework were extended. For example, Spodek (1991a) stated that to be educationally worthwhile, program planning must include the developmental component but also must go beyond to the cultural and knowledge dimensions. Thus, Spodek sees developmental theory as *an* informant of the curriculum but not *the* informant.

The misunderstandings about DAP also led professionals employed by NAEYC to attempt clarification of the problems in interpretation through the publication of *Reaching Potentials: Appropriate Curriculum and Assessment for Young Children* (Vol. 1; Bredekamp & Rosegrant, 1992); however, many issues continued. Thus, the initial

Table 2–12   Different Views of Reconceptualists and DAP Proponents*

Reconceptualists' Views	DAP Proponents' Views
Unlike elementary education, early childhood care and education rely too much on the principles of developmental psychology and child development (Bloch, 1991; Kessler & Swadener, 1994; Stott & Bowman, 1996). Walsh (1991) thinks DAP does not take into account all the recent research on children's learning processes.	Psychological theories have long been used in early childhood care and education as a source of program base. Constructivists have used the theories of Piaget (DeVries & Kohlberg, 1987; Fosnot, 1989) and Vygotsky (1978). Other theories used in early childhood programs include Erikson's (1950, 1951) psychosocial theory, Skinner's (1953) learning theory, and Bandura's (1977) constructs.
DAP leads to a belief in fixed stages and in the individual totally separated from his or her social context (Kessler, 1991b; Lubeck, 1994; Ludlow & Berkeley, 1994; Walsh, 1991).	DAP is based on *both* age and individual appropriateness (Bredekamp & Rosegrant, 1992).
Reliance on child development causes educators to ignore gender, politics, culture, and historical context (Kessler, 1991a; Swadener & Kessler, 1991b). Jipson (1991) thinks DAP considers only one cultural view (European American middle-class values) without regard to cultural issues.	Early childhood programs have served children of lower socioeconomic status (SES) throughout their history (refer to chapter 1). The relationship of DAP and culture can be noted in the use of Bronfenbrenner's (1979) ecological perspective and also in the writings of Bowman (1992).
DAP does not prepare children for life in a democracy (Kessler, 1991a).	Dewey was long associated with early childhood programs (Greenberg, 1987, 1992; Hendrick, 1992). Dewey's philosophy was overwhelmed by Thorndike's ideas (Levin, 1991).
DAP focuses on the how rather than the what of teaching (Walsh, 1991).	DAP is a framework for instruction (Bredekamp & Rosegrant, 1992). Curriculum guidelines are suggested (National Association for the Education of Young Children & the National Association of Early Childhood Specialists in State Departments of Education, 1991).
DAP does not have adult guidance. Teachers prepare the environment and then stand back (Kessler, 1991a; Swadener & Kessler, 1991a). Teachers see DAP as chaotic (Jipson, 1991).	DAP includes both content and process, states that programs must develop their own goals, and uses Vygotsky's ideas of scaffolding (Bredekamp & Rosegrant, 1992). Many have refuted the idea that in DAP, one prepares the environment and then stands back (Burts et al., 1992), never uses direct instruction (Fowell & Lawton, 1992), and ignores academics (Bredekamp & Rosegrant, 1992).

*Before the 1997 revision of the DAP guidelines (Bredekamp & Copple, 1997).

position statement was revised (Bredekamp & Copple, 1997). The position statement revised and expanded DAP in these two ways:

1. In curriculum planning and implementation, a balance is needed between the objectives of instruction or content and attention to the individual child.

2. Because the cultural issue had been raised, the meaning of *developmentally appropriate* was expanded from age or stage and individually appropriate to age or stage, individually, and culturally appropriate.

Research studies are also being used to help resolve the issue. Research shows that DAP and developmentally inappropriate practices (DIP) can be placed along a continuum from one extreme to another (Charlesworth, Hart, Burts, Thomasson, Mosley, & Fleege, 1993; Stipek, Daniels, Galluzzo, & Milburn, 1992). Completing this first step in the research process has enabled researchers to examine DAP and DIP practices. Table 2–13 presents a summary of this research.

IMPLEMENTING THE PROGRAM

After carefully considering all the factors that determine a program base, the director or board must develop a preference for a particular view. The "ideal" program base seems to be the one that best suits the needs of the children and families served. Personal beliefs, whether articulated or maintained as a preconscious set of values, influence decision making. Spodek (1988) discussed how *implicit theories* affect professional behaviors.

Using the program base, administrators need to think through questions pertaining to the pedagogical component of their own programs. They should ask themselves questions such as the following:

1. What are the goals and objectives of my early childhood program—to provide an environment conducive to the development of the whole child? to teach young children academic skills? to provide intensive instruction in areas of academic deficits and thinking skills? to develop creativity? to build a healthy self-concept? to spur self-direction in learning?

2. What provisions for children's individual differences are consistent with my program's goals? Should I expect the same level or varying levels of achievement? Are individual differences acceptable in some or all academic areas? in some or all developmental areas (psychomotor, affective, cognitive)? Are activities child chosen and appropriate to the child's own interest and developmental level, or are they staff tailored to meet individual differences? Are activities presented for one or several learning styles?

3. What grouping strategy is in accord with my program's rationale—homogeneous (chronological age, mental age, achievement, interest) or heterogeneous? fixed or flexible? staff determined or by children's interests? large or small?

4. What schedule format is needed to facilitate my program's objectives—a full- or half-day schedule? the same session length for all children, or length of session tailored to each child's and parents' needs? a predetermined or flexible daily schedule based on children's interests?

Administrators must also consider questions pertaining to the operational components of the program, such as the following:

1. What staff roles are necessary to implement the learning environment as set forth in my program base—persons who dispense knowledge, resource persons, or persons who prepare the environment? persons who use positive or negative reinforcement? group leaders or individual counselors? academic content specialists or social engineers? persons who work almost exclusively with young children or those who provide parent education?

2. What staff positions (director, teachers, volunteers) are needed to execute my program?

Table 2–13   Summary of Research on DAP and DIP

Program Base

DAP is more difficult to incorporate into the public school systems (Espinosa, 1992; Sykes, 1994). Public school prekindergarten programs seemed to have more DAP than privately owned programs (Dunn & Kontos, 1997). More programs are moving toward DAP (A. L. Mitchell, 1993; C. Wood, 1994).

Parents and administrators find it difficult to accept DAP because using DIP often get quick but short-term academic gains; DAP results in long-term gains (Glascott, 1994; Katz & Chard, 2000).

Many administrators are not informed about DAP and thus do not support teachers as they might otherwise do (Rusher, McGrevin, & Lambiotte, 1992). Without positive support, DAP cannot be fully implemented (Heck, Larsen, & Marcoulides, 1990). Teachers, too, need better understandings of DAP because they need to be advocates of DAP, and only teachers can implement DAP (Goffin & Stegelin, 1992).

Between one fifth and one third of classrooms exemplify DAP (Dunn & Kontos, 1997). Most teachers are neither fully DAP nor fully DIP but on the continuum between the two extremes (Charlesworth, Hart, Burts, Thomasson, Mosley, & Fleege, 1993; Mangione & Maniates, 1993). Programs can be DAP and yet come in a variety of styles (Goffin & Stegelin, 1992; Humphryes, 1998; Robles de Melendez & Ostertag, 1997).

Outcomes for Children

Behavioral Outcomes

In comparison to children in DIP programs:

Children in DAP classrooms exhibit fewer behavioral problems (Marcon, 1992, 1994a). DAP preschools and kindergartens were linked to positive behavioral outcomes in the primary grades (Burts et al., 1993).

DAP programs result in desirable social outcomes for children (Charlesworth, Hart, Burts, & DeWolf, 1993; Weikart & Schweinhart, 1991).

Children in DAP classrooms regardless of gender or racial or socioeconomic background exhibited less stress (Burts, Hart, Charlesworth, Fleege, Mosley, & Thomasson, 1992; Burts, Hart, Charlesworth, & Kirk, 1990; Hyson, Hirsch-Pasek, & Rescorla, 1990). Stress is noted most frequently in male, African American, and low socioeconomic children in DIP programs (Hart, Burts, Durland, Charlesworth, DeWolf, & Fleege, 1998).

Academic Outcomes

In comparison to children in DIP programs:

Children in DAP programs were more academically motivated (Hyson, Hirsch-Pasek, & Rescorla, 1990; Hirsch-Pasek, 1991; Stipek, Feiler, Daniels, & Milburn, 1995).

Children in DAP programs scored higher on measures of divergent thinking (Hirsch-Pasek, Hyson, & Rescorla, 1990; Hyson, Hirsch-Pasek, & Rescorla, 1990).

Children in DAP programs have higher academic achievement (Bryant, Burchinal, Lau, & Sparling, 1994; Charlesworth, Hart, Burts, Thomasson, Mosley, & Fleege, 1993; Dunn, Beach, & Kontos, 1994; Frede & Barnett, 1992; Larsen & Robinson, 1989; Marcon, 1992, 1993; Schweinhart, Barnes, & Weikart, 1993).

What academic or experiential qualifications are required or desired? What type of orientation or in-service training is needed? What child–staff ratio is required?

3. What equipment and materials are required—equipment and materials that are self-correcting or that encourage creativeness? that are designed to stress one concept (e.g., color paddles) or many concepts (e.g., blocks)? that require substantial or minimal adult guidance? that are designed for group or individual use? that provide for concrete experiences or abstract thinking?

4. What physical arrangement is compatible with the goals of my program—differentiated or nondifferentiated areas for specific activities? fixed or flexible areas? outside area used primarily for learning or for recess? equipment and materials arranged for self-service by the child or for teacher distribution?

And then the crucial question must be answered: Do the answers have a supportable rationale? Relevant and irrelevant beliefs, appropriate and inappropriate values, and timely and outdated information can be recognized as the administrator considers the alternatives. Bowman (1986) stated that the tremendous increase of knowledge from interdisciplinary sources provides us with a rich base to plan for children, but it also encourages us to "tolerate faddism, quackism, and just plain foolishness" (p. 6).

EVALUATING THE PROGRAM

Administrators are held accountable for the programs under their leadership and direction. With a constant demand for excellence, evaluation has become one of the administrator's most significant responsibilities. Funding and legal sources require evaluation reports. Accreditation (self-evaluation) is based on standards set by the accrediting agencies, such as professional groups.

Furthermore, the staff objectively and subjectively make judgments as they work in the program. Parents question program quality, and public interest in program value is heightened, especially on the part of taxpayers. Administrators must answer to each of these groups.

A discussion of evaluation leads to classification of the types of evaluation. Dopyera and Lay-Dopyera (1990) identified two types of evaluation: intuitive and formal (which they subdivided into objectives-based evaluation, standards-based evaluation, and evaluation research).

Intuitive Evaluation

Intuitive evaluation might be called a personal construct or practical knowledge. Intuitive evaluation is a notion about what constitutes the right way to achieve something. Unlike planned formal evaluation, intuitive evaluation concerns how people perform on a minute-by-minute basis.

Early childhood teachers and administrators have notions about their professional practice. Although these notions guide their day-to-day practice, they are difficult to articulate. These notions come to light when a clash occurs between one's own ideas or actions and those of another who is respected or when the outcomes of what one expects and what ensues differ.

Through studies of intuitive evaluation (Clark & Peterson, 1986; Katz, 1984b; Spodek, 1987), two points seem to be established:

1. Early childhood educators take their book-learned knowledge and guided observations and integrate them with their values and practical knowledge. This knowledge is integrated by each individual teacher from his or her theory-based knowledge, accumulated experience, and understanding of milieu and self.

2. Intuitive evaluation is important because educators must often make judgment calls so quickly that they do not have time to reflect

on theory and empirical findings; thus, intuitive evaluation guides practice.

Formal Evaluation

Planned (or formal) evaluation has its roots in concern over accountability to the funding agencies. With an increasing number of mandates for evaluation, the evaluation profession grew, and activities involving formal evaluation increased. Many educational endeavors require formal evaluation, such as needs assessment, program analysis, cost effectiveness (the effectiveness of a program as it relates to cost per child), and program impact (positive changes in the child or family that affect society).

Administrators must determine the appropriate type of evaluation to serve their needs. Objectives-based and standards-based evaluation are both concerned with accountability. Evaluation research is concerned with the interplay of various aspects of a given program related to outcomes.

Objectives-Based Evaluation.   **Objectives-based evaluation** focuses on what children achieve as a result of participation in a specific program. Objectives-based evaluation is the most common form of formal evaluation. Thus, the criteria used for evaluation are program specific (developed by examining the program's goals and objectives). The analyses of evaluation data provide information on the degree to which program goals and objectives are met.

Evaluation may be conducted at two points in the program. **Formative evaluation** is used to determine the effectiveness of various aspects of the program (e.g., grouping practices) while program changes are still being made. **Summative evaluation** determines the effectiveness of the overall program at some ending point.

Standards-Based Evaluation.   **Standards-based evaluation** is an appraisal of a program based on a set of standards (criteria) developed outside any spe-cific program. These standards may be deemed worthwhile by a professional association (e.g., the National Academy of Early Childhood Programs' Accreditation), the funding or monitoring agency (e.g., Head Start Performance Objectives), or a researcher (e.g., The Early Childhood Environment Rating Scale).

Following are several standards-based evaluations that are comprehensive; that is, they cover all aspects of program quality:

1. **High/Scope Program Quality Assessment (PQA).** The PQA was developed by the High/Scope Educational Research Foundation (1998). The PQA has 72 items that cover these attributes of quality: learning environment, daily routine, adult–child interaction, curriculum planning and assessment, parent involvement and family services, staff qualifications and staff development, and program management. Each item is scored on a 5-point rating scale.

2. **Early Childhood Environment Rating Scale: Revised Edition (ECERS).** The ECERS was developed by Harms and Clifford in 1980 and revised by Harms, Clifford, and Cryer (1998). They see an early childhood program as an ecological system with more parts than just the individual within the program. The ECERS is used to examine 43 attributes that cover these areas of quality: space and furnishings, personal care routines, language and reasoning, activities, interactions, program structure, and parents and staff. Ratings are given for each area, and a total rating can be calculated for each group. Scores on all the groups within a center may be compiled to get a quality score for a center.

3. **Family Day Care Rating Scale (FDCRS).** The FDCRS was developed by Harms and Clifford (1989) and follows the same pattern as their ECERS. The FDCRS is used to examine 32 attributes that cover these areas of quality: space and furnishings for care and learning, basic care, language and reasoning, learning activities, social development, and adult needs. Each item is

described in four levels of quality: inadequate, minimal, good, and excellent. Eight "supplementary items" are provided for homes enrolling children with special needs.

4. **Infant/Toddler Environment Rating Scale: Revised Edition (ITERS).** The ITERS was developed by Harms, Cryer, and Clifford (2003) and follows the same pattern as their ECERS and FDCRS. The ITERS consists of 39 items for the assessment of the quality of center-based child care for children up to 30 months of age. Items are organized under these categories: space and furnishings, personal care routines, listening and talking, activities, interaction, program structure, and parents and staff. Each item is presented on a 7-point scale, with descriptors for 1 (inadequate), 3 (minimal), 5 (good), and 7 (excellent).

5. **School-Age Care Environment Rating Scale (SACERS).** The SACERS was developed by Harms, Jacobs, and White (1995) and follows the follows the same pattern as the ECERS, FDCRS, and ITERS. The SACERS consists of 49 items for the assessment of the quality of child care programs offered by schools and other organizations. Items are organized under these attributes: space and furnishings, health and safety, activities, interactions, program structure, staff development, and supplementary items (for children with special needs).

6. **Assessment of Practices in Early Elementary Classrooms (APEEC).** The APEEC was developed by Hemmeter, Maxwell, Ault, and Schuster (2001) and follows the same pattern as the ECERS, EDCRS, ITERS, and SACERS. The APEEC, designed for kindergarten through grade 3 classrooms, consists of 16 items in these domains of classroom practice: physical environment, instructional context, and social context.

Specific aspects of programs can be checked, too. Some examples include (a) Child's Adjustment to the Program (Nilsen, 2000, p. 265); (b) Early Childhood Work Environment Survey (Professional Development Project of National-

Louis University); (c) Parent Evaluation of Child Care Program (*Child Care Information Exchange,* June 1989, pp. 25–26); and (d) Safety Checklist (Frost, 1992a, pp. 346–350).

Researchers are working on instruments needed for empirical studies of DAP. Different types of instruments have been developed to fit the researchers' investigations. For example, M. Hitz and Wright (1988) developed an instrument to note the degree of change in academic emphasis of early childhood programs (from DIP to DAP). Bryant, Clifford, and Peisner (1991) developed an instrument to determine teachers' knowledge and attitudes about DAP. Similarly, P. Oakes and Caruso (1990) measured teachers' attitudes about authority in the classroom and developed observation instruments to confirm the "self-reports." Charlesworth, Hart, Burts, Thomasson, Mosley, and Fleege (1993) thought of DIP and DAP on a continuum. They developed the Teachers Belief Statements, the Instructional Activities Scale, and the Checklist for Rating Developmentally Appropriate Practice in Kindergarten Classrooms. (Other standards-based assessments are discussed in chapter 3.)

Evaluation Research. Evaluation research examines how various aspects of a program impinge on outcomes for children or families. The purpose of such research is to better understand the interplay of variables. Researchers are concerned about all effects generated by program components; thus, they go beyond specific program goals or objectives and standards that have been deemed worthwhile. Evaluation research studies are often longitudinal, and all are rigorous in their research methodologies.

An Important Consideration

Evaluation generates program changes mandated by external commands (e.g., from regulatory agencies), stimulated by internal (i.e., local) visions or problems, or both. The most meaningful evaluations are most often those stimulated by internal factors rather than those resulting from external mandates. Evaluations mandated by external sources are perceived as useful only when data are also used for local program purposes. Program quality needs to go beyond structural variables (referred to as a top-down approach) that researchers associate with high-quality child and family outcomes (Katz, 1999).

Changes affect programs in the followings ways:

- Change is more difficult if program restructuring rather than program enriching is required.
- Change is more difficult when all staff are affected rather than just a few employees.
- Fast change is as difficult as slow change with staff turnover.
- Change is difficult under staff resistance.

To overcome the negative effects of evaluation, staff must acknowledge the interdependent effects of all program components, and evaluation must include all components, be ongoing, and include all those involved in a program. Pressures for answers from within and without the program will not seem so unbearable, or the difficulties involved in overcoming content and methodological problems so insurmountable, if one keeps in mind the major purpose of program evaluation. If evaluation is seen as a means for program improvement, it becomes a continuous process, and its results become starting points for future planning.

TRENDS AND ISSUES

Curriculum models have had a major impact on program goals, administrative and pedagogical decisions, and program outcomes. However, the very nature of models raises many issues and research uncertainties.

Theory As Program Informant

A question often raised is whether one approach should be selected to promote consistency or whether a curriculum model should be one of several program informants. Some programs are based on several developmental theories, and some professionals call for other disciplines, such as philosophy, sociology, and anthropology, to be used as informants.

Many professionals believe that the cultural context of children's development should be considered; that is, one size does not fit all. The universality of development has been challenged (Gardner, 1999); that is, children develop many valued skills and knowledge in many types of environments (Goncu, 1999). Except during the 1960s and 1970s, the cultural context has been considered important in understanding development. During the 1980s the work of Vygotsky and Bronfenbrenner, which stressed the importance of culture, again aroused interest in the cultural nature of development (Rogoff & Chavajay, 1995). Many researchers are now calling for culturally sensitive approaches that take familial and community cultural values into account in assessing needs for a program service, in planning and delivery services, and in measuring program outcomes. This approach is in sharp contrast to the idea of "cultural deprivation" that was prominent in the 1960s.

Another problem of using developmental theory as an informant is that theory is continually changing. Stott and Bowman (1996) discussed how programs informed by developmental or learning theory thus promote practices based on concepts no longer supported in theory.

Finally, some professionals believe that curriculum models should not be standardized. They see children, teachers, and even families as designers of an emergent curriculum. Conversely, the demand for accountability has led to interest in curriculum models developed by experts and then transported to various sites for implementation. Within-model variation has led to questions as to whether "typical" programs can have the same effects as exemplary programs using the same model (Barnett, 1986; Haskins, 1989). Kagan (1991a) believed that transporting models will not work and that program developers should launch site-specific models. Furthermore, even if a model has been adopted at another site, it is not known how far the program can deviate from its model (e.g., in expenditures per child) before the positive effects disappear. Weikart (1981, 1983) emphasized that the success of a program for young children was based on the quality of the program implementation rather than the model.

Program Quality and Effectiveness of Models

Some professionals believe that the best way to promote program quality is through the adoption of models (Pogrow, 1996). Frede (1998) found the following commonalities in models with long-term effectiveness: (a) coherent programs with curriculum content based on needed school-related knowledge and skills; (b) qualified teachers who use reflective teaching practices aided by qualified supervisors; (c) low teacher–child ratios and small group sizes; and (d) collaborative relationships with parents.

Search for the "Best" Model

Even among high-quality programs, effectiveness must be interpreted with caution. Programs differ in their target populations, duration, and administrative and pedagogical components. Furthermore, the effects of high-quality programs also depend on their reception by children, teachers, and families. Thus, researchers need to determine which aspects of a program (curriculum, other aspects, or both) are beneficial and for whom (Barnett, Frede, Mobasher, & Mohr, 1987; Hauser-Cram, 1990; Horowitz & O'Brien, 1989; F. Jacobs, 1988; D. Powell, 1987a, 1987c; Sigel, 1990). This problem is confounded by the association between the curriculum goals se-

lected and the teaching techniques employed (L. Miller, Bugbee, & Hyberton, 1985). Thus, the question that needs to be answered is, Under what conditions does the model work? (Guralnick, 1988; Meisels, 1985). Other questions still not answered are as follows:

1. Can exposure even to a high-quality program serve as a barrier to environmental risks, or are other efforts needed (e.g., housing) to maximize benefits (Horowitz & O'Brien, 1989)?

2. Can benefits of quality programs accrue to *all* children? (Target populations to receive interventions have been rather limited.)

The search for the "best" model is still an issue. Recently, researchers noted the consistency between program goals and program outcomes. This finding brings us back to philosophical questions. In choosing a model, what outcome is most important? For example, is school success or holistic development the most desired outcome?

Problems with Programmatic Research

Research methodological problems are a major reason for the lack of clarity regarding the effects of different early childhood programs. The major shortcomings include the assessment of program implementation, inadequate measuring instruments, the establishment of comparable experimental and control groups, and limitations in the interpretation of data. Attrition rates have also minimized the effectiveness of many longitudinal studies (Fewell & Vadasky, 1987; Guralnick, 1988; Meisels & Wasik, 1990; D. Powell & Sigel, 1991).

Aside from methodological problems, program evaluation is especially difficult in early childhood care and education programs with broad goals and many service components. These programs are comprehensive (i.e., designed to meet many needs). The complexity is compounded because the services consist of interwoven parts and are designed by various institutions (Knapp, 1995a). Another problem is that programs continue to change as originally unforeseen needs arise and new services are developed (Kagan, 1991b). Finally, professionals must also remember that statistically significant differences cannot necessarily be equated with educational or social significance. L. Shepard (1991) voiced the age-old concern that evaluation often drives the curriculum inappropriately.

Problems with Acceptance of DAP

DAP has certainly become part of every early childhood care and education professional's vocabulary. Although DAP is talked about, it is not being implemented rapidly. The issue continues into the new millennium. Reconceptualists agree that some of their previous concerns were included in the NAEYC (1997a) position statement, such as the social construction of Vygotsky (E. Forman, Minick, & Stone, 1993; A. Smith, 1992) and the added stress on the importance of culture, families, and context-relevant curriculum. However, they still see many problems (Lubeck, 1998), such as the following:

1. The use of categories such as DAP and DIP.

2. The presentation of conflicting ideas such as "norms" and individual rates. The reconceptualists argue that when items are paired, one item becomes subordinate to the other.

3. The use of stages and milestones as a basic framework for DAP. Based on the framework of Vygotsky's work, many researchers now question universal norms or milestones in child development (Cole & Cole, 1993; Rogoff, 1990; Scribner, 1985).

4. The practice of focusing on the DAP guidelines for set situations (Charlesworth, 1998) rather than exploring the range of alternatives in a given context through "reflective practice" (Bowman, 1989).

5. The assertion that the new standards represent a consensus of thinking in the field. The

reconceptualists assert that there is not a consensus and that consensus is dangerous in and of itself. Undoubtedly, more discussion of DAP will and should take place.

Although substantial movement has occurred in the direction of DAP and many seek specifics on its implementation, a significant number of other professionals choose other foci for program planning. Changes undoubtedly will continue to take place in early childhood programs. With regard to the children's program, it is difficult to see a clear trend. In an interview, Spodek noted more individual attempts at innovation but concluded by saying, "I would say that in the last [*sic*] 40 years the ways teachers function and the manners in which schools are organized have not changed all that much" (Allison, 1999, p. 261).

SUMMARY

The administrator's main task is providing leadership in program planning, implementation, and evaluation. The administrator, as a first step, must conduct a needs assessment. The administrator must then understand and choose a curriculum approach from among the various program bases. The factors that should determine a program base are a synthesis of psychological theories, ecological perspectives, and philosophical positions. A curriculum model consists of the program base, the administrative and pedagogical components, and the program evaluation. From the 1960s to the 1980s, the holistic/developmental and the D-I models were the most commonly used. Because these two approaches are diametrically opposed, much controversy arose. Since the 1980s, more program designers have also been looking at ecological perspectives, especially the work of Vygotsky. Controversy over models has led to professional associations' publishing position papers that promoted DAP. The reconceptualists have not agreed. Others within the early childhood profession basically agreed with DAP but believed that additional concerns should be included in constructing a program base. The choice of program base is critical because programmatic research points to a consistent relationship between program base and program outcomes. Every aspect of implementation of the program's administrative and pedagogical components should be in keeping with the program base.

The administrator's final step is making program evaluation plans. Evaluation may be of two types: intuitive and formal. Unplanned, intuitive evaluation is constantly functioning; thus, attempts should be made to understand the criteria being used by all involved in the local program. Formal or planned evaluation may be objectives based, standards based, or outcomes based. The administrator and the staff should jointly determine the reasons for evaluation (e.g., needs assessment, program analysis), the appropriate type of evaluation, the specific instrument to be used, and the timing of the implementation for both formative and summative evaluations. Evaluation results should provide feedback for future program planning.

FOR FURTHER READING

Bredekamp, S., & Copple, C. (Eds.). (1997). *Developmentally appropriate practice in early childhood programs* (Rev. ed.). Washington, DC: National Association for the Education of Young Children.

Elkind, D. (1991). Developmentally appropriate practice: A case study of educational inertia. In S. L. Kagan (Ed.), *The care and education of America's young children: Obstacles and opportunities* (pp. 1–16). Chicago: University of Chicago Press.

Epstein, A., Schweinhart, L., & McAdoo, L. (1996). *Models of early childhood education.* Ypsilanti, MI: High/Scope Press.

Kagan, S. L., & Zigler, E. F. (Eds.). (1987). *Early schooling: The national debate.* New Haven, CT: Yale University Press.

Kliebard, H. M. (1986). *The struggle for the American curriculum, 1893–1958.* New York: Routledge.

Lubeck, S. (1998). Is developmentally appropriate practice for everyone? *Childhood Education, 74,* 283–292.

Roopnarine, J. L., & Johnson, J. E. (2000). *Approaches to early childhood education* (3rd ed.). Upper Saddle River, NJ: Merrill/Prentice Hall.

Spodek, B. (1986). Using the knowledge base. In B. Spodek (Ed.), *Today's kindergarten: Exploring the knowledge base, expanding the curriculum* (pp. 137–143). New York: Teachers College Press.

Spodek, B., & Saracho, O. N. (Eds.). (1991). *Yearbook in early childhood education: Vol. 2. Issues in early childhood curriculum.* New York: Teachers College Press.

Swadener, B., & Kessler, S. (Eds.). (1991). Reconceptualizing early childhood education [Special issue]. *Early Education and Development, 2* (2).

TO REFLECT

1. A local corporation is interested in providing child care for its employees. The personnel manager has been asked to ascertain whether the corporation should plan for an on-site program or make a community investment in child care (through encouraging family satellite programs or using corporate reserve slots). What type of data should the personnel manager collect and analyze before making a decision?

2. A potential proprietor is considering child care as a small business. As the first step, a needs assessment instrument should be devised and implemented. What types of items should be included in the needs assessment instrument?

3. In a final seminar session connected with student teaching, a student teacher asks, "What should a new teacher do if his or her philosophical notions come into conflict with those of an administrator?" Rusher, McGrevin, and Lambiotte (1992) say there are four options: (a) disregard the direction of the administrator, (b) teach in ways that are inconsistent with one's beliefs, (c) leave the profession, and (d) teach using "best practices" and make a concerted effort to change the beliefs of the administrator. What are the pros and cons of each option?

Considering Regulations and Establishing Policies

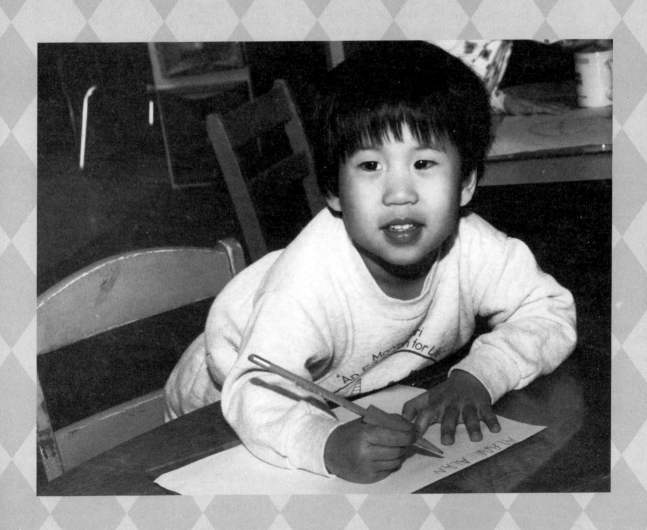

Regulations and policies guide and facilitate the work and life of an early childhood care and education program—its children and their families, its staff, and its director and board. Although regulations and policies may be defined in various ways, these terms will be differentiated in this book as follows: (a) a *regulation* is a rule that is recognized as binding and that emanates from actions of governing bodies outside of the early childhood program, and (b) a *policy* is a written statement that explains a course of action toward achieving the goals of a local program. Regulations and policies are closely linked, because program policies must be based on applicable regulations.

CONSIDERING PROTECTIVE REGULATIONS

As stated, **regulations** are the rules, directives, statutes, and standards that prescribe, direct, limit, and govern early childhood programs. The following characteristics are generally representative:

1. Regulations, taken collectively, cover all aspects of a program—administration, organization, facilities, personnel, funding, and services (e.g., children's program, nutrition, health and safety).

2. Various regulations apply to different types of early childhood programs. Some regulations govern private programs (e.g., licensing and incorporation); others may affect federal and state programs (e.g., direct administration and Head Start Performance Standards). Many regulations must be met by virtually all programs, such as those concerning building codes, fire safety, sanitation, zoning, transportation, staff qualifications, the Civil Rights Act, local board regulations, and laws for populations with special needs.

3. Regulations vary in comprehensiveness; for example, licensing regulations cover the total program, but credentialing requirements affect only the educational preparation of the staff.

4. Most regulations are mandatory. Two exceptions are accreditation, which is self-regulation, and model standards.

5. Regulations come from various sources. Federal agencies regulate some early childhood programs because they provide funds through various grants and subsidies. Most federal funds are administered by a state agency. States fund and regulate some early childhood programs because public education is a state responsibility. Local governments regulate other programs through community ordinances and health and safety codes. The judiciary system even regulates some aspects of early childhood programs through decisions affecting civil rights and the responsibilities of agencies and schools. At times, determining which of several agencies has jurisdiction over programs is difficult. The resistance to national program standards or regulations is a major barrier to quality (Bellm, Burton, Shukla, & Whitebook, 1997).

The various regulatory agencies assume protective roles by assuring parents that the early childhood program meets at least minimum standards. Although this protective role is essential, the regulations have at least five problems:

1. Regulations can keep early childhood programs at minimum levels. Program standards often define goals of achievement for individual programs. Thus, if standards are too low, programs are most often mediocre. Stringent standards can lessen the quality of programs, too, by causing more programs to opt not to be regulated (Hofferth & Chaplin, 1998). The overriding question should be not whether harm or risk has been prevented but whether a child's development is enhanced.

2. Regulations may deter innovation. Regulations are often too concerned with uniformity. Establishing standards for quality that fit all cultural contexts and meet the needs of a rapidly changing society are most difficult.

3. Most states do not have a single agency or legislative committee responsible for early childhood programs. Often, gaps appear in regulations or regulation jurisdictions collide. Establishing state offices of child development may help remedy this situation.

4. Some regulations are simply "on record," with little or no enforcement, such as those that require the registration of family child care homes.

5. Continuous consultation is often omitted. Continuous in-service training opportunities are necessary for providing and maintaining high quality in programs.

Achieving Quality Through Protective Regulations

Regulations are tools that help move programs toward higher quality. G. Morgan (1996) wrote about "regulatory methods" as "levels of standards." The term *standards* implies degrees of excellence along a continuum, with some regulations requiring that programs meet only baseline standards, below which a program's quality is considered unacceptable (and possibly subject to criminal sanctions) and other regulations requiring excellent quality.

Studies of Quality Achieved Through Standards.   In general, early childhood programs that are governed by more effective baseline regulations or meet regulations on the upper end of the standards continuum are of higher quality than programs that meet only baseline standards (and more especially when those standards are set too low or when exemption from the regulations is possible). In short, levels of standards are program quality indicators. For example, states with effective licensing codes (baseline) have a greater number of higher-quality programs (Helburn, 1995; D. Phillips, Howes, & Whitebook, 1992), and this is true in both for-profit and not-for-profit centers (Kagan & Newton, 1989). As compared with nonaccredited programs, accred-

ited (highest level of standards) programs were measured as having the overall higher quality (Cost, Quality, and Child Outcomes Study Team, 1995; Whitebook, Howes, & Phillips, 1990; Whitebook, Phillips, & Howes, 1993). Furthermore, in states in which the baseline is higher, other regulatory methods are even higher (G. Morgan, 1996).

Higher quality in programs is demonstrated in both the pedagogical and administrative components' outcomes. In the pedagogical component, research showed that accredited centers provided more developmentally appropriate activities and higher quality caregiving than nonaccredited centers (Whitebook et al., 1993). High quality is demonstrated in children's increased competence in all areas of development (Barnett, 1995; Helburn, 1995; Herr, Johnson, & Zimmerman, 1993; Peisner-Feinberg, & Burchinal, 1997; Schweinhart, Barnes, & Weikart, 1993; Whitebook et al., 1990). In the administrative component, accredited centers have better trained staff, more extensive professional growth plans, and lower staff turnover than do nonaccredited centers (P. Bloom, 1996; Whitebook et al., 1993). As compared to nonaccredited centers, accredited centers scored higher on clearly written policies (P. Bloom), goal consensus (P. Bloom; Pope & Stremmel, 1992), innovative ideas (P. Bloom), and housing quality (Pope & Stremmel). The more standards a program meets, the higher the child outcomes (NICHD Early Child Care Research Network, 1998a).

Levels of Protective Standards.   Class, as cited by G. Morgan (1996), developed a conceptual framework for levels of standards. Baseline (or the lowest acceptable level of) standards include zoning, fire and various safety regulations, children's rights and protection regulations, regulations governing services for children with special needs, and licensing. Some overlap occurs in regulations imposed by various agencies of the federal, state, and local governments. When regulations of a similar nature are under more than one jurisdiction, an early childhood program must be in compliance with each. For example, a private early childhood program is subject to the fire safety standards of the local city code and the state licensing law. Furthermore, to help ensure that both standards are met, most state licensing agencies require an application for licensure of an early childhood program to include proof of compliance with all applicable city ordinances.

The next level of standards, which are beyond the baseline, are the ones with direct funding oversight, that is, regulations governing public agencies. A **public agency** is an organization that is part of the federal, state, or local government. Three major funded systems that provide child care and education are (a) Head Start, (b) public school early childhood programs, and (c) state social service programs that purchase care and education by contract with privately licensed facilities. Public agencies that provide subsidized programs for young children must meet specified standards to receive funding.

Higher quality is achieved through staff credentialing. One of the eight goals of the Quality 2000: Advancing Early Care and Education initiative was to create various types and levels of staff credentials (Kagan & Neuman, 1997b).

The highest level of standards is accreditation and model standards. Accreditation and model standards assume that all baseline standards have been met and maintained. In addition, programs that meet accreditation and model standards meet other standards of higher quality. Thus, these programs are of good to excellent quality.

Specific Protective Standards

In this section, the protective standards will be arranged from the lowest to highest levels (see Figure 3–1). Some of the regulations apply only to private programs (e.g., licensing), others to public agencies (e.g., public school regulations), and still others to all programs (e.g., regulations governing services for children with special needs and accreditation).

Zoning Regulations. Zoning regulations restrict the use of land. Each city and town is enabled by a state zoning law to divide its land into districts. Within those districts, the city can regulate the use of the land itself and the erection and use of buildings. Regulations are stated in the form of local zoning codes. Generally, zoning regulations become more stringent as population density increases.

Zoning regulates the location of early childhood facilities. Child care facilities, unlike elementary schools, are often not included as a permitted use within a zoning plan. They are treated as "problem use" (excluded from residential sections because of noise and from commercial sections because such areas are not considered good places for children). States are now working to prevent local zoning from outlawing child care.

Building Codes and Requirements for Fire Safety and Sanitation. The statutory basis for building codes and requirements for fire safety and sanitation rests in public safety and health laws. These may be municipal ordinances or state regulations with local enforcement. The Life Safety Code of the National Fire Protection Association provides guidelines for appropriate fire codes for centers, group homes, and family child care. Building codes are concerned with wiring, plumbing, and building materials. Fire regulations cover the type of building construction, alarm systems, sprinkler systems and fire extinguishers, ways to store combustible materials, and evacuation from the building. Sanitation codes are mainly concerned with food service operations; diaper changing and bathroom facilities; and washing toys, equipment, and furniture.

Transportation Requirements. In each state, the agency that regulates matters pertaining to motor vehicles has the legal mandate to protect children transported in buses and private vehicles. Some states have devised special regulations for child care transportation in addition to those required for licensure.

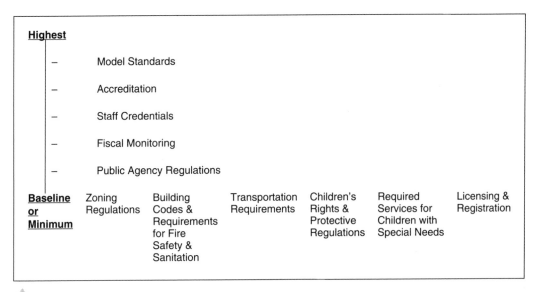

Figure 3–1   Levels of Protective Standards

Children's Rights and Protection Regulations. Historically, children's rights have been viewed in
moral and ethical terms rather than in legal
terms. Several groups have formulated children's
rights. For example, the United Nations Convention on the Rights of the Child, a 1990 international treaty, defined minimum standards for the
economic, social, cultural, and political rights of
children (NAEYC, 1993; Odland, 1995).

Promoting General Rights.   Children's legal rights
are primarily in the form of protection rather
than rights concerning freedom of choice. Protection rights for children are primarily assumed
by parents who have rights of guardianship (e.g.,
they determine the level of financial support,
provide religious and moral teachings, make
choices regarding services such as education and
health care). In some cases, society, through the
law, protects children from the results of their
own lack of judgment (e.g., children are not held
responsible for their contracts), develops laws on
behalf of children (e.g., school attendance and
child labor laws), and intervenes between parents
and children when the courts find that the chil-

dren need more protection—the concept of
parens patriae (e.g., foster care and the administration of health services in life-threatening situations). Children have recently been given some
direct legal rights (e.g., due process and fair
treatment in schools and juvenile courts). Protection rights of children implies responsibilities on
the part of all those involved—parents, society,
and even children themselves.

Handling Custody Issues.   Custody issues arise
when two adults have a right to some degree of
legal or physical custody of a child. **Legal custody**
is the right and responsibility of a person or
agency to make a decision on behalf of a child;
physical custody is the right and responsibility of
a person to provide immediate care. Custody issues arise frequently when children are from single-parent families or under the legal custody of
the state and in the physical custody of foster
parents.

   All early childhood programs need to protect
children involved in custody disputes. Children
can be protected if administrators follow this
procedure:

1. Clarify custody of all children at or prior to time of enrollment. (Information must be in writing, dated, signed, and kept current.)

2. Make sure that the name(s) and address(es) of those authorized to pick up the child are given in writing.

3. Provide a statement to each person enrolling a child that the child will be released only to those persons named on the forms as being authorized to receive the child.

4. If an unauthorized party attempts to receive a child, follow these steps: (a) Tell the person he or she is unauthorized, regardless of theoretical rights; (b) show him or her a copy of the authorization; (c) notify the authorized person of the problem; and (d) if the unauthorized person does not leave, call the police.

Reporting Suspected Child Abuse.   Early childhood educators certainly want protection for children. These professionals are mandated reporters of child abuse in every state and may incur criminal or civil penalties, loss of a job, or loss of a license for not reporting. Thus, early childhood professionals must be familiar with the indications of child maltreatment and state laws regarding reporting suspected cases.

All programs should establish written policies regarding the reporting requirements and internal processes. Policies may include responsibilities for reporting, definitions of reportable cases, descriptions of the internal processes (e.g., who will make the report), and statements about liability. Generally, witnesses write an anecdotal record that documents the episodes and describes any wounds. The witness notifies the administrator, who calls the abuse hotline. A written report (state form) is filed. A copy of the report is kept in the program but not in the child's file.

Child abuse occurring in an early childhood program is a rare but serious event. The National Child Protection Act, as discussed later in this chapter, helps prevent child abuse in centers. The NAEYC (1997b) has a position statement on ways to protect children from abuse within early childhood care and education programs.

Services for Children with Special Needs.   Approximately 5% of children in the United States from birth to age 5 have a disability (U.S. Bureau of the Census, 2001). Services for children with special needs have had a long and varied history (see Decker & Decker, 2001). The history of special education involves the identification of individuals needing special assistance, techniques and equipment and materials used in assisting individuals, and special schools and programs that serve as models for the delivery of services. Today, the inclusion of individuals with disabilities in the mainstream of society has been a growing concern and trend, with about 53% of 3- to 5-year-old children with disabilities spending all or part of their educational day in inclusive settings (U.S. Department of Education, 2001). **Inclusion** is not a legal term; rather, it is a state-of-the-art term for placing individuals with disabilities in integrated settings of all kinds—educational, employment, living arrangements, and others. The history of services for children with special needs is filled with laws that have mandated and encouraged specific services and with litigation.

Individuals with Disabilities Education Act (IDEA). Today, the most important law is Public Law (P.L.) 105-17, more often called IDEA. IDEA supports education and related service programming for children with disabilities.

IDEA has its roots in P.L. 94-142, the Education for All Handicapped Children Act (EHA). Under Part B of the law, all eligible school-aged children with disabilities were entitled to receive a free and appropriate public education (FAPE). In 1986, the EHA was amended by P.L. 99-457 to provide special funding incentives for states that would provide a FAPE for all eligible preschool children (i.e., children ages 3 through 5). Provisions under Part H were included to help early intervention programs for infants and toddlers with disabilities. The EHA was amended in 1990 by P.L. 101-476 to IDEA. IDEA was amended in 1992 by P.L. 102-119 and again in 1997 by P.L. 105-17.

The 1997 revision of IDEA strengthened early childhood services. These three major provisions of IDEA apply to early childhood programs:

1. Part B requires that a FAPE be available for children ages 3 through 21 years who have disabilities. Each eligible child receives services under a written individualized education program (IEP).

2. Section 619 of Part B authorizes grants to all states for services for children ages 3 through 5 who have disabilities and for the continuity of special education services for children moving out of Part C.

3. Part C provides all states with grants for early intervention services and supports for children from birth to age 3 who have developmental delays or who are at substantial risk for delay as a result of diagnosed factors and conditions and for their families. Each eligible child and family receives services under a written individualized family service plan (IFSP).

Americans with Disabilities Act. P.L. 101–336, known as the Americans with Disabilities Act (ADA), is civil rights legislation. As it pertains to children with special needs, this act is concerned with physical access, discrimination, and appropriate program practices. First, ADA requires full physical access to facilities for children or family members with disabilities. Thus, older housing facilities must be changed unless structural changes cause an "undue burden," and new structures (beginning in 1993) must meet ADA accessibility guidelines. Vans or buses must also meet ADA accessibility guidelines. Second, this act prohibits enrollment discrimination based on a child's disability. A program may reject a child only if it can prove that the training of staff or the purchase and use of equipment necessary to ac-

commodate that child would result in an "undue burden." Third, children with disabilities must be provided integrated settings in the least restrictive environment (LRE), and staff must follow P.L. 102–199 in implementing the IEP or the IFSP according to the child's age.

Head Start Amendment of 1993.   The Head Start Amendment of 1993 gives eligibility criteria for the enrollment of children with disabilities. The amendment also offers guidance in providing comprehensive services to children and their families, in screening children, in using evaluative criteria to determine eligibility for special education services, in developing IEPs, and in designating a coordinator of services for children with disabilities.

Litigation Concerning Inclusion.   Before 1990, court cases such as *Briggs v. Board of Education of Connecticut* (1989) and *Barnett v. Fairfax County School Board* (1991) often favored the assertions of school districts that, for specific children, the more appropriate settings were segregated programs. More recently, the courts have been more assertive in rendering decisions favoring inclusion, such as *Greer v. Rome City School District* (1991, 1992) and *Oberti v. Board of Education of the Borough of Clementon School District* (1993). Courts still review specific circumstances, and inclusion may be denied, as in *Clyde K. and Sheila K. v. Puyallup School District* (1994).

Licensing: Minimal Quality Regulations.   Licensing is the procedure by which a person, association, or corporation obtains from its state licensing agency a license to operate or continue operating a child care facility. The state entity has the authority to ensure that standards are met by inspecting the facility and revoking its license if criteria for operation are not met. A state-specified, licensed facility is recognized by the state agency as having met only minimum standards of child care; that is, licensing is a regulation reflecting the criterion of preventing harm to children rather than of providing exemplary care. In some cases, licensing standards do not meet minimum standards for safety (C. W. Snow, Teleki, & Reguero-de-Atiles, 1996).

Although the practice of licensing dates back to 1863, general interest in licensing did not begin until the early 1900s, when public scandals arose over the abuse of children in some child care facilities. This concern led to regulations for minimum standards of care and supervision of the publicly subsidized agencies. Regulation of child care increased with the creation of the U.S. Children's Bureau in 1912 and the Child Welfare League of America (CWLA) in 1920 (Class, 1972). As a result of the federal grants-in-aid funds of 1935, state child welfare departments were able to procure better qualified personnel, child care facilities were brought under child care licensing statutes, social workers took an active interest in protective services, and licensing was identified as a state child welfare function (Class, 1968). In recent years, the numbers of regulated child care centers have continued to increase. For example, data from the Children's Foundation (2002) show that regulated child care centers have increased 24% since 1991.

The regulation of family child care began in Pennsylvania in 1885 (Travis & Perreault, 1983), yet family child care was, for the most part, unregulated. The characteristics and quality of family child care began to be described and researched in the late 1960s and the 1970s by individuals and through the government-sponsored National Day Care Home Study. Thus, most family child care licensing regulations were adopted in the 1960s and 1970s (Travis & Perreault). By the 1980s, many states switched from licensing to registration (A. Kahn & Kamerman, 1987; Travis & Perreault), although today 34% of the states require licensing exclusively (Children's Foundation, 2001).

Registration is a process by which a state's licensing agent publishes regulations, requires providers to certify that they have complied with the regulations, and maintains records on all family child care homes. Providers usually certify that certain health and fire standards are met. Some states also require criminal background checks of registered providers. However, in some states registration is simply a sign-up procedure. A few states use the term *certification* (not to be confused with teacher credentials), which is the same as registration but is often linked to providers receiving public funds.

Nonregulation of family child care is still a problem. Although the Children's Foundation (2001) reported that regulation of group child care homes had increased by 12%, the regulation of family child care homes decreased by one half of 1%. In the study by Galinsky, Howes, Kontos, and Shinn (1994), only 9% of family child care homes were rated "good" and 35% were rated "inadequate" (i.e., "growth harming"). B. Caldwell (1990) stated that the lack of regulation of the family child care system "is one of the factors responsible for the field's slow climb to legitimacy" (p. 4).

States differ in their definitions of what child care facilities must be regulated (Children's Foundation, 2001, 2002). Nonlicensed facilities may include programs operated under public auspices (e.g., public school programs), day camps, programs sponsored by religious organizations, and programs operated by private schools or private agencies (e.g., the YMCA).

The Licensing Agency. The state regulates child care from its constitutional authority to protect the welfare of the child. Licensing of child care facilities falls under the auspices of the Department of Health and Human Services, Human Resources, or the state's equivalent (see appendix 2). According to Class (1968), the licensing agency is a regulatory agency with both quasi-legislative and quasi-judicial authority. The quasi-legislative powers include responsibility for establishing standards; the quasi-judicial powers include responsibility for making decisions to issue or deny a license application and for conducting hearings in grievance cases.

Features of Child Care Licensing Laws. The different types of child care facilities may be covered by a general or differential licensing law. Differential licensing laws have varying standards for these types of programs: child care (family child care homes, group child care homes, and child care centers), foster care (foster homes and group foster homes), child-placing institutions, residential facilities, and children's camps.

An advisory group comprising interested persons, child development and early childhood education experts, politicians, and consumers write licensing codes. The codes are based on new knowledge of how to prevent harm to children and on the number of providers able to meet higher quality regulations. Those with concerns regarding licensing laws look to this task force for action. Public hearings are held on the draft. The agency then issues a legal statement, which becomes the law. Some states aid providers in complying with new rules by postponing the effective date of implementation (i.e., a transition time is built into the code). Licensing codes are often reexamined every 4 or 5 years (G. Morgan, 1996).

Child Care Center Regulations

Regulatory laws governing child care centers differ widely from state to state. To find out about specific regulations of a state, contact the state's licensing agency and request a copy of the regulations (see appendix 2). Areas covered in most licensing codes include the following:

1. **Licensing laws and procedures.** For purposes of licensing, the state says it is illegal to care for another person's child. Then, the state says a person may care for other people's children if he or she applies for and is given permission (a license) by the authorized agency of the government. This section of the code covers terms such as *child care*, programs that must be licensed, policies for obtaining and submitting an application for a license, fees, application approval, duration of license, criteria for revoking a license, policy for posting of license, and conditions requiring

notification of the licensing agency. (General licensing procedures are given in Figure 3–2.)

2. **Organization and administration.** State licensing laws require an applicant to indicate its purposes and the sponsorship of the organization, whether the program is for-profit or not-for-profit, ways in which administrative authority is placed (e.g., boards, director), policies concerning children (e.g., admission, termination, nondiscrimination provision, fees), child–staff ratio, and financial solvency for immediate and continuous operation.

3. **Staffing.** Regulations concerning staffing usually include categories of personnel (director, primary program personnel, and support program personnel); age, education, health, character, and temperament characteristics of staff members; personnel records to be kept; and child–staff ratio.

4. **Plant and equipment.** Licensing codes require applicants to meet local zoning, health, and fire standards and state health department

✓	Request copy of licensing requirements.
✓	Obtain zoning permit.
✓	Contact sanitation, fire, building, and public health inspectors.
✓	Arrange for conferences if problems exist; obtain assistance from state licensing specialist.
✓	Once approvals are obtained from all of the preceding, complete license application and send it to the department.
✓	Expect a visit from a staff member of the licensing department.
✓	Post license.

Figure 3–2 **Licensing Procedure**

standards before applying. The majority of states have regulations concerning the indoor housing (e.g., size, type, and number of rooms needed), environmental control, drinking water sources, sanitary facilities, kitchen facilities, and outdoor space needed. Some equipment regulations are common, such as equipment for naps. Specific regulations on other equipment may not be given but may be listed as "suggested" equipment.

5. **Health and safety.** Health and safety requirements concerning physical facilities, health forms, and nutrition are very specific. Two areas receiving serious attention are (a) sexual abuse, as previously discussed, and (b) concern over infectious diseases in all child care and especially infant programs (G. Morgan, 1986).

6. **Program.** Some states have detailed program specifications. Because child care is not considered educational but a public welfare service in some states, program regulations tend to be more lax than most other licensing regulations. Other state licensing departments desire minimum regulation or believe that parents and staff should have a great deal of autonomy and control over program content and scheduling.

7. **Discipline.** Many states stipulate "no harsh discipline" and give suggestions for the guidance of children. The outlawing of corporal punishment in state codes is the issue behind much effort by certain religious groups to exempt their child care programs from licensing.

8. **Parent involvement.** Most states require that parents be involved in the child care program. Suggested means include serving on boards of advisors, visiting the facility during hours of operation, having parent–staff conferences, and being given materials on the program's goals and policies.

Family Child Care Regulations

Categories for family child care homes are very similar to those for child care centers. The main differences are in the family child care regula-

tions concerning (a) how the number of children will be counted (all children on the premises for supervision, including the caregiver's own children, are counted against the approval capacity); (b) how keeping infants and toddlers affects the count (most family child care homes have mixed-age groups); and (c) how the home, outside area, and personal possessions must be child-proofed for health and safety reasons (some dangerous constructions, such as stairs, or some dangerous items, such as weapons, are found in some homes and thus are part of the accident-prevention regulations). Some professionals question whether center-based regulations should apply to family child care programs (D. Phillips, Lande, & Goldberg, 1990).

Improving Licensing Laws. G. Morgan, Curry, Endsley, Bradford, and Rashid (1985) stated that licensing laws can be judged in terms of whether (a) standards are high or low; (b) the state code covers all forms of child care—infant and toddler programs, family child care homes, and group child care homes; (c) the standards are implemented fully; (d) the licensing system has a broad base of support in the state; and (e) the state has adequate numbers of trained workers in the licensing agency.

Many studies note major problems with licensing coming from the public view of regulations, the licensing codes, and the agency. Following are some of the problems:

1. We live in a deregulation climate. Consumers often think of licensing as determining ideal quality rather than minimum standards (NAEYC, 1998b).

2. In some states, a lack of coordination of requirements between licensing and other codes exists; the two may even be contradictory (Gormley, 1995; NAEYC, 1998b).

3. Too many codes exempt some early childhood programs from licensing in any form (Children's Foundation, 2001, 2002; NAEYC, 1998b). The U.S. General Accounting Office

(2000) found serious problems in allowing programs receiving CC&DBG to "self-certify" (i.e., verify in writing that they are operating a safe and healthy program).

4. Licensing codes often fall below professional standards (e.g., American Academy of Pediatrics, American Public Health Association, & National Resource Center for Health and Safety in Child Care, 2002; NAEYC, 1998a) in critical indicators of quality, such as child–staff ratios, group size, and the education and training of staff members (Children's Foundation, 2001, 2002; NAEYC, 1998b; C. W. Snow, Teleki, & Reguero-de-Atiles, 1996).

5. The Committee on Early Childhood Pedagogy was concerned that states did not include program content quality as part of their codes (NRC, 2001).

6. The licensing agencies also had serious problems in training for licensing staff, caseloads above the recommended level, and infrequent on-site monitoring for effective enforcement and meaningful sanctions (Gormley, 1997; NAEYC, 1998b; U.S. General Accounting Office, 2000).

The profession continues to call for higher licensing standards. For example, the position statement adopted by the NAEYC (1998b) calls for all programs enrolling children from "two or more unrelated families" to be licensed; staff licensure to be separated from program licensure; standards to be in keeping with research; the licensure process to be streamlined; and incentives, knowledge dissemination, and state support to be used to encourage licensing.

Public Agency Regulations.   Publicly funded early childhood programs are not subject to licensing. Instead, all publicly funded programs, such as public school supported and federally supported early childhood programs, are regulated by a state or federal agency. A specified state or federal agency is required by law to prepare regulations.

Legally, public schools are public agencies. Public school education in the United States is a state function. The organizational structure is similar in each state. In most states, the chief state school officer is the superintendent of public instruction or the commissioner of education, who is either elected or appointed. Early childhood education programs in the public schools fall under this officer's jurisdiction. The chief state school officer and the state board of education, composed of elected or appointed board members, make up the policy-making group for public education in the state. With the state board's approval, the chief state school officer selects the personnel and operates the department of public instruction or state education agency. Within the department of public instruction is a bureau concerned with early childhood education programs. Duties of the bureau may include approving requests for state aid, evaluating teacher certification applications, responding to requests for information or assistance, supervising programs in the local school districts, appraising legislative proposals that affect early childhood programs, and publishing information on regulations or trends in early childhood education.

The local school district may be, according to each state's law, a large urban district, a small community district, a cooperative arrangement among several communities, or a county district. The board of education or trustees, an elected group that represents the district's interests, is the policy-making group. As authorized by state laws, the board approves all school expenditures, plans for building projects, makes personnel appointments, and determines the services offered to students and parents. The superintendent, appointed by the school board, is the administrative officer for the school district. The superintendent's function is to execute, within the limits of state law, the board's actions.

Directly superior to the early childhood education teacher is the building principal, who is the instructional leader and administrator of the school physical facility, records, and personnel. Supervisors or supervisor-administrators may be assigned by the superintendent's office to supervise and assist early childhood education teachers. The early childhood education teacher is responsible for caregiving and instruction of the children, for the management of the classroom, and for any assistant teachers or aides placed in the early childhood classroom.

Fiscal Monitoring.   **Fiscal monitoring** refers to standards associated with funding. When the government buys or creates a service through a grant or contract, it establishes specifications for quality. Based on contract law, the relationship of the government to the provider is that of purchaser or contractor; that is, the government sets parameters concerning the dissemination of federal funds, such as allowable expenditures, eligibility, and regulations local and state agencies must adhere to in the dissemination and use of funds. One example of fiscal monitoring is the Head Start Performance Standards, which local Head Start programs must meet for future funding.

Funding standards are the conditions or standards for receiving a grant or contract. If the agency runs its own program, the relationship is even more direct. *Operating standards* are the conditions or standards under which a governmental agency operates a program. The government agency makes sure that services are provided, costs are reasonable, and services are of acceptable quality. Some states require the public program to meet the standard used in licensing; others require a level of quality higher than licensing.

Credentialing Staff.   Recognition of an administrator's and teacher's expertise is called *credentialing, certification,* and *licensure.* Professional preparation is a shortcoming of early childhood care and education because of high demand for early childhood program personnel, inadequate compensation, high turnover of personnel, and

the lack of professional consensus regarding the preparation of personnel. One of the recommendations advanced in the national report of the Quality 2000: Advancing Early Care and Education Initiative (Kagan & Cohen, 1997) is to use this three-tiered approach to credentialing staff: early childhood administrator, early childhood educator, and early childhood associate educator.

Regulations Concerning Administrator Qualifications. G. Morgan (2000b) believes that preparation for directors should be similar regardless of the early childhood program. Directors need proficiency in human development, early childhood programming, and management because the director is the key to quality. G. Morgan prepared a comprehensive list of competencies early childhood program directors should possess (see appendix 3). Because of the histories of various types of early childhood programs, however, required administrative credentialing differs according to program sponsorship.

Administrators of public school early childhood programs must hold a state administrator's certificate that grants legitimate authorization to administer a school program. The state education agency issues various types of administrator certificates (e.g., an elementary principal's certificate). All public school administrators hold teaching certificates, have had teaching experience, and have taken graduate courses in administration.

Directors of Montessori schools are expected to have a bachelor's degree from an accredited institution, Montessori certification, and teaching experience. Competency is expected in teaching, educational administration, and curriculum development.

Head Start does not require any specific training for directors. Most directors come from the ranks of teachers and then work as component coordinators before serving as directors. Those who come from outside of Head Start usually have extensive experience in programs serving low-income children. Head Start does offer new directors workshops, week-long regional training sessions, tailored administrative consultation, and the Head Start Management Fellows program.

Directors of early childhood programs not under the state educational agency must meet the educational and experience requirements of their state's licensing law. Most states require center directors to have some combination of education and experience. In some states an administrator credential is mandatory, especially for those serving publicly funded early childhood programs; in other states, the credential is voluntary. College credit is required for some credentials with the required credit hours ranging from 3 to 36 (Taking the Lead Initiative, 1999b). The vast majority of directors of these programs were classroom teachers (P. Bloom, 1989); they simply learned on the job or by turning to the licensing or funding agency for assistance.

In short, administrators are not well prepared for their jobs. Although public school administrators are well educated and experienced in "school matters," few states require specialized knowledge in early childhood care and education. Conversely, directors of other programs tend to be well versed in the pedagogical components of their programs but are not competent in the administrative components such as organization theory and leadership, management, staff development, legal issues, and fiscal management, including marketing (A. Mitchell, 2000; G. Morgan, 1997, 2000a). Neither principals (Charlesworth, Hart, Burts, & DeWolf, 1993) nor child care directors (Caruso, 1991) have had thorough training in DAP. Those who have had training in early childhood care and education tended to see the importance of DAP (Charlesworth et al.); more female than male principals were DAP oriented (Rusher, McGrevin, & Lambiotte, 1992).

The importance of the director's skills are now being noted. Besides state credentials, these three national director credentials are available: (a) National Administrator Credential sponsored by the National Child Care Association; (b) Christian Director's Child Development Education Credential sponsored by the National Association for Child Development Education; and (c) Professional Administrator National Credentialing sponsored by the National Association of Professional Administrators (Culkin, 2000). Degree programs in early childhood administration are being offered in several colleges (e.g., Carnegie Mellon University's H. John Heinz III School of Public Policy and Management; National Louis University's Center for Early Childhood Leadership; Nova University; University of Missouri at Kansas City's Forum for Early Childhood Organization and Leadership Development). More professional associations are being chartered and are offering various forms of assistance (see appendix 5).

Regulations Concerning Teacher Qualifications. Teachers' qualifications determine children's academic achievement more than any other variable (Darling-Hammond, Wise, & Klein, 1999). Thus, quality programs are to a large extent determined by teacher preparation and career development (Kontos, Howes, & Galinsky, 1997).

Teachers' formal education correlates with overall classroom quality (Phillipsen, Burchinal, Howes, & Cryer, 1997). The teacher's intellectual ability is a predictor of how much a child learns from a teacher (R. Ferguson, 1998). A strong liberal arts background may be helpful, too (Isenberg, 1999). Specialized education (i.e., courses taken in child development and early childhood education) is correlated with classroom quality and especially with positive teacher behaviors, such as teacher sensitivity and responsiveness and positive group management (Darling-Hammond, 1998; A. Epstein, 1999; Howes, 1997; Kontos et al., 1997).

The experience of teachers is not consistently linked to overall classroom quality or positive teacher behaviors (NICHD Early Child Care Research Network, 1996). However, a teacher's formal education including supervised field experiences is a quality predictor, especially of using DAP (Fischer & Eheart, 1991; Kontos & File, 1992; A. Mitchell, 1988; Snider & Fu, 1990). DAP can be implemented only through specialized training (Bredekamp, 1990; Cassidy, Buell, Pugh-Hoese, & Russell, 1995). Burts and Buchanan (1998) developed some ideas about how to prepare teachers to use DAP.

Certification of Teachers in Public School Early Childhood Programs

Education of early childhood teachers has had a long history. Until the first kindergarten training school was established in Boston in 1868, all prospective kindergarten teachers received their training in Germany and other European countries. These schools offered instruction in Froebelian theory and methods and on-the-job training in kindergarten classrooms. "The training given emphasized the kindergarten as a unique form of education apart from and having nothing in common with the school" (Holmes, 1937, p. 270). Although public school kindergartens became common near the turn of the 20th century, kindergarten training schools were continued as private, self-supporting institutions because the normal schools were not able to supply the increasing demand for trained teachers.

Many educators realized the desirability of employing state-certified kindergarten teachers rather than having the kindergarten work "carried on by people who play a piano and love dear little children" ("Marked Kindergarten Progress," 1925, p. 303). Consequently, many colleges and universities reorganized their curricula to meet the needs of students preparing to teach kindergarten. Most of the certificates were based on a high school diploma and a 2-year professional program and were special-subject certificates valid only for teaching in the kindergarten (Vandewalker, 1925). Gradually, almost all states developed certification requirements for teachers of young children (often at the kindergarten level only) that required a bachelor's degree and were patterned after elementary certification requirements.

Today, public school programs include both kindergartens and prekindergarten programs. In all states kindergarten teachers must have a bachelor's degree and a certificate in early childhood education or in elementary education with an endorsement to teach kindergarten. Thirty-five states have similar requirements for public school prekindergarten teachers. Early childhood special education teachers often add specialized education in early childhood special education to a regular early childhood teaching credential (Olson, 2002).

Each state is responsible for certification of its public school teachers. The state department of education (see appendix 2) has the following certification responsibilities: (a) write minimum requirements for each type of certificate; (b) develop guidelines for teacher training institutions to follow in planning degree programs for prospective teachers; and (c) issue, renew, and revoke certification. Although the bases for certification are left to each state, most certification standards specify U.S. citizenship, age and health requirements, earned college degree with special course requirements, and possibly a recommendation from the college or university. Many states also require additional tests of competency (e.g., the National Teacher Exam [NTE]).

Three major problems occur in teachers certification.

1. Each state defines *early childhood education* in its own way. Thus, teachers are prepared for different ages of children, which, in turn, limits certification reciprocity among the states.

2. Specialized training is often limited as a result of standards for certificates. States often endorse the elementary teaching certificate with minimal additional requirements, that is, two to six courses and student teaching beyond the required preparation for the elementary certificate (McCarthy, 1988; G. Morgan et al., 1993). Furthermore, the majority of states have developed alternative certification programs (these programs enroll individuals with a bachelor's de-

gree, usually in the arts and sciences, and offer a curricular shortcut to teaching). Lack of sufficient training is even more evident in those who work with infants and toddlers. Only a few states define early childhood as birth through age 8; the NAEYC (1988) reported three states using this comprehensive definition. Bruder, Klosowski, and Daguio (1991) found few regulatory standards specific to personnel providing services to infants and toddlers.

3. Standardized testing limits the number of students, especially minorities, who complete the requirements for teacher certification, which causes a racial and cultural imbalance between children and their teachers (Meek, 1998).

The early childhood profession has looked at the many issues in the preparation of early childhood teachers. Following are some of the current recommendations:

1. Teachers should have a bachelor's degree with specialized knowledge related to early childhood (e.g., child development and learning; child development knowledge linked to content areas and pedagogical practices; knowledge of integrated curriculum; assessment practices).

2. Preparation should include the history and philosophy of early childhood care and education; inclusive practices; family issues; health, safety, and nutrition; administration of programs; and advocacy.

3. Preparation should include a supervised and relevant student teaching or internship experience (ACEI, 1997; Griffin, 1999; Gundling & Hyson, 2002; NRC, 2001).

The NAEYC addressed the problem of professional content at the associate, bachelor's, and advanced degree levels in the early 1980s. Guidelines for the bachelor's degree were approved by the NAEYC in 1981 and by the National Council for the Accreditation of Teacher Education (NCATE) in 1982. By the mid-1980s, the NAEYC developed guidelines for associate degrees in

early childhood education. In 1986, the NAEYC and the National Association of Early Childhood Teacher Educators (NAECTE) worked cooperatively on developing graduate degree guidelines. These were approved by the NCATE in 1988. These guidelines were revised in 1996 and again in 2001. The standards still encompass the birth-through-8 age range and emphasize the diversity of early childhood care and education settings. The NAEYC still upholds the core values of the 1996 Guidelines (NAEYC, 1996a). The 2001 guidelines place more emphasis on cultural and linguistic diversity, communities in which children live, inclusion curriculum content, teaching strategies, and assessment issues. Field experience is included within each standard (Hyson, 2002).

Similarly, the Division for Early Childhood (DEC) of the Council for Exceptional Children (CEC) developed a position paper on guidelines for the preparation of early childhood special educators. The DEC's guidelines were endorsed by the NAEYC in the same way that the NAEYC's guidelines had been previously endorsed by the DEC (NAEYC, 1996a). A major trend in early childhood special education is to prepare teachers for inclusive educational settings (P. S. Miller & Stayton, 1998, 1999). In 2000, the DEC's new recommend practices were published (Sandall, McLean, & Smith, 2000).

Teacher Qualifications in American Montessori Schools

Because the AMS is a national private agency, the instructional staff of a Montessori school has to meet the licensing code requirements of the state or, in some states, the requirements of the state board of education. In addition to meeting the state's requirements, the AMS has its own certification requirements for working with infants and toddlers and in early childhood (ages 2½ to 6 years), elementary, and secondary programs, as follows:

1. For levels below elementary, high school graduation is required. For elementary and secondary certification, a degree from an

accredited 4-year college or equivalent foreign credential is required, but no specific field of study is stipulated.

2. A minimum of 1 year of study is required for completion of Montessori Accreditation Council for Teacher Education competencies. About 200 clock hours of academic work are required. This may include workshops or seminars in the historical and philosophical foundations of American education and the relationship of Montessori education to current knowledge of child development; knowledge of Montessori theory, philosophy, and materials for instruction as presented in seminars and as seen in observation of laboratory classes; and training in language arts, mathematics, science, art, music, social studies, and motor perception.

3. A practicum of 400 clock hours is required.

Teacher Qualifications in Head Start and Child Care Programs

By September 2003, at least 50% of all Head Start teachers nationwide in center-based programs were required to have an associate, baccalaureate, or advanced degree in early childhood education or in a field related to early childhood education, with experience in teaching preschool children. For each classroom that does not have at least one teacher meeting the degree requirements, the teacher must have the appropriate CDA credential or similar certificate. (The CDA credential is described later in this section.) Preservice and in-service preparation for child care teachers are determined by each state's licensing regulations. In 42 states the head or lead teacher or program director in centers must have some combination of education and experience (Children's Foundation, 2002). Olson (2002) reported that 30 states require no *preservice education* for teachers in child care centers. Few states require that family child care providers and assistant teachers have preservice education or experience (Children's Foundation, 2001, 2002). Furthermore, these facts should be noted about center personnel preservice training:

1. Center directors are more likely than teachers to have preservice learning.

2. States without preservice training requirements often have no orientation requirements, whereas states with preservice training requirements frequently have orientation requirements.

3. Only 10 states have any specialized preparation for working with infants and toddlers and with children who are sick or have disabilities (Children's Foundation, 2002).

Because of the meager requirements, these teachers have far less formal training than teachers in public school programs. For example, the National Child Care Staffing Study (Whitebook et al., 1993) found that only 12% of center staff had bachelor's or graduate degrees in a field related to early childhood education and that 38% had no education related to early childhood education at all. Other staff members had some work in a field related to early childhood education. Generally speaking, licensing codes value experience and may accept it in lieu of academic preparation; however, states have not set standards for the quality of the work experiences. Teachers often lack preservice training if (a) the program is exempt from regulation; (b) the program has not been checked by the licensing agency; and (c) the preservice training requirements are waived as a result staff shortages.

Although child care is still seen by many as an unskilled occupation, states are beginning to strengthen regulations. Many states are now requiring the CDA for lead teachers. As has been mentioned, the CDA credential is used by teachers in a variety of child care settings, including Head Start. The CDA was launched in 1972 as a credential for the entire field of early childhood care and education. It was funded by the federal government and operated by the CDA

Consortium, whose goals are to establish competencies needed for working in early childhood education, to develop methodologies for assessing such competencies, and to issue appropriate credentials (Bouverat & Galen, 1994). On March 25, 1975, the board of directors formally adopted the Credential Award System and authorized the awarding of the CDA credential to anyone who could demonstrate competence by completing the requirements of the consortium.

Because of federal funding cutbacks, the consortium disbanded in 1979, and credentialing was shuffled around until 1985 when the NAEYC took responsibility for credentialing, establishing a separate, not-for-profit corporation—the Council for Early Childhood Professional Recognition, later renamed the Council for Professional Recognition. The council became an independent entity in 1989. In 1992, the council developed the CDA Professional Program (CDA P) for individuals without prior training or experience. The CDA P is often used by higher education institutions preparing CDAs (Council for Professional Recognition, 2000).

Educational prerequisites are now required for the CDA credential. Candidates for the CDA credential must have a high school diploma or its equivalent and have 120 clock hours of education distributed over eight subject areas as shown in Figure 3–3. The CDA credential is now linked to associate-degree-granting institutions with the articulation between CDA training and continuing education units or college credits. Thus, the CDA credential now represents a teacher qualification equivalent to 9 to 12 credits of professional education. For more information, contact the Council for Professional Recognition (see appendix 5).

Besides requiring the training and experience components of the licensing laws, each state now requires a criminal history background check of each employee. The National Child Protection Act of 1993 (H.R. 1237) establishes procedures for national criminal background checks for child care providers. The act requires states to report child abuse crime information to the national criminal history background maintained by the FBI. The act also allows states to conduct background checks on child care providers.

Potential Vulnerability to Legal Actions. Three legal principles often apply in legal actions involving any business:

1. An employee is hired to perform certain types of duties, with certain expectations as to how these duties will be performed. When an employee's actions are consistent with those expectations, an employee is said to be "acting within the scope of authority." An employee is not liable when acting within the scope of authority but is liable when acting beyond it.

2. Except for negligence on the part of employees, employers are responsible for all torts (civil wrongs) committed by employees. The

Figure 3–3   Education Subject Areas Required to Receive CDA Credential

1. Planning a safe, healthy learning environment
2. Advancing children's physical and intellectual development
3. Supporting children's social and emotional development
4. Establishing productive relationships with families
5. Managing effective program operation
6. Maintaining a commitment to professionalism
7. Observing and recording children's behavior
8. Knowing and adhering to principles of child development and learning

legal phrase used for this principle is *respondent superior* ("the boss is responsible"). This principle does not apply to independent contractors, who are responsible for their own torts.

3. Principals (e.g., boards of directors) are responsible for torts committed by their agents (e.g., directors) acting on the business of the principal and within the scope of employment.

Liabilities vary, depending on the form of organization. Programs fully liable are sole proprietorships, partnerships, and for-profit corporations. Liability is limited in some states by the charitable immunity doctrine for programs operated as not-for-profit corporations. Public agency programs, such as public school early childhood programs and Head Start, have generally been immune from full liability as provided by Section 1983 of the Civil Rights Act (Mancke, 1972). Under the Civil Rights Act, immunity was not extended to the following three types of suits: (a) intentional injury (e.g., corporal punishment resulting in lasting injury to body or health; restraint of a person, such as physically enforcing the time-out technique; and defamation, such as implying a student's lack of ability in nonprofessional communication); (b) negligence (e.g., failure to give adequate instruction, failure to take into account a child's abilities, improper supervision, inadequate inspection of equipment); and (c) educational negligence (careless or incompetent teaching practices; L. Scott, 1983).

Several implications can be drawn concerning the potential vulnerability to legal action. First, all employees should have job descriptions spelling out their scope of authority. Second, adequate staffing, safe housing and equipment, administrative diligence, staff awareness and training in care of children, and documentation will do much to reduce the risk of torts. Finally, everyone involved in programs should realize that situations leading to liability are ever-present concerns and that all employees are vulnerable to legal actions.

Accreditation. **Accreditation** is a process of self-regulation; thus, regulations governing programs (e.g., licensing/registration and credentialing of staff) differ from accreditation in several ways. Other regulations are mandatory minimum standards requiring 100% compliance, are determined or set by governmental or funding agencies, and often are imposed at the local and state levels, although some regulations have federal scope (e.g., laws that regulate services for children with special needs). Conversely, accreditation standards are voluntary high-quality standards requiring substantial compliance, are sponsored by professional organizations, and are operated at the national level. Failure to meet compulsive regulation standards can result in legal sanctions, but failure to become accredited can mean failure to gain professional status.

Early childhood programs accredited by a particular association or agency are not necessarily superior to other programs, although they are often superior because staff members have voluntarily pursued a degree of excellence. Because accreditation represents a standard of excellence, the military has 95% of its programs accredited (Howe, 2000; Zellman & Johansen, 1998) and seven states require their prekindergarten programs or other centers receiving state monies to be accredited or working toward accreditation (Jacobson, 2002). Studies have shown that accredited centers were of higher-than-average quality (Cost, Quality, & Child Outcomes Study Team, 1995; Howes & Galinsky, 1996; Whitebook, Sakai, & Howes, 1997).

A study of directors' perceptions of the benefits of accreditation found that 55% of directors of accredited programs thought their programs were more visible, and 38% reported that accreditation made marketing easier. More than 90% of directors reported improvement in their programs, especially in curriculum, administration, health and safety, and the physical environment components but not in staffing and food and nutrition components. The directors also stated that children benefited by better staff morale, improved knowledge and understanding of DAP, and parent understanding of the components and standards necessary for high-quality care (Herr, Johnson, & Zimmerman, 1993). P. Bloom (1996) indicated that accredited and nonaccredited early childhood programs differ in the following areas: innovations and acceptance of change; goal consensus; opportunities for staff development; and clarity about policies, procedures, and communication.

Accreditation, as a process of self-regulation, involves three major steps. The first step involves an application and fee payment to the accrediting association, followed by a **self-study** in which the program attempts to meet the accreditation standards as delineated by interpretive statements, usually called *criteria* (see appendix 4). The self-study is submitted in a specified written format to the sponsoring association. The second step involves on-site **validation,** which is a visit to the program by a team of validators (highly qualified professionals with association training to interpret the accreditation standards and procedures). As their title suggests, these validators verify that the written information is an accurate reflection of daily program operations. The validators then report their findings to the accrediting agency. The third step is the **decision-making process** by the accrediting agency. Programs are informed in writing concerning their accreditation status, along with their strengths and weaknesses.

Accredited programs have a term of accreditation; to stay accredited, program officials must reapply and successfully complete the entire process before the term expires. Furthermore, most associations now require annual reports from their accredited programs regarding each program's current status and maintain the right to revoke accreditation if the program does not maintain quality standards or fails to comply with any procedures. For deferred programs, appeal procedures and association assistance plans are available for helping them to meet the standards and become accredited.

Many programs begin accreditation but stall during self-study either in the initial process or during reaccreditation. Talley (1997) found several reasons for this problem. Almost two fifths of the directors reported a lack of time, and almost one third reported problems with staff turnover or program instability as the major reasons for failure to complete the accreditation process. Three other frequently given reasons for stalling were new directors, seeing the process as overwhelming, and seeing other program concerns as higher priorities. Although a few programs with strong, stable staffs and healthy environments felt accreditation was not important, most programs failed to complete self-study because of quality issues.

Several accreditation agencies are involved in early childhood programs. In 1982, the NAEYC began developing an accreditation system for early childhood programs serving a minimum of 10 children within the age group of birth through age 5 in part- or full-day group programs and ages 5 through age 8 in before- and after-school programs. No family child care programs are included at this time. To accomplish the goals of accreditation, the NAEYC established a new organization—the National Academy of Early Childhood Programs (the Academy). The criteria were revised in 1988. In 2002, a new accreditation organizational structure of the Academy was approved (D. Scott, 2002). Other tasks, especially an update of the accreditation criteria and process along with the needed materials, are projected to be completed by the end of 2004 (Goffin, 2002). Until the new system is fully operational in 2005, programs working toward accreditation join the Academy as "candidate programs" and become members when accredited. The self-study consists of four parts: an Early Childhood Classroom Observation, an Administrative Report, a Staff Questionnaire, and a Parent Questionnaire. The criteria are centered on the following 10 components of group programs for children: interactions among teachers and children, curriculum, relationships among teachers and families, staff qualifications and professional development, administration, staffing, physical environment, health and safety, nutrition and food service, and evaluation (NAEYC, 1998a). To stimulate interest in the NAEYC accreditation system and to provide support during the self-study process, accreditation facilitation projects began in the 1990s (Fils, 2002).

Other professional associations have developed accreditation criteria and procedures for early childhood programs, including the National Association for Child Care Resource and Referral Agencies (NACCRRA), the National Association for Family Child Care (NAFCC), the Ecumenical Child Care Network (ECCN), the National Child Care Association (NCCA), and the National School Age Child Care Alliance (NSACA). Public schools are necessarily accredited by the state education agency. Because early childhood programs in public schools are considered part of the elementary schools, these programs are accredited with the elementary schools in a local school district. In addition to the various state education agencies, early childhood programs that are part of elementary schools may be accredited by the Southern Association of Colleges and Schools. (Among the six regional accrediting associations, only the Southern Association of Colleges and Schools has an arrangement for accrediting elementary schools.) As previously discussed, teacher preparation institutions are often accredited, too.

Model Standards. **Model standards,** developed by experts, are standards of practice based on the most recent knowledge available and the highest standards for the profession. Model standards are not new. For example, the Children's Bureau, established in 1911, described what children's programs could be like as a contrast to the then current conditions (Oettinger, 1964). The U.S. Department of Health, Education, and Welfare (1972) adopted *Guides for Day Care Licensing* as a model licensing standard. More recently, the American Academy of Pediatrics, the American

Public Health Association, and the National Resource Center for Health and Safety in Child Care (2002) developed national health and safety performance standards.

MEETING LEGAL REQUIREMENTS THROUGH REGULATIONS

Some standards do not directly involve the protection of children and their families. These standards concern the business aspects of early childhood programs, such as the legal existence of private programs, fiscal regulations, and staff regulations excluding credentialing.

Legal Existence of Private Programs

Proprietorship, partnership, and corporation are legal categories for three types of private ownership. Legal requirements for operating an early childhood program under any of these categories vary from state to state; this discussion focuses on common features of the laws. Legal assistance should be sought before establishing a private early childhood program.

Proprietorship. Under a **proprietorship,** a program is owned by one person. This person has no partners and is not incorporated. Sole proprietorships may have a single owner and operator or a larger staff with one person as owner. The legal requirements are simple: To create a proprietorship, the owner must file with the city clerk a True Name Certificate or, if the owner is not going to use his or her real name, a Fictitious Name Registration, such as "Jack and Jill Center."

The Assumed Name Law informs clients and creditors of true ownership of the business. In a sole proprietorship, the owner has full decision-making authority as long as decisions are consistent with governmental regulations (e.g., the owner must file a personal tax form). The owner may sell, give away, or go out of the business with no restrictions except the payment of outstanding debts and the completion of contractual obligations. The owner assumes full personal liability, however, for debts, breaches of contract, torts, taxes, and regulatory fees; the liability is not limited in amount and may even exceed the owner's personal funds.

Partnership.   In a **partnership,** two or more people usually join together for purposes of ownership. However, a partnership may involve minor children, a sole proprietorship, or a corporation as a partner. (The sole proprietor and the corporation would be involved in their own business as well as the business owned by the partnership.) A partnership has limited transferability. A partner may sell or give away his or her interest in the partnership only if all other partners consent. If one partner dies, the partnership is dissolved. The law recognizes two types of partnerships:

1. **General partnership.** In this partnership, each partner is a legal coequal. Each partner has the right to make equal contributions, but not necessarily the same kinds of contributions, to the program. Because contribution is a right and not an obligation, it may be worked out in reality on an equal or unequal basis. A general partnership can be risky because each partner has full authority to make binding decisions independently of other partners, sharing equally in any financial obligations, including full personal liability. As with a proprietorship, the partners must file a True Name Certificate. Although partners have individual tax obligations, they also file an information return IRS Form 1065.

2. **Limited partnership.** This partnership must consist of one or more general partners and one or more limited partners. Each general partner faces risks identical to those of a general partnership. Each limited partner is responsible and liable to the extent of his or her financial or service contribution calculated on a monetary basis at the time the partnership was created. Partners must file a True Name Certificate and a Limited Partnership Certificate that spells out the limita-

tions of responsibility and liability. The limited partnership document is written and filed with the secretary of state or is publicized according to the state's laws. Many partnerships find it desirable, although it is not mandatory, to prepare a partnership agreement, a document containing facts about how a program is to be operated and terminated. Because of limited liability, a limited partner participates only in decisions involving finances.

Corporation.   A **corporation** is a legal entity established on a for-profit or not-for-profit basis. Corporations exist as legal entities forever unless dissolved by the board of directors or a court. Most private early childhood programs legally organized as corporations are independent (not part of other businesses). Work site child care programs may be organized as divisions of the parent corporation, subsidiary corporations, or independent not-for-profit corporations.

The corporation protects individuals from certain liabilities by creating a decision-making and accountable board of directors. Although the board may delegate decision-making power to a director, it is still responsible. Individual board members can be held personally liable in certain areas, such as fraud and failure of the corporation to pay withholding taxes on employees' salaries. In short, personal financial liability is greatly diminished in a corporation, as compared with the proprietorship or partnership.

In addition to diminished personal financial liability, regulations governing taxation may provide incentive to operate a program as a corporation. There is often a monetary advantage in paying corporate taxes rather than paying all the taxes on the program's profits as personal income. (Not-for-profit centers must be incorporated to be eligible for tax-exempt status; proprietorships and partnerships are not eligible for tax-exempt status.)

Because the corporation is a legal entity, several documents are required. The forms are usually somewhat different for for-profit and not-for-profit corporations. Three documents are required in the process of incorporating:

1. **Articles of incorporation or certificate of incorporation.** The organization's legal creators, or incorporators, give information about the corporation, such as the name and address of the agency; its purposes; whether it is a for-profit or not-for-profit corporation; its powers, for example, to purchase property and make loans; membership, if the state requires members; names and addresses of the initial board of directors; initial officers; and the date of the annual meeting.

2. **Bylaws.** The IRS requires bylaws if the corporation is seeking tax-exempt status. Bylaws simply explain how the corporation will conduct its business, describe the corporation's power structure, and explain how the power may be transferred.

3. **Minutes of the incorporators' meeting.** After the incorporators prepare the aforementioned documents, an incorporators' meeting is held. The name of the corporation is approved, and the articles of incorporation and bylaws are signed. The incorporators elect officers and the board of directors, who will serve until the first meeting of the members. In for-profit corporations, the incorporators vote to authorize the issuance of stock. Formal minutes of the incorporators' meeting, including votes taken, are written and signed by each incorporator.

These documents, along with payment of a fee, are filed with the secretary of state or are publicized according to state laws. Once the state approves the proposed corporation, a corporate charter is issued. The incorporators no longer have power. Board members carry out the purposes of the organization, and the members own the organization. When corporations dissolve, they must follow state law if they are for-profit corporations and must follow federal regulations if they are not-for-profit corporations.

Early childhood programs may operate either as **for-profit** or **not-for-profit** corporations. Although the titles are somewhat descriptive, they are often misleading, particularly when incorrectly called *profit-making* and *nonprofit* corporations, respectively.

For-profit corporations are organized for purposes of making a profit. Early childhood programs in this category, as well as proprietorships and partnerships, are businesses. A for-profit corporation may be a closed corporation, in which members of a family or perhaps a few friends own stock, or an open corporation, in which stock is traded on exchanges. If the corporation makes a profit, it pays taxes on the profits; individual stockholders file personal income tax forms listing such items as salaries and dividends received from the corporation. In a closed corporation with a subchapter S status, granted by the IRS, the corporation may distribute its profits or losses in accordance with the proportion of stock held by each individual, who in turn pays taxes or files a depreciation schedule.

The main purpose of not-for-profit corporations is other than to make a profit, but such corporations are permitted to make a profit. Any surplus, or profit, however, must be used to promote the purposes of the organization as set forth in the articles of incorporation. In other words, the profit may be used for housing, equipment, or merit raises in the present or future. Proprietary operators of early childhood programs have also organized not-for-profit corporations; such organization gives them certain advantages, such as rent money for the facility, a salary for directing the program, and free surplus food for children in the program. Child care has two types of not-for-profit corporations: (a) those organized for charitable, educational, literary, religious, or scientific purposes under Section 501(c)(3) of the Internal Revenue Code and (b) those organized for social welfare purposes under Section 501(c)(4) of the Internal Revenue Code. Tax-exempt status is not automatic. The not-for-profit corporation must file for and be granted tax-exempt status at both the federal and state levels.

Besides incorporation regulations, several additional regulations should be noted. Separate bank accounts should be obtained for any early childhood program. Corporations are required to have separate accounts, and some governmental agencies will not send funds to a program that does not have a separate account. Also, a banking resolution, stating the name of the person authorized to withdraw funds, is required of corporations (and in some states, of partnerships). Not-for-profit corporations with a certain income level, and other programs receiving monies from certain funding sources, are required to have an audit. In most states, not-for-profit corporations are required to file an annual financial report following the audit.

Franchises and chains may fall under any of the three legal categories of private organizations but are most often corporations. Franchises and chains are differentiated as follows:

1. A **franchise** is an organization that allows an individual or an entity to use its name, follows its standardized program and administrative procedures, and receives assistance (e.g., in selecting a site, building and equipping a facility, and training staff) for an agreed-on sum of money, royalty, or both.

2. A **chain** is ownership of several facilities by the same proprietorship, partnership, or corporation. These facilities are administered by a central organization. Kinder Care Learning Centers is an example of a chain.

Fiscal Regulations

Many fiscal regulations are specific to given programs. Most contracts and Internal Revenue Service (IRS) regulations, however, must be complied with by all early childhood programs. Fraud or failure to comply with fiscal regulations results in serious consequences.

Contracts.   **Contracts** are legally enforceable agreements that may be oral or written (e.g., insurance policies; employment contracts; contracts with parents for fees; contracts for food, supplies, and services; contracts with funding sources; and leases). A contract has three elements: (a) the **offer**—the buyer's proposal to the seller or the seller's invitation to the buyer to purchase a given object or service at a stated price (money or service), (b) **acceptance**—the buyer's acceptance of an offer or the seller's acknowledgment of the buyer's willingness to accept an offer, and (c) **consideration**—the legal term for the price or value of what each party exchanges (e.g., a subscription to a professional journal for $40 per year). Breaking a contract is called a **breach,** and the potential penalty is referred to as **damages.**

IRS Regulations.   Many IRS regulations apply to all early childhood programs:

1. **Employer identification number.** Each organization employing people on a regular salaried basis is required to obtain a federal employer identification number. A program cannot file for a tax-exempt status without first having obtained this number using IRS Form SS-4.

2. **Tax returns.** Employers file quarterly tax returns, IRS Form 941. This form is filed with the regional IRS service center. A penalty is assessed for late filing. Salaried employers of public early childhood programs file the appropriate schedule on IRS Form 1040. All private programs must file tax returns. Sole proprietors and partnerships with other incomes file the appropriate schedule on Form 1040, partnerships without other incomes file IRS Form 1065, for-profit corporations file Form 1120, and not-for-profit corporations file Form 990.

3. **Withholding Exemption Certificates and IRS Form 1099.** A Withholding Exemption Certificate, IRS Form W-4, is required for each employee. The certificates are used for determining the amount to withhold for federal, state, and city income taxes. The form indicates marital status and the number of dependents and must be completed before the first paycheck is issued.

Employees must sign new forms if their marital status or the number of dependents changes or if they want more of their wages to be withheld. An annual statement of taxes withheld from an employee's earnings (Form W-2) is sent to each employee no later than January 31 of the year following the year in which the employee was paid. Occasionally, early childhood programs hire someone to do a temporary job, such as plumbing or electrical work. Because withholding taxes would not have been deducted from the wages, all centers paying $600 or more to any individual who is not a regular employee must file IRS Form 1099.

Staff Regulations Excluding Credentialing

Staff regulations are designed to protect the employee (e.g., prevention of discrimination) and the program (staff qualifications). Staff regulations involve prevention of discrimination, wage-law compliance, board regulations, staff qualifications, potential vulnerability to legal actions, and civil rights of staff with disabilities.

Title VII of the Civil Rights Acts of 1964 and as Amended by the Equal Opportunity Act of 1972. Fair employment practices are mandatory for organizations, companies, and people having contracts with the federal government. The practices are also mandatory for any entity employing or composed of 15 or more people. Employees subject to this act and its amendment must not discriminate against any individual on the grounds of race, creed, color, gender, national origin, or age. Employment practices must be based on relevant measures of merit and competence. The employer must also base job qualifications on bona fide occupational qualifications (BFOQ); thus, job descriptions must clearly specify the tasks to be performed.

Americans with Disabilities Act. The Americans With Disabilities Act (ADA), P.L. 101–336, was signed into law on July 26, 1990. The ADA established civil rights for people with disabilities. The

part of the law concerning employment states that employers with 15 or more employees must avoid job-related discrimination based on the employee's disability. To be protected under the law, the employee must satisfy BFOQ that are job related and be able to perform those tasks that are essential to the job with reasonable accommodations (e.g., making the facility accessible, modifying equipment, modifying work schedules, providing readers or interpreters), if necessary. Furthermore, the employer is legally liable if other employees discriminate or do not make adjustments to accommodate employees with disabilities (Surr, 1992).

Fair Labor Standards Act. The Fair Labor Standards Act of 1938 as amended applies equally to men and women. Employers subject to this act and its amendments must pay employees the current minimum wage; overtime (hours worked over the 40-hour week) at the rate of 1½ times the employee's regular rate of pay; regular wages and overtime pay for attendance at training sessions, whether the sessions are conducted at the place of work or at another site; and equal wages for equal work. The act does not apply to members of one's immediate family.

ESTABLISHING POLICIES AND PROCEDURES

After local program planners have decided on a program base and conducted a needs assessment, they must establish the **goals** or specific purposes of the local program. Goals provide a focus for the entire program. **Policies** are judgments that express a program's intentions for achieving certain goals (e.g., in-service education of staff, budgetary priorities, program evaluation). Policies are written as comprehensive statements of decisions, principles, or courses of action that achieve goals. Policies directly answer the question, "What is to be done and by whom?" (i.e., board or staff position). For example, the policy might state that one of the program director's responsibilities is to "recruit and retain qualified staff."

The rules, regulations, and procedures show how policy is to be implemented. Procedures guide administrators in routine decisions. Thus, in the procedure, the steps for recruiting staff would be delineated.

Public school programs and private centers (except family child care and small child care centers owned by one or two persons or perhaps a family) often operate under the auspices of a board. Because the Board of Directors or Board of Advisors makes and adopts policies and procedures, they are often referred to as local board regulations. Each faculty and staff member employed by an early childhood program is governed by the regulations of its local governing board, which must be in keeping with the restrictions and authorizations of federal, state, and local laws, directives, and regulations.

Reason for Policy and Procedure Establishment

A policy or procedure may be established for several reasons:

1. In many states, the state licensing agency and the state board of education require that programs under their respective jurisdictions have written policies and procedures covering certain aspects of the local program; these policies and procedures must be in keeping with the restrictions and authorizations of state law.

2. Policies and procedures provide guidelines for achieving the program's goals. Inadequate policies and procedures or their absence result in (a) hesitancy on the part of the director because of an inability to judge whether a decision will result in endorsement or admonishment, (b) running from emergency to emergency, and (c) inconsistency in making decisions.

3. If policies and procedures are constant and apply equally to all, they ensure fair treat-

ment. Policies and procedures thus protect the program, staff, children, and parents.

4. Policies and procedures provide a basis for evaluating existing plans and for determining the merit of proposed plans and are usually required by various funding agencies.

5. Policies and procedures may be requested by auditors.

Formulation, Interpretation, and Implementation of Policies and Procedures

The responsibility for policies and procedures is in the hands of the director, the board of directors, or both. Regardless of the program's organization, policy and procedure formulation, interpretation, and implementation are administrative responsibilities.

In small centers, especially those owned and operated as proprietorships, partnerships, or "family-owned" corporations, policy and procedure formulation is often done by the director-owner, who frequently serves as a teacher, too. Many of these small programs would find board-made policies and procedures intimidating, even threatening. Thus, policies and procedures are formulated, interpreted, and implemented in a pattern similar to that of a democratic family organization but with the lead taken and the final decisions made by the director.

Medium-sized centers operated by a local sponsor such as a church may have a board of directors or advisors that works with the director in policy and procedure development. The relationship between the director and the board is often more of a give-and-take relationship than a chain of command or management system. In these medium-sized centers, the director is the "expert" on children's matters and the spokesperson for the staff, whereas the board addresses the sponsor's concerns, such as use of space and utilities, days and hours of operation, and overall program goals that reflect the sponsor's intent in operating the early childhood program.

The chain of command or line of management is the administrative structure used for most large corporate child care programs, chain and franchise types of child care programs, Head Start, and public school programs. In these programs, policy formulation, interpretation, and implementation are formally structured, with the responsibilities of the director and board clearly delineated. In large management types of organizations, the director again serves as an "expert" and spokesperson for the early childhood program but usually through other levels of staff. For example, a superintendent in a public school works with the school board on policies and procedures and sees that the adopted policies and procedures are implemented, but only through other staff levels, that is, assistant superintendents, principals, or both. Unlike in small and even medium-sized programs, informal policy administration in large programs would be chaotic.

By examining policy and procedures formulation, interpretation, and implementation in management types of organizations, it is easy to grasp the nature of this administrative function in all programs. The board of directors is the policy-making and governing body of an early childhood program. More specifically, the board of directors, usually comprising 10 to 12 members who change periodically as new members are elected or appointed, usually performs the following functions with the director under the program's bylaws:

1. **Formulates major policies and procedures for achieving the overall goals of the program.** The board must develop or adopt the program base and provide an outline of services.

2. **Adopts all proposed policies and procedures planned by the director.** Usually, the director formulates policies and procedures, but the board must adopt these prior to execution.

3. **Supports the annual budget.** Usually, the director formulates the budget, and the board approves it before implementation. The board can also authorize expenditures exceeding the specified limits of the budget.

4. **Approves all personnel hired.** The director selects staff within the guidelines set by the board, and the board acts on the director's recommendations and issues the contracts.

5. **Develops criteria for evaluating the program.** The director is expected to inform the board of various evaluation instruments. Once the board selects the instrument, the director implements the evaluation.

6. **Participates in community relations.** The board represents the program in the community.

If the program is especially large and requires a great deal of policy and procedure development, the board, which always has a chairperson, may work on policies through chair-appointed committees. The suggestions of each committee are presented for total board action.

The execution of policies and procedures is the responsibility of the program's director (the local superintendent of schools in the public school system is equivalent to a director in administrative responsibility). The director is selected and hired by the board. The director, who has specialized knowledge in early childhood programs and administration, is charged with furnishing necessary information to the board, relating and interpreting information and policies and procedures back to the staff through the management process, and serving as the administrator of the staff. The board determines the degree of decision-making power delegated to the director and can empower the director to further delegate responsibility.

A great deal of interchange occurs between the board and the director. For example, the director should inform the board of needs for additional policies and procedures or changes in existing policies and procedures, of inconsistencies in policies and procedures, and of the community's attitudes and values The board should provide adequate written and verbal reasons for and explanations of policies and procedures to facilitate execution and should suggest methods of executing policies and procedures.

Characteristics of Viable Policies and Procedures

Developing viable policies and procedures requires that directors or boards examine their potential to achieve a program's goals, overcome the tradition of operating a program by expediency, understand the technique of policy and procedure making, and devote the time required for planning and evaluating policies and procedures. The following are some characteristics of viable policies and procedures:

1. Local program policies and procedures must conform to state law, to the policies of the funding agency, and to the policies of any other regulatory agency. The autonomy of local programs in providing care and education for young children (developing local policy) has given way, in varying degrees, to the policies and regulations of federal and state agencies. Some of these regulations may provide a needed protective role, but they also place serious constraints on local programs. For example, assessing children's progress with a specified assessment device shapes the program accordingly, or limiting funds for staff and equipment makes operating "the best" program impossible.

2. Policies and procedures should cover all aspects of the local program or, at minimum, those situations that occur frequently.

3. Internally consistent (noncontradictory) policies and procedures should be developed for the various aspects of the program. The likelihood of consistency among policies and procedures is greater if the program base and goals have been previously determined.

4. Policies and procedures should be relatively constant. Policy should not change with changes in the membership of the board. Procedures can change without resulting in a change of policy.

5. Policies and procedures should be written and made readily available so that they can be interpreted with consistency by those concerned. A written policy or procedure minimizes the probability of sudden changes and frequent explanations.

6. Generally speaking, policies and procedures should be followed consistently. When exceptions are necessary, they should be stated or allowed for in the policy or procedure. Frequent requests for exceptions often indicate a need for review.

7. Local program policies and procedures should be subject to review and change because their validity rests on current state laws and the regulations of other agencies. Because of the necessity of having adequate and current policies and procedures, a local regulation requiring periodic review of all policies may be written, or certain policies may be written containing a stipulation that they be reviewed by the director or the board one year from the date they go into effect.

Policy and Procedure Categories

As mentioned, policies and procedures should cover all aspects of the local early childhood program. Because of variations in programs, the categories of policies and procedures, and especially the specific areas included in each category, differ from program to program. Most early childhood programs have policies and procedures in the following categories:

1. **Program services.** This states the primary program services to be provided (e.g., care, education), along with other services (e.g.,

food, transportation, social services, parent involvement).

2. **Administration.** Some specific areas included are the makeup of and procedures for selecting or electing members to the board of directors, board committees (e.g., executive, personnel, finance, building, program, nominating), advisory group, parent council, or other councils or committees; the appointment and functions of the director and supervisory personnel; and the administrative operations, such as the chain of command and membership and functions of various administrative councils and committees.

3. **Staff personnel.** Areas covered often involve qualifications; recruitment, selection, and appointment; job assignment; staff training and development; supervision (e.g., statement of purpose of supervision and use of data, steps in supervision sequence, copy of observation and rating forms, guidelines for corrective actions); tenure; promotion; termination process (e.g., circumstances for termination, procedures, and documentation involving firings, along with fair hearings); salary schedules and fringe benefits; payroll dates; absences and leaves; personal and professional activities; and records of policies and procedures. (In addition to being in compliance with the regulations discussed earlier in the section titled "Staff Regulations Excluding Credentialing," personnel policy statements must contain an affirmative action section. For information, contact the Public Information Unit of the Equal Employment Opportunity Commission. In writing staff-personnel policies, the board or the director needs to be aware of the Pregnancy Discrimination Act of 1978 and the Family and Medical Leave Act of 1993 (Gratz & Boulton, 1995).

4. **Child personnel.** This category may comprise requirements for service eligibility, including governmental and agency rules for the determination and documentation of family needs, maximum group (class) size, child–staff ratio, at-

tendance, program services and provisions for child welfare (e.g., accidents, insurance), assessment and reporting of children's progress, and termination of program services.

5. **Health and safety.** This category may cover the evaluation of children before admission, daily admission, the care or exclusion of ill children, medication administration, health services (e.g., screening, immunizations), management of injuries and emergencies, nutrition and food handling, provision for rest or sleep, health and safety education, staff training in health and safety, and surveillance of environmental problems.

6. **Business.** Some areas included are sources of funding, the nature of the budget (e.g., preparation, adoption, publication), procedures for obtaining funds (e.g., fees), guidelines and procedures for purchasing goods and services, persons responsible for financial management and fiscal record keeping, persons involved in the disbursement of money, and a system of accounts and auditing procedures.

7. **Records.** Some areas included are the types of records to be kept, the designation of "official" records versus "staff members'" notes, a place where records are kept, which official will be responsible for records, and basic procedures for handling provisions of the Family Educational Rights and Privacy Act.

8. **Families.** This category may comprise ways of meeting families' needs, family involvement in the program, and basic procedures for family members to follow in making contact with the director or staff for various purposes (e.g., program philosophy; children's admission and withdrawal; days and hours of operation; vacation schedule; what is expected of families; family conferences, meetings, and special events; opportunities for involvement in the program; services for families).

9. **Public relations.** This category relates to participation by the public (e.g., citizens advisory committees, volunteers), the use of program

facilities, relations with various agencies and associations, and communication with the public.

TRENDS AND ISSUES

Throughout the history of regulation, trends can be traced in both forward and backward steps. The need for regulating early childhood programs is evident when one considers the needs of children and their families. Negligence has occurred, however, in protecting our defenseless clients—our children—as seen in the mistaken beliefs that regulations equal quality, in the gaps in regulation, in the lack of administrator's credentials, in the two-tiered system of credentialing teachers, and in the dilemma of affordability versus quality.

Mistaken Belief That Regulations Equal Quality

Unlike accreditation and model standards, compulsory regulations represent minimum acceptable standards. Much variation in licensing standards is noted among the states. Thus, in some states, programs that comply with licensing standards do not actually improve in the standards of quality that matter most for children (D. K. Cohen & Spillane, 1993; Howes, Phillips, & Whitebook, 1992). Today, researchers are making distinctions between **structural quality,** which refers to readily regulatable qualities (e.g., housing size, group size, staff education, adult–child ratio, safety measures), and **process quality,** which refers to variables that are more proximal to children's development (e.g., sensitive caregiving, appropriate activities; Howes, 1992). Regrettably, process quality is not as amenable to regulation as structural quality. Yet, process quality is associated with positive cognitive outcomes, such as higher levels of play (Howes & Stewart, 1987) and higher intelligence and language scores (McCartney, Scarr, Phillips, & Grajek, 1985), and with positive social outcomes, such as attachment to staff (C. Anderson, Nagle, Roberts, & Smith, 1981) and consideration for other children and for staff (D. Phillips, McCartney, & Scarr, 1987).

The results of low standards are very evident in the research (Cost, Quality, and Child Outcomes Study Team, 1995; C. W. Snow, Teleki, & Reguero-de-Atiles, 1996).

Similarly, many states have weak credentialing requirements for college students preparing to work with young children. Broad certification (certification for a wide age and grade span) weakens the education and training of students for work with young children. Furthermore, broad certification standards make building quality programs at the university level difficult. Students simply cannot get adequate training and experience with children from birth to age 8 without extending the length of the baccalaureate training. Without quality programs, excellent students are often reluctant to enter a program, and this situation further damages the early childhood program at the university level (McCarthy, 1988). Narrow certification makes the potential employee less attractive to the employer because of fewer placement possibilities. Furthermore, college students may also find their chances of employment limited with a narrow certification simply because they must compete for fewer openings.

Gaps in Regulation

When it comes to child care and the education of young children, the social norm has always been that parents make the decisions. As discussed in chapter 1, parents do not always act in the best interests of their children. Other studies challenge this assumption but indicate the limitations of choice for many parents (Larner & Mitchell, 1992). Various groups, especially religious groups, oppose regulations against what they deem appropriate for the discipline of children in their programs.

Resistance has led to early childhood programs under certain auspices being exempt from licensing (e.g., religion-operated programs in some states). A few regulations are simply not meaningful for early childhood programs (e.g., general school codes; A. W. Mitchell, Seligson, & Marx, 1989). Some programs fall between the cracks of two regulatory agencies and end up being not regulated. For example, of the 39 states plus the District of Columbia that finance preschool programs, only 16 have standards in place with just 6 requiring preschools to adhere to the standards they have developed. No state holds preschool children accountable for their performance (Spicer, 2002). Only 19 states and the District of Columbia have specific expectations for kindergartners (Olson, 2002). Finally, either most of family child care is not regulated or regulation is not enforced. Although some standards are higher (accreditation and model standards), these standards are met by relatively few programs. Over half of the states are now encouraging accreditation by instituting tiered (i.e., differential) reimbursement rates for programs that move from licensing to accreditation. When the monetary reward equals or exceeds 15% of the market rate, centers are more likely to pursue accreditation (Jacobson, 2002). States that rate programs (e.g., 1 to 5 stars) also boost standards of quality.

Administrator's Credential: Interest and Barriers

The quality of an early childhood program is most dependent on its administrator. Administrators make the decisions that create the conditions for good child outcomes. The Cost, Quality, and Child Outcomes study found that these characteristics of directors are associated with higher quality programs: more years of education, more administrative experience, and greater involvement in curricular planning (Mocan, Burchinal, Morris, & Helburn, 1995). A. Mitchell and colleagues (1989) found that the most effective early childhood administrators had preparation in the field, practiced hands-on responsive management of teaching staff, and had political skills for operating within the school system bureaucracy. Furthermore, professionalism and credibility in the community is related to trained leadership (Jorde-Bloom, 1997).

Most often early childhood administrators are appointed leaders based on longevity in the field and exemplary work with children rather than on administrative training (Jorde-Bloom & Sheerer, 1992). Thus, directors are often viewed as individuals "lost to teaching."

G. Morgan (2000a) suggested an administrative credential or at least specific training as part of licensing. She believes that a director credential that has higher standards than one required for basic licensing should be required for accreditation; furthermore, a qualified director should be included in the definition of rate structure for subsidized programs. A. Mitchell (2000) stated that a credential is supported by the business community (e.g., American Business Collaboration for Quality Dependent Care) and believes a credential would be supported by families and by advocates of universal public school preschools. Directors themselves support a nationally recognized voluntary credential (Poster & Neugebaurer, 1998).

Other professionals see barriers to an administrator's credential. Bredekamp (2000) stated that a certificate should not be made available prior to the availability of academic training requirements, which was an early problem of the CDA. Receiving the needed training may be a problem because of the lack of demand needed to drive offerings by higher education institutions. Furthermore, to plan a national certificate, similar to the CDA, one professional group would have to spearhead the effort as opposed to the several groups that now offer administrator credentials. Assessment systems for credentialing are costly, and procedures must be legally defensible. E. Moore (1997) pointed out that unless a credential is mandated for hiring, it has little impact. Limiting access to jobs may exclude individuals from diverse cultures and thus may affect program quality.

Two-Tiered System of Credentialing Teachers

Historically, two separate agencies have regulated teaching credentials: (a) child care licensing departments and (b) teacher certification

Chapter 3 Considering Regulations and Establishing Policies   93

offices within state departments of education. Thus, licensing has its roots in social welfare, and certification has its roots in education. Licensing accepts experience in place of formal academic preparation (college degrees) and thus encourages employment at the expense of formal education. Conversely, certification places emphasis on formal preparation with some supervised field and clinical experiences at the expense of "real" daily employment experiences. G. Morgan (1994) sees the need for a bridge to span the two tiers—a way to transform the working experiences and pre- and in-service training into some college credit. Grubb (1991) suggested creating a system that allocates different administrative functions to different existing state agencies and then coordinating all of these agencies through an existing state office. Such a coordinated system could help reduce the two-tiered system.

Dilemma of Affordability versus Quality

Some people consider maintaining affordability more important than maintaining quality. On the other hand, early childhood professionals believe families should have a right to expect that the government will assure them that their children will receive a minimum level of protection, just as it assures the population of a minimum level of safety in other areas (e.g., foods and drugs, water supply, police protection). Furthermore, high-quality programs benefit all segments of society—the children whose lives are enhanced; the families who are assured of quality and who are thus better employees; and the populace at large, which profits from its self-sufficient members.

Bredekamp and Willer (1992) believe that accreditation must be part of an articulated professional development system. Trained personnel must be compensated. Higher salaries and good staff–child ratios will make it harder for families to meet child care and education costs. How much accreditation will increase the costs of cen-

ter care is not known, although the Cost, Quality, and Child Outcomes Team (1995) found that high-quality centers cost, on the average, only 10% more than poor-quality ones. Gormley (1991) suggested that microeconomics theory indicates that stringent regulations could reduce the supply of child care services. However, he found that microeconomics theory may not apply because some regulations are costly and some are not and some are enforced and some are not. Regulations affect different types of programs in very different ways. For example, quality child–staff ratios affect center-based programs more than family child care programs because most family providers want to care for only two or three children (Gormley, 1991).

Government funding is being used to promote accreditation. Warman (1998) listed three major public policies that promote accreditation: (a) the use of CC&DBG funds as subsidies to fund child care quality improvement initiatives; (b) minigrants, training, technical assistance, and various bonuses to help programs become accredited; and (c) programs to pursue accreditation in order to be funded or refunded. Limited government funds, however, may not really change the overall picture of quality.

As previously discussed, Talley (1997) found that the accreditation process itself may be self-defeating. Quality perhaps awaits the day when the families demand it for their children.

SUMMARY

Regulations are the rules, directives, statutes, and standards that prescribe, direct, limit, and govern early childhood programs. Regulations, most of which are mandatory, come from governmental and funding agencies. Many regulations are protective in nature. Some of the specific protective regulations represent minimal standards of quality, such as licensing, whereas others represent standards of excellence, such as accreditation. Other standards are not directly protective in nature but permit the legal existence of private programs, regulate the program's fiscal affairs, and govern staff employment practices.

Local early childhood programs need to develop policies and procedures that are the guidelines for achieving local program goals effectively and efficiently. Local policy and procedure formulation, implementation, and evaluation are the responsibilities of the board of directors and the program director.

Many issues pertain to regulations. All of these issues focus on the lack of quality systems and the feasibility of getting public support and funding for needed quality.

FOR FURTHER READING

Barnett, W. S. (1996). Creating a market for quality through NAEYC accreditation. In S. Bredekamp & B. A. Willer (Eds.), *NAEYC accreditation: A decade of learning and the years ahead* (pp. 149–162). Washington, DC: National Association for the Education of Young Children.

Bredekamp, S. (1999). When new solutions create new problems: Lessons learned from NAEYC accreditation. *Young Children, 54*(1), 58–63.

Helburn, S. W., & Bergmann, B. R. (2002). *America's child care problem: The way out.* New York: St. Martin's Press.

Mitchell, A. (1996). Licensing: Lessons from other occupations. In S. L. Kagan & N. E. Cohen (Eds.), *Reinventing early care and education: A vision for a quality system* (pp. 101–123). San Francisco: Jossey-Bass.

Morgan, G., Azer, S. L., Costley, J. B., Genser, A., Goodman, I. F., Lombardi, J., & McGimsey, B. (1993). *Making a career of it.* Boston: Wheelock College, Center for Career Development in Early Care and Education.

National Association for the Education of Young Children. (1991). Early childhood teacher certification: A position statement of the Association of Teacher Educators and the National Association for the Education of Young Children. *Young Children, 47*(1), 16–21.

National Association for the Education of Young Children. (1995). NAEYC position statement on qual-

ity, compensation, and affordability. *Young Children, 51*(1), 39–41.

National Association for the Education of Young Children. (1998). NAEYC position statement on licensing and public regulation of early childhood programs. *Young Children, 53*(1), 43–50.

National Association for the Education of Young Children. (1999). NAEYC position statement on developing and implementing policies to promote early childhood and school-age care program accreditation. *Young Children, 54*(4), 36–40.

Shonkoff, J. P., & Meisels, S. J. (1990). Early childhood intervention: The evolution of a concept. In S. J. Meisels & J. P. Shonkoff (Eds.), *Handbook of early childhood intervention* (pp. 3–32). New York: Cambridge University Press.

Spodek, B., & Saracho, O. N. (Eds.). (1990). *Yearbook in early childhood education: Vol. 1. Early childhood teacher preparation.* New York: Teachers College Press.

TO REFLECT

1. A director has been hired by a local church to establish a not-for-profit preschool program. In using the licensing manual, she is confronted with a regulation that seems unworkable. What options can she exercise?

2. J. Gordon (2000) believes that our field participates in undermining its own quality standards. Two examples he gives are as follows: (1) Because of their focus on parent employment, state welfare departments may subsidize child care programs that do not reach minimum standards; (2) professionals continue to provide in-service training for staff members in programs exempt from licensing. Do you agree with Gordon that we are involved in deprofessionalizing our field and undermining program quality for children?

3. G. Morgan (1996) posed questions about the advisability of being a little more flexible with standards. Should a licensed program be accredited if it fails to meet some accreditation standard and yet seems to be of "good" or "excellent" quality otherwise? For example, could a somewhat

inadequate teacher–child ratio be compensated for by a better qualified staff?

4. Accreditation involves the risk of liability. How do you think the courts would judge these two situations: (a) A formerly accredited center is given a deferral (denied accreditation) and sues for loss of status; and (b) in a state with weak licensing standards, a program is accredited and a child is later seriously hurt?

Leading and Managing Personnel

The staff is the single most important determinant of the quality of early childhood programs. The best programs have highly qualified staff and low teacher turnover (NRC & IOM, 2000). A disparity exists between the professional preparation, access to many roles in the field, and adequate compensation of staff and the growing expectations for optimal care and education of young children. Furthermore, if working conditions are not good for staff members, children do not do well in programs. To ensure job satisfaction for staff as well as program quality, three criteria must be met in staffing: (a) The staff must meet at least minimal qualifications for their specific duties, although an employer hopes to select employees who have the most potential; (b) those selected must understand and be willing to work within the program base; and (c) the staff must feel a personal ownership for and responsibility to the program.

TRENDS IN STAFFING

Advocacy efforts have resulted in an increased recognition of the importance of early childhood education. In addition to the acceptance of kindergartens and primary programs as an integral part of public education, the growing consensus is that enough high-quality infant and toddler and preschool programs should exist to meet the developmental needs of these children and the needs of their families, all at a cost that families and society can afford.

All the characteristics of high-quality programs depend on adequate numbers of well-trained staff members. Early childhood programs need increasingly larger staffs for several reasons. First, more early childhood programs are becoming comprehensive in nature, which necessitates additional staff. Second, an adequate adult–child ratio based on the ages and needs of children served and a small group size are major factors in program quality. Third, with the inclusion of children with special needs in the program, support

staff are needed for screening and identifying these children and for helping to integrate them into regular classrooms (Hebbeler, 1995).

The demographic data on early childhood program staff are not encouraging. Regrettably, as a result of today's economic problems, the tendency is toward fewer staff and larger groups for preschool children (C. W. Snow, Teleki, & Reguero-de-Atiles, 1996). As discussed, several national studies have confirmed the mediocre quality of most early childhood programs. Thus, more and more families are finding child care a constant concern, especially with private quality programs not affordable for most families and with preschool programs unavailable for many children.

Staff Shortage: A Deep-Rooted Problem

The biggest quality issue facing early childhood care and education programs is a lack of ability to recruit and retain staff members. The problem is found primarily in child care programs and Head Start. Public school programs, however, cannot afford to stay unconcerned because the pressure for public school prekindergartens is growing.

Retention of staff especially affects program quality. Staff are leaving child care and Head Start programs at alarming rates. The **turnover rate,** the number of teachers who leave a program during the year, has been extremely high. The turnover rate varies by type of program. For prekindergarten programs the turnover rate is highest in for-profit chains and lowest in public preschool programs. The U.S. Bureau of Labor Statistics (1998) reported a turnover rate of 30% per year for center-based early childhood programs. Some studies report even higher rates (Whitebook, Sakai, & Howes, 1997). The turnover rate varies among relative care and family child care homes; 30% of care arrangements provided by relatives were no longer available after a year, and 25% of unregulated and 8% of regulated family child care arrangements were out of business within one year (Kontos, Howes, Shinn,

& Galinsky, 1995). By comparison, only 6.6% of public school teachers leave their job each year (U.S. Bureau of Labor Statistics, 1998).

The **separation rate,** the percentage of workers who leave the occupation during a year, is also high. Although separation rates are lower than turnover rates, separation rates are highly critical to the staffing crisis because these rates represent a total loss of individuals to the profession.

The **tenure rate,** the amount of time individuals are in a given position or in a given field, is not good. However, the National Child Care Staffing Study found that 67% of staff members viewed child care as a career as opposed to a temporary job, and this seemed to be reflected in tenure rates, which had improved since 1977 (Whitebook, Phillips, & Howes, 1993).

The staffing crisis is not caused by job dissatisfaction. The Worthy Wage Campaign, initiated by the Center for the Child Care Workforce, sought to expose the association of low pay with the difficulty in recruiting qualified staff and the association of high turnover rates among child care workers with low-quality programs. As a group, child care teachers earn less than half as much as comparably educated women and a third as much as similarly educated men (Whitebook et al., 1993). The Bureau of Labor Statistics' data show that preschool teachers earned only 40% of that of kindergarten teachers (Center for the Child Care Workforce, 1998). Predictably, the highest turnover rates occurred in chains that paid the lowest salaries; conversely, the lowest turnover rates were in independent not-for-profit programs that paid the highest salaries ("Quality, Compensation, and Affordability," 1998). Staff compensation and turnover rate are also associated with measured program quality, such as accreditation. For example, the NAEYC-accredited programs had the lowest center turnover rate, but the centers that did not maintain their accreditation did not differ in turnover rate from programs that had never sought accreditation ("Quality, Compensation, and Affordability," 1998). Other causes of the staffing crisis included

(a) lack of benefits (e.g., health, retirement), with many staff members hired on a less than full-time basis at minimum wage so that employers can avoid the costs of benefits (Whitebook et al.); (b) lack of a career ladder; (c) low social status; (d) stressful working conditions (Whitebook, Howes, Phillips, & Pemberton, 1991); and (e) lack of training (Shirah, Hewitt, & McNair, 1993).

The staffing crisis is detrimental to all involved. Children are affected by the change in rituals and by the loss of people associated with the rituals. Insecure children spend less time involved with peers and more time in "aimless wandering" and show drops in cognitive activities (Whitebook, Howes, & Phillips, 1990). Changes in staff are especially detrimental to infants and toddlers. Those who experience more staff turnover do not score as well on cognitive tests (Clarke-Stewart & Gruber, 1984) and develop less secure attachments (Carnegie Task Force on Meeting the Needs of Young Children, 1994; Howes & Hamilton, 1992), as compared with infants and toddlers experiencing no turnovers in care. Families find that it takes time to feel comfortable with new staff. Of course, staff are affected too. For example, directors try to teach and still handle administrative responsibilities. Some centers violate licensing regulations by using unqualified personnel or by violating group size or adult–child ratios.

Staff Diversity: An Urgent Need

Early childhood staff in centers are predominantly female (96% to 98%), under 40 years of age (80%), and members of the majority (95%; Jorde-Bloom, 1992b). Similar percentages are found in public and private school kindergartens and primary grades ("PDK and the Recruitment," 1998–99). The need for more diversity in staff is indisputable because we need to value and support diversity (Derman-Sparks & Ramsey, 2000), provide equal employment opportunity (Sargent, 2001), and promote justice in our world (Elicker, 2002).

The presence of men is advocated more in theory than in practice. Since the 1960s, men have been recruited for different reasons (Decker & Decker, 2001). However important men may be to children's development, relatively few enter and stay in early childhood programs; in fact, the numbers have been declining since the 1970s (Elicker, 2002). Men comprise about 28% of the teachers in public and private elementary through secondary schools (National Center for Education Statistics, 2001). Men comprise even fewer of the early childhood care and education workforce. About 95% to 99% of the center-based child care workforce is female (Center for the Child Care Workforce & Human Services Policy Center, 2002; Whitebook, Howes, & Phillips, 1998). The exodus of men is the result of low wages (A. Mitchell & Morgan, 2001); social isolation; scrutiny and suspicion especially when they nurture young children; being asked to do more than their fair share of heavy and dirty work; and being considered good disciplinarians and macho surrogate fathers, especially for boys from single-mother families (Sargent, 2002). Although some have contended that men often move to higher grades or to administrative positions (C. Williams, 1992), this is not true (National Association of Elementary School Principals, 1996).

Older people can make major contributions to early childhood programs. By 2010, about one in three Americans will be over the age of 60 (U.S. Bureau of the Census, 1992). Many of the elderly are desiring to have part-time employment or to volunteer their services. Older adults in early childhood programs can be beneficial. Margaret Mead (1970) wrote, "[T]he continuity of all cultures depends on the living presence of at least three generations" (p. 2). Early childhood programs could be the ideal place for intergenerational models. The active presence of older adults in the program can help change children's often negative and distorted ideas about the elderly and build positive attitudes toward older people (Aday, Evans, McDuffie, &

Sims, 1996), encourage prosocial behavior (Lambert, Dellman-Jenkins, & Fruit, 1990), and help children form attachments to older adults (T. B. Smith & Newman, 1993). Employment helps older adults by preventing feelings of isolation, supplementing incomes, and using their talents and lifetime experiences (S. Newman, Vander Ven, & Ward, 1992). Older adults can make valuable contributions to the curriculum. Older people are also effective with parents because young parents see older people as surrogate parents (T. B. Smith & Newman).

Many professionals believe that the quality of programs can be improved when the staff as a whole reflects the cultural and racial diversity of the United States. Racial and ethnic diversity is desirable for several reasons: It (a) allows all children to see their own and other groups in various staff roles and helps to reverse the low levels of achievement for children of racial or ethnic minorities, (b) helps families see programs as extensions of their families and communities, (c) permits those aspiring to early childhood care and education careers to see role models, and (d) sensitizes others to the needs of racial and ethnic minority children and their families (E. Moore, 1997).

Since the 1960s, the number of minority staff has waxed and waned. Center-based early childhood programs are staffed primarily in the dominant culture of the local program. Minorities are greatly underrepresented among public school teachers and among administrators (NBCDI, 1993), although the children are increasingly diverse. Racial diversity exists more at the entry levels of the field. The lack of diversity in higher positions on the career ladder may be because minorities lag behind their white peers in academic preparation (Whitebook et al., 1990). Although minorities had more experience at the entry-level positions, for those with college degrees, the rate of advancement to teacher and teacher/director positions was still less than that of their majority peers (NBCDI).

STAFFING AN EARLY CHILDHOOD PROGRAM

After developing a program base and goals on paper, an administrator is faced with the task of determining the staff needed and of matching job requirements with staff members. This task is a continual one; staffing patterns change as a program expands or vacancies occur.

Roles and Qualifications of Personnel

Although all staff members must be in good physical and psychological health and have the personal qualities necessary to work with young children, a person's needed qualifications depend on his or her specific role. And even roles with the same title may vary from program to program.

Personnel may be classified as either primary program personnel or support program personnel. **Primary program personnel** have direct, continuous contact with children. **Support program personnel** provide services that support or facilitate caregiving and the instructional program. Although a staff member is classified by the major role, he or she may occasionally function in another capacity. For example, a teacher may occasionally clean the room or serve food, or a dietitian might discuss good eating habits with children or console a child who drops a carton of milk.

Director.   A **director** is someone who may or may not be in charge of the total program. Directors of early childhood education programs in public schools are often supervisors or resource personnel. In Montessori programs, teachers are traditionally given this title. The title of *director* is frequently given to the person legally responsible for the total program and services. Caruso and Fawcett (1999) used the following terms to define the roles of directors: *executive director* (one who administers a large child care agency that may comprise several social services programs), *program director* (one who runs the day-to-day operations of a program), *educational coordinator* (one who is responsible for the educational component, including staff development and curriculum development, of an agency or a single program), *head teacher* (one who oversees one or more classrooms), and *supervisor* (one who oversees teachers and support personnel). Although this book's focus is primarily on the role of the program director, organizations differ; as programs differ, so do the roles of their directors (see Figure 4–1 for some of the ways program directors' roles differ).

Role.   Regardless of the type of early childhood program or the title of the director, many responsibilities are similar. Professionals have categorized the responsibilities in different ways. For example, Hayden (1996) described the following five administrative roles: technical responsibilities (e.g., regulations and policies, budgets), staff relations, educational planning, public relations (e.g., advocacy, networking, fund-raising, marketing), and symbolic (i.e., director as a symbol for the identity of the group). Carter and Curtis (1998) used the equilateral triangle to conceptualize the role of a director. The roles, which are of equal importance, are managing and overseeing, coaching and mentoring, and building and supporting community. G. Morgan (2000a) listed eight roles of directors and competencies for each role. P. Bloom (2000b) interviewed directors regarding their perceptions of their roles and used linguistic metaphorical analysis of the data. Almost 29% of all directors talked about "leading and guiding"; 28% referred to their role as balancing multiple tasks; and 25% saw their role as "caring and nurturing" of the entire community.

For this text, directors' responsibilities include both a **leadership component** (i.e., the people-oriented or human resources role) and a **management component** or the technical (i.e., organizational, program, business), nonperson aspects of administration. (For more specific examples of leadership and management roles, see Figure 4–2.) P. Bloom (1997c) suggested that

PROGRAM DIRECTORS SERVE IN SIMPLE TO COMPLEX ADMINISTRATIVE ORGANIZATIONS

Program goals
Limited to good care for children — Total services for children — Total services for children and parents

Program operations
Half-day — 8-to-12-hour day — 24-hour program

Delivery system
Family child care — Center or school — Home-visiting — Combination of home-visiting and center

Who the program serves
Infants and toddlers — Preschoolers — Kindergarten and primary-level children — School-age children (before and/or after school including or not including holidays) — Sick children — Special needs children — Combinations of foregoing

(continued)

Figure 4–1   Different Roles of Program Directors

PROGRAM DIRECTORS SERVE IN SIMPLE TO COMPLEX ADMINISTRATIVE ORGANIZATIONS

Work environment

Work alone	Have assistance (e.g., program coordinator, auxillary services coordinators)		

Who they are responsible to

Own their own program (proprietorship, partnership, or family-based corporation)	Parent co-ops	School system or other public agency	Private not-for-profit agency	Corporate system

What they are responsible for (policy making)

All policy	Some policy	No policy

Scope of different roles

Teach part of day	Direct one center (no teaching responsibilities)	Direct more than one center (no teaching responsibilities)

Figure 4–1 *(continued)*

DIRECTOR'S RESPONSIBILITIES

Leadership

Articulates program's mission.

Works with staff to plan entire program component based on goals.

Communicates policies and procedures, needs, program objectives, and problems with all interested parties—board, staff, parents, and their agencies; motivates others to take their responsibilities; resolves conflicts.

Affirms values of program and serves in advocacy roles in concert with various community agencies through communitywide endeavors and through professional organizations.

Serves as a model in terms of the code of ethics (see chapter 11).

Delegates leadership roles and certain responsibilities to others when apopropriate and takes on responsibilities when appropriate to delegate responsibilities.

Continues his or her own professional development.

Management

Writes or adopts and implements all regulations, policies, and procedures.

Abides by all contracts.

Writes program base and overall goals and gets board approval.

Serves as personnel manager by doing the following:

    Conducting a needs assessment

    Recruiting and selecting

    Hiring

    Planning placement

    Filling staff roles with substitutes when needed

    Developing a communications system (e.g., meetings)

    Supervising staff and planning professional development

    Evaluating staff

    Maintaining personnel records

Enrolls and places children and family members.

Plans and maintains records on children and family members.

Develops program calendar and overall daily scheduling (e.g., eating times).

Follows procedures and manages property by doing the following:

    Planning or locating adequate housing and maintaining building and grounds

    Ordering and maintaining equipment, materials, and supplies

    Maintaining all property records (e.g., mortgage or lease payments, insurance, inventories)

Plans finances by doing the following:

    Mobilizing resources

    Developing the budget

    Planning marketing strategies

    Working with funding and regulatory agencies

    Writing proposals for grants and governmental assistance programs

Develops an efficient internal and external (PR) communications system.

Plans program evaluation if needed.

Figure 4–2   Program Director's Responsibilities: Leadership and Management

clear distinctions cannot be made between leadership and management functions in most early childhood programs; most directors have both responsibilities, and the functions themselves overlap. For example, the director may write the program's goals and then articulate the goals to others. The administrative role becomes more complex with the size of the program and the location (i.e., a program located at multiple sites is usually more complex than a program located at one site). The need to balance the leadership and management roles for program success has been studied on a historical basis by Hewes (2000). In stressing the need for a balance among tasks, Neugebauer (2000) likened a successful program director to an orchestra director; that is, he or she must "be able to blend all the talents of the individual performers" (p. 98). In sum, the director has the leadership role in managing quality in the program.

Professional Qualifications. As discussed, the professional qualifications of directors vary, depending on the program's organizational pattern. Several initiatives have examined the director's role and debated the possibilities for credentials as part of the licensing and/or accreditation requirements for center-based sites. Training programs have also been launched.

Essential knowledge and competencies have been identified and continue to be refined. The general consensus is that administrators should have early childhood professional knowledge and administrative competence. More specifically, N. Brown and Manning (2000) identified four areas of knowledge needed by directors, and Neugebauer (2000) and G. Morgan (2000a) developed comprehensive lists of needed competencies (see appendix 3). Many competencies have been described in depth. Some of these competencies include visionary skills (Carter & Curtis, 1998), communication skills and team building (Jorde-Bloom, 1997), human resource management (Stonehouse & Woodrow, 1992), financial management (G. Morgan, 1999), supervision (Caruso & Fawcett, 1999), and culturally relevant leadership and community partnership skills ("Taking the Lead Initiative," 1999a).

In reality, however, many administrators step into their roles without the needed competencies. Less than 20% of all directors have planned a career in administration. Most said they reached their current position because others saw their leadership potential. About 90% come from the ranks of teachers (Bloom, 1997c), often in Katz's (1995b) "Renewal Stage" when teachers are looking for new challenges or in Vander Ven's (1988) "Direct Care: Advanced" stage in which teachers make logical decisions. Thus, competencies are learned through work experience, and work experience becomes a critical factor in program quality (Cost, Quality, and Child Outcomes Study Team, 1995). As new directors learn the needed competencies, they go through stages as shown in Figure 4–3.

Along with work experience, directors use other tools for developing competencies. Many engage in self-study. (Some resources are listed at the end of the chapter.) Besides professional reading materials, other frequently used means of self-study include professional conferences, workshops, and interest groups. Often community business groups conduct forums and other programs of benefit to early childhood program directors. Other directors learn through director mentors ("Taking the Lead Initiative," 2000). Directors also use assessment tools (Freeman & Brown, 2000; Schiller & Dyke, 2001; Sciarra & Dorsey, 1998) for professional development.

Personal Qualifications. Regardless of the program, personal characteristics of effective directors are similar. Because of the numbers and complexities of their responsibilities, successful directors are usually focused and organized. Effective directors must be able to see the program holistically and recognize interconnections. Other characteristics include physical and mental stamina, openness to new ideas, communication skills, flexibility of expression and thought,

STAGES GIVEN BY ANTHONY (1998)

Stage 1: Organizing and Surviving (first year)
   Learn by trial and error
   Learn much new information
   Manage stress
Stage 2: Managing and Focusing (second year)
   Develop expertise in specific program areas
   Extend knowledge and support beyond local program
   Develop time management skills
Stage 3: Leading and Balancing (third or fourth year)
   Develop a vision for the program
   Include others in achieving goals
Stage 4: Advocating and Mentoring (fifth or sixth year)
   Share professional expertise
   Expand current program
   Avoid burnout

STAGES GIVEN BY BLOOM (1997C)

Beginning directors (first year)
   Eager to make a contribution and to be liked
   Face reality shocks (e.g., needed stamina, amount of paperwork, needs of others, lack of support)
   Major problems are lack of management skills, seeing single solutions to complex problems, and
   seeing events from personal perspective
Competent directors (between one and four years)
   Have problems with time management
   Know their strengths and weaknesses
   Often overcome problems of beginning directors
Master directors
   See themselves as change agents, mentors, role models, and advocates
   Engage in reflective practice
   Make role expectations clear to others and use flexible style to meet needs of staff members
   Seek consistency between espoused theory and reality

STAGES GIVEN BY CARUSO AND FAWCETT (1999)

Beginning
   Try to conceptualize roles
   Imitate models from past experiences
   Use different approaches (trial and error)
   Avoid responsibilities by pretending not to have enough time
   Gradually work out authority relationships
Extending
   Somewhat ambivalent about role

(continued)

Figure 4–3   Stages of Directors' Development

Discuss problems and conflicts objectively
See differences in staff members
Understand program better
Maturing
    Make conscious decisions
    Are accountable for their actions
    Are more sensitive to others
    Assess themselves accurately
    Not as burdened by problems

Figure 4–3   *(continued)*

acceptance of capabilities and fallibilities, ability to learn from mistakes, willingness to share credit with others, cheerfulness, warmth and sensitivity to both children and adults, personal sense of security, desire to succeed, and honesty.

Primary Program Personnel. Just as distinctions between care and education should not be made, distinctions between child care workers and teachers are no longer useful. The governing board of the NAEYC (1984) approved the following titles and descriptions:

1. **Early childhood teacher assistant** is a preprofessional with no specialized early childhood preparation who implements program activities under direct supervision.

2. **Early childhood associate teacher** is a professional with minimal early childhood preparation (holds a CDA credential or an associate degree in early childhood education/child development) who independently implements activities and may be responsible for a group of children.

3. **Early childhood teacher** is a professional with an undergraduate degree in early childhood education/child development and is responsible for a group of children.

Role. Except for tasks specific to the age group served, very little distinction can be made among the roles performed by teachers in the various early childhood programs. Roles may include the following responsibilities:

- Serve in a leadership capacity with other staff members.

- Implement the program base by observing and determining children's needs in relation to program goals and by planning activities.

- Communicate verbally and sympathetically with children.

- Respond effectively to children's behavior.

- Model and articulate to families and other staff members practices in keeping with the program's rationale.

Teachers must also be acquainted with, accept, and use children's differences that are the result of special needs and culture. The role of teachers should vary, however, in keeping with the NAEYC's (1984) title and descriptions.

Professional Qualifications. Because the tasks performed by teachers are essentially the same, entry-level qualifications are similar in all programs. Isenberg (1999) stated that a strong liberal arts background seems essential as the base of professional qualifications. Regardless of whether professional development occurs as preservice or in-service or whether it is primarily in the form of formal education or a workshop type of training, it should be knowledge based as opposed to conventional wisdom (Griffin, 1999). A good source for determining the core content of early childhood professionals' knowledge base is the NAEYC's (2001) standards for early childhood professional preparation, which can be revisited at greater depth and breadth at higher levels of preparation. (See appendix 4.)

Early childhood is a diverse field, with people working in various roles and entering the profession at various levels of competence in both experience and education. A career lattice has been proposed (J. Johnson & McCracken, 1994), but concerns about the proposal have been expressed. All agree that professional growth needs to be rewarded, however.

Personal Qualifications. Personal characteristics associated with an effective teacher are difficult to define. Opinion varies as to what constitutes a good teacher of young children. In addition, teaching styles (personality traits, attitudes) are interwoven with teaching techniques (methodology). Characteristics of effective teachers may be specific to the age of the children and vary with the cultural group served. Because teaching is so complex and multifaceted, more research needs to be conducted on personal characteristics and teaching effectiveness (Spodek, 1996).

Characteristics and skills often associated with effective early childhood teachers include warmth, flexibility, integrity, sense of humor, physical and mental stamina, vitality, emotional stability and confidence, naturalness, and an ability to support development without being overprotective (Elicker & Fortner-Wood, 1995). Feeney and Christensen (1979) wrote that the most important characteristic of a good teacher is the ability to be *with* young children rather than do *for* young children. Balaban (1992) described 12 ways in which teachers are with young children; among these ways are as anticipators and planners, listeners and watchers, protectors,

providers of interesting environments, elicitors of language, and smoothers of jangled feelings. In addition to having the foregoing characteristics, teachers who work with infants should be able to develop very close bonds with infants, "read" behavioral cues (e.g., distinguish among cries), and make long-term commitments to programs so that infants are provided continuity (Balaban, 1992; Honig, 1993).

Support Program Personnel. The major role of support program personnel is to furnish services that support or facilitate the program. Support program personnel include dietitians and food service personnel, medical staff, psychologists, caseworkers, maintenance staff, general office staff, transportation staff, and volunteers. A new category of support program personnel is **case manager,** a position created through the Individualized Family Service Plan (IFSP) requirements of Part C of P.L. 105-17. Similar in role to caseworkers, case managers are child and family advocates who serve as a linking agent between families and needed service agencies. Unlike caseworkers, who are traditionally from the social work profession, IFSP case managers are chosen because of expertise in relation to a given child's primary problem and thus may be, for example, nutritionists, physical therapists, or speech pathologists.

Some categories of support personnel are found mainly in public school and government-funded early childhood programs. For example, **early intervention specialists** are teachers or consultants who specialize in the development and learning of children with special needs. Other special education consultants include occupational therapists, physical therapists, and speech-language pathologists (Wesley, 2002). In very small proprietorships, food service, maintenance, and office work are done by the director, teachers, and volunteers.

Support program personnel must have the qualifications of their respective professions. They must also be knowledgeable about age-level expectations of young children. Personal qualifications include the ability to communicate with children and to work with all adults involved in the program.

Substitute personnel should have the same professional qualifications and personal characteristics as the regularly employed personnel whom they replace. To ensure program continuity, careful plans should be made for substitute teachers (see Figure 4–4). Such plans are most essential when substitute personnel will be working alone (e.g., in a self-contained classroom), especially in kindergartens and primary grades.

Assessing Needs and Recruiting Staff Members

The director with a board determines the specific characteristics of the personnel wanted and the minimum accepted. The director may seek a diverse staff through an informal needs assessment or a rigorous affirmative action plan. Because the budget is usually limited, the director must also determine priorities. Other considerations may include the potential staff available and the amount of training and supervision to be conducted. The necessary positions must then be translated into job descriptions.

Figure 4–4   Plans for Substitute Teachers

Prepare children for the possibility of a substitute; for example, have potential substitutes visit the room.

Write these procedures in detail:
• Greeting of children as they arrive
• Meals, snacks, and toileting routines
• Basic activities for each block of time in the schedule and frequently used transitions
• Routines for moving children outdoors and to other places in the building (e.g., library)
• Routines for emergencies
• Administrative duties (e.g., attendance count, meal count, snack money, sending notes home)
• Routines for departure, including a listing of those who ride buses, travel in private cars, etc.

Write plans for 2 to 3 days that do not overburden the substitute; place materials needed for plans in a given drawer or on a given shelf noted in written plans.

Have an up-to-date list of children and note any children with special needs and how those needs are handled (children's name tags can be helpful).

Leave note on desk with semiregular activities such as "duty" responsibilities.

Keep all of the above in a notebook on the desk.

If the substitute did a good job, call and express appreciation. Inform the director or the building principal of the quality of the substitute's work so that a decision can be made about possible rehiring of the substitute. (Also remember that many teachers begin their teaching careers by doing substitute work.)

The director, the personnel administrator, or a committee from the board is responsible for advertising the positions. Programs must follow affirmative action guidelines in recruiting and hiring. **Affirmative action** entails identifying and changing discriminatory employment practices and taking positive steps to recruit and provide an accepting working environment for minorities and women. Manuals on affirmative action programs are available. The ADA outlaws employment discrimination based on disability. The Economic Employment Opportunity Commission will consider the job description and whether reasonable accommodations can be made.

The NAEYC adopted a general (comprehensive) antidiscriminatory policy in 1988 stating that employment decisions must be based solely on the competence and qualifications of persons to perform "designated duties" ("NAEYC Business," 1988). Possible steps in recruiting staff include developing and gathering recruitment materials, advertising, having applicants complete job applications, obtaining documentation of credentials, interviewing, and hiring for a probationary period.

The specifics of recruiting and hiring staff members depend on the type of program and the staff positions sought and potentially available. For example, S. Newman and colleagues (1992) published some guidelines for recruiting and hiring older adults; L. Wallach (2001) discussed methods of recruiting volunteers; and Cunningham and Watson (2002) show how to effectively recruit male teachers.

Developing and Gathering Recruitment Materials. Recruitment materials must include job descriptions that list duties in terms of "essential functions" and how frequently each function must be performed, responsibilities, and authority and must list the qualifications and skills required. Public relations brochures and policy manuals are also good recruitment materials.

Advertising.   The director should first notify persons already involved in the program of an opening and then make the advertisement public. The advertisement should be in keeping with the job description and state all nonnegotiable items, such as required education and experience, so that unqualified applicants can be quickly eliminated. The advertisement should also include the method of applying and the deadline for application. Figure 4–5 is an example of a newspaper advertisement.

The method of applying and the acceptance of applications will depend on the abilities and experiences of applicants and the director's time. Thus, the method of application may vary from a telephone call or completion of a simple application form to a lengthy application form, a résumé, and a letter requesting transcripts and credentials. For example, if written communication abilities are not a part of the job description, applicants could apply in person or over the telephone. A simple application form is given in Figure 4–6 as an example.

Early childhood teachers wanted for a college-sponsored child development center. Responsibilities include planning and implementing developmentally appropriate activities for a group of twelve 3-year-old children. A.A. degree in child development/ early childhood education or a CDA certificate required; teaching experience preferred. Essential functions include constantly maintaining visual supervision of children to ensure safety and occasionally lifting, carrying, and holding children. Write for an application to Mrs. A. Jones, Director, Johnson County Community College Child Development Center, (*address*) or call (*telephone/fax*) Monday through Thursday between 2:00 and 4:00 p.m. Deadline for applications, August 1. We are an Equal Opportunity Employer.

Figure 4–5   Job Advertisement

Application For Teacher Position

JOHNSON COUNTY COMMUNITY COLLEGE CHILD DEVELOPMENT CENTER

Name of applicant _____ _____ _____ _____
                              Last   First   M   iddle or maiden

Address _____ _____
                                  Zip

Telephone number (   ) _____

RECORD OF EDUCATION

High school(s) attended

Name of school	School address	Years attended	Years completed (check)
1. _____	_____	From _____	Fr. ____ Soph. ____ Jr. ____
		to _____	Sr. ____ Graduated ____
2. _____	_____	From _____	Fr. ____ Soph. ____ Jr. ____
		to _____	Sr. ____ Graduated ____

College(s) attended

Name of college	Address	Years attended	Level completed (check)
1. _____	_____	From _____	No degree: _____
		to _____	Degree received: _____
			Major: _____
2. _____	_____	From _____	No degree: _____
		to _____	Degree received: _____
			Major: _____

Teaching certificates: _____

(Name of certificate)

RECORD OF WORK EXPERIENCE

Name and address of employer(s)	Date(s) of employment	Nature of work (Describe)
1. _____	From _____ to _____	_____
2. _____	From _____ to _____	_____
3. _____	From _____ to _____	_____

List names and addresses of three references who are familiar with your educational progress and/or work experiences.

1. _____
2. _____
3. _____

I understand that my signature on this application legally permits authorized administrators of the Johnson County Community College Child Development Center to contact all former employers concerning my work history and character as it pertains to the position for which I have applied.

_____   _____
(Signature)   (Date)

Figure 4-6   Sample Application for Teacher Position

After the deadline for application, the director or other staff member in charge of hiring will screen applications to eliminate unqualified applicants. Those applications eliminated should be retained for affirmative action requirements. Finally, the administrator is required by affirmative action guidelines to list the reasons for rejection and to notify applicants.

Obtaining Documentation of Credentials and Interviewing. The director or person(s) interviewing should obtain the following documents:

1. **References.** The director can legally contact all references given on the application and all former employers concerning work history and character. These references are aids in seeing how the applicant performed in the eyes of others. A sample introductory letter and accompanying reference form are shown in Figure 4–7.

2. **Employment Eligibility Verification.** The U.S. Department of Justice, Immigration and Naturalization Service has a form with instructions for obtaining employment eligibility verification that is used to establish identity and employment eligibility.

3. **Criminal History Records Checks.** Since 1985, many states have passed laws requiring national criminal history records checks for child care center employees. These laws were implemented to comply with federal legislation. Criminal history records checks are the only way to defend against a claim of *negligent hire*, in which an employer is held responsible for injuries to a third party if the injury was foreseeable or if the employer did not investigate before hiring.

Following the screening of applicants and obtaining documentation, all promising applicants should be interviewed. The following steps should be used in the interview process:

1. The director must follow established board policies concerning the nature, setting, and person(s) conducting the interview (e.g.,

board's personnel committee in large programs or the board member, director, or staff member(s) responsible to the new employee), along with determining who will make the final decision regarding selection.

2. The director must be careful to follow Title VII of the 1964 Civil Rights Act prohibiting discriminatory hiring practices. The rule of thumb is that all questions asked of the applicant must have a "business necessity." Some questions to avoid are date of birth or age, marital status, spouse's occupation, pregnancy issues and number of children, child care arrangements, religious affiliation (although inquiry may be made whether the scheduled workdays are suitable), membership in organizations (except those pertaining to the position), race or national origin (except for affirmative action information), arrest record, type of discharge from the military, union memberships, and disabilities (ask only whether the person can perform job specific functions).

3. For teaching positions, the beliefs and values of teachers need to be consonant with those of the program base. The interview should reveal the applicant's ideas and attitudes toward children. To understand what values and beliefs might support an interviewee's teaching practices, the interviewer should ask questions about how the applicant sees his or her role in working with young children. Interviewers who prefer a written discussion guide can use P. Bloom, Sheerer, and Britz's (1991) assessment tool "Beliefs and Values" (pp. 232–233), which is designed to get adults to reflect on their attitudes and beliefs about children, families, and the teacher's role. Some teachers bring professional teaching portfolios that can be used to document interview answers (Hurst, Wilson, & Cramer, 1998). Interview questions should also match the type of candidate (e.g., with older candidates, focus on experiences rather than on career paths; S. Newman et al., 1992).

4. After ascertaining the applicant's ideas and attitudes toward children, the interviewer

Johnson County Community College Child Development Center

TO: _____

FROM: _____

RE: _____
(Name of applicant)

The applicant has given your name as a person who can provide a reference on his or her qualifications. We want to select teachers whose professional preparation, experience, and personality can be expected to produce the best results at our Child Development Center. Please give your full and frank evaluation. Your reply will be kept in strict confidence. Please assist both us and the applicant by replying promptly.

Teaching Position Reference

How would you describe the applicant's ability in each of the following areas?

1. Knowledge of young children's development:

2. Ability to plan developmentally appropriate activities to enrich and extend children's development:

3. Ability to implement planned activities to enrich and extend children's development:

4. Ability to use positive guidance including disciplining techniques with children:

5. Ability to assess children's progress:

6. Ability to organize a physical setting:

7. Ability to work with family members:

8. Ability to work with other staff members as a team:

9. Capacity for professional and personal growth:

On the basis of your present knowledge, would you employ this applicant in a program for which you were responsible? _____

Please explain: _____

What opportunity have you had to form your judgment of this applicant? _____

_____

Additional remarks: _____

_____   _____   _____
Date)   (Signature)   (Title)

Figure 4–7   Sample Introductory Letter and Reference Form

should discuss and answer questions about the program, such as the program base, the ages of enrolled children, the guidance and discipline practices, how children are assessed, the degree of family involvement, a complete description of the job, salary, the length of school day and year, opportunities for promotion, fringe benefits, sick leave and retirement plans, consulting and supervisory services, and the nature and use of assessment to determine job performance and advancement. (For future reference, a staff policy handbook containing such information should be made available to those hired.)

Hiring.   The applicants are informed about the selection at a given date and in a specified manner. The person who is hired must usually sign a contract and other required personnel papers. If no applicant is hired, the recruitment process is repeated.

Many programs give the hired applicant a trial work period in which the director or hiring committee tries to see how compatible the person is with program practices. The conditions of the probationary period must be clearly communicated to the new employee before hiring. The trial period should last 6 months or less, and pay should be slightly less than full salary.

LAYING THE FOUNDATION FOR A COMMUNITY

An early childhood program is an organization that operates within the cultural and community contexts in which it is located. Programs are affected by the local community—its human and financial resources. On the human side, directors interact with other community leaders (i.e., leaders serving various agencies and social interest groups and directors of other early childhood programs), select and hire staff members and recruit volunteers from within the community, and serve community clients (i.e., children and their families). On the financial side, the program is affected by the community economic base and resources devoted to children and families.

Because each community has a culture that affects the early childhood program, directors must understand the local community. In building a knowledge base of the community culture, the director lays the foundation for a quality program (N. Brown & Manning, 2000) by doing the following:

1. Using the type of organizational structure (e.g., democratic) and the definition of leadership (e.g., collaborative) and characteristics (e.g., open communication style) that are most effective

2. Developing program services based on a vision of community needs and values

3. Being sensitive to the needs of staff members and volunteers

4. Providing a welcoming physical environment

5. Promoting a sense of belonging and a sense of community through the involvement of families and members of the broader community

6. Exploring other values, explaining why certain policies are needed, and resolving conflicts between professional and personal values

7. Gaining the insight needed for resource development, marketing, and advocacy and networking within the local community for in-service training of staff members, connecting families to other community resources, and promoting community projects.

BUILDING A POSITIVE AND PRODUCTIVE WORK CLIMATE FOR STAFF

As previously discussed, administrators' responsibilities include both leadership and management components. Leadership is the ability to balance the organization's need for productivity and quality with the needs of the staff. For example, task performance cannot be at the expense of work relationships. Leadership involves the process of making decisions that mold ever-changing goals and of securing the needed commitment to achieve the program's goals. Because leadership directly affects program quality, the term *leadership* seems to be replacing the term *administration*.

Even with great visions and commitment, all programs must function smoothly on a day-to-day basis. Thus, administrators are also responsible for the management component, which focuses on the specific tactics of getting and keeping the program running and provides continuity for program functioning.

Leadership in early childhood care and education is different from leadership in other organizations. Ideas about leadership in early childhood programs have not been based on traditional constructs. Kagan and Bowman (1997) suggested that traditional theories may not have been appropriate because these constructs represent a hierarchical model with a top-down view (i.e., vested right to use unilateral decision making) and a male-oriented (i.e., power-oriented) stance. This hierarchical model emphasizes results, not relations. For over 2 decades, researchers have noted that the leadership styles in fields in which women predominate are more collaborative in nature (Hennig & Jardin, 1976; Lawler, Mohrman, & Ledford, 1992; Morrison, 1992). Collaborative models see leadership as authoritative rather than authoritarian (Rodd, 1998); leaders in these models are committed to the growth of those under their leadership and thus to closing the status gap. These leaders use their authority mainly in implementing ideas coming out of the group process and in handling emergencies. Followers of collaborative leaders are committed to the ideas of the leader because they feel involved and valued (Kelley, 1991). Thus, collaborative leadership emphasizes both results and relations. The early childhood field has had a long history of "shared leader-

ship" (Kagan, 1994b) or "participatory management" (Jorde-Bloom, 1995). Parents and professionals shared leadership in parent cooperatives and Head Start. Today, the emerging effort is toward networking and collaboration, but the team approach is not always carried out in the real world.

People in an early childhood program are not only individuals but also part of a group—called the *faculty* or *staff*. Along with the personalities of these individuals, their roles and positions within the group shape their collective behavior or form the group's personality (L. Barker, Wahlers, Watson, & Kibler, 1987). In all organizations, including early childhood programs, responsibilities are carried out as a result of interpersonal relations more than of formal roles. Interpersonal relations include the way planning is conducted, decisions are made, and conflicts are resolved (Hoy & Miskel, 1987).

Staff members develop perceptions about their program. The collective perceptions are called the *climate* (P. Bloom, 1997b). The climate can be described in terms of the degree to which (a) the group understands and supports the leader's visions for the program, (b) the staff is involved in the collaborative effort and maintains collegiality during the process, and (c) the staff believes the administrator can provide both the expertise and time to manage the program.

Creating and Communicating a Culturally Relevant Vision

Leaders can shape their organizational environment and can transform the lives of those in their program and even the wider community. Carter and Curtis (1998) called for directors to have big dreams about the roles their programs can play in reshaping their communities. Many professionals admire the schools of Reggio Emilia because they were created from a culturally relevant vision.

To have a culturally relevant vision, program directors must constantly reexamine their programs in terms of the changing needs of clients and trends in the field (Schein, 1993). Rapid social changes have occurred in the lives of young children and their families. Drucker (1990) speaks of leaders seeing the connection between the missions of organizations and marketing (Who are your clients? What do they need and value? Do you offer what they need and value?). In response to these changes, a new transdisciplinary knowledge base is forming in early childhood care and education (Stott & Bowman, 1996), and a growing need for family-centered services and collaboration with other community agencies is occurring (Kagan, Rivera, Brigham, & Rosenblum, 1992). Effective leaders have adapted their programs to meet the needs of clients and to make use of "best practices" knowledge.

The constant adaptation of services has required leaders who can create and communicate a culturally relevant vision. Carter and Curtis (1998) provided these practical suggestions for creating such a vision:

- Recall the vision that brought you to this field.
- Share memories of positive childhood experiences.
- Discuss positive experiences portrayed in children's books and how those could be implemented in your program.
- Ask family members to share their hopes for their children who are entering your program.

The vision provides the direction for innovative decisions to bridge the gap between present services and projected needs. Without a vision, the leader will be caught too frequently in *crisis change* (i.e., response to an unexpected occurrence) or *transformational change* (i.e., radical alteration of the organization in order to survive; Rodd, 1998). Visions always involve changes. Unlike reacting to crisis and transformational

changes, initiating innovative changes allows leaders to move their programs in the desirable direction for the following reasons:

1. Leaders can ponder the best- and worst-case scenarios and take only carefully calculated risks. Once they have foresight into the needed changes, they are willing to accept change and convince others to accept it; in short, they are mission driven (J. Collins & Porras, 1994).

2. Leaders can study the entire picture of change from a systems perspective. A systems perspective, according to P. Bloom and colleagues (1991), involves (a) changing people's knowledge, skills, or attitudes; (b) changing the process (e.g., goal setting, decision making); and (c) changing the structure (e.g., goals, policies, housing, budget). If all three are not changed, dysfunction occurs in the system. Looking at changes from a systems perspective allows the leader to look at costs (time, money, disruption) versus positive results (services wanted or needed by clients, effectiveness, efficiency).

3. Leaders can evaluate results. For example, results may be considered positive when they bring status to a program, are cost effective, or produce efficiency. Because change takes time and occurs in stages, Likert (1967) suggested that leaders need to wait a minimum of 2 years to see real change. As noted in longitudinal programmatic research, output can be delayed. Even when the change in programs seems simple, often intervening variables cause delay (e.g., How long would it take to change staff attitudes concerning _____?).

Leaders must communicate—literally sell—their visions to their staff. If innovative change is to be effective, the leader must begin with the vision, identify why the change is needed, set goals and objectives, delegate responsibilities, set standards of performance, and establish time frames. Change through collaborative endeavors takes longer than top-down change. Although some changes may be mandated by a leader, lack of trust in the vision or even in the leader often occurs in authoritarian situations. Many changes require collaboration to be effective because they are often implemented by the staff (e.g., curriculum changes).

Collaborating

Program effectiveness comes from collaborating. Rodd (1998) believes that many early childhood leaders have not developed skills in collaborative decision making. Directors view their early childhood programs as having more effective collaboration than do staff members (P. Bloom, 1995b). Staff perceptions can be checked (P. Bloom et al., 1991, pp. 192–196; Smylie, 1992). Early childhood programs must go beyond a verbal commitment to collaboration to actually using the process. P. Bloom (2000a) provided many helpful suggestions for implementing shared decision making and participatory management.

P. Bloom (2000a) discussed the following four levels of decision making, three of which involve others: (a) *unilateral*—the director makes the call; (b) *consultative*—the director seeks input from others before making the call; (c) *collaborative*—the director and others analyze the problem, generate and evaluate possible solutions, and then decide on the action; and (d) *delegative*—the director provides information, and others make the decision. In business, names for shared decision making include *total quality management, site-based management, quality circles, management by consensus,* and *participatory management.* Leaders must determine whether a decision should be determined by collaboration. Collaborative decision making is more appropriate for novel situations that call for problem solving than for routine decisions. P. Bloom also stated that directors should consider the personal interests or stakes of others in the issue and others' degree of input-competence. Directors must be forthright about how input from others will be used.

Steps in Collaborating.   The steps in decision making through collaborative means are much like the steps involved in any process of decision making. The first step is pinpointing the problem. Assessing needs makes others understand that improvement is a shared responsibility. To pinpoint a problem, one has to realize that the symptoms are not necessarily the problem itself. Thus, one has to collect accurate data on the problem. Data can be collected through anonymous questionnaires or interviews (see P. Bloom et al., 1991) or through documents or records on staff, children, and family members.

The second step involves considering different potential solutions and assessing each one. The main question is, What do we need to do to achieve our goal? Decisions should be based more on research than on personal opinion or tradition. The code of ethics (see chapter 11) should also guide the process when dealing with ethical concerns.

Finally, the group must select the best alternative, develop a plan of action, and implement it. Other decisions must be made, such as who will do each aspect of the plan, what is needed to accomplish the plan (time and monetary resources), and how and when improvements will be measured.

Roles of the Leader During Collaboration.   Collaborative teamwork occurs when individual needs are subordinated to achieve program goals. The director serves as the leader of the team. During the process of collaborating, the leader keeps the task structure clear (i.e., helps the group determine the problem or issue, the goal to be achieved, and the process of attaining the goal or desired results) and ensures constructive relationships. To be successful, a leader must assume several responsibilities.

Motivating Collaborative Efforts.   The leader must encourage the participation of the entire group involved in the proposed change. Rodd (1998) stated that individuals have "the right to be cautious about anything new but not the right to not grow and develop" (p. 132). Several suggestions for motivating are as follows:

1. The leader must convince others that the job itself is important. Because early childhood care and education is inherently important work, leaders find it relatively easy to convince others that their jobs are important. Still, leaders must build a sense of community and foster the "we" feeling of meeting the dynamic needs of children and their families.

2. The leader must know staff attitudes. Several instruments are available to help with this (see P. Bloom et al., 1991, pp. 42, 170–176, 253–255). Shoemaker (2000) developed an "Analysis of Staff Motivation" questionnaire (pp. 158–160).

3. Leaders need to build self-esteem in employees. Bandura (1982) theorized that people must be convinced that they will be successful before they attempt goals. Thus, leaders need to (a) have a democratic organizational climate that provides appropriate autonomy, (b) coach for collaborative work, (c) provide staff needed training and time to learn new skills, and (d) reward individuals with recognition and greater responsibility along with external rewards (e.g., salary increases, job security).

Communicating with Others.   The success of leadership rests almost totally on the ability to communicate because it is the method of attaining shared meanings. During collaboration, leaders must communicate with others their commitment to have an impact on the lives of young children and their families and to implement the visions for their programs. Understanding differences in values and using culturally sensitive communication is important.

To be successful, leaders must recognize barriers to communication (e.g., differences in cultures, staff members working in separate rooms and/or with different age groups of children, interruptions and noise level). To move the collaborative process forward, they must listen, reflect, provide support and objective feedback, and consider the effects their words have on others. See Figure 4–8.

Overseeing Conflicts.   Collaborative decision making leads to fewer conflicts. Conflicts are higher both under authoritarian leadership in which people feel left out of decision making and under permissive leadership in which people want guidance but do not have it. In collaborative decision making, conflicts most often arise because many beliefs are subjective (Clyde & Rodd, 1989) and because collaboration is not majority rule but consensus building.

Leaders can manage conflicts in a constructive way by describing the conflict situation, communicating understandings of the various perspectives, brainstorming for alternatives, and trying and

Figure 4–8   Needed Communication Skills

Reflective Listening Skills

• Understanding content
• Comprehending body language and paralinguistics (tone of voice)

Response Skills

• Setting decision-making parameters
• Stating one's reflections of another's comments as part of the response
• Being sensitive to others' values and feelings
• Using appropriate self-assertion when needed

evaluating alternatives to find the best solution. Sustaining issue-based conflict—not hurting individuals—is desirable because it can lead to "collective wisdom" (E. Jones & Nimmo, 1999).

Delegating Responsibilities. Leaders must distinguish between the tasks the leader must do and those others can do. When delegating responsibilities, the leader must match the tasks to staff members' skills and interests. Rodd (1998) suggested basing the match on Maslow's hierarchy. She believes that staff members at the third level (love and acceptance) can do well in tasks dealing with building or maintaining relationships, such as staff parties; staff members at the fourth (esteem) and fifth (self-actualization) levels accept tasks that require more competence, although those at the fourth level need more recognition than those at the fifth level. People can also volunteer for tasks.

As part of the delegating process, leaders need to be clear about what needs to be done, the deadlines for completion, and the levels of authority and accountability. Leaders must explain that they will not be supervising the tasks but are available to help gather needed tools and information and for support.

Managing

Management skills are necessary for program survival. Managing is the technical aspect of administration. The director is the technical expert who is responsible for the execution of the program. The specific tasks vary from program to program.

Excellent managers are good at time management (getting things done quickly without undue stress). Interruptions and not keeping contacts with others to the point are the main enemies of time management in early childhood programs. Effective time management requires organizing the office, setting goals and matching smaller tasks to goals, establishing priorities among activities and investing maximum time in productive activities, doing the necessary but undesirable tasks, and analyzing impediments to completing tasks.

ENRICHING THE PROFESSIONAL LIFE OF THE STAFF

The most important role of the director is to enable conditions that lead to an enriching professional life for the staff. To enrich the professional life of the staff, directors must assess both collective and individual needs and then plan ways to meet both.

Assessing Staff Needs

Defining competence in terms of the exact background needed is difficult. Certain core knowledge and skills are needed and must be acquired through experience by all early childhood professionals because these are correlated with classroom quality and positive teacher behaviors. Katz and Raths (1986) believe that in addition to background, a certain teacher "disposition" is necessary to be effective. All personnel need to refresh current skills and learn new ones that will help with the changes that are occurring in teaching and with the discarding of inappropriate practices and the rebuilding of appropriate practices.

Because early childhood personnel differ widely in their educational backgrounds and are at different stages in their careers, they experience unique individual needs. Early childhood professionals serve in different roles, too. For example, family child care providers have different needs from personnel in child care centers (Trawick-Smith & Lambert, 1995). Thus, to be effective, leaders must assess both the collective and the individual needs of staff members if they hope to improve the quality of the program.

Identifying Collective Needs.   Orientation to a specific program is needed by all staff members. Orientation should always cover the program base. Staff members cannot work as a team if they do not understand and accept the rationale of the program base and the objectives stemming from the rationale. Other items that orientation should cover include the clientele served, the services of the program, the physical facility, and regulations and local program policies.

Development should continue throughout a staff member's tenure. To be effective, professional development must be seen as an active process of growing and learning, and not a product (e.g., a workshop presented by someone else). Thus, specific group needs must be identified. Abbott-Shim (1990) recommended the use of data from individual job performance assessments, needs assessment surveys, and program evaluations. Data can be collected in the following ways:

1. **Staff job performance assessments** show the strengths and weaknesses of individual staff members. A summary of strengths and weaknesses of staff members can be used to determine potential training areas.

2. **Needs assessment surveys** are surveys in which staff check topics of perceived needs. The director summarizes the responses and identifies training needs. A simple needs assessment survey is given in Figure 4–9. A needs assessment survey has been developed by P. Bloom and colleagues (1991, pp. 211–218).

3. **Program evaluation measures** provide comprehensive evaluation, including sections measuring staff competencies.

Other areas needed by all staff members include the following:

1. **Teachers need combined training in child development and early childhood education.** Research indicates that training in child development and early childhood education is a major predictor of teaching quality (NAEYC, 1996a, 1997a, 2001; NICHD Early Child Care Research, 2000; Shonkoff & Phillips, 2000), especially if child development is understood within a socio-

cultural context. Teachers must learn to integrate what they learn about curriculum, assessment, and group management with what they know about children (Bredekamp & Rosegrant, 1992, 1995b).

2. **Teachers need training in the inclusion of children with special needs.** Most general education teachers have had few opportunities to collaborate with specialists (Joint Committee on Teacher Planning for Students with Disabilities, 1995; Wolery et al., 1994). Special education personnel can help other teachers with concepts and practices concerning holistic development, meeting individual needs, and using a family focus. General education teachers need help in learning use of equipment, warning signs for pending crises, and universal precautions and infection control. General education teachers can share their backgrounds in child development (Rose & Smith, 1993). Staff development opens the doors for ongoing interdisciplinary support of children with special needs and often changes the cautious and even negative attitudes frequently noted when teachers first face inclusion. Many teachers have reported becoming even more aware of the needs of all children following inclusion (Giangreco, Dennis, Coninger, Edelman, & Schattman, 1993).

3. **Teachers need training in multicultural and antibias concepts and practices.** Teachers need to examine their own biases first. Jorde-Bloom (1992a) examined the ways teachers can assess their beliefs and attitudes. *In Our Own Way* (Alvarado et al., 1999) describes how teachers' antibias work shaped their professional and personal lives.

4. **Teachers need training in DAP.** One of the most difficult problems is showing teachers who have theoretical understandings of DAP how to implement the practices in their classrooms (Burts & Buchanan, 1998; Haupt, Larsen, Robinson, & Hart, 1995; Mangione & Maniates, 1993).

5. **Teachers need training in technology.** Technology must be integrated into instruction in appropriate ways. Teachers must also provide

Needs Assessment Survey of
Johnson County Community College Child Development Center

We need some information regarding your specific needs for training. After reading the entire list below, check 6 topics (from the 48 listed) that you would like to have covered in in-service training. After checking, rank the topics in order of importance, with "1" being the most important to you.

Child care

_____ Regulations/legal issues

_____ Evaluation of children

_____ Mainstreaming exceptional children

_____ Health and safety

Child development

_____ Physical development (general)

_____ Social development

_____ Cognitive development

_____ Emotional development

_____ Morals/values development

_____ Language development

_____ Motor skill development

Curriculum (preschool through primary)

_____ Art

_____ Oral language

_____ Writing

_____ Literature

_____ Prereading skills

_____ Mathematics

_____ Social studies

_____ Science

_____ Music

_____ Gross-motor play

_____ Fine-motor play

_____ Incorporating computers

_____ Incorporating multicultural/multilingual learnings

_____ Cooking experiences

_____ Sand/water/mud play

_____ Woodworking experiences

_____ Block-building experiences

_____ Dramatic play experiences

Organization and management

_____ Arranging physical environments

_____ Use of indoor equipment/materials

_____ Use of outdoor equipment/materials

_____ Scheduling problems

_____ Transitions

_____ Grouping

_____ Encouraging effective child–child interactions

_____ Encouraging effective child–adult interactions

_____ Encouraging effective child–material interactions

_____ Guiding children's behavior (discipline)

Staff needs

_____ Credentials/training requirements

_____ Communication skills

_____ Team teaching

_____ Evaluation

_____ Policy development

Families

_____ Family education

_____ Family involvement

_____ Family support

_____ Meeting needs of special families
        (e.g., single parents)

Figure 4–9   Staff Training Needs Assessment Survey

the needed scaffolding for children. Thus, most teachers need training in technology (Haughland & Wright, 1997; NAEYC, 1996b).

Identifying Individual Needs. Staff training has to be individualized, too, because staff members are unique individuals at different stages of development, with different abilities and teaching styles, and with different roles. For example, Katz (1995b) identified four stages of development and the training needs of in-service teachers at each stage:

1. **Survival.** The first year of teaching is filled with self-doubt. Teachers need on-site support and technical assistance.

2. **Consolidation.** During the second and perhaps third year, teachers consolidate the gains they have made and focus on specific skills. They need on-site assistance, access to specialists, and advice from colleagues.

3. **Renewal.** During the third and fourth year, job stress is alleviated through assistance in the analysis of teaching and participation in professional associations.

4. **Maturity.** After the fifth year, teachers benefit from additional formal education, professional conferences, and contributions to the profession (e.g., journal writing).

Burden (1987) identified three career stages that are similar to those of Katz's model. He saw teachers struggling to survive, growing and exploring, and functioning as mature professionals. Instead of using experience stages, Arin-Krump (1981) identified staff needs and training needs for seven age stages based on the work of Erik Erikson, Robert Havighurst, Roger Gould, and Gail Sheehy. For example, Arin-Krump stated that teachers in their 20s are in the stages of identity and intimacy. Marriage and parenting are key concerns, and family life creates much stress. At this age, teachers also want to demonstrate job competence. Thus, staff development for this age group is most successful if it (a) creates a climate that permits discussion of life stresses and (b) defines the parameters of the job and discusses means for effecting change in areas of deficit.

A self-evaluation form is also helpful as a starting point for discussions of individual needs. One example of such a form is a simple open-ended questionnaire covering achievements, challenges, and disappointments ("Staff Self-Evaluation Form," 1992). P. Bloom and colleagues (1991) stated their belief that directors should obtain as much information on each staff member as possible from supervisor assessments, peer assessments, and self-assessments. They developed several assessment tools that could be used for diagnosing individual needs.

Professional roles also determine individual needs. For example, family child care providers serve a wide age range, often care for their own children, live and work in their own homes, have the dual director/teacher role, and work alone (Trawick-Smith & Lambert, 1995).

Improving the Quality of Staff

As previously noted, early childhood care and education is a two-tiered system of teacher regulation. Unlike public school teachers, who have a preservice credential, many other teachers are hired without credential (A. Mitchell, 1996). This has made the field, especially at the preschool level, rely on in-service training. Thus, the director has had to plan and implement **staff development activities** (all activities that aid staff in providing quality for the early childhood program). Staff development is designed to help noncredentialed staff members develop needed knowledge, skills, and attitudes. As has been discussed, even teachers who hold teaching certificates need renewal. Most professionals see staff development as a major catalyst to the development of high-quality programs for young children. Professional associations as well as early childhood leaders in state departments of education have been pushing for more funding for staff development (S. Robinson, 1993/94). The Quality 2000

Initiative called for staff development as a major priority (Kagan & Neuman, 1997b). The NAEYC (1998a) emphasizes building support systems that contribute to professional development and retention.

Regrettably, planning and implementating staff development have not been easy tasks for directors. The Cost, Quality, and Child Outcomes Study Team (1995) found that centers scored low on opportunities for professional growth. Regardless of the difficulties involved, directors play critical roles in the quality of their programs through leadership in professional growth opportunities (Bredekamp, 1990; Jorde-Bloom & Sheerer, 1991). Improving the quality of personnel has been done through encouraging more formal education, mentoring for professional development, providing various group professional development activities, urging professional affiliations, alleviating job stress, and assessing job performance.

All staff development activities need to involve the following:

1. **Active learning.** Active learning involves activities such as collaborating on a project, debating issues, and participating in community activities. Active learning is a way to balance practical and theoretical knowledge, allow adults to learn in the same ways we want children to learn, and stimulate creativity (Cuffaro, 1995; E. Jones, 1986; Piscitelli, 2000).

2. **Reflective practice.** Reflective practice requires teachers to think about their experiences and interactions and adjust activities based on their reflections. Many resources are available to help teachers become more reflective (Rand, 2000; Tertell, Klein, & Jewett, 1998).

3. **Individualized activities.** Staff training must move away from the cookie-cutter approach to an individualized one. Content is determined by assessing collective (i.e., local program) and individual needs. Staff members need to have input into the planning.

Encouraging Formal Education.   From its beginning the kindergarten movement required a course of study for prospective teachers. As kindergartens and other early childhood programs became part of the public schools, teachers were required to obtain degrees from postsecondary institutions and state-granted teaching certificates. Local boards of education also required refresher courses or work toward an advanced degree for renewal of a contract and pay raises. Katz (1995b) indicated that teachers in the stages of renewal and maturity (after 3 to 5 years of experience) are in need of college work.

Unlike public school teachers, preschool teachers, especially those working in child care centers, more often pursue formal education after being employed. To encourage staff members to pursue formal education as an in-service activity, directors must (a) coordinate training offered by institutions and staff members' needs and availability for training; (b) work out other problems associated with training (e.g., classroom coverage during work hours and babysitting and transportation services for after-hours training); (c) supervise field experiences; and (d) provide salary increments or career advancement as recognition for completed work. To encourage staff members to acquire more formal education, a growing number of states have launched initiatives. The best-known initiative is the TEACH (Teacher Education and Compensation Helps) Early Childhood Project, which began in North Carolina in 1990 and has spread to 17 other states. Teachers receive scholarships to attend school and bonus pay when they complete their study; in turn, teachers commit to working in their sponsoring program for at least one more year (Olson, 2002).

Mentoring for Professional Development.   **Mentoring** is the supporting and coaching of a *protégé* (novice staff member) by a *mentor* (educated, experienced, and dedicated staff member). In some cases, mentoring may involve peer coaching (i.e., between two inexperienced teachers), but this model is seldom used. The overall purpose of mentoring is to serve as a bridge between preservice training and early practice or as a way to learn new skills anytime.

Performance supervision is an idea that dates to the 1920s. School supervisors provided help to novice teachers and also evaluated them. Today's mentoring models, which evolved from the industrial concept called *quality circles,* seldom use directors as mentors.

Values of Mentoring. As a result of problems faced by beginning teachers and high rates of teacher turnover and attrition, mentoring is gaining support. Mentoring enhances the work of the mentor and the knowledge and skills of the protégé. More specifically, research on mentoring shows that mentoring builds leadership (Whitebook, Hnatiuk, & Bellm, 1994), helps counter high turnover rates (Kremer-Hazon & Ben-Peretz, 1996), increases feelings of professional growth (Rosenholtz, Bassler, & Hoover-Dempsey, 1986), and instills a sense of community (M. Newman, Rutter, & Smith, 1989). Mentoring seems especially appropriate in predominantly female careers because women appear to benefit from more mentor-initiated contact, more feedback, and more modeling than men (Schneider, 1991). Because of its success, mentoring is now seen in public schools and in many states' early childhood care and education career lattices.

Mentoring Models and Process. Mentoring models may work in various ways as shown in Figure 4–10. For example, some mentors work with one type of program (e.g., family child care), whereas others work with more than one type of program. Some serve as mentors in specific areas (e.g., in the use of assistive technologies or developing literacy skills in children), whereas others work with their protégés on all aspects of their tasks (e.g., in the process of obtaining a CDA credential). Variations in the setting (e.g., the protégé's classroom) and approaches (e.g., one-on-one mentoring, one mentor to several protégés) are also common (Bellm, Whitebook, & Hnatiuk, 1997; Center for Career Development in Early Care and Education at Wheelock College, 2000; "Taking the Lead Initiative," 2000).

The mentoring process usually works this way:

1. The mentor gets to know the responsibilities and program settings of the protégé.

2. With the protégé, the mentor helps establish expectations for the process.

3. The protégé discusses perceived needs. (For example, the protégé might want to use Bellm et al.'s [1997] "Self-Evaluation Checklist" [pp. 91–93].)

4. The protégé and mentor agree on specific goals.

5. The mentor and protégé develop a plan of action (i.e., meeting times and how the mentoring will work).

6. The mentor and protégé prepare a plan of action; the protégé tries out the plan; the mentor observes and gathers data; the mentor and protégé both take some time to reflect on outcomes before discussing the results; the protégé reflects on his or her teaching with the mentor's help (e.g., What do you think happened? How did _____ affect the outcome?). The protégé draws inferences.

7. Together the protégé and mentor decide whether goals and strategies should be incorporated into the teaching repertoire or whether they need to be refined or alternative ideas selected.

Requirements for Effective Mentoring. Following are some requirements of effective mentoring:

1. Select the best mentors possible. Although some qualities of mentors may vary by culture, generally mentors should (a) have

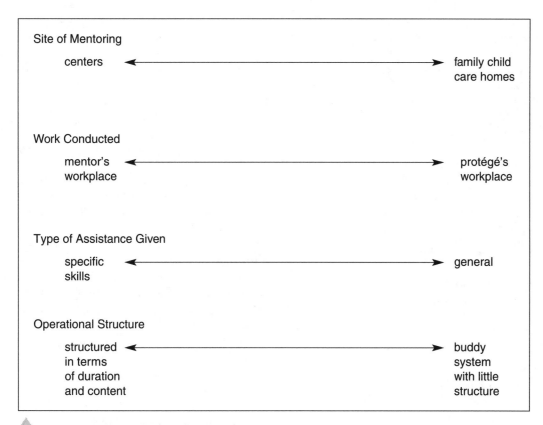

Figure 4–10   Variations in Mentoring Models

training and experience in child development and early childhood education, adult learning, reflective practice, and leadership; (b) have the ability to be supportive of protégés and build a collaborative approach (see "Taking the Pulse of Your Relationship: A Checklist for Mentors" in Bellm et al., 1997, p. 74); (c) use different mentoring methods to match protégés' abilities and learning styles and the goals to be achieved, and be creative problem solvers; (d) have good communication abilities and be able to observe and record protégés' performances; (e) be able to clarify differences in opinions, knowledge-based "best practices," and mandates; and (f) be good role models.

2. Match the mentor with the protégé based on the protégé's needs, abilities, and learning style.

3. Find release time for the mentor, the protégé, or both.

4. Provide necessary coverage of the mentor's and protégé's responsibilities during the process.

5. Collect resources on mentoring (see end of chapter).

6. Budget stipends and wage increases for both mentors and protégés.

Providing Group Professional Development Activities. Group techniques for staff development are also used. Like mentoring, group techniques should fit staff members' abilities, skills, and interests as well as possess appropriate training content. For example, Latimer (1994) gave some pointers on training older adults. The method of presentation should be varied to hold interest. And, most important, staff members must be involved and able to see the direct application of the training to their professional responsibilities.

Finding time for group activities is difficult. Staff development cannot occur during nap time. Staff development needs to occur on a regular basis, with staff receiving release time or appropriate compensation. The following are several ways of handling staff development:

1. The center or school may be closed on certain days for staff development. (Parents should have them on their calendar at the time of enrollment.)
2. The center may close for a week during periods of low enrollment. These are also excellent times for hiring substitute help or getting volunteers.
3. Evening sessions can work. (Serving dinner and having child care for staff are nice touches.)

Discussions.   Staff meetings can be used for discussions (see Figure 4–11 for general tips). Staff should *share* ideas rather than have the director do all the presenting. Staff can learn through discussing and solving problems. Teachers can gain much from reflection on their own work. After sharing ideas, each staff member should try one or more ideas during work.

Staff can also gain from the sharing of personal narratives. Change in teaching occurs through the process of listening and responding (Cinnamond & Zimpher, 1990). Narratives are not new in early childhood education (Ashton-Warner, 1963; Pratt, 1948). Recently published narratives (listed at the end of the chapter) are good for staff development.

Discussions can occur on any aspect of the program. Because of staff diversity, beliefs and values about program goals and policies should be explored through discussions (Carter, 1992). Exchanges of ideas and feelings about issues and role clarification (see P. Bloom et al., 1991, pp. 233–252) are most helpful.

Workshops and Consultation.   Workshops are the most common form of training (Kisker, Hofferth, Phillips, & Farquhar, 1991). They may be provided through outside sources (e.g., professional

---

Divide discussion content into categories (e.g., children's program, parents, administration). Decide which category is covered at a given time (e.g., children's program—1st Tuesday of each month; parents—2nd Tuesday of every other month). Routine announcements may be distributed at the end of each meeting or handled in other ways.

Make meetings relevant to those in attendance. Thus, in some cases, assistant teachers may not need to meet with lead teachers.

Prepare an agenda a few days before a scheduled meeting. Make any needed materials available at this time. The agenda should indicate the amount of time for presentation and for discussion.

Start and stop the meeting on time.

Distribute minutes of the meeting to staff.

Figure 4–11   Tips on Staff Meetings for Discussions

organizations) or developed by staff members themselves. The term *workshop* implies an activity-oriented, as opposed to a presentation-only, session and often centers on one topic. Teachers need to have options on topics. (See Abbott-Shim, 1990; P. Bloom, 2000c; and Carter, 1993 for some ideas.)

If consultation is to yield lasting results, consultants must be viewed as resource people and not as "experts" hired to solve problems. They need to be aware of the real-life concerns of staff (Trawick-Smith & Lambert, 1995) and facilitate staff members in resolving their own problems. If consultant work is to be secured, the administrator must identify potential resource people, describe (in writing) training needs, and provide a format to be completed by potential resource people. Figure 4–12 is an example of a workshop proposal format. Both proposals and presentations should be evaluated as shown in Figure 4–13.

Self-Study in Accreditation and Program Evaluation. The accreditation process is a major avenue for staff development because it involves self-study. Certain items from other program evaluations are appropriate for staff development, too. A very helpful publication is *The What, Why, and How of High-Quality Early Childhood Education: A Guide for On-Site Supervision,* Revised Edition (Koralek, Colker, & Dodge, 1995).

Use of Professional Development Resources. All programs can benefit from the use of professional journals, books, and audiovisual materials. Professional organizations publish many useful materials in many formats.

Urging Professional Affiliations. Membership in professional organizations offers various opportunities for personnel to improve their qualifications. Regrettably, many staff members do not belong to any professional group (Galinsky, Howes, Kontos, & Shinn, 1994; Whitebook et al., 1990).

Figure 4–12   Example of a Workshop Proposal Format

Workshop Proposal

The following information must be submitted for consideration as a resource person for the Johnson County Community College Child Development Center.

Name, address, day and evening phone numbers of individuals submitting request.

Main presenter résumé (title, academic and professional background).

Names and addresses and résumés of other presenters.

Objectives of presentation.

Outline of presentation.

Concept:

Delivery strategy:

Time required:

Method to be used to evaluate workshop effectiveness.

Resource materials provided by consultant.

Special requests (e.g., observation in center before presentation, audiovisual equipment).

Evaluation of_____
Johnson County Community College Child Development Center

Rank each item on a 3-point scale: 1 (Excellent), 2 (Satisfactory), and 3 (Poor).

	Proposal	*Presentation*
Objectives related to training needs	_____	_____
Content related to training needs	_____	_____
Content applicable to work with children	_____	_____
Content organized	_____	_____
Content clearly presented	_____	_____
Delivery strategies held interests of participants	_____	_____
Delivery strategies encouraged give-and-take among staff members and between staff and resource person(s)	_____	_____
Evaluation seemed effective	_____	_____
Resource materials seemed practical	_____	_____

Comments: _____

_____

_____

_____

Figure 4–13   Example of an Evaluation Format for Workshops and Consultation

Professional organizations publish literature such as journals, position papers, and other materials to aid members in professional growth and competence. Almost all professional organizations have regular national, regional, and state meetings that provide a means for hearing and seeing the "latest" and for sharing ideas with others. Professional organizations serve as public representation—advocacy—of members' views to local, state, and national governing bodies. Some organizations offer opportunities for travel and study, research assistance, and consultation. Others provide personal services to members, such as insurance policies and loans. Finally, member-

ship in a professional organization says to families and the community in general, "I am joining with others in an effort to provide the best for our children." See appendix 5 for a list of many professional organizations concerned with the development of young children.

Alleviating Job Stress.   More and more teachers are becoming victims of job stress. **Burnout** can be defined as "a syndrome of emotional exhaustion and cynicism that can occur in individuals who spend much of their time working closely with other people" (Pines & Maslach, 1980, p. 6). Stress comes from several conditions:

- The unexpected is common because of the age of children and the fact that the curriculum designs in many programs are not highly structured (Needle, 1980), and also tedium, or what P. Bloom (1995a) called the "treadmill of activity," can consume energy;

- undesirable working conditions, such as unpaid overtime, the inability to take scheduled breaks because of staff shortage, and the lack of fringe benefits, including medical coverage, often plague teachers (Center for Child Care Workforce, 1998; Whitebook et al., 1993);

- early childhood positions are not considered high-status jobs by some persons who see play activities as less than real teaching (E. Jones, 1994);

- early childhood teachers are so indoctrinated in the importance of the early years of a child's life that they often feel let down when they do not achieve their lofty goals regardless of the underlying cause (Needle, 1980);

- early childhood professionals are often excluded from decision making (P. Bloom, 1997a; Boyd & Schneider, 1997); and

- teachers view themselves as surrogate parents (Needle, 1980). Early childhood professionals are also subjected to health hazards, such as the strain of lifting children, risks of disease, and injuries from biting or kicking children (Townley, Thornburg, & Crompton, 1991).

Most susceptible to burnout are teachers in child care programs. For the most part, these teachers are in the lowest status jobs in the early childhood field, and they receive the least compensation for their work. Stress may come from these teachers' personal lives. Kindergarten through grade 3 teachers reported that the following factors contributed to job dissatisfaction: problems with administrators, too much paperwork, low salaries, problems with families, large class size, not enough time to teach, problems with colleagues, too many meetings, differences in philosophical beliefs about the education of young children, and abuse and misuse of tests (Greathouse, Moyer, & Rhodes-Offutt, 1992). Unlike other occupations, in early childhood care and education, as the level of education increases, disparity is often greater between the perceived expectations of job rewards and actual rewards; thus, job satisfaction often decreases (Kontos & Stremmel, 1988).

As a way to help alleviate some stress, P. Bloom (1997b) suggested improving the organizational climate of the program. The Early Childhood Work Survey measures the organizational climate and may be purchased from the Center for Early Childhood Leadership (see appendix 5). The short form of this instrument is found in P. Bloom and colleages (1991, pp. 177–179). Data from staff exit interviews, such as Olsen's (1993) interview questions, can also help a program look at its organizational climate.

Assessing Job Performance. Directors have the overall responsibility for staff assessment. Sometimes a board member is also involved. Large corporate systems use regional staff administrators to do the assessment. In public schools, principals and central office supervisors assess staff.

Purposes. Assessing job performance provides a mirror for what is happening in the program; that is, assessing job performance can aid in determining the effectiveness of the program in attaining its vision and diagnosing some of its problems. Caruso and Fawcett (1999) stated that "probably no other supervisory process has the *potential* to affect the quality of learning experiences for children as what staff members learn about themselves" (p. 151). The process of assessing job performance aids staff members in realizing that they are professionals (Duff, Brown, & Van Scoy, 1995).

Assessment may be formative or summative. **Formative assessment** is focused on the diagnostic (reflects the strengths and weaknesses of a staff member) and is thus used to promote growth. Formative assessment is usually focused on one problem or a group of related problems at one time (e.g., planning or arranging the physical facility). Teachers want the assessment process to imply that there are always areas in which one can learn and improve. Teachers should also use self-assessment as formative assessment. **Summative assessment** lets persons know how they perform against certain predetermined criteria. Summative assessment "sums up" performance in that it looks at overall performance. Thus, summative assessment is used for such decisions as continuing employment, offering tenure, and advancing merit pay. For the present purposes, only formative assessment is considered because all other purposes of assessment, such as tenure and merit pay, should be based on performance.

Styles of Supervisors. Glickman, Gordon, and Ross-Gordon (1998) noted these three orientations to supervision: directive, nondirective, and collaborative. Several factors affect the styles of supervisors. For example, cultural backgrounds affect factors such as the values placed on dependence/independence, cooperation/individuality, or punctuality. The program base also affects the style of supervision. For example, behaviorist supervisors often have a directive orientation in selecting goals and objectives for staff members and reinforcing these in their efforts to achieve goals, whereas nonbehaviorist supervisors often use a more collaborative approach. Finally, novice staff members generally require more direct supervision than experienced personnel. Supervisors often like to collaborate with experienced teachers on more long-range or difficult-to-achieve goals (Brandt, 1996; Vander Ven, 1988).

Criteria for Assessment. Criteria for assessment should reflect the specific responsibilities of a staff member and be appropriate for the professional level of that person. Generally, personnel who provide similar services should be assessed

according to the same criteria, but personnel serving in dissimilar roles should be assessed according to different criteria, although some assessment items might be the same.

Assessments should be based on observations of performance and the observer's perceptions of the staff member's intentions. Several assessment tools are available and can be adapted to fit local needs. Some sources of criteria include the following:

1. The common elements that "define what all early childhood professionals must know and be able to do" (p. 13) based on a position statement of the NAEYC (Willer, 1994)

2. The CDA competency standards (Council for Early Childhood Professional Recognition, 1996)

3. "Criteria for High-Quality Early Childhood Programs" given in the guide to accreditation by the National Academy of Early Childhood Programs (NAEYC, 1998a) or the adapted version developed by P. Bloom and colleagues (1991)

4. The teacher assessment for constructivist classrooms developed by Stork and Engle (1999)

Besides having the director observe their performance, staff members need to be reflective of their own performance through self-assessment. Although few self-assessment scales are available, the University of South Carolina Children's Center has developed a scale that requires the teacher to reflect on his or her satisfaction with career choice, professional performances, collaborative relations, and long-term career goals (Duff, et al., 1995).

Methods of Observing and Recording. After criteria for assessing personnel performance have been determined, they must be incorporated into an appraisal instrument. Locally devised assessment procedures may include the following:

1. **Narratives** are based on observations. These observations may be open ended or may

focus on specific areas, such as guidance of children or planning. During observations, the director observes the staff member and notes specific strengths and weaknesses of the performance on the basis of the criteria selected for that particular job category. Sometimes a staff member is asked to make a self-assessment based on personal recollections. Videotapes are also becoming a popular means of affirming the director's observations, the staff member's self-assessment, or both. Videotapes do not seem as judgmental as verbal or written critiques.

2. **Portfolios** are also being used in some programs. A portfolio is a collection of materials (e.g., written work, tapes, photographs) that teachers collect and assemble to represent their performance. Thus, portfolios are an extension of narratives.

3. **Interview procedures** may be developed as assessment instruments. On the one hand, an interview may take the form of an open-ended discussion concerning strengths, performance areas needing improvement, and discussions on how to make needed improvements. On the other hand, some interview forms may, in actuality, be verbal rating scales.

4. **Check sheets** and **rating scales** usually list assessment criteria in categories. Many check sheets and rating scales also include an overall assessment for each category of characteristics, for total performance, or for both. Although check sheets and rating scales are written assessment instruments, each instrument has a distinctive style. The check sheet can be used to indicate those behaviors satisfactorily completed by a staff member. The administrator may check "yes," "no," or "not applicable" (see Figure 4–14). A rating scale, a qualitative assessment of performance, represents successive levels of quality along an inferior–superior continuum. The levels of quality may be described in different ways. (See Figures 4–15, 4–16, 4–17, and 4–18.)

Steps in Assessing.   Directors should observe staff members many times before doing a formal observation. Caruso and Fawcett (1999) suggested these steps:

1. Do a preobservation conference to review the purposes of the observation, discuss concerns, and plan procedures.

2. Conduct the formal observation.

3. Conduct the supervisory conference by setting the agenda, reviewing goals, discussing strengths and weaknesses, and making future plans.

4. Do a postconference analysis.

Frequency of Assessment.   Informal assessment, especially self-assessment, should be conducted continually; however, the policy-making body should plan, determine the frequency of, and schedule formal assessment. Formative assessment should be conducted several times per year. Inexperienced teachers often need more assessments than do experienced teachers. Summative assessments are most often conducted annually.

Concerns.   Directors need training and experience in assessing job performance. They must realize that observations are not totally objective but are affected by beliefs and values, stress, and

Figure 4–14   Check Sheet

	Yes	No	Not Applicable
Children have continuous adult supervision	———	———	———
Children were helped with negative emotions	———	———	———

Figure 4–15   Example 1: Rating Scale with Quality Described in Words

A balance between child-initiated and adult-initiated activities was noted

| Excellent | Good | Fair | Poor |

program constraints beyond their control. Directors can also avoid some bias by getting a second opinion (i.e., asking another administrator to observe and look over the completed forms) before conferencing. Directors should ask themselves, Can I prove this statement? In talking about either strengths or weaknesses, directors should be careful about using superlatives, which can be misleading.

Regardless of the criteria chosen and the instruments selected, several basic principles need to be followed out of respect for each teacher and because appraisal records are legal documents. Staff must (a) know they will be assessed, (b) understand that their assessment is based on program goals and their job description, (c) be informed of the process, (d) know they will receive verbal and written results, (e) be informed about how the results will be used, and (f) be assured that their assessment results are confidential and accessible only to those entitled to the information.

PERSONNEL SERVICES AND RECORDS

State boards of education and licensing agencies require that certain personnel services be provided and records kept by early childhood programs

under their respective jurisdictions. In addition to providing those mandated personnel services and records, local boards of education or boards of directors may provide additional services and require other records permitted by state law.

For the most part, public school early childhood programs have more complete services and records than do child care centers. The National Child Care Staffing Study reported that 70% of teaching staff in child care centers worked without a written contract, 40% had no written job description, and 96% had no collective bargaining agreement. Furthermore, only 40% had health coverage, and only 20% had a retirement plan (Whitebook et al., 1990). These working conditions should be changed because they affect job satisfaction.

Contract and Terms of Employment

A **contract** is an agreement between two or more parties. In early childhood programs, a contract is an agreement between each staff member and the director or board specifying the services the staff member must provide and the specific sum of money to be paid for services rendered. Contracts may differ, depending on the job description (e.g., teacher and assistant teacher). All contracts should conform to the following guidelines:

Figure 4–16   Example 2: Rating Scale with Quality Described in Words

```
a   Excellent
b   Above average
c   Average
d   Below average

Creative in teaching        a  b  c  d
```

Figure 4–17   Rating Scale with Quality Described in Numerals

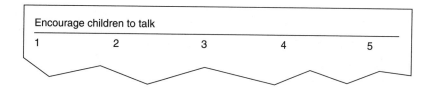

Encourage children to talk

| 1 | 2 | 3 | 4 | 5 |

A written agreement as opposed to an oral one

A specific designation of the parties to the contract

A statement of the legal capacity of the parties represented

A provision for signatures by the authorized agent(s) of and by the teacher

A clear stipulation of the salary to be paid

A designation of the date and duration of the contract and the date when service is to begin

A definition of the assignment

In signing a contract, an employee indirectly consents to obey all rules and regulations in force at the time of employment or adopted during the period of employment. Policies that most directly affect employees may include hours per day and days per week; vacation; specific requirements, such as a uniform or driver's license; sick, emer-gency, and maternity leaves; substitutes; insur-ance; salary increases and fringe benefits; and re-tirement plans. Each employee should have a written copy of all current policies.

The employee may receive a contract for some specified period of time, perhaps an annual or a continuing contract. Contracts for a speci-fied period of time must be renewed at the end of such time period. The two types of continuing contracts are **notification** and **tenure.** An individ-ual having a notification continuing contract must be notified on or before a given date if the contract is not to be renewed. A tenure contract guarantees that an employee cannot be dis-missed except for certain specific conditions, such as lack of funds to pay salaries, neglect of duty, incompetency, failure to observe regula-tions, and immorality. Furthermore, a dismissed tenured employee has the right to a hearing in which the board must prove just cause for the dismissal. Programs offering tenure require that an employee serve a probationary period of a

Figure 4–18   Rating Scale with Quality Described in Words and Numerals

Showed affection and respect to children

| 1 | 2 | 3 |

Usually   Never

Overall assessment

| Superior | | Excellent | | Good | | Average | | Fair |
| 10 | 9 | 8 | 7 | 6 | 5 | 4 | 3 | 2 | 1 |

given number of years (usually 3 or 5) before receiving a tenure contract.

Special service contracts must also be written when a limited service is to be performed by a temporary employee (e.g., consultant). This type of contract must clearly specify the services to be rendered; the date(s) services are to be performed, including any follow-up services; any special arrangements, such as materials to be supplied by a temporary employee (or by the employer); and the fee. The signatures of the temporary employee and the requester should be affixed to the contract, and the transaction should be dated.

Job Description

A job description for each personnel category should be written and kept current and should include the following: (a) job title, (b) minimum qualifications, (c) primary duties and responsibilities, (d) working conditions, (e) additional duties, (f) reporting relationships and limits of authority, and (g) benefits. The Economic Employment Opportunity Commission (EEOC) will examine job descriptions for a section called *essential functions* (a part of the primary duties and responsibilities). This section must also indicate how frequently the function occurs (occasionally—33% or less; frequently—34% to 66%; and continually—67% and over). If someone is not employed because of a disability, the director or board must be prepared to show that the function is essential to the job and cannot reasonably be performed by another staff member. (Essential functions must be in each job description prior to advertising.) Job descriptions should be specific to the particular early childhood program and position rather than adopted from another program. A potential employee should review the job description before signing a contract; all employees should keep their job descriptions in their files. A sample job description is shown in Figure 4–19.

Even with the best of job descriptions, role ambiguity may occur. P. Bloom and colleagues'

(1991) assessment tool is designed to be used with new staff members after they have been on the job about 1 month (pp. 246–247), and another tool is designed for staff after they've been on the job for several months (pp. 244–245).

Insurance and Retirement Plans

Various kinds of insurance and retirement plans protect employees and organizations. Adequate coverage is expensive but essential. Some types of insurance and retirement plans may be mandated by state or federal laws, whereas other types may be voluntary.

Federal Insurance Contributions Act (FICA).   Most centers are required to pay FICA, or Social Security, tax. FICA tax is generally used for retirement purposes. Tax rates are set at a percentage of the employee's salary. The employer deposits quarterly the amount of the employee's contributions collected as payroll deductions plus an equal amount from the employer. (This money is deposited in a separate account because commingling of federal funds is prohibited by law.) A quarterly report on FICA taxes is also required. All organizations, including tax-exempt programs, are responsible for keeping up with current tax laws.

Workers' Compensation Insurance.   Workers' compensation is liability insurance compensating an employee injured by an accident in the course of and arising out of employment. (Independent contractors are not covered. Directors should insist that any contractors doing work for a program certify that they are adequately insured so that they cannot later claim to have been acting as an employee.) Workers' compensation is required in most states, but many states have exceptions for certain classes of employers, such as organizations with few employees or organizations wishing to self-insure. The insurance company pays 100% of all workers' compensation benefits required by state law. Injured employees and, in the case of death, their dependents are eligible

---

Johnson County Community College Child Development Center

Title: Teacher

Qualifications: A teacher shall have at least an A.A. degree in child development/early childhood education or hold a child development associate certificate. A teacher must also meet licensing regulations concerning minimum age and health status. The essential functions include constantly maintaining visual supervision of children to ensure safety and occasionally lifting, carrying, and holding children.

Primary duties and responsibilities: A teacher shall (1) plan and execute developmentally appropriate activities, (2) observe and evaluate children's progress, (3) provide a written report (on the forms provided) to the director and parents at least two times per year, (4) be available for informal parent-teacher contacts at the beginning and end of each session, and (5) perform other duties particular to the program.

Working conditions: A teacher is paid for an 8-hour working day. Reporting time is 7:15 a.m. Monday through Friday. A teacher should be prepared to receive children at 7:30 a.m. A teacher will eat at the noon meal with the children and will have two 15-minute breaks during the 6-hour day. The teacher's planning period is from 1:30 until 3:15 p.m. daily.

The director must be notified in the event of illness or emergencies. Paid vacation periods must be planned 3 months in advance and approved by the director. Other optional benefits include a group health insurance plan, employee retirement fund, and others particular to the program.

Additional duties: A teacher is expected to attend staff development activities on the first Tuesday of each month from 3:30 until 5:30 p.m. and a monthly parent function usually held in the evenings from 7:00 until 9:00 p.m. on the third Thursday of each month.

Reporting relationships and limits of authority: A teacher reports directly to the director of the program. *Prior commitment from the director must be obtained* for purchasing any item, approving additional or terminating any services for children, and releasing information on center activities to the media. A teacher *may take action but must inform* when releasing a child to an authorized adult during normal attendance hours, administering authorized medications, and informing a parent about a child's nonsevere illness. A teacher *may take action without informing* when developing new activities in keeping with the program's philosophy, changing sequence of daily activities except for snack and mealtimes, and talking with parents about children's development.

Benefits: Sick and emergency leave without loss of pay is 12 days for a 12-month period of employment. A 2-week paid vacation plus Thanksgiving and other national holidays are observed.

Figure 4–19   Sample Job Description

for one half to two thirds of their weekly wages, plus hospital and medical benefits. In most states, employees, in turn, give up their right to sue employers for damages covered by the law.

State Unemployment Insurance.   State unemployment insurance is required in most states and varies considerably from state to state. A questionnaire must be completed about the employees' activities and the tax status of the early childhood program. The insurance rates are figured as a percentage of total wages and are different for for-profit and not-for-profit corporations.

Liability Insurance. Liability insurance protects the organization or employee from loss when persons have been injured or property damaged as a result of negligence (rather than accident) on the part of the institution or its employees. However, almost any "accident" that occurs is usually considered the result of negligence. The extent to which an institution or its employees can be held liable varies from state to state, and a liability policy should cover everything for which an institution is liable. In most states, programs providing transportation services are required to have vehicle insurance, including liability insurance.

Health Insurance and Hospital-Medical Insurance. Health insurance, whether fully or partially paid for by the employer or taken on a voluntary basis and paid for by the employee, may assume any of three forms: (a) medical reimbursement insurance, (b) medical service or prepaid medical care, and (c) disability income benefits. Hospital-medical plans fall into three groups: (a) basic hospitalization and medical coverage, (b) major medical insurance, and (c) closed-panel operation (service available from a limited number of physicians, clinics, or hospitals).

Crime Coverages. Protection against loss resulting from dishonesty of employees or others is available under four forms of coverage: (a) fidelity bonds, (b) board-form money and securities policy, (c) "3-D policy" (dishonesty, disappearance, and destruction), and (d) all-risk insurance.

Retirement Programs. Federal Social Security coverage, FICA tax, is usually mandatory. Generally, the tax is used as a federal "retirement program." Most public school program personnel are also under state retirement programs, paid on a matching fund basis by employer and employee. Other programs may also have retirement plans in addition to Social Security coverage.

Personnel Records

Personnel administration involves keeping records and making reports in accordance with state laws, the program's governing body requirements, and federal legislation concerning privacy of personal information. Public and private schools must keep personnel records on each regulation pertaining to employees—both program and support personnel. In most cases, personnel records are kept by the local programs, and reports are submitted to their respective state governing boards (licensing agency or state board of education). However, the governing board may inspect locally kept records.

Personnel records is a collective term for all records containing information about employees. Although these records vary from program to program, they usually embody the following details:

1. *Personal information records* are kept by all early childhood programs. Most of the personal information is given by a potential employee on the application form, and the information is kept current. Personal information includes name, age, gender, address, telephone number, citizenship, Social Security number, and names and addresses of those who will give references.

2. *Personal health records* signed by an appropriate medical professional are required by all early childhood programs. These records may be detailed, requiring specific medical results of a physical examination or specified laboratory tests, or may be a general statement that the employee is free from any mental or physical illness that might adversely affect the health of children or other adults.

3. *Emergency information* is required by many programs. This information includes the names, addresses, and telephone numbers of one or more persons to be contacted in an emergency; the name of a physician and hospital; and any medical information, such as allergies to drugs or other conditions, deemed necessary in an emergency.

4. *Records of education and other qualifications* are required by all programs. They must include the names of schools attended, diplomas or degrees obtained, transcripts of academic work,

and the registration number and type of teacher's or administrator's certificate or any other credential needed by an employee (e.g., a chauffeur's license).

5. *Professional or occupational information records*, including the places and dates of employment, names of employers, and job descriptions, are kept by all programs.

6. *Professional or occupational skill and character references* are included in the personnel records. In most cases, these references are for confidential use by the employer.

7. *Service records* are kept by some programs. These records contain information concerning the date of current employment, level or age of children cared for or taught or program directed, absences incurred or leaves taken, inservice education received and conferences attended, committees served on, salary received, and date and reason for termination of service.

8. *Insurance records* are kept by all programs involved in any group insurance.

9. *Job performance assessment records* are placed on file in many programs. Certain forms must be treated as legal documents, but observer's informal notes should be shredded after they have fulfilled their purposes.

Personnel of many early childhood programs, especially Head Start and others receiving federal funding, are covered under the Privacy Act of 1974 (P.L. 93-579). Because a person's legal right to privacy must be guarded, administrators must keep abreast of the laws pertaining to record keeping and record security. For example, the Privacy Act of 1974 requires federal agencies to take certain steps to safeguard the accuracy, currency, and security of records concerning individuals and to limit record keeping to necessary and lawful purposes. Individuals also have a right to examine federal records containing such information and to challenge the accuracy of data with which they disagree (Title V. Section 522a, 1977).

TRENDS AND ISSUES

The quality of early childhood programs rests on trained administrators and on the knowledge and skills of their staff members. The major trends and issues seem to be centered on improving quality through education and training.

Barriers to the Development of Director Competencies

The development of leadership and management abilities in directors is difficult. One major aspect of the problem is that most early childhood administrators did not actively pursue and prepare for administrative positions but were "selected" from the ranks of teachers (P. Bloom, 1997c; Shakeshaft, 1989). Another major aspect of the problem is mandating credentials and providing the needed training opportunities. Except for public school administrators, few states have mandated credentials for director positions. Until competencies are adopted and training opportunities are widespread, credentialing will likely be voluntary and most directors will learn through experience and self-study and by getting support from others. Regrettably, self-study rarely leads to career progression or recognition.

Effective leadership also requires time. P. Bloom discussed the time it takes leaders to shift their attention from management tasks to vision building, to see issues from less tolerant views, to view them from many perspectives, and to move from the "reality shock" of getting through the day to becoming more reflective of their practices. Certainly, consensus-building teamwork reflects a more diverse information-sharing 21st century and thus is worth the education, training, and time.

Obstacles to the Professional Development of Teachers

The early childhood teaching profession continues to be a two-tiered system in terms of qualifications of personnel and compensation. The field of early childhood care and education is divided between those who believe in total preservice education and those who believe in hiring without credentials and providing in-service education.

Most studies indicate that the levels of education and training for staff in center and family child care have decreased over the past 2 decades (Spodek & Saracho, 1992). Many states are simply registering family child care homes and exempting certain categories of child care centers from licensing codes. Conversely, teacher education programs leading to certification have become increasingly selective because of the increase in admission standards and calls for reforms, such as extended 5-year programs and exit tests (Hilliard, 1991). The entry-level positions and minimum wages available in most programs are not a realistic choice for college-educated people; thus, the trend of hiring without needed credentials will likely continue to worsen.

Unless the quality of personnel and stability in the workforce improve, the early childhood profession will not be able to provide quality programs for all young children. G. Morgan and her associates (1993) said that these forces influence training: mandating qualifications, providing a delivery system for the training, and financing training. Many government and other funding agencies have mandated more qualifications for teachers, but providing and financing training remain major problems for these reasons:

1. Training does not meet the needs of the field in terms of content. Most in-service training is geared to entry-level knowledge and skills, and this training is offered over and over. Furthermore, the training is often targeted to meet the needs of staff working in centers serving 3- to 5-year-old children. Training rarely addresses the needs of staff working in infant and toddler, SACC, or family child care programs. Training to work with children who have special needs is rather scarce, and training to work with culturally diverse and bilingual children is almost nonexistent.

2. The quality of in-service training is not controlled; thus, it is difficult to measure the effectiveness of training (A. Epstein, 1999). The effects of in-service training seem modest (Kontos, Howes, & Galinsky, 1997). To be effective, training must be suited in content and delivery methods to the participants and must provide opportunities to apply the knowledge with mentoring (A. Epstein, 1993; Kontos, Machida, Griffin, & Read, 1992).

3. Training is not readily available. Training needs to be in the late afternoons, evenings, and weekends. The training site needs to be close by and available by public transportation; such training is almost nonexistent in rural areas. Although some programs permit work-hour release time for personnel, scheduling in a way to maintain mandated child–staff ratios is another barrier. To address these barriers, many training initiatives hold some promise (Azer & Hanrahan, 1998). In some institutions **distance programs** (also called *distance education, distance learning,* and *distributed education;* a system in which the educator and students are separated in physical space but brought together in virtual space) offer training that may lead to degrees (e.g., Ivey Tech State College in Indiana, Pacific Oaks College in Pasadena, California). Multimedia techniques are being used to replace some field experiences, such as the program developed by Irving and Tennent (1998).

4. Training is to a great extent a nonsystem. One idea coming from the National Institute for Early Childhood Professional Development is a career lattice. The symbol of a lattice was chosen over a ladder to incorporate the following three ideas:

a. Vertical lines represent diverse settings and roles.

b. Horizontal lines depict levels of preparation, with each ascending level representing greater role responsibility and compensation.

c. Diagonal lines represent movement across roles.

The NAEYC believes that implementation of such a lattice would recognize the diversity of roles, the differing levels of preparation for each role, and the importance of ongoing professional development (J. Johnson & McCracken, 1994). Although there is a professional consensus that each person should have the opportunity for professional development and advancement, many see difficulties with ladders and lattices. Spodek (1991b) likened the early childhood profession to the health profession, a discontinuous field in which training at one level does not prepare the person for the next level (e.g., additional training of a registered nurse does not prepare the nurse to become a physician). Difficulties in considering a continuous field include the following:

a. People employed at one level may not qualify for admission to train at another level.

b. Many people are turned off by formal education and prefer informal training (e.g., workshops).

c. Individuals with specialty work at the associate degree level may be less willing to enroll in general education courses for a bachelor's degree.

d. Transfer of experience or informal training to college course work is most difficult because of lack of standards for content and lack of coordination among training sessions although some institutions are working on *transformations* (the acceptance of Continuing Education Units or evidence of learning gained through noncredit training for college credit).

e. Even transfer of course work from one program to another within an institution or from one institution to another is difficult because of course configurations and the differences in the scope and depth of coverage, although *articulation* (the formal agreement within or between institutions that credits, degrees, or certificates from a given higher education program can be applied to a new program) efforts are also being undertaken.

Thus, the issue of professional development and career advancement remains unresolved. Along with this issue are the catch-22 issues—adequate compensation and benefits and affordability of programs.

SUMMARY

The factors that influence the effectiveness of early childhood programs are incredibly multifaceted and hence complex. All research studies support the contention that the behavior of adults in early childhood programs has an important impact on children.

The qualities of effective staff members have been studied. Although no simple, single response answers the question concerning what professional qualifications (knowledge and skills) and personal characteristics (personality traits and values) people need to work effectively with young children, a great deal of consensus does exist. Directors have the responsibilities of laying the foundation for a community, building a positive and productive work climate for staff, enriching the professional life of staff members, and providing personnel services and keeping records. Better job conditions aid job satisfaction and performance, which, in turn, leads to quality of services.

Trends and issues seem to focus on credentialing directors and teaching staff after they have been employed. Although many attempts have been made at improving the quality of all personnel, the issue of professional development linked with career advancement and compensation is far from resolved.

FOR FURTHER READING

Bloom, P. J. (1997). *A great place to work: Improving conditions for staff in young children's programs* (Rev. ed.). Washington, DC: National Association for the Education of Young Children.

Bloom, P. J. (2000). *Circle of influence: Implementing shared decision making and participative management.* Lake Forest, IL: New Horizons.

Bloom, P. J. (2002). *Leadership in action: How effective directors get things done.* Lake Forest, IL: New Horizons.

Bloom, P. J. (2002). *Making the most of meetings: A practical guide.* Lake Forest, IL: New Horizons.

King, J. R. (1998). *Uncommon caring: Learning from men who teach young children.* New York: Teachers College Press.

Morgan, G. G. (1997a). Historical views of leadership. In S. L. Kagan & B. T. Bowman (Eds.), *Leadership in early care and education* (pp. 9–14). Washington, DC: National Association for the Education of Young Children.

Morgan, G. G. (1997b). *Images of organization* (2nd ed.). Thousand Oaks, CA: Sage.

Stone, J. G. (2001). *The early childhood teacher's role.* Washington, DC: National Association for the Education of Young Children.

Taking the Lead: Investing in Early Childhood Leadership for the 21st Century. (1999). *The many faces of leadership.* Boston: Wheelock College, Center for Career Development in Early Care and Education.

Whitebook, M., & Bellm, D. (1999). *Taking on turnover: An action guide for child care center teachers and directors.* Washington, DC: Center for the Child Care Workforce.

For the Administrator's Library: Books from Other Professions

Autry, J. A. (1991). *Love and profit: The art of caring leadership.* New York: William Morrow.

Bennis, W. G. (1989). *On becoming a leader.* Reading, MA: Addison-Wesley.

Bennis, W. G., & Nanus, B. (1985). *Leaders: Strategies for taking charge.* New York: Harper & Row.

Collins, J. E., & Porras, J. I. (1994). *Built to last: Successful habits of visionary companies.* New York: Harper Business.

Covey, S. R. (1989). *The 7 habits of highly effective people.* New York: Simon & Schuster.

Covey, S. R. (1992). *Principle-centered leadership.* New York: Simon & Schuster.

Denning, W. E. (1986). *Out of the crisis.* New York: Cambridge University Press.

DePree, M. (1987). *Leadership is an art.* Lansing: Michigan State University.

Drucker, P. (1974). *Management: Tasks, responsibilities, and practices.* New York: Harper & Row.

Heifetz, R. A. (1994). *Leadership without easy answers.* Cambridge, MA: Belknap of Harvard University Press.

Hennig, M., & Jardin, A. (1976). *The managerial woman.* New York: Pocket Books.

Hesselbein, F., Goldsmith, M., & Beckhard, R. (Eds.). (1997). *The leaders of the future.* Drucker Foundation Series. San Francisco: Jossey-Bass.

Kelley, R. (1991). *The power of followership: How to create leaders people want to follow and followers who lead themselves.* New York: Doubleday.

McGregor, D. (1960). *The human side of enterprise.* New York: McGraw-Hill.

Mintzberg, H. (1995). *The rise and fall of strategic planning.* New York: Free Press.

Peters, T., & Waterman, R. H. (1982). *In search of excellence: Learning from America's best-run companies.* New York: Harper & Row.

Schwein, E. H. (1985). *Organizational culture and organizations.* San Francisco: Jossey-Bass.

Senge, P. M. (1990). *The fifth discipline: The art and practice of the learning organization.* New York: Doubleday.

Woodcock, M., & Francis, D. (1981). *Organizational development through team building: Planning a cost effective strategy.* New York: Wiley.

Mentoring Resources

Bellm, D., Whitebook, M., & Hnatiuk, P. (1997). *The early childhood mentoring curriculum: A handbook for mentors.* Washington, DC: Center for the Child Care Workforce.

Breunig, G. S., & Bellm, D. (1996). *Early childhood mentoring programs: A survey of community initiatives.* Washington, DC: Center for the Child Care Workforce.

Carter, M., & Curtis, D. (1994). *Training teachers: A harvest of theory and practice.* St. Paul, MN: Redleaf.

Jones, E. (1993). *Growing teachers: Partnerships in staff development.* Washington, DC: National Association for the Education of Young Children.

Whitebook, M., Hnatiuk, P., & Bellm, D. (1994). *Mentoring in early care and education: Refining an emerging career path.* Washington, DC: Center for the Child Care Workforce.

Whitebook, M., & Sakai, L. (1995). *The potential of mentoring: An assessment of the California Early Childhood Mentor Program.* Washington, DC: Center for the Child Care Workforce.

Narratives for Teacher Development

Ayers, W. (1989). *The good preschool teacher: Six teachers reflect on their lives.* New York: Teachers College Press.

Bullough, R. (1989). *First-year teacher.* New York: Teachers College Press.

Chenfeld, M. B. (1993). *Teaching in the key of life*. Washington, DC: National Association for the Education of Young Children.

Davis, D. (1993). *Telling your stories*. Little Rock, AR: August House.

Gillard, M. (1996). *Story teller, story teacher: Discovering the power of storytelling for teaching and living*. York, ME: Stenhouse.

Lipman, D. (1995). *The storytelling coach: How to listen, praise, and bring out people's best*. Little Rock, AR: August House.

Mullan, K. (2000). Teaching storytelling in preservice and professional development programs. In N. J. Yelland (Ed.), *Promoting meaningful learning: Innovations in educating early childhood professionals* (pp. 59–65). Washington, DC: National Association for the Education of Young Children.

Rand, M. K. (2000). *Giving it some thought: Cases for early childhood practice*. Washington, DC: National Association for the Education of Young Children.

Tertell, E. A., Klein, S. M., & Jewett, J. L. (Eds.). (1998). *When teachers reflect: Journeys toward effective, inclusive practice*. Washington, DC: National Association for the Education of Young Children.

Vella, J. (1994). *Learning to teach: The power of dialogue in educating adults*. San Francisco: Jossey-Bass.

Wein, C. A. (1995). *Developmentally appropriate practice in real life: Stories of teacher practical knowledge*. New York: Teachers College Press.

Witherell, C., & Noddings, N. (1991). *Stories lives tell*. New York: Teachers College Press.

TO REFLECT

1. Preschool and kindergarten teachers in public school settings are often at the bottom of a pecking order. Sometimes the discrimination is subtle (e.g., their opinions on schoolwide matters are not acknowledged), and sometimes the discrimination is very open (e.g., they are teased about "playing all day" or majoring in "Sandbox 101"). How can early childhood teachers in public schools gain the respect of their colleagues and administrators?

2. Director X is frustrated because she knows her staff does not particularly respect her as their administrator. She was picked for her position from the ranks of a teacher, although she knew she wasn't the best teacher. She had not actively sought the position and was surprised but pleased when it was offered to her. She has tried three approaches to leadership, and all have failed. First, she tried praise (and very sparse criticism) as a way to please everyone. Next, she tried putting less emphasis on her position (and the authority that goes with it) by taking the smallest office and answering her own phone, and so forth. Finally, she tried to show her staff that she "earned her salary" by becoming a workaholic and working as much as she could—early, late, and on weekends. Why did each approach fail? What should Director X do to gain respect?

3. Director X has four candidates for a teaching position with preschool children. From her interviews, she notes the following: Candidate 1 sees herself in a mothering role. Candidate 2 sees herself aiding children's development, especially their academic development. Candidate 3 wants to build a "little democratic community" in which children's decision making is most important. Candidate 4, who has read some of Montessori's writings, believes in order and organization. What would the classroom be like under each of these four candidates? What criteria should the director use in selecting one of the four candidates?

4. Before taking her position as director of a large corporate early childhood program, Director X has been sent to a weeklong seminar for directors. She is disappointed because she feels that many of the skills she is learning are not applicable to early childhood program leadership. How is leadership in early childhood programs different from leadership in other organizations? What are the implications?

Planning the Physical Facility

Places speak to us in powerful ways. To children, a place immediately suggests a repertoire of potential behaviors. Open spaces urge children to "run like the wind"; tiled bathrooms say, "I'm a megaphone—use your voice"; colors stimulate or calm; and objects seem to say, "Play with me; I'm strong" or "Touch carefully because I'm fragile." Sounds and fragrances repel or attract. To adults, the organization and aesthetics of an environment communicate a program's culture—the goals and lives of those who live there. What early visitors to the Reggio Emilia schools reported was the beauty of the environment. The physical environment either helps or hinders adults' abilities to facilitate the program's goals and do so in comfort.

Many of today's facilities are the result of a profound understanding of how children develop and accurate interpretations of child–child, child–material, and child–adult interactions. A. Olds (1998) said that the environment must be more than adequate; it must be beautiful.

Before contemplating the specifics of housing, one must remember the following:

1. The location of the building is an important aspect of planning because local zoning regulations may include restrictions.

2. Regardless of the type of program, most of the occupants will be young children who often spend 2,000 or more hours per year in the environment, so the facility should be child-oriented and also comfortable for adults.

3. The safety of the children and the staff is of maximum importance.

4. Housing is an important consideration in planning for those with disabilities. Programs receiving direct or indirect federal assistance of any kind must be accessible to students and employees with disabilities. Zoning laws in many areas also require that buildings accommodate those with disabilities. Special architectural plans and room arrangements are needed for those with physical disabilities and visual impairment. Also, noise and activity levels must be controlled when children with learning disabilities and hyperactivity are integrated into the program.

5. Variations in the arrangements of space and materials contribute to the effectiveness of housing. There should be differences in the placement of objects in space (e.g., high, eye-level, low), sizes of areas (e.g., large areas for running, small areas for squeezing through), sound levels (e.g., noisy places, quiet areas), interesting areas (e.g., alcoves, skylights, special ceilings, porches), and light and color (e.g., cheerful, busy color schemes; quiet, relaxing hues). A. Olds (1998) suggested that nonpoisonous plants and flowers, artwork, and beautifully textured fabrics used for curtains, wall hangings, and tablecloths all add to the aesthetics. In short, design should be aesthetically pleasing.

6. Flexibility is essential. Housing should be planned to accommodate children's changing interests and individual and group pursuits both inside and outside.

7. Decisions about equipment and materials are vital when planning the physical facility. Because equipment and materials are housed and used within the facility, their selection must be a part of the initial planning.

8. Costs must be considered. The building or physical facilities require a large initial investment but are amortized over many years.

For over 2 decades, early childhood researchers have discussed the impact of the physical environment on the behaviors of its inhabitants and showed how facilities can help meet the specific goals of a program (D. Day, 1983). Determining the specifics of housing begins with a collective vision for the local program (i.e., based on the needs of the community of children, families, and staff members). Program goals must be defined in terms of environmental features that make the program possible.

Housing a child care center is the responsibility of the director or the director and the board. Planning for a large center or a multisite program often begins with the appointment of a committee from the board to conduct preliminary plans. In smaller programs, the director does the planning. Corporate chains and franchises usually have employees who manage the construction and renovation of their centers based on a prototypical design. Housing a public school prekindergarten and kindergarten is planned by the local board with input from the principal and sometimes teachers of the local school. Regardless of who does the planning, the following steps should be taken:

1. The specific needs of the program, including maximum enrollment, the ages of the children, the special needs of the children, and the program objectives, must be outlined.

2. Input should be sought through reading or be obtained from individuals and organizations specializing in housing programs, and trips should be planned to facilities housing similar programs. The director needs to work with the licensing agent, architect and contractor, accountant, and attorney (who examines all contracts).

3. Plans should be compared with regulations, accreditation, or model standards. Regulations usually determine the type of building, number of exits, nature of exits (signs and door/window hardware), decorative materials (type of carpet and wall coverings), location of hot water heaters and furnace in relation to the activity room, type and number of fire extinguishers, and type and placement of alarm systems.

4. Programs requiring board action must submit their plans to the board for approval.

Not every early childhood program will be so blessed as to have a new building. Many will be housed in old structures or in new additions to older buildings. Renovated buildings are fine if they meet the needs of the program and are not just hand-me-downs or castoffs. The foregoing steps for planning new buildings often apply when planning an addition to an existing building. Some early childhood programs must share their children's activity room or building with other groups, such as religious or civic groups. A major problem in a shared facility is cleaning the room or building, storing equipment, and then setting up again. Vergeront (1987) gave many ideas for managing housing in programs that must share facilities. Some programs cannot own their own buildings but must lease them. Directors who lease buildings need to seek long leases and consider whether the lease is renewable, who is responsible for repairs, and how the building can be altered (e.g., ramps built, walls painted, fence erected).

ENTRY/EXIT AREA

Because the entry/exit area serves as the first and last picture of the facility that children and family members see every day, the area may be a major factor in communicating the attitude "It's nice here!" or "This is a good place for my child!" The entry/exit area is also the view most often seen by the public, and the public's opinion of a program may be based on what it sees—even from street distance.

Foyers are helpful for keeping cold or hot air out of the main activity room and are a good place to wipe feet and shed dripping outdoor wear. The entry/exit area could also be a mall with views of indoor and outdoor activity areas, a porch, a courtyard, or a gaily decorated interior room. Regardless of the design, the area should be a bright, welcoming area because blind corners and dimly lit places are frightening to young children. A sense of belonging can be created by displays of children's photos and work, photos of families, and information and photos of staff members. This area should provide a view of the activity room and have a transition space (a place to say good-bye to family members and to watch from) so that young children can gradually join the activities of the program. Such a view also enables family members returning for their children to make a quick scan of the activity room to locate their children. In buildings that house several activity rooms, the entry/exit area should be close to each child's classroom. Sussman (1998) believes corridors should be more than mere passageways. They should be inviting, perhaps centered on a theme, with each room entrance decorated distinctively.

Heavy doors at the entry/exit bring family members inside and make it more difficult for "child-fugitives" to flee. For school-age children, entry/exit doors should operate easily. Near the entry/exit area should be a parking lot for family members; Greenman (1988) stated that without a parking lot family members will not linger. To accommodate young children with disabilities, a ramp into the building should be provided. The ramp should be located near the parking lot. (The curb must be cut to enter the parking lot, or the ramp should lead directly from the street.) Other specifications for the ramp include a slope of no less than 12 ft for each 1 ft of drop, a 36-in. minimum width for wheelchairs, and handrails. Thresholds to entrances should be no higher than 3 in. Doors should open readily and have 32-in. clearings.

For safety purposes, the entry/exit area should be designed to establish control over access to the center. For example, staff should be near the entry area when most family members are arriving, and a receptionist office or desk should be near the entrance. Some programs have installed observation cameras near all entry/exit areas and in the parking lot.

INDOOR SPACE

The amount and types of indoor space vary from program to program. Child care centers are usually housed in multiple-room buildings. In all but the smallest centers, separate activity rooms house different age groups. Other areas of the building are used for children's feeding and eating, diapering and toileting, isolation, storage, and napping. Early childhood classrooms housed in schools often have a single activity room that is also used for napping and storage. Children in several classrooms often share rest rooms and sometimes additional space for certain activities. Generally, one cafeteria is used on a rotation basis by all of the age groups housed in the building. Both centers and schools have additional areas for adults, such as offices, kitchens, workrooms, janitor's area, and storage areas. Because housing varies with the program, some of the following suggestions are not equally applicable to all early childhood programs.

Arranging and Furnishing the Activity Room

The children's activity room is perhaps the single most important area of the building because children work and play in this room for most of their day. Space affects the quality of living and learning within a center.

Building Design and Directional Orientation. Buildings must be designed in keeping with the climate, topography, and surrounding area (e.g., nearby large trees and buildings can block light). Directional orientation is important because of light and temperature. Generally, a southern or eastern exposure is better than a western exposure. Of course, programs housed in renovated buildings will not have a choice as to directional orientation; however, if the orientation is incorrect, the resulting light-reflection problems can be partially overcome by using certain color schemes and lighting techniques.

Room Size. Room size can be considered in three ways: (a) the number of square feet per child, (b) the total dimensions of the room, and (c) the spatial density, which is related not only to square feet per child but also to the availability of toys and equipment. Many states use 35 sq ft per child as the minimum square footage in licensing regulations. This minimum refers *only* to the activity area and is a minimum protective regulation below which a program cannot be licensed. Greenman (1988) pointed out that residences have 10 to 20 times the amount of square feet per occupant compared with centers.

For nonwalking infants, 35 sq ft per child is adequate (Lally, Provence, Szanton, & Weissbourd, 1986). Because mobile infants and toddlers need an "action room," 35 sq ft per child is just too small (Bergen, Reid, & Torelli, 2001). A more adequate room size is 75 sq ft per child (Lally, Griffin, Fenichel, Segal, Szanton, & Weissbourd, 1995). For preschool children, 35 sq ft per child is not adequate. A. Olds (2001) stated that 42 sq ft per child is workable, but recommended 50 sq ft per child. Larger rooms allow several adults to work in the same room and provide more space for the physically disabled. Generally speaking, if the group of children is small, the space per child should be increased (use 60 sq ft or a little less). If the group of children is large, the space per child should be less (40 sq ft or a little more). One can readily see that using 60 sq ft per child with a large group would result in a very large room. Regardless of the number of children or the length of the session, the children's activity room should be a minimum of 900 sq ft of clear floor space, exclusive of rest rooms, dining area, and separate napping area. Designs for many new classrooms call for 1,200 to 1,500 sq ft (C. Hohmann & Buchleitner, 1992).

Limited indoor space may be offset by sheltered outdoor space (e.g., a covered porch) where climate permits. When floor space is small and ceilings are high, space can be stretched vertically. Balconies with panels or cargo nets can be built over storage; they can be the second floors of two-story houses; or housekeeping centers can be arranged on balconies with block centers below. On the one hand, a balcony built against a wall, particularly corner walls, is the most stable and economical construction; on the other hand, a freestanding loft gives more freedom of placement. Stairs and ramps for ascending and descending to lofts take up additional floor space, however. Safety is a problem with vertical spaces,

also. For safety purposes, a handrailing should be provided for stairs greater than three steps. Stationary ladders are safer than rope ladders, and ladder rungs should extend above a platform for easy mounting and dismounting. Ramps covered with friction material and with handrailings are safer than stairs or ladders, but ramps can be used only with platforms less than 4 ft high.

Space affects play and other behaviors. The activity room should be small enough to be intimate. Children interact more and dramatize fantasy themes more in smaller rooms than they do in larger rooms (Howes, 1983). Negative and idle behavior is common in situations with a high density of children and few resources or equipment; thus, the quality and quantity of resources should be increased if high density is unavoidable. On the other hand, positive and constructive behavior is prevalent in child care centers with low density (at least 48 sq ft per child) of children and plentiful resources. Too much space can cause problems, such as more running and chasing and less cooperative behaviors (Clarke-Stewart & Gruber, 1984) and fewer adult–child interactions (Howes, 1983).

Room Arrangement.   The room arrangement can affect comfort, security, autonomy, style of learning, and self-discipline. Several criteria must be considered.

1. *The room arrangement should have no hidden areas because such areas cannot be supervised.* Children still have privacy and staff can supervise as long as dividers and storage cabinets are not over 4 ft high. When two rooms are joined by a wall or when a small room opens off the main room, Plexiglas panels or openings in the wall at adult height facilitate supervision.

2. *The room arrangement should facilitate reaching the program's goals.* Facilities designed for programs adhering to the D-I view have smaller, more enclosed (e.g., with high dividers) areas in which teacher-directed activities take place. Because the areas are enclosed and seem small, children focus their attention on "large" adults

and on teacher-prescribed activities. Some less-enclosed centers may be available for children's use during free times (see Figure 5–1). Programs that adhere to the holistic/developmental point of view need a roomy environment—calculated to give much more mobility. The room is often divided with low partitions into learning centers, with the size of each work space compatible with the number of children in the area at one time and the space required for both use and storage of equipment and materials. The enclosures suggest the nature of the activities (e.g., block building, art, dramatic play) and the space in which the activity is to take place. Low and less-enclosing partitions (open shelves or tables instead of high walls) allow adults to observe from a greater distance and suggest to children that they are free to engage in self-initiated activities. (See Figures 5–4 through 5–17 in later sections of this chapter.)

3. *A somewhat enclosed space is easier to organize than a totally open space.* The height and placement of partitions affect the appearance of openness. If partitions are over 4 ft high and if they almost surround an instructional area or learning center, the room appears to be closed. In addition to partitioning, room shape and dimensions affect the appearance of openness. An activity room slightly longer than it is wide is less formal looking and easier to arrange. Long, narrow activity rooms encourage running and sliding. The tunnel-like appearance can be minimized by (a) placing learning centers at either end, (b) conducting activities in the center of the room, and (c) using equipment (e.g., tables, shelves) to break straight pathways. Square rooms often have dead space in the center because activity areas are placed along walls instead of toward the center of the room.

4. *Somewhat closed room designs prevent negative behaviors and provide children with needed privacy.* Negative social behaviors, such as aggression, withdrawal, and a tendency to wander about the room (Neill & Denham, 1982), are seen more often in open than in closed room designs.

Open spaces do not offer the privacy children need to construct a sense of self (Laufer & Wolfe, 1977), to "cocoon" when the noise and other stimuli overwhelm them (Greenman, 1988; Hyson, 1994; NAEYC, 1998a), to be cuddled (Hyson, 1994), and to focus on their special endeavors (Meltz, 1990) before gradually moving into the group (A. Olds, 2001). Chaotic and frantic child behaviors are associated with centers that do not have privacy areas. Window seats, special corners, alcoves, platforms, small closets with the doors removed, and a few learning centers or workstations for one child all help meet indoor privacy needs (Greenman, 1988; L. Johnson, 1987; D. Kennedy, 1991; A. Olds, 2001). Cozy places can also be created with rocking or gliding chairs, pillows, and beanbag chairs, but do not include sleeping areas. Prescott, Jones, and Kritchevsky (1972) measured privacy in programs by using a continuum of seclusion–intrusion features (insulated units—protected areas for small groups; "hiding" areas—places that cozily house one or two children; and softness measures—rugs, cushions, and pillows).

5. *How much of the floor space is covered with furniture and materials affects room arrangement.* Most professionals believe that good space organization is found where the surface is between 50% and 67% covered.

6. *The needs of children with disabilities should be considered when a room is being arranged.* The child with a physical disability requires more space for movement. Wheelchairs require an aisle of 36 in. and corners of 42 in. minimum. Room arrangement must permit *all* children **accessibility,** the ability to enter all parts of the environment and to access equipment and materials (Winter, Bell, & Dempsey, 1994), and **availability,** the ability to participate in all experiences (Cavallaro, Haney, & Cabello, 1993).

Floors, Ceilings, and Walls. Floors, ceilings, and walls must be both functional and durable. The materials used on their surfaces should be coordinated so that they are aesthetically pleasing and comfortable.

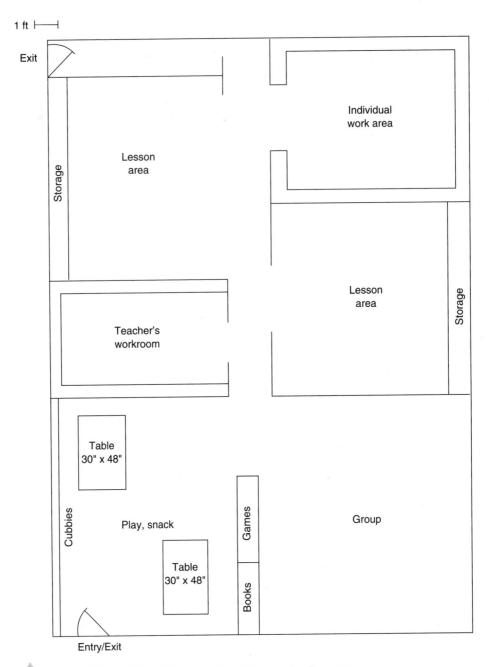

Figure 5–1   Typical Floor Plan for a Direct-Instruction Program

Floors.   Young children are accident prone; they get floors wet from play activities, spilling, and bathroom accidents. When choosing floor coverings, keep in mind that floors must be kept dry, sanitary, and warm for children's play. Flooring materials should be easy to clean, suited to hard wear, and noise absorbing, and should not give off toxic fumes. Because children enjoy working on the floor, good floor coverings can reduce the number of tables and chairs needed. In fact, floors should be viewed as part of the furniture.

Resilient flooring and carpet are the most prevalent materials used. Resilient flooring includes various types of vinyl floors and linoleum. Vinyl tile, which varies in quality, is the best resilient flooring. Carpet is superior to resilient flooring in softness, noise absorption, and minimizing injuries and breakage. Carpet presents problems, however; for example, difficulty of spill cleanup, retention of germs, buildup of static electricity, difficulty in moving cabinets or bins equipped with casters or in using toys with wheels, and children's possible allergic reactions to carpet fibers. The best carpet is thick, dense, made of wool or long-lasting synthetic, woven or tufted, and laid on a thick pad of natural materials without the use of latex glue. High pile or shag carpet causes problems for children in wheelchairs. Of the soft floor coverings, wall-to-wall carpet is probably the most desirable, but large carpets, area rugs, and throw rugs may be suitable.

Two things must be kept in mind when choosing whether to use carpet or vinyl tile:

1. For most programs, the best choice is to use both. Usually 33% to 50% of the floor area should not be carpeted. Carpet is best for infant and toddler rooms. Carpet with large pillows offers a safe floor environment for nonwalkers and toddlers. Toddlers may need a bit of play space on resilient flooring for block building and for play with wheel toys. Resilient flooring is preferred under feeding and diapering areas. Similarly, programs for older children use resilient

flooring for areas that get stained or that have rugged use and carpet for areas that have passive (cozy book corners) or noisy activities. Indoor/outdoor carpet is best used for preventing slipping on floors where water or sand may be spilled.

2. When one cannot choose *both* carpet and vinyl tile or when one does not know which is best for a certain area of the room, vinyl tile is the better choice. Carpet can always be laid over resilient flooring. The carpet must not cause slipping, and the edges must not cause tripping. Carpet can be covered temporarily, but it is rather difficult to manage. To cover, lay down plastic sheeting and then inexpensive, splinter-free boards such as plywood sheets.

Many programs use lofts (and platforms) or wells to facilitate the floor as a place to work and play. Some infant and toddler rooms use a few-inch raised area with low side panels and a gate of Plexiglas. This area protects nonwalkers from the more active toddlers. Older children enjoy learning centers created by raised and sunken areas, but such areas are less flexible in use. Platforms or wells can be built into the activity room during its construction; less-permanent structures can be built with wooden boxes attached to a plywood base and carpeted, or a platform can have locking casters. If platforms or wells are used, consider the following recommendations: (a) Raised or lowered areas should be out of the main flow of traffic; (b) changes in floor levels should not exceed 2 or 3 ft, and the steps should not be steep—five or six steps for a well 2 ft deep; (c) Plexiglas panels need to partially surround the well; and (d) electrical outlets should be provided near the wells or platforms if electrical teaching equipment will be used.

A final problem is keeping floors warm and free from drafts. Radiantly heated floors have been used, but this kind of heat does not solve draft problems. A perimeter wall system as a supplementary heating source provides floor warmth and freedom from drafts.

Ceilings. Ceilings should be of differing heights to accommodate equipment of various heights. Variation in ceiling height helps with noise control and is aesthetically pleasing. A 7-ft ceiling is too low unless the space is for children only. Low ceilings make staff members appear excessively large because of their nearness to the ceiling. Such an illusion makes children feel dominated by adults. The recommended ceiling height is 10 to 11 ft.

To provide visual interest and to minimize the presence of adults, some play areas should have low-ceilinged spaces, approximately 4 ft, that exclude adults. Low-ceilinged areas may be created by building a two-story playhouse; by using a balcony; or by hanging parachutes, canopies, or fabric hangings that can be changed from time to time. Skylights, beams, and fluttering materials (e.g., dangling little mirrors, glass beads, crystals, pretty paper) are interesting to young children.

Walls. Although permanent walls provide acoustic privacy, fewer interior walls give greater flexibility in room arrangement. Supervision becomes less of a problem when low dividers and storage units delineate space. Fewer walls also minimize the presence of adults.

Much of the color in a room comes from walls. Color choice depends on several criteria:

1. **The amount of light in a room.** Soft pastels may be chosen for a southern or western exposure, but a northern exposure may need a strong, light-reflecting color such as yellow. Sussman (1998) likes using lightly pigmented pastels with a few intense highlight colors.

2. **The size and shape of the room.** Bright colors make walls look closer and thus are more appropriate in large rooms. Mirrors and light colors on walls make rooms look larger. If slightly different shades of the same color are used on opposite walls, narrow rooms appear wider (Olds, 2001).

3. **The perception of clutter.** Early childhood programs often use too much color, which

can be a stressor. Bright colors and permanent murals or graphics may look fine in empty rooms. Once these rooms are occupied, however, they often look cluttered because equipment, artwork, and children's clothing add to the room's brightness.

4. **The influence of color on academic achievement.** A limited amount of research has been reported on this topic. Research does indicate, however, that red is a good choice for areas planned for gross-motor activities and concept development activities; yellow is good for music and art activities; and green, blue, and purple are effective in reading areas. The use of various colors may be most important in infant and toddler programs because children have a perception of color over form (shape) until 4 years of age. In rooms with young infants, yellow may be a good choice because it is the first color perceived.

5. **The psychological impact of colors.** Bright reds create excitement. Yellows, deep purples, and greens are restful. "Ethnic" color pallets may help create a sense of belongingness (Caples, 1996).

Walls may be covered with various types of materials. Washable wallpaper and high-quality latex paint are the overall best choices. Paneling or wainscoting in block areas or other areas with rugged use may be a good choice. Wall finishes of soft, porous materials can deaden sound, tackboard finishes can permit the use of walls for display, and various wall treatments can be aesthetically pleasing.

Storage and Display Facilities. Every early childhood program facility must have storage. The amount of storage is positively associated with the richness of the program (Prescott, 1984) because storage allows one to accumulate and use resources and reduce room clutter. For children, storage extends their play ideas, logical concepts (e.g., sorting, classifying, sequencing), and understanding of responsibility for things. Display aids the visual environment and enhances the learning process.

Storage.   Isbell and Exelby (2001) described storage as (a) open and closed and (b) fixed, movable, and portable. A balance needs to be achieved between open and closed storage areas for children's items. Open storage gives children some choices, and closed storage allows staff to regulate choices. Generally speaking, programs housing older children and those following the holistic/developmental program base have more open storage. Programs housing infants and toddlers and those following the D-I view have more closed storage. Some items, such as cleaning supplies, medicines, professional library items, teaching aids, personal records on children and staff, business records, and personal items of staff, always need to be in closed or secured (locked) storage.

Storage units that are built-in (fixed) cannot be altered. Freestanding units (movable) allow for flexible arrangement and can serve as room dividers; some freestanding units can tip, however. (For safe storage units, see Isbell and Exelby, 2001, pp. 137–159, for ideas.) Portable storage units (baskets, tote bags, boxes) are good for some items.

For infant and toddler programs, 2-ft-high shelves are appropriate for open storage, but they must be very sturdy because babies pull themselves up on them. For preschool and primary programs, shelf height should be approximately 3 ft for open storage items. Bins are unsuitable except for moving heavy materials (e.g., hollow blocks). To aid the flow of traffic and eliminate unnecessary additional steps, shelves or racks should be placed near the area where they will be used. The design and materials used in storage units should be compatible with their purpose, such as slanted shelves for books, resting-cot closets with louvered doors to allow air circulation, and shelf materials resistant to water damage in water play centers. Different storage designs (slanted, vertically and horizontally partitioned cabinets, drawers and shelves of varying depths) help in arranging, finding, and protecting materials and equipment; they are also aesthetically pleasing.

Display.   Equipment and materials should be displayed like wares in a market so that children can "window shop" or "buy." Arrangement and accessibility of materials are almost as important as the materials themselves. Displays of children's work in progress and completed work and of photographs of their work enable children to expand on their work and to affirm learnings in their own eyes, serve as a means of assessment, and help family members and other adults understand what children are doing.

The Cost, Quality, and Child Outcomes Study Team (1995) found that display boards were often too high for children's viewing. For infants, items should be placed on the walls, near the floor. These items include low bulletin boards covered with simple pictures or even household objects that contrast between object and field, unbreakable mirrors, and texture/color boards. For older children, an abundance of "pinning space" near eye level is desirable. Seefeldt (2002) provided many ideas on displaying children's work.

Furniture and Other Essentials.   The Cost, Quality, and Child Outcomes Study Team (1995) found that preschool programs scored high in furnishings (i.e., furnishings were child sized and in plentiful quantity). Furniture should fit the objectives of the program. For example, programs for infants and toddlers and for older children following the holistic/developmental view use fewer pieces of traditional school furniture and more soft pieces (e.g., pillows, hammocks, couches, beanbag chairs, even carpeted floors). Programs for older children, especially those programs following the D-I view, are more apt to be equipped with traditional school furniture (tables and chairs, or desks). Regardless of the program base, the furniture used in early childhood programs should be comfortable for both children and staff, cleanable (e.g., upholstered couches and chairs can be covered in washable slipcovers or throws), and aesthetically pleasing.

Infants and toddlers have some special needs, including the following:

Feeding

Car seats with trays

Feeding chairs (high chairs, low chairs)

Feeding implements (bibs, bottles, cups, plates, spoons)

Storage units

Tables (about 15 in. high) and nontip chairs

Wastebasket (covered)

Changing and Toileting

Changing table or counter

Sink with spray nozzle

Stools (11 in. for toddlers)

Storage units

Toilet-training chairs

Wastebasket (covered)

Napping

Bed linens (brightly colored patterned sheets, blankets, stuffed toys; no stuffed toys for very young infants)

Cots ($24'' \times 42''$ for toddlers)

Cradles

Cribs ($30'' \times 54''$ for children under 18 months)

Other Furniture and Essentials

Barrels (carpeted)

Chairs (infant seats, soft stuffed chairs, reclining baby chairs, rockers)

Couches

Cubbies (hooks at child's shoulder level, not eye level)

Evacuation crib and mattress (or $3' \times 4'$ canvas wheeled cart used in hotels and hospitals for collecting linen)

Pillows (large, throw)

Play yard (some are portable; some may be elevated for less floor draft problems, for easier adult accessibility, and for play space underneath)

Mattresses (including air)

Storage cabinets (approximately $11\frac{1}{2}'' \times 15'' \times 24''$; open and closed)

Strollers

Tables (for infants, 12-in. high with raised edges; for toddlers, 14- to 15-in. high) and chairs (8-in. seat height)

Toddler wagons (for transporting toddlers on "walking excursions")

Furniture for preschool (ages 3 years through 5 years) and primary-grade children (ages 6 years through 8 years) should be of the proper height and proportions, be durable and lightweight, and have rounded corners. If space is at a premium, furniture, especially children's chairs, should be stackable.

Tables accommodating from four to six children are advisable. Although tables are designed in many geometric shapes, rectangular tables accommodate large pieces of paper for art and craft work, and round tables are attractive in the library center. Trapezoidal tables are quite versatile because they can be arranged in many configurations. All table surfaces should be "forgiving surfaces" (easy to clean and repair) because of children's intensive use (Vergeront, 1987). Portable drawing and writing surfaces, such as clipboards and Formica-covered boards, can also be used. Formica countertops are excellent for artwork (e.g., finger paints, Play-Doh) and cooking.

Children's chairs should have a broad base to prevent tipping and a full saddle seat with a back support approximately 8 in. above the seat. The distance between the seat height of the chairs and the table surface should be approximately 7½ in. So that children can safely carry the chairs, chair weight should not exceed 8 to 10 lb.

In addition to regular school chairs, soft furniture (e.g., couches, easy chairs, beanbag chairs, hammocks) and stools and benches should be provided. Storage units and display facilities are also a necessity. Specific furniture includes the following:

Chairs (10- to 12-in. seat height)

Children's rocking chairs, easy chairs, stools, and benches

Dividers (bulletin boards, flannel boards, screens)

Storage units (approximately 15″ × 28″ × 48″; portable, built-in, or both and open, closed, or both) and cubbies

Tables (16 to 20 in. high)

Furniture for school-age child care must accommodate varying sizes of children. All types of furniture are needed for the many types of activities (e.g., arts and crafts, cooking, table games, homework, watching videos). Most programs prefer that the emphasis be on soft, homelike furniture because many children have been sitting at desks in hard chairs all day. Much storage space is needed for children's personal items and for program materials during nonprogram hours.

Staff and visiting adults need adult furniture for comfort. Children can also use some of the adult furniture. This furniture includes the following:

Chairs (soft and wood)

Closets and low cabinets with locks (for personal possessions)

Desks, work tables, or both

Filing cabinets

Other furnishings include clocks, wastebaskets, and nonpoisonous plants. Window treatments need to be included, too. Curtain fabrics can add softness, color, texture, and pattern to rooms. Duo-tone blinds (dark on the inside and reflective on the exterior side) are probably best for control of light and window heat.

General Criteria for Learning/Activity Centers

Certainly, the age of the children served and the program objectives determine whether learning/activity centers are to be used. Programs following the holistic/developmental view often use learning/activity centers as the basis for room arrangements. Conversely, programs following the D-I view use such centers to a lesser degree. Most early childhood programs use some centers. The types and arrangement of centers must be in keeping with the local program's objectives. Although a professional may think in many ways about centers in relation to program objectives, one way is through Jones and Prescott's (1978) seven dimensions of activity settings, as shown in Table 5–1. Similarly, Greenman (1988) used these dimensions: comfort, softness, security, safety and health, safety and risk, privacy and social space, order, autonomy, and mobility. He pointed out that some dimensions are mutually exclusive; for example, soft items can compromise health.

Learning/activity centers are a series of working areas that have a degree of privacy but are related to the whole activity room. Their distinctiveness and integrity can be maintained by using the suggestions described in the following subsections.

Defining Space. Organizing space and making clear boundaries between activity areas is important. The space should remain flexible but have enough definition to provide a feeling of place. All definitions should permit traffic flow but also provide containment.

Space can be defined by placing dividers (e.g., sheer curtains hung from the ceiling or wood dividers 2 ft high to 4 ft high provide enclosure for sitting or standing children, respectively); by arranging storage units in various

Table 5–1   Dimensions of Activity Settings

Dimension	Explanation	Example
Dimension 1: Open/Closed	Open activity involves the use of materials with no correct outcome and no set stopping point, encourages creative experimentations, and supports interaction.	Sand play and art activities
	Closed activity involves the use of materials with "correct" outcomes and involves right-wrong feedback with a possible sense of accomplishment.	Puzzles and lotto
Dimension 2: Simple/Complex	Simple activity involves the use of usually one material with only one possible use.	Swings
	Complex activity involves the use of two or more play materials with the potential for active manipulations and alteration by children.	Sand table with digging equipment, sifters, sand molds, and water
Dimension 3: High/Low mobility	High-mobility activity requires large-muscle mobility.	Climbing equipment
	Low-mobility activity requires little to no mobility.	Puzzles
	Intermediate-mobility activity requires moderate mobility using both large and small muscles.	Blocks
Dimension 4: Social Structure	Individual activity	Looking at a book
	Small-group activity	Blocks
	Intermediate-group activity	Music activity
	Whole-class activity	Listening to a story
Dimension 5: Soft/Hard	Softness is based on the presence of soft textures.	Malleable materials: Sand Lap to sit on Single sling swings Grass Rug/carpet Water Messy activities (finger paints) Cozy furniture Dirt to dig in Animals to hold
	Hardness is based on the presence of hard textures.	Lack of the above
Dimension 6: Intrusion/Seclusion	Intrusion is "interruption" by other children.	On a climbing apparatus, a child may show off skills to another child by saying, "See me" or "Watch."
	Seclusion is the lack of intrusion by others.	Reading a book while sitting in a chair "off the beaten path" does not invite intrusion.
Dimension 7: Risk/Safety	Risk activity tests the child's skills; the child sees apparent risks.	Climbing activity
	Safe activity involves no risk.	Finger painting

configurations; or by using dividers or storage units in conjunction with corners and walls to create two or more areas. Space can also be defined by differences in colors or shades of wall paint or carpet in adjoining centers, by differences in light intensity in adjacent centers, by manipulation of the floor planes with lofts (and platforms) or wells, and by varied ceiling heights.

Before deciding how to define space for a learning/activity center, one must decide whether the space is to be permanent. Differences in colors or shades of wall paint, carpet colors, and manipulation of floor planes are somewhat permanent, but placement of movable dividers or storage units and light intensity are not. Being able to add, eliminate, or change centers has advantages.

Allowing Sufficient Space. Sufficient space should be allowed for the type of activity that a particular center is intended to accommodate. More space is required in centers with group play, large items of equipment or materials to spread out, or materials or equipment tending to cause aggressive acts among children. The amount of needed storage determines space needs, also.

Providing Acoustic Isolation. The noise level from one center should not interfere with activities in another; noise is often a problem in small activity rooms. Seclusion may be achieved by using adequate acoustic materials on the floors, walls, or ceilings; by providing headsets; by locating centers with similar noise levels (e.g., library and concept centers) adjacent to each other; and by placing extremely noisy centers (e.g., workshops) outside. Most of the literature suggests separating noisy and quiet areas, but a less marked separation may help prevent areas of the activity room from appearing to be more for boys or for girls.

Arranging Equipment and Materials. Equipment and materials should be arranged in the appropriate center. Open shelves encourage children to select and return their items. Finding the "homes" of various materials, both a self-help skill and a visual discrimination skill, is aided by such cues as pictures or silhouette labels placed on storage shelves for matching items and by distinctiveness created by various types of shelving (inclined, slotted, stepped, drawers). Tote bins or boxes that are transparent or clearly child-labeled are most helpful.

In arranging some items, children's safety and the prevention of object damage is a concern. In general, heavy but portable items (e.g., quadruple unit blocks) should be placed on the lower shelves of cabinets. Heavy or nonportable objects should be placed on tables or shelves where they can be used without being moved.

Equipment and materials for regular but not daily use should be readily available and stored to prevent deterioration and damage. If space permits, they should be stored in or near the center where they will be used. Labeling also helps staff locate equipment and materials quickly. Special care must be exercised in storing *consumable* (short-life) items (e. g., food, paper, paste, paints), audiovisual equipment, science materials, musical instruments, recordings, and any breakable objects.

Considering Other Criteria. Other factors enter into the arrangement of learning/activity centers, such as the type of floor covering required, the size and quantity of equipment and materials, special requirements (e.g., a water source, an electrical outlet, a specific intensity of light, a certain type of storage), and the maximum number of children working in each center at one time. To prevent problems of overcrowding, popular centers may be widely separated to distribute children throughout the room. Furthermore, pathways throughout the activity room should be clear and wide enough to prevent congestion. The edges of pathways can be defined by furniture or changes in floor covering.

Activity Centers for Infants and Toddlers

For infants and toddlers, the curriculum is tied to the physical environment (Torelli & Durrett, 1998). The infant and toddler activity center must be an interesting place full of beautiful sights, sounds, and textures that capture these babies' attention and lead them to explore and problem-solve in their sensory and motor world. The room needs to be arranged and equipped to provide a safe and virtually restriction-free environment for babies and to promote the effective and comfortable functioning of adults.

Infant and toddler rooms should not simply be scaled-down versions of preschool rooms (Dodge, Dombro, & Koralek, 1991). Primarily, infant and toddler environments need to give these very young children a sense of security and provide autonomy (Lowman & Ruhmann, 1998). In studying materials in infant and toddler rooms, the Cost, Quality, and Child Outcomes Study Team (1995) found that ethnic and racial variety in materials was not evident, pretend play toys were rarely available, and sand and water materials were not often included.

Infant and Toddler Rooms. Infants and toddlers need a room organized into distinct areas that reflect a range of activities. Several principles need to be kept in mind:

1. *Infant and toddler rooms should be designed both to "baby scale" and "adult scale."* For infants and toddlers, most items are placed from floor level to 14 in. to 16 in. off the floor, but some things need to be higher for babies to see when elevated. Adults who provide physical care and a lap for these babies need adult-size furnishings.

2. *Infants and toddlers need an aesthetically pleasing environment of beautiful colors, sounds, forms, textures (especially softness), and patterns.* A. Olds (1998) stated that young children will "feast upon the nuances" of sensory stimuli.

3. *Smaller activity centers for one or two children are more appropriate than the larger centers typical of programs for older children.* Some centers for one infant or toddler can be as small as a throw rug, mat, or window (Greenman & Stonehouse, 1996).

4. *Activity centers can surround a large play area that becomes the center of action.* To expect infants and toddlers to play exclusively in the activity areas is a DIP. By 2 or 3 years of age, children recognize differences in space and know what types of behaviors are expected in certain areas. Toddlers who are ready to play in centers must have spatial areas sharply defined if order is to be maintained.

5. *Activity centers need to house items in multiple quantities.* Children at this age rarely share; they spend most of their time playing alone but in the presence of others.

6. *Infants and toddlers need many secluded places.* An elevated area with protective panels may separate infants from active toddlers for short periods of time. Toddlers need couches, low sturdy shelves, barrels, and other secluded places.

7. *Infants and toddlers especially need an activity room that permits high mobility, has mainly open activities, and provides materials for complex activities* (as defined in Table 5–1). Lowman and Ruhmann (1998) stated that the following are excellent open materials for toddlers: household items; art materials; soft blocks; and sensory stimulating items for listening, smelling, and touching.

8. *Infants and toddlers need stability.* Lowman and Ruhmann suggested that "loveys" (objects to which children are attached) stay in the environment with other materials rotated slowly.

9. *Infants and toddlers need stimulation.* Infants and toddlers need materials that appeal to but do not overload the senses (Lowman & Ruhmann, 1998).

10. *Infants and toddlers need safety and sanitation.* Because very young children pull up and climb on furniture and explore toys with fingers and mouth, safety is a priority. Diapering, toileting, feeding, napping, and mouthing of things require that the whole environment be regularly washed and sanitized.

11. *Some storage units and equipment are inappropriate and even dangerous.* Infant and toddler

play items should not be housed in bins or toy boxes. Windup swings or walkers should not be used.

12. *Adult-sized couches, upholstered chairs, benches, and rocking chairs should be widely separated in the activity room.* Because babies stay near adults, bunching (clustering of adults and children) occurs when adults sit near each other (Greenman & Stonehouse, 1996).

Cataldo (1982) listed the following centers for infants and toddlers: block and vehicle area, small manipulative toy area, quiet area, and art center. P. Adams and Taylor (1985) suggested the following activity areas: listening, seeing, touching, fantasy, water and sand, quiet, gross-motor, creativity, and construction. Stewart (1982) added a music area. Lowman and Ruhmann (1998) called for a simplified environment with four major centers: large-motor, dramatic play,

messy, and quiet. Because Greenman and Stonehouse (1996) considered one-child spaces as centers, they listed more centers; some of their center names suggest the activity (e.g., "Infant Peek-a-Boo") and others indicate materials (e.g., "Mirror Area").

Figure 5–2, an example of a floor plan of an infant and toddler activity room, illustrates some of the principles discussed. Napping, feeding, and changing and toileting areas are discussed later in this chapter.

Materials for Infants and Toddlers.   Very young, nonwalking infants explore with their senses. Stimulation with materials is important. Items needed may include the following:

Balls (clutch, nipple, and texture)
Bells (to firmly attach to wrist or shoes)

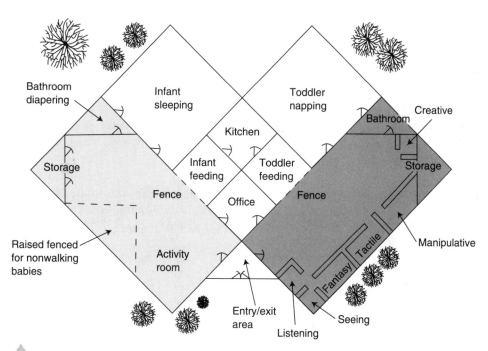

Figure 5–2A   Infant and Toddler Activity Center (The lightly shaded area is detailed in Figure 5–2B. The darkly shaded area is detailed in Figure 5–2C.)

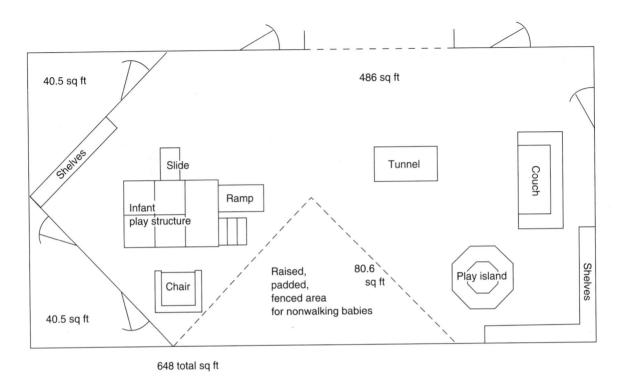

Figure 5–2B, *continued*

Dolls (soft-bodied and rag) and stuffed toys

Faces (pictures and the live human face)

Keys (plastic, on a ring)

Mirrors (unbreakable, crib and wall)

Mobiles (facing downward and slowly moving)

Pictures and designs (e.g., on walls, crib linens)

Puppets (for adults to use)

Rattles

Recordings (of lullabies)

Rings including interlocking rings (for grasping and mouthing)

Squeak and squeeze toys

Teethers

A wide variety of materials are used in centers for older infants and toddlers. The materials may include the following:

Listening

Banging and shaking materials

Musical toys

Percussion and rhythm instruments (e.g., drums, bells, wooden blocks, sticks, tambourines, xylophones)

Rattles

Recordings (tapes or CDs of books, rhymes, music, and animal sounds)

Tape or CD players

Wind chimes

Seeing

Aquariums

Banners or streamers (especially for outside)

Books (picture books of cloth, vinyl, and cardboard)

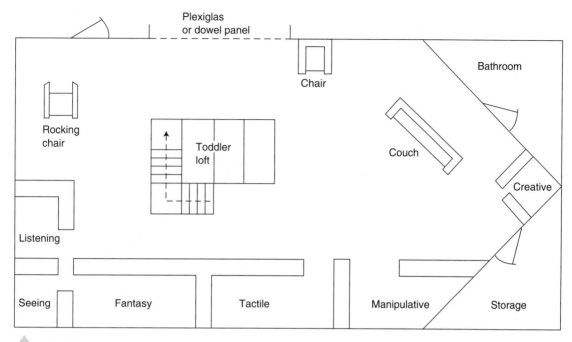

Figure 5–2C

Flannel or magnetic boards with rather large pieces for placing on board

Lotto games (with only a few pictures to match)

Mirrors (unbreakable; handheld and hung on wall)

Mobiles (at eye level or with objects or pictures hung facing downward)

Pictures and wall hangings

Puzzles

Sponges (cut into different shapes)

Terrariums

Tactile

Books with "feely" pictures

Cuddly toys

"Feely" balls and boxes

Mouthing toys

Textured cards and wall hangings

Manipulatives

Activity boards (manipulative boards and latch-and-lock boards)

Beads (wooden beads, wooden spools, and snap beads)

Block props (animals, people, small vehicles)

Blocks (lightweight plastic or foam for stacking and large interlocking blocks, such as Lego)

Containers (pails, margarine tubs with lids, shoe boxes with lids, muffin pans with items to fit into cups)

Cradle gyms

Dressing boards (button and zipper)

Funnels and colanders

Gadget boards

Hole punch

Kitchen items (pots, pans, spoons, cups, egg beaters)

Lacing cards

Peg-Boards with large pegs

Push/pull toys

Puzzles (simple with knobs)

Rattles

Sand and sand toys (pail, sieves and sifters, measuring cups and spoons, funnels, sand wheels)

Sewing and lacing cards with yarn and laces

Shape sorters

Stacking or nesting toys

Water and water play toys (for pouring, straining, floating)

Fantasy

Bags (e.g., tote)

Blankets

Blocks (lightweight)

Cars/trucks/trains/planes

Dolls (washable) with easy-to-dress clothes

Dress-up clothes, especially hats

Housekeeping furniture and other items (refrigerator, sink, stove, table and chairs, buggy, high chair, play food, empty and clean food containers, pots and pans, plastic dishes, housecleaning tools such as mop and broom)

Miniature settings (dollhouse, farm, airport)

Mirrors

Pillows

Play animals (soft, rubber or vinyl)

Puppets

Purses (including bags, totes, and small suitcases)

Scarves (to wave around)

Shopping cart

Stuffed animals

Telephones

Creative

Crayons (large-size and nontoxic)

Easel

Glue

Magazines (for cutting)

Markers (watercolor and nontoxic)

Paintbrushes

Paints (watercolors, finger paints, tempera)

Paper (construction, manila and white drawing paper, newsprint, and finger paint)

Scissors (blunt-ended and soft-handled)

Sponges (for painting)

Stamp pad and stamps

Gross Motor

Balls (large rubber, soft beach, or balls designed for infants and toddlers)

Beanbags and target

Blocks (large vinyl or other lightweight blocks)

Bowling ball and pins (plastic)

Boxes, cardboard (to carry and crawl in)

Bubble-making materials

Climbers (low)

Exercise mats

Jump-off platforms with good padding

Platform with panels (raised about 15 in. off the ground to make a bridge)

Pounding bench

Push/pull toys

Ramps

Riding toys (steerable, pedal, scoot)

Ringtoss

Rocking toys (rocking boat and rocking horse)

Sand and sand toys (especially outside)

Slide (low or placed on slightly inclined terrain)

Steering wheels (attached to platforms with sides or other stable structures for pretend play)

Steps (two or three, not steep, with handrailings and panels)

Swings (special swing with straps for infants; sling type of seat for toddlers)

Troughs with moving water and floating objects

Tunnels

Wagons

Walking rails (attached 15 in. off the floor)

Wheelbarrows

Learning/Activity Centers for Older Children

Learning/activity centers are common in preschool programs and in kindergarten and primary-level programs using the holistic/developmental approach. Several common learning/activity centers for preschool and kindergarten children are described in the following subsections.

Block Center/Area. A **block center/area** is the space that is used for building with unit, hollow, or both types of blocks and for playing with the created structures and accessories (e.g., transportation toys, people and animal figures). Construction with smaller building materials takes place in the manipulative/constructive center. Block centers/areas may be housed inside or outside, on a terrace or other firm, flat surface. Block centers/areas are often located in noisy areas of the classroom because of the noise created by handling blocks and the accompanying dramatic play. Various group sizes may be accommodated in several ways, including the following:

1. A small block center, about 75 sq ft, can accommodate two children. Small block centers, if protected by storage units or if spatially defined by a low platform (but never a loft) or a pit, may be placed near the room entrance for timid children needing to make the home-to-program transition. Sometimes, these centers use reduced-size unit blocks (replicas of unit blocks whose dimensions are about two thirds of the dimensions of standard unit blocks), mini-hollow blocks, or both. These blocks may be built on a table as well as on the floor. Usually, about 100 to 150 blocks and a few accessories are shelved in the small block center.

2. A large block center, about 260 sq ft, can accommodate up to seven children. Because blocks require such a large area, the space may be referred to as a *block area* instead of a *block center.* From 700 to 1,000 standard unit blocks or 80 or more hollow blocks are recommended for a large block area. Because block constructions are easily knocked over by fast-moving traffic, the large block area should be located in the section of the room where traffic moves at a slower pace and where structures can be left up. Shelves are usually at the back and the left and right sides of the area; a movable divider (screen) can provide protection from the front and can be adjusted to the fluid nature of block construction. The large block area should be adjacent to the dramatic play center. Occasionally, large block areas can be subdivided for multiple construction sites.

3. A small set of hollow blocks (e.g., 10 long, 10 square, 10 boards), used in conjunction with dramatic play, are often housed in dramatic play centers, especially those that change themes throughout the year (e.g., store, post office, farm or ranch).

4. Large outside block areas, for building with a full set of hollow blocks or unit blocks, are usually temporary in nature. Because wooden blocks must stay dry, they are transported in block carts or bins and even children's wagons to and from the block building area.

Acoustic materials, such as a dense, low-pile carpet, should cover the floor and block shelves. Even outside, indoor/outdoor carpet protects children from either rough cement or possible splinters. Storage shelves are open. A well-equipped block center takes three or four storage shelves ($4' \times 3' \times 1'$), with three horizontal divisions creating shelves 1 ft apart. Vertical subdivisions create cubicles. Small cubicles (about 13 in. wide) are for half units, pillars, cylinders, ramps, and floorboards. Medium cubicles (about 18 in. wide) are for triangles, switches, curves, arches, and small accessories. Large cubicles (about 24 in. to 37 in. wide) are for units, double units, quad units, roof boards, and accessories. The arrangement of blocks and accessories should be attractive and well thought out; for example, (a) store blocks lengthwise for quick identification (blocks cannot be identified by their ends or narrow faces); (b) label each section of the shelves with silhouette drawings; (c) emphasize the size of the blocks by shelving blocks seriated by length, with larger blocks on the bottom shelf; (d) do not pack shelves too tightly; (e) arrange a set of same-size blocks in widely separated shelves to facilitate traffic movement to and from the shelves; and (f) rearrange shelves and vary accessories from time to time to attract attention.

In block centers/areas in which the floor rather than a platform is used for building, approximately 18 in. to 24 in. in front of all storage shelves must be defined as a "no-building zone" so that the shelves remain accessible. (The no-building zone can be defined by a change in floor covering or color or by marking off with colored tape.) On the walls, pictures of buildings, bridges, and other constructions (e.g., cut from magazines, photographs of field trip sites, photographs of children's constructions) can be displayed. Figure 5–3 is an example of an indoor block center/area.

The main materials for indoor block areas are unit blocks, so named because each block is the unit size ($1\frac{3}{8}'' \times 2\frac{3}{4}'' \times 5\frac{1}{2}''$ for standard-size unit blocks) or a multiple or fraction of one of the dimensions of that unit. Hollow blocks are the main materials for outdoor block areas. Factory-made accessories designed specifically as accessories for block play are better than those

not so designed because they are in correct proportion to the blocks. Figures of people and other accessories, if appropriate, should be multicultural. Children can also make their own accessories. Materials to include in the block center/areas are as follows:

Accessories (art materials for making accessories or for decorative purposes; figures of people or animals; farm products; minifurniture; traffic signs; transportation items; miscellaneous materials—colored cubes, empty wooden thread spools, small sticks, pretty stones and shells; samples of carpet and tile squares)

Block shelves (for indoors) and bins or carts (for outdoors)

"Blueprints or house plans" and "construction hats" (play props)

Books related to building

Pencils, paper, and so on, for drawing or writing about building

Pictures of buildings

Outdoor hollow blocks (see Bender, 1978) or polyethylene or corrugated cardboard blocks

Steering wheel (attached to a stable structure for pretend play)

Unit blocks (see Hirsch, 1996, p. 149)

Dramatic Play Center. The **dramatic play center** is an area of the room designed specifically for children's spontaneous pretend play. In dramatic play, children act out the roles of family members and community workers, reenact school activities and story plots, and learn such social amenities as table manners and telephone courtesy. Dramatic play may occur in almost any learning/activity center; however, one or more centers are usually arranged specifically for dramatic play.

Unlike other learning centers that provide space, storage, and materials, dramatic play centers are more like stage settings (Beaty, 1996). The most common stage setting is housekeeping, with the "house" divided into one to three

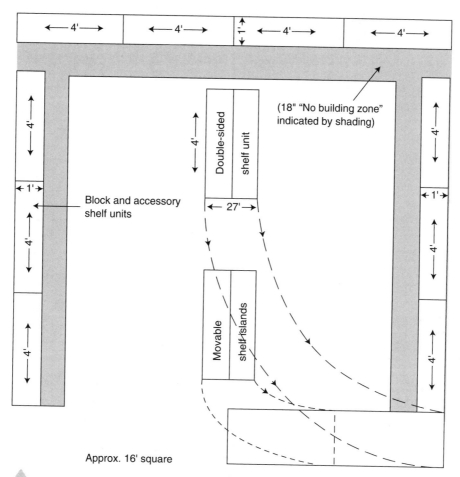

Figure 5–3   Large Indoor Block Center/Area

"rooms." The almost universal room is the kitchen, followed by a bedroom, and then a den or living area. These rooms within the housekeeping center should look distinctive, with enclosures to give a homelike atmosphere. (Openings between the rooms must be wide enough to accommodate doll buggies, however.) A loft bedroom above the downstairs kitchen or living room is very effective. Because of the size of the furniture and the mobility of children during play, suggested room sizes are 80 sq ft for the kitchen, 40 sq ft for the bedroom (more space if

dress-up is included in this room), and 40 sq ft for the living room (see Figure 5–4).

In programs housing older preschoolers and primary-level children, dramatic play should be expanded beyond the prestructured housekeeping area. The Cost, Quality, and Child Outcomes Study Team (1995) found that most programs had only housekeeping centers. Because housekeeping play is still valuable, the center is retained but often as a one-room house (e.g., mainly kitchen and perhaps a doll bed or couch). Additional dramatic play space (approximately

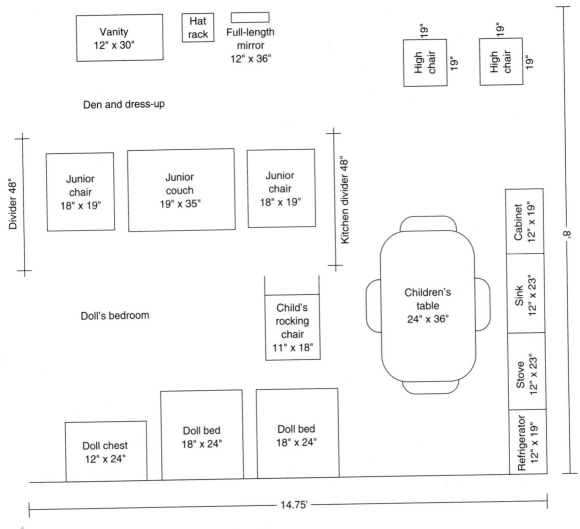

Figure 5–4   Dramatic Play Center: Housekeeping

60 sq ft) is provided for multipurpose use. In this space, children dramatize different themes (e.g., farms, stores, parks) throughout the year. This multipurpose dramatic play center is primarily floor space and storage until children create their own stage settings through the use of such materials as hollow blocks, boxes, gadgets, miniature dollhouses, farms, and other replicas, and theme-specific materials found in prop boxes (see Figure 5–5). Examples of floor plans for specific themes are provided in many teacher's resources (e.g., Isbell, 1995; Warner & Craycraft, 1991).

Many early childhood programs also have a puppet theater housed near the dramatic play center or the language center. Usually, storage and display shelves and a freestanding puppet theater, are all that is needed.

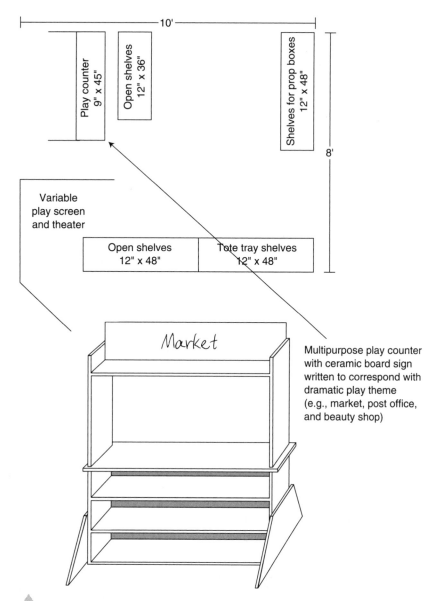

Figure 5–5   Dramatic Play Center: Multipurpose and Puppet Theater

Besides requiring adequate floor space, all dramatic play centers need adequate storage for the many pieces of equipment and materials. Carpet, although not essential, aids acoustic control and gives warmth and softness.

The needed dramatic play equipment and materials depend on the themes introduced. Dolls, puppets, books, and pictures should fulfill multicultural and antibias criteria. Preschool children prefer realistic to nonrealistic props

(Haight & Miller, 1993). The Cost, Quality, and Child Outcomes Study Team (1995) found a lack of needed variety in dramatic play materials. Categories of equipment and materials to consider include the following:

Cameras (toy, and an instant camera with film)

Costumes, especially hats and tools of the trade of community workers (e.g., doctor's bag and stethoscope) and costumes for reenacting stories

Doll items (table and two to four chairs; doll furniture—high chair, bed or cradle, carriage, chest of drawers, refrigerator, stove, sink, cabinet for dishes, washer/dryer; doll wardrobes and linens; pots, pans, dishes, flatware—all items should be unbreakable; ironing board and iron; housecleaning articles—broom, dust mop, dustpan, and dust rag; artificial food; clothesline and clothespins; dishpan; pictures and other home-decorating items)

Dolls (baby and teenage dolls)

Dress-up clothes for men and women (long skirts, blouses, dresses, shirts, pants, shoes, caps, hats, boots, small suitcase, scarves and ribbons, flowers, jewelry, purses, neckties)

Fabric (several strips 2 or 3 yd in length that can be used imaginatively)

Gadgets (rubber hose, steering wheels, PVC pipe, old faucets, door locks, springs, keys, pulleys, bells, scales, alarm clocks, cash registers and play money, cartons and cans, paintbrushes, paper bags, light switches, paper punch for tickets)

Miniature dollhouse, community, farm, service station, and so on

Mirrors (full-length and handheld)

Pictures of community workers

Play screens, cardboard houses, and so on

Puppets and puppet theater

Reading/writing materials (appropriate for theme)

Rocking chair

Stuffed animals

Telephone

Specific prop equipment and materials are suggested in the following references:

Barbour, A., & Desjean-Perrota, B. (2002). *Prop box play*. Beltsville, MD: Gryphon.

Boutee, G. S., Scoy, I. V., & Hendley, S. (1996). Multicultural and nonsexists prop boxes. *Young Children, 52* (1), 34–39.

Myhre, S. (1993). Enhancing your dramatic play area through the use of prop boxes. *Young Children, 48* (5), 6–11.

Soundy, C. S., & Gallagher, P. W. (1992). Creating prop boxes to stimulate dramatic play and literacy development. *Day Care and Early Education, 21* (2), 4–8.

Suskind, D., & Kittel, J. (1989). Clocks, cameras, and chatter, chatter, chatter: Activity boxes as curriculum. *Young Children, 44* (2), 46–50.

In addition to these suggestions, make prop boxes based on the occupations of the program's family clientele.

Art Center. The **art center** is the section of the room devoted to the making and displaying of the visual representations of children. Through art and craft materials, young children develop their sensory and perceptual concepts of color, form, size, texture, and light and dark and their aesthetic sensitivities; represent their mental thoughts in visual products rather than in words; display their creativity; express their emotions; and refine their small-motor skills with the tools of artists.

The art center must be a little studio that ignites children's interests through offering a comfortable place to work without unrealistic constraints (e.g., "Don't get a drop of paint on the floor because it will stain the carpet!"); through storing, drying, and displaying furnishings designed for much self-directed activities; and through providing a wide variety and quantity of media to explore. Specific criteria include the following:

1. The art center should look like a cheerful studio. It should be appropriately located where ample light is available from lighting fixtures or windows that provide sun-free directional light. A center near the door to the playground allows art activities to expand to outdoor areas. Cheerfulness is further enhanced by the display of children's products on walls or display boards that are painted (or covered) in a pleasing color.

2. The art center should have places for individual and group work. Work surfaces include the wall (porcelain boards and murals), tilted surfaces (easels), and flat surfaces (tables). Movable stand-up tables should be approximately 20 in. high, and sit-down/stand-up tables should be about 18 in. high. Built-in work surfaces should be 20 in. high and between 2 and 3 ft deep. The art center needs many storage shelves for supplies. To protect paper from light and dust, storage shelves for paper should have doors, although other storage shelves may be open. Drying art products will require lines or racks for paintings and mobiles, and shelves for three-dimensional products.

3. Surfaces in the art area should be impervious to water, paint, paste, and clay and be easy to clean. Pretest materials for red paint staining before selecting surface coverings. Floors should not be slippery when wet, and all surfaces should dry quickly. Linoleum, Formica, or a vinyl cloth should cover the tables; ceramic tile, vinyl-coated wallpaper, or waterproof paint should cover the walls; and the floor should have a vinyl tile covering.

4. A sink in the art center or in an adjacent rest room with plenty of counter space on both sides is essential for mixing paints and cleanup. The sink should have a faucet 23 in. above the floor and should be equipped with a disposal drain for catching clay and paste. The sink counter and the wall behind the sink should be covered with an easily cleaned surface.

5. The "studio" may be rather open or cozy, although cozy centers must be roomy enough to accommodate space-consuming tables and floor easels and children moving about with wet paintings. Thus, the art center will need to be approximately 190 sq ft. (See Figure 5–6 for a layout of an art center.)

Much variety in art equipment and materials is needed but is often not available in early childhood programs (Cost, Quality, and Child Outcomes Study Team, 1995). Art equipment and materials include the following:

Aprons (snaps or Velcro is preferred because ties can knot)

Chalk (various colors, 1/2- to 1-in. diameter)

Chalkboards

Clay (powdered or Play-Doh or Plasticine)

Clay boards

Cookie cutters

Crayons

Design block sets

Display boards and tables

Drying rack

Easels (two or three working sides with a tray for holding paint containers on each side)

Food coloring

Geometric shapes (e.g., insets)

Gummed paper in assorted shapes for making designs and pictures

Junk materials for collage work (beads, buttons, cellophane, cloth, flat corks, sewing trims, wallpaper scraps, wrapping paper scraps, yarn)

Magazines for collages

Markers (felt-tip, various colors)

Mosaics

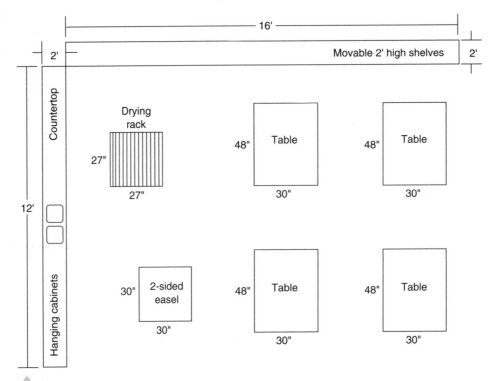

Figure 5–6   Art Center

Mounting board (approximately 22″ × 28″)

Pails (plastic with covers for storing clay)

Paint (fluorescent paint, finger paint, powdered or premixed tempera paint, watercolor sets)

Paintbrushes (camel hair or bristle, 1/2 in. and 1 in. thick with long handles)

Paint jars (some that do not spill are now made)

Paper (cellophane; construction paper, 18″ × 24″; corrugated paper; crepe paper; drawing paper, 18″ × 24″, white and manila; finger paint paper or glazed shelf paper; metallic paper, 10″ × 13″; newsprint, 18″ × 24″; poster board; tissue paper; tag board)

Paper bags

Parquetry blocks and cards

Paste and glue

Paste brushes and sticks

Pencils (colored)

Pictures of children engaging in art activities, reproductions of famous paintings, and pictures of sculpture and architecture

Pipe stems

Plastic canvas

Plastic squeeze bottles

Printing blocks or stamps

Recipes for finger paints, modeling materials, and so on

Rolling pins

Rulers

Scissors (adult shears and right- and left-handed scissors for children)

Scissors rack

Sorting boxes for sorting colors and shapes

Sponges

Staff supplies (art gum erasers; felt erasers; fixative; glue; hole punch; correction fluid; masking, mystic, and transparent tape; paper cutter; pins for bulletin boards; rubber cement; shears; stapler)

Stories and poems with themes of color, shape, size, beauty of nature, and so on

Templates

Textured materials (for tactile experiences)

Weaving materials

Yarn (various colors) and yarn needles

Music Center.   The **music center** is the area of the room devoted to children's explorations of tone and rhythm. Some activities are rather passive, such as listening to music and looking at books and pictures associated with music and dance. Other activities are more active and involve music expression, such as singing, playing instruments, and creating dances. Besides the music center, additional space is devoted to whole-group musical activities; this area is usually the same area as used for other whole-group activities. Locating the music center adjacent to the whole-group makes music materials easily accessible for whole-group activities. However, music carts are available for easy transport of such items. Furthermore, if space permits, it is fun to open the music center (e.g., move a portable screen) to expand the space for marching or dancing.

The music center is often rather small (e.g., 80 sq ft may be adequate), especially if the activities can easily expand into the whole-group area. Because singing, playing instruments, and dancing are noisy, the center should be somewhat enclosed and acoustically treated to contain sound. Carpet helps in acoustic control and minimizes the danger of falls when dancing; resilient flooring, on the other hand, permits more freedom of movement. The piano and Autoharp should not be placed near windows, doors, or heating or cooling units. Tapes must be kept away from anything with a magnetic

field and stored within areas having moderate temperature (50°F to 77°F) and humidity (40% to 60%) ranges.

The arrangement of the music center can be quite simple. One side of the center should have a table or counter equipped with listening stations. Space between each station is helpful for looking at books or drawing while listening. Space for stools or chairs must be included. A place to store tapes and CDs and to display and store records and books should be nearby. Another side needs tables or counter areas for holding xylophones, Autoharps, tape players, and other "sound makers." The third side needs to be equipped with a Peg-Board or shelving for other rhythm and percussion instruments and hooks for scarves, capes, and other dress-up clothes for dancing or marching. A portable screen can be used to enclose low-mobility activities and can be pulled back to allow for more room to dance. The screen can also double as a Peg-Board for holding rhythm and percussion instruments (with silhouette drawings of instruments aiding children in putting them away) or as a pinning space for pictures or drawings (see Figure 5–7).

Equipment and materials for music may include the following:

Autoharp

Books—picture books about music, dancing and marching, and environmental sounds, and illustrated song books (for children), music song books and music appreciation books (for teacher use)

Capes, full skirts, scarves (3′ × 5′), band uniforms for marching and dancing

Computer music programs (software)

Listening stations (with tape and CD players and headsets)

Melodic instruments (chromatic bells, electronic keyboard, xylophones)

Music cart

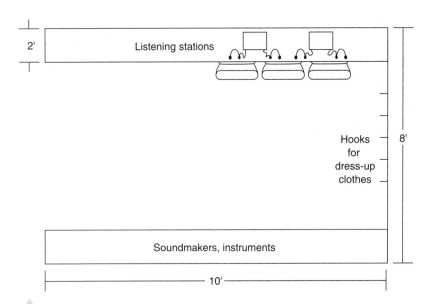

Figure 5–7   Music Center

Piano (and piano bench)

Pictures (of musicians, musical instruments, dancers, bands, orchestras)

Racks or other containers for tapes and CDs

Rhythm instruments (drums, claves, triangles, tambourines, cymbals, tom-toms, hand bells, jingle sticks, wrist bells, ankle bells, shakers, maracas, rhythm sticks, tone blocks, castanets, sand blocks, sounder, finger cymbals, gong bell)

Whistles

Water and Sand Center.   The **water and sand center** is the area of the room in which children explore two of nature's raw materials—water and sand. Besides the properties of water and sand, the type of water and sand materials will lead to other concepts (e.g., containers lead to concepts of empty and full, heavy and light, more and less, shallow and deep, and measurement). Sand and water tables can be used for other messy activities, too (e.g., S. West & Cox, 2001).

The water and sand area is relatively small (approximately 60 sq ft is sufficient), enclosed, and simple in arrangement. The center is often located in the noisy section of the room because children often interact in excited ways in this area. Because a water source is needed for both water and sand tables, the center is often close to the art or science center. If the center is near an outdoor terrace, the tables may be pushed outdoors on some days.

Because of the water and sand, floors will be slippery. Sand also tracks and can remove floor finishes. Thus, the best floor covering is an indoor/outdoor carpet that can be vacuumed with a wet/dry vacuum. If resilient flooring is used, rubber mats with tapered edges will prevent slipping. Some teachers simply keep their resilient floors dry and clean with sponge mops, sponges, and brooms and dustpans. (Preschoolers can help with cleaning if brooms and mops have short handles.) Concrete and outside flooring materials will also be very slippery; thus, terrace floor coverings must be carefully considered.

Shelving for water and sand play must be unaffected by water. Large items need open shelves.

However, many water and sand play enhancers are small; thus, some shelving that is designed to hold tote boxes is excellent. Tote boxes can be labeled with picture or words (e.g., *floating, measuring*). These boxes also allow for the needed rotation of items for this center (Figure 5–8 shows a center plan example).

Water and sand items include the following:

Aprons and smocks (plastic)

Dishwashing detergent or bar soap

Food coloring

Gloves (rubber for water play)

Mops, brooms, sponges (for cleanup)

Sand (white and brown)

Sand table

Sand toys (blocks, small; cans; cartons; cookie cutters; cups; dishes, plastic; figures, plastic animals, and people; flowers, plastic; funnels; gelatin or sand molds; ladles; marbles; measuring cups, plastic; pans; pitchers; planks, short; rocks, small; salt or spice shakers, plastic; sand combs; sand dolls; sand pails; sand wheels; screens, plastic; shells; shovels; sieves; sifters; spoons; strainers; tubes, cardboard, plastic, PVC; vehicles—trucks, bulldozers, tractors; watering cans)

Water play table

Water play toys (aquarium nets; balls—Ping-Pong, plastic, and rubber; bath toys; bowls, plastic; bulb baster; cooking whisk; corks; detergent squeeze bottles; dolls, washable; fishing bobbers; funnels; hose; marbles; measuring cups, plastic; medicine droppers; pitchers, small plastic; rocks, small; shaving brushes; shells; sponges; strainers; Styrofoam trays; watering cans, plastic; water wheels)

Water pump for indoor water play table

Carpentry or Woodworking Center. The **carpentry or woodworking center** is an area of the room in which older preschool and primary-level children enjoy sensory stimulation (e.g., handling wood and tools, hearing the sound of cutting and hammering, and smelling sawdust), derive physical exercise, develop logico-mathematical understandings (as they measure, cut, and fit the "bits and pieces"), and represent the real world through their constructions.

The carpentry or woodworking center requires ample space (approximately 60 sq ft) and must be convenient for constant adult supervision. It must be enclosed or at least out of the way of traffic flow. Because the center is so noisy and because children working in the center do not need distractions, many programs place the center in an empty room or hallway or on an outside terrace. If located in the room, the center is often placed near the block area. Plenty of light is needed for the center.

The area must be equipped with a sturdy workbench. Some centers also have a sawing bench. Tools are stored in a tool rack with a silhouette drawing of the tools on the backboard to enable children to put away tools independently. The tool rack must be either portable for storing tools when not in use or a locking wall-mounted type, such as one of the styles shown by Skeen,

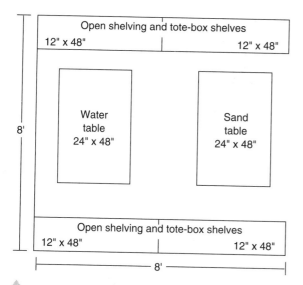

Figure 5–8 Water and Sand Play Center

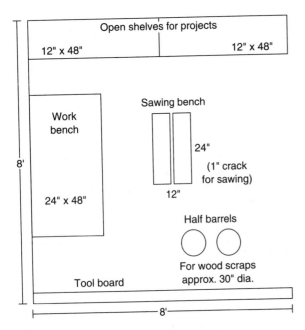

Figure 5–9 Carpentry or Woodworking Center

Garner, and Cartwright (1984). Wood scraps are stored in boxes, baskets, and wooden bins. Figure 5–9 is an example floor plan for this center.

Good-quality carpentry and woodworking equipment is important (Sosna, 2000). Young children cannot handle and do not need a rasp, screwdriver and screws, a plane, a brace and bits, a file, an ax or hatchet, metal sheets, tin snips, or power tools. Equipment and materials needed for carpentry or woodworking are as follows:

Bar clamps

C-clamps (variety of)

Cloth, leather, Styrofoam, cardboard, cork, bottle caps, and other scraps to nail on wood

Hammers (claw) of differing weights and sizes

Hand drill and assorted drill bits

Hard hats

Magnet (tied to a string for picking up dropped nails)

Nails (thin nails with good-sized heads because thick nails tend to split wood)

Paints (water-based)

Pencils (heavy, soft-leaded)

Pliers

Ruler and yardstick used as a straightedge more than for measuring

Safety goggles

Sandpaper of various grades (wrapped around and tacked to blocks)

Sawhorses

Sawing bench—design shown in Skeen, Garner, and Cartwright (1984)

Saws (crosscut and coping)

Soap bar (rubbed across the sides of a saw to make it slide more easily)

Tacks

Tri-square

Vises (attached to workbench)

Wire (hand-pliable)

Wood (scraps of soft wood, such as white pine, poplar, fir, and basswood with no knots), doweling, wood slats, wooden spools, and cross-sections of tree stumps (see Leithead, 1996)

Wood glue

Workbench or worktable (drawers for sandpaper and nails are desirable)

Science and Mathematics Center. The **science and mathematics center** is the area of the room in which children wonder, reflect, and problem-solve in their scientific and mathematical world, see how science and mathematics are part of their everyday lives, learn to respect and appreciate their beautiful world, and develop physical and logico-mathematical concepts. In many early childhood programs, however, the science and mathematics center often consists simply of a window ledge with a plant and a small table, often called the "discovery table."

Because of the diversity of science and mathematics learnings and the many different materials, some science and mathematics materials are housed out of the center. For example, plants are often housed throughout the room. If the center has too much sunlight, the aquarium may be located elsewhere to avoid algae buildup. Many science and mathematics learnings take place in the cooking, block, water and sand, and manipulative centers, as well as outdoors.

Generally speaking, science and mathematics centers should be moderate in size (approximately 60 sq ft) and enclosed. Because the care of animals and plants as well as other activities may be messy, the floor covering should be resilient. A sink should be in the center, or the center needs to be adjacent to the art center or another area with water. (Check state licensing standards concerning food preparation areas and the proximity of animals in cages.) Electrical outlets are a must for aquariums and incubators.

Some science and mathematics materials are left out throughout the year, but other materials are changed regularly. Thus, the following criteria must be considered in planning:

1. Display and working areas should be plentiful. Counter space and tables encourage children to observe and interact with their environment. A counter at children's sitting or standing height can hold an aquarium, terrarium, plants, or animal homes. Tables or counter space can also hold materials that are not out all the time—magnets, prisms, seeds, rocks, sound makers, various models (e.g., spaceships, dinosaurs), and mathematics manipulatives. A centrally located table draws children's attention to the current interest (e.g., getting seeds from a pumpkin). A book display rack is also effective, with a small area rug or floor cushions making for a nice reading area. Plenty of pinning space is needed for beautiful science pictures and posters.

2. Closed storage space is also needed. For example, a built-in closet can have open shelves at the top and built-in drawers to store the many science and mathematics items. Units with tote bins can

also be used for storage. Figure 5–10 shows an example of a science and mathematics center layout.

Equipment and materials needed for the science/mathematics center include the following:

Animal cages (for animals such as small mammals, insects, amphibians)

Animals (e.g., mammals, insects, fish)

Aquarium (equipped with air pump and hose, filter, gravel, light, thermometer; fishnet; aquarium guide)

Beads (for pattern work and for developing an understanding of geometric concepts)

Binoculars

Bird feeder (for the outside space)

Books and pictures (with science and mathematics themes)

"Broad Stair" and "Pink Tower" (Montessori)

Bubble-making materials

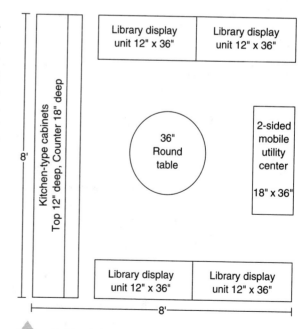

Figure 5–10   Science and Mathematics Center

Calculators (for young children)

Cameras

Chick incubator

Collecting nets

Collections (e.g., rocks, bird nests, insects, seashells)

Compass (directional)

Computer programs (software)

Counting discs

Counting frame

Cuisenaire rods

Cylinders graduated in diameter, height, and both diameter and height (Montessori)

Design cubes and cards

Dominoes (number)

Dowel rods in graduated lengths

Fabric, wallpaper, and cabinet- and floor-covering samples (patterns)

Flannel board objects (for science and mathematics concepts)

Flashlights

Gardening tools (child-sized)

Geoboards

Geometric shape insets and solids

"Golden Beads" (Montessori)

Kaleidoscope

Lotto (for science and mathematics concepts)

Magnets (bar, horseshoe, bridge)

Magnifying lenses (handheld and tripod)

Measuring equipment (linear measuring—rulers, yardsticks, tapes; measuring cups and spoons; scales—balance, bathroom, postal or food; time instruments—sundial, egg timer, clocks; weather gauges—rain gauge, thermometer)

Mirrors (unbreakable)

Miscellaneous materials (string, tape, plastic containers of assorted sizes, boxes, buckets, sponges, straws, dippers, bags, and hardware gadgets)

Models (e.g., animals, space equipment, simple machines)

Number cards (sets)

Numerals (e.g., cards, insets, kinesthetic, puzzles, numerals to step on)

Objects to count

Parquetry blocks and cards (also called attribute blocks)

Peg-Boards and pegs (for developing number and geometric concepts)

Pictures (with science themes)

Plants, seeds, and bulbs (with planting pots, soil, fertilizer, and watering cans)

Prisms

Puzzles (with science and mathematics themes)

Seed box (a transparent container for viewing root growth)

Simple machines

Sorting box

Sound-producing objects

Stacking and nesting materials (for size concepts)

Terrariums (woodland and desert)

Tubing (plastic or PVC)

Vases

Weather vane

Writing materials

Cooking Center.   The **cooking center** is an area of the room in which children prepare and eat food items. Cooking activities are not designed to teach children how to cook; rather, they are designed to promote the learning of many concepts (nutrition, health, safety, language, mathematics, science, multicultural) and skills (social interaction, fine-motor, decision-making, problem-solving) through enjoyable firsthand experiences. Cooking is a real activity and not a pretend one, too!

Many early childhood programs do not have space for a separate cooking center. With the use of small appliances, most teachers can provide for cooking activities. The cooking area can be successfully combined with the art center. If the art center is enlarged, storage units can divide the art and the cooking centers. The area in which snack and meal preparation takes place can also make an excellent cooking center, especially if one counter is built at child height. An ideal cooking center, whether a shared area or a separate area, would require approximately 30 sq ft, be enclosed, and look like a small kitchen (see Figure 5–11).

The center needs a stove with a see-through glass door, a refrigerator, a sink, and storage cabinets. Some storage cabinets need to be closed and even locked if they house potentially dangerous items (e.g., knives, electrical appliances, cleaning agents). Carts may be used to remove these items if lockable storage within the cooking center is not available. Pantry items need to be stored carefully to prevent bacterial growth and insect and rodent infestations.

Equipment and materials for the cooking center include the following:

Air freshener

Aluminum foil

Aprons

Baking pans (various sizes)

Blender

Can opener

Centerpieces for special occasions

Cookie sheet

Cooling racks

Counter saver

Cutters (biscuit and cookie)

Cutting board

Dishcloths and towels

Dish drainer

Dishpan

Dishwashing detergent

Egg separator

Electric griddle

Electric mixer

Electric skillet

Flatware, plastic (knives, forks, spoons)

Garbage bags

Gelatin molds

Grater

Ice cream maker

Kitchen scissors

Knives

Measuring cups (liquid and dry)

Microwave oven

Mixing bowls (metal and plastic)

Mixing spoons

Muffin pans

Napkins

Nutrition charts

Pantry items (foodstuffs)

Paper dishes (plates, bowls, cups)

Paper towels

Peelers (vegetable and apple)

Pictures of foods, kitchens, and people eating in different settings

Pitchers

Place mats, tablecloths, table runners

Plastic bags (resealable)

Popcorn popper

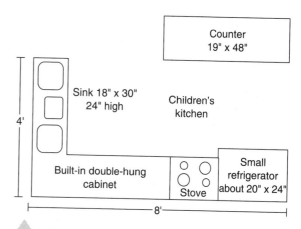

Figure 5–11   Cooking Center

Popsicle sticks

Pot holders

Pot scrubbers

Recipe books for children

Recipe cards (individual cards for each step; poster with entire recipe)

Refrigerator with freezer

Rolling pin

Rotary eggbeater

Rubber scraper

Sauce pans (various sizes)

Serving trays

Sifter

Skillet

Spatulas

Sponges

Storage containers (canisters, microwave dishes, refrigerator dishes)

Stove (hot plate and electric oven may substitute)

Strainer

Straws

Thermometer

Timer

Toothpicks (round)

Warming tray

Wax paper

Wet wipes

Whisk

Manipulative and Small Constructive Toy Center.
The **manipulative and small constructive toy center** is the area of the room in which children handle small objects. This center serves to develop fine-motor skills, eye–hand coordination, and spatial concepts (e.g., noting how to turn a puzzle piece to get it to fit), as well as many other concepts.

The center does not need to be very large (approximately 100 sq ft) because of the size of materials and the relatively low mobility of children. The center is usually very enclosed and is located in the quieter part of the room. The floor may be resilient flooring or low-pile carpet.

The center needs some open floor space for building with Tinkertoys, Junior Erector sets, miniature hollow blocks, or miniature unit blocks; for playing with a marble chute; or even for working a jigsaw puzzle. Tables are needed for using interlocking blocks, parquetry blocks, and design cubes and perhaps for lacing a sewing card or working a puzzle. One table should have a plain surface; some of these tables, especially designed for this center, have "wells," in which one or more recessed tote trays hold manipulatives such as beads. If Legos or Duplos are used, a second type of table should be considered that has Lego- or Duplo-compatible surfaces. Storage cabinets with open shelves and with cubicles for clear plastic tote bins that keep materials in view are needed.

Because of the need for both open floor space and tables, the center could be subdivided by a double-sided storage peninsula. Open shelves of this unit could face the open floor side, and cubicles for tote bins could face the tables. Additional storage could be located at the back or sides of the center (see Figure 5–12 for a layout of this center).

Equipment and materials for the manipulative and construction center include the following:

Accessories for small construction toys (e.g., Lego vehicles)

Banks ("piggy" or boxes with small slots or holes for dropping small disks or marbles)

Beads (for stringing)

Bolt and nut boards

Construction toys (interlocking blocks, snap blocks, Junior Erector set, miniature hollow blocks, miniature unit blocks, Tinkertoys)

Cylinder boards (Montessori)

Design materials (design cubes and cards, parquetry blocks and cards, plastic mosaics)

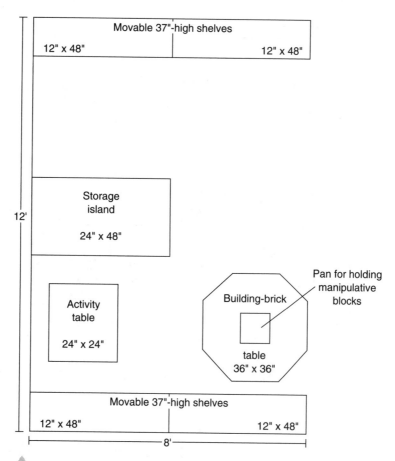

Figure 5–12 **Manipulative and Small Constructive Toy Center**

Dressing materials (e.g., dolls, frames, shoes with laces)

Insets (also called shape boards)

Lacing cards

Latch frames or lock boxes

Paper punch

Pegs and Peg-Boards

Puzzles (with storage racks or cases)

Sectioned boxes

Sewing cards or plastic canvas

Emerging Literacy and Book Center. The **emerging literacy and book center** is an area of the room designed to focus on looking and listening activities and to offer children hands-on experiences with communication-developing materials. The ideal center would be large (approximately 150 sq ft) but should be subdivided to give a cozy atmosphere. The center should be enclosed and located in the quiet section of the room. The language center could be divided into the following three subsections as shown in Figure 5–13:

1. A loft could provide space for two book nooks. The loft itself could be equipped with a small book rack, puppet storage, and a small puppet theater. Beneath the loft, cozy

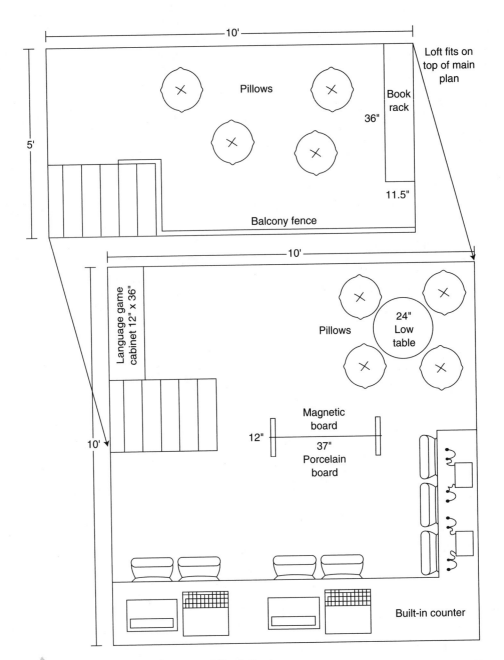

Figure 5–13   Emerging Literacy and Book Center

floor pillows could serve as a book nook for one or two children.

2. Adjacent to the loft could be an area equipped as a communications center, with computers, listening stations, language masters, projectors, and a place for writing by hand.

3. The third area could be equipped as a reading and storytelling room with book storage and display; flannel and magnetic boards; a wall pocket chart; and places to sit at a table, on a couch, or on the floor. The back of the reading room could serve as a language game area, with storage cabinets, a low table with floor cushions, a chalkboard room divider, and a magnetic board.

Items needed for the emerging literacy and book center include the following:

Alphabet letters (e.g., alphabet insets, kinesthetic letters, magnetic letters, letters to step on)

Books and recordings of stories

Computers and software

Flannel boards and magnetic boards

Games and materials for developing letter and sound awareness

Globes (primary) and maps (simple)

Lotto (covering many subjects)

Numerals (e.g., numeral insets, kinesthetic numerals, magnetic numerals, numerals to step on)

Perceptual and conceptual development games and materials (absurdities, missing parts, sequencing, opposites, classification)

Picture dominoes

Pictures and flannel or magnetic representations of finger plays, poems, and stories

Projector, slides, and filmstrips

Puppets and a puppet theater

Puzzles for developing literacy knowledge (e.g., having story themes; rhyming words, sequencing)

Signs and labels

Writing materials (e.g., paper, chalkboards, porcelain boards, markers, crayons)

Other Areas.   A children's room should have private areas (NAEYC, 1998a). The Cost, Quality, and Child Outcomes Study Team (1995) found that preschool programs were low in "space to be alone" and "furnishings for relaxation." The team concluded that centers were too hard, not cozy and homelike. Private areas serve as places to tune out, to enjoy being by oneself for a few minutes, or to reduce excitement (Isbell & Exelby, 2001). Kielar (1999) suggested ways to provide quiet places in our early childhood programs.

Cozy areas with soft textures are needed in facilities for young children and may be critical to the development of children with disabilities (Prescott, 1987). Private areas also serve as places to watch from, such as a small block center, a rocking horse, a window seat, a playhouse, or a riding toy. A place to watch from should be close to ongoing activities while providing the child with a sense of enclosure.

Children also enjoy special-interest areas, such as an aquarium or terrarium; a rock, mineral, or shell collection; a garden seen from a window; a hanging basket; an arboretum; books; and displays connected with specific curriculum themes. Special interest areas can also be used to display "treasures" of the homes.

Learning Centers for Primary-Level Children.   Learning centers for primary-level children (ages 6 through 8) do not have to be as sharply defined (separated in appearance) as centers for younger children. Such centers, which resemble workshops, may include different combinations of centers used at the preschool–kindergarten level. For example, one primary program has these learning centers: cooking/science/art, dramatic play/music, reading, and mathematics/block construction. Another program uses these clusters of centers: art/cooking, construction, mathematics/computer, and language/reading.

Similar to preschool/kindergarten room design, messy and noisy areas are separated from less messy and quieter areas. The requirements for each center (e.g., floor coverings, furniture) are the same as those for centers previously described.

School-Age Child Care Activity Centers.   SACC activity centers are unique for three reasons. First, SACC programs must accommodate a wide age range (often ages 5 through 10 or 12). Second, programs are for shorter periods of daily time (an average of 2 to 3 hours) during the school session and sometimes all-day care during holidays and summer vacation periods. Third, SACC programs are often shared-space areas (space shared with regular school programs, religious programs, or preschool child care). It is too costly to set up a permanent, nonshared center for the fewer hours of the SACC program, as compared with other early childhood programs.

Activity centers for SACC programs are often created by mobile shelves and dividers. A large storage closet or storage–workroom combination is most helpful. SACC programs are often designed with activities that are similar to quality home life for school-age children. The centers can include (a) quiet areas for reading, doing homework, listening to music with headphones, creative writing, or just resting; (b) creative areas for art and craft work, possibly including woodworking; (c) table games and manipulative areas; (d) cooking or snack areas; and (e) high-technology areas. Other fun areas are block construction, science centers, and larger table games such as Ping-Pong.

School-age child care programs need a variety of materials, such as the following, to accommodate various ages, interests, and needs:

Quiet

Books (reference books or materials on CDs for doing homework and a selection of trade books for leisure reading)

Listening station (with headphones)

Magazines (children's)

Mazes

Newspapers

Recordings (music and stories)

Word puzzles (e.g., crossword puzzles)

Games and Manipulatives

Board games (e.g., Monopoly, Scrabble, chess, checkers, Chinese checkers, Life, Clue, bingo, and tic-tac-toe)

Card games (e.g., cards for Fish)

Interlocking blocks (e.g., Lego)

Jacks

Magnetic building sets

Parquetry blocks, design blocks, and design cards

Puzzles (jigsaw with 100 to 500 pieces)

Woodworking

See the list given for older children on page 172.

Arts and Crafts

See the list given for older children on pages 167–169.

Materials for Hobbies

Items needed would depend on specific hobbies.

Writing Supplies

Chalk

Chalkboards or porcelain boards

Computer and printer

Marking pens

Paper (various types)

Pencils with pencil sharpeners

High Tech

Calculators

Computers with selected software

Projectors, slides, and filmstrips

Tapes and CDs

Television with DVD and VCR players

Outside

Ball game equipment (e.g., basketball, softball, dodgeball, kick ball, volleyball, soccer)

Marbles

Riding equipment (e.g., bicycles, skates, skateboards)

Sand/water/mud (see the list for older children on page 171)

Developing an Activity Room Layout Plan

Before drawing a floor plan, these steps may need to be taken:

1. Look at space from many environments. Can you identify who works and lives in the space? List elements that you like (e.g., lighting, color, softness, organization of space), and file pictures of these elements for later reference (Carter & Curtis, 1998).

2. Decide on the centers that best fit program goals. A minimum of six activity centers is needed for a group of children (C. Hohmann & Buchleitner, 1992). Calculate the number of center activity places needed. To calculate the number of center activity places needed, multiply the number of children by 1.5; for example, 20 children require 30 activity places. Having more choices than children lessens waiting time and offers a reasonable number of options.

3. List the centers and give the maximum activity places (maximum number of children who can be in a center at the same time) for each center, as shown in Table 5–2.

Table 5–2   Determining Maximum Activity Place

Center	Maximum Activity Places
Cooking	3
Dramatic play	4
etc.	etc.
	Total of 30 places

4. Develop a matrix of centers and the requirements for each. Requirements would need to be developed. (We used the Jones and Prescott [1978] dimensions and a few additional criteria as an example; see Table 5–3). Cluster centers that share compatible criteria as shown in Figure 5–14. These centers may be housed near each other if possible. For example, using a plumbing core is economical but may be impractical when dealing with a great deal of floor space.

Figure 5–15 is a floor plan for a preschool or kindergarten (especially for ages 3 through 5)

Table 5–3   Center Criteria

Criterion	Center		
	Block	**Art**	**Library**
Open	X		
Closed			
Simple			
Complex	X		
High mobility			
Intermediate mobility	X		
Low mobility			
Individual			
Small group	X		
Intermediate group			
Whole class			
Soft	X (carpeted)		
Hard			
Intrusion			
Seclusion	X		
Risk			
Safety	X		
Electricity			
Water			
Quiet			
Noisy	X		
Open storage	X		
Closed storage			
Display			

Figure 5–14   Clustering Centers with Compatible Criteria

Figure 5–14   Clustering Centers with Compatible Criteria

All of these centers need a water source.	Cooking Water play Art Snack
These centers are conceptually related and may be used together.	Dress-up Housekeeping

children's activity room. Figure 5–16 is a floor plan for a primary-level (especially ages 6 through 8) children's activity room. Figure 5–17 is a floor plan for an SACC activity center. Because floor arrangements must fit the needs of the local program, the floor plans are intended for illustration.

Additional Areas for Children

Learning is going on all the time in an early childhood program both in and outside of the children's activity room. Additional areas are for shared activities, and others are used to take care of children's physical needs and to assist children in becoming self-reliant in taking care of these needs. Thus, designing additional areas must be done with as much care as planning the children's activity room. A. Olds (2001) found 20 sq ft per child workable but 22 sq ft per child desirable for these additional spaces; otherwise, adults and children in these areas often infringe on the space of the activity room. Toys, wall hangings, mirrors, and other interesting items should be available in the napping, feeding and dining, and changing and toileting areas, although the emphasis is on adult–child interactions during care routines.

Shared Activity Areas. In some early childhood programs, several activity rooms open into a shared activity area (e.g., a large room, a very long and wide hallway, or a covered patio). Shared activity areas are often used for gross-

motor activities, music, rhythmic activities, and drama.

Children's Cubbies. Children should have their own individual cubbies (also called lockers) for storing personal belongings because this emphasizes personal possessions and respecting others' possessions, helps children learn proper habits for caring for their belongings, and reduces the danger of spreading contagious disease. The cubbie area should not be part of the entry/exit area but should be close to this area and the outdoor space. The area should be large enough to facilitate easy circulation of staff. The floor covering in this area should be easily cleaned because it will get quite dirty during inclement weather.

Cubbies usually provide space for outer garments. The overall dimensions of such cubbies are approximately $56'' \times 12'' \times 15''$. Cubbies seldom include doors because these catch little fingers, are always in the way, and are never closed. Such cubbies may be modified by adding one or two top shelves to accommodate a tote tray (usually $7'' \times 8'' \times 15''$) for personal possessions. Another shelf about 10 in. from the bottom of the cubbies provides a place for the children to sit while putting on overshoes or changing clothes. Garment hooks (never use racks) are attached to the bottom of the lower top shelf or to the sides or back of the cubbies. Overshoes are placed under the bottom shelf.

Infants' Diapering Areas and Children's Rest Rooms. The diapering and rest room areas should be

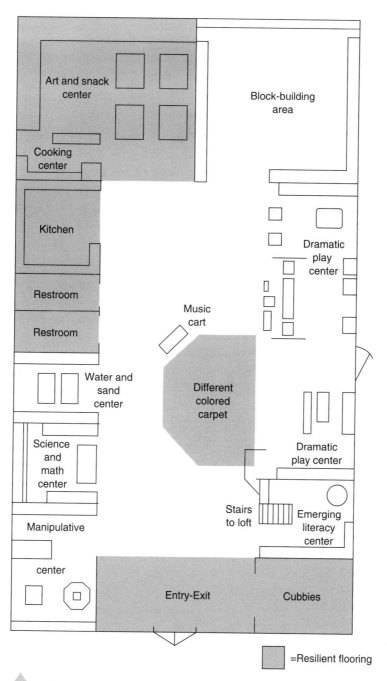

Figure 5–15   Preschool/Kindergarten Children's Activity Room

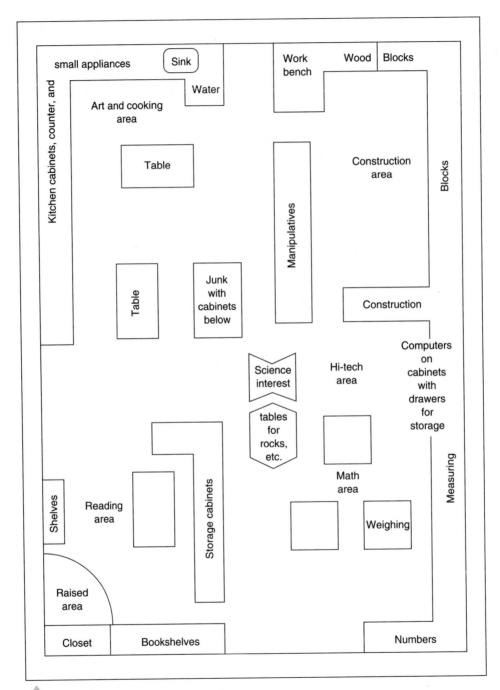

Figure 5–16   Primary-Level Children's Activity Room

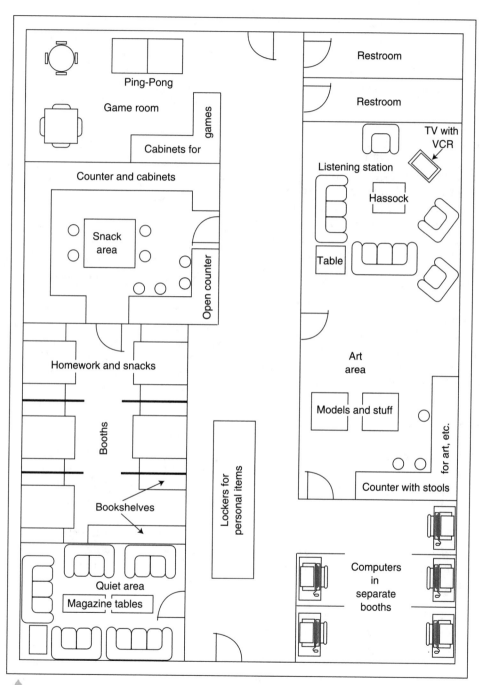

Figure 5–17   School-Age Child Care (SACC) Activity Center

spacious enough for children and the adults who are supervising and helping them. They should be easy to clean and disinfect (e.g., seamless floors), and they should be cheerful with windows for sunlight and ventilation, bright colors, and potted plants.

Diapering Area. The diapering area for infants should be spatially separated from the kitchen and feeding areas but should be close to the activity room so the teacher and babies can maintain visual and auditory contact. (A mirror on the wall above the table can aid the caregiver in keeping an eye on the other babies.) One diapering table is needed for every six to eight infants. The diapering table or counter should be adjacent to (a) a sink with running hot and cold water for immediate staff hand washing and (b) a closed-closet storage for soap, washcloths, diapers, and counter disinfectants. Diapers and other trash must be disposed of in containers inaccessible to both infants and older children. Although the main interaction should be between the adult and the child, washable toys can also be provided.

Children's Rest Rooms. Children's rest rooms should be located adjacent to each activity room and to the outside play area with doors leading to both. The ratio of the number of toilets to the number of children should be 1:5 for toddlers and 1:10 for preschoolers. Toilet seat heights must be scaled down for toddlers and scaled down or adapted (e.g., flooring raised in front of stools) for preschool children. For children with a disability, toilet seat height must be appropriate for wheelchair users, and toilet tissue should be not more than 6 in. from the front of the toilet bowl. Handrails should be mounted on the wall for additional safety. Urinals, especially trough rather than floor-mounted types, keep the toilet seats and floors clean. Some children like privacy; unlocked, low partitions between and in front of toilets provide this feature and permit easy supervision. Partitions rather than doors are especially helpful for children with a physical disability. Because young children flush many objects, multiple clean-outs, easily accessible U-traps, and separate shutoff values for each toilet are also needed.

Lavatory sinks should be adjacent to but outside the toilet areas and near the door. The ratio of the number of sinks to the number of children should be about 1:8. Sink heights should vary between 18 in. and 2 ft. A blade or lever rather than a knob water control should be used to help the child with a disability become independent. Water temperature must be set low enough to prevent scalded hands. (Because the thermostatic control must be set higher for the dishwasher, another water heater must be installed for kitchen water.) Sinks must be equipped with disposal drains to catch clay, sand, and so forth; mirrors, preferably of safety glass or metal, should be placed at child's height over them. Paper towels in a dispenser or electric blowers (with the bottom edge mounted about 24 in. above the floor) should be used. A bathtub with a flexible shower hose is necessary in all-day programs or those serving younger children.

Drinking fountains should be located near the rest rooms and out of the path of fast-moving traffic. They should be made of stainless steel and be between 20 and 23 in. high. Fountains must be selected to accommodate the needs of children with disabilities. Water-bubbling level should be controlled. Because it takes time for young children to learn to get enough water from a fountain to quench their thirst, paper cups should be available for children just learning to drink from a fountain.

Feeding and Dining Areas. Kitchen facilities need not be extensive for programs in which only snacks are served. A kitchen needs a few heating elements, a refrigerator with a small freezer compartment, a sink with hot and cold water, a dishwasher, counter space, and storage units. The Department of Agriculture publishes guides for the selection of food service equipment for programs serving main meals. Kitchens equipped with a half-door (Dutch door) and a Plexiglas panel in the bottom half allow for visual contact between children and adults and permit children to see food preparation activities. (Regulations do not permit children in the kitchen area.)

The feeding area for infants and toddlers should be equipped with feeding chairs and some toddler-sized tables and chairs for family-style eating. The feeding area should be near the kitchen. The dining area for older children should be bright, cheerful, and airy, with screens on the windows. Tables and chairs should be the correct size and allow plenty of space for each child. Dishes and cutlery should be sized for small hands. All surfaces should be made of materials that are soap-and-water scrubbable and resistant to water damage.

Napping Areas. Infant and toddler napping areas should be spacious, with a separate crib for each child. The napping area should be adjacent to the playroom, with an observation window in the sleeping room. The room should appear cozy, with carpet, shaded windows, and rocking chairs. A ceiling fan increases air circulation and masks outside noises. Soft music is also desirable.

Napping area should be considered for all-day preschool programs. Sleeping areas should be isolated from noise in adjacent areas, and lighting should be controlled. If a separate napping room is used, efficient use of space can be achieved by placing cots end to end in rows, with an aisle approximately 4 ft wide between the rows.

Schools rarely have separate napping areas. All-day school programs must provide for resting in the children's activity room. Because cots take up so much floor space and must be stored, children often sleep on mats or thick towels placed on the floor of the classroom. If draft is not a problem, the arrangement seems to work for the typical 60- to 90-minute rest.

Isolation Area. An isolation area is necessary for caring for ill or hurt children until family members arrive. The isolation area often contains a bed or cot and can be equipped with a few toys and books. A small bathroom adjacent to the isolation area is helpful.

Adult Areas

Working as a staff member in an early childhood program is demanding both physically and psychologically. The quality of work life directly affects an adult's abilities to deliver effective early childhood programs. Yet, ironically, many programs fail to provide a comfortable place for staff, family members, or visiting adults even though some of these same programs provide a wonderful physical environment for children. Cryer and Phillipsen (1997) found that preschool centers scored low in meeting adults' personal needs, such as separate rest rooms, a comfortable staff lounge, and a safe and adequate storage area for teachers' belongings. Family members and other community members should also feel welcome in a world comfortable and inviting for adults as well as children. The two major criteria to meet in planning adult areas is that they be scaled to adult size and that the type and specific design of each area fit the needs of the program.

Family Reception Area. A family reception area should make families feel welcome and encourage the exchange of information between family members and staff. A separate area adjacent to the children's activity room has the following advantages: (a) Family members have a place to sit and wait until their children complete an activity or put on wraps; (b) family members do not have the feeling of being stranded in the middle of the children's room while waiting; (c) interruptions of children's activities are minimized; and (d) family members can speak confidentially with staff members. The family reception area should be well defined and comfortable and invite visiting and the viewing of children's work and information materials for families.

Throughout the activity room there should also be inviting places for family members to observe ongoing activities or to enjoy a transition time with their children. A. Olds (1999) believes that space should invite people to gather, explore, and be comforted.

Adult Lounge/Rest Room. An adult lounge should be provided for resting and visiting. Comfortable chairs and a place for preparing and eating a snack should be considered in the design. Reading materials should also be provided. For greater privacy, adult rest rooms should not be part of the lounge but should be located nearby.

Office and Workroom. The design of the office and workroom area should fit the needs of the local program. For most early childhood programs, space will be needed for desks or tables and chairs, cabinets for filing professional materials and records, office machines (e.g., paper cutter, laminator, photocopier, computer and printer), large work tables, high stools, a sink, and storage units for office supplies and other work materials. If some materials or equipment for the program are shared by several classrooms, they should be stored in or near the workroom. Each staff member needs a spacious locker (with a lock) for personal items.

Professional Library. An early childhood program should have a professional library to keep staff informed and to help them in planning. The library is usually a storage and display area located in or adjacent to the office or workroom. The library should contain catalogs from suppliers of equipment and materials; curriculum materials; journals and other publications of professional associations; advocacy materials; and professional books, software, and audio visuals.

Environmental Control

An important consideration in constructing any early childhood facility is environmental control, including lighting, heating, cooling, ventilating, and acoustics. Lack of adequate environmental control results in a number of problems, such as eyestrain from glare or discomfort from heat or cold. It can also contribute to poor behavioral patterns, not only in children but also in adults. Adequate environmental control promotes energy and money savings, too.

Lighting. A. Olds (2001) believes that light affects physical well-being and also has a psychological and aesthetic impact on children and adults. Light also changes a person's perceptions of color and form.

Natural light from large windows, balconies, and porches is preferred over artificial light. Natural light is healthy; it destroys bacteria and mold, is a source of vitamin D, contributes to a sense of optimism, and connects people with their natural world. Children learn many things by looking through windows at frost, rain, and snow; light and shade patterns (which they can connect with the passage of time); natural and social scenes; and sources of light. Too often windows are blocked because of problems with heating, cooling, or glare or to solve storage and display problems.

Placement of windows is important for environmental control of heat and cooling as well as excessive light and hence glare. Placement is also important for children's learnings. For children to see outside, windowsills should be 18 to 24 in. high. When standing on balconies and lofts, children find higher windows interesting, too. Even skylights are fascinating for young children.

Facilities also need artificial lights even with ample window area (about 20% of floor area). Artificial lighting should be incandescent (A. Olds, 2001) or full-spectrum (Schreiber, 1996). Centers need flexibility in lighting rather than flooding the entire center with light. For example, lighting should be direct and indirect, come from various heights, and be concentrated in certain areas. Regulatory agencies frequently specify the minimum amount of light intensity, usually

50 to 60 foot-candles of glare-free illumination. Because lighting should be tailored to the needs of children working in each center, variable light controls should be provided in each area.

Reflective surfaces in the room determine the efficiency of illumination, such as light-colored shades on walls, ceilings, and floors. Tables and countertops should reflect light, too. Reflective surfaces can produce a glare, however. Glare can be controlled by louvers, blinds, and overhangs that control excessive light at windows, by peripheral artificial lights, and by matte finishes on furnishings. Properly placed windows soften the shadows cast by overhead lighting.

Heating, Cooling, and Ventilating. The temperature of the room should be between 68°F and 72°F (20°C and 22°C) within 2 ft of the floor; thus, thermostats should be at the eye level of seated children. Because windows can cause heating and cooling problems, many facilities have reduced the amount of window area. The circulation of air should be 10 to 30 cu ft of air per child per minute. For comfort, the humidity should be from 50% to 65%. If a humidifying system is not installed, an open aquarium or an uncovered water table will add humidity to the room.

Acoustics. Sounds can soothe or jar. Extreme noise impedes development and is most harmful for babies and children with learning disabilities and hearing loss.

A moderate amount of noise is expected in programs for young children. To prevent excessive noise, acoustical control is a must. A nearly square room has better acoustic control than a long, narrow room. Acoustic absorption is more effective and thus more economical underfoot than overhead. Learning/activity centers that generate the greatest amount of noise should be designed and decorated for maximum acoustic absorption. Sand and grit on the floor increase noise as well as destroy the floor covering. Using tablecloths on luncheon tables, area rugs, remov-able pads on tabletops when hammering, and doors to keep out kitchen noises all aid acoustics.

OUTDOOR SPACE

Outdoor play has been an integral part of early childhood programs and hence housing facilities. Early childhood educators need to spend as much time planning outdoor space as they do planning indoor space. Outdoor play is important to children. In fact, when adults were asked about their favorite play experiences as children, over 70% reported outdoor play experiences (Henniger, 1994).

Brief History of Playground Design

Concepts about the values of certain types of play have changed over the years. Along with these changing concepts has come an evolution in playgrounds. Ideas about how to design playgrounds stem from theories of play. When play was conceived of as using up surplus energy or for relaxation, children engaged in free play. When play was seen as helping children develop the skills needed for adulthood, gardening and other activities were included in the outdoor program.

Early childhood educators were especially interested in play. Froebel's playgrounds for kindergarten children were more than "sites for physical fitness." To Froebel, children's playgrounds "were nature itself." Children tended gardens, built stream dams, cared for animals, and played running games. Besides Froebel's kindergartens, also coming from Europe was Zakerzewska's "sandgarten," which influenced G. Hall to write a book called *The Story of a Sand-Pile* (1897). By the 1900s, the progressives (headed by Dewey) and the Froebelians were at odds over many issues, although outdoor play was not an issue. Play was most important in the progressive kindergartens, and training in play was part of teacher education (Parker & Temple,

1925). Nursery schools placed a major emphasis on play (H. Johnson, 1924; Palmer, 1916). By the mid-1940s, less emphasis was placed on play; thus, equipment in schools and parks became more unsafe and of little play value (Frost & Klein, 1983; Frost & Wortham, 1988).

Theorists such as Piaget and Vygotsky recognized play as important for children's holistic development. Today, outdoor play is seen as important for motor development (Poest, Williams, Witt, & Atwood, 1990), sensory stimulation (A. Olds, 2001; Tilbury, 1994), language and problem solving (Rivkin, 1995), cognitive development (Sallis et al., 1999), and social skills (Frost, Wortham, & Reifel, 2001). Although play is seen as important, Rivkin (1995) stated, "Children's access to outdoor play has evaporated like water in sunshine" (p. 2).

Types of Playgrounds

Frost and Klein (1983) identified four contemporary types of playgrounds:

1. **Traditional playgrounds** are located primarily in public parks and public schools. The equipment is selected for exercise purposes. Metal and wood structures, chosen for their durability and ease of maintenance, are the main pieces of equipment.

2. **Contemporary playgrounds** are designer made and are primarily located in public parks. Like traditional playgrounds, they are mainly for climbing, swinging, and sliding, but the equipment is more aesthetically pleasing.

3. **Adventure playgrounds** have raw materials and tools for children to build their own structures with adult guidance (Pederson, 1985).

4. **Creative playgrounds** have structures built from discarded materials. Many complex units can be used for climbing, swinging, and fantasy play. Many loose materials (e.g., blocks, sand, and props) are also available. Creative playgrounds are popular in preschools.

General Criteria and Specifications for Outdoor Space

Regardless of the type of program, outdoor space should meet the following criteria:

1. Outdoor space should meet safety guidelines (as discussed in later sections of this chapter).

2. Outdoor space should preserve and enhance natural features (A. Olds, 2001).

3. The design should be based on the needs of children as determined by local program goals. Frost and Wortham (1988) summarized how each aspect of development is enhanced through play and listed the types of materials suited for each developmental outcome. Research studies have been designed to examine children's play on various types of playgrounds. Some of the findings are as follows:

a. Physical exercise and games with rules occur over 75% of the time on traditional playgrounds. Dramatic play occurred almost 40% of the time on creative playgrounds, with boys engaging in dramatic play twice as frequently as did girls (although the opposite trend occurs indoors). Constructive play is also popular on creative playgrounds (Frost, 1992a).

b. On traditional playgrounds, children like action-oriented swings and seesaws more than they like climbers and slides. Movable props and materials were popular on creative playgrounds and enabled children's play to spread out over a wide range of equipment as they adapted the materials to the play situation (Frost, 1992a). Children like adventure playgrounds the most and traditional playgrounds the least. Complex social and cognitive behaviors occur more frequently on creative than on traditional playgrounds (Hartle & Johnson, 1993).

c. Differences in playgrounds may be only cosmetic. Thus, research studies have been designed to look at desirable features. Desirable features include equipment that can be rearranged and linked into different patterns; encapsulated spaces; multifunctional play structures; equipment for dramatic play; loose parts; action-oriented equipment, especially swings (for primary-level children); wheeled toys (especially for kindergartners); moderately structured, as opposed to highly structured, materials to allow for creativity; equipment that accommodates diverse skill and ability levels; and places for solitary, parallel, and group play (Hartle & Johnson, 1993). Similarly, J. E. Johnson, Christie, and Yawkey (1987) found that two playground design features associated with high levels of play are flexible materials (materials that children can manipulate, change, and combine) and materials providing a wide variety of experiences. Interestingly, children preferred the inexpensive play environments to the more expensive varieties (Frost, 1992a).

d. Playgrounds must meet the needs of children with disabilities, as discussed later in this chapter.

4. Outdoor space should be aesthetically pleasing and appeal to all the senses. Talbot and Frost (1989) proposed some design qualities (e.g., sensuality, brilliance, "placeness," and juxtaposition of opposites) that should be considered in designing playscapes that address the child's sense of wonder and awareness. Many nature-related elements can be incorporated into a basic playground to make it aesthetically pleasing (Wilson, Kilmer, & Knauerhase, 1996).

Specifications for the outdoor space should be sufficiently flexible to meet local needs and requirements. Other considerations include location, size, enclosure, terrain, surface, shelter, and storage.

Location. Outdoor activity areas should not surround the building because supervision would be almost impossible. The area is best located on the south side of the building, which will have sun and light throughout the day. The outdoor space should be easily accessible from the indoor area.

To minimize the chance of accidents as children go in and out, a facility should have (a) a door threshold flush with the indoor/outdoor surfaces, or a ramp if an abrupt change in surface levels is present; (b) adjoining surfaces covered with material that provides maximum traction; (c) a sliding door or a door prop; and (d) a small Plexiglas panel in the door to prevent collisions.

Indoor rest rooms and cubbies should be adjacent to the outdoor area. If this arrangement is impossible, one rest room should open off the playground. The sometimes difficult problem of managing clothing makes speedy access to a rest room important. A drinking fountain should also be easily accessible to children during outdoor play.

Size. Most licensing regulations require a minimum of 75 sq ft per child for outdoor activity areas. The amount of space varies according to the age of the children, with infants and toddlers requiring less space than older children. The NAEYC (1998a) stated that 75 sq ft per child is the minimum, but the calculation can be based on the maximum number of children who will be using the space at one time. (This necessitates scheduling outdoor time for all children in the program, which is not the way to put children's needs first.) A. Olds (2001) recommended between 100 and 200 sq ft per child. A minimum of 15 sq ft per child should be added for a sheltered area or terrace. Approximately 33% of the square footage of the outdoor area should be used for passive outdoor play, as in a sandpit or outdoor art center, and the remainder for active outdoor play, such as climbing and running. The type of playground can affect size, too; adventure or junk playgrounds may be ½ to 2½ acres in size.

Enclosure. Enclosure of the outdoor area relieves teachers of a heavy burden of responsibility, gives children a sense of freedom without worry, and prevents the intrusion of stray animals. Non-climbable barriers 4 to 6 ft high are adequate as boundaries that adjoin dangerous areas (parking lots, streets, ponds), but minimal barriers such as large stones or shrubbery are adequate in areas where the outdoors has no potential dangers. Besides safety, consider what children will hear and see on the other side of the "fence" in choosing enclosures. Beauty may be enhanced by flowers or plants along the "fence" line.

In addition to having an entry from the building, the outdoor area should have a gate opening wide enough to permit trucks to deliver sand or large items of play equipment. If children are allowed to use the outdoor area for after-program hours, a small gate should be installed and benches placed on the periphery to give adults a place to relax while watching and supervising.

Terrain.   Flat terrain with hard surfacing is dangerous because it provides no curb for random movement. A gentle rolling terrain has several advantages. Mounds are ideal for active games of leaping and running and are a natural shelter for such passive games as sand or water play. Mounds can be used in conjunction with equipment; for example, slides without ladders can be mounted on a slope so that children can climb the mound and slide down the slide. Ladders and boards can connect the mounds. Tricycle paths can wind on a rolling terrain. Hills should be relatively small (no more than 3 ft measured vertically, with no more than a 10° slope) and located at the back or the side of the play area.

Surface.   Surfaces for infants and toddlers should be mainly grass, wood, sand, and dirt. Outdoor activity areas for older children should also have a variety of surfaces and be well drained, with the fastest drying areas nearest the building. Low areas should be filled in with topsoil; however, if permanent equipment is placed over these areas, feet will recreate the basin. Approximately 50% to 67% of the total square footage should be covered with grass, and about 1,000 sq ft should be covered in hard surfaces for activities such as wheeled-toy riding and block building. Some areas should be left as dirt for

gardening and for realizing "a satisfaction common to every child—digging a big hole!" (Baker, 1968, p. 61). Areas underneath equipment need special resilient materials (as discussed in "Safety" under "Other Considerations").

Shelter.   The building, trees and shrubs, or a rolling terrain should protect children from excessive sun and wind. Knowledge of snow patterns and prevailing winds may lead to the use of snow fences or other structures to provide snowy hills and valleys. A covered play area, such as a verandah, should be planned as an extension of the indoor area. The shelter's purpose is for passive play during good weather and for all play during inclement weather. A covered shelter should be designed to permit a maximum amount of air and sunshine but may have blinds for light or weather protection; seating, even cushions, needs to be provided.

Storage.   Outdoor storage can be attached to the main building, perhaps next to a terrace where the storage can provide shelter. If detached from the building, outdoor storage should be of a design and material to fit and not detract from the main building. If a separate building is used, the outdoor storage should serve as a windbreak to the outdoor activity area. A single storage unit 12 ft long, 10 ft wide, and 7 to 8 ft high is sufficient for most early childhood programs. The doorway should be 6 ft wide and should be a tilt- or roll-a-door garage type of door. Hooks or pegs for hanging can be installed 4½ ft above the floor along one side of the storage shed, and shelves for storing equipment in daily use can be built 2 or 3 ft above the floor along the back of the shed. A high shelf can be used for storing seasonal items or items for staff use. Outdoor storage areas should have slightly raised flooring to prevent flooding after a substantial rainfall. A ramp facilitates moving equipment into and out of the storage shed and minimizes tripping over different levels. This type of storage unit can also serve as a prop for dramatic play.

Smaller storage areas located near certain centers, such as sand, block building, and dramatic play, are preferable for some materials. These storage areas are usually closed/locked storage cabinet structures, at child height, made of materials that can withstand moisture (e.g., cedar), and mounted to a concrete surface for stability and to prevent flooding.

Outdoor Space Arrangement

The outdoor space needs to be appropriate for the local program goals for each age group. The indoor space should be extended outdoors, and the outdoor space should be extended indoors. Outside areas should also reflect the local community; for example, Rivkin (1995) described how playgrounds in different neighborhoods model the communities' existing social life (pp. 36–40).

Before planning an outdoor space, talk with staff members, family members, and older children and see what they would like to do outside, visit other playgrounds, and analyze the current area. In planning or redesigning outside areas, evaluation tools are also most helpful (DeBord, Hestenes, Moore, Cosco, & McGinnis, 2002; Dempsey, Strickland, & Frost, 1993).

Outdoor Space Arrangements for Infants and Toddlers. Many people think of playgrounds as areas for rough-and-tumble play. Thus, when one says an "infant and toddler playground," it almost sounds oxymoronic. Infants and toddlers need fresh air and sunlight, however, and they delight in exploring their outside environment. Perhaps it would seem less strange to call the planned outdoor environment an *outdoor place* or *park* complete with benches for adult sitting and supervision and for holding infants and toddlers.

Although general specifications for outdoor space have already been discussed, four criteria are extremely important in planning an outdoor place for the infant and toddler. First, the area must be scaled to the size of these very young

children to be safe, comfortable, and rich for exploring. Second, it must be safe—that is, it should provide a gentle terrain for crawling, walking, running, and stepping up and down; have no high play structures; be free of materials that would be harmful if eaten (e.g., no gravel, only sand protected from animals, plant life safe in all stages of growth; American Academy of Pediatrics, American Public Health Association, & National Resource Center for Health and Safety in Child Care, 2002; R. Moore, 1993); and be free of foreign objects. Third, the outdoor place must meet the sensory motor explorations of the very young. Differences in hardness, textures, light, and temperatures (sun and shade) are needed, as well as contrasts in colors, in open and breezy areas and encapsulated and still areas, and in high areas and low areas. Fourth, infants and toddlers need loose materials for play.

Noncrawling Infant Space. For noncrawling infants, an enclosed area should have a surface that encourages reaching, grasping, and kicking. These infants also enjoy baby sit-up swings and swinging cradles. The area should stimulate visual and auditory senses with colorful streamers, soft wind chimes, prisms and mirrors, and natural sounds (e. g., breeze in the trees, birdsongs). A stroller path would also be appropriate.

Older Infant and Toddler Space. According to Frost (1992a), four design principles should be used in planning a play environment for older infants and toddlers: (a) Allow for a wide range of child-initiated movement via pathways, hills, ramps, and tunnels; (b) stimulate the senses; (c) provide for novelty, variety, and challenge; and (d) make the area safe and comfortable. Wortham and Wortham (1992) thought of three cells of possibilities in the design of infant and toddler playgrounds: (a) structures that lead to specific types of play, such as a slide; (b) natural environment experiences, such as examining living things and weather; and (c) areas for open-ended activities that promote creativity, such as sand and water areas, and that use construction types of toys and dramatic play props.

Older infants and toddlers either ignore or do not comprehend the function of separate play centers; thus, they will attempt to push a trike up a climber or pour sand on a crawling baby. A creative use of barriers will restrict children to developmentally appropriate, and thus safe, areas by requiring certain skills in order to reach an area and will serve to help keep certain activities within a play zone. For example, two or three steps can lead to a 15-in.-high platform, half-buried tires can form minitunnels around the sand area, a small gate can lead to the garden, and shrubs can curb the push/pull toy path.

Crawling and walking pathways in an infant and toddler outdoor place not only assist traffic flow but also can serve as a means for exploring. The surfaces of these paths should be a mosaic—changing from dirt to grass with "cobblestones" of slatted plank squares, patterned rocks, colored bricks, and half logs buried along the way. Raised (15 in. maximum) walkways with railings are also exciting.

Various structures are effective in an infant and toddler outdoor place, such as the following:

Block-building areas

Dirt-digging areas

Elevated trough with moving water

Garden

Logs or low, anchored benches to straddle or climb over

Minitunnels (half-buried tires) and longer tunnels to crawl through

Mirror wall (vertical, unbreakable mirror)

Objects that react with movement and sound to wind or touch, such as colorful banners, bells, canopies, tree branches, wind chimes, and pans for hitting

Pathways for push/pull and ride-on toys

Pet hutches

Platforms (14- or 15-in. maximum height with ramps that have boarded sides or handrailings; floor of platform has a safety surface; paneled sides of the platform have (a) shape holes (e.g., squares, circles, octagons) large enough to stick one's head and shoulders through to "survey one's world" or a bubble panel (a clear, plastic concave panel), (b) pull-up bars, and (c) activity panels

Roofs for playhouses

Sand areas—the favorite material

Set-in-the-ground ladders

Slides inset into the slope of a hill

Swings with baby seats, porch swings, and swinging platforms for looking at the "moving ground" or the clouds

Wobbly structures, such as a board with springs or a low swinging bridge

The safe, natural environment—trees, shrubs, flowers, pine cones, and tree stumps—should be left undisturbed. As much as possible, play areas for older infants and toddlers need to integrate sensory, exploratory, and action-oriented devices. For example, a structure can have panels to look at and feel, objects to manipulate (e.g., pulleys, drums, steering wheels), and structures that promote action (e.g., climbers and slides).

Figure 5–18 is a plan for an infant and toddler outdoor place. It illustrates some of the principles discussed.

Outdoor Areas for Older Children. Older children need playgrounds that fit their developing motor skills, their advancing cognitive skills, and their growing peer interactions. They need a smooth transition in playgrounds from infancy to preschool. For example, preschoolers still need structures that integrate sensory, exploratory, and action-oriented activities, but the structures should be more complex than those seen on toddler playgrounds. Like toddlers, preschoolers

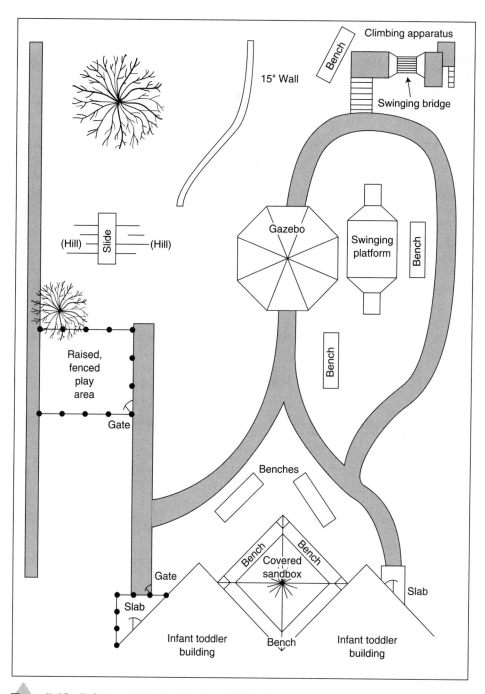

Figure 5–18   Infant and Toddler Outdoor Activity Area

need dramatic play materials, but their props need to encourage more advanced symbolism and more cooperative play than do props for toddlers. Likewise, a smooth transition in playground design must occur in programs serving preschool and primary-level children. Primary-level children need more open grassy areas, more gymnastic types of apparatuses, and more pretend toys than do preschool children (Frost, 1992a).

Play Experiences and Zones. Outdoor play needs to meet the holistic developmental needs of children. For challenging older children's total development, J. E. Johnson, Christie, and Yawkey (1987) listed four types of play experiences: (a) functional play or exercise that involves practice and repetition of gross-motor activities, (b) constructive play that involves using such materials as paints or sand to create, (c) dramatic play or pretend play that is often conducted in enclosed places, and (d) group play or play that involves more than one child (e.g., seesaws, rule games, often dramatic play).

Like indoor activity rooms, playgrounds are designed on a zonal or center basis. Esbenstein (1987) suggested the following seven areas: (a) transition, (b) manipulative/creative, (c) projective/fantasy, (d) focal/social, (e) social/dramatic, (f) physical, and (g) natural element. The five play zones given by Guddemi and Eriksen (1992) are (a) a nature zone with plants, animals, and rocks housed in an active or quiet area; (b) an adventure zone for construction and digging that requires close and continuous adult supervision and is fenced in (because it is unsightly); (c) an active play zone for chase and ball games on open grassy areas for preschoolers and on both grassy and hard-surface areas for primary-level children, for sand/water play, and for play on play structures; (d) a quiet learning zone with easels, water/sand tables, a book area, and a snack area; and (e) a quiet play zone for dramatic play. Centers can also integrate more than one type of play. Henniger (1993) suggested that outdoor centers should duplicate indoor en-

vironments, but Jensen and Bullard (2002) called for centers housed outdoors to be uniquely different from those inside.

General Criteria for Arranging Zones. Although some consider the indoor environment to be more or less an extension of the outdoors, outdoor centers are different from indoor centers. Outdoor centers are often less structured; the divisions between centers are less clear (e.g., a "car wash" involves water play, dramatic play, and push/pull and riding toys); centers may be located in several areas (e.g., dramatic play may be in a playhouse under a play structure, in tents under the trees, or in the garden); children have more freedom to move; there are fewer restrictions on the number of children allowed per center; and more seasonal changes are obvious in outdoor centers (e.g., water play in warm weather) than in indoor centers (Vaughn, 1990).

Because the outdoor space is an extension of the indoor area in some way, areas must be provided for **active** and **passive play.** (No clear-cut distinction is made between the two types of play. Large-muscle play is usually active, but walking on a balance beam may be passive; water play is usually passive, but running from a squirting hose is active.) Active and passive play areas must be separated, and space must be left around each activity area for safety reasons (as discussed in the subsection "Safety" under "Other Considerations"). Active play areas require more space because of the vigorous, whole-body movement. In passive play, children need protection from excessive wind or heat and from other fast-moving children. Passive play areas should be enclosed and protected from more active play areas. Enclosure may be accomplished with shrubbery or large stones, with small openings between these areas, by changing the terrain, or by providing a sheltered area. Additional protection may be obtained by building a slightly winding path or by separating the two types of play areas. Often, a great deal of physical inactivity occurs in outdoor areas; thus, children need places to cluster and sit. Boulders or logs are perhaps more enjoyable than park or picnic benches.

Compatible zones, such as social and creative, should be located near each other. The natural topography often determines the best zone use; for example, a slopping area is good for running and sledding.

Children need pathways to minimize conflict and prevent accidents (e.g., getting too close to swings). Pathways should lead to places of interest (e.g., a garden) and should connect play zones and even equipment within a zone. Pathways can be made interesting by using curves and intersections, by including bridges, by having doors and gates to open and close, by varying the composition of the path (e.g., stepping stones, mosaics of pavers or pretty rocks, timber rounds), and by including special things along the path (e.g., flowers, a butterfly or ladybug house, a wind chime, and weather station), and by including places to sit.

Specific Zones and Equipment. In the outdoor area, five play spaces per child is recommended. Each zone must be carefully planned. The following suggestions should be considered in planning these play zones:

1. **Open area.** The open area needs to be large for playing with balls, Frisbees, and hula hoops, as well as for just running.

2. **Road for vehicles.** A hard-surfaced area can form a tricycle, wagon, or doll buggy road extending through the outdoor space and returning to its starting point. The road should be wide enough to permit passing. A curving road is more interesting, and right-angle turns should be avoided because they cause accidents. Like pathways, the road should have some challenges (e.g., a slight rise) and be aesthetically attractive (e.g., flowers and plants along the side, archways to ride through).

3. **Sandpit.** Berry (1993) noted that sand play was the most popular outside play activity of preschool children. A sandpit can be a large

mound or a narrow, winding river of sand. Children should have flat working surfaces, such as wooden boards or flat boulders, beside or in the sand. An outdoor sandpit should have a boundary element that "should provide a 'sense' of enclosure for the playing children, keep out unwanted traffic, protect the area against water draining from adjacent areas, and help keep the sand within the sand play areas" (Osmon, 1971, p. 77). Boundaries can be built or created by a rolling terrain. The sandpit should be partially shaded but with exposure to the purifying and drying rays of the sun. Water should be available through a "vandal-proof" tap (i.e., a tap in which water cannot be turned on or off when the tap is removed). Shade cloth held down by heavy objects can be used to protect the sandpit from animal use. (The sand that packs the best has granules of different sizes; do not use crushed stone.)

4. **Water areas.** Outdoor water play activities should allow for more energetic play than indoor water activities. Water places can include birdbaths, fountains, elevated streams, water tables, sprinklers, and splash and wading pools. Concrete wading pools must have slip-proof walking surfaces and a water depth of 6 in. Water temperature should be between 60°F and 80°F (16°C and 27°C). In colder weather, a drained wading pool makes an excellent flat, hard surface for passive play. For programs on a meager budget, an inflatable pool can be used, and a garden hose with a spray nozzle or water sprinkler attached can serve as a water spray.

5. **Gardens.** Gardens can have almost any kind of living plant life—flowers, herbs, vines, shrubs, trees, and even weeds! An outdoor garden should be fenced to protect it from animals or from being accidentally trampled. The garden should be narrow, perhaps 2 ft wide, to minimize the need for the child gardener to step into the garden (especially important when the plot is muddy). A narrow garden can take on an aesthetically pleasing shape as it parallels straight fences or encircles large trees. Raised garden beds allow children in wheelchairs to participate.

6. **Play structures.** Complex play structures, discussed in detail by Vergeront (1988), have almost totally replaced the separate, large-muscle pieces of equipment (e.g., climbing frame, slides, gliders) seen on traditional playgrounds. Children use these structures not only for developing gross-motor skills but also for engaging in dramatic play.

Figure 5–19, a plan for an outdoor activity area for older children, illustrates some of the principles discussed and is only one example of an outdoor area. For more open space for primary-level children or SACC programs, the dirt mound and the sandpit could be designed as "rivers." If the storage unit were relocated, much more open space would be available.

Equipment and materials must be carefully planned for the outdoor area. Some items include the following:

Art materials

Assorted toys for open area play (e.g., balls, hoops)

Construction materials (e.g., blocks, woodworking equipment)

Dramatic play props (see Odoy & Foster, 1997)

Musical game recordings

Nature materials (e.g., animals, binoculars, cages for animals, feeders, gardening bulbs, plants, seeds and tools, magnifying lenses, weather instruments; see McGinnis, 2002; Wilson, Kilmer, & Knauerhase, 1996)

Play structures (for criteria, see Vergeront, 1988)

Sand/water toys

Wheeled toys

THE EARLY CHILDHOOD FACILITY

As part of planning the early childhood facility, assessing the site size is highly important. The site must house the building, the outdoor play space, paths and parking spaces, and additional "green areas." A. Olds (2001) recommended 325 sq ft to 574 sq ft per child for the site.

For large centers the needed site size can seem formidable to young children and can be tiring for adults. Large centers may need to use a cluster or campus plan with multiple entrances and exits (and nearby parking spaces). The buildings should be linked. Most sites, however, are too small to meet program goals, to house children for long hours, or to grow.

Figure 5-20 illustrates one possible arrangement of the children's activity room, the outdoor activity area, and the other children's and adults' areas of an early childhood facility. The figure is not intended as a model layout but is presented to graphically depict some of the ideas discussed in this chapter.

OTHER CONSIDERATIONS

Designing the indoor and outdoor space and selecting equipment is only one aspect of the planning process. Early childhood administrators must always be mindful of whether their facility meets safety standards and accommodates the needs of children and adults with disabilities. Early childhood administrators should make wise decisions in purchasing and caring for equipment and materials and in securing insurance coverage for the facility and its contents.

Safety

The safety of children, staff, parents, and others is of maximum importance. A safe environment encourages children to work and play without heavy restrictions that wear on both children and adults and that prevent maximum program benefit. The outdoor play area is the most hazardous area in most facilities. Problems come from many sources.

Regulations. Regulations for outdoor areas lag behind those for indoor areas (Runyan, Gray, Kotch, & Kreuter, 1991; F. Wallach & Afthinos, 1990). Public school outdoor play areas are

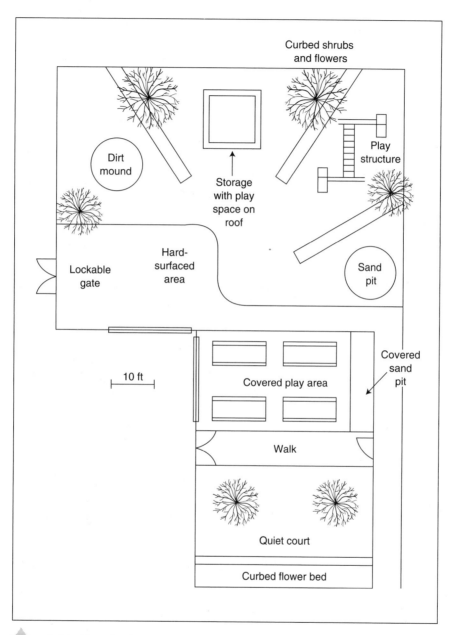

Figure 5–19   Preschool, Kindergarten, and Primary-Level Outdoor Activity Area

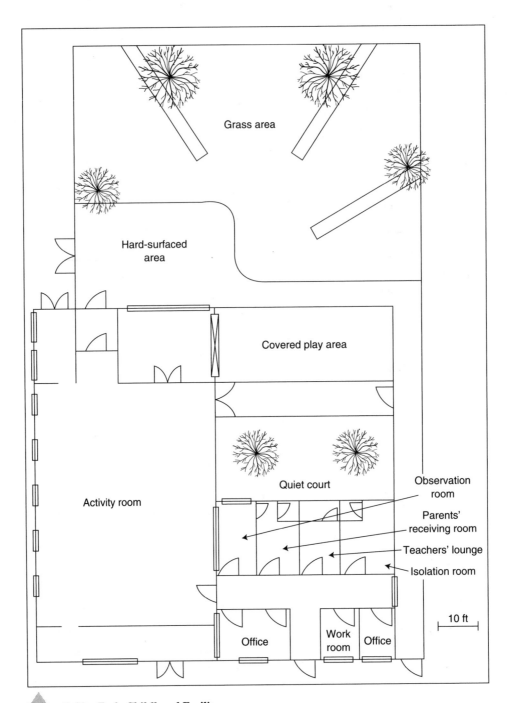

Figure 5–20   Early Childhood Facility

virtually unregulated (F. Wallach & Edelstein, 1991). Regulations are not always consistent either.

Supervision.   Teachers need to be aware of the potential seriousness of playground injuries. The U.S. Congress, Office of Technology Assessment (1995) reported that each year approximately 200,000 preschool- and elementary-age children receive emergency care from injuries that occurred on playground equipment. Of these, about 36% are severe. For children under age 5, injuries to the head and face account for nearly 60% of all injuries. For children ages 5 and older, injuries to the arms and hands account for 43% of all injuries. Of the 9 to 17 children who die each year, strangulation accounts for 47% and falls for 31%. Playground equipment most associated with injuries are swings, climbers, and slides. Head injuries are primarily the result of falls, and strangulation and asphyxiation result from loose items of clothing (e.g., hoods on coats, cords, and frayed materials), improperly used equipment (e.g., ropes, hoops), or equipment that entraps (spaces between 3½ and 9 in.). For more information on playground hazards, see the National Playground Safety Institute's compilation of injuries (www.nrpa.org/playsafe/dirtyd~1.htm).

Adequate supervision requires the following:

1. Teachers need training in playground safety. Although some center sites have developed playground safety programs, these programs rarely exist, even in public schools. The National Program for Playground Safety is offering a *Safe Playground Supervision Kit*, which includes a video on the importance of supervision, an instruction guide, and a first aid pack (see www.PlaygroundSupervision.org).

2. Adequate supervision also requires that teachers be able to see the entire play area. Playground arrangement, especially of storage units, fences, shrubs and trees, and large play structures, must not block vision. Passive play zones must not be hidden between two active play zones.

3. Playground supervision requires the same adult–child ratio as do indoor activities, and even more adult help is preferred. Although teachers need breaks, outdoor playtime is highly inappropriate as a break time or even an adult visitation time. Beyond the safety concern, outdoor areas are learning areas too; in quality programs, teachers are interacting with children, including teaching them safe play practices.

Separating Play Areas.   Play areas must be separated for safety reasons. The space around each piece of equipment must be equal to the child's potential action outward or the maximum distance children can jump, slide, or swing forward from any position on the equipment. Children also need space to bypass a piece of equipment. Paths should be 3 to 5 ft wide, adjoin safety areas, and be slightly curving. If paths are too curvy, children tend to cut through one play area to reach another play area, and supervising staff may not be able to adequately supervise all play areas.

Equipment Hazards.   Safety includes proper design for the age of the children and for children with disabilities, proper spacing and installation, and adequate maintenance of equipment. Equipment must also be of high-grade construction, nontoxic, and appropriate for climate conditions. A complete discussion of safe equipment is beyond the scope of this book, but a few recommendations are given in Table 5–4 for the more potentially dangerous pieces of equipment. A listing at the end of this section also provides sources for further information. The American Society for Testing and Materials (1999) provides national safety standards for equipment for children ages 2 through 12.

Surfacing Under Fall Zones.   A major safety problem is hard-packed surfaces under and around outdoor equipment. Changes in types of surfac-

Table 5–4   Safety Specifications for Selected Playground Equipment

Swings

Tire or shrub barrier around swings

24″ between swings; 36″ between swings and
    support posts; greater distance for tire swings

Swing seats fitted to child and lightweight
    (e.g., canvas)

Infant swings with safety straps and special swing
    seats, exergliders, and wheelchair swings for
    children with disabilities

No animal types of swings

S-hooks completely closed

8″ to 10″ soil underneath

Slides

Slope—no more than 30°

Side height—minimum of 2.5″, safest at 7.5″

Platform deck—10″ wide at top

Exit surfaces—16″ long, parallel to ground, exit
height of 8″ to 12″, 24″ of loose soil underneath

Climbing equipment

Maximum height 24″ (toddler) to 54″ (primary level)

Vertical barriers 30″ to 38″ high on walkways
    and decks that are over 30″ high

Access to decks and climbers (use all three)—
(a) ladders with rungs at 75° to 90° angles;
(b) ladder steps with rungs at 50° to 75° angles;
(c) stairway with steps at 35° angles or less

Protective caps over bolts

4″ to 6″ of loose soil underneath for 24″ stuctures,
    and 12″ of loose soil underneath for 54″ structures

ing should be level to prevent children from tripping. Special surfacing is needed under any equipment from which a child might fall. When a child falls, either the surface gives to absorb the impact or the child gives with a resulting bruise, broken bone, spinal injury, head injury, or even death. The following are three types of surfaces, each with its disadvantages, used under equipment:

1. **Organic loose material** (e.g., pine bark, mulch) maintained at a depth of 6 to 12 in. Organic materials must be kept fluffed up and at the maximum depth to be effective. However, the material scatters and decomposes.

2. **Inorganic loose material** (e.g., sand, pea gravel, shredded tires) maintained at a depth of 6 to 12 in. Animals may use sand as a litter box, and sand loses its resiliency in wet, freezing weather. Gravel is hard to walk on, and shredded tires stick to clothing. Pea gravel surfaces are unsuitable for children under 5 years of age and dangerous for children under 3 years of age because pea gravel gets into small children's eyes, ears, and noses.

3. **Compact materials** (e.g., rubber and foam mats). These materials require a flat surface and professional installation. They are costly and are also subject to vandalism.

A 6-ft zone with a protective surface in all directions as well as underneath stable equipment and a 7-ft zone with a protective surface around and under equipment with moving parts, such as swings (Vergeront, 1988), should be provided. Guidelines on surfacing safety are published by the U.S. Consumer Product Safety Commission (1997).

Other Safety Considerations.   Safety can be provided by doing the following:

1. **Fencing the play area** (4 ft high around most hazards and 6 ft high around water hazards) **and making all electric equipment inaccessible to children.** One third of family child care homes had no enclosure around the outside play area (Wasserman, Dameron, Brozicevic, &

Aronson, 1989). Electrical equipment (boxes, transformers, outlets, connections for underground utilities, heat pumps and air conditioners) must be located outside the outdoor playground.

2. **Providing physical supports** such as Plexiglas or wood panels on platforms, decks, and walkways *and* **color-coding complex features** (e.g., rungs of ladders that require spatial judgments).

3. **Removing toys and playing children from obstructing landing or fall zones around equipment.**

4. **Keeping sandboxes covered and following Aronson's (1993) cleaning and disinfecting procedures.**

5. **Correcting and removing all hazards.** (*Hazards* are accident-causing problems that a child cannot identify or cannot evaluate the seriousness of. *Risks* are challenges that are not "hidden" and can be evaluated by the child. Children develop because of managed risks but suffer most of their injuries because of hazards!) Resilient fall-zone surfacing must be maintained. Protrusions and sharp edges must be repaired. Broken or rusting equipment or equipment with potential pinch or crush areas must be removed. Frost (1992b) recommended a thorough inspection weekly. He suggested using a checklist, making repairs immediately, and documenting inspections and repairs.

6. **Avoiding toxic vegetation.** Check with local botanical garden personnel or landscape architect or call the local poison control center to avoid placing toxic plants in children's play spaces (see R. Moore, 1993).

7. **Following safety regulations and recommendations published by the following organizations:**

American Society for Testing and Materials (ASTM) www.astm.org

National Program for Playground Safety (NPPS) www.uni.edu/playground

U.S. Access Board www.access-board.gov

U.S. Consumer Product Safety Commission (CPSC) www.cpsc.gov

Planning Facilities for Accommodating Special Needs

The need for early childhood programs to accommodate children and adults with special needs comes from a body of literature supporting the benefits of inclusive settings and from legal mandates. Many questions arise concerning what are "reasonable steps" (as required by the ADA) and whether all disabilities must be addressed in a given program.

The indoor and outdoor facilities and the various areas within the facility (e.g., learning centers and play zones, rest rooms, eating areas) must be accessible for all children and adults. Accessibility is often achieved by more open space; doors and paths that accommodate wheelchairs; ramps with appropriate slopes; grab bars and handrails; raised tables with wheelchair indentions; and lower shelves, water fountains, and doorknobs. Accessibility to facilities is a priority because without accessibility, inclusion cannot occur and because students with physical disabilities are the fastest growing population of children receiving services (T. Caldwell, Sirvis, Todaro, & Accouloumre, 1991).

Housing and equipment must also allow those with disabilities to safely take part in activities and to make choices from the range of activities provided for those without disabilities. Fully integrating the program is much more difficult than merely providing basic accessibility. Furthermore, integrated outdoor environments are more difficult to achieve than integrated indoor environments (Aronson, 1991). Permanent structures, most of which are located outdoors, require the most expensive adaptations; however, these adaptations are being incorporated into the designs for lofts and small play structures used indoors and in play structures and other equipment used outdoors. Loose materials are easy and appropriate ways to provide a more integrated setting, but these materials are mainly used in indoor activities and are only recently being incorporated into quality, creative playgrounds.

Specific environmental design features for integrated settings are beyond the scope of this book. The following sources provide most of the basics for planning:

Barbour, A. (1999). The impact of playground design on the play behaviors of children with differing levels of physical competence. *Early Childhood Research Quarterly, 11,* 75–98.

Eichinger, J., & Woltman, S. (1993). Integration strategies for learners with severe multiple disabilities. *Teaching Exceptional Children, 26*(1), 18–21.

File, N., & Kontos, S. (1993). The relationship of program quality to children's play in integrated early intervention settings. *Topics in Early Childhood Special Education, 13*(1), 1–18.

Flynn, L. L., & Kieff, J. (2002). Including everyone in outdoor play. *Young Children, 57*(3), 20–26.

Goltsman, S. M., Gilbert, T. A., & Wohford, S. D. (1993). *The accessibility checklist: An evaluation system for buildings and outdoor settings. User's guide* (2nd ed.). Berkeley, CA: MIG Communication.

Ross, H. W. (1992). Integrating infants with disabilities. Can "ordinary" caregivers do it? *Young Children, 47*(3), 65–71.

Theemes, T. (1999). *Let's go outside! Designing the early childhood playground* (Appendix B, pp. 89–93). Ypsilanti, MI: High/Scope Press.

Wolery, M. (1994). Designing inclusive environments for children with special needs. In M. Wolery & J. S. Wilbers (Eds.), *Including children with special needs in early childhood programs* (pp. 97–118). Washington, DC: National Association for the Education of Young Children.

These websites are helpful, too:

www.access-board.gov/play/guide/intro.htm

www.indiana.edu/%7enca/playground/play/htm

www.boundlessplaygrounds.org

Purchasing Equipment and Materials

The purchasing of equipment and materials is of immeasurable significance. To facilitate the program, items must meet the needs of the program and be in sufficient quantities for the activities planned. Moreover, careful purchasing of equipment and materials helps to ensure the selection of quality items that last longer. Careful planning for purchases also eliminates costly returns. (Companies may charge up to 30% of the cost of the items returned as well as shipping costs.) In today's inflationary world, careful planning is essential if items are to be secured within budgetary limitations. Fortunately, many purchases can be made over time. Major purchases are made with start-up monies and at the beginning of each budget year. Supplementary purchases can be made throughout the year. Monies must be laid aside for purchases of replacement items and for different materials and equipment should program goals change.

Purchasing Guidelines. Many considerations must be given to purchasing equipment and materials. The following suggestions are only minimal guidelines:

1. The buyer should purchase equipment and materials that will facilitate program goals. For example, programs following the D-I models and the Montessori model will use materials that are task-directed, autotelic (self-rewarding), and self-correcting in the skill areas of reading readiness and mathematics (refer also to Tables 2–3 and 2–6). Conversely, the holistic/developmental models use materials that encourage creativity, experimentation, and peer social interaction. For example, these less-teacher-directed approaches use more raw or primitive materials (any materials that do not duplicate reality—e.g., a lump of clay, a scrap of cloth, a bead). Children with varying degrees of competence and differing

interests can work with such materials. Raw materials also permit children to use various symbols to stand for real objects (refer also to Tables 2–2, 2–4, 2-5, and 2–7). Materials must meet the needs of children with disabilities and be usable to teach multicultural, nonsexist concepts. These items include dolls and hand puppets with a range of skin tones or characteristic features and books, puzzles, and pictures depicting various ethnic and racial groups and nontraditional sex-role behaviors. The buyer should consider equipment and materials that can be used in a variety of situations, that reflect individual differences, and that need to be stored infrequently. Finally, as long as program goals are being met, teacher preferences should be considered.

2. The buyer should check on the amount of money available and the procedures for purchasing. Material and equipment needs are determined by the director in small programs or through staff input in larger programs. Needs should be determined before developing a budget. Once the budget is written by the program director (in small programs) or by the executive director and approved by the board (in large corporate programs and in public school or federally funded programs), purchasing can begin. Restrictions are placed on the purchasing authorizations in large and tax-supported programs. For example, specifications may have to be prepared to determine whether bidding will be used. In cases in which purchases do not involve substantial amounts or in cases with no prospect of competition in the bidding, purchases are negotiated. Small centers in close geographic proximity should consider purchasing as a group to obtain better prices and reduced shipping costs.

3. The buyer should keep a perpetual inventory and a list of items needed. The inventory record is an essential aspect of the purchasing procedure. The **inventory** is a record of the quantity of materials purchased and of the location of items; it becomes the basis for preventing duplication, determining what equipment and materials

need to be replaced, deciding insurance needs, calculating loss or theft of items, and assisting in budget planning with yearly readjustments. The inventory should be kept on a computer disk with a backup disk kept in another building. This record should list and identify all equipment and materials that have been purchased and delivered with the date of acquisition. For nonconsumable items, the inventory record should provide the current cost of replacement (often more than the initial cost) and the maintenance provided. Inventoried equipment should be marked with the name of the program and an inventory number. In multiclass programs, the number of the room in which the equipment belongs should also be placed on the item.

4. The buyer should be economical by negotiating prices or requesting bids. In comparing costs, the bottom line is total delivered costs. Differences in prices may be offset by freight charges. Service is as important as low prices. The buyer should also be economical by determining whether the item can be adapted from a previously purchased item or made by the staff and whether a nonconsumable, expensive item can be shared.

5. The buyer should not overbuy consumable items. As a general rule, consumables are more susceptible to deterioration than are permanent pieces of equipment and materials.

6. A buyer should purchase only from reputable companies (see appendix 6).

7. The buyer should consider building space for using and storing equipment and any additional building specifications for use of any item (e.g., electrical outlet, water source).

8. The buyer should select only safe, durable, relatively maintenance free, and aesthetically pleasing equipment and materials.

Purchasing Kits and Sets. The available kits and sets of early learning materials cover a range of skills and embody the contents of various curricular areas. Kits and sets differ from singly packaged items in several ways: (a) The materials are collected and arranged to provide for a range of individual and group activities; (b) various learning methods are employed while working with materials (listening to recordings of stories; manipulating objects; viewing books, pictures, and filmstrips; and talking); (c) a manual or teacher's guide provides guidance in using the kit; (d) materials of the kit or set are sold as a unit, although components may be sold separately; (e) kits are rather expensive; and (f) the materials are encased in a drawer, cabinet, or luggage type of storage container. Some kits are published with staff training materials, supplementary materials for children's activities, and assessment materials.

As is true of all instructional materials, the user should carefully evaluate kits or sets. Before purchasing a kit or set, a person should ask the following questions:

1. Do *all* the materials match the goals of the program and the developmental level of children both in content and in format?

2. How does having the kit benefit teachers (e.g., Does it save time in collecting or making materials? Do teachers need the kit or set as a guide in presenting concepts or skills?)?

3. What is the total cost (e.g., Can several teachers in the program use the same kit or set with their groups of children? Are special services such as training of staff and installation and maintenance needed, and are they covered in the cost? What is the cost of replacement or consumable parts? Is other equipment, such as audiovisual equipment, needed for using the kit or set? What is the cost of shipping?)?

4. Are the materials and storage case durable, easily maintained, and safe?

5. How much space is needed to use and store the kit or set?

Purchasing Children's Books. Children's books are used extensively in most early childhood programs. Selection of books is important for two reasons: (a) Because of the varying quality of published books, children can have a steady diet of poor to mediocre books, and (b) books should enhance the specific goals of the local early childhood program. Books are usually selected by using one or more of the following criteria:

1. Like all curriculum activities, the book "promotes the development of knowledge and understanding, processes and skills, as well as dispositions to use and apply skills and to go on learning" (Bredekamp & Copple, 1997, p. 20). For example:

a. The book has a theme considered interesting to most young children (e. g., nature, machines, holidays).

b. The book has a theme that can help young children overcome some general concerns (e.g., common fears, making friends, cooperative play) or can help specific children cope with their particular problems (e.g., divorce, working mothers, minority group membership, a disability, mobility). Using books to meet children's social and emotional needs is referred to as **bibliotherapy.**

c. The book has a theme that correlates with a thematic unit or project. Books to extend and enrich almost every concept are available.

d. The book has a theme that can teach a value (e.g., sharing, fair play).

e. The book promotes rather specific literacy skills (e.g., predictable outcome, rhyming words, alliteration).

f. The book has good possibilities for follow-up activities (e.g., dramatic play, artwork, story writing).

2. The book is considered high-quality literature (i.e., received awards, such as the Caldecott Award). Early childhood educators may use several sources in finding titles of quality books, as given in appendix 6.

Purchasing Computer Hardware and Software. In providing microcomputer technology for both administrative and curricular use, careful purchasing is important. The potential of computer technology for use in educational settings is increasing. Furthermore, from the cost perspective, technology represents a major investment, and from the standpoint of advances in technology, technology that is "in" today may be obsolete tomorrow. Thus, purchasing decisions should match the needs of the director and the goals of the children's program and should be on the cutting edge of the technology market. Care must be taken in purchasing both *hardware* (physical components of a computer system, such as a central processing unit [CPU], the monitor, and the keyboard) and *software* (computer program packaged as one program or as two or more related programs).

Hardware. An early childhood program needs one computer for administrative purposes and a minimum of one computer for every 10 preschool children and one computer for every 5 older children enrolled if the computer is to be truly integrated into the early childhood curriculum (Thouvenelle & Bewick, 2003). The brand choice is optional because Macintosh and the IBM-compatibles are getting more difficult to distinguish in terms of ease of use. More manufacturers and suppliers produce IBM-compatibles as opposed to the one company that manufactures Apple/Macs, which may affect price, maintenance, and the availability of software (Haughland & Wright, 1997; Thouvenelle & Bewick, 2003).

Directors need to purchase CPUs with large capacities of RAM (Random Access Memory) for two reasons. First, good computers last only about 3 years before becoming inadequate. Second, software requirements for children's programs are higher than for most word processing and for many business applications. Disk drives, both a diskette drive and a CD-ROM drive, and a sound card to play music and other sounds are needed.

Peripheral devices (input/output devices that are not part of and hence are peripheral to the CPU) must be carefully chosen, too. A color monitor, one or more input devices (e.g., keyboard, mouse or track ball, switch, touch window screen, touch tablet, Muppet Learning Keys), and an inkjet or laser printer are not optional. Some optional peripherals are *modems* (devices that allow computers to communicate or network via telephone lines) and stereo speakers. Software dealers can inform potential buyers of the hardware demands for specific programs.

Special devices are made for small hands and children with special needs. P.L. 105-17 (IDEA) mandates that all students with disabilities be considered for assistive technology as part of their IEPs or ISFPs. The Technology-Related Assistance for Individuals With Disabilities Act of 1994 (P.L. 103–218) requires that states develop comprehensive programs of technology-related assistance for all persons regardless of age. Assistive technology devices are defined by the Technology-Related Assistance for Individuals With Disabilities Act of 1988 (P. L. 100–407) as any piece of equipment or product system that can improve the functional capabilities of those with disabilities. Many companies provide information on available assistive hardware and its use. Assistive technology ranges from a smaller mouse or a larger track ball to computerized interactive language systems.

Software. As has been mentioned, when selecting software, one must be sure that the computer's hardware components (called the *configuration*) and the software match in terms of (a) the size of the hard disk drive and the amount of space available, (b) the type of disk drive, (c) the amount of RAM, (d) the version of the operating system, (e) the type of graphics display and speech/sound enhancement, (f) the type of input device (e. g., touch window screen, keyboard, mouse), and (g) the need for/type of printer. If the buyer knows the computer configuration, the software producer can determine the match.

Software for children's programs must be chosen with just as much care as other materials for three reasons:

1. Software is expensive. Software can range in price from a few dollars to thousands of dollars for super software packages. Administrators can save money by making careful choices, by checking software specialty stores or mail-order companies, or by using shareware (freeware). Teachers may exchange titles or borrow titles from libraries (but it is illegal to copy software except shareware, just as it is illegal to copy copyrighted print materials).

2. The software should meet quality criteria; that is, it should (a) make effective use of computer capacity, (b) be easy to install, (c) be child-proof, (d) be easy to use (simple to operate, with few commands that allow children to work independently of adults), (e) have correct content, (f) have quality design features, and (g) provide for differences in children's interests and abilities. Shade (1996) said that the primary question to ask about software for children is this: "Can the child make decisions about what he wants to do and operate the software to accomplish that task, with minor help from the adult?" (p. 18).

3. Software must match the goals of the program. The types of available software are (a) open-ended, discovery software programs—*simulations* (programs that model real-life situations so that children can use their skills and concepts in lifelike settings that are close to the "real thing") and *microworlds* (programs in which children act on software to make something happen rather than respond to close-ended questions or situations); (b) drill-and-practice programs in which the child is rewarded for selecting the correct answers to the problems; and (c) books on CD-ROM that have colorful graphics, animation, music, and "hot spots"—areas that can be activated by clicking. Microworlds and simulations are used by the holistic/developmental programs, and drill-and-practice programs are used by D-I approaches. Microworlds and simulations are becoming increasingly popular, but the majority of software releases are still of the drill-and-practice type.

Haugland and Shade (1994a) asked early childhood teachers what they wanted software publishers to know. Teachers indicated that they wanted to have software in many content areas so that they as teachers may infuse technology into the local program's curriculum rather than have complete programs (super software packages). These teachers also wanted to see less drill-and-practice software and more microworlds and simulations software. Haugland and Shade (1994b) estimated that only about 25% to 30% of the available software is DAP. The NAEYC (1996b) developed a position statement on technology and young children, which should be reviewed before selecting software.

Software must be carefully evaluated. Software evaluation systems use different criteria for their evaluations; thus, the evaluation system's philosophy must be consistent with the chosen program base. (See Haughland & Wright, 1997, pp. 23–24, for a listing of software evaluation systems.) Besides referring to software ratings, teachers need to take a comprehensive look at the program itself. Teachers need to view themselves as test pilots who push the software to its limits and who see the software through the eyes, hands, and minds of children in the program.

Many early childhood programs purchase a *database management system*—software that allows the user to create, maintain, and access data on a database for administrative functions. Common database applications are children's records; accounts receivable/payable; payroll; meal planning (USDA); personnel management; general ledger; scheduling children and staff; online check-in/out; and report, letter, and label writing. Many producers sell these applications in individual modules because an entire package can cost several thousand dollars. Many software packages are now available (see appendix 6). Small early childhood programs often use word processing programs, spreadsheet programs, or both to do their administrative record keeping.

Caring for Equipment and Materials

Caring for equipment and materials teaches children good habits and helps prevent expensive repairs and replacements. Teachers should keep the following suggestions in mind:

1. The room and shelves should be arranged to minimize the chance of accidents and to maximize housekeeping efficiency. Equipment and materials should be shelved close to the working space; objects susceptible to damage should be used in areas out of the main flow of traffic; and breakable items or those likely to spill should be placed on shelves within easy reach (if frequent accidents involving the same item occur, try setting the item in a different place). Enough open space should prevent accidents.

2. Children should be taught how to care for equipment and materials. Staff should establish a routine for obtaining and returning equipment and materials and for using facilities. To establish a routine, every item must have a place, and time must be allowed for returning all items there.

3. Spilled materials should be cleaned up. In some cases, a teacher can create a science lesson on cleaning.

4. Staff should set good examples in caring for equipment and materials.

5. Staff should station themselves properly for adequate supervision.

6. Plenty of equipment and materials should be available so that each child has something to do and does not have to wait too long for a turn. Tempers flare and damage occurs when children are not constructively involved. Children should

be removed from an area when they deliberately destroy or damage equipment or materials.

7. Damaged equipment and materials should be repaired as soon as possible. Items should not be used until they are repaired.

8. Equipment should be cleaned regularly. Toys for infants and toddlers should be cleaned daily with a disinfectant, and equipment for preschoolers should be cleaned weekly.

9. Staff should periodically check equipment and materials. They should tighten loose nuts, bolts, clamps, and other hardware; replace or sand rusted parts; repaint rusted tubing; oil metal parts; sand wooden equipment where splinters are found; paint or use clear protective coatings on wooden equipment and remove loose paint; repair torn fabric and secure fasteners on doll or dress-up clothes; and replace broken-off or sharp plastic equipment.

10. Staff should consider what heat, light, moisture, and storage methods might do to the equipment and materials.

11. Poisonous or dangerous items should be stored where children cannot get to them. To request information about a product, call your local poison control center.

12. To report a product one believes to be unsafe, write to:

Consumer Product Safety Commission (CPSC)

www.cpsc.gov/ or call 800–638–2772

Purchasing Insurance

Adequate insurance for a facility as well as for equipment and materials is of utmost importance. Coverage is required for mortgaged buildings and is recommended for all owned buildings and for the contents of rented buildings. Basically, fire insurance covers fire and lightning. Most policies can have an extended-coverage endorsement attached that covers such things as losses from wind, hail, explosion (except from steam boilers), civil commotion, aircraft, vehicles, smoke, vandalism, and malicious mischief. If the program moves equipment and materials to various buildings, the insurance should include a floater policy to protect against loss resulting from such transportation. To have adequate fire insurance (basic or extended-coverage endorsement), the administrator must maintain up-to-date property records that reflect current values. Other types of insurance may also be necessary. If the program owns vehicles, insurance should be secured to protect against losses from material damage or the destruction of the vehicle and its material contents (liability insurance is usually required by law). Theft insurance may be needed in some areas but is usually expensive.

TRENDS AND ISSUES

The body of literature on designing children's environments is growing. Dempsey and Frost (1993) referred to the environment as the "interface between the teacher and the child" (p. 306). The issue centers on a question of quality. Where do we want our children to live and work for 8 or more hours daily? Are we willing to settle for a child care center with a postage-stamp-size building, often elevated and portable; two small, metal doors; a tin roof; vinyl siding in tan or gray or occasionally crayon-bright colors; high windows with print curtains at each end; in front of the building, a yard of well-trodden ground scattered with a few pieces of backyard type of play equipment, a sand patch, and a few deserted tricycles; a chain link fence with a few sprigs of grass standing along the fence line enclosing the play yard and building and giving a squirrel-cage effect to the whole scene? Are we willing to allow our school buildings with a fence enclosing a sea of asphalt and its island building slip into further decline? Although we need much more research on housing design, we know that centers and schools need to be safe and comfortable, uniquely designed for their child and adult occupants, and aesthetically beautiful.

The appearance of the microcomputer in the early childhood environment is the most recent major trend in equipping the child's environment. Some serious hurdles in technology, such as the high cost, the provision for teacher training, and the creation of hardware and software products designed with young children in mind (e.g., products that are not simply electronic ditto sheets) need to be overcome. As described by Char and Forman (1994), the future of interactive technologies can offer powerful tools for young children's development.

SUMMARY

Careful planning is required for housing an early childhood program. The program base and objectives of the local program should determine the housing facilities. To a great extent, housing determines the quality of an early childhood program. Housing can be thought of as the stage upon which all interactions take place—child–child, child–adult, and child–material. Housing involves (a) the entry/exit area in which children makes the transition from home to program and from program to home and the area from which family members most frequently view the program; (b) the children's activity room, with its planned arrangement designed to meet the children's needs as defined by the program objectives; (c) the additional areas for children (shared activity areas, cubbies, diapering areas and rest rooms, feeding and dining areas, napping area, isolation area); (d) adult areas (family reception area, lounge, office/workroom, professional library); and (e) the outdoor space—a unique extension of the activity room. Because of the wide variety of equipment and materials available for use in early childhood programs, many people may believe that the early childhood curriculum is entirely contained in such materials. Certainly, the uses of equipment and materials are powerful regulators of children's experiences. Thus, selection of the types of equipment and materials purchased and the ways in which they will be used must be carefully determined by the local program.

Once housing facilities are constructed or selected and materials and equipment chosen, they determine the staff members' abilities to work with and supervise children, the types and convenience of activities, the accessibility of equipment and materials and of places to work and to play, and the safety of children. In short, one should never have to adapt the program to the physical setting; rather, the physical setting should always serve the purposes of the program.

FOR FURTHER READING

Bronson, M. B. (1995). *The right stuff for children birth to 8: Selecting play materials to support development.* Washington, DC: National Association for the Education of Young Children.

Ceppi, G., & Zini, M. (1998). *Children, spaces, relations: Metaproject for an environment for young children.* Reggio Emilia, Italy: Reggio Children.

Dempsey, J. D., & Frost, J. L. (1993). Play environments in early childhood education. In B. Spodek (Ed.), *Handbook of research on the education of young children* (pp. 306–321). New York: Macmillan.

Eskensen, J. B. (1987). *The early childhood playground: An outdoor classroom.* Ypsilanti, MI: High/Scope Press.

Feldman, J. R. (1997). *Wonderful rooms where children can bloom! Over 500 innovative ideas and activities for your child-centered classroom.* Peterborough, NH: Crystal Springs Books.

Frost, J. L. (1989). Play environments for young children in the USA: 1800–1990. *Children's Environments Quarterly, 6*(4) 17–24.

Greenman, J. T. (1988). *Caring spaces, learning places: Children's environments that work.* Redmond, WA: Exchange Press.

Hart, C. H. (Ed.). (1993). *Children on playgrounds.* Albany: State University of New York Press.

Peck, N., & Shores, E. F. (1994). *Checklist for diversity in early childhood education and care.* Little Rock, AR: Southern Early Childhood Association.

Rivken, M. S. (1995). *The great outdoors: Restoring children's right to play outside.* Washington, DC: National Association for the Education of Young Children.

Sanoff, H., & Sanoff, J. (1988). *Learning environments for children: A developmental approach to shaping activity areas.* Atlanta: Humanics Press.

Sloane, M. W. (2000). Make the most of learning centers. *Dimensions of Early Childhood, 28*(1), 16–20.

Topal, C. W., & Gandini, L. (1999). *Beautiful stuff! Learning with found materials.* Worcester, MA: Davis Publications.

Wardle, F. (1997). Playgrounds: Questions to consider when selecting equipment. *Dimensions of Early Childhood, 25*(1), 9–15.

Whitehead, L. C., & Ginsberg, S. I. (1999). Creating a family-like atmosphere in child care settings: All the more difficult in large child care centers. *Young Children, 54*(2), 4–10.

TO REFLECT

1. Planning the physical environment to match program goals enhances the chances of fulfilling one's goals. List the goals of a local program or use the sample goal statements provided by Bredekamp and Rosegrant (1992, p. 18). How could each goal be promoted through the physical environment? For example, the first sample goal given by Bredekamp and Rosegrant is to "develop a positive self-concept and attitude toward learning, self-control, and a sense of belonging" (p. 18). Learning centers in which children have choices would be *one* way to promote the first goal.

2. Planning often involves compromises. For example, how can a director plan (a) for physical challenges on the preschool playground without creating undue risks for the young children and (b) for a hygienic yet soft environment for infants?

3. A director of a child care center realized that some of the children with special needs could profit from assistive technology. Thus, she ordered some new equipment. Unfortunately, she realized the special needs children were not really profiting from the new equipment.

Disappointed, she wondered what had gone wrong. What other changes could likely be needed to effect the desired outcome? Knowing how one change affects and often requires changes in other aspects of a program is referred to as looking at proposed changes from a *systems perspective*. What other examples have you seen in which the lack of a systems perspective caused a valuable idea to fail?

Financing and Budgeting

Early childhood programs are expensive. The total revenue base for early childhood care and education programs is about $56 billion (Casper, 1995; Hill-Scott, 2000). Preschool early childhood programs are mostly a private-market approach with families paying 60%, the government paying 39%, and the private sector paying 1% of the costs (A. Mitchell, Stoney, & Dichter, 1997; Olson, 2002). Conversely, user tuition and fees constitute only 23% of the total revenue used in public higher education (Sandham, 2002).

Both the scope and the quality of services are related to the financial status of a program, although programs with similar hourly costs range in quality from poor to excellent. Even with careful budgeting, good programs cannot operate effectively for long depending on donations and volunteers without weakening the quality and quantity of their services and without damaging the morale of those involved. In general, the highest quality centers had the most resources per child (Helburn, 1995). A strong relationship exists between staff wages and program quality in both center-based and family child care programs (Kontos, Howes, Shinn, & Galinsky, 1995; Whitebook, Sakai, & Howes, 1997) because as wages increase, turnover of staff declines (Whitebook & Bellm, 1999b).

The NAEYC stated that the crisis facing early childhood programs is rooted in this nation's failure to recognize the interrelatedness of three basic needs: (a) children's need for services, (b) staff's need for adequate compensation, and (c) families' need for affordable programs. The Association's governing board adopted a position statement that all children and their families should have access to high-quality programs and that staff should be offered salaries and benefits commensurate with their qualifications (NAEYC, 1987). In 1995, the NAEYC (1996c) reaffirmed its previous position but stated that if both quality and compensation improve, these programs will cost more. Based on several studies, the Center for Child Care Work Force concluded that often the indirect costs of turnover are equivalent to an improved compensation package for staff (Whitebook & Bellm, 1999a). The Quality 2000 Initiative recommended that the early childhood field (a) estimate the actual costs of initiating and sustaining a comprehensive quality early childhood care and education system; (b) implement revenue-generating mechanisms; and (c) develop a model for distributing funds to families, such as vouchers, tax credits, and direct payments (Kagan & Neuman, 1997b). In 2000, the NAEYC determined that the financing of a high-quality early childhood system must be a public priority of the NAEYC (NAEYC Policy Brief, 2001).

Because directors must manage local programs' resources, they need financial management skills. J. Greenman and Johnson (1993) indicated that directors are weak in financial management ability and have very limited skills in market assessment. Few early childhood administrators receive adequate training in fiscal management. Such training is important for two reasons. First, fiscal tasks take about 50% of a director's time (Cost, Quality, and Child Outcomes Study Team, 1995). Second, families, funding agencies, and taxpayers who believe that their early childhood programs are properly managed are more likely to subsidize the program. As is true of all other aspects of planning and administration, fiscal planning begins with the goals of the local program. Unless the proposed services and the requirements for meeting those services (in the way of staff, housing, or equipment) are taken into account, how can a budget be planned? And although program objectives should be considered first, probably no early childhood program is entirely free of financial limitations.

Fiscal planning affects all aspects of a program; consequently, planning should involve input from all those concerned with the local program (e.g., the board of directors or advisory board, the director, staff members, families). By considering everyone's ideas, a more accurate conception of budgeting priorities, expenditure level, and revenue sources can be derived. Furthermore, planning and administering the fiscal aspects of an early childhood program should be a continuous process. Successful financing and budgeting will only come from evaluating current revenue sources and expenditures and from advance planning for existing and future priorities.

Fiscal affairs are probably the most surveyed aspect of an early childhood program. A central criterion used to evaluate the worth of a program is often economic, that is, using funds efficiently and showing benefits that exceed costs. As described in chapter 2, many federally financed early childhood programs that began in the 1960s and 1970s conducted longitudinal studies that showed these programs' economic worth to society.

Not-for-profit programs are responsible to their funding agencies, for-profit programs are accountable to their owners and stockholders, and all programs are accountable to the Internal Revenue Service. Even if the average citizen does not understand the problems of fund management, any hint of fund misuse will cause criticism. Administrators must budget, secure revenue, manage, account for, and substantiate expenditures in keeping with the policies of the early childhood program in a professional and businesslike manner.

COSTS OF EARLY CHILDHOOD PROGRAMS

High-quality early childhood care and education programs are labor intensive and expensive. Most programs, except publicly funded ones, operate in a price-sensitive market. They are financed primarily by working parents and are only supplemented by public and private contributions.

Estimates of Program Costs

Reported costs of early childhood programs show extensive variation. Costs may vary with the type of program, the level of training and size of the staff, sponsorship (whether it is a federal program, a public school, or a parent cooperative), the delivery system (center based, home visitor), and the children enrolled (their ages and whether or not they have disabilities). Another factor contributing to variations in costs is whether the program is new or is offering new, additional services and thus has start-up costs or whether the program is already under way and has continuing costs. Geographic location, the amount of competition, and the general economy also contribute to the varying costs.

Varied Costs of Different Programs.   Different types of programs vary in their costs. Neugebauer (1993b) conducted a national survey of fees charged to parents. He used as the baseline the fees charged for 3- and 4-year-olds attending centers full time (all day for 5 days per week). For full-time care, the fees for toddlers were 15% higher and the fees for infants were 28% higher than the baseline. The percentages were rather consistent from center to center. School-age child care (SACC) fees for before- and after-school care were 26% lower than the baseline, and fees for after-school care were 55% lower than the baseline. SACC fees, however, were reported to vary "dramatically" from center to center; thus, the percentages are less meaningful. Facilities in continuous use (e.g., preschool child care) are cost effective in comparison with facilities with downtime (e.g., half-day nursery schools, SACC programs).

Meeting the needs of children with disabilities is also expensive. Costs are functions of the type and degree of exceptionality—with intellectually gifted the least expensive and those with a physical disability the most expensive—and of the type of services offered (e.g., transportation for children with physical disabilities is often more expensive than tutors for children identified as having learning disabilities). On the average, costs for centers that enroll children with disabilities are 15% higher than those for centers that do not enroll special needs children

(I. Powell, Eisenberg, Moy, & Vogel, 1994). However, the total costs per service hour is about 8% less for inclusive programs than for traditional special education programs (Odom, Wolery, Lieber, & Horn, 2002).

Program sponsorship has little bearing on costs. For example, the Cost, Quality, and Child Outcomes Study Team (1995) found that for-profit and not-for-profit centers charge similar fees per child hour and both receive about 3.7% in profit or surplus, respectively. The costs vary some by affiliation and profit status. The estimated costs are highest in public schools, followed by not-for-profit private centers. The costs are lower in religiously sponsored centers (I. Powell, Eisenberg, Moy, & Vogel, 1994).

Cash Costs versus Full Costs of Programs. **Cash costs** (the amounts charged and paid for services) and the **full costs** (the amounts actually required to operate programs when all costs are included) are different. The Cost, Quality, and Child Outcomes Study Team (1995) found that cash costs for centers meeting minimal standards (but not those with good to excellent ratings) was $2.11 per child hour ($95 per child week, or $4,940 per child year). Geographic differences in cash costs ranged from $1.50 per child hour in North Carolina to $2.88 per child hour in Connecticut. The Northeast has the highest child care costs in the United States, and the South and West have the lowest (I. Powell, Eisenberg, Moy, & Vogel, 1994). Urban areas are more expensive than rural areas.

The Cost, Quality, and Child Outcomes Study Team (1995) found that the full cost for child care services was $2.83 per child hour ($127 per child week, or $6,604 per child year). The U.S. General Accounting Office (1999) estimated that the cost of care in accredited centers was about $7,000 per year for 50 weeks of full-time care. The average cost per child in Head Start was just over $5,000 in 1998; however, Head Start is a 34-week, part-day program.

Program Quality and Costs. The costs of high-quality programs have also been considered. The Cost, Quality, and Child Outcomes Study Team (1995) estimated that the difference in today's cash (not full) costs of going from minimal to quality services was 10% (from $4,940 to $5,434 per child year). This percentage assumes that 10% is spent on items related to quality enhancement. Willer (1990) estimated the full cost of high-quality center care to be $8,000 per child year for children under age 5. The Washington Quality Child Care Think Tank estimated that quality child care cost $8,300 per child per year (Packard Foundation, 1996).

Cash costs of programs, however, seem to remain low at the expense of program quality. Some of the reasons for this include the following:

1. The government contributes to low-quality care when its agencies impose payments at *market rate* (i.e., subsidies are capped at levels determined by what families with average incomes are supposedly willing to pay) for child care services or fail to provide higher reimbursement for higher quality care. Generally speaking, governmental agencies use estimated cash costs to determine what they will pay for services, and thus, to some degree, circularity results. In other words, because agencies pay a certain number of dollars, program designers plan their programs on the basis of expected amounts of money. If funded the first year, program designers write a similar program the next year in hopes of being refunded. Thus, the agency pays approximately the same amount again, and the cycle continues. The program is thus designed around a specific dollar value whether or not it makes for the "best" program.

2. Labor is the most expensive aspect of early childhood programs. In the highest quality programs, about 70% of the budget is in salaries and benefits. The easiest way to make a program more affordable and to ensure profit/surplus is to decrease wages and increase the number of children per staff member. Low wages result in

less qualified employees at the point of entry, less incentive for employees to increase skills because of the lack of significant monetary reward, and greater employee turnover rates. The trade-off for low salaries and benefits is a low-quality program. Yet, research points to a positive relationship between program quality and budget allocations for teacher salaries and benefits; that is, programs that spent approximately two thirds of their budgets on salaries and staff benefits tended to be of high quality, and quality diminished considerably in programs spending less than one half of their budgets on salaries and staff benefits (Olenick, 1986). Similarly, Whitebook, Howes, and Phillips (1990) stated that the single best predictor of teacher effectiveness was salary.

The real earnings by child care teachers and family child care providers have decreased by nearly one fourth since the mid-1970s (Bellm, Breuning, Lombardi, & Whitebook, 1992; Willer, 1992). Family- and center-based teachers pay about 19% to 20% of the full costs of child care through foregone earnings (Cost, Quality, and Child Outcomes Study Team, 1995; Helburn, 1995). More specifically, the U.S. Bureau of Labor Statistics (1996) reported that the average hourly wage of child care workers was $6.12 and that of family child care providers was $3.37. The Center for the Child Care Workforce (2000) found that family child care providers earned about $10,500 annually, and center child care teachers earned about $15,000 annually. Salaries of center teachers in the NAEYC-accredited programs are one half those of public elementary school teachers. The gap widens as the years of experience increase (I. Powell, Eisenberg, Moy, & Vogel, 1994). Furthermore, non-public-school programs seldom provide pension plans or health benefits for staff.

3. As discussed in chapter 1, inadequate consumer knowledge on the part of families reduces incentives for centers to provide high-quality programs. Families should not only seek quality programs but also understand the full costs of such

programs and become advocates for subsidies that move program incomes closer to full costs. Thus, Carter and Curtis (1998) showed two methods of calculating the full costs of their programs and provided a sample mock invoice that can be sent to families yearly reflecting these costs.

4. Directors also rely on volunteer help and other donations to help absorb the differences between the cash costs and the full costs of their programs. Volunteer services and donated goods absorb about 2% of full costs, and donated occupancy (e.g., programs using facilities of religious organizations) absorbs about 6% of full costs (Cost, Quality, and Child Outcomes Study Team, 1995).

Costs to Families

Programs primarily supported through user fees are expensive for families. Families pay about 60% of all expenditures for child care, with the federal, state, or local governments paying most of the remaining expenses (Stoney & Greenberg, 1996). In constant dollars, the average cost of family child care has increased steadily since 1990 (Casper, 1995), and family child care is almost totally paid through family fees. In 49 of the 50 states, the annual cash cost for child care was more than the annual tuition fees at a public college, and in cities in 15 states, child care costs twice as much as public college tuition (Schulman & Adams, 1998). Because child care costs have risen to compensate programs for their loses in subsidies (Willer, 1992), child care has become less affordable for most families. Families do not have equitable financing either. Child care expenses are often the second or third largest item in a low-income working family's household budget. The average monthly costs for nonpoor families were higher in absolute terms but lower in terms of the percentage of the household budget; that is, 18% to 25% for lower income families and 7% for higher income families (U.S. Bureau of the Census, 1997; U.S. Department of Health and Human Services, 1999).

Because families living in poverty can have their child care fees subsidized, their children are as likely to be enrolled in high-quality early childhood programs as those children coming from high-socioeconomic families. Struggling families whose incomes are just above the poverty level are often priced out of quality programs. Subsidies that lower the price of child care often induce low-income families to work. However, as their incomes rise, assistance with child care is decreased or cut off. Even if assistance were available, most states do not have enough child care program openings available to serve families eligible for assistance (G. Adams, Schulman, & Ebb, 1998). Affordable programs for low-income families are of lower quality than government-subsidized ones (Blau & Hagy, 1998). Besides income, other factors also preclude low-income families from higher quality programs, such as nonday shifts (41% of low-income mothers work these shifts) and residence in low-income neighborhoods that do not have high-quality programs (Queralt & Witte, 1998; U.S. Bureau of the Census, 1997).

Costs to families differ for the following reasons:

1. Programs differ in costs because of the quality of services, geographic location, age of the children served, and ability of the program to take advantage of scale economics (i.e., serve more children or provide more hours of service than competing programs).

2. Even in programs that charge similar fees per child hour, the costs per family may vary because of various types of subsidies. The subsidies include the following:

a. **Multi-child discounts.** About half of for-profit centers offer multi-child discounts; however, the fee discount varies greatly (Neugebauer, 1993b).

b. **Fees subsidized by public funds.** Some programs provide care for children whose fees are subsidized mainly through public funds. These government-funded subsidies are provided for children of low-income working families through the Child Care and Development Fund (CCDF) and Temporary Assistance to Needy Families (TANF). Rohacek and Russell (1998) found that (a) child care subsidy acts to keep families from ever needing welfare; (b) moves families from welfare to work; (c) pays for itself in real dollars; and (d) helps develop the regulated child care system. They found that the best subsidy system gives more help to families with the lowest incomes—those with the greatest risk of returning to welfare.

c. **Tax credits and deductions.** At both the state and federal levels, *tax credits* (taken against taxes owed) and *deductions* (amounts subtracted from income before computing taxes owed) reduce child care costs for eligible families who claim them. Families should determine their eligibility to claim the Dependent Care Tax Credit, Child Tax Credit, Earned Income Tax Credit, and the Dependent Care Assistance Program (DCAP). Because few eligible families claimed their tax credits, the National Women's Law Center launched the Child Care Tax Credits Outreach Campaign. (Both the National Women's Law Center and the National Center for Children in Poverty provide excellent information on taxes and child care; see appendix 5.)

Although child care is expensive, not working can also be expensive because of a family's foregone income. The amount of foregone income when a family member provides child care services rather than obtains outside employment is another expense that varies from family to family. The income is considered foregone when a family member provides child care services either without payment or on an intrafamilial income transfer. In either case, the amount of foregone income depends on the caregiver's employable skills and the availability of employment or on the caregiver's potential income. (Calculating foregone income also requires considering the cost of outside employment, such as transportation, clothing, organization or union dues, and higher taxes.)

Cost Analysis of Programs

The decision to fund an early childhood program and the kind of investment to make depend on cost analyses. Given today's economic situation, programs applying for public monies are reviewed in terms of costs versus savings (i.e., social benefits to the individuals involved and to society in general). Early childhood care and education seem to be warranted on economic grounds alone. Social benefits quantified in economic terms are always difficult to calculate and, especially in the case of early childhood programs, are almost impossible to gauge because many of the benefits cannot be measured until young children reach adulthood.

Cost analyses are of several types. The reason for doing a cost analysis determines the type of analysis employed. **Cost-effectiveness analysis,** the preferred analysis of researchers (Barnett, 2000), compares the costs of two or more programs that have the same or similar goals to find the least-cost method of reaching a particular goal. Programs that offer a low-cost approach compared with other approaches to achieve certain objectives are referred to as cost-effective programs.

Cost-efficiency analysis, also called *functional cost analysis,* usually follows cost-effectiveness analysis. Cost-effective programs can further reduce costs by developing a least-cost, within-program management plan. Cost efficiency is achieved when all program components are optimally used. These functions are usually analyzed: administration, care and education, food, health services, transportation, facilities, training and special events, and family services (G. Morgan, 1999).

One of the issues today is how much to spend on preschool programs to achieve positive eco-nomic benefits to the general public (i.e., taxpayers) and to the participants that exceed the costs of the programs. **Cost-benefit analysis,** the most difficult analysis, measures the value of the program to the child and his or her family (e.g., better jobs) and to society (e.g., savings to public schools as a result of fewer grade repetitions or special education placements; lower crime rates; taxes on higher incomes) minus the costs of the program. Placing a dollar value on such benefits is difficult. However, a program is referred to as a cost-beneficial program when the monetarily calculated benefits exceed the monetarily calculated costs. For example, a cost-benefit analysis has been done on the long-term benefits of the Perry Preschool Program. Although the program was much more expensive than the typical public school prekindergarten or Head Start, the Perry Preschool Program generated cost-benefit programs in excess of 7:1 (Barnett, 1993a). The national costs of not providing 2 years of high-quality early childhood care and education programs is about $100,000 for each child born in poverty, or a total of $400 billion for all poor children under age 5 today (Barnett, 1993a, 1993b). Lewis (1997) reported that each dollar spent in high-quality preschools saves the public $7.16 in later services. In short, high-quality programs have long-term benefits for the child, the family, and society (Packard Foundation, 1995).

Costs of Local Programs

Local program administrators often think of costs in terms of budget items. Budget items are usually the program functional items used in cost-efficiency analysis. The following distinctions must be made in an analysis:

1. **Start-up costs.** Start-up costs are the monies that must be available before a program is under way. Even after the program begins, most programs underenroll for 6 months of operation, and monies from promised funding sources are often delayed. Start-up costs include monies for the building, equipment and

supplies, 3 months of planning, and the first 6 months or longer of operation.

2. **Fixed and variable costs.** Fixed costs (e.g., program planning) do not vary with the number of children served, but variable costs (e.g., building, teacher salaries, equipment) vary with the number of children served.

3. **Marginal costs.** Marginal costs are the increased cost "per unit" (total program costs divided by the number of recipients) of expanding a program beyond a given enrollment. Marginal costs may decrease to a given point and then increase when additional staff or housing is required.

4. **Capital versus operating costs.** Capital costs (e.g., building) are basically one-time costs, whereas operating costs (e.g., salaries, consumable materials) are recurrent.

5. **Hidden costs.** Hidden costs are costs free to a program but paid by someone else (e.g., the donor of a facility). **Joint costs** are somewhat "hidden" too because they are shared costs (e.g., two separately funded programs that share a staff workroom or audiovisual equipment). **Foregone income costs** (e.g., income foregone because of services or goods provided a program) are difficult to calculate.

FINANCING EARLY CHILDHOOD PROGRAMS

Financing early childhood programs is a measure of worth. High price tags most often speak of high quality and great worth. As a nation, we acknowledge the importance of child care and education more in rhetoric than with the pocketbook. The amount of money available to early childhood programs and the stability of these funds directly influence their quality. Money also speaks more subtly in terms of the values we place on the care and education of young children and of the documented risks we are willing to take if the early years of childhood are neglected.

The specific ways early childhood programs are paid for by families, government, and corporations are referred to as **financing mechanisms.** The way the financing mechanism is administered (e.g., grants, contracts, loans, vouchers) is called an **administrative mechanism.** An administrative mechanism is governed by policy concerning the eligibility for and use of any funds (Brandon, Kagan, & Joesch, 2000). Although many early childhood programs receive funds from parents (e.g., fees, tuition, and donated goods and services), most programs are subsidized with monies from governments, philanthropic organizations, and corporations. These subsidies can be *direct* (i.e., paid directly to a given program, such as a grant) or *portable* (i.e., paid by users who had choices among programs enrolling children whose fees are subsidized—hence, portable).

Various regulations govern (a) a program's eligibility to receive revenue from a source such as the federal government; (b) procedures for obtaining revenue; (c) the use made of the revenue; and (d) which personnel are accountable for the expenditure. Because of the many types of programs and the intricacies and variations involved in funding, only a brief description of the sources of financing is given here.

Government and Foundation Financing

Financing strategies for early child care and education programs are embedded in the rationale for high-quality programs, such as school readiness, brain development research, economic development, and welfare-to-work reforms. Thus, early childhood programs are becoming more publicly supported. To expand their current financing mechanisms for early childhood programs, the federal, state, and local governments are using these two revenue sources:

1. **Direct revenue sources.** Direct revenue sources are primarily monies from tax sources— sales, income, and other taxes—planned for government spending. Although most states subsidize early childhood programs through

general revenue dollars, some are funding through "sin tax" revenues, such as taxes on alcohol sales and the gambling industry and from tobacco company settlements (Sandham, 2002).

2. **Indirect revenue sources.** Indirect revenue sources are foregone government monies due to claims made by individuals or corporations through the tax system (i.e., tax exemptions, deductions, and credits).

Government funding results in several ongoing concerns. Funds are not stable and fluctuate with government budget as choices are made among many needs. Another concern is the bewildering array of funding agencies and assistance programs. Because, at present, no federal centralized program of child care exists, the extent of federal involvement in early childhood programs is not easily determined. Along with the problem of dealing with the number of federal sources, a jumble of rulings from agencies results in many different standards. Assistance programs are constantly being deleted and added, and appropriations may fall below congressional authorization. A final concern has to do with the regulations that accompany funding, especially federal funding. Federal funds can be **categorical grants** (grants used for specified, narrowly defined purposes) or **general revenue sharing** (funds provided on a formula basis to state and local governments, with few or perhaps no limits to how the money is spent). The trend has been toward federal "deregulation." The middle ground is achieved through **block grants.** In a block grant, federal aid is provided for more broadly defined activities so that state or local groups can have greater discretion in designating programs to meet local needs. Recipients must comply with some federal regulations (e.g., fiscal reporting and nondiscrimination requirements).

Public School Financing of Kindergartens and Primary Programs.   Public school programs are supported by local, state, and federal monies. Taxation is the major source of monies available for funding; consequently, revenues for public school programs are closely tied to the general economy of the local area, the state, and the nation.

Local Support.   Tax funds, usually from real and personal property taxes, are used to maintain and operate the schools, and the sale of bonds is used for capital improvements and new construction expenses. According to the National Center for Education Statistics (1997), the richest districts spend 56% more per student than do the poorest. These "poor schools" have less qualified teachers, fewer resources, and more distressed housing. The local school board's authority to set tax rates and to issue bonds for school revenue purposes is granted by the state; that is, authority is *not* implied. When granted the power to tax, the local school board must follow state laws concerning tax rates and procedural matters in an exacting manner. In this way, the state protects the public from the misuse and mismanagement of public monies.

State Support.   The amount of state support for public schools varies widely from state to state. Almost every state has some form of foundation program designed to equalize the tax burden and educational opportunities among school districts. Generally, the foundation program begins with a definition of minimum standards of educational service that must be offered throughout the state. The cost of maintaining the standards is calculated and the rate of taxation prescribed. The tax rate may be uniform or based on an economic index ability—the ability of a local school district to pay. If local taxes do not cover the cost of maintaining minimum standards, the balance of the costs is provided via state monies. States vary considerably in the machinery they use for channeling state monies to local school districts, the most common plans being flat and equalization grants. In the last decade, the issue of equalizing funding among school districts within a state has resulted in a rash of school finance litigation (Verstegen, 1994).

Federal Support.   Since the 1940s, the federal government has become the chief tax collector. Until recently, the trend had been toward unprecedented expenditures for education. Consequently, public schools (as well as other institutions, agencies, and organizations) relied more and more on federal assistance programs to supplement their local and state resources. Federal funding of public schools is used for two purposes: (a) to improve the quality of education (e.g., research, experimentation, training, housing, and equipment) and (b) to encourage greater effort by state and local districts to improve the quality of education by providing initial or matching funds for a program. Federal expenditures in education declined because of reductions in the types of programs funded or the amount of funds available in retained programs. However, the No Child Left Behind Act of 2001 (NCLB), signed into law on January 8, 2002, is a major reform of the Elementary and Secondary Education Act (ESEA) and redefines the federal role in K-12 education. The Act encompasses 45 programs. (Highlights of the Act are given in a later section.)

State Financing of Prekindergarten Programs.   Beyond commitment to financing kindergarten and primary grade programs in public schools, state investment in the financing of other early childhood programs is greater than ever before. States have long been involved in programs for young children. With the passage of welfare legislation, the Personal Responsibility and Work Opportunity Act of 1996, the state's role in early childhood services greatly expanded.

Most of the programs financed are center based, including the public schools, although some include home-based components. Doherty (2002) reported that four states are phasing in universal prekindergarten programs for 4-year-

olds and that many other states are providing programs for at-risk 4-year-olds. Some states are expanding Head Start programs. Many states are investing in child care through both direct and portable subsidies; however, gaps exist in every state's child care subsidy system (Schulman, Blank, & Ewen, 2001).

Although state commitment to support early childhood programs is growing, the support is far from adequate. G. Adams and Poersch (1997) measured state commitment to early childhood by looking at state funding practices. They found that (a) the amount of commitment varied widely across the nation and even between neighboring states; (b) many states with high rates of poverty did not secure available funds; (c) state wealth was not associated with commitment; and (d) early childhood programs are not high on the list of priorities to receive state funds (e.g., almost three fifths of the states invested less than 50 cents out of every $100 of state tax revenues on early childhood services; two thirds of the states spend 10 times this amount on corrections and prisons, and more than one half of the states spend 30 times as much on highways). Similarly, the National Center for Children in Poverty reported an overall increase in state investments, yet identified an uneven progress across states. For example, 33 states report funding increases of 10% or more, 5 states report increases of less than 10%, 10 states report no change in funding, and 2 states report overall decreases in funding. Furthermore, significant differences among states exist in per capita investment with 6 states spending more than $200 per child and 14 states spending $20 or less in fiscal year 2000 (Cauthen, Knitzer, & Ripple, 2000).

The cost per child in state-sponsored early childhood programs varies considerably, too. Sandham (2002) reported that the variables that determine the cost are (a) the maximum income level at which a family is eligible, (b) the age at which a child is eligible, (c) the relationship between the family's income and the level of the subsidy, and (d) teacher salaries. Brandon and

Wilson (1999) are developing a financing model that will enable states to estimate the costs of programs under different conditions (e.g., length of daily session) and for different populations of children.

States also use various financial administrative mechanisms. For example, some states allocate early childhood funds to school districts on the basis of school finance formulas; others use a categorical aid system. The most common method of state funding of early childhood education, however, is through grants or contracts awarded on a competitive basis by a state administrative agency, usually the department of education. For example, grants may go to school districts or private agencies whose programs are approved by the state board of education or who meet other regulatory guidelines. In some states, grants are used for pilot programs only. A few states use noncompetitive ways of awarding grants, such as school districts that have high concentrations of low-income students or elementary students with low standardized achievement test scores. Several states require that state money be matched with local, federal, or in-kind services because of statutory restrictions on state spending for these programs. Reviews of the research show **competitive discretionary grants** (grants awarded on the basis of the merits of the competing project proposals) to be the weakest funding method and the **index of need allocation** strategy (the index is a proxy for the magnitude of the need rather than number of students) to be the strongest funding method (Jordan, Lyons, and McDonough, 1992).

States are attempting to tie financing with the quality of programs. For example, 4% of a state's allocation under the CCDF block grant and 25% of all new Head Start dollars must be spent on initiatives to enhance quality (Olson, 2002). For the most part, state standards for quality are weak. For example, only 20 states and the District of Columbia require a college degree for teachers of prekindergarten children; 30 states require only a high school diploma for teachers

in child care centers; and only 7 states require that state-subsidized prekindergarten programs meet accreditation standards (Doherty, 2002).

Federal Financing. In addition to providing some federal fiscal support to certain programs, such as the public schools, the federal government remains the primary source of support for some comprehensive early childhood programs. The federal government pays for early childhood services in two ways:

1. **Contracts and grants.** Monies from contracts and grants flow directly to the program. The funds are awarded based on a specific service to be provided and a given number of recipients or targeted level of enrollment. Government agencies typically negotiate contract rates with a specific provider or group of providers. Rates are based on the amount of money that is available to purchase care and an assessment of the cost of providing the service (i.e., cash costs incurred in running the program).

2. **Vouchers.** A voucher is a payment mechanism whereby funds are given to the family rather than the program and follow the child to the family-selected program. Vouchers include both purchase-of-service systems and cash payments. Voucher systems base reimbursement on the market rate.

The modern era of federal support for early childhood care and education began with Head Start in 1965. Other programs soon followed. Federal funding, targeted primarily for low-income families and including programs for young children, continued to grow until 1977. Although federal support for social programs declined from 1977 to 1988, federal support for early childhood programs (e.g., Head Start) remained rather constant in dollar amounts; in actuality, federal support declined because the number of children living in poverty increased (Einbinder & Bond, 1992) and inflation took its toll on the value of the dollar. After 1988, federal support increased. At the current levels of federal spending, about 50% of all children eligible for Head Start are being served, about 12% of all eligible children are receiving assistance from Child Care and Development Block Grant (CCDBG), and about 66% of children eligible for Title 1 are being served (Washington Update, 2001).

Federal Assistance Programs. Throughout the modern era of federal financing, the purpose of most federal assistance programs has been to accomplish particular educational objectives or to meet the needs of specific groups. Most federal assistance programs (a) require early childhood programs to meet specified standards; (b) give priority or restrict services to certain client groups; (c) require state or local support in varying amounts; and (d) specify funds to be used for certain purposes (e.g., food, program supplies), which in turn curtail programs' flexibility. Some of the major federal assistance programs, whose total funds dwarf state financing, include Head Start and Early Head Start, CCDBG, TANF, Early Learning Opportunities Act, Children's Day Care Health and Improvement Act, IDEA, and various food programs. The NCLB Act of 2001 is a $19 billion investment. Seven of the 10 title programs under the NCLB are described as follows;

1. **Title I—Improving the Academic Achievement of the Disadvantaged.** The stated purpose of Title I is to ensure that all children have fair, equal, and significant opportunity to obtain a high-quality education and reach a minimum proficiency level on challenging state academic standards and assessments.

2. **Title II—Preparing, Training, and Recruiting High-Quality Teachers and Principals.** The purpose of Title II is the preparation and training of principals and teachers.

3. **Title III—Language Instruction for Limited English Proficient and Immigrant Students.** The purpose of Title III is to help students attain English language proficiency to meet the challenges of Title I.

4. **Title IV—21st Century Schools.** Title IV funds programs to prevent school violence and to foster drug-free environments. Title IV also funds the creation of Community Learning Centers (before- and after-school opportunities) to complement the school academic program.

5. **Title V—Promoting Informed Parental Choice and Innovative Programs.** Title V includes educational block grants, charter schools, magnet schools, and funds for the improvement of education in local areas.

6. **Title VI—Flexibility and Accountability.** Title VI funds are designed to enhance state and local assessment systems and to improve the dissemination of information on student achievement and school performance to families and community members.

7. **Title VII—Indian, Native Hawaiian, and Alaska Native Education.** Title VII authorizes expenditures to meet the unique educational needs (e.g., language) of these groups.

Obtaining Federal Assistance. Federal funding sources are in a state of constant change. The latest edition of the *Catalog of Federal Domestic Assistance* describes the federal agencies administering various assistance programs and the projects and services funded under these agencies. (Many specific federal programs that provide funds for early childhood programs are listed in appendix 7.)

Securing Federal Funds

Most federal funds are obtained by writing and submitting a grant proposal and having the proposal approved and funded. One person on the early childhood staff can best oversee the entire writing of the proposal, although input should be obtained from all those involved in the program. In fact, early childhood programs that plan to seek regular federal assistance may find it advantageous to hire a staff member with expertise in the area of obtaining federal as well as other funds, such as foundation grants, that require proposal writing. Proposal writing can vary according to an assistance program's particular requirements, but most use a similar format.

A certain terminology is used in obtaining federal funds and must be understood by those involved in locating appropriate grants and writing proposals. The following terms are frequently used:

1. **Assets.** The amount of money, stocks, bonds, real estate, or other holdings of an individual or organization.
2. **Endowment.** Funds intended to be kept permanently and invested to provide income for support of a program.
3. **Financial report.** A report detailing how funds were used (e.g., a listing of income and expenses).
4. **Grant.** A monetary award given a program. Grants are of several types:
   a. **Bricks and Mortar Act.** An informal term for grants for building or construction projects.
   b. **Capital support.** Funds for buildings (construction or renovation) and equipment.
   c. **Declining grant.** A multiyear grant that grows smaller each year in the expectation that the recipient can raise other funds to make up the difference.
   d. **General-purpose grant.** A grant made to further the total work of the program, as opposed to assisting a specific purpose.
   e. **Matching grant.** A grant with matching funds provided by another donor.
   f. **Operating-support grant.** A grant to cover day-to-day expenses (e.g., salaries).
   g. **Seed grant** or **seed money.** A grant or contribution used to start a new project.
5. **Grassroots fund-raising.** An effort to raise money on a local basis (e.g., raffles, bake sales, auctions.)
6. **In-kind contribution.** A contribution of time, space, equipment, or materials in lieu of a monetary contribution.
7. **Proposal.** A written application for a grant.

Proposal Planning

Proposal planning is, in essence, research. And as is true with any research, problem identification is the first step. What is needed? If the assistance program sends out a request for a proposal (RFP), the need is already defined in broad or general terms.

The second step is gathering documented evidence in the population or potential population served by the early childhood program. Also, assessment must be made as to how critical or extensive the need is. Most proposals require that needs and the degree of these needs be described in terms of demographic, geographic, and socioeconomic distribution as well as racial and ethnic makeup. Because proposals often have to be written quickly (perhaps in 2 to 4 weeks), a notebook should be kept with current data available. Data may be secured from the following and other sources:

- Community action associations (local)
- Department of Health and Human Resources (local and state) federal publications (found in the *Monthly Catalog of U.S. Government Publications*)
- U.S. Department of Commerce, Bureau of the Census
- U.S. Department of Labor, Bureau of Labor Statistics
- U.S. Department of Labor, Employment and Training Administration

The literature must be reviewed to see whether others have handled the problem and with what results. To prevent duplication of services in a local area, the administrator must also present evidence as to whether the same or similar needs are being met by other local programs. The duplication check needs to be made with local social services organizations, which can be identified through the telephone directory, the Department of Health and Human Services, and agencies served by the United Fund or Community Chest.

The final step is the writing of a two- or three-page proposal prospectus. The prospectus should contain a statement of the proposed problem, what will be done about the problem, the target group to be served, the number of people to be served, and whether the proposed early childhood program is needed. The prospectus is helpful in clarifying thinking and in getting the opinions of others, including reviewers of funding agencies. (Some federal agencies require a prospectus before accepting a complete proposal.)

Funding sources must also be identified. Federal assistance and other funding sources are listed in appendix 7.

Writing the Proposal

Federal agencies have their own guidelines for writing a proposal; they differ from agency to agency, but the guidelines should be followed exactly. Most guidelines want the following points to be covered in the body of the proposal:

1. **Title page.** Title of project; name of agency submitting application; name of funding agency; dates of project; and names, addresses, and signatures of the project director and others involved in fiscal management.

2. **Statement of problem.** General and specific objectives, documentation of needs and degree of needs, review of literature of programs that have tried to meet the specified needs, and description of any local programs currently involved in meeting specified needs.

3. **Program goals and objectives.** Description of broad program goals and specific, measurable outcomes expected as a result of the program.

4. **Population to be served.** What qualifications will children and families need for inclusion in the program? Will all who qualify be accepted? If not, how will the participants be chosen from those who qualify?

5. **Plan of procedure.** Were several alternative approaches available for solving the problem? If so, why was a particular alternative selected? How will each objective be accomplished?

6. **Administration of project.** What staffing requirements are being proposed? How will the program be managed? What is the program's capability to conduct the proposed project? Does the program have community support? Show a time schedule of activities that will occur from the day of funding until project termination.

7. **Program evaluation.** What assessment devices will be used? Who will conduct the assessment? How and in what format will the evaluation be submitted?

8. **Future funding.** How will the operation of the program be continued at the conclusion of federal assistance?

9. **Budget.** Must show sound fiscal management.

10. **Appendixes.** Include job descriptions, director's vita, organizational structure of the early childhood program.

Some agencies also require completion of an application form that usually asks for information about the general subject; to whom the proposal is being submitted; the legal authorization; the project title; the name of the person submitting the proposal; the program director's name, address, and telephone number; the probable budget; the amount of funds requested; and the date the application is transmitted. Some agencies have a form for a proposal abstract, and usually agencies require that this summary be no longer than 200 words. Forms assuring protection of human subjects and nondiscrimination may be required.

Foundation Support. Many fields, including education, have benefited from foundation giving.

Foundations are one of several kinds of non-governmental, not-for-profit organizations that promote public welfare, including that of young children, through the use of private wealth operated under a federal or state charter and administered by trustees. Other similar organizations are trusts and endowments. Foundation aid is typically given to support research. Because of increased federal support of education, foundation grants to education have decreased in the past few years. Large foundations have many goals that change periodically. Smaller foundations are often limited to specific goals or specific geographic areas. A good source of support may be foundations from local corporations. Nevertheless, administrators of early childhood programs should investigate foundations as potential sources of funds (see appendix 7).

Similar to federal funds, foundation funds are obtained through submission and approval of a proposal. The foundation's board of directors determines the guidelines for submitting proposals, sets a deadline for application, reviews proposals, and selects recipients.

Employer Assistance

Employers can provide child care assistance to their employees. Employer assistance includes some of the following methods:

1. Employers may contract with individual vendors to create a discount rate for specific programs.

2. Employers may subsidize costs by providing vouchers to employees.

3. Employees may receive assistance through a Dependent Care Assistance Plan (DCAP). DCAPs can enable employees to use pretax dollars to purchase dependent care services if they are offered through a flexible benefit program (i.e., employers offer a choice of benefits from which employees choose). The federal Internal Revenue Code allows employers who have established a DCAP to exclude child care benefits pro-

vided to their employees in an amount up to $5,000 per employee from federal income, FICA, and unemployment taxes and often from state income taxes. Benefits may come as cash, a voucher, or free or subsidized care in a child care facility. Usually the DCAP is a salary reduction that is returned to the employees as a reimbursement for child care expenses. (Any money *not* used for child care is *not* returned to the employee.) In short, a DCAP makes child care a nontaxable benefit. As a nontaxable benefit, salary reduction under a DCAP is more beneficial to higher income employees. To be beneficial to lower income employees, employers need to create a matching amount reduced from the employee's salary or to provide child care vouchers. Administrative costs of DCAPs are paid by employers.

Fees, Tuition, and Miscellaneous Sources of Funds

For-profit programs operate almost exclusively on tuition and fees and are usually the most expensive. Families who must pay more than 10% of their gross income for one or more children need subsidies. Directors should also inform families on how to apply for tax credits.

Although child care is costly, for-profit independent centers do not make substantial profits; in fact, many centers do not break even. Financial problems are often the result of underestimating income from fees and tuition. Optimal fees and tuition for early childhood programs may be determined in several ways. One method is to determine costs and the amount of profit (or surplus) needed. The cost is distributed among the children on a fixed fee, a sliding scale fee, or two fixed fees for different income brackets. Because children are not in attendance all the time, the tendency is to underestimate income from fees. Budgets must allow for a 3% to 8% vacancy rate. The administrator may also compensate by using G. Morgan's (1999) method of calculating last year's **utilization rate** (i.e., divide last year's actual income by the maximum potential income from fees). A well-run center operates at 95% or greater utilization rate; thus, the utilization rate is a good estimate to use even if fees are increased. A more accurate **break-even analysis** (a managerial tool that identifies the point at which a program generates enough revenue to cover expenses) is also explained in detail by G. Morgan (1999). A director should use the break-even point to evaluate the impact of various changes, such as raising or lowering tuition.

In addition to carefully calculating fees and tuition, an early childhood program must have definite policies on fee payment. Loss of income may occur as a result of absenteeism or child turnover. The following suggestions might be considered in establishing a fee policy:

1. Set a deposit fee at the time of enrollment, to be returned at the time of withdrawal if all monetary policies have been met. Two or three weeks' tuition or fees is reasonable.

2. Several weeks' notice should be given to withdraw a child. (The fee deposit covers this if notice is not given in advance.)

3. Children on the waiting list must be enrolled within a stated period of time after notification or their place on the waiting list will be forfeited.

4. Payments may be no more in arrears than the amount of the initial deposit.

5. Payments must be made when a child misses a few days, or a withdrawal notice should be given for an extended absence.

Neugebauer (1993c, 1993d) gave specific examples of fee policies in for-profit centers.

Some funds for early childhood programs can come from several miscellaneous sources. A few examples of these sources are as follows:

1. Public support via a community campaign can help make up the difference between the program's anticipated income and its expenses. For example, some programs qualify for United Way funds (which may be called by some other name). Specific eligibility requirements must be met to qualify for such local funds.

2. In-kind contributions are often available through some community resource, such as a charitable organization.

3. Endowments may be given in someone's memory, or scholarships may be awarded.

4. The early childhood program may engage in fund-raising projects to supplement income from other sources. A cash-benefit analysis should be done before mounting a fundraiser. Yields from $10 to $25 per hour, after expenses, are of marginal value; raising funds above $25 per hour is worthwhile.

BUDGETING

A **budget** is a list of all goods and services for which payment may be made. Because the budget determines the planned allocations of a program's resources, G. Morgan (1999) stated, "Budget is policy" (p. 11). Budgets are important because no matter how good a program is, it cannot continue to operate if it is not on a sound fiscal foundation. Limited funds require making decisions about priorities, and funding and regulatory agencies require information about monetary functions.

Regulations Governing Budget Making and Adoption

Budgets of small, privately owned programs are developed by their owners/directors and are not subject to regulations unless the program receives some subsidies from public funds. Budgets of larger private and publicly funded programs are usually developed by local program directors or the superintendents of schools for public school programs. Efforts are usually made to include the opinions of various personnel in the first draft of the proposed budget. However, in some of these large programs, such as a corporate chain or community action association, the budget is often created at the level of the larger organization, and the director only monitors expenditures and submits financial reports. Budgets of larger private and publicly funded programs are subject to many budgetary regulations. Once created, the budgets are presented to their respective boards of directors or advisors for approval. In addition to requiring the board's approval, regulations may require that the budget be presented to licensing or funding agency personnel before approval. In publicly funded programs, funds and thus fiscal control may come from several governmental agencies that will be involved before the adoption process ends.

Developing a Budget

The budget serves as a financial plan for a given period of time. Budgets itemize income (revenues) and expenses (expenditures). Directors often prepare several types of budgets.

Types of Budgets.   Directors of early childhood programs often work with two types of budgets. A budget projection and start-up budget are used in the beginning of the budgeting process. Operating budgets are used after a program is under way.

Budget Projections and Start-Up Budgets.   A *budget projection* (also called a *pro forma budget*) projects how the operation of a business will turn out based on certain assumptions. Often loans from banks or start-up grants require that a financial plan be submitted. Although a *financial plan* requires a description of the program, a management summary, and many supporting documents (e.g., licensing status, insurance coverage, tax status, contracts), the major aspect is the financial data. Financial data will include a projected start-up budget, funding requests and repayment plans if applicable, a break-even analysis, a projected monthly cash flow for a year, and a projected timetable for self-sufficiency.

A **start-up budget** includes all the income and expenses incurred in starting a program.

G. Morgan (1999) listed these categories of items in a start-up budget: (a) the capital cost of land, building, and equipment; (b) personnel costs for planning and implementing program; and (c) *lag costs* (costs between the time one provides the service and gets paid). Other start-up expenditures may include training, meetings, publicity, and repayment of the loan. Start-up budgets vary depending on whether one initiates a completely new program or buys a currently operating program. G. Morgan put dollar amounts to categories of start-up expenses.

Operating Budget.   An **operating budget** includes items on which money will be spent once a program is operating near the planned capacity. The operating budget includes all the income and expenses for one calendar year (January 1 through December 31) or for one fiscal year (often July 1 through June 30 or September 1 through August 31). Operating budgets usually have three components: (a) a synopsis of the program; (b) specifically itemized expenditures for operating the program, including direct costs (items attributed to a particular aspect of the program, such as personnel salaries) and indirect costs (overhead items not attributed to a particular aspect of the program, such as interest on bank loans, utility costs, and advertising); and (c) anticipated revenues and their sources, including in-kind contributions. Before writing the budget, the administrator should list the program's objectives and needs. The program's goals and needs and the fiscal plan should be carefully related and reflected in the written budget.

Budget Formats.   Proposed revenues and expenditures must be presented in an effective way. Budgets are organized by headings, either determined by the funding agency or the local program. The headings are referred to as the **budget format.** Two types of format are as follows:

1. **Functional classification.** This format assembles data in terms of categories for which money will be used, such as administration, child instruction, family education, food and health

services, and transportation. The advantage of the functional classification format is that one can readily link expenditure categories to program purposes. One disadvantage to this approach is that functional categories tend to be somewhat broad and thus raise questions regarding the expenditures within a classification. Another disadvantage is the lack of distinct classifications for some items; for example, health services may be listed under several classifications.

2. **Line-item classification.** This format lists the sums allocated to specifics of the program (e.g., salaries of designated personnel, gas, electricity, water, telephone, postage). The major advantage of this approach is that it shows specific accountability for expenditures. A disadvantage occurs if the categories are narrow because the director has little power to exercise changes in expenditures.

Many computer-assisted finance programs are available for use in preparing budgets and in performing and recording financial transactions. Often these have to be adapted to fit local needs.

Writing the Budget. The first step in writing a budget is to create an estimate of income or receipts. This section should clearly indicate expected monies from specified services, such as tuition, fees, contributions, and fund-raising projects. G. Morgan (1999) offered excellent examples of how to maximize a program's income by balancing full-time and part-time children, monitoring enrollment and attendance, having waiting lists, and determining fees and collecting them. For purposes of income calculations, in-kind donations should only be recognized when the good or service would have had to be purchased if it were not given. (Some programs, such as Head Start, however, must recognize nonessential donations.)

The next step is to estimate costs. Estimated costs given as percentages of the total operating budget for the highest quality programs are as follows: salaries—65%; rent or mortgage—11%;

food—7%; educational equipment and materials—3%; insurance—2%; telephone, utilities, office supplies, maintenance and repairs, and health and social services—14%; and supplementary services (screening/referral for children; family education and support)—3% (I. Powell, Eisenberg, Moy, & Vogel, 1994). Of the total operating budget for salaries, which may vary from 60% to 85% of the total budget in high-quality programs, 74% is for instructional staff, 13% is for noninstructional staff, and 13% is for benefits for all employees (Hayes, Palmer, & Zaslow, 1990). As shown, salaries account for the major part of the budget. In reality, for-profit centers making the most profits spend a lower percentage of their revenues on salaries (53.7%) than do centers making the least profits (62.4%; Stephens, 1991). Yet, as previously discussed, the quality of programs and salaries are highly correlated. Income must increase dramatically to provide the recommended level of compensation for early childhood professionals. For a quick estimate of operating costs, begin by considering salaries at least equal to 50% of the budget. The full cost per child is then calculated by this formula:

$$\text{Full cost per child} = \frac{\text{Teacher's annual salary}}{\text{\# of children in the group}} \times 2$$

After completing the expenditure section, the administrators should furnish actual figures for the current fiscal year. Any significant difference between current services and expenditures and those proposed should be explained. In planning the expenditure section, directors should keep the following points in mind:

1. Wages or salaries must be paid on time.

2. A desirable inventory level is one that will carry a program through 2 months of operation.

3. A program may have cash flow problems. Federal funds do not pay ahead of time for expenses; receipts and proof of money spent

are required for reimbursement, and even reimbursement checks may come irregularly.

To prevent cash flow problems, the director should observe the following practices:

1. Initial enrollment should not be overestimated.

2. Equipment should not all be purchased at the beginning. Equipment estimates should be calculated on cost per use rather than on the purchase price. For example, it is more expensive to spend $100 on equipment and then not use it than it is to spend $500 on equipment that will be in constant use.

3. The number of staff hired should correspond to initial enrollment.

4. Enrollment variations—for example, a summer lull—should be expected.

5. The director should check with the governmental agency for its reimbursement schedule, which may be 6 months or longer, and then determine whether the local bank will give credit or a short-term loan to state or federally funded centers that receive governmental reimbursements.

6. Accrual accounting is the best. Expenses should be reported when monies are encumbered rather than when paid.

A budget may be written in many ways, with only one absolute rule of budget formulation: Planned expenditures cannot exceed projected income. An example of an annual budget format is given in Figure 6–1. (Petty cash is not a budget item; petty cash is a way of spending money from any line.) G. Morgan (1999) offered excellent case examples that can be used for study.

Reporting the Budget

Directors are required to give budget reports. Some common types of reports are (a) a *budget comparison report,* in which one compares the previous month to the current month in each category; (b) an *annual report,* which lists the amount budgeted and the amount spent during the calendar or fiscal year; and (c) a *statement of financial position,* which reflects revenues earned and expenses incurred for a calendar or fiscal year.

To prepare reports accurately, all financial transactions should be recorded immediately. A checking account is the safest way to handle financial transactions and provides the audit trail. Directors need to be aware of the new financial accounting standards required for not-for-profit organizations (Lukaszewski, 1996).

TRENDS AND ISSUES

Although most people agree that early childhood care and education yield direct benefits to young children and their families as well as public benefits, a crisis is emerging that centers on financing. The problem has two facets: (a) quality of programs and (b) affordability to families. The problem is simply defined: If quality goes up in terms of wages, child–staff ratios, and program services, programs become less affordable, and vice versa. All professionals agree that no trade-off should exist between quality and affordability; however, the reality is that trade-offs are occurring and that quality is, more often than not, the loser. The Carnegie Institute (Carnegie Corporation of New York, 1996) reported that the United States provides some of the worst services for children in Western society. As more and more programs fail to meet even minimum standards, a new question arises: Will the money not spent today, along with major interest, be used to pay the piper in a not so distant future?

Providing Adequate Subsidies

In child care and education, portable aid substitutes for, rather than supplements, any direct support to a program (Stoney, 1999). The opposite is true in other consumer areas, such as paying for housing or higher education; in these areas, support is provided through direct financial assistance to programs and through portable subsidies that are made available to help users

ANNUAL BUDGET FORMAT

Income

Annual tuition (tuition for each X number of children)   _____

Application/registration fees   _____

Government monies   _____

Investment income   _____

Cash donations and funds raised   _____

Volunteer work and in-kind donations calculated as income   _____

Other: _____   _____

_____   _____

   Total income   _____

****

Staffing Expenses

Salaries

   Director or director/teacher   _____

   Teachers & assistants   _____

   Workers' Compensation, retirement, & other fringe benefits   _____

   Substitutes   _____

   Food service personnel   _____

   Secretary/receptionist   _____

   Custodian   _____

   Others: _____   _____

Taxes   _____

Payroll-related expenses   _____

Bank charges & loan payments   _____

Licensing and accreditation fees   _____

Staff training including consultant fees   _____

Professional memberships & fees   _____

Health insurance   _____

Advertising (for enrollment)   _____

Loss of property & uncollectable accounts   _____

Figure 6–1   Example of an Annual Budget Format

Other: _____   _____

_____   _____

Total staffing expenses   _____

****

Operating expenses

   Rent/mortgage   _____

   Building insurance   _____

   Children's equipment/materials/supplies (excluding food)   _____

   Field trips   _____

   Food and snacks   _____

   Meetings, special events   _____

   Vehicle purchase and maintenance   _____

   Utilities   _____

   Communication (telephone, fax, Internet service provider, & postage)   _____

   Business expenses: _____

      Office machines: computers, copiers, etc.   _____

      Service fees on office machines   _____

      Office supplies   _____

      Accounting and bookkeeping   _____

   Building repairs & maintenance costs   _____

   Publicity & fund-raising   _____

   Hygienic, health, & custodial supplies   _____

   Laundry   _____

   Other: _____   _____

_____   _____

Total operating expenses   _____

****

Total expenses before contingencies   _____

Allowance for contingencies (3% of budget)   _____

Total expenses   _____

Net cash flow from operations   _____

_____

Figure 6–1   *continued*

purchase the needed goods and services (Barbett & Korb, 1999; Stoney, 1999). To enhance program quality and to serve all children, both direct and portable subsidies are needed by child care and education programs (A. Mitchell & Morgan, 2001).

Problems exist with portable subsidies, too. First, government portable subsidies for child care and education are based on the going market price rather than on the full costs per child. Quality improvements require paying above the market rate. Differential subsidy rates should be based on the child (i.e., program costs are higher for infants and toddlers and for children with special needs) and on the overall quality of the program (i.e., accredited programs should have the highest subsidy rates). Second, gaps also exist in every state's subsidy system (Schulman, Blank, & Ewen, 2001). Because of restrictive eligibility, many families do not qualify for subsidies. Many eligible families do not receive aid because 33% of the states do not have the funds needed to serve all eligible families (Schulman & Blank, 2002). As previously explained, even families who receive aid often lose eligibility as soon as their income changes. Without experiences in high-quality programs, children from low-income families are at an increased risk for school failure. The Committee on Early Childhood Pedagogy recommended that the federal government fund high-quality center-based programs for all children who are at high risk for school failure (NRC, 2001).

Compensating a Skilled and Stable Workforce

Because early childhood care and education is essentially a service, high-quality programs depend on a skilled and stable workforce (Howes, Smith, & Galinsky, 1998; Vandell & Wolfe, 2000). Stagnant, low wages result in a nonstable supply of workers with inadequate skills and education. Funds to support professional training are limited. Most funds provide entry-level training only. Some potential sources include the following:

- Child and Adult Care Food Program
- CC&DBG
- Child Care Improvement Grants (Family Support Act)
- Job Training Partnership Act
- Title II (NCLB)

Although investments in education have a positive effect on program quality, investments in education have not had the same effect on compensation. As previously discussed, teachers subsidize early childhood programs with foregone wages. Now that the link between the staffing crisis and teacher compensation is understood, *compensation initiatives* (initiatives that result in dependable and ongoing wage increases) are under way (Whitebook, 2002). Initiatives vary with respect to the emphasis on the link between compensation and education/training (Whitebook & Eichberg, 2002). Some initiatives focus on wage increases or benefits tied to individual education/training; others focus on program eligibility to participate; and a few are system-based initiatives (e.g., U.S. Military's Personnel Pay Plan; Head Start Quality Improvement Act). (See the last section of this chapter for sources of summaries of some of those initiatives.) Finally, Zonder (1997) made some practical suggestions to aid directors in improving both staff compensation and quality.

Financing a System of Early Childhood Education

Without a coordinated system of services supported by financing strategies that provide needed resources, the goal of accessible, affordable, and high-quality programs for all children will not be fulfilled. The NAEYC (NAEYC Policy Brief, 2001) called for financing a system of early childhood education that includes (a) providing direct services to children in families with low incomes, (b) compensation for staff as a reward for additional education and a commitment to remain in a program for a longer period of time, and (c) funding the *infrastructure* (functions that support direct services).

Today, a major problem is the lack of financing coherence. The lack of coherence begins at the federal level, where the government cannot decide on one funding mechanism (e.g., tax credit or expansion of direct funding to early childhood programs) and thus has compromised by doing a little bit of everything. This lack of coherence in funding is perpetuated by the literally countless federal agencies that administer federal funds and by the two major state divisions (Department of Health and Human Resources and the Department of Education) that administer some of the federal funds and handle state supplementary revenues. By the time the paltry funds reach the local level, often there is no longer a good match between local needs and the goals of programs and no connection (transition) among programs. In all likelihood, there will be duplication of many program services, confusion for families who will find either too many program options or no viable program for their children, and children who will be placed in programs with inappropriate practices. A tripartnership among the federal, state, and local levels is needed to create a coherent funding policy that can make the most out of these bits and pieces. Kagan (2000a) stated that financing an early childhood education system begins with obtaining concrete data on how much it will cost; how revenues should be generated and disbursed; and the appropriate balance of contributions from public, private, and family sectors.

SUMMARY

Programs for young children are expensive. A quality program will cost $6,000 or more per child per year. Although families seldom pay the full costs, early childhood programs can be a large expenditure of the family budget, especially for middle- and low-income families. For many families, high-quality early childhood programs are simply not affordable.

Public early childhood programs are financed through local, state, and federal funding sources. For-profit early childhood programs are supported primarily through tuition and fees.

Budgets must be carefully made in keeping with program goals; that is, expenditures should reflect the goals of the program. Fiscal planning is important for several reasons. First, the quality of a program is determined to a great extent by expenditures, especially staff compensation. Regrettably, inadequate staff compensation has resulted in a staffing crisis in child care programs. Second, the central criterion for evaluating a program is often economic (benefits should exceed costs). Third, administrators must show fiscal responsibility.

A major crisis centers on financing. Decisions about funding are decisions about program quality. Any trade-off between affordability and quality will result in a loss of benefits to young children, their families, and all segments of society. Without adequate staff compensation linked to training and experience, early childhood programs will continue to be of mediocre quality and experience high staff turnover rates. Funding diversity outside some framework of coherence, such as a system of early childhood education, further erodes the judicious use of funds for the creation and maintenance of high-quality programs for all children.

FOR FURTHER READING

Center for Child Care Workforce. (1998). *Worthy work, unlivable wages: The National Child Care Staffing Study, 1988–1997.* Washington, DC: Author.

Ewing Marion Kauffman Foundation. (1999a). *Stepping up: Financing early care and education in the 21st century* (Vol. 1). Kansas City, MO: Author.

Ewing Marion Kauffman Foundation. (1999b). *Stepping up: Financing early care and education in the 21st century* (Vol. 2). Kansas City, MO: Author.

Helburn, S. W., & Bergmann, B. R. (2002). *America's child care problem: The way out.* New York: St. Martin's Press.

Mitchell, A. (1998). *Prekindergarten programs funded by the states: Essential elements for policy makers.* New York: Families and Work Institute.

Morgan, G. G. (1999). *The bottom line for children's programs: What you need to know to manage the money.* Watertown, MA: Steam Press.

Stevenson, M. F. (1995). *Fund raising for early childhood programs* (Rev. ed.). Washington, DC: National Association for the Education of Young Children.

Stoney, L. (1994). *Promoting access to quality child care: Critical steps in conducting market rate surveys and establishing rate policies.* Washington, DC: Children's Defense Fund.

Stoney, L., & Greenberg, M. (1996). The financing of child care: Current and emerging trends. Special issue on financing child care, *Future of Children, 6* (2), 83–102.

Initiatives for Child Care Compensation

Bellm, D., Burton, A., Shukla, R., & Whitebook, M. (1997). *Making work pay in the child care industry: Programming practices for improving compensation.* Washington, DC: Center for Child Care Workforce.

Kinch, A. F., & Schweinhart, L. J. (1999). Making child care work for everyone: Lessons from the Program Recognition Project. *Young Children, 54*(1), 68–73.

Mitchell, A., & Morgan, G. G. (2001). *New perspectives on compensation strategies.* Boston: Wheelock College, Institute for Leadership and Career Initiatives.

Mitchell, A., Stoney, L., & Dichter, H. (2001). *Financing child care in the United States.* Kansas City, MO: Ewing Marion Kaufman Foundation.

Montilla, M., Twombly, E., & DeVita, C. (2001). *Models for increasing child care worker compensation.* Washington, DC: Urban Institute.

Quality, Compensation, and Affordability. (2000). Promoting strategies for increasing compensation. *Young Children, 55*(3), 58–59.

Sources of Sample Business Documents and Management Tools

Bush, J. (2001). *Dollars & sense: Planning for profit in your child care business.* Albany, NY: Delmar.

Copeland, T. (1995). *The basic guide to family child care record keeping* (5th ed.). St. Paul: Redleaf.

Copeland, T. (1997). *Family child care contracts and policies: How to be businesslike in a caring profession* (2nd ed.). St. Paul: Redleaf.

Pruissen, C. M. (1998). *Start and run a profitable day care: Your step by step business plan.* North Vancouver: Self Counsel Press.

Stephens, K. (1991). *Confronting your bottom line: Financial guide for child care centers.* Redmond, WA: Exchange Press.

TO REFLECT

1. As an employee with a small business development program, you have been assigned to assist a potential proprietor of a child care program. What types of information should you encourage the prospective child care owner to have when he or she approaches the local bank for a loan?

2. Parent X has had her child enrolled in your program for 3 years. Her child's tuition has always been paid on time. Recently, the parent lost her job when a local plant closed. Although you have a fee policy, she asks that you make an exception for her child until she can find another job. You also note that you have a waiting list of three other families who have steady employment. What should you do—keep the child whose parent cannot pay or follow your fee policy and enroll a child whose parents can pay?

3. Teachers subsidize early childhood programs with foregone wages. For example, the Cost, Quality, and Child Outcomes Study Team (1995) found that center-based teachers' foregone income was $5,200 a year, and a national report (Education Week, 2000) stated that public school teachers' foregone income was $7,894 per year. What would this amount to in a lifetime of earnings? Many teachers work (e.g., planning, assessing, recording, attending meetings) beyond paid hours and spend out-of-pocket money on equipment and materials for their classrooms. As a professional advocate, how would you face the

perverse equation of care costing too little to achieve worthy staff compensation and too much to be affordable for many families? Do you think capable teachers who like teaching are justified in leaving the profession for better pay? In striking for better pay?

4. With many government budget crunches, funding sources for early childhood programs are limited. Under these circumstances should more affordable (and hence minimal quality) programs be offered to more children and families or should high-quality (and hence more costly) programs be offered to fewer children and families?

Planning the Children's Program

The focus of planning and administering an early childhood program is on planning and implementing children's activities. All other administrative tasks—meeting regulations, establishing policies, leading personnel, planning the physical facilities, and financing—are performed in reference to planning and implementing the children's program. The role of the director is to serve as the local program leader in defining the program base (by considering the knowledge and interests of children, the physical and social environments including the concerns of families and staff members, and standards for curriculum content), in defending the pedagogy (being knowledgeable and sensitive to program implementation), and in collaborating with those agencies in the community that provide support services (e.g., health care, family support, social services).

PROGRAM PLANNING

Curriculum is a way of helping teachers think about children and organize children's experiences in the program setting. Young children learn from every experience; thus, curriculum involves individual and group activities, physical care routines, supportive relationships, and all other aspects of a child's day in the program. Because of its comprehensive nature, the term *curriculum* is often replaced with the word *program* (Almy, 1975). In short, the curriculum that professionals select is the "actual membrane between the world and the child" (Weikart, 1989, p. 28).

Stating the Program Base

A major decision must be made about the local program base—the program's psychological (theoretical tenets about what and how children learn or develop), ecological (how learning and development are influenced by the uniqueness of a person's multiple environments), and philosophical (social purposes served) orientations. As discussed, the most commonly used program

bases come from the D-I and the holistic/developmental models. The children's program in the D-I approach is basically a teacher-determined fact- and skill-driven approach focused on the content of the three Rs. Conversely, the holistic/developmental approach selects curriculum goals based on broad-based developmental and cultural content and implements this curriculum through a combination of child-initiated and teacher-supported activities in a classroom community environment consistent with democratic values. The director's choice of a program base has an impact on all planning involved in early childhood programs (review Figure 2–1).

Developing Program Rationale

The rather theoretical program base leads to statements of program rationale. Some programs refer to these statements as their "program philosophy." Many local programs adopt rationale from published ideas and curriculum materials of the various models as shown in appendix 1. Local programs are also using the professional associations' position statements, referred to as DAP. DAP is not a program-based prescription; rather, it is an assertion that programs for young children should consider (a) present knowledge about child development and learning; (b) what we know about the strengths, needs, and interests of enrolled children; and (c) knowledge about the social and cultural contexts of the local community (Bredekamp & Copple, 1997). Because these three dimensions of knowledge are dynamic, the stated program base will change as knowledge changes. Besides resources from model programs and position statements about DAP, curriculum standards, developed by various regulatory and funding agencies, are being used to develop rationale.

Knowledge of Children. Although a lack of consensus exists about whether child development and learning can be used as a conceptual basis for curriculum planning, most professionals believe that knowledge of children should in- form program rationale. The NAEYC identified 12 principles of child development and learning that inform practice (Bredekamp & Copple, 1997). Age-related human characteristics lead proponents of DAP to assert that they can make general and reliable predictions about achievable and challenging curriculum for most young chil- dren in a given age/stage range (Katz, 1995b). For knowledge of children to be relevant, re- search must be current (e.g., National Center for Education Statistics, 2000) and be conducted in different cultures (Lynch & Hanson, 1998).

Interests and Needs of Children.   All educators re- alize that children have different needs and in- terests, and that these differences must be con- sidered in planning. Teachers in D-I programs often meet the problem of differences through testing and homogeneous grouping or place- ment. Conversely, teachers in holistic/develop- mental programs use continual observations of each child to determine challenging content and encourage child-initiated activities to implement much of the curriculum. Limited direct instruc- tion is implemented with individuals or small groups rather than with whole groups, for the most part.

In addition, the education of young children with special needs must be considered. Today over half of all preschool children are in inclu- sion programs. The roots for the practice of in- clusion began in the 1980s with the Regular Edu- cation Initiative (REI) movement. The REI began to gain support within special education (Bricker, Peck, & Odom, 1993; Division for Early Childhood Task Force on Recommended Prac- tices, 1993) and the early childhood professions (Wolery, Strain, & Bailey, 1992).

Children with special needs are a diverse group, and planning for these children is a chal- lenge (D. Ferguson, 1995; Fuchs & Fuchs, 1998; P. Hunt & Goetz, 1997; T. E. C. Smith & Dowdy, 1998). The IEP is composed of tailor-made goals for the child. According to Wolery, Strain, and

Bailey (1992), these goals must be very specific and will usually require adult assistance for chil- dren to attain them. Services focusing on measur- able, specified outcomes are highly compatible with the D-I view. Intervention can also be imple- mented in holistic/developmental classrooms, however, because the curriculum is already so in- dividualized. Several early childhood special educators have designed strategies that combine DAP of the early childhood care and education programs with the more teacher-determined environment of the special education class- room (Hemmeter & Grisham-Brown, 1997; B. Mallory, 1998; Russell-Fox, 1997). Under the IDEA amendments of 1997, professionals are calling for a developmentally appropriate frame- work for writing IEPs (Edmiaston, Dolezal, Doolittle, Erickson, & Merritt, 2000; Yell & Shriner, 1997). (See appendix 1 for readings on inclusion of children with special needs.)

Environment of Local Programs.   The child has to be seen in terms of himself or herself (the *microsystem*); the child's immediate or extended family (the *mesosystem*); and the child's neighbor- hood, school, and community (the *macrosystem*). The United States is becoming a more diverse na- tion, and children come to early childhood pro- grams from all cultural backgrounds. Children are being socialized in home and classroom set- tings that are a microcosm of the world. Now, more than ever before, curriculum must mirror *all* young children (King, Chipman, & Cruz- Jansen, 1994). Thus, diversity is a hallmark of quality early childhood programs.

Physical Environment.   Young children's experi- ences are tied to their local physical environ- ment. Successful curricular activities are based on prior experiences and are more likely to be successful when they involve an abundance of firsthand, direct experiences and real objects to manipulate. For example, the theme "winter ac- tivities" is not a good long-term topic in some cli- mates. Furthermore, nearby sites are essential for conducting investigations when using the project approach.

In quality programs, the social and cultural environment is closely tied to the program's physical environment. The general decor of the space should look "homey," not "foreign." For example, the visuals displayed, music listened to, literature read, and dramatic play props should reflect the social and cultural composition of the families, staff, and community of the local program.

Social Environment.   Directors must also analyze the strengths and needs of families in the local programs. Cultural manifestations include (a) language (verbal and nonverbal) and conventions about its use; (b) intellectual modes, such as learning styles; and (c) social values, such as daily child-rearing tasks, skills nurtured in children, guidance ("discipline") practices, and attitudes about delays and exceptionalities seen in children.

Early childhood programs are becoming more culturally sensitive and responsive to the families they serve (B. Mallory & New, 1994). Three documents were especially influential in creating a greater sensitivity to the social environment of early childhood programs:

1. Bias was brought into the spotlight through the publication, *The Antibias Curriculum: Tools for Empowering Young Children* (Derman-Sparks and ABC Task Force, 1989).

2. The NAEYC's (1995b) recommendation that "the nation's children all deserve an early childhood education that is responsive to their families; communities; and racial, ethnic, and cultural backgrounds" (p. 1).

3. The NAEYC's revised statement concerning DAP, which included basing program practices on what is culturally appropriate in addition to what is developmentally and individually appropriate (Bredekamp & Copple, 1997).

The local program rationale should reflect the needs and strengths of families and the views of the staff. For example, Chipman (1997) called for

1. using various cultural learning styles (e.g., cooperative rather than competitive environments),

2. assessment that focuses on potential as well as performance and relies on multiple measures,

3. awareness of multiple intelligences,

4. greater cultural sensitivity when disciplining,

5. acceptance of children with special needs, and

6. correcting subtle stereotypical messages.

Program directors must realize there may be more than one path to high-quality programs (Bromer, 1999; Modigliani, 1990). Wardle (1999) believes that some culturally embedded practices would never be considered DAP; yet he sees some practices that might be developmentally inappropriate in some cultures but appropriate in others.

Besides developing program rationale based on the culture of the local community, all children need multicultural/antibias education. Local programs are often uncertain about which goals to pursue (Derman-Sparks & A.B.C. Task Force, 1989). Many experts realize that merely adding multicultural content to a traditional curriculum is not enough; they believe that what is needed is content approached from many cultural perspectives. The Quality 2000 Initiative (Kagan & Neuman, 1997b) called for programs that promote cultural sensitivity and pluralism (C. Phillips, 1994b; D. Phillips & Crowell, 1994). Derman-Sparks (1992) sees the following four goals for a multicultural/antibias curriculum for young children: (a) developing personal and group identity; (b) seeing similarities as well as differences; (c) identifying unfair or untrue images, speech, or behaviors and realizing that such things hurt; and (d) confronting bias by "speaking up." C. Phillips (1994a) described three distinct ways to plan: (a) Programs can focus on changing negative responses to cultural diversity; (b) programs can begin with the culture of the home and build transitions to mainstream lifestyle; and (c) programs can embrace biculturalism by asking family assistance in maintaining home cultural values and lifestyles. Swick, Van Scoy, and Boutte (1994) suggested several appropriate opportunities for promoting multicultural sensitivity: (a) educating families about building children's self-esteem, (b) helping children explore their own culture through family and school activities, (c) training families and teachers to assess their multicultural competence, (d) supporting the development of skills needed to promote multicultural understandings, and (e) promoting intense teacher education concerning multicultural education. The many readings under "Multicultural/Antibias Understandings" listed in appendix 1 should help local programs in developing their program rationale.

Directors must realize that programs cannot be totally preplanned without considering the abilities and interests of a particular group of children. Vygotsky (1978) pointed out that children's cognition is contextualized; that is, it emerges out of and derives meaning from particular activities and social experiences. He felt that learning experiences that do not make use of the social histories of particular children result in difficulties. Using the observations of children engaged in program activities as a resource for program planning has been called *emergent curriculum* (E. Jones & Nimmo, 1994).

Standards. Early childhood programs have recently become a standards-based environment. In general, *standards* can be defined as expectations for learning and development. More specific terms used to refer to standards include the following:

- **Program standards** (expectations for the quality of a program)
- **Content standards** (what a child should be able to do within an academic area, such as mathematics)
- **Benchmarks** (the knowledge and skills a child should have by a given time in school, such as the first semester of kindergarten)

- **Performance standards** (quality levels of performance with respect to the knowledge or skill described in a benchmark)

Program standards have been part of early childhood care and education for many years. For example, program standards were written for nursery education in 1929. More recently, program funding standards were written for Head Start (called "Head Start Performance Standards") and for other grant-funded programs. Several professional early childhood associations have published accreditation standards for early childhood programs for several years, too.

Early Learning Standards.   The NAEYC refers to content standards for young children as *early learning standards*. Early learning standards are new to early childhood care and education. Although the standards movement, in which student outcomes on performance standards were linked to placement and retention decisions and to a program's accountability, began in elementary and secondary education in the 1980s, the development of the National Education Goals of 1989 led to a standards movement affecting all levels of education (Bredekamp & Rosegrant, 1995a). Many states are developing early learning standards that are linked to the state's curriculum for school-age children. For example, 19 states and Washington, DC, have specific expectations for kindergarten children; 15 states and Washington, DC, have standards for prekindergarten children, but only 6 states require adherence to the standards; and no state has early learning standards for child care programs (Doherty, 2002). Head Start has also developed new standards, called the "Head Start Child Outcomes Framework," intended to guide the assessment of 3- to 5-year-old children enrolled in Head Start (Head Start Bureau, 2001).

Several factors have contributed to the movement for early learning standards, including the following:

1. Many states want their kindergartens and prekindergartens to have standards in alignment with state standards for older children as part of an effort to improve school readiness.

2. Studies of brain development have increased the understanding of young children's capacity for learning (Bergen & Coscia, 2001).

3. A recent longitudinal study showed that many children had learned traditional kindergarten subject matter in literacy and mathematics in preschool programs (National Center for Education Statistics, 2000) and were thus prepared for more challenging content in kindergarten.

4. The Committee on Early Childhood Pedagogy recommended that federal and state departments of education develop, field test, and evaluate curricula and companion assessment tools based on what is known about children's development. They recommended that content standards for the early years address these often omitted areas: phonological awareness, number concepts, methods of science investigations, and cultural knowledge and language (NRC, 2001).

Literacy and Mathematics Standards. The early childhood years are the most important period for literacy development. The NRC (1999b) stated that *functional literacy* is now defined as reading for information and interpreting ideas. This definition has increased literacy expectations. The International Reading Association (IRA) and the NAEYC (2000) adopted a joint position statement in 1998 on literacy development in young children. This statement included (a) a call for developmentally appropriate goals and expectations, (b) a developmental continuum for reading and writing development to be used for identifying literacy goals, and (c) a cautionary reminder for program designers to take into account developmental variation. The emphasis on early learning standards for literacy development has resulted in state involvement in literacy initia-

tives not only for kindergartens and primary grades but also for younger children. Some of these initiatives are family literacy programs, but others are focused on the training of preschool and child care teachers (Jacobson, 2002). These initiatives are being funded by a mix of federal, state, and private monies (see appendix 7).

Similar to the joint position statement on literacy, the National Council of Teachers of Mathematics (NCTM) and the NAEYC (2002) adopted a joint position statement in which the associations affirmed that high-quality and challenging mathematics for 3- to 6-year-old children is a vital foundation for later learning. Although the statement has many recommendations, a goals continuum was not developed. However, the NCTM (2000) had developed standards for prekindergarten through second-grade children prior to the position statement.

In addition to the goals developed for literacy and mathematics, many other quality resources are available for curriculum planning in all areas. Appendix 1 and the last section of this chapter provide some excellent resources for program planning.

Stating Goals

Goals for a local program are rather broad and general statements about what the designers hope to achieve. Katz (1995a) believes curricula at every level should address the acquisition and strengthening of these dimensions of growth:

1. **Knowledge.** Children should have knowledge the culture deems important. Knowledge includes representational knowledge (ideas, concepts, constructs) and behavioral knowledge (how to perform certain skills or enact certain procedures).

2. **Skills.** Children should develop general intellectual skills (observing, gathering information, problem solving), more specific academic skills (decoding words, writing letters), and social skills (communicating, negotiating).

3. **Dispositions.** Children should acquire positive dispositions or enduring habits of the mind (a desire to understand, a striving for accuracy, persistence, open-mindedness).

4. **Feelings.** Children should develop positive feelings, which are subjective emotional or affective states (feel competent, feel accepted).

Only a few statements (often fewer than 18) will constitute the goals of a program. An example of a **goal statement,** the collection of written goals, is provided by the National Association for the Education of Young Children and the National Association of Early Childhood Specialists in State Departments of Education (1991).

Translating Goals into Child Outcomes

Local programs further delineate goal statements by identifying *child outcomes* (competencies children need to acquire or strengthen). Curricular competency lists may also include actions teachers may take to assist children.

Generally speaking, the competencies most often identified by D-I programs come from the three Rs. For example, competencies may include physical knowledge concepts, visual and auditory skills, language development, number concepts, and small-motor coordination skills. Competencies may also concern attitudes, such as persistence and delay of gratification. Broad competencies are often further defined by writing as narrower concepts and skills which are then sequenced for implementation. Table 7–1 is an example of one of these

Table 7–1   Sample Competency Writing for D-I Programs Age Group: Preschoolers

Needed Competencies	Sample Curriculum for Preschoolers
Preschoolers need to	**For *preschoolers,* adults need to**
Identify eight basic colors (red, orange, yellow, green, blue, purple, black, and brown) by	
(1) matching	Provide materials for matching like colors.
(2) pointing to (3) naming	Using colored paper, (a) name colors and ask child to point to color and (b) point to colors and ask child to name.
(4) making secondary colors	Ask child to name primary colors and then secondary colors. Provide paints, color paddles, or crayons and paper and ask child to make secondary colors.
(5) coloring/painting with colors as directed	Provide a color sheet with directions for child to follow (e.g., color the ball "red").
(6) sorting color "families"	Provide materials showing various shades/tints of each of the eight basic colors. Ask child to group these into color families or to seriate shades/tints into color families.

concepts written in a competency format. In this example, "identify eight basic colors" is the broad concept, and the six narrower concepts are numbered and listed in sequential order of difficulty.

Competencies in holistic/developmental programs are often broad in comparison with D-I programs. Competencies cover all domains (i.e.,

physical, cognitive, language, social, and emotional) and may also cover Katz's (1995a) dimensions of development. Broad competencies permit the offering of a wide range of activities. Varying levels of skills and interests are accommodated through a range of performance criteria. Tables 7–2, 7–3, and 7–4 show examples of

Table 7–2   Sample Competency Writing for Holistic/Developmental Programs Age Group: Infants and Toddlers

Needed Competencies	Sample Curriculum for Infants and Toddlers	
Infants and toddlers need to	For *infants,* adults need to	For *toddlers,* adults need to
Develop a sense of trust and a loving relationship.	Read infant cues and meet infants' physical and psychological needs quickly and warmly.	Support attempts to accomplish tasks, comfort when tasks are frustrating, and express joy at successes.
		Respect security objects, such as a favorite toy.
Develop a sense of self.	Call infant by name.	Name body parts.
	Place mirrors at eye level, including near the floor.	Respect children's preferences (e.g., toys and food).
		Support attempts at self-care.
Have social contact.	Engage in face-to-face contacts, use physical contact, and have vocal interactions.	Help children control negative impulses and comfort when they fail.
		Help children become aware of others' feelings.
		Model interactions for children to imitate.
Explore their world.	Take children to their world of experience or bring objects and activities to them.	Provide support for active exploration (be near but refrain from too many adult suggestions for play).
Sample sensory experiences.	Provide pictures and objects to touch, taste, and smell.	Place books and objects on shelves.
		Decorate room with pictures and objects.
Undertake motor experiences.	Provide safe places for movement. Encourage movement (e.g., place objects slightly beyond reach).	Provide safe places and equipment and materials that aid large-muscle development (e.g., stairs, ramps, large balls, push/pull toys).
	Express joy at successes.	Express joy at successes.

Table 7–3   Sample Competency Writing for Holistic/Developmental Programs Age Group: Preschoolers and Kindergartners

Needed Competencies	Sample Curriculum for Preschoolers and Kindergartners
Preschoolers and kindergartners need to	**For *preschoolers* and *kindergartners*, adults need to**
Feel reassured when fearful or frustrated.	Use positive statements.
	Provide comfort when frustrated and repeatedly demonstrate needed rules.
Become more independent.	Provide opportunities for practicing self-help skills, such as having dressing dolls and providing time and just the needed assistance in toileting and eating.
Make friends.	Permit children to form their own play groups.
	Encourage onlookers to join a play group by suggesting roles for them (e.g., a grandmother in housekeeping center in which the other roles are already taken).
	Model positive social interactions for them to imitate.
Explore their world.	Provide many materials that children can manipulate (e.g., water, sand, blocks, latches) in order to discover relationships.
	Provide dramatic play props for children to use in trying on roles.
Exercise their large muscles and control their small muscles.	Provide equipment to climb on, "vehicles" to ride on, and balls to throw and catch.
	Provide materials to manipulate (e.g., art tools, puzzles, pegs and Peg-Boards, beads to string).
Engage in language experiences.	Talk to, read to, sing to, tell and dramatize stories, and play singing games (e.g., Farmer in the Dell).
	Write children's dictated stories.
	Have classroom charts and other printed materials in view.
	Provide materials (e.g., paper and writing tools) for children to draw, scribble, write, copy signs, etc.
Express themselves creatively.	Provide a variety of art media and various forms of music for creative expression.
Develop concepts of themselves and the world around them.	Provide opportunities to learn skills (e.g., mathematics) and content areas (e.g., social studies, science) in integrated ways (while working on projects instead of times set aside to concentrate on each area).*
Become familiar with symbols.	Provide props for dramatic play.
	Provide books for "reading."
	Write children's dictated stories.
	Provide art and writing materials.
Make choices and implement their ideas.	Permit children to select many of their own activities.
	Provide a physical setting that encourages individual or small, informal groups most of the time.

*Key readings on the content of and teaching strategies for skill and content curricular areas are listed under the heading "Readings on Curriculum Development" at the end of this chapter.

Table 7–4 Sample Competency Writing for Holistic/Developmental Programs Age Group: Primary Grades/Levels

Needed Competencies	Sample Curriculum for Children in Primary Grades (Levels)
Children in primary grades (levels) need to	For *children in primary grades (levels),* adults need to
Show more self-control.	Prevent overstimulation when possible and help children deal with fears and excitements (e.g., talking about them).
	Set clear limits in a positive way and involve children in rule making.
	Use problem solving to manage discipline problems.
Gain more independence.	Permit children to identify areas needing improvement.
	Support children in their work toward mutually established goals.
Work with other children.	Provide opportunities through small groups for children to cooperate with and help other children.
Explore their world.	Provide materials that are concrete and relative to ongoing projects.
	Plan for field trips and resource people to enhance classroom projects.
Use large and small muscles.	Provide appropriate materials.
Use language as a way of both communicating and thinking.	Provide materials for both reading and writing that will enhance ongoing projects.
	Provide quality literature.
	Read aloud stories and poems each day and ask child readers to share in the oral reading.
	Plan projects, such as preparing a class newspaper or making books.
Express themselves creatively.	Plan ways to integrate art, music, dance, and drama throughout the day.*
Develop concepts.	Integrate curriculum (skill and content areas) in such a way that learnings occur through activities such as projects rather than in an isolated format.*
Use symbol systems.	Provide manipulatives.
	Assist children in developing skills in reading, writing, and mathematics when these are needed to explore or solve meaningful problems.*
Make choices.	Provide opportunities to work individually and in small groups with self-selected projects and materials for a greater part of the time.
	Involve children in their own self-management (e.g., setting their own goals, budgeting their time, evaluating their own efforts, cooperating with others).

*Key readings on the content of and teaching strategies for skill and content curricular areas are listed under the heading "Readings on Curriculum Development" at the end of this chapter.

some of the competencies that might be used in these programs. Another example of competencies is the "Head Start Child Outcomes Framework" (Head Start Bureau, 2001).

Organizing the Curriculum

Curriculum activities must be organized in some manner. Children want to make sense of their physical and social world and to do so must build on their prior knowledge and skills. Thus, children cannot profit from a "grab bag" of experiences. Curriculum organizers are either separate concepts and skills or integrated approaches. Because the advantages of one organizer becomes the disadvantages of the other, only advantages will be discussed.

Separate Concepts and Skills. To organize a curriculum by separate concepts and skills, key concepts are identified and carefully sequenced. (The sequenced key concepts, along with teaching suggestions, are often provided in manuals.) Teachers help develop the concepts in the prescribed sequence using the children's acquired competencies as the bridge to the next concept. For example, teaching number concepts may begin with rote counting followed by activities involving one-to-one correspondence, rational counting, recognition of written numerals, and number combinations (adding by using objects only, objects and symbols, and symbols only).

Curriculum organization by separate concepts and skills has long been used with older children who are often taught separate academic content even by different teachers during the school year. Early childhood program designers of the D-I models often incorporated this method of organizing the curriculum.

Organizing the curriculum by separate concepts and skills has its advantages, including the following:

1. For some subject matter, researchers have identified a sequence of how particular concepts and skills build on others (Clements, Sarama, & DiBiase, 2003).

2. Children develop concepts in a coherent manner (according to academic logic).

3. In this age of standards and accountability, this method of organizing the curriculum ensures engagement with and hopefully mastery of important ideas. (The method is often seen as an efficient way to master standards that are important for program accountability.)

4. Untrained or inexperienced teachers may not know the rich possibilities of other materials (e.g., materials housed in learning centers) for children's learnings. Thus, they feel more comfortable and possibly more successful using separate concepts and skills as a curriculum organizer than the integrated curriculum approaches.

Integrated Curriculum Approaches. An **integrated curriculum approach** involves choosing a topic or concept for extended investigation from which activities can be planned that draw from one or more academic disciplines (e.g., mathematics, science). Several strategies can be used in the integrated approaches: (a) choosing topics that permit the exploration of content across subject-matter disciplines, (b) identifying concepts that are meaningful across the disciplines (e.g., literacy, patterns), and (c) identifying processes that are applicable to many disciplines (e.g., representation, scientific method). Many resources are now available on the integrated curriculum (Dodge, Jablon, & Bickart, 1994; Hart, Burts, & Charlesworth, 1997; Hohmann & Weikart, 1995; A. Mitchell & David, 1992).

Integrated curriculum approaches are not new. Correlated curriculum approaches and the project approach have long been used for school-age children. Integrated curriculum has been more or less *the* approach used in early childhood programs until D-I models were designed in the 1960s. The introduction of D-I models resulted in a reaction by the holistic/developmental program designers, who do not think of curriculum as specific skills and content to be "covered" by teachers and "absorbed" by children.

Integrated curriculum approaches have many advantages, including the following:

1. Young children are active, self-motivated learners who learn best through self-initiated experiences rather than decontextualized teaching (Fromberg, 2002; Isenberg & Quisenberry, 2002).

2. Cognitive learning efforts foster the construction of knowledge and skills (Chaille & Britain, 1997), promote more social interactions (DeVries, Reese-Learned, & Morgan, 1991), and encourage children to take more responsibility for their own work (B. Jones, Valdez, Norakowski, & Rasmussen, 1994).

3. Children learning through integrated curriculum approaches showed high-level mastery of basic reading, language, and mathematics skills (Marcon, 1992). This finding was particularly significant for boys (Marcon, 1992) and for children from low-income families (Knapp, 1995b).

4. High-involvement and low-stress activities promote the best learning (Rushton & Larkin, 2001; Santrock, 2003; Wolfe & Brandt, 1998).

5. In integrated approaches, children can use different combinations and degrees of each of the eight intelligences or avenues for learning (Carlisle, 2001; Gardner, 1993).

6. Children develop social competence best through cooperative efforts (Katz & McClellan, 1997) and feel successful when they engage in meaningful learning and learn in a safe way (Fromberg, 2002; Isenberg & Jalongo, 2000).

7. Integrated approaches permit the curriculum to be based on the needs and interests of children in the group and thus would not look the same from year to year or from one classroom to another. Rather than be preplanned, curriculum is said to emerge from children's needs and interests, teachers' interests, things and people in the environ-

ment, unexpected events, and values of the culture (E. Jones & Nimmo, 1994; K. Williams, 1997).

8. Making conceptual connections across diverse academic disciplines reduces the volume of standards.

Units and Themes. Two approaches to integrating the curriculum are units and themes. Both are teacher planned, for the most part, although children may participate in the planning and in choosing some activities. Usually, the *unit* has a narrower or more focused topic with more specific learning objectives than the *theme*. However, the approaches are so similar that many programs call this approach, a *thematic unit*.

Thematic units often last one to two weeks. Teachers choose the topics, plan the activities, and prepare the materials for various learning centers and other activities to correspond with the topics. During implementation, information on the topic is given by the teacher to the whole group in a daily unit lesson. Usually, art, music, cooking, and literature, as well as other activities, more or less reflect the unit theme. Because teachers design these activities, children may not see the connection. Often, literacy and mathematics competencies are presented as contrived thematic activities. For example, during a "Fall" unit, children may match capital and lowercase letters written on laminated paper pumpkin shells and on "detached" laminated paper pumpkin stems, respectively. The child places the correct stem on each pumpkin. Matching is seldom learned in a week or even in a semester; thus, the matching will continue but the patterns will change to correspond with the thematic units.

Teachers often repeat units year after year. In some schools, all the teachers on a given level (e.g., kindergarten) teach the same unit lessons using many of the same materials. Teachers could make thematic units more DAP by carefully observing the needs and interests of the children who are currently enrolled and by allowing ideas to emerge from the children as well as the teachers.

Projects. The *project,* an integrated curriculum approach, involves choosing an area of interest or a problem and incorporating curriculum areas into it (Katz & Chard, 2000). The project approach had its roots in progressive education (Dewey, 1916; Kilpatrick, 1918). The approach was recently revitalized by the Reggio Emilia schools.

Ideally, project ideas emerge as opposed to being preplanned. Project ideas can result from children's natural encounters with the real environment, the mutual interests of children and teacher, and the teacher's response to an observed need in children (Helm & Katz, 2001; E. Jones & Nimmo, 1994). The topic of the project is written as a narrative line used to convey the direction of children's investigation (e.g., instead of using the broad thematic unit topic of "Water," a project topic might be "How We Use Water" or "The River in Our Town"; Katz & Chard, 2000). Criteria used for determining project topics include the following:

1. Topics must be related to children's own everyday experiences.
2. The study must involve real objects.
3. Opportunities must exist for collaboration, problem solving, and representation (e.g., artwork, block building, dramatic play).
4. Competencies in all domains must be applied as needed.

According to Helm and Katz (2001), projects go through three phases. In Phase 1, teachers begin thinking about a project topic and may even "web" to see the possibilities. A **web** is a visual representation (a diagram resembling a spider web) of curriculum possibilities. An *anticipatory web* is one to which children add their own ideas. If the program has early learning standards, expected child outcomes may be added to the web or just listed (see Figure 7–1; additional readings on webbing are listed at the end of the chapter). The teacher checks for children's

knowledge and interests by having the children verbally share their experiences about a topic and express them through representation. Phase 1 lasts about 1 week and forms the basis for modifying plans. During the 2nd and 3rd weeks, Phase 2 occurs. Children gain new information. They get firsthand, real-world experiences and are led to recall and represent details. Children have many opportunities to reflect on their expanding and refining knowledge through multiple representations. A project grows from the input of children, teachers, and families and through the introduction of materials. Phase 3 allows children time to further assimilate their ideas through play or share their understandings. Often, Phase 3 leads to new ideas and new projects. (See the end of this chapter for key books on project planning.)

IMPLEMENTING THE CURRICULUM

After planning the basic approach of the local program, the director and staff must implement the program (i.e., decide how the specific features of the program will be carried out). To help all children reach their potentials, planning must be done for a particular group of children, in a particular place, and at a particular time. Planning requires constant observation of children and a willingness to adjust program implementation.

Designing Teaching Strategies

Teaching strategies have to do with how teachers interact with children during instructional time. Similar to the lack of consensus on content, a lack of consensus on the best pedagogical strategies also exists. Teaching strategies are closely tied to the way the curriculum is organized.

Teacher-Directed Activities. Teacher-directed activities occur mainly in D-I early childhood programs, kindergartens, and programs for school-age children. Direct instruction is the preferred

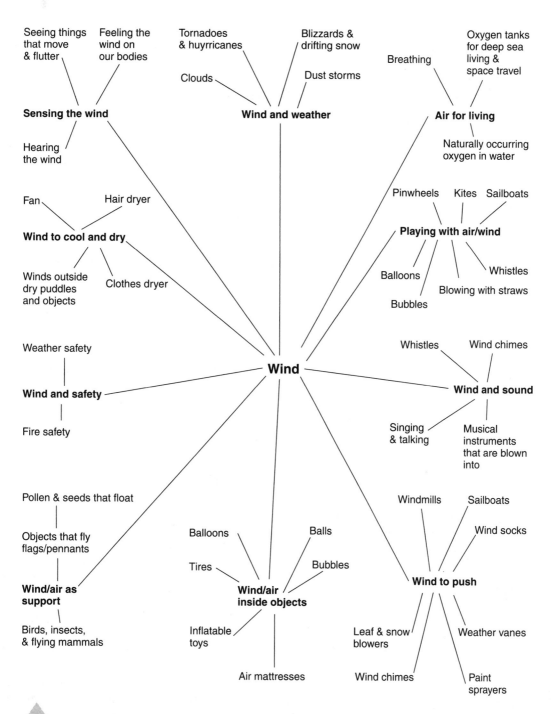

Figure 7–1A   Anticipatory Concept Web

Figure 7–1B   Abbreviated Anticipatory Concept Web with Expected Child Outcomes

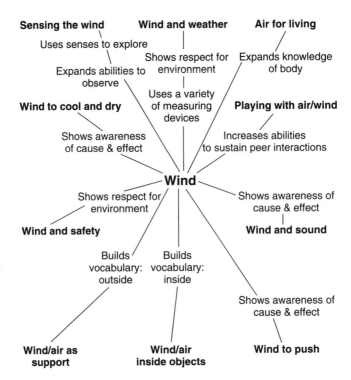

method of those teachers who organize curriculum as separate concepts and skills and is often used to teach "academic" content, especially language, reading, and mathematics.

The instructional plan, often written as a lesson plan, usually includes clearly stated performance objectives, a procedure, and an assessment of the children's performance. Objectives and corresponding materials are based on sequenced concepts. Drill is often part of the procedure.

Child-Initiated Activities and Scaffolding. Child-initiated activities occur mainly in holistic/developmental early childhood programs. Child-initiated activities and scaffolding are the preferred method of those who use integrated curriculum approaches.

In this teaching strategy, children engage in child-initiated activities approved by the teacher. For example, High/Scope children plan and get

teachers approval before beginning daily activities (Hohmann & Weikart, 1995). Another type of assistance comes from Vygotsky's theory. Children are aided in their pursuits by scaffolding, a direct support system provided to a child to perform in his or her *zone of proximal development* (ZPD; the distance between where the child is functioning and where he or she can profit from assistance by an adult or more advanced peer).

Program planners who prefer child-initiated activities cite these reasons for their preference:

1. Teacher-directed activities on a large- or whole-group basis make it almost impossible to provide for various developmental levels, interests, or learning styles.

2. Child-initiated activities enhance all areas of development (Frost, Wortham, & Reifel, 2001).

3. Teachers can provide the needed structure for children's learning by (a) structuring

materials, space, and time; (b) engaging in coplanning with children; and (c) providing scaffolding or short periods of direct instruction.

Using Computers and Other Technologies

Computers have been in early childhood programs for over 2 decades, and many young children have computers in their homes. Program designers often debate whether the gains in children's development justify the costs (Healy, 1998). Undoubtedly, technology is here to stay, and if used correctly, will affect children's learning by extending and enriching many concepts being offered in the classroom.

Connecting Technology to Young Children's Development. Because development changes over the early childhood years, DAP with technology also changes. Because computers do not match the way infants and toddlers learn, computer use is not recommended for this age group (Elkind, 1998; Haugland, 1999). Three- and four-year-olds need to explore computers. Teachers may ask questions and propose problems to expand children's computer experiences but should provide minimal help. For these preschool children, computer activities should be one of many classroom experiences. Kindergarten and primary-age children need to continue to make choices about computer activities but should also have some teacher-planned activities that match desired program outcomes. For this age group, important skills include learning how to seek out information and gathering and integrating knowledge from various sources (Haugland, 1999; Haugland & Wright, 1997).

Noting the Benefits. Research indicates that computer activities can supplement other activities and also provide unique avenues for learning. Program designers must understand the connection between the types of computer activities and their benefits.

General Benefits. Regardless of the program orientation, computers and other technologies will provide several benefits. First, children will learn about technology (e.g., people control technology by making up rules that in turn control how technology works; different programs work by using different rules; technology is part of the everyday world). Second, new hardware and software features are permitting children with disabilities to use these technologies (Behrmann & Lahm, 1994). Third, some objects (e.g., shapes, pictures) can be manipulated more easily on the computer than their concrete counterparts (e.g., actual blocks) in a child's hand (P. Thompson, 1992). Fourth, technologies allow teachers to meet the diverse needs of children (Haugland & Wright, 1997). Finally, computers can aid social competence, such as communication, cooperation, and leadership, and help develop positive attitudes about learning (Cardelle-Elawar & Wetzel, 1995; Denning & Smith, 1997; Haugland & Wright, 1997).

Benefits of Selected Software and Integration. Because computers can also be misused, educators must take responsibility for using this learning tool to the advantage of children. To help teachers in making critical judgments, the NAEYC developed a position statement on technology and young children (NAEYC, 1996c). The statement calls for teachers to carefully evaluate software, integrate technology into the regular learning environment as only one tool of learning, and provide equitable access to technology.

The curricular values of these technologies are dependent on the selected software and the degree of technology integration into the curriculum. Thus, program orientation must be considered in all decisions. Programs with D-I orientations have primarily used **drill-and-practice software,** a form of software that resembles a ditto sheet or workbook page and is sometimes referred to as an "electronic ditto sheet." Some drill-and-practice software programs are small, separate programs, but others are drill-oriented

integrated learning systems (ILSs), a super-software package that provides a complete curriculum in a subject, especially reading or mathematics, through an extensive sequence of lessons. Much research has been conducted on the effects of using drill-and-practice software. Children who used these programs increased their reading skills (Hess & McGarvey, 1987) and showed even greater gains in mathematics (Clements & Nastasi, 1992). On the negative side, drill-and-practice use may diminish children's feelings that they control technology (Papert, 1993), may cause a loss of creativity (Haugland, 1992), and will not improve children's conceptual skills (Clements & Nastasi, 1993). In the affective domain, drill-and-practice software encourages turn taking (*not* collaboration) and competition (Clements & Nastasi, 1992).

Those who advocate holistic/developmental programs prefer **open-ended software,** software in which children are free to do many different things (e.g., drawing but not "coloring in" predrawn pictures, word processing, and programming in Logo). Because children do not accomplish much when asked to "freely explore" (Lemerise, 1993), distinctions must be made between open-ended projects and "freely exploring" the computer; however, research has shown that the use of open-ended software results in gains in intelligence quotients, nonverbal skills, structural knowledge, long-term memory, manual dexterity, and self-esteem (Haugland, 1992). Haugland also found that the gains were greater when children used supplemental activities (activities beyond the computer). For example, when compared with a drill-and-practice group of children, the "off-and-on" group showed gains of more than 50% over the drill-and-practice group in verbal, problem-solving, and conceptual skills, although the drill-and-practice group had worked on the computer three times longer. Research has also shown that open-ended software aids critical thinking (Clements & Nastasi, 1992; Kromhout & Butzin, 1993; Nastasi & Clements, 1994) and allows for the connection of ideas from different content areas (Bontá & Silverman, 1993). Unlike drill-and-practice software, open-ended programs encourage collaboration (Clements, 1994). Nastasi and Clements (1994) also reported higher scores on *effectance motivation* (believing one can affect the environment).

Other high-technology opportunities can be provided through digital videos and cameras, computer-controlled robots, and objects that communicate with computers. Internet use is also providing intriguing possibilities. These new technologies may significantly enhance young children's learning.

Creating Classroom Transitions

Transitions occur with changes of activity, location, or caregiver (e.g., when a parent leaves or picks up a child). The way transitions are handled either makes the day go smoothly and positively for children or causes chaos and negative reactions. Well-executed transitions incorporate the teachers' knowledge of individual and group needs (B. Taylor, 1999). Some general suggestions are as follows:

1. Begin the day on a calm and happy note. Early morning greetings and sharing are important.

2. Have a consistent daily routine and reduce the number of "between activity" transitions with large blocks of time.

3. When making a transition, do the following: (a) Prepare children by announcing the upcoming transition; (b) keep signals low-key (e.g., soft bell or quiet voice) and make the transition activity interesting but not too stimulating (see resources at the end of the chapter); (c) position oneself appropriately to offer assistance; and (d) begin new activities right away.

4. Use realistic expectations and provide some choices to diminish child resistance.

5. Avoid developmentally inappropriate transitions if possible. If impossible, teach the

activity as a game (e.g., walking in a line can be a "parade").

6. Prepare children in advance of moving them to a new location.

7. End the day pleasantly and calmly. Plan easy and quick ways to distribute notes or items to be sent home. Warmly acknowledge the departure of the group or each child.

Providing for Physical Care Routines

Teachers in D-I programs help children follow set procedures in physical care activities (e.g., children gather for snacks at a given time, children are seated, snacks are distributed in a predetermined way, cleanup procedures are followed). In the holistic/developmental programs, physical care activities are used for socialization (e.g., table manners are emphasized during eating) and for cognitive enrichment (e.g., children discuss nutrition and the properties of foods—color, size, texture, and shape).

Planning for Special Times

Special plans must be suitable to children's needs and be as carefully developed as daily plans, although they require even more flexibility. Certain routines—especially eating, toileting, and resting—should always be followed as closely as possible.

First Days.   Whether the first days represent children's first experiences in early childhood programs or denote their entry into different programs, children view the first days with mixed feelings of anticipation and anxiety. The first days should be happy ones because they may determine children's feelings of security and their attitudes toward programs.

A baby or a toddler needs a week to make a gradual transition to a program (L. Miller & Albrecht, 2000). This time is called *inserimento* in the Reggio Emilia program (Bove, 1999). Initiation of preschool and even kindergarten children is best done gradually, too. This time allows

for the preliminary orientation of children to the program. If all children enter on the same day, additional adult assistance should be secured for the first days.

Generally speaking, planning for first days requires that more time and individual attention be given to greeting children and their families, establishing regular routines, and familiarizing children with teachers and the physical plant. For the first days, use equipment and materials and plan activities that most children of the particular age group are familiar with and enjoy and that require minimum preparation and cleanup time. Teachers need to enjoy this time of becoming acquainted with the children.

Field Trips.   A field trip is a planned journey to somewhere outside the school building or grounds. Early childhood programs have long used community resources. Field trips and resource people are used extensively in projects. Thoughtful planning of field trips and for resource people is important both because of benefits to children's learning and because of the added dangers of taking children beyond the building and grounds. The teacher must do the following:

1. Help children achieve the goals of the program.

2. Make arrangements with those in charge at the point of destination. Staff should keep a perpetual inventory of local places to visit and resource people suitable to their program's needs. In compiling such an inventory, list the name of the place, the telephone number, the person at the location in charge of hosting visitors, age limitations, the time of day visitors are welcome, the number of children the place can accommodate, how long a tour takes, and additional comments. Preferable apparel, whether advance notice is required, what children can see or do and what the host provides for children, and the number of adults requested to accompany the group should also be stated. Refer to this inventory in making

plans. Make arrangements for the visit, and if the host is to give explanations, make sure he or she can communicate with young children. Make arrangements for the care of the physical needs of children, staff, and other adults assisting with the field trip, such as locations of places to eat and rest rooms. One staff member should visit the destination before final plans are made.

3. Provide enough qualified volunteer aides to supervise. Good judgment and experience in working with young children are qualities to look for in volunteers. The ratio should be one adult for every four or five children. Volunteers should have a list of the names of the children under their care; when they do not know the children,

name tags should be worn for easier identification.

4. Obtain written parent consent for each field trip and keep the signed statement on file. Notice the example of a field trip form in Figure 7–2. The signed form is essential because the parent's signature serves as evidence that the parent has considered the potential dangers of his or her child's participating in the field trip. No statement on the form should relieve the teacher and director of any possible liability for accidents. Such a statement is worthless because a parent cannot legally sign away the right to sue (in the child's name) for damages, nor can staff escape the penalty for their own negligence, as

---

Dear _____ ,

Our class will be making a field trip to the _____ bakery on May 13. A baker will take us on a tour of the bakery. We hope to learn how bread and rolls are made. We will be leaving school at 9:00 a.m. and will be returning in time for lunch. We will ride on a bus to the bakery and back to our school. We all think it will be fun to ride on the bus with our teacher, Mrs. Smith, and three mothers. Please sign the form below to give your permission for me to take the trip.

                                                                    Jody

- -

I, _____ , give my permission for
              (Name of parent)

_____ to attend a field trip to
              (Name of child)

_____ .
              (Destination)

My child has permission to travel _____ .
                                              (In a parent's car, on a school bus)

I understand that all safety precautions will be observed.

Date _____ Signature _____

Figure 7–2   Field Trip Form

shown in judicial decisions (*Fedor v. Mauwehu Council of Boy Scouts,* 1958; *Wagenblast v. Odessa School Dist.,* 1988).

5. Obtain permission from the director or building principal for the children to participate in the field trip. Policies of early childhood programs often require that teachers complete forms giving the specifics of the field trip.

6. Become familiar with the procedures to follow in case of accident or illness. Take children's medical and emergency information records in case emergency treatment is required during the field trip.

7. Make all necessary arrangements for transportation and determine whether all regulations concerning vehicles and operators are met.

8. Prepare children by helping them understand the purposes of the field trip and the safety rules to be observed.

9. Evaluate all aspects of planning the field trip and the field trip itself.

Class Celebrations. Class celebrations are traditional in early childhood programs and require special planning. Celebrations should relate to the program's objectives because "tacked on" celebrations could be counterproductive. Directors need to consider the beliefs and preferences of families and staff members and local community customs concerning various celebrations. If celebrations are to be observed, specific policies should be written and provided to families.

Developing Supportive Relationships

Although many directors are aware of the importance of early brain development, fewer realize the importance of social and emotional competence. Recent research has confirmed that social and emotional competence is critical for a child's early school success and for later accomplishments in the workplace. Lack of social and emo-

tional competence is linked to behavioral, social, and emotional problems.

School involves social relationships with adults and peers. Children who are successful in school are confident, use friendly approaches with peers, can communicate emotions, are able to concentrate on and persist in tasks, can follow directions, and are attentive. Yet data from a recent survey showed that up to 46% of kindergarten teachers reported that half their class or more had specific problems in a number of areas in making the transition to school (Peth-Pierce, 2001).

Because the early childhood years, beginning in infancy, are critical to the development of social and emotional competence, directors must give a great deal of attention to this aspect of children's development in their programs. The quality of the adult–child relationships is the most important aspect of the quality of the children's program. Children whose teachers are sensitive and responsive and who give them attention and support are more advanced in all area of development compared with children who do not have these positive inputs (Lamb, 1998; NICHD Early Child Care Research Network, 1998a, 2000).

Caring as Infant/Toddler Curriculum. Close and caring relationships between very young children and significant adults provide the context for all aspects of growth, development, and learning (R. Thompson, 1997). Programs must stress continuity of care (Essa, Favre, Thweatt, & Waugh, 1999). Continuity can be accomplished by assigning each child to a primary and secondary caregiver and having these caregivers stay with a group of infants and toddlers until the preschool years. Caregivers must also build a supportive relationship with families to provide for continuity of care. Because culture is so involved in early child-rearing practices, cultural issues are becoming more important as programs enroll infants (Lally, 1995).

For infants the development of a secure attachment with their mother, father, and/or other primary caregiver is the major social and emotional milestone (Raikes, 1996). To facilitate this attachment, caregivers must be able to show empathy and develop rapport with babies. Babies share their emotions, and adults must be able to read the cues, engage in mutual gazes, and communicate with gurgles and coos and with language, including happy and lulling songs (Honig, 1995). Reciprocal responsiveness between the adult and the baby has been likened to a dance (Honig, 2002; Thoman, 1987).

By age 2, toddlers become more self-aware and want to gain some independence and self-control. Good teachers show an attitude of total presence ("I am interested in you; I am here for you."). Teaching and caring for emotionally fragile toddlers requires calmness and and a sense of knowing when to do "more" and when to do "less" (Rofrano, 2002). Additional resources are listed at the end of the chapter.

Nurturing Emotional Literacy.   Peth-Pierce (2001) noted that young children, especially boys, enter school with emotional illiteracy. These children often misinterpret their own emotions and those of others. They often lack the ability to manage their emotions properly. Emotional literacy (intelligence) is based on three skill levels—perception, understanding, and managing (Salovey & Sluyter, 1997).

Although a universality of emotions exists, the culture affects the expression of emotions and the contexts in which they are expressed (Small, 1998). Thus, families and teachers often see "problem" behaviors and temperaments in different ways (National Center for Education Statistics, 2000). In talking about some behaviors, teachers and families may see that emotional literacy is using the appropriate emotional expression for a given social context.

To be effective, emotional literacy skills must be interwoven into the daily curriculum. Some ideas include the following:

1. Empower children by helping them feel successful. Teachers can begin empowering by (a) using both child-initiated and teacher-determined activities, (b) encouraging both interdependent and independent activities, (c) recognizing the uniqueness and contributions of each child, (d) focusing on achievements in all domains, (e) working individually with children, (f) saving and displaying products of achievement, and (g) encouraging peers to say positive things about class members.

2. Read stories that discuss emotions. Follow up with reflective questions (e.g., "How did _____ feel when _____?"). Relate the stories to children's lives (Sullivan & Strang, 2002/03).

3. Extend children's vocabulary of "feeling" words.

4. Help children make inferences about expressions, body language, and tone of voice.

5. Create a "comfort corner" in which children can express feelings by writing, drawing, using puppets, and dictating into a tape recorder (Novick, 1998). Other resources are listed at the end of this chapter.

Encouraging Social Competence.   **Social competence** is the ability to initiate and maintain good relationships with peers (Katz & McClellan, 1997). Children who are not competent are often labeled as aggressive or loners. Competent participation in a group is developmental and can be encouraged in the preschool years. Emotional literacy is tied to social competence. Understanding one's emotions and those of other's as well as the ability to regulate one's emotions allows for the development of social competence. Beyond nurturing emotional literacy, teachers can aid social competence by reducing external controls and building a sense of community.

Reducing External Controls.   *Discipline* and *punishment* are terms that focus on external control by adults. Child development specialists and early childhood professionals have warned of the harmful effects of punishment, especially corporal punishment (Hyman, 1997). Any form of shame reinforces a negative self-label and leads to a self-fulfilling prophecy (Gartrell, 1995). Regrettably, external control is still used by many teachers.

Today, "time-out" has become the major means of dealing with class problems. The rationale for time-out is that children need to be separated from peers to regain emotional control and to think about the effects of their behaviors. Time-out is a technique that punishes rather than teaches strategies for handling impulsive behaviors (Gartrell, 1998). Using time-out diminishes the child's feelings of self-worth and deprives the child of group membership (Marion, 1999). In fact, the threat of time-out makes the class apprehensive and leads to a feeling of conditional acceptance (Clewett, 1988).

Although praise is not punishment, it is a form of external control. Teachers praise when children "jump through their hoops" (Kohn, 2001b). Praise is ineffective and harmful for these reasons:

1. Children may stop positive activities once attention is withdrawn.
2. Praise creates stress because one must continue doing good to maintain love.
3. Praise only occurs for observed actions (some actions are missed).
4. Praise makes children dependent on adult appraisal, as opposed to self-appraisal, of their efforts.
5. Praise may be used to control others (e.g., "I like the way _____ is sitting" means that others are not doing what the adult wants).

Effective praise can be used to promote self-confidence. Effective praise is delivered privately (Marshall, 1995) and focuses exactly on what the child did as opposed to a generalization of "goodness" (e.g., "Thank you for picking up your

books" rather than "You are a good helper"; R. Hitz & Driscoll, 1988).

Building a Sense of Community. Teachers need to build a sense of community instead of using practices that single out individual children or small groups of children for punishment or praise. Building a sense of community involves facilitating the learning of democratic life skills (i.e., seeing oneself as a worthy individual, working cooperatively as a member of the group, expressing emotions in nonhurtful ways, seeing the viewpoints and feelings of others, and solving problems in ethical ways; Gartrell, 1998). Some suggestions for building a sense of community are as follows:

1. Form teacher–child attachments to build trust (Betz, 1994).
2. Model openness and empathy. Champion all children as equal participants including those who may be stigmatized.
3. Work on projects and other small-group activities in which all children plan together, share responsibilities, and acknowledge each other's contributions.
4. Use class meetings to (a) make agreements that ensure an atmosphere free from exclusionary practices and ridicule, (b) work on biases, and (c) problem-solve (Vance & Weaver, 2002).
5. Be a facilitative coach for conflict resolution. Gartrell (2000) recommended this five-step approach to resolving conflicts: (a) Cool down, (b) help children state problem, (c) brainstorm for ways to resolve the issue, (d) try one alternative, (e) and follow up.
6. Use guidance talks with individual children. Discuss how their behaviors affect others, how positive approaches should work better for all concerned, and ways to make amends (Marion, 1999).

Other resources for encouraging social competence are listed at the end of the chapter. For children who have exceptionally challenging emotional or behavioral difficulties, special interventions are needed (see chapter 8).

Supporting Children Who Experience Stressful Events. Young children experience *stressors* (situations and events that cause stress) in their lives. Some stressors involve illnesses; others involve loss, such as parental separation or the death of a loved one; and others involve violent acts. Even school activities, especially program transitions and assessment, can be stressful. New information coming from brain research shows that all information is sent not only to the functionally appropriate place in the brain (e.g., the speech center) but also to the lower brain, which sorts its emotional significance. If the information is threatening, the normal thinking abilities are blocked (Wolfe & Brandt, 1998).

Teachers can work to create low-stress activities in the classrooms and to support children during stressful events in their lives. Some suggestions are as follows:

1. Acknowledge children's feelings and accept reactions that may seem "wrong." (A child's developmental stage affects reactions.)

2. Provide caring words to defuse upsetting things (Rushton & Larkin, 2001) and physical contact to help assure ("Helping Young Children in Frightening Times," 2001).

3. Emphasize familiar routines at home and at school.

4. Avoid letting children see the event replaying many times. For example, turning off the television or getting children involved in activities away from the television can prevent them from seeing replays of certain events.

5. Express your own fears and sadness. Remain calm while talking to children and assure them that people are there to help those in need (Greenman, 2001).

6. Engage in classroom activities that release stress (discussions; physical activities; story-

telling and dramatic play; sand, water, and block play; play with clay; and reading books that deal with these stressors).

7. Communicate with families about any changes noted in a child's development and provide suggestions concerning what families may do. Other resources are listed at the end of this chapter.

Considering Other Aspects of Implementing the Curriculum

Regardless of the program goals, several other points need to be considered before implementing: For each planned activity, adequate staff, space (and its arrangement), materials and equipment, and time must be provided. Plans must consider the needs of all children. For some children, activities may need to be modified by using a different learning modality or by changing the challenge level. McCormick and Feeney (1995) provided an example of a checklist form for "activity customization." Finally, planning also requires considering alternative activities to forestall problems that result from a lack of interest, inclement weather, unforeseen scheduling changes, or breakage of materials or equipment.

CREATING APPROPRIATE PROGRAM SUPPORTS

Decisions about grouping, scheduling, and staff responsibilities are the backbone or support of planning and implementing the local program. These decisions involve management within a group and thus directly affect how care and education services are delivered.

Grouping

U.S. society acknowledges the importance of the individual; yet, a chaos-free society must have some conformity—some group-mindedness. From birth until a child enters an early childhood program, the child's individuality is fostered, tempered only to some extent by the "group needs" of the child's family. In contrast, because of the number of children involved and the time limits imposed, the early childhood program is forced to put some emphasis on group needs except in infant and toddler programs. (Infants and toddlers function totally as individuals in quality programs.) Although the individual is most important throughout the early childhood years, group needs become more important as children advance in age. In fact, it is often said that a child enrolling in an early childhood program is entering a "group setting."

The NAEYC (1998a) defines **group** as the number of children assigned to a staff member or to a team of staff members occupying an individual classroom or a well-defined physical space within a larger room. All grouping decisions are used to facilitate adult–child and child–child interactions in the program.

Size of Group.   Group size is not directly related to program base. Regardless of the program base, the literature is replete with the benefits of small group sizes. Small classes are associated with more adult–child interaction, more individual attention, more social interactions, more complex play, and more teacher time given to fostering children's language and problem-solving skills (Howes, 1997; Kontos, Howes, & Galinsky, 1997). Small class size increases school-age children's achievement in reading, mathematics, and science; decreases grade repetitions; and increases graduation rates (Krueger, 1999). Small group size is critical to children needing more individual attention—infants and toddlers, children with special needs, and children who are experiencing a lack of continuity in their lives.

The National Academy of Early Childhood Programs recommends a maximum group size of 8 for infants; 12 for toddlers up to 30 months; 14 for toddlers between 30 and 36 months; 20 for 3-, 4-, and 5-year-olds; 30 for 6- to 8-year-olds; and 30 for 9- to 12-year-olds in SACC programs (NAEYC, 1998a). To determine the size of the group, the director must also consider the needs of the children, the skills of the staff, the housing facilities, and the grouping plan.

Adult–Child Ratios.   The **adult–child ratio** is the number of children cared for by each adult. Data from Howes, Phillips, and Whitebook (1992) showed that programs that met the NAEYC-recommended adult–child ratios were more DAP than programs not meeting the NAEYC recommendations. The NAEYC (1998a) concluded that smaller group sizes and lower adult–child ratios are strong predictors of program compliance with indicators of quality, especially appropriate curriculum and positive adult–child interactions. Improving the ratio without reducing group size yields less positive results (Mosteller, 1995). In achieving quality in programs, the adult–child ratio is more important than the educational level of staff in infant and toddler programs; conversely, the educational level of the staff is more important than the adult–child ratio in programs for preschool and school-age children (NICHD Early Child Care Research Network, 1996).

The recommended adult–child ratio within group size is detailed in Table 7–5. Preschool model programs rarely exceed 1:7, but most states use a ratio of 1:10 to 1:20 for preschoolers, and kindergarten and primary classes often exceed 1:20 (Gormley, 1995). Even minor changes in group sizes and adult–child ratios affect program quality (Burchinal, Roberts, Nabors, & Bryant, 1996; Howes & Norris, 1997).

Grouping Patterns.   **Grouping,** or organizing children for learning, is an attempt to aid individual development in a group setting; that is, to make caring for and teaching children more manageable and effective. Once curricular plans are formulated and the basic delivery system is chosen, decisions about grouping patterns follow.

Moving Children from Program to Program.   Two approaches are used to move children from program to program. The **graded** system, which began at the turn of the 20th century, is based on the concept that children of similar ages are homogeneous in ability. The graded system in which children enter at a legally specified age is the most typical practice of elementary schools.

Table 7–5   Recommended Adult–Child Ratios Within Group Size*

Age of Child	Group Size										
	6	8	10	12	14	16	18	20	22	24	30
Infants (birth to 12 months)	1:3	1:4									
Toddlers (12 to 24 months)	1:3	1:4	1:5	1:6							
2-year-olds (24 to 30 months)		1:4	1:5	1:6							
2-1/2-year-olds (30 to 36 months)			1:5	1:6	1:7						
3-year-olds					1:7	1:8	1:9	1:10			
4-year-olds						1:8	1:9	1:10			
5-year-olds						1:8	1:9	1:10			
Kindergartners								1:10	1:11	1:12	
6- to 8-year-olds								1:10	1:11	1:12	1:15
9- to 12-year-olds										1:12	1:15

*Smaller group sizes and lower adult–child ratios have been found to be strong predictors of compliance with indicators of quality such as positive interactions among staff and children and developmentally appropriate curriculum. Variations in group sizes and ratios are acceptable when the program demonstrates a very high level of compliance with criteria for interactions, curriculum, staff qualifications, health and safety, and physical environment.

Source: National Association for the Education of Young Children. (1998). *Accreditation Criteria and Procedures of the National Academy of Early Childhood Programs—1998 edition.* Washington, DC: Author. Reprinted with permission. A review and revision process of these standards is taking place.

Many nonpublic early childhood programs group children in the same way based on the assumption that children should be grouped according to their stage and that age is the best predictor of stage.

Recognizing that children of similar ages are not necessarily homogeneous in achievement, other educators called for a **nongraded** approach, a plan that enables children to advance in the sequenced curriculum at their own rate. Self-pacing simply refers to the fact that some children will progress through the required curriculum either faster or slower than their age peers in all or some of the curriculum areas.

Grouping Within the Classroom.   **Ability grouping** is really achievement-level grouping. It is based on the assumption that both children and teachers profit from a homogeneous achievement group. Ability grouping is common in programs adher-

ing to the D-I position. Thus, it is widely practiced in elementary schools and particularly during reading and mathematics instruction. Even nongraded approaches may use ability grouping, although the children in the group could be of different ages (Bingham, 1995). In an attempt to get their instructional groups even more alike, many teachers place children in three or four intraclass groups for prereading, reading, or mathematics instruction.

In opposition to the homogeneity of ability groups, a resurgence of interests in mixed-age grouping is occurring. **Mixed-age grouping,** also called **multiage grouping** and **family grouping,** is defined as placing children who are at least 1 year apart in age in the same classroom group. Mixed-age grouping appears to be identical to the nongraded concept, which also groups children of mixed ages; however, unlike the nongraded approach, which may group according to ability, mixed-age grouping is designed to keep the groups heterogeneous in all ways (Bingham, 1995). In fact, the rationale for such programs rests on the benefits of heterogeneity itself. Multiage grouping is more common at the preschool level than at the elementary level, although it was the "dominant model of education until the arrival of the industrial revolution and urbanization" (Veenman, 1995, p. 366). Early childhood programs using mixed-age groupings include Froebelian kindergartens, Montessori schools, the more recent "open education" models (e.g., British Infant Schools, the New Zealand schools), some child care centers, family child care homes, and the Reggio Emilia schools.

Holistic/developmental programs note that Piaget (1959) and Vygotsky (1978) both saw mixed-age peers as important for the learning process. DAP are based on the concept that curriculum is matched not only to the child's stage but also to the child's individual needs. Katz (1991b) believes that early childhood programs must be responsive to a wide range of developmental levels and to the individual backgrounds and experiences of children. Individual needs can be met more readily in family groups.

A great deal of research has been conducted on family versus ability grouping. The cognitive and social advantages of family grouping over ability grouping are given by Bailey, Burchinal, and McWilliam (1993); DeBord and Regueros-de-Atiles (1991); Katz, Evangelou, and Hartman (1990); and Theilheimer (1993).

Family grouping does have some difficulties that must be worked out. Family grouping requires more skill on the part of the teacher as a diagnostician of what children need to enhance their development, more planning in terms of managing schedules and equipment and materials, and a greater ability to operate in a team-teaching situation. Family grouping also requires family education because many families think their older children are not being stimulated because of the presence of younger children in the group. Several excellent readings on strategies

for programs implementing mixed-age groups are available (Katz, Evangelou, & Hartman, 1990; L. Moore & Brown, 1996).

Persistence Grouping. **Persistence grouping** is a form of grouping in which the teacher has the same group of children for consecutive years, usually infants and toddlers or kindergarten and first grade. Persistence grouping is also called **multiyear assignment** and **looping.**

The rationale for persistence grouping is that (a) children will do better in school if secure (Burke, 1996); (b) in the 2nd year, more instructional time is created because teachers "know" the children and the children know their teachers' expectations (Kuball, 1999); and (c) teachers have more curriculum flexibility that can result in more individualized instruction and a greater ability to monitor the child's work (Bellis, 1997). Because persistence grouping involves change, many things must be considered. Do parents like the idea? Do teachers feel comfortable with teaching two grade levels? May a teacher or parent opt out? An excellent source for explaining implementation of such grouping is *The Looping Handbook* (J. Grant, Johnson, & Richardson, 1996).

Scheduling

Decisions about scheduling greatly influence children's feelings of security, the accomplishment of program goals, and the staff's effectiveness. **Scheduling** involves planning the length of the session and timing and arranging activities during the session.

Length of Session. Early childhood programs traditionally have been half-day sessions with the exception of child care programs. Because of the awareness of the needs of young children who are considered at risk, Head Start and other preschool programs for at-risk preschool children are often full-school-day programs. As noted, more kindergartens are opting for a full-day schedule.

Although controversy has surrounded the length of the session, maternal employment and the growing emphasis on early learning standards will result in more and more full-day programs. It is obvious, however, that the quantity of time spent in school is not as significant as the quality of the experience.

Timing and Arranging Activities. Regardless of whether the session is half-day or full-day, good schedules for early childhood programs have the following characteristics:

1. A good session begins with a friendly, informal greeting of the children. Staff should make an effort to speak to each child individually during the first few minutes of each session. A group activity, such as a greeting song, also helps children feel welcome. This is also a good time to help children learn to plan their activities.

2. Children's physical needs, such as toileting and eating, should be cared for at regular intervals in the schedule. For older children, special times should be set aside for toileting early in the session, before and after each meal or snack, and before and after resting. Meals should be served every 4 or 5 hours, and snacks should be served midway between meals; however, each child's individual needs must be considered. This aspect of the schedule must remain very flexible.

3. The schedule should fit the goals of the program and the needs of the children as individuals and as a group. A balance should be maintained between physical activity and rest, indoor and outdoor activities, group and individual times, and teacher-determined and child-initiated activities.

4. The schedule must be flexible under unexpected circumstances, such as inclement, weather, children's interests not originally planned for, and emergencies.

5. A good schedule should be readily understandable to the children so that they will have a feeling of security and will not waste time trying to figure out what to do next.

6. A good session ends with a general evaluation of activities, straightening of indoor and outdoor areas, a hint about the next session, and a farewell. Children need to end a session with the feeling of achievement and with a desire to return. These feelings are important to staff, too!

Schedules must fit the length of the program day, week, and year. However, *scheduling* usually refers to the timing of daily activities. Local programs should devise their own schedules. Programs that serve children of different age groups must prepare more than one schedule to meet each group's needs.

In general, schedules are often referred to as fixed or flexible. Programs place more emphasis on group conformity through using **fixed schedules;** that is, by expecting children to work and play with others at specified times and by taking care of even the most basic human differences—appetites and bodily functions—at prescribed times except for "emergencies." Often, programs for kindergarten and primary-grade (level) children have fixed schedules. (State departments of education/instruction often specify the total length of a school day and the number of minutes of instruction in each of the basic subjects). D-I preschool programs are very time oriented, too. An excellent example of a fixed schedule is that used in Bereiter and Englemann's (1966) program.

Conversely, **flexible schedules** allow for individual children to make some choices as to how to spend their time and require children to conform to the group for only a few routine procedures (e.g., the morning greeting and planning session) and for short periods of group "instruction" (e.g., music, listening to stories). Infant programs have perhaps the most flexible schedules of all early childhood programs because infants stay on their own schedules. Child care programs often have flexible schedules because of their longer hours of operation, children's staggered arrivals and departures, and the varying ages of children the center serves. Flexibility is a must for children with special needs, too. McCormick and Feeney (1995) provided excellent suggestions for helping these children prepare for program transitions and follow transition directions. Furthermore, the health care services provided for children with special needs (e.g., ventilating, breathing treatments, tube feeding) should be planned to meet the individual needs of these children and when it causes least disruption to peers. Programs adhering to the holistic/developmental approach, including open education primary-level programs, also have long, flexible time periods. Flexible schedules are more appropriate with emergent and integrated curricula (E. Jones & Nimmo, 1994; Rosegrant & Bredekamp, 1992). Rigid schedules undermine children's decision making and play (Wien, 1996). Of course, children need guidance in programs with flexible schedules; Wien and Kirby-Smith (1998) showed how two teachers used collaborative reflection to know when an adult-imposed change in activities is and is not appropriate.

Because almost all programs use schedules, a few examples for different age groups follow. Examples are not given for infants, who follow their own schedules, or for public school kindergarten and primary programs because they adhere to state and local regulations regarding scheduling. Feeding, toileting, and resting were placed on all the foregoing schedules; however, health needs should be provided on an as-needed basis but also should be offered at regularly scheduled times. The schedules are only suggestions; they are not prescriptive.

1. **Toddler schedules.** Toddler schedules usually revolve around the children's feeding and sleeping periods but should include lots of time for play activities both inside and outside. An example of a schedule for a full-day session is shown in Figure 7–3.

2. **Nursery school schedules.** Nursery schools serve children of prekindergarten age (usually exclusive of infants) and are frequently operated for half-day sessions. Children arrive and depart at approximately the same times. Generally, nursery school schedules have short group times for stories and songs and longer blocks of time for

Figure 7–3   Toddler Schedule

7:00–8:30 a.m.	Arrival, changing or toileting, dressing babies who are awake, and individual activities
8:30–9:00 a.m.	Breakfast snack, songs, stories, and finger plays
9:00–10:00 a.m.	Manipulative toy activities conducted by staff, and changing or toileting
10:00–11:00 a.m.	Naps for those who take morning naps and outside play for others. (Children go outside as they awaken.)
11:00–11:45 a.m.	Lunch and changing or toileting
11:45–1:00 p.m.	Naps
1:00–2:00 p.m.	Changing or toileting as children awaken and manipulative toy activities
2:00–2:30 p.m.	Snack, songs, stories, and finger plays
2:30 p.m. until departure	Individual activities

Figure 7–4   Nursery School Schedule

9:00–9:15 a.m.	Arrival, group time activities, such as attendance count, greeting song, and brief exchange of experiences
9:15–10:15 a.m.	Active work and play period with child-selected activities in the activity centers
10:15–10:30 a.m.	Toileting and snack
10:30–10:45 a.m.	Group time for story, finger play, music, or rhythmic activities
10:45–11:15 a.m.	Outdoor activities
11:15–11:30 a.m.	Rest
11:30–11:45 a.m.	Cleaning up and discussing the next session; "What we will do tomorrow . . ."
11:45–12:00 noon	Quiet activities and farewells as children depart

active work and play periods. An outline of a nursery school schedule is shown in Figure 7–4.

3. **Child care center schedules.** Child care centers have perhaps the most flexible schedules of all early childhood programs. An example of a child care center schedule is shown in Figure 7–5.

4. **School-age child care program schedules.** School-age child care (SACC) programs usually follow very flexible schedules. An outline of an SACC program is shown in Figure 7–6.

Determining the Responsibilities of Staff

In making daily plans, coordination of the responsibilities of staff is essential. Without careful planning, the program will have duplication of tasks, omissions in services, and a general lack of staff efficiency. Following are some criteria to consider in planning the responsibilities of the staff:

1. The goals of the local program
2. Specific organizational policies (the way children are grouped for care or instruction)
3. The number of staff involved and the qualifications and skills of each individual

4. The layout of the building and grounds and the nature of equipment and materials
5. The specific plans for the day

The responsibilities of staff must be in keeping with legal authorizations (e.g., certification) and with the policies of the governing board. The director usually determines the responsibilities of staff, although in some cases, teachers may assign duties to assistant teachers and volunteers. Specific responsibilities may be delegated by the director or lead teacher, but mutually agreed-on responsibilities in keeping with the basic job descriptions are usually more satisfactory. A periodic exchange of some duties lessens the likelihood of staff burnout and the frustration of always having less popular responsibilities, such as straightening the room. Staff morale will be higher and the program will function more coherently and smoothly when all staff members are involved in the program from planning to implementation.

TRENDS AND ISSUES

Three major trends and issues seem to be occurring in planning the children's program. One concern is planning a quality curriculum within

Figure 7–5   Child Care Center Schedule

7:00–9:00 a.m.	Arrival, breakfast for children who have not eaten or who want additional food, sleep for children who want more rest, and child-initiated play (which should be relatively quiet) in the activity centers
9:00–9:30 a.m.	Toileting and morning snack
9:30–11:45 a.m.	Active work and play period, both indoor and outdoor. Field trips and class celebrations may be conducted in this time block
11:45–12:00 noon	Preparation for lunch, such as toileting, washing, and moving to dining area
12:00 noon–1:00 p.m.	Lunch and quiet play activities
1:00–3:00 p.m.	Story, rest, and quiet play activities or short excursions with assistants or volunteers as children awaken from naps
3:00–3:30 p.m.	Toileting and afternoon snack
3:30 p.m. until departure	Active work and play periods, both indoor and outdoor, and farewells as children depart with parents
5:00 p.m.	Evening meal for those remaining in center, and quiet play activities until departure

today's standards-based environment. A second concern, closely tied to the first, is how to implement the curriculum using balanced teaching strategies. The third concern is the debate about inclusion.

Defining Quality Curriculum: The Standards Movement

As discussed in chapter 1, concern about quality programs, including quality curricula, has been growing. Release of data from several national

Figure 7–6   SACC Schedule

6:30–7:00 a.m.	Arrival, and activities such as quiet games or reading
7:00 a.m. until departure for school	Breakfast, grooming, and activities such as quiet games or reading
3:00–3:15 p.m.	Arrival from school
3:15 p.m. until departure	Snack, and activities such as homework, tutorials, outdoor play, craft projects, table games, and reading

studies showed the poor to mediocre quality of early childhood programs (Friedman & Haywood, 1994; Helburn, 1995; Kontos, Howes, Shinn, & Galinsky, 1995). The importance of curriculum quality as a foundation for lifelong academic and social competence was confirmed by two reports: *From Neurons to Neighborhoods: The Science of Early Childhood Development* (Shonkoff & Phillips, 2000) and *Eager to Learn: Educating Our Preschoolers* (NRC, 2001). Additionally, a call for early learning standards became part of an effort to improve school readiness by improving content and pedagogy in the early years.

Seeing the Benefits. Early learning standards can be part of a high-quality system of program services to children. Curriculum standards can help identify important educational outcomes and can help build a coherent system of learning opportunities for children, even resolving some of the barriers to program transitions (B. Caldwell, 1991). Developing local curriculum standards can also be a means of building consensus between schools and families.

Noting the Risks. Although every professional agrees on "quality," curricular issues are far from resolved. Adopting standards can be beneficial, but doing so can be risky because standards reflect preferences. Several professional associations see the risks of early learning standards as being basically the same as the risks expressed about the trend toward "academic" programs that led to position statements about DAP. Following are some of the concerns about early learning standards:

1. Standards may focus on children's achievements rather than content and pedagogical improvements (Hatch, 2002).
2. Test scores can be used to penalize children (L. Shepard, Kagan, & Wurtz, 1998a).
3. Because of developmental variability and heightened risks for some children, bench-marks are an added risk (Neuman, Copple, & Bredekamp, 2000).
4. Standards themselves can be too narrow if they are a fact- and skill-driven approach. Nonacademic strengths, such as emotional literacy, social competence, and positive approaches to learning, also predict success in school and in later life (Peth-Pierce, 2001; Raver, 2002).
5. Standards are not beneficial without highly qualified teachers and comprehensive school resources.

Issuing Standards on Standards. Because of the risks of early learning standards, the NAEYC and the National Association of Early Childhood Specialists in State Departments of Education (2002) approved a joint position statement, "Early Learning Standards: Creating the Conditions for Success." These associations recommend that early learning standards be (a) significant, developmentally appropriate content and outcomes; (b) informed by research and developed and reviewed by all stakeholders; (c) implemented and assessed by ethical and appropriate means; and (d) supported by adequate program resources, professional development, and a partnership with families and other community members.

Balancing Teaching Strategies

As previously discussed, D-I and holistic/developmental programs use different teaching strategies, as shown in Table 7–6. The D-I approach uses more teacher-determined and whole-group activities to teach separate concepts and skills. Conversely, the holistic/developmental approach emphasizes child-initiated and small-group activities presented as integrated content. Guidelines for DAP emphasize self-directed learnings. However, DAP also recognizes some direct instruction; for example, teachers may use direct instruction as a scaffolding strategy for individuals or small groups.

▲ **Table 7–6   Teaching and Learning Activities in D-I and Holistic/Developmental Programs**

D-I	Holistic/Developmental
Content is often written in lesson plan format.	Content is written as units/themes and projects.
Curriculum is compartmentalized (taught as separate subjects).	Curriculum is integrated.
Content or skills presented in teacher-prescribed lessons are often foreign to children.	Understandings are built as children recall past events to understand new ideas.
Skills often do not meet individual needs because the same competencies are deemed necessary for all children and the lessons are teacher prescribed without child input or choice.	Projects are collaboratively planned. Children choose among the activities.
Competencies learned through separate subject lessons may seem useless beyond the classroom doors.	Competencies gained through projects are learned in the real-world setting and thus seem more relevant now and in the future.

The benefits of DAP are well researched, but the implementation of DAP is more of a goal than a reality. Some professionals who work with at-risk children see DAP as inappropriate (Stipek & Byler, 1997); however, others do not agree, saying that "children destined to be leaders of tomorrow are not being educated in skill and drill" (Hale, 1994, p. 207). Many teachers are simply not implementing DAP. For example, over 67% of teachers questioned in one study thought that what they did each day was in conflict with their personal beliefs favoring DAP (Hatch & Freeman, 1988b). Many researchers felt that full-day programs, especially full-day kindergartens, would offer more child-initiated activities; however, the greatest percentage of time in both full-day and half-day programs is consumed by teacher-determined, whole-group activities (Elicker & Mathur, 1997; Morrow, Strickland, & Woo, 1998).

Several causes contribute to the lack of implementation of DAP. Teachers admit that their practices are influenced by families and school administrators (Stipek & Byler, 1997). Other causes for the lack of implementation of DAP may include (a) the national mania for accountability, (b) inexperienced staff whose feelings of insecurity lead to dependence on prescribed activities (Galley, 2002), and (c) the cost of quality programs.

Considering Inclusion

Early childhood professionals are continuing to debate the best placement practices for children with disabilities, although the debate is not as vociferous as it is among those who work with older children. **Inclusion** means many things and can be seen on a continuum. **Full inclusion** means that *all* children are in the regular classroom, with both regular and special educators working together in various ways. **Partial** or **optional inclusion** means that children with special needs are in the regular classroom part of the day. **Special education** means that children with special needs are in self-contained classrooms with no inclusion. Educators who believe all children should be educated in the same environment are called **full inclusionists.** Those who prefer partial inclusion are referred to as **responsible inclusionists** (Palloway & Patton, 1997). Fuchs and Fuchs (1998) used the terms *full inclusionists* and *inclusionists* for the two ideas. Table 7–7 lists the major arguments given by inclusionists and responsible inclusionists. Shonkoff and Phillips (2000) indicated that the individualization of

Table 7–7   **Positions on Inclusion**

Full inclusionists believe. . .

Full inclusion placements (a) prevent differences from being as obvious to peers as they are in part-time inclusion programs and (b) prevent regular educators from using special education classrooms as "dumping grounds" for difficult-to-teach children (D. Ferguson, 1995; D. Ferguson, 1995; Lipsky & Gartner, 1991).

Standard curricula and universal standards should be deemphasized. Self-paced education should be emphasized for *all* children (Stainback & Stainback, 1992).

Changing stereotypic thinking about disabilities and strengthening social skills of *all* children should be goals of the school (Fuchs & Fuchs, 1998).

Special education placements often become terminal arrangements (Dillon, 1994).

Responsible inclusionists believe. . .

Children's needs should determine placement decisions (Byrnes, 1990; Byrnes, 1990; Fuchs & Fuchs, 1995; Hilton & Liberty, 1992). Even many in the disability community want placement options (Maloney, 1995).

Schools are most important for helping children learn concepts and master skills needed for success in later school years and in life (Fuchs & Fuchs, 1998).

Full inclusion may not support all children with disabilities (P. Hunt & Goetz, 1997). More effort has been placed on defining compliance with various laws concerning disabilities rather than achieving a research base on educational outcomes (Fuchs & Fuchs, 1998).

Many teachers have not been trained for early intervention programs (Hanson & Lovett, 1992).

service delivery and making the intervention a coordinated family-centered one are essential features of intervention.

Full inclusion seems to be easier to implement at the preschool level than at any other level because (a) the educational goals recommended for early childhood and special education are similar (NAEYC, 1996a), (b) early childhood and special education teachers have used team teaching (Bergen, 1994), and (c) some teachers hold dual certificates or have had some course work in both areas. At the kindergarten and primary levels, partial inclusion may work

best for all concerned because of (a) a lack of additional personnel, (b) higher adult–child ratios, (c) inadequate housing, and (d) state-mandated curriculum standards that do not conform to DAP and are thus inappropriate for young children with disabilities.

SUMMARY

Curriculum is a way of helping teachers think about children and organize children's experiences in the program setting. The first step in program planning is to establish the program base. The director must then make statements concerning the local program's curriculum or program rationale, which is often called the "program philosophy." The rationale should be based on a knowledge of children, the interests and needs of children, and the physical and social environment of the local program. Often, early learning standards have to be considered, too. From these sources, goal statements must be generated. Goal statements are then translated into written program competencies that further refine the broad goal statements. The basic organization of the curriculum must be determined.

Plans must be made for implementing the curriculum. Deciding on the basic teaching strategies is most important. Other aspects of implementation include decisions about how computers will be used, classroom transitions, physical care routines, and special times. Plans for developing supportive relationships, both adult–child and child–child, are necessary to aid children in reaching program goals.

Directors and teachers must make decisions about group size and adult–child ratios, grouping children, and scheduling activities. These plans must conform to regulations and should be compatible with program goals. Finally, equitable staff responsibilities must be determined.

Three trends and issues seem to be occurring in program planning: (a) defining program quality in light of the standards movement, (b) implementing curriculum activities through balanced teaching strategies, and (c) planning the best settings for children needing special interventions. Attempts are being made to resolve all of these issues, but many barriers are still to be removed.

FOR FURTHER READING

Bredekamp, S., & Rosegrant, T. (Eds.). (1992). *Reaching potentials: Appropriate curriculum and assessment for young children* (Vol. 1). Washington, DC: National Association for the Education of Young Children.

Bredekamp, S., & Rosegrant, T. (Eds.). (1995). *Reaching potentials: Transforming early childhood curriculum and assessment* (Vol. 2). Washington, DC: National Association for the Education of Young Children.

Chafel, J. A., & Reifel, S. (Eds.). (1996). *Advances in early education and day care: Theory and practice in early childhood education* (Vol. 8). Greenwich, CT: JAI.

Chandler, P. A. (1994). *A place for me: Including children with special needs in early care and education settings.* Washington, DC: National Association for the Education of Young Children.

Hart, C. H., Burts, D. C., & Charlesworth, R. (Eds.). (1997). *Integrated curriculum and developmentally appropriate practice: Birth to age 8.* Albany: State University of New York Press.

Haugland, S. W., & Wright, J. L. (1997). *Young children and technology: A world of discovery.* Boston: Allyn & Bacon.

Kendall, J. S., & Marzano, R. J. (1997). *Content knowledge: A compendium of standards and benchmarks for K-12 education* (2nd ed.). Alexandria, VA: Mid-continent Regional Educational Laboratory. Website: www.mcrel.org/standards-benchmarks/

Perry, G., & Duru, M. S. (Eds.). (2000). *Resources for developmentally appropriate practices.* Washington, DC: National Association for the Education of Young Children.

Thouvenelle, S., & Bewick, C. J. (2003). *Completing the computer puzzle: A guide for early childhood educators.* Boston: Allyn & Bacon.

Von Blanckensee, L. (1999). *Technology tools for young learners.* Larchmont, NY: Eye of Education.

Projects and Webbing

Berk, L. E., & Winsler, A. (1995). *Scaffolding children's learning: Vygotsky and early childhood education.* Washington, DC: National Association for the Education of Young Children.

Chard, S. C. (1998a). *Project approach: Developing the basic framework. Practical guide 1.* New York: Scholastic.

Chard, S. C. (1998b). *Project approach: Developing the basic framework. Practical guide 2.* New York: Scholastic.

Edwards, C. P., Gandini, L., & Forman, G. (Eds.). (1998). *The hundred languages of children: The*

Reggio approach—Advanced reflections (2nd ed.). Greenwich, CT: Ablex.

Helm, J. H., & Beneke, S. (Eds.). (2002). *The power of projects: Meeting contemporary challenges in early childhood classrooms—Strategies and solutions.* New York: Teachers College Press.

Helm, J. H., & Katz, L. G. (2001). *Young investigators: The project approach in the early years.* New York: Teachers College Press.

Hendrick, J. (1997). *First steps toward teaching the Reggio way.* Upper Saddle River, NJ: Merrill/Prentice Hall.

Katz, L. G., & Chard, S. C. (2000). *Engaging children's minds: The project approach* (2nd ed.). Norwood, NJ: Ablex.

Classroom Transitions

Feldman, J. (1995). *Transition time: Let's do something different.* Beltsville, MD: Gryphon.

Feldman, J. (2000). *Transition tips and tricks.* Beltsville, MD: Gryphon.

Hayes, K., & Creange, R. (2001). *Classroom routines that really work for preK and kindergarten.* New York: Scholastic Professional Books.

Henthorne, M., Larson, N., & Chvojicek, R. (2000). *Transition magician 2.* St. Paul, MN: Redleaf.

Larson, N., Henthorne, M., & Plum, B. (1994). *Transition magician.* St. Paul, MN: Redleaf.

Developing Supportive Relationships

Caring as Infant and Toddler Curriculum

Greenberg, P. (1991). *Character development: Encouraging self-esteem and discipline in infants, toddlers, and two-year-olds.* Washington, DC: National Association for the Education of Young Children.

Honig, A. S. (1992). Dancing with your baby means sometimes leading, sometimes following. *Dimensions of Early Childhood, 20*(3), 10–13.

Honig, A. S. (1993). Mental health for babies: What do theory and research teach us? *Young Children, 48*(3), 69–76.

Honig, A. S. (2002). *Secure relationships: Nurturing infant/toddler attachment in early care settings.* Washington, DC: National Association for the Education of Young Children.

Raikes, H. (1996). A secure base for babies: Applying attachment concepts to the infant care setting. *Young Children, 51*(5), 59–67.

Szanton, E. S. (2001). Viewpoint. For America's infants and toddlers, are important values threatened by our zeal to "teach"? *Young Children, 56*(1), 15–21.

Nurturing Emotional Literacy

Association for Supervision and Curriculum Development. (1997). *Social and emotional learning: Guidelines for educators.* Alexandria, VA: Author.

The Center on the Social and Emotional Foundations for Early Learning http://csefel.uiuc.edu

Curry, N. E., & Johnson, C. N. (1990). *Beyond self-esteem: Developing a genuine sense of human value.* Washington, DC: National Association for the Education of Young Children.

Eaton, M. (1997). Positive discipline: Fostering the self-esteem of young children. *Young Children, 52*(6), 43–46.

Goleman, D. (1995). *Emotional intelligence.* New York: Bantam.

Hechtman, J., Grove, S. F., & Mester, T. (1994). *I'm glad I'm me—Self-esteem for young learners.* Cypress, CA: Creative Teaching.

Encouraging Social Competence

Buzzelli, C. A. (1995). The development of moral reflection in early childhood classroom. *Contemporary Education, 66,* 143–145.

Carlsson-Paige, N., & Levin, D. E. (2000). *Before push comes to shove: Building conflict resolution skills with children.* St. Paul, MN: Redleaf.

Da Ros, D. A., & Kovach, B. A. (1998). Assisting toddlers and caregivers during conflict resolutions: Interactions that promote socialization. *Childhood Education, 75,* 25–30.

Essa, E. (1999). *A practical guide to solving preschool behavior problems* (4th ed.). Albany, NY: Delmar.

Evans, B. (2002). *You can't come to my birthday party: Conflict resolution with young children.* Ypsilanti, MI: High/Scope.

Gartrell, D. J. (2000). *What kids said today.* St. Paul, MN: Redleaf.

Gartrell, D. J. (2003). *A guidance approach for the encouraging classroom.* Albany, NY: Delmar.

Greenberg, P. (1992). Ideas that work with young children. How to institute some simple democratic practices pertaining to respect, rights, roots, and responsibilities in any classroom (without losing your leadership position). *Young Children, 47*(5), 10–17.

Harris, T. T., & Fuqua, J. D. (2000). What goes around comes around: Building a community of learners through circle times. *Young Children, 55*(1), 44–47.

Honig, A. S., & Wittner, D. S. (1996). Helping children become more prosocial: Ideas for classrooms, families, schools, and communities (Part 2). *Young Children, 51*(2), 62–70.

Katz, L. G., & McClellan, D. E. (1997). *Fostering children's social competence: The teacher's role.* Washington, DC: National Association for the Education of Young Children.

Kohn, A. (1999). *Punished by rewards.* New York: Houghton Mifflin.

Kreidler, W. J., & Whittall, S. T. (1999). *Early childhood adventures in peacemaking: A conflict resolution guide for early childhood educators* (2nd ed.). Boston: Work/Family Directions.

Logan, T. (1998). Creating a kindergarten community. *Young Children, 53*(2), 22–26.

McClurg, L. G. (1998). Building an ethical community in the classroom: Community meeting. *Young Children, 53*(2), 30–35.

Rand, M. K. (2000). *Giving it some thought: Cases for early childhood practice.* Washington, DC: National Association for the Education of Young Children.

Saifer, S. (1990). *Practical solutions to practically every problem: The early childhood teacher's manual.* St. Paul, MN: Redleaf.

Schreiber, M. E. (1999). Time-outs for toddlers: Is our goal punishment or education? *Young Children, 54*(4), 22–25.

Slaby, R. G., Roedell, W. C., Arezzo, D., & Hendrix, K. (1995). *Early violence prevention: Tools for teachers of young children.* Washington, DC: National Association for the Education of Young Children.

Stone, J. G. (2001). *Building classroom community: The early childhood teacher's role.* Washington, DC: National Association for the Education of Young Children.

Styles, D. (2001). *Class meetings: Building leadership, problem-solving, and decision-making skills in the respectful classroom.* Markham, Ontario: Pembroke.

Vance, E., & Weaver, J. J. (2002). *Class meetings: Young children solving problems together.* Washington, DC: National Association for the Education of Young Children.

Wittmer, D., & Honig, A. (1994). Encouraging positive social development in young children, Part 1. *Young Children, 49*(5), 4–12.

Supporting Children Who Experience Stressful Events*

*Alat, K. (2002). Traumatic events and children: How early childhood educators can help. *Childhood Education, 79,* 2–7.

Castle, K., Beasley, L., & Skinner, L. (1996). Children of the heartland. *Childhood Education, 72,* 226–231.

Dumas, L. (1992). *Talking with your child about a troubled world.* New York: Fawcett.

Farish, J. (1995). *When disaster strikes: Helping young children cope.* Washington, DC: National Association for the Education of Young Children.

Greenberg, J. (1996). Seeing children through tragedy: My mother died today—When is she coming back? *Young Children, 51*(6), 76–77.

*Greenman, J. (2001). *What happened to the world? Helping children cope in turbulent times.* South Watertown, MA: Bright Horizons Family Solutions.

Helping young children in frightening times. (2001). *Young Children, 56*(6), 6–7.

Jones, E. (1997). *A circle of love: The Oklahoma City bombing through the eyes of our children.* Oklahoma City, OK: Feed the Children.

Miller, K. (1996). *Crisis manual for early childhood teachers.* Beltsville, MD: Gryphon.

Stanford, B. H., & Yamamoto, K. (Eds.) (2001). *Children and stress: Understanding and helping.* Olney, MD: Association for Childhood Education International.

READINGS ON CURRICULUM DEVELOPMENT

Literacy

Adams, M. J., Foorman, B. R., Lundberg, I., & Beeler, T. (1998). *Phonemic awareness in young children: A classroom curriculum.* Baltimore, MD: Paul H. Brookes.

Armington, D. (1997). *The living classroom: Writing, reading, and beyond.* Washington, DC: National Association for the Education of Young Children.

Bowman, B. (2003). *Love to read: Essays in developing and enhancing early literacy skills of African American*

* Websites are provided in these sources.

children. Washington, DC: National Black Child Development Institute.

Burns, M. S., Griffin, C., & Snow, C. (Eds.). (1999). *Starting out right: A guide to promoting children's reading success*. Washington, DC: National Academy Press.

Dickinson, D. K., & Tabors, P. O. (2002). Fostering language and literacy in classrooms and homes. *Young Children, 57*(2), 10–16.

Gable, S. (1999). Promote children's literacy with poetry. *Young Children, 54*(5), 12–15.

Gambrell, L., Morrow, L. M., Neuman, S. B., & Pressley, M. (Eds.). (1999). *Best practices in literacy instruction*. New York: Guilford.

Greenberg, P. (1998a). Some thoughts about phonics, feelings, Don Quixote, diversity, and democracy: Teaching young children to read, write, and spell, Part I. *Young Children, 53*(4), 72–82.

Greenberg, P. (1998b). Warmly and calmly teaching young children to read, write, and spell: Thoughts about the first four of twelve well-known principles, Part 2. *Young Children, 53*(5), 68–81.

Greenberg, P. (1998c). Thinking about goals for grownups while we teach writing, reading, and spelling (and a few thoughts about the "J" word), Part 3. *Young Children, 53*(6), 31–42.

International Reading Association (IRA) & NAEYC. (1998). *Position Statement. Learning to read and write: Developmentally appropriate practices for young children*. Washington, DC: National Association for the Education of Young Children.

Isbell, R. T. (2002). Telling and retelling stories: Learning language and retelling stories: Learning language and literacy. *Young Children, 57*(2), 26–30.

National Research Council. (1999). *Starting out right: A guide to promoting children's reading success*. Washington, DC: National Academy Press.

Neuman, S. B., Copple, C., & Bredekamp, S. (2000). *Learning to read and write: Developmentally appropriate practices for young children*. Washington, DC: National Association for the Education of Young Children.

Neuman, S. B., & Roskos, K. A. (Eds.). (1998). *Children achieving: The best practices in early literacy*. Newark, DE: International Reading Association.

Raines, S. C., & Canady, R. J. (1989). *Story s-t-r-e-t-c-h-e-r-s: Activities to expand children's favorite books*. Mt. Rainier, MD: Gryphon.

Raines, S. C., & Canady, R. J. (1991). *More story s-t-r-e-t-c-h-e-r-s*. Mt. Rainier, MD: Gryphon.

Roskos, K. A., & Christie, J. F. (2002). "Knowing in the Doing"—Observing literacy learning in play. *Young Children, 57*(2), 46–54.

Schickedanz, J. A. (1999). *Much more than the ABCs: The early stages of reading and writing*. Washington, DC: National Association for the Education of Young Children.

Snow, C., Burns, M. S., & Griffin, P. (Eds.). (1998). *Preventing reading difficulties in young children*. Washington, DC: National Academy Press.

Soundy, C. S., & Stout, N. L. (2002). Fostering the emotional and language needs of young learners. *Young Children, 57*(2), 20–24.

Wuori, D. (1999). Beyond letter of the week: Authentic literacy comes to kindergarten. *Young Children, 54*(6), 24–25.

Mathematics and Science

Andrews, A., & Trafton, P. R. (2002). *Little kids—Powerful problem solvers*. Portsmouth, NH: Heinemann.

Baroody, A. (2000). Research in Review. Does mathematics instruction for 3- to 5-year-olds really make sense? *Young Children, 55*(4), 66–77.

Bodrova, E., & Leong, D. J. (1996). *Tools of the mind*. Upper Saddle River, NJ: Merrill/Prentice Hall.

Clements, D. H. (2001). Mathematics in the preschool. *Teaching Children Mathematics, 7*, 270–275.

Clements, D. H., & Sarama, J. (2000). Standards for preschoolers. *Teaching Children Mathematics, 7*, 38–41.

Copley, J. V. (Ed.). (1999). *Mathematics in the early years*. Reston, VA: National Council of Teachers of Mathematics.

Copley, J. V. (2000). *The young child and mathematics*. Washington, DC: National Association for the Education of Young Children.

Diezmann, C., & Yelland, N. J. (2000). Developing mathematical literacy in the early years. In N. J. Yelland (Ed.), *Promoting meaningful learning: Innovations in educating early childhood professionals* (pp. 47–58). Washington, DC: National Association for the Education of Young Children.

Fosnot, C. T., & Dolk, M. (2001). *Young mathematicians at work: Constructing number sense, addition, and subtraction*. Portsmouth, NH: Heinemann.

Fuson, K. C., Grandau, L., & Sugiyama, P. A. (2001). Achievable numerical understandings for all children. *Teaching Children Mathematics, 7*, 522–526.

Gallenstein, N. L. (2003). *Creative construction of mathematics and science concepts in early childhood.* Olney, MD: Association for Childhood Education International.

Geist, E. (2001). Children are born mathematicians: Promoting construction of early mathematical concepts in children under five. *Young Children, 56*(4), 12–19.

Greenberg, P. (1993). Ideas that work with young children. How and why to teach all aspects of preschool and kindergarten math naturally, democratically, and effectively (for teachers who don't believe in academic programs, who do believe in educational excellence, and who find math boring to the max)—Part 1. *Young Children, 48*(4), 75–84.

Greenberg, P. (1994). Ideas that work with young children—Part 2. *Young Children, 49*(2), 12–18, 88.

Grieshaber, S., & Diezmann, C. (2000). The challenge of teaching and learning science with young children. In N. J. Yelland (Ed.), *Promoting meaningful learning: Innovations in educating early childhood professionals* (pp. 87–94). Washington, DC: National Association for the Education of Young Children.

Hinnant, H. A. (1999). Growing gardens and mathematicians: More books and math for young children. *Young Children, 54*(2), 23–26.

Kamii, C. (1982). *Number in preschool and kindergarten.* Washington, DC: National Association for the Education of Young Children.

Kamii, C. (1983). *Young children reinvent arithmetic.* New York: Teachers College Press.

Kamii, C. (1989). *Young children continue to reinvent arithmetic: Second grade.* New York: Teachers College Press.

Kamii, C., & DeVries, R. (1978). *Physical knowledge in preschool education: Implications of Piaget's theory.* Englewood Cliffs, NJ: Prentice Hall.

Lind, K. (1997). *Science in the developmentally appropriate curriculum. Integrated curriculum and developmentally appropriate practice—birth to age 8.* Albany: State University of New York Press.

Meriwether, L. (1997). Math at the snack table. *Young Children, 52*(5), 69–73.

Moyer, P. (2000). Communicating mathematically: Children's literature as a natural connection. *The Reading Teacher, 54,* 246–258.

National Association for the Education of Young Children and National Council of Teachers of Mathematics. (2002). *Early childhood mathematics: Promoting good beginnings. Joint position statement.* Washington, DC, and Reston, VA: Authors. www.naeyc.org/resources/position_statements/psmath.htm.

National Council of Teachers of Mathematics. (2000). *Principles and standards for school mathematics.* Reston, VA: Author.

National Research Council. (1996). *National science education standards.* Washington, DC: National Academy Press.

Rakow, S. J., & Bell, M. J. (1998). Science and young children: The message from the National Science Education Standards. *Childhood Education, 74,* 164–167.

Sgroi, L. A., Gropper, N., Kilker M. T., Rambusch, N. M., & Semonite, B. (1995). Assessing young children's mathematical understandings. *Teaching Children Mathematics, 1,* 275–277.

Simon, M. A. (1995). Reconstructing mathematics pedagogy from a constructivist perspective. *Journal for Research in Mathematics Education, 26,* 114–145.

Thatcher, D. H. (2001). Reading in the math class: Selecting and using picture books for math investigations. *Young Children, 56*(4), 20–26.

Whitin, D. J. (1997). Collecting data with young children. *Young Children, 52*(2), 28–32.

Social Studies

Bisson, J. (1997). *Celebrate! An anti-bias guide to enjoying holidays in early childhood programs.* St. Paul, MN: Redleaf.

Haas, M., & Laughlin, M. (1997). *Meeting the standards: Social studies readings for K-6 educators.* Washington, DC: National Council for Social Studies.

Lenhoff, R., & Huber, L. (2000). Young children make maps! *Young Children, 55*(5), 6–12.

Maxim, G. W. (1997). Developmentally appropriate map skills instruction. *Childhood Education, 73,* 206–211.

Seefeldt, C. (1997). *Social studies for the preschool/primary child* (5th ed.). Upper Saddle River, NJ: Merrill/Prentice Hall.

The Arts

Althouse, R., Johnson, M. H., & Mitchell, S. T. (2003). *The colors of learning: Integrating the visual arts into the early childhood curriculum.* New York: Teachers College Press.

Dighe, J., Calomiris, Z., & Zutphen, C. V. (1998). Nurturing the language of art in children. *Young Children, 53*(1), 4–9.

Engel, B. S. (1995). *Considering children's art: Why and how to value their works.* Washington, DC: National Association for the Education of Young Children.

Engel, B. S. (1996). Learning to look: Appreciating child art. *Young Children, 51*(3), 74–79.

Honig, A. S. (1995). Singing with infants and toddlers. *Young Children, 50*(6), 72–78.

Honigman, J. J., & Bhavnagri, N. P. (1998). Painting with scissors: Art education beyond production. *Childhood Education, 74,* 205–212.

Schirrmacher, R. (1998). *Art and creative development for young children.* Albany, NY: Delmar.

Seefeldt, C. (1995). Art—A serious work. *Young Children, 50*(3), 39–45.

Taunton, M., & Colbert, C. (2000). Art in the early childhood classroom: Authentic experiences and extended dialogues. In N. J. Yelland (Ed.), *Promoting meaningful learning: Innovations in educating early childhood professionals* (pp. 67–76) Washington, DC: National Association for the Education of Young Children.

Thompson, C. M. (Ed.). (1995). *The visual arts and early childhood learning.* Reston, VA: National Art Education Association.

Wright, S. (1997). Learning how to learn: The arts as core in an emergent curriculum. *Childhood Education, 73,* 361–365.

Zimmerman, E., & Zimmerman, L. (2000). Research in Review. Art education and early childhood education: The young child as creator and meaning maker within a community context. *Young Children, 55*(6), 87–92.

Block Building; Dramatic Play; and Mud, Sand, and Water Play

Barbour, N., Webster, T. D., & Drosdeck, S. (1987). Sand: A resource for the language arts. *Young Children, 42*(2), 20–25.

Betz, C. (1992). The happy medium. *Young Children, 47*(3), 34–35.

Cartwright, S. (1990). Learning with large blocks. *Young Children, 45*(3), 38–41.

Crosser, S. (1994). Making the most of water play. *Young Children, 49*(5), 28–32.

Davidson, J. I. (1996). *Emergent literacy and dramatic play in early education.* Albany, NY: Delmar.

Ferguson, C. (1999). Building literacy with child-constructed sociodramatic play centers. *Dimensions of Early Childhood, 27*(3), 23–29.

Gura, P. (Ed.). (1992). *Exploring learning: Young children and block play.* New York: Paul Chapman.

Hirsch, E. S. (Ed.). (1996). *The block book* (3rd ed.). Washington, DC: National Association for the Education of Young Children.

MacDonald, S. (2001). *Block play: The complete guide to learning and playing with blocks.* Beltsville, MD: Gryphon.

Wellhousen, K., & Kieff, J. (2001). *A constructivist approach to block play in early childhood.* Albany, NY: Delmar.

West, S. & Cox, A. (2001). *Sand and water play: Simple, creative activities for young children.* Beltsville, MD: Gryphon.

Play

Buchanan, M., & Cooney, M. (2000). Play at home, play in the classroom. *Young Exceptional Children, 3*(4), 9–15.

Council on Physical Education for Children. (2000). *Appropriate practices in movement programs for young children ages 3–5. A position statement of the National Association for Sport and Physical Education (NASPE).* Reston, VA: NASPE.

Fromberg, D. P. (2002). *Play and meaning in early childhood education.* Boston: Allyn & Bacon.

Frost, J., Wortham, S., & Reifel, S. (2001). *Play and child development.* Upper Saddle River, NJ: Merrill/Prentice Hall.

Greenberg, P. (1992). How much do you get the children out? *Young Children, 47*(2), 34–37.

Isenberg, J. P., & Jalongo, M. R. (2001). *Creative expression and play in early childhood* (3rd ed.). Upper Saddle River, NJ: Merrill/Prentice Hall.

National Association for Sports and Physical Education. (1995). *Moving into the future: National standards for physical education—A guide to content and assessment.* St. Louis: Mosby.

Payne, V. G., & Issacs, L. (1995). *Human motor development: A lifespan approach.* Mountain View, CA: Mayfield.

Pica, R. (1997). Beyond physical development: Why young children need to move. *Young Children, 52*(6), 4–11.

Roskos, K. A., & Christie, J. F. (Eds.). (2002). *Play and literacy in early childhood.* Mahwah, NJ: Erlbaum.

Sanders, S. W. (2002). *Active for life: Developmentally appropriate movement programs for young children.* Washington, DC: National Association for the Education of Young Children.

Sanders, S. W., & Vongue, B. (1998). Challenging movement experiences for young children. *Dimensions of Early Childhood, 26*(1), 9–17.

Saracho, O. N., & Spodek, B. (Eds.). (1998). *Multiple perspectives on play in early childhood education.* Albany: State University of New York Press.

Wardle, F. (1995). Alternatives . . . Bruderhof education: Outdoor school. *Young Children, 50*(3), 68–73.

Werner, P., Timms, S., & Almond, L. (1996). Health stops: Practical ideas for health-related exercise in preschool and primary classrooms. *Young Children, 51*(6), 48–55.

TO REFLECT

1. An early childhood director is faced with many families wanting an academic program (referred to as a DIP) for their children. What can the director say to explain the risks and lack of benefits of such a program? If the director's explanation is not accepted, what should the director do? Should the director do as the families wish as a way of possibly ensuring the enrollment for the program? Should the director follow what he or she feels is "best practices" and hope that most families will stay with the program?

2. The director of a preschool center has called a meeting of the lead teachers for each of the five classrooms. According to their job description, lead teachers must take the responsibility for the development of curriculum plans that will be implemented in their own classrooms. The director wants the group to develop a list of criteria that they can use in deciding on the appropriateness of themes or projects and the corresponding activities. What criteria could be used? (Be specific enough to be helpful.)

Providing Nutrition, Health, and Safety Services

Increasing emphasis on nutrition, health, and safety in society has resulted in expanded programs for young children. Nutrition, health, and safety are highly interrelated. For example, long-time inadequate nutrition affects health status, and inadequate nutrition even for a short period of time can affect a child's alertness and thus safety. A comprehensive approach to nutrition, health, and safety services in early childhood programs requires the provision of services to children; a healthy and safe environment; and education to children, staff, and families. This comprehensive approach is supported by the third objective of Goal 1 of *America 2000* (U.S. Department of Education, 2001), which states, "Children will receive nutrition and health care needed to arrive at school with healthy minds and bodies, and the number of low birth weight babies will be significantly reduced through enhanced prenatal health systems" (p. 61). Thus, today's emphasis is on total health and safety rather than on only control of contagion.

PROMOTING NUTRITION

Because of the effects of hunger and malnutrition on young children, early childhood programs are becoming more concerned about nutrition. Adequate nutrition is essential for the fulfillment of one's potential for physical or biological growth and development and for maintenance of the body.

During periods of rapid growth, a child is especially unprotected against malnutrition. For many children, malnutrition begins in the prenatal period. Nutritional adequacy is essential for optimal brain development (B. Morgan & Gibson, 1991; Strupp & Levitsky, 1995). Born with low birth weights, malnourished newborns are more likely to have physical disabilities and learning problems than normal birth weight babies.

More American children suffer from *misnourishment* (underconsuming important nutrients and overconsuming calories through high-fat and sugary foods; Bhattacharya & Currie, 2001). In fact, most children's diets are in need of improvement. The Federal Interagency Forum on Child and Family Statistics (2002) reported that 73% of 2- through 5-year-old children and 87% of 6- through 9-year-old children have poor diets. Inadequate growth, iron deficiency, and overweight are three common problems of inadequate nutrition.

Inadequate growth, called *stunting* or *wasting* (when a child is below the 10th percentile in height for age and/or below the 10th percentile in weight for height) often results from inadequate nutrition (Korenman, Miller, & Sjaastad, 1995). Poverty is associated with malnutrition. Inadequate growth is twice as high among preschoolers from poor families as compared with preschoolers from nonpoor families (Cook & Martin, 1995). Toddlers who grow up in poverty suffer from high rates of malnutrition and anemia; that is, poor toddlers are 40% more likely than nonpoor toddlers to be underweight and clinically malnourished. This figure increases to 60% in the winter when heating costs peak (Carnegie Corporation of New York, 1994). Lags in cognitive development are associated with inadequate growth; more specifically, these children lag in visual-motor skills, early mathematics skills, phonemic awareness, aural comprehension, and general knowledge (Karp, Martin, Sewell, Manni, & Heller, 1992). When combined with poverty, nutrition has the greatest negative impact on achievement (Duncan, Yeung, Brooks-Gunn, & Smith, 1998).

Iron deficiency is positively associated with malnourishment. Similar to inadequate growth, iron deficiency is not seen in isolation. The insults from iron deficiency with and without anemia are increased for children who are from certain ethnic groups and who grow up in poverty. For example, Ogden's (1998) data showed that nonpoor Anglo infants had the lowest prevalence of iron deficiency (3%), and that Mexican American toddlers—both nonpoor (12%) and poor

(18%)—had the highest risk. Iron deficiency results in lower test scores on cognitive processes (e.g., spatial memory, selective recall), mental functioning (e.g., arithmetic achievement, written expression), and motor development (Lozoff, Jimenez, Hagen, Mollen, & Wolf, 2000; Nokes, van den Bosch, & Bundy, 1998). Behavior is also affected by iron deficiency. For example, children with iron deficiency were shown to be fearful, anxious, and depressed. Similarly, families reported that these children had cognitive problems (i.e., shortened attention span and failure to focus on tasks) and social problems (Lozoff, Jimenez, Hagen, Mollen, & Wolf, 2000; Lozoff, Klein, Nelson, McClish, Manuel, & Chacon, 1998). Furthermore, cognitive and behavioral problems tended to persist even with treatment (Lozoff, Jimenez, Hagen, Mollen, & Wolf, 2000).

Misnourishment is on the rise among all children in the United States. Most commercials are for foods high in fat, sugar, and sodium. Eating meals away from home at fast-food places contributes to the junk-food intake. Along with sedentary activities (Bar-Or, 2000), misnourishment with high fat and sugar foods leads to obesity in children. Javernick (1988) warned about the growing problem of obesity in children many years ago; it has now reached 25% (Gabbard, 2000). Obesity and low physical activity increase the risk of early hypertension and diabetes (Perry, 2001; Stoneham, 2001) and damage children's self-esteem (Loewy, 1998). Skipping meals, especially breakfast, is common, with about 4 out of 30 students missing breakfast each day (Burghardt & Devaney, 1993). Skipping meals reduces the speed and accuracy of response on problem-solving tasks (E. Kennedy & Davis, 1998). Most important, misnourishment habits, like many other habits, are formed early in life and continue into adulthood.

Four broad objectives seem to be an integral part of early childhood nutrition programs: (a) assessing children's nutritional status, (b) providing and serving nutritious meals and snacks, (c) hiring staff and meeting other requirements of the food service program, and (d) planning nutrition education for children and families.

Assessing Children's Nutritional Status

Much concern has been raised about the role of nutritional problems in physical health, learning disabilities, and behavioral disorders. Medical and dental examinations and laboratory tests reveal nutrition conditions (e.g., overweight, underweight, iron deficiency anemia, food allergies) that need remediation. Marotz, Cross, and Rush (1997) listed these four methods of nutritional assessment: *dietary assessment* (assessment of nutrient intake), *anthropometric assessment* (comparison of height, weight, and head circumference with standard norms), *clinical assessment* (observation of physical signs of malnutrition), and *biochemical assessment* (laboratory tests of blood, etc.). The authors provided a form for families to complete as part of a child's dietary assessment. Besides awareness of health records, families and staff members need to watch for vomiting and diarrhea, consuming excessive amounts of liquids or solid foods, frequent dawdling over foods or refusal to eat, and persistent food sprees (wanting the same food every day or even several times a day).

As discussed, malnourishment combined with poverty has a maximum negative effect on children's development. Good nutrition may serve as a buffer for poverty. Thus, teachers should be very observant of children in poverty—noting their eating habits in the program, checking their growth, and being aware of listless behaviors because active play behaviors are beneficial to all developmental domains (Pellegrini & Smith, 1998).

If treatment is necessary, staff should follow the recommendations while the child is in the program. If necessary, they should assist the family in carrying out the care plan and ascertaining whether the child has received follow-up assessment. Staff should have in-service training concerning specific nutrition problems.

Providing and Serving Nutritious Meals and Snacks

Meals served in early childhood programs must contribute significantly to each child's nutrient needs. The specific fraction of the child's total nutritional requirements would be in proportion to the total amount of time the child is in the program each day and the requirements of the funding agency of the specific program. Many children will receive four fifths, and possibly more, of their nutritional requirements through their early childhood programs. Any special dietary needs of children should also be met. Nutrition programs should not only meet the nutritional needs of children but also expose children to a wide variety of foods so that they will develop a taste for many foods (Birch, Johnson, & Fisher, 1995), provide for direct dietary consultation to meet the needs of children, and provide menus to families to aid in food selection for the remaining part of the child's diet. Finally, meals and snacks should provide an opportunity for the child to learn about new foods, new ways foods can be served, and social amenities.

Because nutrition standards for early childhood programs come from several sources, the regulations are confusing. All standards are based on the Recommended Dietary Allowances (RDA) published by the Food and Nutrition Board of the National Academy of Sciences. The RDA represents the values of optimal nutrient need categorized by age and gender and also provides a margin of safety for all nutrients. Because many states' licensing codes and the NAEYC's (1998a) center accreditation follow the meal and snack service requirements of the U.S. Department of Agriculture's (USDA) Child and Adult Care Food Program (CACFP), these meal and snack patterns will be used in this text. The meal and snack patterns are based on the USDA's 1992 Food Guide Pyramid and the Food Guide Pyramid for Young Children (ages 2 to 6; U.S. Department of Agriculture, 2000).

The food part of the early childhood program budget is expensive but can be reduced by participating in the USDA's CACFP. To do this, however, programs and the children they serve must both be eligible. Generally speaking, not-for-profit programs and for-profit programs that serve a significant number of "needy children" (up to age 12) receiving government foods are eligible. Programs involved in the meal service of the CACFP have a great deal of detailed paperwork. For specific information, the program director should contact the USDA's Public Information Office at 703-305-2276, the National Food Service Management Institute's (NFSMI) "Help Desk" at 800-943-5463, or the CACFP director in each state's Department of Education (see appendix 2).

Some general guidelines follow. However, it is imperative to check all regulations to avoid costly mistakes and delayed implementation.

Infants.   Because infants are so vulnerable nutritionally, program directors should seek medical advice for each infant. The USDA Infant Meal Pattern is given in Table 8–1. When infants are ready to begin solid foods, offer only one new food at a time and continue for 3 or 4 days before introducing another food. Start with 1 to 2 tsp and gradually work up to the recommended amounts. Introduce cereals first, then strained fruits and vegetables, and finally strained meats. Fruit juices must also be offered one at a time. Dried bread or a teething biscuit helps teething babies. Mashed and finely chopped foods are introduced once babies can chew.

Practices to follow in feeding infants include the following:

1. Wash your hands before getting formula, food, or items used in feeding.

2. Change the infant's diaper. Then, wash your hands again.

3. Before feeding, place a bib under the infant's chin.

4. Hold infants under 6 months of age comfortably in a semisitting position. Eye contact and cuddling are essential to effective

Table 8–1   Child Care Infant Meal Pattern—CACFP

Birth–3 Months	4–7 Months	8–11 Months
Breakfast		
4–6 fluid ounces of formula[1] or breast milk[2,3]	4–8 fluid ounces of formula[1] or breast milk[2,3] 0–3 tablespoons of infant cereal[1,4]	6–8 fluid ounces of formula[1] or breast milk[2,3]; and 2–4 tablespoons of infant cereal[1]; and 1–4 tablespoons of fruit or vegetable or both
Lunch or Supper		
4–6 fluid ounces of formula[1] or breast milk[2,3]	4–8 fluid ounces of formula[1] or breast milk[2,3] 0–3 tablespoons of infant cereal[1,4]; and 0–3 tablespoons of fruit or vegetable or both[4]	6–8 fluid ounces of formula[1] or breast milk[2,3] 2–4 tablespoons of infant cereal[1,4]; and/or 1–4 tablespoons of meat, fish, poultry, egg yolk, cooked dry beans or peas; or 1/2–2 ounces of cheese; or 1–4 ounces (volume) of cottage cheese; or 1–4 ounces (weight) of cheese food or cheese spread; and 1–4 tablespoons of fruit or vegetable or both
Supplement (Midmorning or Midafternoon Snack)		
4–6 fluid ounces of formula[1] or breast milk[2,3]	4–6 fluid ounces of formula[1] or breast milk[2,3]	2–4 fluid ounces of formula[1] or breast milk[2,3], or fruit juice[5]; and 0–1/2 bread[4,6] or 0–2 crackers[4,6]

[1]Infant formula and dry infant cereal must be iron-fortified.

[2]Breast milk or formula, or portions of both, may be served; however, it is recommended that breast milk be served in place of formula from birth through 11 months.

[3]For some breastfed infants who regularly consume less than the minimum amount of breast milk per feeding, a serving of less than the minimum amount of breast milk may be offered, with additional breast milk offered if the infant is still hungry.

[4]A serving of this component is required when the infant is developmentally ready to accept it.

[5]Fruit juice must be full-strength.

[6]A serving of this component must be made from whole-grain or enriched meal or flour.

Source: United States Department of Agriculture. (2000). *Building blocks for fun and healthy meals: A menu planner for the child and adult care food program.* Washington, DC: Author.

development. Never prop bottles. Babies taking bottles in a reclining position are more prone to choking and developing ear infections and dental caries than infants who take their bottles in a semisitting position. Older infants may be fed in low chairs or at feeding tables. Adults must supervise at all times.

5. If solid foods are to be offered, present them before the major portion of the formula or breast milk is given.

6. Discard opened or leftover formula.

7. Keep infants upright for 15 minutes after feeding to help avoid regurgitation of formula, breast milk, or food.

8. When returning young infants to bed, place them on their right sides to prevent aspirating formula or breast milk if they cannot roll over. All infants should sleep on their backs, which lowers the incidence of Sudden Infant Death Syndrome.

9. Allow older infants to explore and handle food and try to feed themselves.

10. Use great patience in beginning spoon feeding. Babies push food from their mouths as a reflexive action of the tongue.

11. Clean the infant's hands, face, and neck after feeding. Resources providing additional information on infant feeding are given at the end of the chapter.

Young Children. Young children must learn to eat a variety of nutritious foods. Table 8–2 is a meal and snack plan developed by the USDA. Some studies show that staff frequently plan the meals in child care settings although they have little training in nutrition (Drake, 1992; Pond-Smith, Richarz, & Gonzalez, 1992). Resources for menu planning are provided at the end of the chapter. Written menus are often required in the licensing and auditing processes.

The following are some other practices for planning enjoyable meals and snacks:

1. Avoid foods that can lead to choking, such as foods with small bones, grapes, hard candies, hot dogs, peanuts, and popcorn. (Staff must be trained in the Heimlich maneuver.)

2. Large portions of food are overwhelming to children; serve food in small portions and permit second helpings.

3. When serving a new or unpopular food, try the following: (a) Serve a tiny portion with a more generous portion of a popular food, (b) introduce only one new food at a time, (c) introduce a new food when children are hungry, (d) eat the food yourself, (e) have children prepare the food, (f) keep offering the food because the more often children are offered a food, the more they are inclined to try it. Before putting foods on the menu, teachers can use them as snack foods.

4. Plan special menus for holidays and birthdays but avoid junk foods (Wardle, 1990).

5. Do not serve the same food, or virtually the same food, such as meatballs and hamburgers, on consecutive days.

6. Consider children's ethnic backgrounds and plan meals to include familiar foods.

7. Take advantage of children's likes and dislikes as to how foods are prepared and served. Young children generally like a variety of foods (different sizes, shapes, colors, textures, and temperatures), foods prepared in different ways, foods served in bite-sized pieces or as finger foods, vegetables with mild flavors, strong-flavored vegetables served only occasionally and in small portions, fruit (but not vegetable) combinations, good textures (fluffy, not gooey, mashed potatoes), and foods that are not too hot or cold. (Cool foods quickly so as to avoid holding foods between 45 and 140°F or 7 and 60°C.)

8. Provide a good physical and emotional climate by having adults set a good example of eating; by having an attractive room setting with furniture, dishes, silverware, and serving utensils suited to young children; by either avoiding serving delays or using activities such as singing

Table 8–2   Meal Pattern for Young Children—CACFP

Breakfast Meal Pattern

Select All Three Components for a Reimbursable Meal

Food Components	Children Ages 1–2	Children Ages 3–5	Children Ages 6–12[1]
1 milk fluid milk	1/2 cup	3/4 cup	1 cup
1 fruit/vegetable juice,[2] fruit and/or vegetable	1/4 cup	1/2 cup	1/2 cup
1 grains/bread[3] bread or	1/2 slice	1/2 slice	1 slice
cornbread or biscuit or roll or muffin or	1/2 serving	1/2 serving	1 serving
cold dry cereal or	1/4 cup	1/3 cup	3/4 cup
hot cooked cereal or	1/4 cup	1/4 cup	1/2 cup
pasta or noodles or grains	1/4 cup	1/4 cup	1/2 cup

[1]Children age 12 and older may be served larger portions based on their greater food needs. They may not be served less than the minimum quantities listed in this column.

[2]Fruit or vegetable juice must be full-strength. Juice cannot be served when milk is the only other snack component.

[3]Breads and grains must be made from whole-grain or enriched meal or flour. Cereal must be whole-grain or enriched or fortified.

and simple games while waiting; by providing a quiet time before meals; by making mealtime pleasant; by offering children choices and recognizing that young children occasionally go on food sprees; and by understanding that young children do not have an adult's sense of time and are not prone to hurry to finish.

Children with Special Needs. In providing and serving nutritious meals and snacks, the program must meet the special needs of a child with a disability. For example, children with delayed feeding skills may need special help, and children with metabolic problems and food allergies will need a carefully planned diet. Excellent information on the nutrition and feeding of children with special needs is provided by Pipes and Glass (1989). Specific written instructions must be pro-

vided by the parent or legal guardian and by the health care provider.

Hiring Staff and Meeting Requirements for the Food Service Program

Planners of food services must consider more than the nutritional needs of children. They must also consider the staff needed for food service responsibilities; the availability of housing space and food preparation equipment, including storage; and costs. Some food service options include the following:

1. Catered meal service, a very expensive option and not under the program's direct control

2. Prepackaged convenience foods, which are expensive, have limited appropriate selections,

Lunch or Supper Meal Pattern

Select All Four Components for a Reimbursable Meal

Food Components	Children Ages 1–2	Children Ages 3–5	Children Ages 6–12[1]
1 milk			
fluid milk	1/2 cup	3/4 cup	1 cup
2 fruits/vegetables			
juice,[2] fruit and/or vegetable	1/4 cup	1/2 cup	3/4 cup
1 grains/bread[3]			
bread or	1/2 slice	1/2 slice	1 slice
cornbread or biscuit or roll or muffin or	1/2 serving	1/2 serving	1 serving
cold dry cereal or	1/4 cup	1/3 cup	3/4 cup
hot cooked cereal or	1/4 cup	1/4 cup	1/2 cup
pasta or noodles or grains	1/4 cup	1/4 cup	1/2 cup
1 meat/meat alternate			
meat or poultry or fish[4] or	1 oz.	1–1/2 oz.	2 oz.
alternate protein product or	1 oz.	1–1/2 oz.	2 oz.
cheese or	1 oz.	1–1/2 oz.	2 oz.
egg or	1/2	3/4	1
cooked dry beans or peas or	1/4 cup	3/8 cup	1/2 cup
peanut or other nut or seed butters or	2 Tbsp.	3 Tbsp.	4 Tbsp.
nuts and/or seeds[5] or	1/2 oz.	3/4 oz.	1 oz.
yogurt[6]	4 oz.	6 oz.	8 oz.

[1]Children age 12 and older may be served larger portions based on their greater food needs. They may not be served less than the minimum quantities listed in this column.

[2]Fruit or vegetable juice must be full-strength. Juice cannot be served when milk is the only other snack component.

[3]Breads and grains must be made from whole-grain or enriched meal or flour. Cereal must be whole-grain or enriched or fortified.

[4]A serving consists of the edible portion of cooked lean meat or poultry or fish.

[5]One-half egg meets the required minimum amount (one ounce or less) of meat alternate.

[6]Yogurt may be plain or flavored, unsweetened or sweetened.

(continued)

and require large freezers for storage and large ovens or microwaves for heating

3. Cafeteria service, which is less expensive but is not under the program's direct control and often provides serving sizes that are too large for young children

4. Meal and snack preparation at the program site, which requires hiring more staff and purchasing more equipment

Hiring Staff. Enough personnel should be employed so that meals and snacks can be prepared and served in the time allowed. According to the

Table 8–2   *(continued)*

Supplement (Midmorning or Midafternoon Snack)

Select Two of the Four Components for a Reimbursable Meal

Food Components	Children Ages 1–2	Children Ages 3–5	Children Ages 6–12[1]
1 milk			
fluid milk	1/2 cup	1/2 cup	1 cup
1 fruit/vegetable			
juice,[2] fruit and/or vegetable	1/2 cup	1/2 cup	3/4 cup
1 grains/bread[3]			
bread or	1/2 slice	1/2 slice	1 slice
cornbread or biscuit or roll or muffin or	1/2 serving	1/2 serving	1 serving
cold dry cereal or	1/4 cup	1/3 cup	3/4 cup
hot cooked cereal or	1/4 cup	1/4 cup	1/2 cup
pasta or noodles or grains	1/4 cup	1/4 cup	1/2 cup
1 meat/meat alternate			
meat or poultry or fish[4] or	1/2 oz.	1/2 oz.	1 oz.
alternate protein product or	1/2 oz.	1/2 oz.	1 oz.
cheese or	1/2 oz.	1/2 oz.	1 oz
egg[5] or	1/2	1/2	1/2
cooked dry beans or peas or	1/8 cup	1/8 cup	1/4 cup
peanut or other nut or seed butters or	1 Tbsp.	1 Tbsp.	2 Tbsp.
nuts and/or seeds or	1/2 oz.	1/2 oz.	1 oz.
yogurt[6]	2 oz.	2 oz.	4 oz.

[1]Children age 12 and older may be served larger portions based on their greater food needs. They may not be served less than the minimum quantities listed in this column.

[2]Fruit or vegetable juice must be full-strength. Juice cannot be served when milk is the only other snack component.

[3]Breads and grains must be made from whole-grain or enriched meal or flour. Cereal must be whole-grain or enriched or fortified.

[4]A serving consists of the edible portion of cooked lean meat or poultry or fish.

[5]One-half egg meets the required minimum amount (one ounce or less) of meat alternate.

[6]Yogurt may be plain or flavored, unsweetened or sweetened.

Source: United States Department of Agriculture. (2000). *Building blocks for fun and healthy meals: A menu planner for the child and adult care food program.* Washington, DC: Author.

standards established by the American Academy of Pediatrics, the American Public Health Association, and the National Resource Center for Health and Safety in Child Care (2002), the food service staff should comprise the following:

1. The caregiver in a family child care home

2. One full-time child care food service worker in centers enrolling up to 30 children

3. One full-time child care food service worker and a part-time aide in centers enrolling up to 50 children

4. One full-time child care food service worker and a full-time aide for centers enrolling up to 125 children

5. One full-time food service manager, one full-time cook, and a part-time aide for centers enrolling up to 200 children

6. One part-time or full-time staff member if vendor services are used

Each state's licensing standards for private programs or state and federal regulations for public programs indicate the qualifications necessary for food service personnel. If a staff dietitian, registered with the American Dietetic Association, is not available for the program, one should be hired as a consultant. For staff needing training in food service management, many training resources are provided by the National Food Service Management Institute (NFSMI; see contact information at the end of the chapter).

Providing Facilities and Equipment. A local child care nutrition specialist or food service expert should work with the architect on the design of the food service parts of the facility. Food service equipment must be purchased, installed, and operated according to the standards of the National Sanitation Foundation (NSF), applicable public health authority, or the USDA (see the end of the chapter for contact information). Planning resources, available from the NFSMI, include *Food Service Equipment Guide,* 1999; *Guide for Purchasing Food Service Equipment,* 1998; *Guidelines for Equipment to Prepare Healthy Meals,* 1996; and *The New Design Handbook for School Food Service,* 1997.

Purchasing Food. Planning food purchases helps control costs and reduces waste. These suggestions should be considered:

1. Check several food companies or stores in the area for quality food at reasonable prices and for such services as credit or delivery.

2. Know food products. Purchase government-inspected meats, fish, and poultry; pasteurized, grade A milk and milk products; properly sealed breads and pastries; and frozen foods that are kept hard-frozen and perishable foods that are kept under refrigeration. Notice which brand names prove most satisfactory.

3. Carefully calculate the quantities of food needed. Use standardized recipes that always yield a specific quantity. A standardized recipe can be adjusted to provide the number of servings needed for a meal or snack (see the resources at the end of the chapter).

4. Carefully consider the types of food (perishable or nonperishable) and the amount of storage space in determining when to purchase food.

5. Keep accurate records of the type and quality of food purchased, when and how food was used in the program, cost, and any other notes useful for other purchases. An excellent guide is *First Choice: A Purchasing Systems Manual for School Food Service* (2nd ed., 2002), which is available through NFSMI.

Meeting Sanitation Requirements. All sanitation requirements must be rigidly enforced to avert disease. Sanitation must be considered in all aspects of food service. Local programs should check the resources available through the NSF, NFSMI, and USDA.

Following are a few examples of protective measures:

1. All food service employees must meet state and local health requirements and must be clean and free of infections on the skin and contagious diseases each time they prepare or serve foods.

2. Preparation and serving utensils and dishes must be thoroughly washed, sterilized, and properly handled. A dishwasher should be set for a water temperature of 160–165°F (66–74°C), using 0.25% detergent concentration or 1 oz of detergent per 3 gal of water. Follow these four steps if washing by hand:

a. Wash with soap or detergent in hot water (110–120°F or 43–49°C).

b. Rinse in warm water.

c. Sanitize by immersing for at least 1 minute in clean, hot water (at least 170°F or 76°C) or by immersing for at least 3 minutes in a sanitizing solution of 1 tbsp household bleach per 2 gal of water.

d. Air dry; do not wipe.

3. Foods should be checked on delivery, protected in storage, used within the specified time, and kept at appropriate serving temperatures: hot foods at 140°F (60°C) or above and cold foods at 45°F (7°C) or below.

4. Wash raw foods carefully and cook other foods properly.

5. Dispose of all foods served and not eaten.

6. Help children develop habits of cleanliness.

Planning Nutrition Education

Early nutrition experiences have a major impact on how a child will be nourished physically and emotionally in the future. Children's current and later eating habits and health are affected by diet and nutrition education (Fuhr, 1998). Eating is also a social experience in which one is nourished by the company of family and friends (Murray, 2000). Thus, nutrition education is extremely important.

Implementing Nutrition Education for Children. Early childhood programs should include nutrition education for young children. In the past, nutrition has been a part of the health component of the curriculum or has centered on specific food activities rather than being an integral part of the total curriculum. Nutrition learnings can be readily integrated into the curriculum because the content is broad. More specifically, nutrition education can involve children in the following:

1. Developing concepts about foods and good diets and how foods promote health, growth, and development (see the resource list that follows).

2. Connecting the foods they eat with food origins, storage, and preparation. Wonderful projects with visits to local community sites could readily emerge.

3. Planning, preparing, and serving nutritious snacks. Cooking experiences will help them learn to measure, follow directions, cooperate with others, coordinate eye–hand movements, use language as a means of expression, recognize the differences in the food preferences of the various ethnic groups, and eat foods prepared in different ways. Cooking will also foster creativity using food products (Cosgrove, 1991; Dahl, 1998; Howell, 1999; Klefstad, 1995). Many cookbooks, such as those listed later, are designed for young children.

4. Having opportunities to socialize and develop socially acceptable eating behavior and adaptability to various meal settings—at home, in restaurants, or on picnics.

Many resources are available for nutrition education. The following is a list of some available resources:

Nutrition Education Resources (all available from NFSMI)

Exploring Foods with Children, 1995

Food and Me: Teacher's Kit for Grades PreK-K, 1995

Food Time: Teacher's Kit for Grades 1 and 2, 1995

More Than Mud Pies: A Nutrition Education Curriculum for 3- to 5-Year-Olds in Day Care Centers and Preschools, 1998

Nifty Nutrition with Skill Integration Activities (separate versions available for kindergarten, first grade, second grade, and third grade), 1998

Pyramid Pursuit, K-3, 1993

Tickle Your Appetite for Child Care, 1998

Cookbooks for Children

Appleton, J., McCrea, N., & Patterson, C. (2001). *Do carrots make you see better?* Beltsville, MD: Gryphon.

Barchers, S. I., & Rauen, P. J. (1997). *Storybook stew: Cooking with books kids love.* Golden, CO: Fulcrum.

Barchers, S. I., & Rauen, P. J. (1998). *Holiday storybook stew: Cooking through the year with books kids love.* Golden, CO: Fulcrum.

Betty Crocker Series. (1999). *Betty Crocker's kids cook!* New York: Wiley.

Braman, A. N. (2000). *Kids around the world cook! The best foods and recipes from many lands.* New York: Wiley.

Bruno, J., & Herrera, R. E. (1991). *Book cooks: Literature-based classroom cooking.* Cypress, CA: Creative Teaching Press.

Ellison, S., & Gray, J. (2001). *365 foods kids love to eat: Fun, nutritious and kid tested* (2nd ed.). New York: Gramercy.

Foote, B. J. (2001). *Cup cooking: Individual child portion picture recipes.* Beltsville, MD: Gryphon.

Gold Medal Flour. (1997). *Gold Medal alpha-bakery cookbook.* Minneapolis: General Mills.

Good, P. P., Good, R., & Good, K. (2000). *Amish cooking for kids.* Intercourse, PA: Good Books.

Harms, T. (1991). *Learning from cooking experiences.* Menlo Park, CA: Addison-Wesley.

Hodges, S., Warren, J., & Bittinger, G. (1995). *Multicultural snacks.* Everett, WA: Totline Publications.

Jenest, V. (1996). *Food for little fingers.* New York: St. Martin's Press.

Katzen, M., & Henderson, A. L. (1994). *Pretend soup and other real recipes: A cookbook for preschoolers and up.* Berkeley, CA: Tricycle Press.

Kingham, J. L. (2002). *Cooking kids!* Lincoln, NE: iUniverse.

Kohl, M. F., & Potter, J. (1997). *Cooking art: Easy edible art for young children.* Beltsville, MD: Gryphon.

Kourempia-Cowling, T. (2000). *Cooking with kids: Recipes for year-round fun.* Torrance, CA: Frank Schaffer.

Lund, J. M. (2000). *Cooking healthy with the kids in mind.* New York: PenguinPutnam.

Pulleyn, M., & Bracken, S. (1995). *Kids in the kitchen.* Asheville, NC: Lark Books.

Rudloff, S. (2000). *Cooking with your kids.* San Leandro, CA: Bristol.

Warren, J. (1992). *Super snacks: Seasonal sugarless snacks.* Everett, WA: Warren.

Webb, S., & Myler, T. (1998). *Kids can cook.* Dublin: Anvil.

Wilkes, A. (2001). *Children's step-by-step cookbook.* New York: DK Publishing.

Williams, C. (2002). *The kid's cookbook.* Birmingham, AL: Oxmoor House.

Serving Families' Needs. Families as well as early childhood educators have an impact on children's nutrition habits (S. Swadener, 1995). Although children decide how much (or even whether) to eat, adults are responsible for the foods children are offered. Family members can help their children develop appropriate nutrition concepts and attitudes (Nahikian-Nelms, Syler, & Mogharrehan, 1994). They need to be informed on various topics concerning nutrition for children, including (a) foods needed for a healthy child; (b) planning, buying, storing, and preparing varieties of foods; (c) common eating problems of children; (d) children who need special diets; and (e) money savers.

Staff need to know the social realities of the families with whom they work; otherwise they may make nutrition demands that families cannot meet. Families can be reached in meetings, demonstration classes, and home visits and through newsletters. Some specific suggestions follow:

1. Staff can aid families in planning nutritious meals by using the Food Guide Pyramid.

2. Newsletters can include information about food planning and preparation and recipes as a way of developing the young child's interest in foods and snacks. Resources, available from NFSMI, for nutrition education in the home include the following:

    Food, Family, and Fun: A Seasonal Guide to Healthy Eating, 1998.

    Food Guide Pyramid for Young Children Booklet, 1999.

    Go, Glow, Grow: Food for You, 1996.

3. Printed program menus should be sent home so families can better plan home meals.

4. Other information on nutrition, such as the nutrient content of foods in relation to cost, the nutrient content of food after storage and preparation, and the relationship between nutrition and the health of infants and young children, should be made available

through educational programs and articles in newsletters.

5. Ask family members to participate in the children's nutrition program or in cooking activities. Remind them of ways to involve children in food preparation at home and ways to promote good dietary habits.

6. Make a list of federal nutritional services that may help meet family needs (see the list at the end of the chapter).

SUPPORTING HEALTH

Attention to health issues in programs for young children dates back to 1945 (Child Welfare League of America, 1945). Research concerning health has been sporadic until recently. Today, the definition of *health* has expanded from the absence of disease to a state of total physical, mental, and social and emotional well-being. Each of the three aspects of health contribute equally to a person's overall health. For example, physical health problems often cause young children to be listless, which results in less exploration and play; this decreases interaction in one's physical and social worlds and adversely affects cognitive and social and emotional development. Conversely, a stressful cognitive, social, or emotional environment can lead to physical health problems. As a result of our increased understanding of this interactive relationship, early childhood professionals are giving increased attention to health.

Program directors must be concerned about the health of all those involved in early childhood programs. More specifically, directors must develop health policies for children and staff in keeping with current information and must plan and oversee the implementation of the policies.

Assessing Health Status

Assessment of health is an appraisal of an individual's state of health. Because health is a dynamic quality, appraisal must consist of an in-depth periodic assessment by a specially trained health professional and continuous staff observations conducted in a variety of day-to-day activities.

Staff. Working in an early childhood care and education program is physically demanding, results in heavy exposure to children's illnesses, and can be emotionally stressful. The health of adults is a key element in the quality of an early childhood program. A staff member's illness can become a health hazard to children and other staff members, is costly to a program when substitutes must be hired, and can cause a lack of consistent child care.

Planning for staff members' health assessment begins with the wording of the job descriptions. Each job description needs to be explicit about the health attributes required for each staff position; otherwise a refusal to hire or a dismissal may be discriminatory. Although some aspects of health are required by all (e.g., being free from contagious diseases), others are more job specific (e.g., the ability to lift).

Policies should be written and shared with potential employees concerning (a) the content of the health history and medical examination including any specific examinations for a given role; (b) who can perform the examination, where it can be performed, and who pays for it; (c) who at the local program receives the information; and (d) when it must be received. For protection of the local program from liability problems, the health assessment should be completed and reviewed before the job offer is made final and before the hiree comes into contact with children. Samples of staff health assessments are found in *Caring for Our Children* (American Academy of Pediatrics, American Public Health Association, and National Resource Center for Health and Safety in Child Care, 2002, p. 413) and in *Model Child Care Health Policies* (Early Childhood Education Linkage System, 2002, appendix U).

Children. Children's health status prior to enrollment must be considered. For program admission purposes, children should have a medical examination within 6 weeks of initial enrollment and be on the current vaccination schedule. Samples of child health assessments are found in *Caring for Our Children* (American Academy of Pediatrics, American Public Health Association, and National Resource Center for Health and Safety in Child Care, 2002, p. 440) and in *Model Child Care Health Policies* (Early Childhood Education Linkage System, 2002, appendix B). These samples forms ask for pertinent information on the child's health history, current medical examination results, allergies, immunization record, results of screening tests, and the date of the child's last dental examination. The physician is also asked to list any health problems or special needs and recommended care.

Advocating Preventive Health Care

The early childhood program can have considerable influence on children's health. Many opportunities exist for strengthening the concept of preventive health care by securing health services, preventing infections in the program, and communicating with families.

Securing Health Services.   All children need to receive high-quality health services. Early childhood programs are required by various regulatory agencies to provide some health services, such as health consultation (Dooling & Ulione, 2000). In addition, early childhood directors need to locate available resources and obtain their criteria for child and family assistance. For starters, directors need to check health departments; clinics operated by hospitals and medical schools; voluntary groups such as the United Fund, the American Red Cross, civic clubs, religious groups, and family service associations; medical assistance under Medicaid (Title XIX); armed forces medical services; and insurance and other prepayment plans.

Preventing Infections in Programs.   Protection from infectious diseases is a daily concern of early childhood staff, families, and health professionals. Although it is unrealistic to prevent the spread of all infectious diseases in any group (including a family), much can be done to reduce the risk of transmission.

Vulnerability of Children.   Infections are transmitted through direct contact (touching), blood contact, the fluids of the respiratory tract, and the stool of the intestinal tract. Children are highly vulnerable because of the following:

1. Close physical contacts among children and adults—feeding, diapering and toileting, sharing objects including moist art media and water tables, and affection giving and receiving

2. Children's lack of immunity

3. Children's small body structures, such as the distance between the nose and throat and the middle ear

4. Children's bumps and scrapes on the skin that afford entry of infectious agents into the body

5. Children's lack of understanding of how to protect themselves from infectious agents

Health concerns are great for infants and toddlers in group programs. These very young children do show an increased incidence of respiratory illness and diarrhea as compared with infants and toddlers not in group settings (Harms, 1992).

Environmental Protection Practices.   Safe environments for both children and adults can be achieved by following certain health practices. The Cost, Quality, and Child Outcomes Study Team (1995) found that in infant and toddler programs, diapering and toileting and personal grooming did not meet requirements for minimal-quality scores. They found that in preschool programs, standards for hand washing were not consistently met. Some of the basics are as follows:

1. Safe programs have fewer than 50 children, consist of small groups of non-toilet-trained

infants and toddlers, and separate children in diapers from other children.

2. Food service must meet health standards.

3. The diapering area is the most dangerous area for the growth of illness-causing microorganisms. The following practices reduce risks in diapering:

   a. Change a child on a table with a plastic-covered pad that has no cracks and that has a restraint device.

   b. Place paper bags or wax paper squares under each child before changing. Special paper is now available on rolls that can be attached to some changing tables (like that used in a physician's examination room). Also use paper to pick up the diaper.

   c. Use disposable gloves to augment hand-washing procedures.

   d. Wash the diapering surface twice daily and after any diaper leaks. Scrub with detergent and water. Rinse with clean water treated with a disinfectant (1/4 c chlorine bleach to 1 gal water) kept in a spray bottle. The disinfectant must be made fresh daily and stored away from children. Leave the solution on the surface for 2 minutes prior to wiping it dry with paper towels.

   e. Wash your hands after diapering, using running water. If a sink with elbow controls, which is desirable in this area, is unavailable, use a paper towel to turn off the faucet.

   f. Post procedures for diapering in the diapering area. Warrick and Helling (1997) list detailed procedures for diapering.

4. Require consistent attention to hand washing. Children and adults should wash their hands before serving or eating food, after each diaper change or use of rest rooms, and after wiping a nose. Proper hand washing requires the following:

   a. Use soap in soft-water areas and detergent in hard-water areas. Liquid soap is more sanitary than bar soap. Liquid soap dispensers should be cleaned and refilled on a regular basis. If bar soaps are used, the bar should be rinsed before and after use and kept dry.

   b. Work the soap in the hands for 2 to 3 minutes, rinse with running water, clean under the nails, keep the elbows higher than the hands, turn off the faucet with a paper towel, and dry hands with a disposable paper towel.

   c. For hand washing of infants and young toddlers, wipe the hands with damp towels moistened with a liquid soap solution, wipe with disposable towels moistened with clean water, and then dry with paper towels. For older children, squirt drops of liquid soap onto their hands from a squeeze bottle; children then rinse their hands under running water and dry them with a paper towel.

5. Follow universal precautions to prevent transmission of blood-borne diseases (e.g., HIV/AIDS), which have been adapted for child care programs. The precautions are as follows:

   a. Wash hands for 2 to 3 minutes after contact with blood or other body fluids contaminated with blood.

   b. Cover cuts and scratches with a bandage.

   c. Use disposable absorbent materials (e.g., facial tissue, paper towels) to stop bleeding.

   d. Use disposable latex gloves when you encounter bleeding and wash hands as soon as you remove your gloves.

   e. Clean blood-soiled areas and disinfect with a solution of 1 part chlorine bleach and 9 parts water.

   f. Discard blood-stained materials in a plastic bag and place in a lined, covered garbage container.

g. Put blood-stained laundry in sealed plastic bags. Machine wash separately in cold soapy water and then wash separately in hot water.

6. The facility and equipment must be cleaned regularly. The following are suggestions for cleaning:

   a. General cleaning of the building should be done daily when children are gone.

   b. Clean cribs, strollers, and tables daily, using the same procedure and cleaning materials as described for cleaning the diapering table. This should also be done with wooden toys and laminated books.

   c. Wash high-chair trays in a dishwasher.

   d. Daily, wash toys that are put in the mouth. This can be done more quickly if toys are placed in nylon mesh bags (used for hosiery), washed, and rinsed. Soak toys in 3/4 cup bleach to 1 gal water for 5 minutes. Rinse again and hang to dry.

   e. Rinse rattles and other dishwasher-safe mouth toys before placing in the dishwasher. (Saliva forms a film when heated, aiding in the growth of microorganisms.)

   f. Use bedding with one child only; wash weekly or after soiling.

   g. Clean and disinfect bath fixtures daily or after soiling.

   h. Remove trash daily.

   i. Dispose of soiled diapers or hold them for laundry in a closed container.

   j. Never place dishes or bottles on the floor.

   k. Clean floors and other surfaces after feeding.

See other sanitation standards given by the American Academy of Pediatrics, the American Public Health Association, and the National Resource Center for Health and Safety in Child Care (2002).

A local sanitation checklist of health practices should be developed. Items should be checked off by date and time and initialed by the person fulfilling the requirement.

Communicating with Families. Early childhood program staff members must regularly communicate with families on health care issues. Following are some of the basic areas of communication:

1. Reflecting on family concerns regarding health, such as exclusion of children from the program for certain contagious diseases and the costs of health care. Directors of programs should help families find ways to resolve some of these concerns.

2. Explaining, before the enrollment of a child, the policies concerning exclusion for certain illnesses and why these policies are needed.

3. Sharing information daily between staff members and families as each child is passed from family caregiver to staff member and back again. A daily written form should be provided for all infants and toddlers and for preschoolers and young school-age children if symptoms of illness appear. All instructions by medical professionals should be included. Various sample forms for family–staff communication are provided by Godwin and Schrag (1996, pp. 119–126).

4. Helping families make contact with health care professionals and services.

5. Informing parents about exposure to communicable disease. The program should share information concerning how the disease is spread, how it is prevented or controlled, the symptoms of the disease, what the program is doing, and what the family should do. A letter is sent for more serious contagious diseases, not for colds. A sample letter is provided in *Model Child Care Health Policies* (Early Childhood Education Linkage System, 2002, appendix K).

Providing Health Care

The health care provided in a local program must be viewed from many perspectives, such as individual child needs, children's collective needs, family needs and those of their employers, and staff needs. The program facility (i.e., the space and equipment needed to provide care) must also be considered in providing health care. Sometimes these needs or situations are not compatible. For example, a mother may need to work, but her ill child may need individual care or may have an illness that can spread to other children. The *Code of Ethical Conduct and Statement of Commitment* requires that the program place the welfare of an enrolled child or the group of children before other needs (Feeney & Kipnis, 1998).

Caring for Children with Mild Illnesses.   Until recently, most regulations required children with any communicable disease be removed from the group setting. Such regulations and policies have been debated on the basis of the following questions:

1. *Does removing an ill child reduce the spread of infection?* Programs with stringent policies for excluding ill children, compared with less strict programs, showed no difference in the amounts or kinds of illnesses. For many illnesses, it is difficult to determine the risk of spread of infectious diseases for the following reasons: (a) Children with no symptoms may spread infection; (b) children often spread infection several days before and after symptoms; and (c) the presence or absence of certain symptoms, including fever, is not correlated with the amount of infectious disease a child is spreading.

2. *Can family members afford to stay home with a mildly ill child?* Adult family members may feel unable to lose work time and thus may leave an ill child at home under the care of an older sibling or under the care of a neighbor who is to "check" on the child. Family members may try to cover the illness by trying to cover the symptoms. They may also feel guilty about not providing total care of their child and supposedly exposing the child to an illness spread in the program.

3. *What is best for an ill child?* Ill children do not need to feel guilty about the inconvenience their illness causes their families or their caregivers. Ill children may need more comfort, but often not much more care than well children. If an ill child is to be kept in the program, staff need to (a) maintain information on the onset of the illness and current symptoms, possible contributing factors (e.g., vaccinations), complicating illnesses (e.g., chronic illnesses), intake (food and drink) and output (times urinated and number of bowel movements), and care given; (b) follow basic health practices, especially hand washing; (c) follow approved practices for caring for children with fever, vomiting, or diarrhea; and (d) provide a place to play and play materials suited to an ill child.

4. *Can families pay for short-term special care when their children are ill?* Directors have special-care options: (a) hiring additional staff for ill children, (b) providing a "get well room" with a familiar caregiver, and (c) forming a linkage with nearby families that provide temporary family home care or with a sick-child center. In each of these options, families pay for the special care.

Today, ill children are usually excluded from group programs if they cannot participate in routine activities, if the illness requires staff care that in turn compromises the care of the other children, and if the ill child poses increased risks of spreading the illness to others (Early Childhood Education Linkage System, 2002, pp. 4–5). Based on these standards, directors of programs must develop policies for specifying limitations on the attendance of ill children, provisions for the notification of families, and plans for the comfort and care of ill children.

Some communicable diseases must also be reported to the health department, which in turn will make recommendations for informing families of children who may have been exposed. For example, HIV/AIDS must be reported. Directors should handle the situation by (a) educating the staff on the causes, transmission, and prevention of HIV/AIDS; (b) training staff to use universal precautions in handling all children (and other adults involved in the program); (c) determining how best to address fears and concerns; and (d) following states' guidelines on confidentiality and disclosure.

One designated staff member must make decisions concerning the care of ill children based on policy. For example:

1. **Mildly ill child admitted to program.** If a mildly ill child is admitted to a program, a symptom record (see Figure 8–1) must be kept and a copy given to the family each day. The family member and caregiver must consult on treatment. Medication administration policies must be followed.

2. **Child becomes ill after program admission.** The teacher must complete a symptom record and notify the designated staff member to make a decision concerning the continued care of the child. If the child is allowed to stay, the family is called, and the same procedure is followed as given for a mildly ill child admitted to the program. If the child is too ill to stay, the family is called, and the child is carefully supervised until a family member arrives.

Caring for Children with Noninfectious Chronic Illnesses and Disabilities. Many children who have a chronic illness or a disability are eligible for services under P.L. 105-17. Planning needs to be done prior to accepting these children. Following are some points to consider:

1. The prognosis of the illness or disability
2. Adaptations in program activities or in the schedule
3. Special housing arrangements needed
4. Special equipment needed
5. Special dietary needs

6. Coordination of home and program administration of medication
7. Possible special care and emergency procedures (e.g., replacement equipment should failure occur, backup power source, supplemental oxygen, resuscitator bag, and suctioning catheter)

Although some children require intensive services beyond the usual early childhood program, most children with a chronic illness or a disability will require only minor adaptations.

Administrating Medication. Legally, the administration of medication is an act by an adult that can alter the metabolism of a child in a way not always susceptible to immediate control. Before making a policy, the program director should check licensing or other regulations. In writing a policy, the following points should be considered:

1. A parent or guardian provides the written order of a physician authorizing the use of the medication for a specified length of time for a particular child.

2. The parent provides a written request that a staff member administer the medication (see appendix 8).

3. The medication is labeled with the child's name, the name of the drug, and directions for administration.

4. Staff maintain a written record of the date and time of each administration and the name of the staff member administering the medication (spills and refusals to take medication should be noted on a log; see Figure 8–2).

5. Safe and appropriate (e.g., refrigerated) storage places for medications are designated.

Staff members need to know possible side effects, how to recognize them, and specific action to take.

Child's Name _____

Date _____

SYMPTOMS

Major Symptoms

    Respiratory: runny nose; sore throat; difficulty in breathing; cough; other

       (Please describe) _____

       _____

    Skin: itch; rash; oozing; lesion; other

       (Please describe) _____

       _____

    Gastrointestinal: nausea; vomiting; diarrhea; trouble urinating; frequent urinating with pain; other

       (Please describe) _____

       _____

    Body movement: stiff neck; limp; other

       (Please describe) _____

       _____

When symptom began _____

CHILD'S REACTIONS

    Food/fluid intake

       (Please describe) _____

       _____

    Urine, bowel, and/or vomiting

       (Please describe) _____

       _____

    Crying, sleeping, other behavior

       (Please describe) _____

       _____

Figure 8–1a   Symptom Record

EXPOSURE

Ill children or staff

(Please describe) _____

_____

Ill parent or sibling

(Please describe) _____

_____

New foods

(Please describe) _____

_____

Ingestion of or contact with potentially harmful substance (e.g., art materials, cleaning materials, room paint, plants, animals)

(Please describe) _____

_____

CARE AND ADVICE

First aid, emergency care, or other care

(Please describe) _____

_____

Health provider advice

(Please describe) _____

_____

Parent consultation

(Please describe) _____

_____

_____
(Signature of person completing form)

Figure 8–1b   Symptom Record

Child's name ————————————————

Date ————————————————————

Time	Safety Check of Label and Storage	Notes	Staff Member's Initials

(Give copy to parent when child is picked up.)

Figure 8–2   Medication Administration Log

Helping Children Develop Good Mental Health. Health has many dimensions, and perhaps the most important is mental health. Each day problems resulting from mental health stressors enter early childhood programs through the emotions and challenging behaviors of young children. The risk factors are biological, such as perinatal stress, birth trauma, and congenital defects (Brennan, Mednick, & Kandal, 1991; Shore, 1997) and environmental, such as the social conditions arising from poverty, exposure to violence, and even the lack of a caring environment in low-quality programs (Kaplan, 1998; Simmons, Stalsworth, & Wentzel, 1999; Slaby, Roedell, Arezzo, & Hendrix, 1995; Stanford & Yamamoto, 2001).

The emotional domain is perhaps the most compelling aspect of development in young children. Honig (1993) stated that the most serious problems for infants and toddlers "lie in the domain of social/emotional functioning" (p. 69). During these early years, children must build secure relations and develop independence. Honig sees family and staff education, professional resources, and environmental changes aimed at reducing stress as all important in ensuring these young children's mental health. Even for preschoolers, group programs can be sources of great tension. All young children often feel "one among many" for very long hours and lonely and separated from their families. Primary-age children are coping with the stress of "school" and often with the daily transition of school to child care programs or school to "home alone."

Striving for mental health in group programs and in the homes of children must be a top priority. Directors and staff members can employ many strategies that will help, including the following:

1. Provide staff in-service education about stressors that staff members will confront in early childhood programs. For example, family members feel the anxiety of separating from their babies and young children and of meeting the dual and often conflicting demands

of employment and parenting. Staff often feel frustrated with distressed infants, defiant toddlers, and aggressive or withdrawn preschoolers; with family members they believe could do better jobs of parenting; and with the human and physical qualities of the workplace. Finally, some children and adults are also experiencing less than optimal and even abusive home lives; these "from home" stressors will be played out on the stage of the group setting.

2. Combat violence in the community. Directors and staff members should work with families, business leaders, and social agency professionals in promoting activities aimed at reducing the risks of violence within the community.

3. Recognize the risk factors (see Figure 8–3) and signs of possible neglect and abuse (see Figure 8–4) in children, know how to respond to child disclosures of neglect or abuse (Austin, 2000), and have written policies on reporting suspected child neglect or abuse.

4. Develop program policies that lessen the chances of hurtful discipline and/or abuse within the program. Directors must be vigilant in the implementation of these policies (Mikkelsen, 1997; NAEYC, 1997b).

5. Establish a team approach with families in working toward building home–program continuity and maintaining consistent expectations for children's behaviors.

6. Provide family education information on topics such as resolving conflicts within the home including sources of professional and emergency assistance, making television and computers a less dominant aspect of family life (for ideas, see Hoffman, 2002), and controlling the contents of media seen by children.

7. Prepare staff with constructive coping strategies for dealing with children's challenging behaviors by

a. using positive guidance (see chapter 7);

b. implementing strategies for dealing with persistent and very challenging behaviors (see the resource list at the end of the chapter); and

c. recognizing children's behaviors that need assistance by mental health professionals (Division of Early Childhood of the Council for Exceptional Children, 2001).

Protecting Staff Members' Health. As discussed, medical examinations are an important means of protecting staff health. Staff members also need first aid training; precautionary training for situations involving blood-borne pathogens; and information on protecting their backs while lifting, safeguarding themselves during pregnancy, and knowing when not to work. (See *Caring for Our Children* by the American Academy of Pediatrics, the American Public Health Association, and the National Resource Center for Health and Safety in Child Care, 2002, for detailed information.)

Adequate paid sick leave protects the health of adults. When sick leave is not available, staff might not leave when they are ill or may return before they should resume their duties. Fully paid health insurance in child care programs is rare (Whitebook, Howes, & Phillips, 1998).

Keeping Health Records. Licensing and other regulations usually require that each child have a recent medical examination and an up-to-date immunization record before admission to a program. Health records should be on file about 1 month before the child's admission. Records are updated every 6 months for children under 2 years of age and every year for those over 2. The contents of health records were described in the section "Assessing Health Status."

Because children are being cared for more and more frequently in early childhood programs, staff need to work with children's physicians. A staff member may have important information to convey to a child's physician or may wish to obtain the physician's advice on handling

Figure 8–3   Risk Factors for Neglect and Abuse

Society
◆ Poverty
◆ Overcrowding
◆ Illegal drug culture
◆ High crime area
◆ High unemployment rate
◆ Few social services
◆ Unaffordable health care

Parent/Family
◆ Unwanted pregnancy
◆ Single parent
◆ Teen parent
◆ Physical, sexual, or emotional abuse as a child
◆ Emotional neglect as a child
◆ Use of violence to express anger
◆ Lack of self-esteem
◆ Emotional immaturity
◆ Poor coping skills
◆ Alcohol or illegal drug abuse
◆ Marriage problems
◆ Financial stress
◆ Recent stressful events (divorce, recent move, death in family)
◆ Illness (physical or mental health, especially depression)
◆ Lacks parenting skills including no preparation for the extreme stress of a new baby
◆ Lacks knowledge of child development; thus has unrealistic expectations for the child
◆ Heavy parenting responsibility (multiple births or single children less than 18 months apart in age)
◆ Weak bonding or attachment to a child (often due to child's care in ICU after birth)
◆ Use of physical punishment (called corporal punishment)
◆ Isolation (lack of family or friend support)

Child
◆ Under the age of five years, especially under age of one year
◆ Low birthweight or premature
◆ Looks like or has traits like a disliked relative
◆ Irritable or cries a great deal (colic; ADHD)
◆ Disobeys parents or argues a great deal (older child)

Source: Decker, C. A. (2004). *Children: The early years* (p. 676). Tinley Park, IL: The Goodheart-Willcox Company, Inc. Reprinted with permission.

Neglect

A child may be physically neglected when he or she
♦ is malnourished
♦ fails to receive needed health care without a parental objection
♦ fails to receive proper hygiene (is not washed or bathed; has poor oral hygiene; has ungroomed skin, nails, and hair)
♦ has insufficient clothing or clothing that is dirty, tattered, or inappropriate for the weather
♦ lives in filthy conditions and/or inadequate shelter

A child may suffer mental or educational neglect when he or she
♦ lacks moral training
♦ lacks constructive discipline
♦ fails to receive positive examples from adults
♦ fails to have adequate supervision
♦ is left alone for hours
♦ fails to attend school regularly because of parents
♦ fails to receive parent stimulation toward learning or education suited to his or her ability
♦ is not allowed to take part in wholesome recreational activities

A child may be emotionally neglected if he or she
♦ experiences constant friction in the home
♦ is denied normal experiences that produce feelings of being wanted, loved, and protected
♦ is rejected through indifference
♦ is overly rejected, such as through abandonment

Abuse

A child may be physically abused if he or she
♦ seems fearful or quiet around parents but has no close feeling for them
♦ is wary of physical contact initiated by an adult
♦ has little or no reaction to pain and seems much less afraid than most children the same age
♦ has unexplained injuries or shows evidence of repeated injuries, such as having bruises in various stages of healing or repeated fractures
♦ is dressed inappropriately, such as an injured child dressed in pajamas who was reportedly injured on a bicycle or a child dressed in a turtleneck in the summer to cover bruises
♦ has long bones that, when x-rayed, show a history of past injuries
♦ has injuries not reported on previous health records
♦ has parents who have taken the child to many hospitals and doctors without appropriate explanation
♦ has parents who refuse further diagnostic studies of their child's injuries
♦ has parents who show detachment or see the child as bad or "different" during medical treatment
♦ has parents who give too many minute details about the cause of injury
♦ tries to protect parents when they are questioned about the child's injuries

A child may suffer verbal abuse if he or she
♦ lacks self-esteem
♦ is either too quiet and polite or uses harsh and improper language when dealing with others, especially those who are smaller or younger
♦ expresses long-term feelings of damage and isolation *(continued)*

Figure 8–4   Signs of Child Neglect and Abuse

A child may be sexually abused if he or she
- has extreme and sudden changes in behavior, such as loss of appetite or sudden drop in grades
- has nightmares and other sleep problems
- regresses to previous behaviors, such as renewed thumb sucking
- has torn or stained underwear
- has infections (with symptoms like bleeding or other discharges and itching) or swollen genitals
- fears a person or shows an intense dislike of being left alone with that person
- has an STD or pregnancy
- has unusual interest in or knowledge of sexual matters

Source: Decker, C. A. (2004). *Children: The early years* (pp. 679–680). Tinley Park, IL: The Goodheart-Willcox Company, Inc. Reprinted with permission.

Figure 8–4   *continued*

a particular health problem in the center. S. Dixon (1990) provided some guidelines that make communication easier.

PRACTICING SAFETY

Safety is no longer seen as just sheltering the child. Safety includes environmental care, emergency preparedness, child protection, and safety consciousness. Thus, safety is an integral part of the daily early childhood program.

Planning Environmental Safety

Environmental safety needs close attention. Environmental safety includes setting limits for children, facility safety, vehicular safety, and sanitation and hygienic practices.

Setting Limits for Children.   Children will take risks—many of which are good learning experiences. At other times, though, an adult must stop or redirect a child in a potentially harmful situation. Children must begin learning how to predict hazards and choose safe alternatives. Staff must decide on a few rules based on the population of children (e.g., younger children and children with special needs often need more precisely defined limits), facilities and equipment, activity, and the supervision available. These rules should always be stated in positive ways, with the alternative behavior given (e.g., "Fences are to keep us safe. Climbing is fun. If you want to climb, you must climb only on the gym. The gym is made for us to climb").

Implementing Facility and Vehicular Safety.   General facility safety and environmental protection practices are given in chapter 5 and in an earlier section of this chapter, respectively. Each program needs to establish environmental safety policies and procedures to fit its own special needs. Each program should develop a safety checklist based on the local facility. Staff should continually scan for safety hazards and do a thorough safety check once a month and after any program disruption or vacation time. Different people should do the safety check. Noted repairs should be made immediately, or actions should be taken to prevent children's contact with the hazard.

Transporting children requires additional safety precautions. Each driver must be a responsible person, possess a current license appropriate for the number of passengers, and have liability insurance in keeping with state law. Vehicles must have current safety inspection stickers in states requiring such inspections. The vehicle must be equipped with appropriate restraint systems for age/size/special needs of children and for adults (For Your Information, 2002). Obtain the latest information on transporting children safely from the Department of Transportation Hotline (888-327-4236), the National Highway Transportation Safety Administration, the American Academy of Pediatrics, or the Healthy Child Care America Campaign (see the contact information at the end of the chapter).

For each field trip, special safety plans must be made. For example, how and where to load and unload must be preplanned. A copy of each child's emergency information form (see appendix 8), blank accident forms, and first aid kit must be taken on the field trip. A minimum of two adults must be with each group of children at all times. On field trips, teachers should determine group sizes that allow for appropriate supervision.

Using Hygienic Practices. When families and teachers work together on the assumption that preventive measures rigorously practiced are in the best interests of all children and adults, those involved in group programs are less vulnerable to disease. A health care professional is needed as a resource person for advising on policies, occasionally monitoring practices, and providing in-service education to parents and staff. Effective ways to interrupt the transmission of infectious agents are hand washing, environmental cleaning (for specifics, see Aronson, 2002, p. 128), and using group-limiting strategies (e.g., small groups, grouping by toileting status, designating toys for certain groups of children).

Preparing for Emergencies

Emergencies arise even when early childhood programs take every possible measure to protect children's health and safety. To minimize the risks to children, procedures for handling them must be developed. The key elements in handling emergencies include the following:

1. Preplan necessary action for evacuating children in the event of a fire or explosion and preplan measures to take during tornadoes, hurricanes, flash floods, earthquakes, smog alerts, and civil defense emergencies. Consult with the local fire department and local Red Cross chapter or Civil Defense chapter in developing guidelines (see Copeland, 1996). Have the exit route and procedures posted near or on exit doors. Have flashlights, a first aid kit, a cell phone, a battery-operated radio, food and water, blankets, children's books, paper and crayons, completed emergency information forms, and class lists on a shelf by each exit door. Plan a designated meeting place and procedures for checking on the presence and well-being of each person at the designated area. Practice the desired plan (and alternative plan) once a month or more often if necessary. Tell family members your emergency site(s).

2. Have on hand a first aid kit (see Figure 8–5) and current references for handling emergencies. The kit should be carried to the playground, on field trips, and during evacuations.

3. Staff need to be trained and informed of their responsibilities for administering first aid. They must also recognize when an accident or illness requires immediate medical help.

4. Parents or legal guardians must be notified in case of an accident or illness. They should be given the opportunity, if possible without endangering the child, to participate in making decisions and aiding in the treatment procedure.

5. The child's records should contain a consent form authorizing emergency medical treatment and transportation if parents cannot be reached. The emergency information form usually includes the names, addresses, and phone numbers of parents and other persons who can accept responsibility for the child when parents cannot be contacted; the name and phone number of the physician to be contacted; and the name and address of the hospital to which the child may be taken (see appendix 8). Once a month, perhaps with the fee statement or during check-in, parents should be asked to verify information on the emergency information forms.

Figure 8–5 Contents of First Aid Kit

Ammonia (for bee stings)
Antiseptic (solid packages)
Bandages (assorted sizes, including triangular and eye dressing)
Cash for emergencies
Cold pack
Container for carrying insect, plant, or spider specimens (for medical identification)
Cotton balls (for applying pressure)
Emergency information forms and medication for children with chronic problems (see appendix 8)
Eye irrigation solution
Facial tissues
First aid books and charts
Gauze (pads—2″ × 2″ and 4″ × 4″; flexible roller gauze—1″ and 2″ widths)
Gloves (disposable latex)
Injury report forms (see Figure 8–6)
Insect sting preparation (if needed by anyone in program) and baking soda (to soothe insect stings and bites)
Notepad and pen/pencil
Plastic bags
Pocket mask for CPR
Safety pins
Scissors and tweezers
Soap (preferably liquid)
Splints (plastic or metal)
Syrup of ipecac
Tape (adhesive—1/2″ and 1″ widths)
Telephone numbers for emergency aid and cell phone
Thermometer (nonglass)
Towels (1 large and 1 small)
Water

6. Forms should also be available for staff to document the procedures they followed in handling an injury or illness. Careful documentation helps prevent mistakes in caring for children and also lessens the potential liability to the program (see Figure 8–6).

Providing Child Protection

As previously discussed, child neglect and abuse in families or in programs cannot be tolerated. Staff must also protect children in cases of disputes over custody. Staff must remember the stress of all those involved—the child, both parents (or biological and adoptive parents), and even other family members. Staff must realize they cannot take sides in these issues but must perform their responsibilities on behalf of the child in accordance with legal decisions.

Promoting Safety Consciousness and Education

Safety awareness is highly important for the entire early childhood program community.

1. **Staff members.** The Consumer Product Safety Commission (1999) noted pervasive

Child's name _____

Birth date _____

Parent location information _____

_____

Child's physician _____

(Telephone) _____

- -

Injury

    Date _____ Time _____

    General description (e.g., bite, burn, cut) _____

    _____

    Where/how injury occurred _____

    _____

    Staff supervisor (at time of injury) _____

    Other adult witnesses to the injury _____

    _____

Action Taken

    Child's apparent symptoms and reaction _____

    _____

First Aid (if any)

    Nature of _____

    _____

    _____

    Administered by _____

    Assisted by _____

Figure 8–6a   Injury Report Form *(continued)*

Medical Help Sought (if any)

From whom _____

Time of contact _____

Advice _____

_____

_____

Parent Contact

Attempts _____

Parent advice _____

_____

_____

Follow-up Care

Description _____

_____

_____

Condition of Child at Time of Release

Description _____

_____

_____

_____
(Signature of person completing form)

Note: For quick reference and as a time saver, always have a form with information above the dotted line completed on each child.

Figure 8–6b   *continued*

health and safety violations even among licensed centers. Among the hazards were fire code violations, unsafe use or storage of toxic chemicals, unsanitary conditions, and lack of playground safety.

2. **Children.** Young children are receptive to developing concepts and attitudes. Because children are prone to unsafe behaviors, safety information is useful to them now and can be readily incorporated into their current daily living activities. Furthermore, habits developed in the formative years are often carried over into adulthood.

3. **Families.** Providing safety information to families is a way to increase family understandings, influence children's actions, and provide a greater continuity between home and school.

Assessing Risks and Protecting Children. Early childhood professionals must never become complacent about safety. Each staff member must learn to assess risks, including the activity, the setting (e.g., learning center), and how a specific group of children will respond. Even teacher stress can increase risks. Accurate assessment cannot guarantee safety, however. Every situation has risks. For example, some directors do not understand outdoor dangers; thus, they often allow some teachers to take breaks when children are outside. Other directors think the most serious accidents occur outdoors; thus, they become complacent about play indoors. (Yet in family child care settings, most accidents occur indoors.) Two other examples of recently stressed safety precautions are (a) that children can drown in 2 inches of water (thus children must be carefully supervised while playing with or in water, and sprinklers are safer than wading pools for water play), and (b) the 1992 recommendation by the American Academy of Pediatrics that "healthy infants born at term" be placed on their backs or sides for sleep (Gershon & Moon, 1997), which is now called "back to sleep."

Professionals are expected to provide for children's safety. Thus, they are legally responsi-

ble. Failure to be responsible is considered negligence. Negligence has two categories:

1. **Acts of omission,** in which adults fail to take precautionary measures needed to protect children (e.g., failure to inspect facility for safety, failure to supervise or provide adequate supervision)

2. **Acts of commission,** in which adults' actions or decisions involve risks (e.g., taking a field trip even though several needed volunteers did not show up to accompany the children)

Directors can protect children while also protecting themselves and their staff from liability judgments by carefully writing job descriptions, obtaining safety training for staff, maintaining appropriate records (especially accident report forms), and securing liability insurance. Although safety management is challenging because of the ages of children, acting responsibly can save lives and prevent negligence from being found by the courts.

Teaching Safety Education to Children. Children also need health and safety education. Most education for young children is done through incidental learning experiences and imitation of adults. For example, safety education for young children is often embedded in other curriculum content (e.g., school bus safety may be used as part of an orientation to a program or preparation for a field trip; kitchen safety may be part of classroom cooking experiences). Other safety practices are promoted during various national educational campaigns (e.g., Fire Prevention Week). Although these teachable moments are the most meaningful for children, they need more specific instruction on coping with emergencies, how to get help, and even first aid basics in the case of older preschool and primary-level children.

Resources for safety education are not plentiful. Most resources feature a few activities on one theme, such as "Play Safe! Be Safe!" a preschool program on fire safety sponsored by the BIC Corporation (http://www.fireproof-children.com/resources_besafe .htm). A few comprehensive curriculum resources are available, however, such as *Growing, Growing Strong* (C. Smith, Hendricks, & Bennett, 1997).

Providing Information and Training to Adults. Family members and early childhood professionals are very aware of their responsibilities to protect children. Most adults, however, are deficient in health and safety information. Information is needed in many areas, such as the following:

1. The relationship of health to total well-being
2. Prenatal care
3. The characteristics of the child's developmental stage associated with health problems and safety hazards
4. Nutrition and exercise for the growing child
5. Injury prevention
6. Stress management in children and adults
7. The detection and management of symptoms of common childhood infectious diseases
8. The prevention of child abuse and detection and the reporting of suspected child abuse and neglect
9. Agencies and resources for health and safety education and assistance
10. Emergency preparedness

Training must be provided in these and other areas of need and interest. Staff training on various topics must be repeated so that new staff members can receive training and all other staff members can replenish their knowledge and skills. One advocacy effort is the Healthy Child Care America Campaign (1996).

TRENDS AND ISSUES

Health concerns are still great for young children in early childhood programs. Especially vulnerable to infectious diseases are infants and toddlers and the adults who care for them. The care of some children with special needs also presents problems to staff. With the great increase of these children in group programs, professionals are calling for better education and more consistent monitoring of health and hygienic practices.

Early childhood professionals are asking regulatory agencies to write and enforce more comprehensive regulations. Particular needs include a focus on infants and toddlers and on children with special needs, on dangerous and improperly installed outdoor equipment, and on child-proofing family child care homes.

Many see the need for greater and more consistent health and safety consciousness among early childhood professionals and family members of young children. Teachers' responsibilities for children's nutrition, health, and safety are greatest during the early childhood years. However, training in these areas is much less extensive than other aspects of preservice and in-service teacher preparation.

SUMMARY

Nutrition, health, and safety practices and education are essential ingredients of quality early childhood programs. Nutrition is highly important in programs for young children for two reasons: (a) Early childhood programs need to provide up to 80% of a young child's total nutrition requirements, and (b) children develop lifelong eating habits as a result of early eating experiences. Thus, staff members need to know the nutritional requirements of young children, how to provide a nutritious diet, and how to create an appropriate eating environment. Health affects each area of a person's development. The health goals in early childhood programs are to assess the health status of staff members and children, advocate preventive health care, communicate with families, and provide some health care. Child safety includes planning environmental safety, preparing for emergencies, providing child protection, and promoting safety consciousness and education. Thus, both health and safety are broad in scope in quality programs.

Trends and issues include concern about the control of infectious diseases in early childhood programs and about the care of children with chronic health conditions. Many also see the need for more comprehensive and enforced health and safety regulations and for greater health and safety consciousness among those who have direct contact with young children— professionals and family members.

FOR FURTHER READING

American Academy of Pediatrics, American Public Health Association, & National Resource Center for Heath and Safety in Child Care. (2002). *Caring for our children* (2nd ed.). Elk Grove Village, IL: American Academy of Pediatrics.

Aronson, S. (2002). *Healthy young children: A manual for programs.* Washington, DC: National Association for the Education of Young Children.

Clark, M., Holt, K., & Sofka, D. (Eds.). (1998). *Early childhood nutrition resource guide.* Arlington, VA: National Center for Education in Maternal and Child Health.

Early Childhood Committee of the Pennsylvania Chapter of the American Academy of Pediatrics. (1997). *Preparing for illness: A joint responsibility for parents and caregivers* (Rev. ed.). Washington, DC: National Association for the Education of Young Children.

Early Childhood Education Linkage System. (2002). *Model child care health policies.* Rosemont, PA: Author.

Healthy Child Care America Campaign. (1997). *Blueprint for action: 10 steps that communities can take to promote safe and healthy child care.* Elk Grove Village, IL: American Academy of Pediatrics.

Papert, S. (1996). *The connected family: Bridging the digital generation gap.* Marietta, GA: Longstreet.

Shallcross, M. L. (1999). Family child care homes need health and safety training and an emergency rescue system. *Young Children, 54*(5), 70–73.

READINGS IN SPECIFIC AREAS

Nutrition

Infant Feeding

American Academy of Pediatrics, American Public Health Association, & National Resource Center for Heath and Safety in Child Care. (2002). *Caring*

for our children (2nd ed., pp. 155–162). Elk Grove Village, IL: American Academy of Pediatrics.

Aronson, S. (2002). *Healthy young children: A manual for programs* (pp. 47–50, 65, 68–69). Washington, DC: National Association for the Education of Young Children.

Committee on Nutrition, American Academy of Pediatrics. (2001). The use and misuse of fruit juice in pediatrics. *Pediatrics, 107,* 1210–1213.

Missouri Department of Health. (1992). *Breastfed infants and you: A manual for child care providers.* Jefferson City, MO: Author.

U.S. Department of Agriculture. (2002). *Feeding infants: A guide for use in the child nutrition programs.* Washington, DC: USDA, Food and Nutrition Service, Child and Adult Care Food Program.

Warrick, J., & Helling, M. K. (1997). Meeting basic needs: Health and safety practices in feeding and diapering infants. *Early Childhood Education Journal, 24*(3), 195–199.

Resources for Program Menu Planning and Standardized Recipes

Berman, C., & Fromer, J. (1997). *Meals without squeals: Child care feeding guide and cookbook* (2nd ed.). Palo Alto, CA: Bull Publishing.

Bomba, A. K., Oakley, C. B., & Knight, K. B. (1996). Planning the menu in the child care center. *Young Children, 51*(6), 62–67.

Dunkle, J. L., & Edwards, M. S. (1992). *The (no leftovers) child care cookbook: Kid-tested recipes and menus for centers and home-based programs.* St. Paul, MN: Redleaf.

Edelstein, S. (1992). *Nutrition and meal planning in child care programs: A practical guide.* Chicago: American Dietetic Association.

National Food Service Management Institute. (1996). *Connecticut cooks for kids.* University, MS: University of Mississippi.

USDA's Team Nutrition. (1996). *Assisted numenus guidance: School lunch and breakfast menus.* Alexandria, VA: Author. (Available from NFSMI)

USDA's Team Nutrition. (1999). *Child care recipes: Food for health and fun.* Alexandria, VA: Author. (Available from NFSMI)

USDA's Team Nutrition. (2000). *Building blocks for fun and healthy meals.* Alexandria, VA: Author. (Available online: http://www.fns.usda.gov/tn/Resources/buildingblocks.html)

U.S. Department of Agriculture. (2002). *Menu magic for children*. Washington, DC: USDA, Food and Nutrition Service, Child and Adult Care Food Program.

Federal Food Programs for Families

Afterschool Snack Program
http://www.fns.usda.gov/cnd/Afterschool/default.htm

Child and Adult Care Food Program (CACFP)
www.fns.usda.gov/cnd/care/cacfp/cacfphome.htm

Commodity Supplemental Food Program (CSFP)
www.fns.usda.gov/fdd/programs/csfp/csfphome.htm

The Emergency Food Assistance Program (TEFAP)
www.fns.usda.gov/fdd/programs/tefap/tefaphome.htm

Food Stamp Program (FSP)
http://www.fns.usda.gov/fsp/

National School Lunch Program (NSLP)
www.fns.usda.gov/cnd/Lunch/default.htm

School Breakfast Program (SBP)
www.fns.usda.gov/cnd/Breakfast/default.htm

Special Supplemental Nutrition Program for Women, Infants, and Children (WIC)
www.fns.usda.gov/wic

Summer Food Service Program (SFSP)
www.fns.usda.gov/cnd/Summer/default.htm

Exceptionally Challenging Behaviors

Chrisman, K., & Couchenour, D. (2002). *Healthy sexuality development: A guide for early childhood educators and families*. Washington, DC: National Association for the Education of Young Children.

Curry, N. E., & Arnaud, S. H. (1995). Personality difficulties in preschool children as revealed through play themes and styles. *Young Children, 50*(4), 4–9.

Education Development Center. (1997). *Supporting children with challenging behaviors: Training guides for the Head Start learning community*. Washington, DC: Department of Health and Human Services, Head Start Bureau.

Kaiser, B., & Rasminsky, J. S. (1999). *Meeting the challenge: Effective strategies for challenging behaviors in early childhood environments*. Ottawa, Ontario: Canadian Child Care Federation.

Kaiser, B., & Rasminsky, J. S. (2003). *Challenging behaviors in young children: Understanding, preventing, and responding effectively*. Boston: Allyn & Bacon.

Koplow, L. (Ed.). (1996). *Unsmiling faces: How preschools can heal*. New York: Teachers College Press.

Pianta, R. C., & Walsh, D. J. (1996). *High-risk children in schools: Constructing sustaining relationships*. New York: Routledge.

Quinn, M. M., Osher, D., Warger, C. L., Hanley, T. V., Bader, B. N., & Hoffman, C. C. (2002). *Teaching and working with children who have emotional and behavioral challenges*. Longmont, CO: Sopris West.

Sandall, S., & Ostrosky, M. (Eds.). (1999). *Practical ideas for addressing challenging behaviors*. Denver, CO: Division for Early Childhood of the Council for Exceptional Children. (Available from NAEYC)

Slaby, R. G., Roedell, W. C., Arezzo, D., & Hendrix, K. (1995). *Early violence prevention: Tools for teachers of young children*. Washington, DC: National Association for the Education of Young Children.

NATIONAL RESOURCES FOR NUTRITION, HEALTH, AND SAFETY INFORMATION

Nutrition

Child Nutrition Division
www.fns.usda.gov/cnd

Food Distribution Division
www.fns.usda.gov/fdd

Food and Nutrition Information Center
www.nal.usda.gov/fnic

Food Research Action Center
www.frac.org

Healthy School Meals Resource System
http://schoolmeals.nal.usda.gov

National Dairy Council
www.nationaldairycouncil.org

National Food Service Management Institute
www.nfsmi.org

Nutrient Database for Standard Reference
www.nal.usda.gov/fnic/foodcomp

Team Nutrition
www.fns.usda.gov/fn

U.S. Department of Agriculture, Agricultural Marketing Service
www.ams.usda.gov

U.S. Department of Agriculture, Center for Nutrition Policy and Promotion
www.cnpp.usda.gov

U.S. Department of Agriculture, Food and Nutrition Service
www.fns.usda.gov

U.S. Department of Agriculture, Food Safety and Inspection Service
www.fsis.usda.gov

U.S. Department of Agriculture, National Agricultural Library
www.nal.usda.gov

Health

American Academy of Family Physicians
www.aafp.org

American Academy of Pediatrics
www.aap.org

American Association for Health Education
www.aahperd.org/aahe

American Professional Society on the Abuse of Children
www.apsac.org

Centers for Disease Control and Prevention
www.cdc.gov

Child Care Bureau, Administration for Children and Families, U.S. Department of Health and Human Services
www.acf.dhhs.gov/programs/ccb

Childhelp USA
www.childhelpusa.org

Healthy Child Care America Campaign, American Academy of Pediatrics
www.aap.org/advocacy/hcca/materials.htm

National Center for Education in Maternal and Child Health
www.ncemch.org

National Clearinghouse on Child Abuse and Neglect Information
www.calib.com/nccanch

National Foundation to Prevent Child Sexual Abuse
www.childsexualabuse.org

National Healthy Mothers, Healthy Babies Coalition
www.hmhb.org

National Institute of Health, National Institute of Child Health and Human Development
www.nichd.nih.gov

Safety

American Red Cross
www.redcross.org

American Society for Testing and Materials
www.astm.org

Drowning Prevention Foundation
http://drownprevention.com

Juvenile Products Manufacturers Association
www.jpma.org

National Fire Protection Association
www.nfpa.org

National Highway Transportation Safety Administration
www.nhtsa.dot.gov

National Program for Playground Safety
www.uni.edu/playground

National Safety Council
www.nsc.org

National Weather Service
www.nws.noaa.gov

Occupational Health and Safety Administration
www.ohsa.gov

Playground Safety Institute (National Recreation and Park Administration)
www.opraonline.org/playgrnd/institut.htm

Safe Kids Campaign
www.safekids.org

TO REFLECT

1. In a prekindergarten through Grade 6 public school, the early childhood teacher realizes the foods are difficult for "little hands" to handle. What are some reasonable requests that the teacher could make to the cafeteria workers?

2. You have just attended a workshop on nutrition and foods in early childhood programs. The presenter made the following points: (a) Providing nutritious meals and snacks is not enough, children have to eat the foods to get the benefits; and (b) many learnings can take place during meals and snacks—nutrition education, vocabulary development, sensory learnings, table manners, etc. As a novice teacher, you are eager to implement all you've heard. However, your mentor colleague suggests that doing all of this could be overwhelming. What does the mentor mean? Who is right? Can teachable moments become pressure situations?

3. As a director of a preschool program, you are writing a policy concerning ill children. What criteria should you use to achieve the balance between a child's need to be cared for by a family member and the family member's need to meet the demands of a job?

Assessing, Recording, and Reporting Children's Progress

Assessing, recording, and reporting children's progress is one of the most controversial aspects of program development for young children. Among the various types of early childhood programs, greater diversity appears in the area of assessment than in almost any other aspect of the programs. The controversy centers on (a) the purposes of and the methods used in assessment; (b) the staff time spent in recording children's progress, the possibility that records will negatively stereotype children, and the indiscriminate release and use of information about children and their families; and (c) the problem of what and how to communicate assessment results to families about their children and to the community or sponsors about the program.

ASSESSING AND DOCUMENTING IN EARLY CHILDHOOD PROGRAMS

Assessing and **documenting** are the methods by which professionals gain understandings of children's development and learnings. When assessing is used correctly, the process is linked to program goals. Assessing and documenting involves four separate processes. First is determining the need and thus the purpose of assessing. Second is gathering evidence by the appropriate method. Third is processing the information (documenting) so as to permit the formation of judgments. Fourth is making professional judgments; that is, using assessment results as a tool in the decision-making process.

History of Assessing Young Children

Until recently, observations have been used almost exclusively in assessing and documenting young children's development and learning. The earliest recorded observations were probably the baby biographies, such as Pestalozzi's *A Father's Diary*, written in 1774, and Tiedemann's work, published in 1878. Darwin also published a diary of the development of his infant son in 1877. Most baby biographers were not content to sim-

ply describe natural observations but also tried little experiments with their children. Teachers, too, wrote of their observations, such as Elizabeth Peabody's descriptions of children's thinking in the Alcott school (Peabody, 1835). Early childhood programs established for research purposes also used systematic observations of young children. For example, preservice teachers at the Normal School in Worcester, Massachusetts, kept observational records of children as suggested by G. Stanley Hall (Haskell, 1896). Harriet Johnson, Caroline Pratt, and Lucy Sprague Mitchell, who organized the Bank Street Bureau of Educational Experiments Nursery School in New York City, kept observational records on children in their natural settings (Greenberg, 1987). Louise Woodcock (1941) published her observations of 2-year-olds at Bank Street. Susan Isaacs (1930, 1933), the gifted teacher in Cambridge, England, published many of her insightful observations.

Since the beginning of formal education, teachers have tested schoolchildren's knowledge of subject matter by using both oral and written formats. The beginning of the science of statistics and the child study movement of the 20th century, however, resulted in the development of standardized tests. Some tests designed for young children included the *Gesell Developmental Scales,* the *Merrill-Palmer Scale of Mental Development,* the *Minnesota Preschool Scales,* the *Goodenough Draw-a-Man Test,* the *Iowa Test for Young Children,* and the *Cattell Infant Intelligence Scale.* Because the early childhood years were considered a special time in a child's life—a time when individual growth patterns were highly respected—standardized tests had little impact on young children's lives until the 1960s. A wave of standardized tests swept over early childhood programs with the launching of Head Start and the model preschool programs. Most of these tests were achievement standardized tests and were used as measures of program effectiveness. Standardized tests were also used to identify children at risk as mandated by P.L. 105-17.

School Accountability and High-Stakes Testing

The level of testing soared to new heights with the publication of *A Nation at Risk* (National Commission on Excellence in Education, 1984). As discussed, the National Education Goals of 1989 led to the standards movement affecting all levels of education (Bredekamp & Rosegrant, 1995a). Curriculum and assessment are given more importance in early childhood programs as a result of national reports on the poor quality of many early childhood programs and a recognition of the importance of the early years for overall development and as a result of the growth of state-supported prekindergarten programs. Thus, many states are developing early learning standards that are linked with the state's curriculum for school-age children. Along with the early learning standards, many states are mandating testing in the early childhood years. For example, 17 states mandate kindergarten readiness testing as a first step in identifying children in need of special services or as a means of planning instruction, and 6 states use readiness test data to monitor statewide trends in how prepared children are for formal schooling. Furthermore, 15 states and Washington, D.C., require developmental or diagnostic testing of prekindergarten children (Olson, 2002).

Tests are often instruments of child, teacher, and program accountability (NRC, 1999a). Because of the accountability factor, the practices are called *high-stakes assessment;* that is, assessment that carries serious consequences for those deemed accountable. For example, a test score can be used as the sole criterion for placement or retention of a young child, and aggregate results can determine merit pay for teachers and the status of the program.

Call for "Responsible Assessment"

Professional reactions to high-stakes testing and calls for appropriate assessment began to emerge in the 1990s. The following professional associations have issued position statements supporting appropriate assessment:

American Educational Research Association. (2000). *Position statement on high stakes testing.* Washington, DC: Author.

American Educational Research Association, American Psychological Association, & National Council on Measurement in Education. (1999). *Standards for educational and psychological testing.* Washington, DC: American Educational Research Association.

Association of Childhood Education International. (1991). On standardized testing. *Childhood Education, 67,* 132–142.

National Association for the Education of Young Children. (1988b). NAEYC position statement on standardized testing of young children 3 through 8 years of age. *Young Children, 43*(3), 42–47.

National Association for the Education of Young Children & National Association of Early Childhood Specialists in State Departments of Education. (1992). Guidelines for appropriate curriculum content and assessment in programs serving children ages 3 through 8. In S. Bredekamp & T. Rosegrant (Eds.), *Reaching potentials: Appropriate curriculum and assessment for young children* (Vol. 1, pp. 9–27). Washington, DC: National Association for the Education of Young Children.

National Association of Early Childhood Specialists in State Departments of Education. (2001). *Still unacceptable trends in kindergarten entry and placement.* Denver, CO: Author.

National Association of School Psychologists. (1999). *Position statement on early childhood assessment.* Bethesda, MD: Author.

The NAEYC (2001) has called assessment that is ethically grounded and supported by sound professional standards *responsible assessment.* Some specific characteristics of responsible assessment are as follows:

1. The overall purpose of assessment is to benefit children and families, help teachers in their work, and aid the improvement of programs.

2. Assessment instruments and data use should be tailored to a specific purpose and be valid, reliable, and fair for that use.

3. Assessment practices should be collaborative. Teachers and families need to be involved in decisions about assessment practices.

4. Assessment needs to be "developmentally valid" (Meisels & Atkins-Burnett, 2000). To be developmentally valid, assessment practices must be
   a. age and stage appropriate in content and method of collection,
   b. culturally and linguistically appropriate,
   c. adapted as needed, and
   d. focused on children's strengths and best performances.

5. Assessment must be closely connected or aligned with the goals of the local program. If appropriate, assessment practices will be
   a. broad based (i.e., covering all domains of development and learning),
   b. performance oriented,
   c. embedded in classroom activities, and
   d. drawn from multiple sources over many points in time (L. Shepard, Kagan, & Wurtz, 1998b).

PURPOSES OF ASSESSMENT AND DOCUMENTATION

The purpose of assessment determines all other aspects of assessment and documentation. Purposes determine what is measured, how it is measured, and even the acceptable levels of validity and reliability (L. Shepard, Kagan, & Wurtz, 1998b).

Promoting Children's Learnings and Development

Assessment designed for the purpose of promoting children's learnings and development is called **formative assessment.** Formative assessment is used to (a) determine a child's progress in attaining program goals and objectives and thus may also identify children who need further help; (b) serve as a tool in family–staff communication (e.g., families learn about the curriculum,

appropriate expectations for children, and their child's performance in the program); and (c) improve the quality of the program by helping teachers assess what is working and not working and hence to modify curriculum, to determine methodology, and to provide feedback in a mastery-learning strategy and by identifying needs for professional training.

Effective formative assessment requires teachers to understand each child's performance through knowledge of child development, cultural and linguistic competencies, and age and grade expectations (i.e., know when a given response is precocious performance, expected performance, or below expected performance). Validity and reliability are achieved because teachers do multiple assessments over various points in time that allow for the emergence of patterns or consistencies in each child's performance (L. Shepard, Kagan, & Wurtz, 1998b).

Authentic Assessment and Documentation Methods. **Authentic assessment and documentation,** also called *performance assessment and documentation,* require children to demonstrate what they know and what they can do; that is, they apply knowledge within the context of a real or simulated situation (Bergen, 1993/94; Meisels, Dorfman, & Steele, 1995).

Authentic assessment is a relatively new term but not a new concept. Observations of young children, the assessment method used in authentic assessment today, were used exclusively until standardized tests were developed. Along with the call for DAP, authentic assessment has come into greater use in early childhood programs for the following reasons:

1. Authentic assessment operates on the assumption that children should be evaluated according to the criteria important for the performance of a given task (Bergan & Field, 1993).

2. Authentic assessment provides teachers with a comprehensive picture of the child (Goodwin, 1997).

3. Authentic assessment promotes skill in self- and peer assessment; tests promote competition (Osin & Lesgold, 1996).

4. Authentic assessment allows children to focus on the entire process rather than an "end product"—the test (Osin & Lesgold).

Authentic or performance assessment has the following characteristics:

1. Assessment areas are based on the total curriculum content that was designed to meet each child's needs in all domains of development and learnings (as opposed to testing isolated "bits and pieces" of the curriculum covering the cognitive domain almost exclusively).

2. Assessment data are gathered by observing children in their day-to-day tasks and in the familiar setting or by examining the products of children's performance (e.g., the art creation). Figure 9–1 shows how assessment and documentation activities can be planned while writing an anticipatory web.

3. Assessment is part of the continuous teaching–learning process rather than a separately scheduled event. (Summary records are completed periodically, however.)

4. Qualitative criteria are used in making professional judgments. For example, if the teacher references the child's performance to its position on a path of development, the term *developmental assessment* is frequently used. (Two authentic assessment tools will be described in a later section.)

Observations.   Observation has been the most common method of child study over the years (R. Dixon & Lerner, 1992). Recently, we are seeing a resurgence of interest in observations (Bronson, 1994; D. H. Cohen, Stern, & Balaban, 1997). The reason for the renewed interest in observations is the growth of authentic assessment methods.

Observations are also the most rewarding method of assessing children's development and learnings because they are appropriate and accurate (younger children do not hide their feelings). Other reasons for the popularity of observation may be the following factors:

1. A person can simultaneously work and observe children (regrettably, many look and do not see!).

2. Observations may be conducted by teachers as well as by researchers.

3. Observations may be conducted for long or short intervals of time.

4. Observations may be used in conjunction with any other assessment method.

5. Observations are suitable for use in any type of program because one child or a group of children may be observed and any aspect of development can be assessed.

Disadvantages in using observations for assessment are as follows:

1. The validity of observation depends on the skill of the observer.

2. The observer's biases are inherent in observations.

3. The soundness of observations may depend on the behaviors observed because some aspects of development (e.g., motor skills) are easier to observe than others (e.g., thinking processes).

4. When a person is simultaneously working with children and observing them, it can be difficult to "see the forest for the trees."

5. One-way mirrors used in observation rooms and hidden audio- or videotapes may not be ethical.

The observer must be unobtrusive. Observers should not have interactions with or reactions to children's activities. Observers must never discuss their observations casually if children can be identified or professionally if any child or any adult (except adults involved with

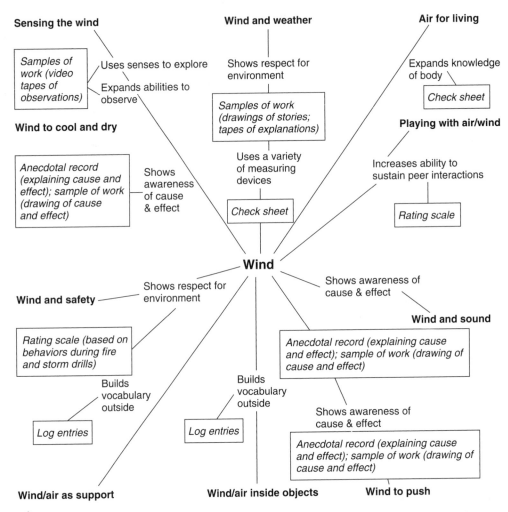

Figure 9–1 Assessment and Documentation Methods Included on Anticipatory Web (review Figures 7–1A and B)

the child in the program) is within hearing distance. Written records must also be kept secure.

The purposes of the observations determine the method of observation and the recording system. Several popular methods of observing young children and some of the recording possibilities used by teachers (and researchers) are described in the following subsections.

Naturalistic Observations

Naturalistic observations are observations of a child engaged in regular day-to-day activities within the natural setting. These open-ended observations allow the child options that in turn permit the teacher (or researcher) to see the uniqueness of the child more clearly (Rhodes & Nathenson-Mejia, 1992). These researchers refer to it as a "story of an individual" (p. 503). However, biases occur in what we record.

Naturalistic observations may be recorded as an anecdotal record or a running record. An **anecdotal record** is a record of an incident in a child's life that occurred during participation in program activities or during a home visit. Characteristics of a good anecdote are as follows:

1. It gives the date, the place, and the situation in which the action occurred. This is called the *setting*.

2. It describes the actions of the child, the reactions of other people involved, and the responses of the child to these reactions.

3. It quotes what is said to the child and by the child during the action.

4. It supplies "mood cues"—postures, gestures, voice qualities, and facial expressions that give cues to how the child felt. It does not provide interpretations of the child's feelings but provides only the cues by which a reader may judge what the feelings were.

5. The description is extensive enough to cover the episode. The action or conversation is not left incomplete and unfinished but rather is described until a little vignette is created.

Below the narrative account, space should be left for comments. These comments may be interpretive (what the observer believes about the incident) and/or a written professional judgment (what the observer believes should be done to help the child developmentally).

See an example of an anecdotal record in Figure 9–2. Other examples are given by Beaty (2002), Bentzen (2000), Nicholson and Shipstead (2002), and Nilsen (2000).

A **running record** is similar to an anecdotal record except that it is more detailed with a total sequence of events. The running record was popularized by Piaget (1952). In a running record, the observer records everything without screening out any information. See the example in Figure 9–3. Other examples are given by Beaty (2002), Nicholson and Shipstead (2002), and Nilsen (2000).

Figure 9–2   Anecdotal Record of Behavior

Child's name: _Susie_   Date: _2/12/2004_

Setting: _Block center in a child care center; activity child-chosen._

Incident: _Susie was building a block tower. When the seven-block tower fell, she tried again. This time, she succeeded in getting only six blocks slacked before they fell. She kicked her blocks and walked over to John's nine-block tower and knocked it over. When the teacher approached, she cried and refused help with the tower. (John left the center after his tower was knocked over.)_

Comments: _Susie is showing more patience by rebuilding—a patience not seen last month. However, her crying and destructive responses are not as mature as they should be for a 5-year-old. She must be shown ways to cope with common frustrations._

Child's name: _Susie_   Date: _5/5/2004_

Setting: _Block center in a child care center; activity child-chosen._

Incident	Comments
9:25 Susie watches three or four children play with the blocks.	Susie is interested in the blocks.
9:30 She calls to John, "What are you doing?" John replies, "I'm building a tall, tall building, the biggest one ever." Susie says, "I can build a big one."	She especially likes John's tower. Susie is apparently challenged.
9:31 Susie stacks seven blocks. They fall. (She counts the blocks in John's tower.) She again starts stacking blocks—with the sixth block, they fall.	Susie knows she almost got the same height tower again. Susie is willing to try again.
9:35 She kicks at her blocks three times and then walks over to John's tower and strikes it with her hand.	Her aggression spreads to John.
9:37 Mrs. Jones approaches Susie. Susie turns her back on Mrs. Jones and cries. Mrs. Jones kneels and talks to Susie. Then Mrs. Jones picks up a block, but Susie runs away.	She is not yet willing to be comforted or helped. Teacher's approach was calming —no more aggression.

(John left the center earlier.)

Figure 9–3   Running Record of Behavior

A **specimen description,** often written by researchers, is a method in which the observer records all the events within a given situation. One records the entire "stream of behavior," which is so complete that it can be dramatized. Specimen records "require more rigorous detail and predetermined criteria" (Irwin & Bushnell, 1980, p. 103). The technique is described in detail by Wright (1960), and one example is R. Barker's (1951) *One Boy's Day.* Another specimen record completed in a preschool classroom is given by Bentzen (2000).

Structured Observations

Structured observations are structured in terms of bringing children into contrived environments (e.g., how infants react when a stranger is present and the mother is present and then absent) or identifying a specific, defined behavior,

observing it in the natural environment, and keeping quantitative records (e.g., Sarah had two biting episodes on Monday and one biting episode on Tuesday). Two types of structured observations are event sampling and time sampling.

Event sampling is a narrative of conditions preceding and following a specified behavior. For these observations, a behavior is preselected (called a *target behavior),* defined very specifically, and then observed. To record, the observer usually knows when to expect the behavior (e.g., time of day, during a certain activity, in a certain grouping pattern, with a given adult). In event sampling, the observer is trying to confirm a hypothesis about what triggers the behavior. Thus, three items are recorded: (a) the antecedent behavior (what led to the target behavior), (b) the targeted behavior (complete description of the incident), and (c) the consequent event (reac-

Child's name: _____ *Mike* _____ Date: ___ *2/1/2004* ___

Behavior: ____ *Biting a child on exposed skin areas* ____

Time	Antecedent	Behavior	Consequent Event
8:00	*Children eating breakfast as they arrive. Ann has finished breakfast but takes a piece of apple off Mike's plate*	*Mike tries to get it back. When unsuccessful, he bites Ann's hand.*	*Ann cries, and Mike calls out, "I didn't bite."*

NOTE: Other behaviors are recorded as they occur.

Figure 9–4   Event Sampling Behavior Record

tions of the child, such as crying). Describing the event in detail is most important. See Figure 9–4. Other examples are found in Beaty (2002) and Bentzen (2000).

Time sampling is tallying a specified behavior while it is occurring. In time sampling, a target behavior is preselected, carefully defined, and then observed at specified intervals. These time intervals may be preset at uniform time periods or at randomly selected time intervals. For discrete behaviors, a simple frequency tabulation is recorded. Several types of coding systems may be used (Irwin & Bushnell, 1980). The observer can write a narrative in addition to coding. See Figure 9–5. Other examples are given by Beaty (2002), Bentzen (2000), and Nilsen (2000). Because the amount of writing is reduced, the observer can record observations on several

Child's name: _____   Date: _____

Target Behavior: _*Types of interaction in the housekeeping center.*_

Time 1	Time 2	Time 3	Time 4	Time 5
9:00	9:05	9:10	9:15	9:20
V+	V+	NV–	V–	0

V = verbal interaction
NV = nonverbal interaction
0 = no interaction
+ = positive
– = negative

Figure 9–5   Time-Sampling Behavior Record

children in one session by rotating observations in a predetermined and consistent manner among the children. Using the time periods in the example in Figure 9–5, Child A would be observed during the 1st minute of each time frame—9:00 to 9:01, 9:05 to 9:06, and so on; Child B would be observed during the 2nd minute of each time frame—9:01 to 9:02, 9:06 to 9:07, and so on; and in a similar way, three other children would be observed.

For nondiscrete behaviors (e.g., crying, clinging to adult, wandering around the room), the length of occurrence or duration is often recorded (see the example in Figure 9–6). Both frequency and duration recordings may be summarized in graphs, which give visual representations. Even two complementary behaviors may be plotted on the same graph for a better picture of a child (e.g., daily totals of aggressive and sharing acts).

Interviews.   Interviews with families are now used with greater frequency in early childhood programs. The interview method permits a more comprehensive picture of the child's life at home and with peer groups. The *interview method of assessment* generally has the following characteristics:

1. Questions used in an interview are usually developed by staff.

2. Family members of the child are usually interviewed; others familiar with the child are occasionally interviewed.

3. Specific questions in the interview commonly include background information about the child and sometimes the family. Interview data help in assessing needs and potential program services.

Advantages of the interview as an assessment technique are as follows:

1. Valuable information—both verbal and emotional—may be gleaned.

2. Interviews can be used in conjunction with other assessment methods.

3. Interviews are suitable for use in any type of early childhood program.

4. Interviews can help clarify and extend the information found on written forms.

Child's name: _____   Date: _____

Behavior: Wandering from center to center. (Child stays less than 2 minutes at an activity in one "stretch.")

Days	Time	Subtotal	Total
1	9:04–9:08	4	
	9:12–9:13	1	5
2	9:01–9:04	3	3
3	9:04–9:07	3	
	9:13–9:15	2	5
4	9:01–9:05	4	
	9:12–9:13	1	5
5	9:02–9:07	5	
	9:10–9:11	1	6

Average: 4.8 minutes per day

Figure 9–6   Duration Record of Behavior

The interview method also has disadvantages:

1. The information obtained may not be comprehensive or accurate because the questions were unclear or not comprehensive or because the interviewee was unable or unwilling to answer.

2. The interviewee's and interviewer's biases are entwined in the information given and in the interpretation of the information, respectively.

3. The interview method is very time consuming.

Samples of Children's Work. Samples of children's work serve as an excellent authentic method of assessment if they meet the following criteria:

1. Samples of various types of children's work should be collected: dictated or tape-recorded experiences told by children; drawings, paintings, and other two-dimensional art projects; photographs of children's projects (e.g., three-dimensional art projects, block constructions, a completed science experiment); tape recordings of singing or language activities; and videotapes of any action activities.

2. Samples are collected on a systematic and periodic basis.

3. Samples are dated, with notes on the children's comments and attitudes.

Advantages to using samples of children's work as an assessment technique are as follows:

1. The evidence is a collection of children's real, ongoing activities or products of activities and not a contrived experience for purposes of assessment.

2. Collecting samples is not highly time consuming.

3. Collecting samples works for all aspects of all programs.

4. Samples can be used as direct evidence of progress.

5. If samples are dated and adequate notes are taken about them, interpretations can be made later by various people.

6. Some samples can be analyzed for feelings as well as for concepts.

7. Samples can be used in conjunction with other assessment methods.

Disadvantages of using samples of children's work are as follows:

1. Samples may not be representative of children's work.

2. Samples of ongoing activities are more difficult to obtain than two-dimensional artwork.

3. Some children do not like to part with their work.

4. Storage can be a problem.

5. Photographs, magnetic tapes, and videotapes are relatively expensive.

In-Depth Authentic Assessment Methods. Children's learnings and development are very complex. Because of the complexity, both Piaget and Vygotsky objected to the analysis of children's understandings based on standardized testing methods that allowed no flexibility in pursuing the thought processes of children. In an effort to make the competencies of young children of today more transparent and thus supportive of further learnings, researchers are again exploring the child-study methods of Piaget and Vygotsky, working on in-depth methods of authentic assessment, and advocating that teachers use these methods.

Using the Clinical Interview. The clinical interview method was developed by Piaget. The **clinical method** is a procedure for assessing a child's level of knowledge with respect to a particular concept. Piaget wanted to pursue interesting responses and establish the stability of answers (i.e., Was the response simply a guess?). Although Piaget liked and used naturalistic observations, he realized they were too time consuming because a child may not deal with a particular concept while being observed. The clinical interview approach avoided the time problem but maintained the open-ended nature of naturalistic observations.

Unlike naturalistic observations, clinical interviews present the child with a verbal question or a concrete problem. At first Piaget used more abstract verbal questions but later used cognitive problems (tasks) stated in terms of concrete materials or events. Thus, the success of the interview did not totally depend on the child's ability to verbalize thoughts. The revised approach allowed the interviewer to observe the child's actions and to listen to the verbalizations.

Because the goal of the clinical interview is to identify the child's underlying thought processes about a specific concept, the child is asked to reflect on and explain thinking processes (i.e., "think aloud"). The interview begins with general questions. The development of the interview is determined by the child's responses. Generally, tasks and questions become more specific to focus on a particular aspect of thinking and more difficult to test the limits of the child's thinking. During the interview, both correct and incorrect responses are followed by a request to explain the reason. The reasoning the child gives is most important; a "mature" answer is a correct, stable response with a correct reason.

Several researchers (Ginsburg, Jacobs, & Lopez, 1993; Kamii & Peper, 1969; Moon & Schulman, 1995) described clinical interview assessment techniques teachers can use. However, the method is not widely used beyond research because it is time consuming and requires professional preparation to be familiar with the typical thinking about a specific concept and to adopt the language level of the child and question without suggestions that deform the child's thought processes. Ginsburg (1997) brought current insight into this approach.

Assessing Emerging Learnings and Development. Vygotsky had a somewhat broader interpretation

of developmental readiness for new concepts and skills than Piaget had. Unlike Piaget, Vygotsky saw development and learnings as being constructed more through children's interactions with peers and adults than through personal experiences. He believed that a child who is about to learn a new concept or skill can benefit from "instruction" by others.

Vygotsky believed that standardized tests only measure what children already know and can do by themselves. He believed that teachers need insight into the types of assistance children need in order to extend their emergent learnings. Teachers must observe children to determine what they have mastered and what they can do with a little help (i.e., teachers must find each child's constantly changing ZPD). More specifically, to provide an appropriate **scaffold,** a support in terms of information or modeling, a teacher must assess what a child can do with different levels of assistance and how children use these levels. Children with even the same test scores often differ substantially in the breadth of their ZPDs. If the ZPD is narrow, a child can perform with assistance only slightly above his or her independent performance level; however, if the ZPD is wide, support can help the child perform at a substantially higher level than he or she could while working independently on the task. In short, Vygotsky believed that teaching was most effective in the dynamic ZPD (Berk & Winsler, 1995; Bodrova & Leong, 1996; Burns, Delclos, Vye, & Sloan, 1992). To do this, teachers must pretest, teach, and retest to determine the child's responsiveness (Missiuna & Samuels, 1989).

Tools for Structuring Authentic Assessments. Although authentic assessment resolves the conflict between program goals and what is measured, a gap does exist between idealized portrayal of authentic assessment and its implementation. Teachers need a framework for systematically collecting and documenting children's performance on program activities. Such a framework allows assessment to be worthwhile for promoting children's learnings and development and to be understood by family members and policy makers.

Two major assessment tools have been developed by researchers. Because researchers have identified the important constructs of children's learnings and development, the tools mesh assessment procedures with the educational goals of many quality early childhood programs. Both tools provide a comprehensive picture of how the child is performing in the program and thus allow teachers to connect assessment results to decision making about curriculum content and teaching strategies.

High/Scope Child Observation Record (COR). The COR (High/Scope Educational Research Foundation, 1992) is used to assess children ages 2½ to 6 years in developmentally appropriate programs. Using notes taken over several months that describe episodes of a child's behavior in six COR categories (initiative, creative representation, social relations, music and movement, language and literacy, and logic and mathematics), the teacher rates the child's behavior on 30 five-level COR items. Teachers score the COR two or three times each year, with the initial ratings given after children have been in the program 6 to 8 weeks.

The Work Sampling System. The Work Sampling System (Meisels, Jabalon, Marsden, Dichtelmiller, Dorfman, & Steele, 1994) is a performance assessment system designed for children from preschool through Grade 5. The approach is used to assess and document children's skills, knowledge, behavior, and accomplishments in seven domains (personal/social development, language and literacy, mathematical thinking, scientific thinking, social studies, the arts, and physical development) performed on multiple occasions. The Work Sampling System comprises the following components: developmental guidelines and checklists, portfolios of children's work, and summary reports completed by teachers. Assessment takes place three times a year.

Identifying Children Needing Additional Intervention Services

The identification of children needing additional intervention services is a two-stage process. The first stage, usually called **screening,** involves a brief assessment to determine whether referral for more in-depth assessment is needed. The second stage, usually called **diagnostic assessment,** consists of a more complete assessment. If the child is identified as needing intervention, special plans are made.

Screening Assessments. Developmental screening is the first step in an assessment/intervention process (Nuttall, Romero, & Kalesnik, 1999). Screening is performed individually on large numbers of children and is often done by nonspecialists. Two common problems occur with screening assessments. First, often tests other than developmental screening tests are administered. In many early childhood programs, readiness tests instead of developmental screening tests are used supposedly to assess the child's ability to acquire skills. (Readiness test results often lead to placement and retention decisions.) Readiness and screening tests can never be used interchangeably. Screening tests must be valid for the purpose and reliable (Meisels & Atkins-Burnett, 1994). Second, screening tests should never be used to deny services or for placement. Many children, especially minority students, have been "mislabeled" based on screening test results (Burnette, 1998).

Diagnostic Assessments. According to federal law, diagnostic assessments, administered following screening, must be conducted in a team setting that uses multiple sources of assessment data and must be a part of a system of intervention services. Diagnostic assessments should consider the child's biology, interactions with others, and patterns of cultural and linguistic environment (Greenspan & Weider, 1998). These criteria should be rigorously used to prevent children from being misclassified and receiving intervention that do not meet their needs (Burnette, 1998). Although diagnostic assessment data are used to create IFSPs and IEPs, monitoring the provision and effectiveness of services is a must.

Determining Program Effectiveness and Making Policy Decisions

Assessment designed for the purpose of determining program effectiveness and making policy decisions is called **summative assessment.** More specifically, summative assessment is the evaluative process that is used to determine the effectiveness of curriculum and methodology and to provide a product measurement (i.e., a judgment about the overall worth of a program). Program evaluation permits the planning of additions to or revisions of services and even determines changes in program rationale. Since the mid-1990s, a shift toward summative evaluation has occurred. Researchers are looking at the results of quality early childhood programs (Council of Chief State School Officers, 1995; Schorr, 1994). Although the information about the connection between effective services and desired outcomes for young children and their families can assist in holding decision makers accountable for investing in quality early childhood programs and meeting specified outcomes (Kagan, Rosenkoetter, & Cohen, 1997), high-stakes testing, as previously discussed, can be damaging (NRC, 1997, 1999a). Damage is not distributed equitably across the population because the vast majority who fail the tests are poor, minority, and male (Meisels, 2000).

For purposes of determining program effectiveness and making policy decisions, children, teachers, and schools are almost always measured by standardized achievement tests. Every state in the nation has adopted standardized tests in these four core areas: reading, mathematics, social studies, and science.

Description of Standardized Tests. **Standardized tests** can be thought of as "store-bought" tests developed by people familiar with test construction and as more formal assessment devices than authentic assessments. Standardized tests have the following characteristics:

1. Specific directions for administering the test are stated in detail, usually including even the exact words to be used by the examiner in giving instructions and specifying exact time limits. By following the directions, teachers and counselors in many schools can administer the test in essentially the same way.

2. Specific directions are provided for scoring. Usually, a scoring key is supplied that reduces scoring to merely comparing answers with the key; little or nothing is left to the judgment of the scorer. Sometimes, carefully selected samples are provided with which a student's product is to be compared.

3. Quantitative data are usually supplied to aid in interpreting the part and composite scores. Generally, the test is referred to as a **criterion-referenced measure** (a measure in which a person's behavior is interpreted by comparing it with a preselected or established standard or criterion of performance) or a **norm-referenced measure** (a measure in which a person's behavior is interpreted against the behavior of others—one would hope, but not always—of similar backgrounds on the same testing instrument).

4. Information needed for judging the value of the test is provided. Before the test becomes available for purchase, research is conducted to study its reliability and validity.

5. A manual that explains the purposes and uses of the test is supplied. The manual describes briefly how the test was constructed; provides specific directions for administering, scoring, and interpreting results; contains tables of norms; and provides a summary of available research data on the test.

Standardized tests are often classified on the basis of content. For example, standardized tests may be classified as follows:

1. **Aptitude tests. Aptitude tests** measure a person's capacity for learning. These tests are designed to evaluate a person's ability to progress in cognitive activities; they may measure an aggregation of abilities or one or more discrete abilities. Items on aptitude tests are "(1) equally unfamiliar to all examinees (that is, novel situations) or (2) equally familiar (in the sense that all students have had equal opportunity to learn, regardless of their pattern of specific courses"; G. S. Adams, 1965, p. 182). Aptitude tests for (a) general mental ability, (b) special aptitudes (e.g., motor performance, articulation), and (c) screening tests are available.

2. **Achievement tests. Achievement tests** measure the extent to which a person has mastered certain information or skills as a result of specific instruction or training. Achievement tests are given most frequently in the areas of reading, language, and mathematics but may also be given in other school subjects. *Readiness tests* focus on current skill acquisition. *Diagnostic components* of achievement tests pinpoint specific areas of weakness on the basis of item analysis of achievement tests.

3. **Personal/social adjustment tests. Personal/social adjustment tests** are, in reality, tests of good mental health. Generally, a person is considered to have good mental health if his or her behavior is typical of his or her own age and cultural group.

Not all tests fit into one of these categories. Tests may be classified on other bases. Classification is not as important as the description of the purpose as given by the test developer.

Concerns About Standardized Assessment Practices. With the explosion of standardized tests and testing, professionals, especially those in the holistic/developmental camp, became vocal concerning how some assessment uses and practices have the potential for doing harm. The following recent concerns should be taken seriously by early childhood program directors:

1. The assessment instrument may not match the program's rationale. One of the greatest dangers is that assessment itself can determine a program rather than a program determining the how and why of assessment. It is almost as though the cart is placed before the horse. For example, some program planners take the content of standardized tests and plan activities to teach these items. Teaching to a test encourages a narrow academic program (Peel & McCary, 1997). "Curriculum based on tests is narrow and fails to embed knowledge in meaningful contexts, thus making it virtually unusable for the learner" (Bowman, 1990, p. 30). Warnings that standardized tests are altering the curriculum continue to be given (Dahlberg & Asen, 1994). Kohn (2000) stated that when high-stakes testing is employed, instruction becomes less DAP. He explained that important practices and policies (e.g., caring communities, emergent curriculum) are threatened by "top-down, heavy-handed, corporate-style, standardized version of school reform that is driven by testing" (Kohn, 2001a, p. 20). The order should be reversed. A program should be rationally planned and based on current and accurate information about children; tests should be selected to fit the program's goals and objectives.

2. Assessment instruments may not reflect the current theory used in the program. For example, the whole language approach to reading instruction is advocated by many, but reading achievement tests focus on narrow subskills (Teal, Hiebart, & Chittenden, 1987). Reading readiness tests are not aligned with what kindergarten teachers think are important (National Center for Education Statistics, 1999). Likewise, achievement tests in mathematics look at subskills rather than at the construction of number concepts. Finally, standardized tests do not measure deep understandings or children's attitudes and dispositions.

3. As previously discussed, tests may be used for purposes other than those for which they were designed.

4. Tests may not meet the standards given in the current editions of reference books providing technical qualities of tests (e.g., acceptable levels of validity and reliability, statistics appropriate to the program's purpose, lack of inherent cultural and linguistic biases; NRC, 1999b). The psychometric quality of most standardized measures designed for young children has been and continues to be inadequate (Langhorst, 1989). Scoring errors can also occur (Meisels, 2000).

5. Testing can be stressful and/or inappropriate for all those involved.

   a. Testing may be stressful for children (Charlesworth, Hart, Burts, & DeWolf, 1993; Greenspan & Weider, 1998). Testing itself is always a problem with young children because young children do not have a repertoire of test-taking skills. Some of the problems these children have are inadequate motor skills for taking paper-and-pencil tests; short attention spans; problems in following directions; and the problem of being influenced by the tester, the physical setting, or both. Staff need to be aware of children's feelings.

   b. Family members are also under a great deal of stress. Many families are apprehensive of decisions based on testing and on labels that may be placed on their children if "inadequacies" are noted. Placement and retention decisions should not be based on data from one assessment source. Stiggins (1991) referred to this use of tests as the "ultimate sorting tool" (p. 2). Darling-Hammond and Falk (1997) stated that retention is not appropriate if children do not learn the material when it is first taught.

   c. Teachers are under stress when testing is the predominant indicator of teachers' accountability. Regrettably, this situation has led to teachers' basing their curriculum on certain tests and, in some instances, teaching the test items themselves, helping children with the answers during the testing session,

and even tampering with recorded responses.

   d. Directors of programs are often stressed, too. Testing drains learning time and funds. Some school systems and states use aggregate scores as a way of comparing schools. Standardized tests are designed to produce variances. Thus, statistically, some children and some schools will fall at the lower end of the performance range. High scores are most often correlated with high family incomes.

Position Statements on Standardized Testing. As discussed, various professional associations issued strong statements about standardized testing because of these concerns in assessment practices. The goal is not to prohibit all standardized testing but for early childhood directors to recognize the following:

1. Assessment instruments should be used only for their intended purposes.

2. Assessment instruments should meet acceptable levels of quality (e.g., validity, reliability).

3. Placement and retention decisions should be made from multiple sources of data.

4. Assessment instruments should be used only if children will benefit and the benefit does not come from reduced group variation. (Schools must be more adaptive to normal variance.)

L. Shepard (1994) added two principles to the NAEYC's guiding principle of assessment— that any assessment practice should benefit children or else it should not be conducted: (a) "the contents of assessments should reflect and model progress toward important learning goals" (p. 208), and (b) the methods of assessment must be developmentally appropriate. To understand how these principles are applied, 30 questions for program administrators to affirm in making assessment decisions were included in the position statement of the National Association for the Education of Young Children and the National Association of Early Childhood Specialists in State Departments of Education (1991).

L. Shepard, Kagan, and Wurtz (1998b) stated that if standardized testing is mandated, early childhood programs should make efforts to use sampling methods rather than subject all children to testing. For example, the use of *matrix sampling*, a statistical technique whereby each child takes only part of the test, is helpful because the method lessens the testing burden on each child and makes it impossible to use individual scores to make high-stakes decisions. They stated, "Before age eight, standardized achievement measures are not sufficiently accurate to be used for high-stakes decisions about individual children and schools" (p. 53). Kohn (2001a) suggested various short-term and long-term responses to the current assessment situation.

RECORDING

Record keeping, the documentation of assessment, has always been an important aspect of a staff member's duties; today, record keeping is becoming even more important and prevalent. Many advantages come from record keeping, such as the following:

1. Teachers who document children's learnings make more productive planning decisions; documentation informs teaching.

2. Records can help staff see each child's progress. Staff who work daily with a child may better see progress through a review of the records. By documenting, the teacher can tell whether expected skills and concepts are emerging as they should or whether significant lags without progress are occurring in which specialized professional assistance may be needed. Through records, specialists can determine whether a problem is transient or continuous, when a problem began, and how pervasive its ef-

fects are on the child's development. On the basis of the evidence found in the records, specialists can suggest possible solutions to the problem. Good records also permit the independent assessment of a child by more than one person.

3. Documentation communicates to children that their learnings are important. Thus, children become more evaluative of their own work. They can see their own progress in records—especially in collected, dated, and sequenced samples of work.

4. Documentation is needed because of greater involvement with families. Records can be used as a basis for discussions with family members.

5. Records are also beneficial to a child who changes programs frequently. Records of a recently transferred child make it easier for staff to assist the child in the new situation.

6. Because funding agencies, citizens' groups, boards of directors or school boards, and parents often require "proof" of the early childhood program's effectiveness in meeting its goals, the evidence is often best demonstrated by the records that have been kept. The local program's regulatory agency requires various records as a basis for subsequent funding.

7. Records also help teachers see the results of new teaching techniques or services. Records can also be used as data for research.

Possible disadvantages to record keeping are as follows:

1. A staff member can spend more time keeping records than planning and working with children.

2. A staff member can make a prejudgment based on records and become positively or negatively biased toward a child.

3. Because of the requirements of the Family Educational Rights and Privacy Act, staff need special training in developing accurate, appropriate, and relevant records and in

developing record protection and handling procedures.

4. Record keeping may become a meaningless activity because the types of data required to be kept may not be congruent with the goals of the local program or because records may be filed and forgotten or may not be used effectively.

Computers are helping programs overcome some of these problems. For example, microcomputers can store information, maintain and generate files, and ensure privacy of records (by coding the computer so that only specified people have access to certain parts of a child's file). Producers of software have noted teachers' needs for quick and accurate record keeping.

Types of Records

Records may be classified in many ways. For purposes of this book, we classify records as background information records, performance records, referral records, and summary records.

Background Information Records. **Background information records** include information gathered from various sources outside the local program. Early childhood professionals are realizing that early experiences in the home and neighborhood and previous early childhood program (or school) experiences provide important "pictures" of a child. Many programs now ask for considerable information from families. Sometimes, these records are supplemented by additional information obtained by a caseworker or specialist or are volunteered at a later date by the family members or the child.

Basic information about a child and the child's family is always part of background information records, including the child's legal name, home address, and telephone number; birth date, birthplace, and birth certificate number; number of siblings; and parents' or guardians' legal names, home address and telephone number, occupation(s), place(s) of business, and business telephone number(s).

Medical information is also included in the background information records, and completion of medical information records is required before a child is admitted to a program. (See chapter 8 and the forms in appendix 8.) Finally, records on the child's personal and social history are frequently included as part of the background information records. This information may be supplied by a family member or by another adult who knows the child. Family members may record the information on forms, or a staff member may record the information during an interview. The child's personal and social history is likely to include information about birth history (birth weight, problems associated with birth, or birth defects); self-reliance; development, especially affective development and motor skills; previous experiences that aid concept development, such as places the child has visited in the community, trips taken beyond the community, and previous group experiences; problems, such as disabilities and illnesses, fears, and accident proneness; and interests, such as television programs, computers, books, toys, pets, and games. Occasionally, questions are asked about the family situation, family relationships, and family member attitudes and may encompass family income, housing, occupations, educational level, aspirations for their children, and views of child rearing, including guidance methods family members have found to be effective. Martin (1998) provided an example of such a questionnaire.

Performance Records. **Performance records** include any documentation regarding children's development and learnings. A given performance record may be used as an entity, such as a composite score on an achievement test. Conversely, a performance record may be used as a professional note, such as an anecdotal record, contributing only one piece to the child's blueprint.

Most early childhood programs keep perform-ance records, and these records are mandated in many programs. The contents of performance records differ according to the goals of the local program. D-I programs tend to assess perform-ance in the three Rs. For the most part, profes-sionals in these academic programs use various types of standardized tests. For example, screen-ing, diagnostic, or intelligence tests may be used for placement decisions; readiness tests may be used for making instructional decisions; and often achievement tests are used for measuring each child's progress toward a criterion or for comparing the achievement of a child with that of the norming group. Occasionally, these pro-grams use more informal methods if designed to measure observable program objectives. Con-versely, in holistic/developmental programs, pro-fessionals want to assess knowledge, skills, dis-positions, and certain affective expressions in all domains and in many contexts. Holistic/developmental programs find authentic assess-ment techniques and the performance records generated from these techniques compatible with their beliefs.

Performance records take several forms. The chosen form depends on the nature of the obser-vation. For example, if a teacher wants to assess whether a child can name certain colors, a check sheet makes a more appropriate record than a rating scale. Conversely, a social competence, such as "getting along with others," exists on a continuum and thus is better described by using a record that has a continuum format, such as a rating scale. Common forms of performance records include the following:

1. **Log entries. Log entries** are short, dated notes. A single entry may not be significant, but multiple entries in one area of development spanning weeks and months often provide useful information. Many teachers find it easier to write logs on several children (and possibly in several domains) on pages that have been divided into eight rectangles or on pages of white, adhesive la-bels. (The log notes will measure approximately $1\frac{1}{2}''$ to $2\frac{3}{4}'' \times 4''$.) Each note or label is then transferred to an individual child's record sheet devoted to a specific domain of development (see Figure 9–7). The COR uses log entries (High/Scope Educational Foundation, 1992).

2. **Anecdotal entries.** Anecdotes often give more information than logs. Similar to a series of log entries, a series of well-written anecdotes in one domain can reveal patterns of development. As previously discussed, a running record is an even more thorough account of performance. Figure 9–8 is an example of an anecdotal record.

Figure 9–7   Individual Child's Log Entries

Domain: _Mathematics_____   Child's name: _____

10/3/2004 *Placed a napkin at each child's plate but returned to the napkin holder for each separate napkin.*	10/27/2004 *Watched E.M count the number of napkins needed for her table. Then imitated E.M. at her table. In putting napkins on the table, she returned to napkin holder for each separate napkin*

Figure 9–8   Anecdotal Record

> *Sept. 27*   Tim and two other boys (Stefan and Binh) were in the sandbox using dump trucks for hauling sand. Stefan remarked that his lot needed more sand than the lot to which they had just delivered one dump-truck load. Tim looked and asked, "How much more sand?" "Twice as much," replied Stefan. "Then I'll drive my truck up once and give them a load and come back for one more load of sand," Tim commented.

3. **Check sheets.** A **check sheet** is a prepared list of behaviors based on program goals. The teacher simply indicates the presence or absence of these behaviors in a child. Dating (rather than merely checking) observed behaviors provides more information. Check sheets may be completed while actually observing children because information can be recorded rather quickly, or check sheets with more summary types of state-

ments (e.g., "Uses physical one-to-one correspondence") can come from narrative records, such as a series of log entries. Some records, called *checklists* by some professionals, are really more like rating scales because teachers are given the behavioral descriptors and then are asked to check on a continuum (e.g., "no evidence, beginning, developing, or very secure"). An example of a check sheet in shown in Figure 9–9. Using

---

(Child's name)

Art Concepts

Can recognize these colors: red   _____

                              yellow   _____

                              blue   _____

                              green   _____

                              orange   _____

                              purple   _____

                              black   _____

                              brown   _____

Can arrange four varying grades
of sandpaper from rough to smooth.   _____

Can name the colors and point to
rough and smooth fruit in a
reproduction of Cezanne's painting
Apples and Oranges.   _____

Figure 9–9   **Check Sheet**

check sheets is discussed in detail by Bentzen (2000) and Nilsen (2000).

4. **Ratings. Ratings** assess the quality of an attribute with the judgment indicated on a quality-point scale. Only behaviors that can be described according to the degree to which the competence or trait exists can be recorded on rating scales. Judgments are based on either observations or impressions; thus, the validity of rating scales is based mainly on the adequacy of the observations. Three popular rating scales are as follows:

a. **Forced-choice.** Observers must choose among predetermined (spelled-out) behaviors on a continuum (see Figure 9–10).

b. **Semantic differential.** The observer is given descriptions of the two extremes, which are opposites on the continuum. The observer chooses any marked point between the extremes. Often, the number of points between the extremes (see Figure 9–11) is an odd number (3, 5, 7, or 9).

c. **Numerical.** Numerical scales use numerals on a continuum (often 1–3, 1–4, or 1–5). Each numeral may be verbally described, or only certain numerals may be described (e.g., endpoints or endpoints and middle numerals; see Figure 9–12). Other examples of rating scales used in early childhood programs are given by Beaty (2002), Martin (1998), Nicholson and Shipstead (2002), and Nilsen (2002).

5. **Samples of children's work.** Samples of children's work can take many forms. Common samples are drawings and paintings and papers showing language and mathematics skills. Less common but very important samples are (a) pictures of three-dimensional art products, block structures, and even two-dimensional materials too large to keep easily; (b) printouts from computer work; (c) audiotapes of verbal performances; and (d) videotapes of other performances (e.g., motor skills, interactions with others in the program). Helm, Beneke, and Steinheimer (1998) and Nilsen (2000) provided many ideas for documenting samples of children's work.

6. **Test scores and diagnostic profile information.** These records are often raw or converted scores or other graphic or descriptive information coming from performance on staff-constructed or standardized instruments.

Referral Records. All early childhood programs that employ specialists to work with children who need unique assistance need **referral records.** Specialists hired as full-time staff or as part-time consultants may include medical professionals, psychometrists, counselors, speech pathologists, and physical therapists. If the program does not employ specialists for support services, the director should develop a community resource directory. In some cases, a directory may be available through the local Chamber of Commerce, the

Figure 9–10   Forced-Choice Rating Scale

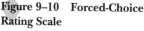

_____
      (Child's name)

1. Can put on his or her outdoor clothes

               _____
               Not   Sometimes   Always
               Yet

Figure 9–11   Semantic Differential Rating Scale

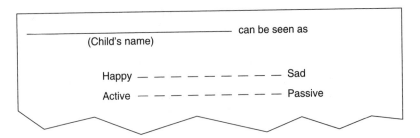

United Fund, the Community Council, or the state's Department of Social Services. Directors who must compile their own file of community resources should include in each description the basic service; whether it is physical health, mental health, or recreation; the name of the agency, its address, and telephone number; the days and hours of operation; and a detailed explanation of the services it provides, eligibility requirements, and the name of the person to contact.

The contents of referral records must be in keeping with the law. Local early childhood programs should develop a separate referral form for each type of referral (different forms for referral to medical specialists, speech pathologists, and so forth). The items on each form differ, but each type should include the signed permission for referral from a parent or legal guardian; the date and the person or agency to which the referral is being made; the name of the staff member referring the child; the specific reasons for the referral; either a digest of or the complete reports from other referrals; the comments or attitudes of family members, peers, or the child him- or herself if they are available; the length of time the staff member has been aware of the problem; and what staff or family members have tried and with what success. Many referral records allow space for the specialist's report after assessment and support services are provided.

Summary Records. **Summary records** are records that summarize and interpret primary data. No new information is added, but primary data are studied and interpreted. Background information records and referral records, on the one hand, are kept intact and updated but are rarely summarized. Performance records, on the other hand, written or collected by using various formats and encompassing a length of time, must be

Figure 9–12   Numerical Rating Scale

(Child's name)

1. Motor skills can best be described as:

	1 = Poor skill < — — — — —> 5 = Excels in skill

hops	1	2	3	4	5
skips	1	2	3	4	5
climbs steps (ascending)	1	2	3	4	5

reviewed and reduced to a summary format in order to analyze them for either formative or summative purposes.

Summary records are completed several times a year to aid teachers in better understanding each child's progress and interests for the purposes of curriculum planning and communicating with families. Summary records are used to abstract aggregate data (with individual children's identification removed) for aiding program directors in their periodic reports to their funding or sponsoring agencies.

Thus, summary performance records often use broad descriptors of behavior, such as "Likes to write" or "Knows that print is read left to right and top to bottom." These summary statements can be developed from the program's goals for children's development and learning in each domain. Roskos and Neuman (1994) gave an example of this type of summary record. In a way, check sheets and report cards given to parents are also summary records. Other summary instruments, designed to assess many domains, are called *developmental assessment systems* (discussed in detail by D. H. Cohen, Stern, and Balaban, 1997). The Work Sampling System (Meisels, Jabalon, Marsden, Dichtelmiller, Dorfman & Steele, 1994) uses summary records.

Record Collections

Most family child care programs and small child care centers have not kept any record collections. Public school programs have kept cumulative records on children from entrance to graduation. Head Start and other government-funded programs keep records on children from year to year. The most common type of record collection is the cumulative record. The portfolio is now becoming a recommended method for documentation collection.

Cumulative Records.   A **cumulative record,** a summary record of the entire school career, was often reduced to a card the size of a file folder. The cumulative record was limited to the child's name,

birth date, and birth certificate number; parents' or guardians name's and addresses; the child's immunization records; and each year's attendance record, summary grades, standardized test information, and a digest of any major actions taken by the school or family (e.g., referrals). Many university-sponsored child study and teacher training programs and some government- and foundation-supported early childhood programs have kept voluminous records on young children's growth and development.

Portfolios.   Danielson and Abrutyn (1997) identified three types of portfolios:

1. **Display portfolios** are photographs and general descriptions of what children do in the classroom, but these portfolios do not focus on an individual child.

2. **Showcase portfolios** show an individual child's best work; however, because the work is only the "best" work, the portfolio may not be an accurate picture of that child.

3. **Working portfolios** show the individual child's process of learning skills and concepts; evidence of typical work with both the strengths and weaknesses is included, with all samples clearly connected to program goals.

In this text, the **portfolio,** defined as a method of gathering and organizing evidence of a child's interests, skills, concepts, and dispositions over time with documentation clearly connected to program goals, is a summary record. Thus, the text definition fits Danielson and Abrutyn's definition of a working portfolio. Most programs will use both **process portfolios** (several items collected to document each goal) and **archival portfolios** (final item or items put in the portfolio) for each predetermined sampling date (e.g., September, January, and April).

Constructing a portfolio involves the following steps:

1. Plan with all staff members the types of data that can document specific criteria being

used as the learning goals of the local program. Each child's work sample may be different because children can demonstrate their understandings and skills in many ways. A chart could be made of program goals, typical activities, and types of authentic assessment samples that would fit each type of activity. Some excellent samples were suggested by Dodge, Colker, and Heroman (2002) and Meisels, Dichtelmiller, Jabalon, Dorfman, and Marsden (1997). A general listing of types of contents for working portfolios is given in Figure 9–13. Samples and documentation should come from many sources, including teachers and other professionals, family members, and the children (who should be encouraged to select some of the items).

2. Document each item collected. Collection alone is not enough. The documentation should contain the date, whether the child worked independently or with others, and the amount of work required. Gronlund (1998) offered an example of a "Portfolio Documentation Checklist" (p. 6), which saves time documenting each item.

3. Decide how frequently samples should be taken. Samples are often taken in September (baseline documentation), January, and April.

4. Identify criteria for judging samples as evidence that children are progressing toward goals. For example, neatness of handwriting should not be a criterion of creative writing.

5. Decide how the portfolios will be used. A portfolio from the previous year with the name and other identifying information removed can be used to explain the working portfolio to family members, teachers, and board members; portfolios can be used in conjunction with family–teacher–child conferences; a few pages of the portfolio can be removed and sent to the family

Figure 9–13   Contents of Working Portfolios

Background information

Health information

Teacher observations

    Logs, anecdotal records, running records, etc.

    Check sheets

    Rating scales

    Samples of child's work, such as writing,
       drawing, painting, scissor work,
       audiotapes (storytelling, show and tell, etc.),
       videotapes (projects, gross-motor activities, fine-motor activities,
       dramatic play, etc.), and photos (artwork—especially 3-D, block
       building structures, etc.)

Test scores

Activity chart (shows centers child chose)

Interviews with child

Parent information

    Parents' observations

    Parent–teacher and parent–teacher–child conference summaries

    Parent questionnaires

    Parent notes

member along with a note for families not attending conferences or for nonconference times (the pages are to be returned); portfolios can be sent to the next teacher; and portfolios can be used to prepare various reporting documents.

6. Decide how both a process and an archival portfolio will be "housed." Process portfolio materials are initial records usually kept in several folders or an expandable file folder with about 12 pockets for each child. (The file folders or pockets should be labeled background information records, anecdotal records, artwork, and so forth.) Archival portfolio materials are perhaps best kept in an individual three-ring binder with materials displayed in clear vinyl page-sized pockets. Confidential information should be stored in a secure place elsewhere. Because the literature on portfolios is so extensive, some readings on portfolios are given in a separate listing at the end of the chapter.

Family Educational Rights and Privacy Act (FERPA)

Children's records are protected under the Family Educational Rights and Privacy Act (FERPA). This law provides the following:

1. Parents or legal guardians of children who attend a program receiving federal assistance may see information in the program's official files. This information includes test scores, grade averages, class rank, intelligence quotient, health records, psychological reports, notes on behavioral problems, family background items, attendance records, and all other records except personal notes made by a staff member solely for his or her own use.

2. Records must be made available for review within 45 days of the request.

3. Parents may challenge information irrelevant to education, such as religious preference or unsubstantiated opinions.

4. Contents of records may be challenged in a hearing. If the program refuses to remove material challenged by parents as inaccurate, misleading, or inappropriate, the parent may insert a written rebuttal.

5. With some exceptions (e.g., other officials in the same program, officials in another program to which the student has applied for transfer, some accrediting associations, state educational officials, some financial aid organizations, the courts), written consent of parents is required before program officials may release records. Programs must keep a written record as to who has seen or requested to see the child's records.

6. Parents have the right to know where records are kept and which program officials are responsible for them.

7. Unless a divorced parent is prohibited by law from having any contact with the child, divorced parents have equal access to official records.

8. Most of the foregoing rights pass from parent to child when the child is 18 years of age.

9. Program officials must notify parents (and 18-year-olds) of their rights.

REPORTING

Reporting is becoming a more important aspect of early childhood programs as programs seek to involve family members in their children's development and as the programs become more accountable to families, citizens' groups, and funding and regulatory agencies. As is true of all aspects of an early childhood program, reporting practices should be based on program goals. Planning reporting requires administrators to think in terms of four steps in developing a reporting practice: (a) determining the purposes of reporting, (b) facilitating reporting through assessment data, (c) selecting the methods of reporting, and (d) rethinking reporting practices. Because reporting is so tied to the assessing and recording process, it is best considered before assessment plans are completed.

Determining the Purposes of Reporting

The first step in developing a reporting practice is to determine the purposes of reporting. For most early childhood programs, a major purpose of reporting is to provide information to family members about their child's progress. Families and staff jointly discuss the child's strengths and needs and plan the next steps in the educative process. Another major purpose of reporting is to meet the requirements of funding and regulatory agencies. Although funding and regulatory agencies require reports on many aspects of programs, program success as measured by children's progress is a major component in the reports made to all regulating and sponsoring agencies.

Facilitating Reporting Through Assessment Data

Once the specific purposes of reporting have been determined, the next step is to make a connection between assessment data and purposes. Several important questions are as follows:

1. *What type of assessment meets the purposes of reporting?* More specifically: (a) What information do family members need to know about their child's progress? (Likely, much of this information will be the same as teachers need for curriculum decisions), and (b) what information does the regulatory or funding agency expect to know about the collective progress of children that in turn will demonstrate the program's value? (These data can be used in rethinking program goals, too.) Basically, the desired information for both families and agencies should be directly linked to the program goals. Programs with narrower, academic goals will assess and report children's progress in academic areas; programs with more holistic/developmental goals will gather and report data in many domains of children's development and learnings.

2. *In what format will assessment data be recorded?* Generally, standardized tests yield quantitative data—numerical raw scores (e.g., number

correct) and numerical converted scores (e.g., percentiles, stanines, developmental ages), and authentic assessment techniques yield qualitative data (e.g., anecdotes, samples of children's work). If one considers assessment data from the standpoint of the ease of reporting only (not in terms of their appropriateness for program goals and the ages of children involved, although these are critical criteria), quantitative data are more difficult to explain to families, who want to know what the scores mean. Furthermore, composite scores yield no information about the specific strengths and weaknesses in each child's progress; thus, reporting requires a careful interpretation of subscore data. Quantitative data, however, lend themselves to the concise summary data often expected by funding and regulatory agencies; in fact, many standardized achievement tests provide class record/profile data that can be easily incorporated into agency reports. In some cases, however, quantitative scores may not be understood by those reading the agency reports. Conversely, qualitative data are much easier for families to understand but are more difficult to summarize and definitely do not lend themselves to tables and graphs. If both quantitative and qualitative assessment data have been collected, the teacher must explain each type of data and also show how the data relate to each other.

3. *Against what criterion will assessment outcomes be measured?* For example: Is progress being compared with that of a norming group? Is progress measured against specific program goals? Is progress being compared with developmental landmarks? This information must be reported.

4. *How will data be assembled?* The ways data are assembled determine the ease of access and the need to summarize before reporting.

Selecting the Methods of Reporting

The third step in planning reporting is to determine the method or methods of reporting, especially to families. (Agencies usually have their own reporting formats.) Reporting methods are diverse. The types of methods are both oral and written. Most families prefer some of each type. Common methods include informal reports, report cards, check sheets, narrative report letters, and individual conferences.

Informal Reports.   Informal reports are perhaps the most common way of reporting—so common that staff may not even be aware that they are communicating information about children's progress. This kind of report may be a casual conversation with a family member in which a staff member mentions, "Lori excels in motor skills," or, "Mark is learning the last step in tying his shoes." Family members may note their child's progress while volunteering in the program. Samples of children's work with or without teachers' comments are often sent home. Children, too, report on themselves, such as, "I learned to skip today," or, "I shared my boat with everyone at the water table."

Report Cards.   **Report cards,** written progress reports recorded on heavyweight paper or card stock, have been the traditional form for reporting children's progress. Because the items assessed supposedly represent school objectives and because the recorded data become part of the child's permanent record, report cards are seen as legal or quasi-legal documents.

Traditional Report Cards.   The traditional report card is more frequently used in early childhood programs that enroll kindergarten or primary children (programs that have an educational focus) than in programs that enroll children of prekindergarten age. Because the predominant marking system on report cards presents assessments of work habits, reading readiness, and mathematics readiness, report cards are used mainly in programs with the academic, D-I perspective. Although rumors circulate that the report card is dead, or at least dying, it in fact survives, finding its way into homes at monthly to semiannual intervals.

Traditional report cards usually list such items as academic subjects or activities and areas of personal or social adjustment and have a blank space opposite each item for recording a symbol denoting progress. A key on the report card interprets the symbols, whether they are the traditional A, B, C, D, and F symbols (rarely used) or others. Other specifics frequently included are the child's attendance record, a space for comments, and a parent's signature line for each reporting period. Because the items selected for inclusion on the report card should fit program goals, the items vary. The following list indicates the wide range of assessed achievements:

General well-being (e.g., alertness and the ability to rest)

Identity (e.g., writes name, knows address)

Social maturity (e.g., friendly, shares, controls temper)

Eye–hand coordination (e.g., able to use art and hand tools, able to trace shapes)

Perception of direction (e.g., shows consistent handedness, knows right and left)

Work habits (e.g., has adequate attention span, follows directions)

Language development (e.g., speaks clearly, has adequate vocabulary, makes up stories)

Reading readiness (e.g., understands sequence, shows interest in stories, recognizes likenesses and differences both visually and aurally)

Mathematics (e.g., counts rationally, recognizes numerals)

Science (e.g., shows curiosity, classifies)

Music (e.g., enjoys listening and singing, participates in rhythmic activities)

Art (e.g., enjoys arts and crafts, recognizes colors, handles tools correctly)

Health, safety, and physical education (e.g., practices good health habits, obeys safety rules, participates in physical activities, shows good sportsmanship)

Traditional report cards come in various styles. One style may require the staff member to check a child's achievements. An understanding or skill the child has not developed is left unchecked. This style closely resembles the check sheet and is shown in Figure 9–14. Another style may require staff to mark both understandings and skills the child has achieved and not achieved. A report card style that might be used for a program that serves children of bilingual families is shown in Figure 9–15. The example shown in Figure 9–16 requires the teacher to denote each child's progress by marking one of three choices. Another style calls for the teacher to assess both effort and progress on each item, as shown in Figure 9–17. Yet another style requires the teacher to assess progress on each item on an inferior–superior continuum; such a style is actually a rating scale, as shown in Figure 9–18.

Newer Report Cards. The traditional report card does not fit the needs of the holistic/developmental programs, which often assess children's progress by authentic methods (S. Robinson, 1997). Good (1993) described a report card that could be used by programs adhering to the holistic/developmental rationale. The four major areas she included on these report cards are (a) the *identification section* (e.g., name of school, year, grade or level, child's name, and teacher's name), which is typically included on traditional report cards, too; (b) the *educational philosophy section,* in which both the general philosophy and the specific features of the program are described; (c) the *progress report section,* which is tied to actual practices rather than to "subject areas," uses checklists as shown in Figures 9–14 and 9–16, and has a place under each developmental area (e.g., fine motor, emergent literacy) for teacher comments; and (d) the *response*

Figure 9–14   Report Card with Achievements Checked

A Message to Parents

In kindergarten, your child lives, works, and plays with other children of his or her age. He or she has learning experiences that are a foundation for all that follows in later school years. This card is a description of your child's development at this time. Each quality checked is evident in your child. You, as a parent, will help and encourage your child by your interest in his or her growth.

BEHAVIOR IN LARGE- GROUP SITUATIONS	Participates with confidence	
	Usually follows others	
	Participates in activities	
	Gets along well with others	

RESPONSE TO RULES	Cooperates when encouraged	
	Accepts group decisions	
	Follows rules of the school	

Figure 9–15   Bilingual Report Card

Name (Nombre) _____

S   Satisfactory growth at this time.
    Desarrollo satisfactorio al presente.

N   Not yet.
    Todavia no es satisfactorio el desarrollo.

Can hop Puede saitar		Puts on wraps Se pone el abrigo
Knows age Sabe su edad		Knows address Sabe su domicilio

section, which provides space for a family member to comment. A space should also be provided in which a family–teacher conference can be requested by either the teacher or a family member.

Check Sheets.   **Check sheets** contain lists of desired behaviors. The teacher indicates that the child has developed a particular skill or has shown understanding of a particular concept by using a check mark—hence, the name. Some

Figure 9–16   Report Card with Level of Progress Checked

Progress Report

Name_____

A check shows the child's performance	1st Semester			2nd Semester		
	Most of the time	Part of the time	Not at this time	Most of the time	Part of the time	Not at this time
WORK HABITS						
Takes care of materials						
Has good attention span						
Is able to work independently						
Follows group instruction						

Figure 9–17   Report Card with Effort and Progress Checked

EDUCATIONAL GROWTH	EFFORT		PROGRESS	
	Adequate	Needs to improve	Shows development	Shows strength
PERSONAL ATTITUDES AND SKILLS				
Is interested and contributes				
Can put on outdoor clothing				
Can tie shoes				
Can wait his or her turn				
Keeps hands to himself or herself (doesn't bother others)				
STORY PERIOD				
Retells stories and rhymes				
Refrains from disturbing others				
Sits quietly				
Shows interest in story				
Listens while story is read				

programs use check sheets as the only method of reporting, but check sheets are more frequently used in conjunction with other methods of reporting. These sheets may be given to a family member during an individual conference or may be enclosed in the report card. Check sheets generally differ from report cards in the following ways:

1. They are usually printed on sheets of paper rather than on cards.

2. Categories of items on check sheets are similar to those on report cards, but the items on check sheets tend to be more specific. An item on a report card might read as shown in Figure 9–19. The same item listed on a check sheet might look like the example in Figure 9–20.

3. Items on report cards may rate a child as to his or her degree of accomplishment (e.g., "satisfactory," "progressing," "needs improvement"), whereas check sheets indicate whether the child has accomplished a specific task.

Narrative Report Letters.   Programs using **narrative report letters** usually provide forms on which teacher write a few brief comments about a child's progress under each of several headings, such as psychomotor development, personal and social adjustment, cognitive development, language growth, work habits, problem-solving growth, aesthetic growth, self-reliance, and general evaluation. An example of a narrative report letter form is shown in Figure 9–21. Narrative report letters are highly appropriate for

Figure 9–18   Progress Rating Scale

Your Child's Progress

Name of child _____   Year and class _____

School _____   Teacher _____

GROWTH AND DEVELOPMENT

		Rarely	Constantly

A.   Considers ideas and points of view of others   _____|_____

B.   Demonstrates good health habits   _____|_____

C.   Expresses ideas and feelings   _____|_____

Figure 9–19   Progress Report Card

Puts on outdoor clothing   Always   Sometimes

Figure 9–20   Progress Check Sheet

Can button clothes . . . . _____
Can put on overshoes . . . . _____
Can zip a coat . . . . _____
Can lace and tie shoes . . . . _____

Figure 9–21   Narrative Report Letter

Your Child's Progress

Name _____   Level _____

Psychomotor development (motor skills):

George can gallop, skip, run, and throw and catch a rubber ball. He enjoys all games that use movement, and his skills indicate that his attainment is high in this area of development.

Personal/social adjustment:

George does not initiate many aggressive acts; however, he still has trouble keeping his hands to himself. He responds to negative overtures from his classmates by hitting.

Language growth:

George appears to enjoy new words. He uses rhyming words and makes up words to fit the rhymes. He has not been able to express negative feelings toward others with words, however.

General evaluation:

George is progressing nicely. More opportunities to talk with others would help him learn to express himself. He performs well in the room and on the playground as long as he is kept busy and as long as others leave him alone.

---

summarizing authentic assessment records. The advantage of report letters is that teachers can concentrate on a child's specific strengths and needs without giving letter grades or marking "satisfactory/unsatisfactory" and without noting progress in highly specific areas, such as "knows his address" or "ties her shoes." The two disadvantages to report letters are that (a) report letters are highly time consuming, but the use of computers lessens the time spent in preparing them (the computer generates the report form and permits the word processing of the narrative itself); and (b) unless teachers carefully study their records on each child, they may slip into writing stereotypical comments, especially after writing the first few reports.

Individual Conferences.   Many programs schedule **individual conferences** with each child and the child's family members. Conferences permit face-to-face communication among children, families,

and teachers. A teacher must plan intensively for a successful conference. (General guidelines for planning the conference are given in chapter 10.)

To effectively discuss children's progress, teachers need to plan the conference by using a written guide sheet that lists the topics and main points to be discussed. The teacher should consult all records on the child and carefully transfer to the guide sheet any information to be shared with family members. A report card, check sheet, developmental profile, or selected materials from the portfolio given to family members can be used as the guide sheet. Time is provided for family members to express their concerns as topics listed on the guide sheet are covered. Additional concerns of family members need to be addressed, too. Conferences should end on a positive note, with plans for follow-up in areas of concern at home and at school. Family members and children can look at the other items in the portfolio at the end of the conference. Many program directors are finding that if teachers give a copy of the guide sheet to each family member a few days before the conference, family members have time to think about the contents and to prepare questions and comments for the conference.

Rethinking Reporting Practices

The final step in developing a reporting practice is to experiment with the reporting plans and revise them if necessary. Reporting practices must not only work for program personnel but also open dialogue between staff and the recipients of reports, especially families. In short, the only purpose of reporting to families is to establish collaboration on behalf of children.

TRENDS AND ISSUES

Assessment reform seems to be lagging behind the push to modify the curriculum. Kagan (2000b) believes that early childhood professionals must design an assessment system that will determine children's full range of development and learnings (i.e., physical well-being and motor development, social and emotional development, approaches toward learning, communication and language development, and cognitive development) and provide needed safeguards (e.g., unnecessary assessment, improper techniques, misuse of data).

In 1994, the National Education Goals Panel convened the Goal 1 Early Childhood Assessments Resource Group. The following purposes for assessment in early childhood were identified: (a) to promote children's learnings and development; (b) to identify children for health and special learning services; (c) to monitor trends and evaluate programs and services; and (d) to assess academic achievement and hold individual students, teachers, and schools accountable. L. Shepard, Kagan, and Wurtz (1998a) outlined how appropriate uses and technical accuracy of assessments for the foregoing purposes change across the early childhood age continuum.

More research is needed on the efficacy of authentic assessment in reporting children's progress (Herman & Winters, 1994). Many directors and teachers agree with the concept of authentic assessment. Teachers need help in using authentic assessment and will need intense training in in-depth authentic assessment methods, such as the clinical interview and assessing emerging learnings and development. Furthermore, many teachers are not familiar with making professional judgments based on broader pictures of children and may even be hesitant in assuming this responsibility. Several authentic assessment systems, such as COR and the Work Sampling System, provide a structure for the assessment data and inform teachers of criteria that may be used in making inferences about what children can do. In addition, the systems have the qualities of strong standardized tests—that is, a strong reliability and predictive validity.

Many professionals are questioning screening practices and the use of the data. Teachers need training in recognizing whether a child's departure from a developmental benchmark is a sign of a learning problem or is consistent with cultural and linguistic differences. Perhaps programs should provide more high-intensity intervention to *all* children coming from high-risk backgrounds.

Another problem in assessment comes from trying to combine the purposes of assessment and use the data in many ways. Often, standardized achievement tests are used for assessment. Although combining purposes saves money and time, such combining often results in the misuse of data, such as using readiness tests for screening or using assessment for determining program effectiveness and also for holding individual children accountable.

SUMMARY

Assessing, recording, and reporting are integral parts of an early childhood program. Thus, these components must be thoughtfully and carefully planned, in keeping with program goals. Providing quality assessment and recording and reporting assessments is not a simple matter but requires a highly trained staff and leadership by directors.

Similar to the professional concerns about inappropriate curriculum content and teaching strategies are concerns about assessment. Assessment can support children's development or undermine it. Abuses and misuses have occurred in how assessment methods have been selected and administered (e.g., a disconnect between curriculum/teaching strategies and assessment practices); by the lack of a user-friendly format for young children (e.g., the use of the paper-and-pencil format); by the misassessment of young children with disabilities and those from culturally and linguistically diverse families; by the use of single measurements for making high-stakes decisions about children, staff competencies, and program effectiveness; and by the way scores have been interpreted to family members.

Professional associations have called for many changes in assessment, recording, and reporting practices. The major changes recommended include the following:

1. The almost exclusive use of ongoing, unobtrusive observations of children in actual classroom situations (authentic or performance assessment), and the use of special sampling techniques when standardized tests are mandated to determine program effectiveness.

2. Documentation of authentic performance assessment done by the writing of logs and anecdotes, the checking and rating of certain specified behaviors, and the gathering of samples of children's work. Other records can include notes taken during interviews and home visits and the summaries of assessments and services provided by specialists.

3. The development of reporting purposes and practices that mirror local program goals and that are verified by authentic performance assessment and appropriate observation rec-

ords. Usually, the contents of reports are summarized performance records with samples of actual performance used to document the summary data and collected to form a portfolio. The format for reporting may be written, oral, or a combination of the two.

Several trends and issues were noted. Assessment reform seems to be lagging behind curriculum reform. Professionals are calling for an appropriate assessment system to fulfill the various purposes of assessment and to provide needed safeguards.

FOR FURTHER READING

Day, J. D., Englehardt, J. L., & Bolig, E. E. (1997). Comparison of static and dynamic assessment procedures and their relation to independent performance. *Journal of Educational Psychology, 89,* 358–368.

Ginsburg, H. P. (1997). *Entering the child's mind: The clinical interview in psychological research and practice.* New York: Cambridge University Press.

Hemmeter, M. L., Maxwell, K. L., Ault, M. J., & Schuster, J. W. (2001). *Assessment practices in early elementary classrooms.* Washington, DC: National Association for the Education of Young Children.

Kagan, S. L., Rosenkoetter, S., & Cohen, N. (1997). *Considering child-based results for young children: Definitions, desirability, feasibility, and next steps.* New Haven, CT: Yale Bush Center in Child Development and Social Policy.

Kamii, C. (Ed.). (1990). *Achievement testing in the early grades: The games grown-ups play.* Washington, DC: National Association for the Education of Young Children.

Lidz, C. S. (1991). *Practitioner's guide to dynamic assessment.* New York: Guilford.

McAfee, O., & Leong, D. (2001). *Assessing and guiding young children's development and learning.* Boston: Allyn & Bacon.

Meisels, S. J., & Atkins-Burnett, S. (2000). The elements of early childhood assessment. In S. P. Shonkoff & S. J. Meisels (Eds.), *The handbook of early childhood intervention* (2nd ed., pp. 231–257). New York: Cambridge University Press.

Popham, W. J. (2000). *Testing! Testing! What every parent should know about standardized testing*. Boston: Allyn & Bacon.

Sacks, P. (1999). *Standardized minds: The high price of America's testing culture and what we can do to change it*. Cambridge, MA: Perseus.

Shepard, L. A., & Bliem, C. L. (1995). Parents' thinking about standardized tests and performance assessments. *Educational Researcher 24* (5), 25–32.

Shepard, L. A., Kagan, S. L., & Wurtz, E. (1998). *Principles and recommendations for early childhood assessments*. Washington, DC: National Education Goals Panel.

Wiggins, G. (1998). *Educative assessment: Designing assessments to inform and improve performance*. San Francisco: Jossey-Bass.

Wortham, S. C. (1995). *Measurement and evaluation in early childhood education*. Upper Saddle River, NJ: Merrill/Prentice Hall.

Readings on Authentic Assessment

Beaty, J. J. (2002). *Observing development of the young child* (5th ed.). Upper Saddle River, NJ: Merrill/Prentice Hall.

Benjamin, A. C. (1994). Observations in early childhood classrooms: Advice from the field. *Young Children, 49*(6), 14–20.

Bentzen, W. (2000). *Seeing young children: A guide to observing and recording behaviors*. Albany, NY: Delmar.

Boehm, A. E., & Weinberg, R. A. (1997). *The classroom observer: Developing observation skills in early childhood settings* (3rd ed.). New York: Teachers College Press.

Bredekamp, S., & Rosegrant, T. (Eds.). (1995). *Reaching potentials: Transforming early childhood curriculum and assessment,* (Vol. 2). Washington, DC: National Association for the Education of Young Children.

Cohen, D. H., Stern, V., & Balaban, N. (1997). *Observing and recording behavior of young children* (4th ed.). New York: Teachers College Press.

Gullo, D. F. (1994). *Understanding assessment and evaluation in early childhood education*. New York: Teachers College Press.

Helm, J. H., Beneke, S., & Steinheimer, K. (1998). *Windows on learning: Documenting young children's work*. New York: Teachers College Press.

Nicholson, S., & Shipstead, S. G. (2002). *Through the looking glass: Observations in the early childhood classroom* (3rd ed.). Upper Saddle River, NJ: Merrill/Prentice Hall.

Nilsen, B. A. (2000). *Week by week: Plans for observing and recording young children*. Albany, NY: Delmar.

Puckett, M. B., & Black, J. K. (1999). *Authentic assessment of the young child: Celebrating development and learning*. Upper Saddle River, NJ: Merrill/Prentice Hall.

Wortham, S. C. (1996). *The integrated classroom: The assessment-curriculum link in early childhood education*. Upper Saddle River, NJ: Merrill/Prentice Hall.

Readings on Portfolios

Danielson, C., & Abrutyn, L. (1997). *An introduction to using portfolios in the classroom*. Alexandria, VA: Association for Supervision and Curriculum Development.

DeFina, A. A. (1994). *Portfolio assessment: Getting started*. New York: Scholastic.

Grace, C., & Shores, E. (Eds.). (1994). *The portfolio and its use: Developmentally appropriate assessment of young children* (3rd ed.). Little Rock, AR: Southern Early Childhood Association.

Graves, D. H., & Sunstein, B. S. (Eds.). (1992). *Portfolio portraits*. Portsmouth, NH: Heinemann.

Gronlund, G. (1998). Portfolios as an assessment tool: Is collection of work enough? *Young Children, 53*(3), 4–10.

Helm, J. H., Beneke, S., & Steinheimer, K. (1997). *Teacher materials for documenting young children's work: Using Windows on Learning*. New York: Teachers College Press.

Martin, S. (1998). *Take a look: Observation and portfolio assessment in early childhood*. Reading, MA: Addison-Wesley.

McDonald, S. (1997). *Portfolio and its use: Book II*. Little Rock, AR: Southern Early Childhood Association.

Potter, E. F. (1999). What should I put in my portfolio? Supporting young children's goals and evaluations. *Childhood Education, 75,* 210–214.

Shores, E. F., & Grace, C. (1998). *The portfolio book*. Beltsville, MD: Gryphon.

Smith, A. F. (2000). Reflective portfolios: Preschool possibilities. *Childhood Education, 76,* 204–208.

TO REFLECT

1. Authentic assessment requires teachers to match the content and the technique (instrument) with local program goals. List the goals of a local program or use the sample goal statements provided by Bredekamp and Rosegrant (1992, p. 18). What types of content could a preschool teacher assess for each goal? For each type of content, which technique(s) would be appropriate?

2. A primary school principal changed the program policy of giving letter grades (A, B, C, etc.) to authentic assessment and portfolio documentation. Several of the children's family members were upset at the change. What could have been done to prevent some of the conflict from arising?

Working Within the Family and Community Contexts

10

Early childhood programs cannot work effectively in isolation. Children learn and develop in three contexts—families, early childhood programs and schools, and communities. For this reason, families, early childhood programs, and communities are connected through their shared and complementary roles as facilitators of a quality life for young children that will help them succeed now and in the future. Because early childhood staff are in regular contact with families and programs are a visible agency in the community, staff must take the responsibility for stronger, sharing connections within the family and community contexts.

HISTORICAL PERSPECTIVE ON COLLABORATION

Parent involvement has had a long history in early childhood care and education. Where no programs or schools were available, nurturing and educating children were family functions. Early childhood programs were designed to support families in this socializing function, although families are considered the primary nurturers and teachers of their young children.

Similar to the role of families in early childhood programs is the family's role in public school education. The public school system of the United States was founded, financed, operated, and regulated by parents and other citizens of the local community. In cases in which professionals and families have had different perspectives on children's education, legislation and court decisions, for the most part, have upheld families as the major decision makers concerning their children's upbringing.

Early Involvement of Parents

Historically, many early childhood programs had parent involvement (K. White, Taylor, & Moss, 1992). Froebel developed activities for mothers to do with their infants. From the late 1800s through the early 1900s, kindergarten teachers in the United States taught children in the mornings and spent the afternoons visiting parents in their homes (Weber, 1969). English nursery schools valued and promoted parent involvement (McMillan, 1919). Nursery schools that operated in the prestigious academic institutions of the United States involved parents. Parents were dependent on the nursery school programs under the Works Progress Administration of the Depression years and the Lanham Act Centers during World War II. Parent cooperatives, which were modeled after the English nursery schools, began in the United States in 1916 (K. Taylor, 1981). Montessori highly valued the role of parents and believed that the "mission of parents" was to "save their children by uniting and working together for the improvement of society" (Montessori, 1966, p. 215).

Changing Philosophy of Recent Years

Although early childhood programs have had a long history of parent involvement, professionals have been slow to embrace full collaboration. D. Powell (1989) stated that in the 1960s, program designers felt that parents should be involved to the "maximum feasible participation" (p. 5). For example, by the 1960s, intervention programs such as Head Start mandated parent involvement. Instead of parent involvement being defined as solely parent education in child rearing, now education was concerned more broadly with supporting the family. In the 1970s, goals for parent involvement centered on improving communication and developing positive relationships. During this decade, laws for children with disabilities were written. With the inclusion of children with disabilities into early childhood programs, parents' views, abilities, and difficulties had to be considered in program decisions, and parents themselves became more vocal (Comer, 1988; Fantini, 1970). Parent involvement goals of the 1980s centered on professionals needing to be sensitive to the needs and wants of parents, such as discussing program policies with parents. Finally, in the 1990s, parent involvement came to mean seeing parents in real partnership and collaboration. The primary goal of parent involvement was to coordinate the efforts between home and program (D. Powell, 1998). Thus, early childhood programs were no longer seen as compensating agents for deficit environments (D. Powell & Diamond, 1995). The idea of full collaboration led Galinsky and Weissbourd (1992) to say that the parent–child relationship, rather than the child, is the primary client. D. Powell (1998) stated that professionals should not see the child and family as separate entities but as a *family*. (Because of the changes in the terminology concerning collaboration, in this text the term *parent* will be used to denote involvement in historically earlier programs and the terms *family* and *family member* will refer to adults who are involved on behalf of a given child in today's programs.)

As early childhood programs have continued to expand their focus beyond the child to the entire family, the terminology for involvement has changed. The term *parent involvement* implied the primary role of parents in children's education. *Parent education* focused on the educational needs of parents. *Parent participation* emphasized the idea of collaboration; that is, parents were seen as co-decision makers on policy boards. With *collaboration* the current watchword, *family empowerment* became the term that denoted the change. S. Minuchin's (1984) family system framework provided the ideas on which family empowerment is based. Family empowerment involves developing the self-confidence to advocate for children and to take assertive steps on behalf of children (S. White & Coleman, 2000). J. Epstein (2001) prefers the idea of a partnership, not power. (*Partnership* is cooperative, but *power* is adversarial.) She further extended the term *partnership* to "school, family, and community partnerships."

Collaboration: A Crucial Element of Quality Programs

Program–family–community collaboration is a crucial element in the provision of quality early childhood programs (Larner, 1996; Raab & Dunst, 1997). The importance of collaboration is based on Vygotsky's (1978) sociocultural theory of development and Bronfenbrenner's (1979) ecological systems theory. Beyond these theoretical constructs, collaboration is supported in these ways:

1. P.L. 105-17 (IDEA) requires collaboration for making referrals to assess children for exceptionalities and for planning intervention strategies. Another law, P.L. 103-227 (the Goals 2000: Educate America Act), calls for schools to promote partnerships that encourage parent involvement and participation.

2. Position statements on DAP (Bredekamp & Copple, 1997), ethical conduct (Feeney & Freeman, 1999), linguistic and cultural diversity (NAEYC, 1995b), and interventions for children with special needs (Division for Early Childhood Task Force on Recommended Practices, 1993) call for program–family–community collaboration.

3. Standards for teacher preparation include training standards in establishing productive relationships in the family and community contexts (NAEYC, 2001; see Standard 2, p. 12).

4. Early childhood centers accredited by the NAEYC (1998a) must meet criteria in the component, "Relationships among Teachers and Families."

5. Many research studies of early childhood programs support collaboration as beneficial for the program, child, and family. Implications of research studies led the Committee on Early Childhood Pedagogy to recommend that "all early childhood programs build alliances with parents to cultivate mutually reinforcing environments for children at home and in early childhood programs" (NRC, 2001, p. 318).

LEGAL RIGHTS OF FAMILIES

Education of children is not mentioned in the Constitution of the United States; however, through interpretation of the Tenth Amendment, education became the responsibility of the states. Generally speaking, states require tax support and personnel credentialing, determine minimum curriculum standards, and establish and mandate attendance policies. Many other aspects of authority are delegated to local school systems with local school boards acting as agents of the state. The concept of local control is fundamental to public school organization, and parents, as citizens and taxpayers, have a right to be involved in the decision-making process. All educational agencies that receive funds under any federal program must follow certain statutes in addition to state statutes and local policies.

Parents and legal guardians have the legal authority for the upbringing of their children, including their children's education. The authority of the schools to educate (and keep children safe) is granted through state statutes. In the statutes of most states, the teacher stands **in loco parentis** (in the place of the parent) to the child. This legal terminology is replaced in some state statutes by other phrases meaning the same thing. In states without such a provision, the court affirms the in loco parentis position of the teacher. To more appropriately assume this role, teachers should know what parents want for their children.

When disputes arise and cannot be settled, the judicial system is asked to balance the fundamental rights of parents and the delegated role of the school. Few court cases occurred before the 1950s. Because of greater diversity of families, more and more judgments are being made by the courts. Court cases have dealt with matters such as compulsory attendance, school fees, civil rights, services to children with disabilities, religious and moral beliefs (e.g., vaccinations, religious education, prayer, curriculum content), and liability (e.g., injuries, failure to report abuse, harassment).

BENEFITS AND CHALLENGES OF WORKING WITH FAMILIES

Results of research studies support family involvement as a crucial element in the provision of high-quality early childhood programs. Because of the benefits of family–program collaboration, this partnership is supported through legislation, various position statements, standards for teacher preparation, and criteria for accreditation of early childhood centers. Family involvement is also seen as a source of tension.

Benefits of Working with Families

Families serve as the first and most important nurturers and teachers of their children. To meet their children's needs, families of today use other resources, too, especially early childhood programs and schools. On the basis of Bronfenbrenner's (1986) ecological model, two of the most significant environments for the child are the home and the school. Although these two environments affect the child separately, they also overlap to form an environment in which events in one environment affect the other. Thus, all children benefit from family–program collaboration.

Benefits for the Program.   Early childhood programs can benefit from family involvement. Benefits for the program include the following:

1. When families are able to explain family structures and family cultures to teachers, teachers may become more empathetic and able to work from family strengths.

2. Family members who are involved in the program better understand the program rationale, the curriculum content, and the teaching strategies. The roots of advocacy always begin with a knowledge base. For example, some of the program designers of the 1960 model programs found that parents had a unique empathy in explaining the program's services and problems to other parents.

Some of these programs had a parent educator component in which parent educators (a) trained new parents in specific activities (e.g., toy making), (b) modeled language patterns to be used with activities, (c) explained the program rationale, and (d) stressed the importance of involvement.

3. Family involvement frequently enables the school to comply with federal and state guidelines. For example, the Head Start program mandates that the local advisory boards have parent representatives and that parents serve in the classroom as paid employees, volunteers, and observers. Federal guidelines established for programs serving children with disabilities require parents to be involved in the writing of the IEPs for their children.

4. Through family volunteers, schools achieve a better adult–child ratio. Family members' assistance often enables teachers to conduct program activities that would be impossible without such assistance.

5. Family members can serve as resource people. Their special talents and interests can be useful to the program.

6. Family members can serve as program decision makers (discussed in a later section).

7. Family involvement results in higher staff morale for directors, and teachers see collaboration as a sign of respect (J. Epstein, 2001).

Benefits for the Child.   A major premise is that goals for children are best achieved if families and teachers agree on these goals and the basic ways of achieving them. B. Caldwell (1985) suggested that early childhood programs function as an extended family. Benefits for the child include the following:

1. Bronfenbrenner and Morris (1998) pointed out how demographic and economic changes have interrupted and undermined the relationships essential for healthy psychological development of the family. Schools and communities can serve as support systems.

2. Family–program partnerships can enhance program quality, a benefit to the child (K. White, Taylor, & Moss, 1992).

3. Quality family involvement results in the child's increased cognitive growth, improved language and academic achievement, and growth of problem-solving skills (Bermudez & Marquez, 1996; Marcon, 1994b; Pena, 2000).

4. Family involvement allows children to see that family members and teachers are working together for them. This relationship affects children's affective functioning, leading to a positive self-image and a productive orientation to social relations (Marcon, 1994a) and to positive attitudes about school (J. Epstein, 2001).

Benefits for the Family.   Planned family participation in early childhood programs is viewed as a means of enhancing family members as adults and as parents. Benefits for families include the following:

1. Participation in early childhood programs can enhance family members' feelings of self-worth and contribute to increased education and employment (Bermudez & Marquez, 1996; J. Epstein, 2001).

2. Involvement can help family members gain confidence in their nurturing and educating roles (J. Epstein; D. Powell, 1989). B. White (1988) found that family members can profit from the educational expertise the early childhood program offers in child development and guidance by bringing the knowledge into the home.

3. Family involvement leads to families' better understanding their importance in their children's education. This helps families help schools maximize educational benefits (J. Epstein, 2001).

4. Family involvement helps the process of securing needed interventions for children (Pena, 2000). D. Powell (1989) reported that in some programs, families of children with and without disabilities formed informal support networks.

5. Involved family members may even become an early childhood program's strongest advocates.

Challenges of Working with Families

Many benefits have been stated, although family involvement in an early childhood program may present some challenges. In the Cost, Quality, and Child Outcomes Study (1995), the score for parent relations in infant and toddler programs was below the mean (Cryer & Phillipsen, 1997). P. Edwards and Young (1992) saw families and schools as having a history of tensions and mistrust. Challenges were also noted by N. Jacobs (1992), who stated that the greatest ethical concerns of teachers pertained to their relationships with families.

Moreover, early childhood programs are not meeting the needs of all families. Higher levels of family involvement are associated with families who have a high educational status (D. Stevenson & Baker, 1987), families from affluent communities (J. Epstein, 1995), families with younger children (J. Epstein), and families with special needs children (Shriver & Kramer, 1993).

Boundaries Between Home and Program Are Blurred. Elkind (1994) described two major transformations in family life. The Industrial Revolution brought families to cities and changed the family unit to a nuclear family. The family was child centered, and roles within the family and between the family and other institutions were distinct. Today, families are no longer child centered as adults seek relief from family functions. The boundaries within the family and between the family and other social institutions are more permeable and blurred.

Early childhood programs are assuming responsibilities for children that once were considered family responsibilities. Families and programs are now seen as having a joint responsibility for nurturing and teaching. The responsibilities of the home and program are difficult to separate. Stamp and Groves (1994) referred to the unique relationship between families and schools as the "third institution."

Sociologists theorize that an optimal social distance exists between home and school. The distance protects the unique characteristics of each (Litwak & Meyer, 1974). Finding the balance in early childhood education is difficult, however, because teachers must do traditional parenting types of tasks and even feel a strong attachment to children in their programs. When the boundaries are blurred, tensions occur (D. Powell, 1989). Haseloff (1990) called these tensions, "power-struggles." Two examples are (a) Kontos's (1984) findings that teachers saw parents as having far poorer parenting skills than the parents felt they had and (b) Galinsky's (1990) findings that mothers who expressed guilt about working were more likely to be seen as inadequate parents than those who worked but did not express guilt. Galinsky reported that parents and teachers felt possessive about children, and often jealousy was noted.

Family-Structural and Cultural Diversity Often Lead to Discontinuities. Families and program staff may have different values and beliefs that stem from their respective personal perspectives based on family and community structures and other cultural influences. Differences between families and program staff often lead to serious discontinuities and expectations for children's development and learnings.

Family Structure. Program staff work with families from all types of *family structures* (family composition types). Family structure may cause certain family stressors to affect program involvement and to result in some problems for children. For example, single-mother families have high rates of poverty and more time constraints, which often reduce participation in program involvement, including home support of children's development and learnings. Children from single-parent families often have diminished emotional supports and lower levels of cognitive stimulations (Levine-Coley, 1998). Thus, children raised by single parents may have lower levels of social and academic well-being (Cherlin, 1999).

Socioeconomic Status.   Low-income families experience many negative life events and have fewer resources for coping with these experiences. This often leads to stress (Edkin & Lein, 1997). Children from low socioeconomic families often show behavioral and academic problems (Brody & Flor, 1997). Families with higher socioeconomic backgrounds show more family involvement (D. Stevenson & Baker, 1987). The more positive home learning environments of high-income versus low-income families account for as much as half the gap in test scores of preschool children (J. Smith, Brooks-Gunn, & Klebanov, 1997).

Ethnic/Linguistic Culture.   Culture is embedded through family belief and value systems and modes of family interactions. Families transmit values and behaviors from one generation to another. Children may accept, modify, or resist cultural influences (P. J. Miller & Goodnow, 1995).

E. Hall (1977) distinguished between low-context cultures (Western European and United States mainstream) and high-context cultures (Asian, Southern European, Latino, African American, and Native American). In low-context cultures, the individual is valued over the group, independence of individuals is a virtue, individuals are encouraged to assert themselves and achieve, and communication is verbal and precise. By contrast, in high-context groups, interdependence (extended family and community) is valued, contributions to the group are prized, and language involves more nonverbal and contextual cues. Child rearing and daily routines are imbued with cultural expectations. For example,

in low-context cultures, the child sleeps alone; is comforted by objects; is put in swings, in infant seats, and on the floor to play; and is encouraged to self-feed at an early age. Thus, families' expectations about the various forms of young children's achievement differ by culture (Goodnow, 1996). The way children are taught (i.e., adult engagement with children versus children learning through observation) is also cultural (Goodnow, 1996).

Many families are non-English-speaking. Language is a major barrier. Whitebook, Sakai, and Howes (1997) found that 50% of directors and 33% of teachers in 92 California child care centers had difficulty communicating with family members because of language differences.

When program and family cultures are similar, home values are reinforced. Conversely, when dissimilarities occur, program goals, curriculum content, and teaching strategies may be unrealistic. Dissimilarity of program and home values may lead to children's competencies going unrecognized and to incorrect interventions. Children may also feel isolated (García Coll & Magnuson, 2000). Greenberg (1989) stated that when families feel alienated, children often believe that they must choose between home and school or compartmentalize their two worlds, and these children often become major discipline problems. "Expected school behavior may be quite alien to what's needed by some children at home and in the neighborhood where they live" (Gonzalez-Mena, 2002, p. 293). Children do much better in programs in which family members and teachers hold similar perceptions of a given child's competencies and engagement in program activities (Peet, Powell, & O'Donnel, 1997).

Family and Staff Feelings and Conflicts Create Tensions.   Collaborative efforts may be difficult as a result of tensions and conflicts. Some families may feel inhibited or even inferior around staff members because of their family-structural or cultural differences or because of their limited and unsuccessful school experiences. If communication with staff members is difficult, these feelings are even more pronounced. Staff members who lack respect for all families may respond negatively, often discounting what families do for their children (Greenberg, 1989). Kontos and Wells (1986) concluded that the families needing the most staff support were least likely to get it. Conversely, professionals can feel threatened by families, especially those who are highly educated. Staff see the children of these families coming to programs already "knowing," having been taught by uncredentialed family educators (Greenberg, 1989).

Conflicts may also arise over the curriculum content and teaching strategies. As discussed, many families prefer a structured, academic program; conversely, teachers are professionally urged to use a more holistic/developmental approach. Although both families and teachers want children to achieve, conflicts are caused by disagreements about how to achieve certain goals (Stipek, Rosenblatt, & DiRocco, 1994).

Family members and staff bring their stress to the relationship (Galinsky, 1988; Leavitt, 1987). Stress often results in conflict over program policies. For example, on the one hand, family members expect staff to take into account the lack of anyone to care for sick children at home, to understand the difficulty of getting to the center by bus before closing time, and to understand their need to "pay later." On the other hand, staff members expect families to understand the limitations of group care (e.g., caring for individual children, hours of operation, and payment of fees).

The attitudes of program staff and families about collaboration itself may impede it. Family rights and jurisdiction to make decisions about the education of their children are difficult realities for some staff members. Perhaps the attitude is the result of a long tradition in which family involvement alarmed many professionals. Some professionals have seen home teaching of

academics as confusing to the child, family member visits to the program as disruptive, and family members' critiques of the program's curriculum and methodology as unqualified judgments of professionals by nonprofessionals. Thus, before the 1960s, working with parents was primarily parent education—the school communicating to parents but parents not involved in major decisions. Teachers' negative feelings about family rights are supported in research. For example, Gargiulo (1985) found some professionals not wanting to share responsibilities with families. Schulz (1987) stated that some professionals may even deny family members' knowledge about their own children. Vander Ven (1988) found that teacher perspectives are based on the teacher's stage of professional development. In the early stages of their professional life, teachers often view families from a somewhat deficit theory. Thus, in dealing with families, they tend to be authoritarian or paternalistic. With experience, teachers develop an awareness of the importance of working collaboratively with families. Similarly, family members' attitudes can undermine collaboration. For example, Kraft and Snell (1980) identified four types of such families: (a) the family member who constantly calls attention to the school's shortcomings, (b) the family member who takes no initiative, (c) the family member who abuses the teacher's time, and (d) the family member who claims that he or she has greater educational expertise than the professional.

Collaboration Is a Weak Component of Teacher Training. Family involvement is not a strong aspect of preservice teacher training. Staff members rarely have specialized training in working with families (Brand, 1996; Coleman & Churchill, 1997; Honig, 1996), although this situation is changing as a result of new standards in professional preparation. Training should aid staff members' sensitivity to all families' needs and develop their abilities to design ways to better meet those needs

(Alexander & Entwisle, 1988; Galinsky, 1987; D. Powell, 1989; D. Stevenson & Baker, 1987; H. Stevenson, Chen, & Uttal, 1990).

Meeting the Challenges of Collaboration

Although directors and staff members experience challenges in working with families, many of these problems may be overcome. Professionals must develop understandings about the sources of these differences and show as much acceptance for the variety of family views as they do for differences in children. Following are several suggestions:

1. Those working in early childhood programs need to be trained to work with families.

2. Staff members need to develop certain knowledge, skills, and attitudes about family involvement. Teachers often see families as clients who need redirection. Advice delivered in this way has never been effective (Henry, 2000). Many programs are changing their approaches. For example, High/Scope no longer provides "knowledge" to families but tries to deliver a climate respectful of diversity in family attitudes and beliefs (M. Hohmann & Weikart, 1995). See Table 10–1 for more specific information on the concepts, skills, and attitudes needed by teachers.

3. Program expectations should be realistic (J. Epstein, 2001). Families need many activities from which to choose (D. Stevenson & Baker, 1987; Workman & Gage, 1997). Contrary to some professionals' beliefs, most families want to help their children (Daniel, 1996). Families may not be able to participate in the traditional family activities, but many want to be involved. For example, families from lower and higher income groups may differ in the ways they are willing to be involved in their children's education. Higher socioeconomic families prefer individual conferences and volunteering (D. Stevenson & Baker, 1987), whereas lower socioeconomic families

prefer tutoring their children at home (Hoover-Dempsey, Bassler, & Brissie, 1987). Thus, programs should implement a family involvement component tailored to the needs of all families.

4. J. Epstein (2001) believes that family involvement is a developmental process that is built over time. Because involvement is developmental, directors of early childhood programs need to begin the process by developing a family involvement philosophy and determining specific goals and objectives. Developing a philosophy and specific goals and objectives helps to prevent activities from being disconnected (Davies, 1991; D. Powell, 1991). Coleman (1997) offered the following suggestions as possibilities: (a) reflect an understanding of and a respect for diversity, (b) assess the local family–program and teacher–family relations, (c) know what local families want for their children, (d) know how local community agencies are involved with families, and (e) evaluate the family involvement program.

5. Professionals need to learn to work with "difficult" families just as they work with "difficult" children. Families' judgments about the knowledge and skills of teachers are often based on "friendly communication" with teachers (Kontos, Howes, Shinn, & Galinsky, 1995). Professionals are most interested in communication focused on the child, but family members want communication focused on a broader range of topics, including the family (Elicker, Noppe, Noppe, & Fortner-Wood, 1997; D. Powell, 1998). Although the literature on techniques for working with these families is rather scarce, some effective techniques are discussed by Boutte, Keepler, Tyler, and Terry (1992). Families feel vulnerable and sensitive about their children, especially when the communication is negative. Professionals need to consider how bewildered families feel when their children are not achieving program goals or when their children have been diagnosed with disabilities.

6. Programs need to work for total support of families (discussed later in the chapter).

Table 10–1   Concepts, Skills, and Attitudes Needed by Teachers for Sensitive Family Involvement Programs

Teachers need to

—know more about the families they serve

Many variables affect the values and needs of families that in turn influence communication between teachers and families, such as home routines; home communication/instructional strategies; guidance values and techniques; expectations for children's self-help skills; children's important relationships, including grandparents and other extended-family guardians; community involvement; challenges that confront families as a result of socioeconomic status, racial/ethnic minority group, etc.; and stressors, including homelessness, joblessness, serious illness, death, divorce, single parenting, parenting special needs children, etc. (Murphy, 1997; Neuman, Hagedorn, Celano, & Daly, 1995; D. Powell, 1987b; 1991).

—know potential challenges to family involvement

Barriers may prevent full participation. (Refer to "Challenges of Working with Families.")

Parents need to know it is all right to choose *not* to be involved (Sciarra & Dorsey, 1998), although they should be encouraged to suggest ways they could possibly be involved.

—convey the similarities of goals

Both parents and teachers are committed to supporting the development of the child (J. Epstein, 1991; Stipek, Milburn, Clements, & Daniels, 1992). Both want the child's development to be addressed in the context of the family, the early childhood program, and the community (Comer & Haynes, 1991; Garbarino & Abramowitz, 1992; D. Powell, 1991; Zigler, 1989). J. Epstein (2001) described the following five types of mutually supportive endeavors: (a) child rearing and children's health and safety, (b) family–school communication, (c) parent participation, (d) support of children's learning, and (e) advocacy efforts to advance children's education and development.

Teachers need to be aware of what parents believe about early childhood development (Melmed, 1997).

Where goals of parents and teachers differ, they must be identified and reconciled by looking for options that meet the needs of both (Murphy 1997).

—convey the importance of the family

Parents must be convinced that they play *the* most important role in their children's lives. For example, the National Institute of Child Health and Human Development Study of Early Child Care found that parent relationships were a stronger predictor of children's development than the quantity and quality of care in early childhood programs ("Study Releases New Findings," 1997).

COLLABORATION WITHIN THE FAMILY CONTEXT

Early childhood programs are experiencing increased family involvement. This movement has occurred for several reasons. First, throughout the history of public education in the United States, citizens have professed and defended the benefits of community control over educational policy and decision making. Second, as discussed, collaboration benefits the program, the child,

and the family. Bronfenbrenner (1979) suggested that a setting's (e.g., home or school) developmental potential is improved when linkages exist between settings (e.g., homes and early childhood programs). Third, families as purchasers of children's services influence the type of care and education offered within the community.

Families want to be involved in early childhood programs (Daniel, 1996). They want program staff to show them how to get involved (J. Epstein & Sanders, 1998). Families are more likely to be involved if they believe the invitation for involvement is sincere, if the program climate shows respect and empathy for families, if the family–program relationship is inclusive (e.g., staff represents community diversity; children's home culture is incorporated into the curriculum), and if alternative ways of being involved are available (Coleman & Wallinga, 2000b; Hoover-Dempsey & Sandler, 1997).

Family–Staff Communication

Communication between family and staff members is necessary for the optimal development of the child and is thus associated with higher quality programs. Achieving optimal family–program communication is a challenge. These basic suggestions are important for staff members achieving effective communication:

1. Make yourself available for all families. Kontos and Dunn's (1989) study showed that mothers held in low esteem by teachers had fewer contacts with teachers than mothers held in high esteem. Program staff must be inclusive of families as well as children.

2. Match communication to the family's cultural and educational backgrounds but focus on each family, not on the "group" to which the family belongs. For example, staff members should talk in the family's primary language, use appropriate communication speed, avoid educational jargon, and use appropriate physical distance while talking face-to-face.

3. Promote comfortable exchanges. Staff members should be open and welcoming. In discussing a child's problem, state the issue using anecdotes to describe specifics, listen to the family's perspective, and respond in a professional way that is perceived as a team relationship.

4. Provide various communication channels. The best communication is individually directed and face-to-face rather than group directed and printed. However, families cannot always arrange for two-way communication. Thus, maximum re-

turns in the area of family–staff communication require the use of various information channels: conferences, home visits, and written communication; various ways of promoting dialogue, such as individual and small-group conferences, demonstrations, and formal programs; and plans for acting on the information received—that is, methods of adjusting the services of the program to fit the needs of the child.

Family Area. The family area should invite relaxed communication among families and between families and professionals. Such an area should be well defined and inviting, with adequate lighting and ventilation, comfortable chairs, and a place to write. Using **documentation panels** (presentation panels that represent children's learnings by showcasing their work, such as photos and samples of work, and that provide information linking children's achievements to program goals) are pleasant ways for families to learn about the program (Brown-DuPaul, Keyes, & Segatti, 2001). Helburn (1995) found that families often have no idea what children are experiencing in centers. Photos and bits of information on program families and staff members help develop a sense of community.

Family members appreciate materials with information about child development and about the early childhood program. Suggested materials include the following:

1. Periodicals published by organizations concerned with young children

2. Guidelines for helping families choose appropriate literature, toys, and other materials for young children

3. Suggestions for good movies, television programs, Internet sites or children's software, local events, and any community happenings designed for children, families, or both

4. Information about the program's services, basic schedule, names of staff members, special events, and vacation periods

5. Directions for making things, such as finger paint, flannel boards, and bulletin boards

6. Materials that serve as preparation for or follow-up to meetings with program staff

7. Information of concern to all families on childhood diseases, safety in the home and play areas, warnings on products used by children, and discipline and guidance. Free or inexpensive booklets can be secured from the American Red Cross, local pediatricians, and insurance companies.

In addition to the family area, a few family places can be incorporated into the children's activity room. For example, a bench or small couch in a couple of pleasant places in the room can provide a place for a family member to observe the program in action or participate in transitions between home and program with their child. Providing a snack or refreshments from time to time is also welcomed by many family members.

Spring or Autumn Orientation. Many early childhood programs, especially school-based programs, have an orientation meeting in the late spring or early autumn for families who will be enrolling children. This is an excellent means of establishing a cooperative relationship between families and staff. The purpose of the meeting is to orient families to the program's services and requirements for admission to the program and to the techniques they can use in preparing their children for entrance.

After greeting family members, a multimedia presentation of sample activities of the local program, an informal presentation of typical activities by currently enrolled children, or a video presentation of a program with a similar rationale (see videos distributed by the NAEYC or Educational Productions' *Kindergarten, Here I Come!*) gives families insight into the program. In some orientations, teachers may involve enrolling children in a few activities, such as a story, songs, or finger plays.

Admission requirements and other major policies should be briefly described and also provided in a written format (see appendix 8). For example, in school-based programs, families need information on food, transportation, supplies, and fee policies. Staff members need to show families how to mark supplies and send money to school.

Families, especially those with children enrolling in prekindergarten and kindergarten programs, want to know how to prepare the child for an early childhood program. They should be discouraged from engaging in a "crash course" of academic preparation because young children are less likely to gain long-lasting knowledge and may develop an unfavorable attitude toward learning. Teachers, however, must stress the importance of family involvement in their child's development and learnings. Families often like a list of activities (with simple teaching strategies) that can be done at home. Families should be given an opportunity to ask general questions (but should save questions concerning their child for one-on-one communication).

The meeting should last no longer than an hour. A social time following the meeting gives families a chance to visit with each other and with staff. A tour of the facility is appropriate during this time.

Family Member's First Individual Visit. For programs with continuous enrollment (e.g., child care centers), the first individual visit to an early childhood program is often to see the program firsthand and to register the child. The initial individual contact between the family and a staff member must go beyond the mechanics of registration, however. The family's first visit to the program's facility is a time of direct learning and impressions for both family and staff members.

Usually, the family member and child meet with the director, who conducts an interview. The family member should obtain from the director (a) an overview of the goals of the program, (b) an explanation of major policies, (c) application/

enrollment forms, and (d) receipts of required fees if the family member has made the decision to enroll the child. The director should obtain important information from the family member about the child. Hanhan (2003) called this an "intake interview." During the interview, the director can obtain (a) an impression of the relationship between the family member and the child, (b) an impression of how the child reacts to the new situation and how the family member feels about putting the child in the program, (c) a personal and social history of the child, and (d) the family member's impressions of the child's developmental strengths and weaknesses.

The director often gives the family member and child a tour of the facility and introduces them to the teacher. The family member and child should be invited to observe and even become involved in some of the activities. Observation and participation give the family member and child time to become comfortable in the setting and allow the teacher an opportunity to observe the family member and child informally.

Handbook for Families and Volunteers.   The major purposes of the handbook are to help the families become oriented to the program and to serve as a reference during the child's first year of enrollment. In planning a handbook, several points should be considered:

1. Information in the handbook should be consistent with the program's goals and policies.

Because goals and policies differ from program to program, the staff of each program must develop their own handbook.

2. At a minimum, the handbook should contain (a) an introduction to the goals and services of the program; (b) information about the program's policies that directly concern families, such as the days and hours of operation and fees; and (c) information on requirements that must be met before admission to the program. Other information the handbook might contain includes (a) the developmental characteristics of young children, (b) the ways families can help their children's development and learnings, (c) health and safety guidelines for young children, (d) the methods used to report children's progress, (e) a list of needed program supplies, (f) how families can be involved in the program, and (g) a calendar of program events (see appendix 8).

3. Before writing the handbook, the frequency of revision should be determined. If annual revisions are not planned, a minimum of variable information, such as names of staff members, fees, and hours of operation, should be included. Because much of the variable information is essential, blank spaces can be left in the handbook and completed in handwriting each year or easily revised on the computer. An example is shown in Figure 10–1. For partial revision, a plastic

Figure 10–1   **Handbook Style Written for Easy Revision**

Lunch Period

A hot lunch will be served in the cafeteria every day. It costs_____¢ a day, or you may pay $_____a week. (Checks may be made payable to _____.) If your child wishes to bring his or her lunch, milk will cost_____ ¢ a day. Those who wish to know whether their children qualify for free or reduced-cost lunches may secure forms in the central office.

spiral binding or a stapled handbook can be easily dismantled and reassembled.

4. Information in the handbook should be arranged logically. Having a table of contents, printing each section on a different color paper, and cutting each section longer or wider than the preceding section for a tab effect are ways to facilitate locating specific information.

5. Information in the handbook should be concise. The handbook is a reference—not a novel!

6. The writing should be in the primary language of and at the reading-skill level of families served by the program. The writing should be clear and free from educational terminology.

7. The handbook should be attractive and the writing style interesting. Various colors of paper, readable type, photographs, cartoons, or children's drawings help make it attractive. Writing style may vary.

8. In designing a handbook, costs must be considered. Because the handbook can become expensive, various printing techniques should be explored. Several estimates should be obtained. Computer-processed and printed material is cost effective and attractive if carefully word processed and if a laser printer is used.

9. The handbook can also be made available at a designated website.

Large-Group Meetings.   Although individual conferences are most common, large-group meetings are worthwhile, especially for programs not conducting orientation sessions. A popular type is the "get-acquainted" meeting. Unlike the spring or autumn orientation, the get-acquainted meeting is held a few weeks after the beginning of the term. For a get-acquainted meeting, the following guidelines should be followed:

1. **Send invitations to families.** If you include an RSVP, you can follow up on families who do not respond, perhaps by telephone for a personal touch. A night meeting is preferable to an afternoon one because it permits more working families to attend. Tuesdays, Wednesdays, and Thursdays are usually the best days for meetings, but check the community calendar before setting a date. Plan a meeting to last a maximum of 1 hour followed by a social period, or plan an easy "supper" followed by a conference. Child care services for the conference time almost always ensure a better turnout.

2. **Set the meeting date after you know the children.** A meeting after the program begins helps you associate family members with children.

3. **Arrange the room to show your program to best advantage.** For example, show the program's schedule, arrange materials and equipment around the room, and display some of the children's work.

4. **Make a specific outline of your presentation;** for example:

   a. After most of the guests have arrived, greet them as a group.

   b. Introduce other staff members.

   c. Briefly describe your background and the program's history and express confidence in the year ahead.

   d. Outline the purpose of the meeting. Explain that individual conferences will be scheduled and that family members can call anytime about their children.

   e. Explain the purposes of the program by using specific examples. An excellent way to communicate goals and activities is to take families through a typical day. A multimedia presentation of currently enrolled children engaged in activities is very effective. (All children must be shown in at least one activity.)

   f. Review the policies of the program. Families may be asked to bring their handbooks for reference.

g. Suggest ways families can help their children.

h. Have a short question-and-answer period, but remind families that particular concerns are discussed in individual conferences.

i. Invite families to have refreshments, to visit with each other, and to look around the facility. Thank them for coming.

In addition to being a get-acquainted meeting, a large-group meeting is an appropriate setting for explaining new policies and changes in previous policies, for introducing new program services, and for outlining and explaining new methods or curricular content. The large-group meeting is also an excellent medium for sampling families' opinions about and attitudes toward the program.

Special-Topic Meetings.   Families often have interests in certain topics. Articles, brochures, and videotapes are available from professional associations that provide quick, concise, down-to-earth messages for families on often-requested topics. (Some of these materials are sold in multiple copies at reasonable prices.) Program directors should assess needs by contacting family members about convenient times for meetings and about topics in which they are interested. Sometimes, directors compile a list of topics to consider but also encourage others to add their own topics to the list. Small committees of family members need to be involved in planning. Delgado-Gaitin (1991) offered many ideas for how the planning phase should be conducted.

Special-topic meetings may be for all families. If interests or needs vary considerably, however, directors should consider small-group meetings of three to six family members. The general topic is predetermined and announced. Some family members prefer to describe the situation in relation to their own children. A discussion follows among the families, with professionals providing some additional insight as suggestions are made. Another option for a special-topic, small-group meeting is to invite an authority to lead the discussion.

Many suggestions previously described for large-group conferences are appropriate for small-group meetings, such as a well-planned agenda with a total meeting time of 60 to 75 minutes, child care services, and refreshments. Small-group meetings have these advantages over large-group meetings: (a) They are easier to schedule because fewer families are involved, (b) they help those who feel uneasy in an individual or large-group meeting, and (c) they meet the special needs and interests of families and reassure families that others have similar concerns. The major disadvantage is to the director and other professionals, who have more of their own time invested, especially if the meetings are in the evenings or on weekends.

Scheduled Individual Conferences.   Individual family–staff conferences help families understand the program and how their child is developing. Scheduling conferences early in the program year will allow family participation in the planning and help avoid problems later (Neilson & Finkelstein, 1993). Although the conference setting may be informal, families can expect staff to discuss the program's goals and methodology in depth and how the child relates to the program. If questions or problems are not under the teachers' jurisdiction, teachers should direct families to appropriate channels. Many scheduled individual conferences concern the progress the child is making toward meeting his or her planned goals. Suggestions for preparing and conducting individual conferences are as follows:

1. Send out a brief newsletter explaining what individual conferences are, what families can contribute, and what teachers hope to accomplish as a result of the conferences. (It is not necessary to send a newsletter if information about scheduled individual conferences is included in the handbook, although a reminder is

important.) The point of the conferences is to share with families the ways teachers are helping children meet program goals and to elicit family concerns for their children. If certain topics are to be covered, inform the families. As noted in chapter 9, if a child's progress is the topic of the conference, the teacher should prepare a guide sheet before the conference.

2. Construct a schedule of appointments specifying conference times and inviting families to choose an appointment time. Appointments are never made back-to-back. Allow a few minutes' break between conferences to allow teachers time to jot down notes and prepare for the next conference. Although the example schedule is designed for 20-minute conferences, many teachers find 30 minutes minimal time to cover the purposes of the conference and to avoid an assembly-line appearance. If possible, schedule only a few conferences each day—perhaps some during the hour before the program opens and some in the late afternoon and evening (see Figure 10–2). Confirm the conference time.

3. Prepare your conference carefully. For example:

a. In your letter requesting family members to make appointments, explain whether they are to bring their enrolled child and other young children. If child care is provided, more families may be able to participate in individual conferences.

b. Provide an attractive, private place for the conference. The teacher should not sit behind a desk. It might be advantageous to hold the conference in one of the family members' homes rather than in the school. (Individual conferences with all families in one home are not to be confused with home visits.)

c. Provide early-arriving family members with a place to wait and have another employee or volunteer chat with them until the conference time. If no one can wait with them, provide professional or popular reading material.

d. Have a clear picture of the child in terms of the goals of the program. Also, list information to collect from family members; for example, you may want to obtain a developmental history of the child. Plan to elicit family members' concerns for the child early in the conference; E. Morgan (1989) has helpful insights into "reading" these concerns.

4. When conducting a conference, the following suggestions may help:

a. Greet family members cordially.

b. Explain what you are doing with and for the child. In talking about the child, use the child's portfolio. Point out strengths or positive areas first and then areas in which greater focus is needed.

c. Never put a family member on the defensive. A teacher needs to be aware of the attitudes a family member may take when the child is having problems so as not to respond argumentatively. Family members may blame the teacher or the program content or believe that their child is simply going through a stage. Family members can be especially unprepared to hear or accept the fact that their child needs special interventions. Abbott and Gold (1991) provided some suggestions that may apply in many difficult situations.

d. Use good communication techniques as previously described.

e. Do not expect to have an answer to every problem or expect family members to solve all problems. Decisions should be reached during the discussion by active listening, problem solving, and making arrangements to follow up. Follow-up is most important. If family members know they have your assistance, they will not feel helpless.

f. Practice professional ethics as stated in the *Code of Ethical Conduct and Statement of Commitment* (Feeney & Freeman, 1999).

Date _____

Let's get together and talk. I would like to discuss with you

1. Developmental gains _____   5. Sharing toys _____

2. Eating habits _____   6. General adjustment _____

3. Bathroom habits _____   7. _____

4. Crying _____

Please list below some of the things you would like to talk with me about.

_____

_____

Child care will be available to your enrolled child and younger children. Please indicate the day(s) and times(s) you could come for a 30-minute conference by circling one or more of the following time periods:

Oct. 7 Mon.	Oct. 8 Tues.	Oct. 9 Wed.	Oct. 10 Thurs.	Oct. 11 Fri.
6:30–7:00 a.m.	6:30–7:00 a.m.	6:30–7:00 a.m.	6:30–7:00 a.m.	6:30–7:00 a.m.
7:15–7:45 a.m.	7:15–7:45 a.m.	7:15–7:45 a.m.	7:15–7:45 a.m.	7:15–7:45 a.m.

8:00 a.m.–5:00 p.m. Program in session

5:00–5:30 p.m.	5:00–5:30 p.m.	5:00–5:30 p.m.	5:00–5:30 p.m.	5:00–5:30 p.m.
5:45–6:15 p.m.	5:45–6:15 p.m.	5:45–6:15 p.m.	5:45–6:15 p.m.	5:45–6:15 p.m.

If these times are inconvenient, please suggest a time or times. _____

_____

I will confirm a time for your appointment.

Sincerely,

_____

Figure 10–2   Invitation to Scheduled Individual Conference

g. Do not make family members feel rushed; however, in fairness to others who are waiting, conferences must end on schedule. If necessary, family members can make another appointment to continue the discussion.

5. Make notes on the conference and file them in the child's folder.

A new trend in family–teacher conferences is the "child–family member–teacher" conference. Young children are usually excluded from family–teacher conferences. Including children in conferences in which goals for their education are being determined is helpful in securing children's cooperation in meeting current goals for development. Children will also become increasingly skillful in self-assessment and decision making. For an excellent source that addresses the techniques of incorporating children in conferences, consult Shores and Grace (1998).

Informal Individual Conferences. Unlike scheduled individual conferences, which are usually staff initiated and noted on the program calendar, informal conferences may be initiated by a family member or professional and held when the need arises. These conferences should be encouraged for any number of reasons: (a) learning more about the program, (b) questioning the meaning of activities observed, or (c) discussing a present or foreseeable concern.

Most communication between family member and staff occurs at the transition points when children are dropped off and picked up. In some programs, however, the family members cannot identify a staff member with whom they have a significant relationship. If nonscheduled individual conferences are to be meaningful, one consistent person needs to reach out to families during transition times, and that person should receive training in family–staff communication.

If a professional initiates the conference to discuss a specific concern (and certainly, many conferences have been initiated for that reason

only!), the teacher and family member collaborate on ideas to solve the problem. Usually the procedure for collaboration involves the following:

1. Defining the concern and showing evidence to support statements
2. Agreeing on a goal
3. Gathering information about the problem and what has been done in the home or in other programs to solve (or attempt to solve) the problem
4. Enlisting help in resolving the problem

Excellent suggestions are given by O'Hanlon and Weiner-Davis (1989) and Manning and Schindler (1997). In discussing a sensitive issue or concern, concentrate only on the concern and use professional communication skills and ethics.

Home Visits.   Home visits have had a long history and are still a prevalent family–staff communication option in almost 100% of Head Start programs, 45% of school-based programs, 18% of not-for-profit programs, and 7% of for-profit programs (U.S. General Accounting Office, 1995). Home visits are conducted for various reasons, such as explaining the goals of the program, conducting an "intake interview," and educating family members. Home visits can promote quality programs for these reasons:

1. Professionals are seen as people who care enough about the child to visit the family.
2. The professional can learn a great deal about the home and community by simple observation.
3. Because family members often feel more comfortable in their own homes than at the program site, they may provide more information and discuss more of their concerns.
4. The child may find the transition to the new program easier if the teacher visits before his or her beginning day. In some programs, a family member takes a photograph of the

child and teacher together for the child to keep at home.

Home visits require careful planning. All visits must be prearranged for a mutually satisfactory time. (A few family members may not want to participate in home visits, and such a decision must be respected.) Teachers should call the home a day before the visit to see whether the previously scheduled time is still satisfactory. (Family members do not like to be surprised!)

Most home visits last about 1 hour. The first 5 to 10 minutes is a greeting time for family member(s), child, and teacher. The teacher and the child interact for another 20 to 30 minutes in the child's room or in a place suggested by the family. A parting "ritual" is preplanned, such as taking a few photographs, offering a small school gift to the child, or walking to the car together. Other practical suggestions are given in many sources (e.g., Fox-Barnett & Meyer, 1992; L. Johnston & Mermin, 1994).

Family Visitation. Family visitation of the program gives the family member the opportunity to observe the program and to see the child functioning with peers and adults. The staff member has the opportunity to observe adult–child interactions in the program setting and the family's expressed attitudes toward the program.

Family members should be encouraged to visit the program, although many families do not visit. Sending a special invitation often results in more visitations and may even initiate greater family involvement in the program. A sample invitation is shown in Figure 10–3. Family members should be made to feel welcome as observers or participants in activities even if they come unannounced.

During an open house, family members may view samples of the children's work (e.g., artwork, stories children have written, block structures they have built), examine equipment and materials, and visit with staff and other guests. The open house is held at a time when the program is not in session. An example of an invitation to an open house is shown in Figure 10–4.

Workshops. Workshops are a prevalent family involvement option in almost 100% of Head Start programs, 64% of school-based programs, 40% of not-for-profit programs, and 23% of for-profit programs (U.S. General Accounting Office, 1995). Workshops are great for more informal group communication among families and staff. The following are two common types:

1. Materials workshops in which adults and staff analyze instructional materials for concepts

Figure 10–3 Invitation for Program Visitation

Dear _____

    Your child has been in our program for 6 weeks and has made gains in development, such as sharing with friends, handling a long-handled paintbrush, building with large floor blocks, stringing tiny beads, listening to those wonderful real and pretend stories, and so many more things. Won't you please come and enjoy being part of our day? Your child will welcome the most special people in his life—you.

                        Sincerely,

                        _____
                        (Teacher's signature)

Figure 10–4   Open House
Invitation

Dear _____

    We are having an Open House on Thursday, October 24, at 7:30 p.m. Examples of your child's work will be on display. We hope you will come and see some of the things your child has done in school.
    We will be looking forward to visiting with you. Refreshments will be served in the auditorium.

                       Sincerely,

                     _____

                     (Staff member's signature)

---

and develop original equipment and materials for presenting these instructional concepts. Teachers should determine the types of activities families are willing to take part in and provide choices for families. Dodd and Brock (1994) provided many practical suggestions.

2. Workshops may also be held in the evening for repairing the building and grounds or equipment and materials.

Newsletters.   Newsletters are designed for helping family members communicate with their children about program activities, for meeting the developmental and learning needs of their children in the home setting (see Figure 10–5), and for developing a liaison between staff and families.

    Following is information that might be included in newsletters:

1. Announcements about the program or about daily or special activities in the program

2. Suggestions for home learning activities and methods that may be conducive to learning (Harms & Cryer, 1978)

Figure 10–5   Newsletter

Dear _____

    Television plays a big part in children's lives. Children enjoy watching television in their spare time. Of course, it is important that they do not stay glued to the television. Playing outdoors in the fresh air, visiting with friends, looking at books, and getting to bed early are important.
    Because many television shows are educational and enjoyable, television can be a wise use of some leisure time. Each week, I will send home a schedule of some shows from which your child might profit. Your child might tune in these programs if they are shown at a convenient time for your family.

                       Sincerely,

                     _____

                     (Teacher's signature)

---

3. Information on new books, play materials, Internet sites, and television programs for children

4. Reprints of articles to help family members

5. Announcements about community events

6. Ideas for summer fun

7. Future plans for the program

8. Updates on staff changes and profiles on staff and families

9. Notes of appreciation to family and community volunteers

Newsletters should be no longer than two pages. Like all written communication to family members, newsletters need to be in the primary language and reading-skill level of the family. Sharing information about good home and program practices must be very concise and clear. Diffily and Morrison (1997) offered 93 messages that may be copied or adapted for inclusion in newsletters. Newsletters are duplicated and sent to family members most often on a biweekly or monthly basis.

Telephone Conversations. Telephone conversations may be initiated by either a family member or a staff member. Families may use telephone conversations to help staff better understand the child during the day. Perhaps the child was sick during the night, is worried, or is excited. Some families may be more at ease talking over the telephone than in a face-to-face communication. Telephone conversations allow for quick, unplanned contacts.

Staff can use telephone conversations to make positive contacts, which can serve as pleasant events for the child, too. The following are examples of positive telephone contacts:

1. The staff member explains to the family member something interesting or successful the child did; the family member is then able to reinforce the child immediately.

2. The staff member can call to inquire about the health of family members or to congratulate a family member on the arrival of a new baby, a work promotion, or an honor.

Other Methods.   Several other methods aid family–staff communication. The following are some examples:

1. **Informal notes.** Notes are very effective and quick ways to communicate. Many varieties of notes are effective, such as the following:

a. A short note praising a child's effort, a "happy note," can be sent to the family member. An example is shown in Figure 10–6.

b. Families need thanks too. Show your appreciation when families support the goals of your program.

c. Because families want to share their children's days, a photograph of an activity with a note written on the back is enjoyed by any family member.

d. Stamp and Groves (1994) suggested an "Ask Me About" badge. These badges let families know their children have reached milestones, and they should ask their children about these important events.

e. Families know you care when you send cards or notes for children's birthdays or when family members are ill.

f. For families with e-mail service, informal notes may be sent. (Due to the lack of privacy, sensitive concerns or information considered personal should not be sent by e-mail.)

2. **Program website.** A website can list the program's goals, information on policies, a calendar, a newsletter, and e-mail addresses of staff members.

_____ was a good helper.
She helped a friend pick up the spilled pegs.

Figure 10–6   **"Happy Note"**

3. **Program videos.** Videos of program activities, including special events, can be shared with family members.

4. **Family bulletin boards.** Family bulletin boards can display children's work, general information on nurturing and educating children, notices of community and program events, and special achievements and events in the lives of family and staff members.

5. **Social events.** Social meetings, such as picnics for the whole family, adult/child breakfasts or going-home snacks, or a recognition event for volunteers, stimulate good relationships between families and staff.

Family Participation

Involvement with families includes family participation in the program. Family participation has had a long history. In parent cooperative programs, parents learned about child development through classroom involvement. Head Start called for parents to be involved as employees and volunteers and to serve on advisory councils. Like Head Start, some government-sponsored early intervention programs had parent involvement. More recently, programs serving children with disabilities require family involvement. Thus, most of the regular family participation occurs in not-for-profit centers, especially those receiving government support.

Regrettably, only just over half of all centers have family participation. Fathers are not as apt as mothers to be involved in early childhood programs (Fagan, 1994) except for the transporting of their children to and from the program (Atkinson, 1987). Studies seem to support the idea that early childhood programs should develop separate male-involvement programs (Cunningham, 1994; Fagan, 1994, 1996). Grandparents are becoming involved in early childhood programs; thus, many materials are being written on intergenerational programming (Seefeldt & Warman, 1990). The early childhood program must initiate and maintain programs that enlist the worthwhile services and resources of family members. Communication is linked to family participation; the more staff members communicate formally with family members, the more likely families will be to participate (Endsley, Minish, & Zhou, 1993).

Families as Members of Policy Advisory Committees and Boards of Directors. Many early childhood programs include families as members of planning and advisory groups. Some programs may operate under two boards—one at the program level and the other at the agency level if the program is part of a community service agency. The ultimate form of family participation occurs when family members serve on the board of directors. In Head Start, all parents of enrolled children are members of the Head Start Parent Committee. The committee meets to discuss issues relating to policy and curriculum. The committee elects parent representatives to the Head Start Policy Council, the governing body of the program. Parents may also be elected to serve as officers on Policy Councils at the local, state, and national levels. Most state licensing laws require that a not-for-profit, private early childhood organization operate under a governing board composed, at least in part, of the people it serves. Public school early childhood programs are under the jurisdiction of the local board of education or trustees, an elected policy-making group representing the community's interests.

Including family members in planning and advisory groups or on governing boards is in accordance with the democratic principles of citizens' rights and responsibilities in formulating public policy, works as a two-way public relations committee, and constitutes a partnership between professionals and families. For families to be effective members of planning and advisory groups, committees and councils must have the following characteristics:

1. The committee or council must be an educational group, not a pressure group. Although politically minded individuals may serve on

the committee or advisory council, their input should not necessarily be considered the thinking of the majority.

2. The director must show members of the committee or council how a decision will affect the program and make sure families have appropriate information on which to base their decisions. Families must then have input into the decision-making process because one cannot convince families to become involved if the most important decisions (those regarding the goals of the program, the program's delivery system, staffing policies, fiscal matters, and program evaluation) have already been made.

3. The family members and all other board members must be trained. Programs have failed because of problems at the committee or council level. Training must be given in identifying problems, investigating possible solutions, understanding regulations, learning decision-making processes, and communicating recommendations to the power structure.

4. The committee or council must be small enough to be manageable (12 or fewer members), and membership should be rotational.

Family Members as Volunteers. Family members can also participate as volunteers on a regular, semiregular, or occasional basis. Volunteering is a prevalent family involvement option in 88% of Head Start programs but is prevalent in only 45% of school-sponsored programs, 27% of not-for-profit programs, and 12% of for-profit programs serving prekindergarten children (U.S. General Accounting Office, 1995). Family members are more involved in social activities and fund-raising than as regular volunteers. For a volunteer program to work, the director must support it by providing general guidance in planning, although family members can organize and operate the program itself. In effective programs, all families are given a chance to participate, a choice of

roles, and the freedom to determine the extent of their participation. Some will choose not to participate.

Program and Support Program Volunteers. Family members are valuable as program volunteers because they (a) know and understand family members' working hours, transportation situations, and community mores; (b) can serve as cultural models for children; (c) help staff members understand children's likes and dislikes, strengths and weaknesses, and home successes and failures; (d) act as interpreters in bilingual programs; and (e) assist staff in program activities, such as storytelling, art, music, and gardening. As volunteers they also (a) assist in the positive guidance of children; (b) accompany staff members in home-visiting programs; and (c) serve as ambassadors to the neighborhood.

Specific expectations of volunteers should be determined by the program's needs and the volunteers' abilities. Some basic considerations are as follows:

1. Volunteers should have an orientation to the program's facility and staff, to professional ethics, and to state and local laws regarding personnel qualifications and activities. Orientation could include a broad overview of the program's goals, rules and regulations, specific tasks and limits of responsibility, classroom management (if involved with children), and a hands-on experience with materials. Volunteers' response to the orientation will benefit future programs.

2. Professionals should be oriented toward using volunteers. Teachers cannot delegate their responsibility of supervision of the children to volunteers. (The program is liable if a volunteer or child under a volunteer's supervision is injured.) After orientation, staff should be given a choice of whether or not to use volunteers.

3. A handbook is helpful for staff and volunteers, reiterating much of the information given during the orientation program.

4. Professionals should plan specific activities for volunteers. Greenberg (1989) reported that when volunteers are given menial jobs or are asked to perform tasks no one else wants to do, they may develop a negative attitude and become less involved. Teaching activities require careful planning. Teachers should set up the activities for the volunteers so that only a child or small group of children works with a volunteer at one time. Before demonstrating teaching techniques, a teacher should briefly explain the rationale for and the plan of the activity, the materials to be used, and the possible learnings. An effective way to plan is to develop a web showing possible tasks for volunteers (Coleman & Wallinga, 2000a).

5. Volunteers must be assessed by the director and should be encouraged to discuss their involvement.

Family members can also serve as support program volunteers, such as lunchroom workers, assistants to program nurses, assistants in the library/media center, assistants in distributing equipment and materials, workers in transportation services, office workers, and people who gather information on support services.

Occasional Volunteers. Many family members cannot serve as volunteers on a regular or even a semiregular basis; however, they often can and are willing to help on several occasions during the year. Family members can be very valuable as volunteers for special services. These special services can include the more traditional volunteer areas of field-trip supervisors, contributors to fund-raising projects, and assistants during special occasions (e.g., as a helper during class celebrations; or a greeter for an open house or family–teacher conferences). Also, volunteers can serve as resource persons representing various occupations and hobby groups. Staff should survey family members for their special talents and encourage them to share their talents with young children.

Parent Education and Family Resource and Support Programs

Parent education has had a long and exciting history (Berger, 2000). The child study movement of the early 1900s made child rearing a science. Parent education and home visitations began early in the century as a way to help immigrants. With the development of the progressive education movement, parent and lay programs, such as the child study movement, the Parent–Teacher Association, mental health associations, and parent cooperative nursery schools, developed during this period.

In the 1960s, the shift of emphasis was away from the middle class. Lower-class children were seen as needing better parenting. Almost all early intervention programs of the 1960s and 1970s had a parent education component. Parents were educated in child development and in their role as their child's primary teacher who needed to collaborate with the early childhood program or school. A major movement toward family resource and support programs began in the 1980s. Family resource and support services differ from the more traditional education programs in that they offer a wide array of services and thus serve as a support system for families rather than as a change agent, and they work to prevent problems rather than repair damage in family–child relations.

Purposes of Parent Education and Family Resource and Support Programs. The basic assumption of parent education is that if the parent's role as a teacher is enhanced, the parent will be able to maximize the child's level of functioning. Studies support the idea that a positive self-image as a parent leads to confidence in the parent-educator role (Swick, 1987). Thus, specific purposes of parent education are as follows:

1. To become more positive about oneself as a change agent within the family.

2. To learn more about child growth and development.

3. To develop general concepts of effective child-rearing practices.

4. To acquire an understanding of the local early childhood program's rationale, program content and methodology, and support services.

5. To become an important part of the educative process by expressing positive attitudes about the program and staff and about education in general, by reinforcing the child's achievement, by providing continuity between activities at home and activities in the program, and by extending the child's knowledge and skills.

Family resources and support programs grew as a result of research of the importance of the family's influence on children's development and the success of parent education and self-improvement programs (Davies, 1991). The U.S. Department of Education (1994) encouraged family resource and support programs in its paper, *Strong Families, Strong Schools: Building a Community Partnership for Learning.* Unlike the more traditional programs, family resource and support programs are based on the following premises: (a) The validity of a variety of child-rearing styles and of the significance of the contexts (e.g., community and special relations) in which families are embedded should be recognized and accepted, and (b) adult behaviors do not affect children in a unilateral way (Weissbourd, 1983). Most of these ideas are similar to Gage and Workman's (1994) family strengths model, which is based on the following beliefs:

1. Because the family is the most important institution for the growth and development of children, the home should have access to the resources that foster children's development.

2. The family is the best determiner of its own needs.

3. Family support is a shared responsibility among family, early childhood program, and community.

4. Activities are designed to help family members recognize their own strengths and resolve their own problems.

Types of Parent Education and Family Resource and Support Programs. Parent education and family resource and support programs are of many types (J. Epstein, 2001; National PTA, 2000). Their nature depends on program needs, family needs and wishes, and program goals. Techniques may vary as well. Services for families may be either staff directed or family initiated; they may have one focus or be multifaceted; and they may be direct, using organized classrooms, or indirect, with family members observing teaching and guidance techniques during program visitations. Programs may be sponsored by school systems, universities, or various community agencies or be handled through a cooperative, interagency approach.

Orientation Programs. Perhaps the most common service offered to parents of children enrolled in an early childhood program is orientation—through handbooks, newsletters, and meetings. Orientation programs are designed by the staff in local programs.

Home-Visiting Programs. Home-visiting programs were designed to help family members learn how to teach their young children, including how to prepare and collect educational materials. The exact nature of home-visiting programs depends on the program objectives, the number of families to be visited, the number and frequency of visits per family, and the program's financial resources (refer to chapter 1).

Family Discussion Groups. The basic goals of family discussion groups are to define the role of families in child development, extend family members' knowledge and understanding of the needs of children, and clarify misconceptions about the functions of child rearing. Structured discussion programs, such as T. Gordon's (1970) *Parent Effectiveness Training* and Dinkmeyer and McKay's (1976) *Systematic Training for Effective*

Parenting, were very popular parent education approaches. Unstructured parent discussion groups, in which family members identify an area of concern and a knowledgeable resource person leads the discussion group, also became popular. Peer support groups emerged among families of children with disabilities. Today, parenting seminars, online discussion groups, and family support groups are popular.

Resource Centers. A common type of resource center for children is the toy-lending library designed to develop concepts and verbal fluency in young children. Such libraries offer guidelines in using toys and thus help families provide intellectual stimulation for their children. These resource centers were originally established as part of the compensatory education programs of the 1960s and 1970s (Nimnicht & Brown, 1972). Adult resource centers have also been used for providing child-rearing information. Today, resource centers for children and adults are seen in some public libraries and as part of some comprehensive early childhood programs.

Self-Improvement Programs. Self-improvement programs were designed to empower adult family members as individuals to improve their own lives. Services may include instruction for family self-improvement in the areas of basic adult education, English for speakers of other languages, consumer education, nutrition, clothing, health, community resources, home repairs, and family life. Such instruction may be in the form of formal courses for high school credit or informal workshops and are usually offered by the public school system for the benefit of all adult residents of a community.

Family Resource and Support Programs. Family resource and support programs are for all families. To be effective, however, the services must be individualized to support different stages in the family life cycle and to meet other concerns (e.g., work/family issues, family crises). Services could include the following:

1. Programs for children, including a home-visiting program, a home-care program, and a center-based program

2. Programs for adults in such areas as family and consumer sciences, child development, adult education, and job counseling

3. Health and nutrition services, including medical services for children and adult family members and classes in child care, safety, and nutrition

4. Social services, such as referral, recreational, and assistance in finding adequate housing and in providing food and clothing

Gage and Workman (1994) provided an example of a menu of support services and family involvement activities from which families may choose.

COLLABORATION WITHIN THE COMMUNITY CONTEXT

Communities have always played an important role in the support of families and educational programs in the United States. Demographic and social factors, such as population growth, diversity within communities, mobility of families, and fewer extended families, have diminished the feeling of community. Because our society has become fast-changing and turbulent, collaboration within the local community is seen as crucial for both families and early childhood programs (NAEYC, 1994b).

Early childhood professionals may hold an important key to community support through collaboration because they see families regularly over long periods of time and are knowledgeable of and visible within the community. Early childhood professionals can serve as advocates and service brokers for meeting family needs for economic assistance (e.g., TANF, child welfare services, subsidized child care), child health services (e.g., Medicaid, nutrition programs, local health services), and special child care needs (e.g., Head Start, family violence prevention and treatment, adoption and foster care, homeless services; Allen, Brown & Finlay, 1992).

Early childhood programs need community support, too. As noted in chapter 1, many business leaders are seeing the need for employer-supported child care for their employees and for quality education for children as the basis for maintaining a competitive workforce for the future. Recently, community support of early childhood programs in other nations is influencing U.S. programs, such as the principle of local community support (*gestione sociale*) in the work of the Reggio Emilia schools (C. Edwards, Gandini, & Forman, 1998).

Kirst (1991) called for a complete overhaul of family services. The combined efforts of all agencies that work for families would prevent the fragmentation of services and lead to a cumulative impact on families (Kagan, 1994a; C. Stone, 1995).

TRENDS AND ISSUES

Family and community involvement has had a long history in early childhood education. Yet, the field lacks a consensus on the meaning of *family involvement,* which often results in disconnected program activities (Coleman & Churchill, 1997) and less than effective results (Gomby, Culross, & Behrman, 1999; K. White, Taylor, & Moss, 1992). The accumulation of research in parent education, the primary way of working with families until the 1970s, and the ecological views of Bronfenbrenner (1979) held that children could not be viewed separately from their families. Although many farsighted professionals had long held this view, family involvement became more widely accepted. Recently, early childhood professionals began to respond to even greater demographic changes, such as (a) society's becoming more culturally diverse, (b) a changing workforce in which mothers of infants and toddlers are the fastest growing segment, and (c) a changing family and community structure in

which mutual support within and among families is often lacking. Early childhood professionals began to recognize that both the child and the family are consumers of early childhood care and education and of various related services. Thus the terms *partnership* and *collaboration* became the watchwords of the 1990s. In fact, among professionals, the term *early childhood education* has a collective meaning that includes not only the care and education of young children but also programmatic attention to families' needs and goals. However, in practice, with the exception of government-sponsored programs, early childhood programs rarely involve families beyond occasional meetings and scheduled conferences (U.S. General Accounting Office, 1995; Lynn, 1997), and family involvement is not a major component of program evaluation (Raab & Dunst, 1997).

Evidence continues to mount that families need interventions that go beyond parenting skills (Cowan, Powell, & Cowan, 1998). Programs with a family and child component, called **family-centered models,** seem to be the most successful in achieving long-term developmental and learning gains for children from low-income families (Yoshikawa, 1995), especially if adult family members perceive that they and their children need help (D. Olds, Henderson, Kitzman, Eckenrode, Cole, & Tatelbaum, 1999). Table 10–2 presents an outline of the principles and components of these collaborative efforts. Some programs with integrated services are Early Head Start, Head Start, and Even Start. Besides these federally funded programs, other models are under way in local communities and states.

SUMMARY

Working with families has had a long history in early childhood education. The early kindergartens and nursery schools had parent education as one of their program services. Early child-

◆ **Table 10–2   Family-Centered Models**

Principles Underlying Model	Components of Programs
Families are viewed within their community contexts, which promote or curtail family strength.	Target the overall development of parents as individuals by contexts acknowledging all their roles and responsibilities and by encouraging and providing empathic and many supportive relationships with other adults.
Parents are seen as individuals with roles and responsibilities in which child rearing is only one role.	
The parent–child relationship is influenced by parenting knowledge but, more important, by parent self-esteem, family background, socioeconomic status and other cultural factors, and the community setting.	See the parent–child relationship (rather than the child) as the primary client of the program and thus work to strengthen this enduring relationship.
A specific event that influences any member of the family has some effect on the family system.	Seek full collaboration with parents in planning and policy making and take a "facilitator" professional role rather than "expert" professional role in the collaborative process.
	Offer comprehensive services or provide community links to those needing services.

hood kindergartens and primary grades (levels) housed in the public schools became more involved in communicating with families and having them occasionally assist in the classroom than in having them as close allies in the educative process. By the 1960s, however, researchers involved in the early intervention programs found that an involvement and education program component, in addition to children's services, was necessary for maximum benefits to the child. Since the 1980s, the movement has been toward family resource and support programs that serve not as agents of family change but rather as a support system for preventing problems while accepting family diversity.

Even greater demographic and social changes occurred in the 1990s. Partnership and collaborative views altered the more traditional views of working with parents. Programmatic attention is now being given to the entire family's needs. To meet each family's needs, supportive efforts and resources are shaped collaboratively (among professionals and family members) and are met through family-centered programs and other

linkages to community resources. However, these family-centered models are not common among early childhood programs.

FOR FURTHER READING

Barbour, C., & Barbour, N. H. (2001). *Families, schools, and communities: Building partnerships for educating children* (2nd ed.). Upper Saddle River, NJ: Merrill/Prentice Hall.

Coleman, M. (1997). Families and schools: In search of common ground. *Young Children, 52*(5), 14–21.

Coleman, M., & Churchill, S. (1997). Challenges to family involvement. *Childhood Education, 73,* 144–148.

Cryer, D., & Burchinal, M. (1997). Parents as child care consumers. *Early Childhood Research Quarterly, 12,* 35–58.

Diffily, P., & Morrison, K. (Eds.). (1996). *Family-friendly communication for early childhood programs.* Washington, DC: National Association for the Education of Young Children.

Epstein, J. L. (1995). School/family/community partnerships: Caring for the children we share. *Phi Delta Kappan, 76,* 701–712.

Epstein, J. L. (2001). *School, family and community partnerships: Preparing educators and improving schools.* Boulder, CO: Westview Press.

Epstein, J. L., Coates, L., Salinas, K. C., Sanders, M. G., & Simon, B. S. (1997). *School, family, and community partnerships: Your handbook for action.* Thousand Oaks, CA: Sage.

Feinberg, W., & Soltis, J. (1998). *School and society* (3rd ed.). New York: Teachers College Press.

Flynn, L., & Wilson, P. (1998). Partnerships with family members: What about fathers? *Young Exceptional Children, 2*(1), 21–28.

Henderson, A. T., & Berla, N. (Eds.). (1994). *A new generation of evidence: The family is critical to student achievement.* Washington, DC: Center for Law and Education.

Hoover-Dempsey, K. B., & Sandler, H. M. (1997). Why do parents become involved in their children's education? *Review of Educational Research, 67,* 3–42.

Knapp, M. S. (1995). How shall we study comprehensive, collaborative services for children and families? *Educational Researcher, 24,* 5–16.

Levine, J., Murphy, D., & Wilson, S. (1993). *Getting men involved: Strategies for early childhood programs.* New York: Scholastic.

Levine, J., & Pitt, E. (1995). *New expectations: Community strategies for responsible fatherhood.* New York: Families and Work Institute.

Lynn, L. (1997). Teaching teachers to work with families. *The Harvard Education Letter, 13*(5), 7–8.

McLane, M. L. (1995). *A model handbook for child care administrators to increase parent involvement.* Fort Lauderdale, FL: Nova Southeastern University.

Melaville, A. I., Blank, M. S., & Asayesh, G. (1993). *Together we can: A guide for crafting a profamily system of education and human services.* Washington, DC: U.S. Government Printing Office.

National Association for the Education of Young Children. (1994). *Principles to link by: Integrated services systems that are community-based and school-linked.* Washington, DC: Author.

National PTA. (2000). *Building successful partnerships: A guide for developing parent and family involvement programs.* Indianapolis: National Educational Service.

Powell, D. R., & Diamond, K. E. (1995). Approaches to parent-teacher relationships in U.S. early childhood programs during the twentieth century. *Journal of Education, 177,* 71–94.

Ryan, B. A., Adams, G. R., Bullotta, T. P., Weissberg, R. P., & Hampton, R. L. (Eds.). *The family-school connection: Theory, research, and practice.* Thousand Oaks, CA: Sage.

Swap, S. M. (1993). *Developing home–school partnerships: From concepts to practice.* New York: Teachers College Press.

Swick, K. J. (1991). *Teacher–parent partnerships to enhance school success in early childhood education.* Washington, DC: National Education Association and the Southern Early Childhood Association.

Washington, V., Johnson, V., & McCracken, J. (1995). *Grassroots success: Preparing schools and families for each other.* Washington, DC: National Association for the Education of Young Children.

Family Diversity

Gonzalez-Mena, J. (2000). *Multicultural issues in child care* (3rd ed.). Mountain View, CA: Mayfield.

Lock, D. (1998). *Increasing multicultural understanding.* Thousand Oaks, CA: Sage.

Lynch, E., & Hanson, M. J. (Eds.). (1998). *Developing cross-cultural competence: A guide for working with children and their families* (2nd ed.). Baltimore: Brookes.

Nieto, S. (2002). *Language, culture, and teaching: Critical perspectives for a new century.* Mahwah, NJ: Erlbaum.

O'Shea, D. J., O'Shea, L. J., Algozzine, R., & Hammittee, D. J. (2001). *Families and teachers of individuals with disabilities: Collaborative orientations and responsive practices.* Boston: Allyn & Bacon.

Sturm, C. (1997). Creating parent-teacher dialogue: Intercultural communication in child care. *Young Children, 52*(5), 34–38.

Turnbull, A. P., & Turnbull, H. R. (2001). *Families, professionals, and exceptionality: A special partnership* (4th ed.). Upper Saddle River, NJ: Merrill/Prentice Hall.

Organizations Supporting Collaboration

Alliance for Parental Involvement in Education
www.croton.com/allpie

Center on Families, Communities, Schools and Children's Learning (Johns Hopkins University)
www.jhu.edu/news_info/educate/experts/epstein

Family Support America (formerly Family Resource Coalition of America)
  www.familysupportamerica.org

Institute for Responsive Education
  www.responsiveeducation.org

National Coalition for Parent Involvement in Education
  www.ncpie.org

National Parent Teacher Association
  www.pta.org

Parents as Teachers National Center
  www.patnc.org

Partnership for Family Involvement in Education
  http://pfie.ed.gov/

TO REFLECT

1. Allan (1997) referred to the imaginary line that still separates schools and families and prevents families from truly participating in the school lives of their children. What is the symbolism inherent in that demarcation? How do professionals make hard-drawn lines even in subtle ways? How can we recognize and erase these barriers?

2. How can we decide when it is appropriate for families to have "the" say in policy decisions and when the director or board should have "the" say? How might staff members respect the delicate balance of shared family–program responsibilities?

3. Families often bring their own adult concerns (e.g., divorce, stress of being a single parent, financial problems) into formal and informal family–teacher conferences. As a director, how would you advise your teachers to address such concerns?

4. One of the most difficult situations for directors in working with families is dealing with families who do not believe they have the time, abilities and skills, or interests to help their children. When families lack confidence in their child-rearing roles, how does the program build on their strengths? Can all families be empowered? Can cooperation be defined in different ways to accommodate different family-life pressures?

Contributing
to the Profession

The role of the early childhood administrator, regardless of the official title, is one of leadership. As a leader, the administrator must be concerned with the quality of early childhood care and education. The concern for quality must go beyond the local program to an interest in the overall excellence of early childhood programs. Consequently, administrators as leaders can contribute to their profession by promoting the professionalization of early childhood education, engaging in informed advocacy, becoming involved in research, and helping others find a place in the profession.

PROMOTING PROFESSIONALIZATION

"*Professionalization* refers to the public recognition of and demand for a specialized service that can only be provided by some people prepared to do it" (Vander Ven, 1988, p. 138). Professionalization is also seen as a dynamic process in which an occupation can be observed to change certain crucial characteristics in the direction of a profession (Vollmer & Mills, 1966).

The word **profession** is defined in terms of certain occupational characteristics, such as the following (D. Thompson, 1984):

1. Having an existing knowledge base

2. Focusing on service

3. Performing a unique function for clients and society

4. Having a monopoly of knowledge in the field

5. Internally determining standards of education and training

6. Having professional practice recognized by some form of license or certification

7. Shaping most legislation of the profession by the profession

8. Gaining in power, prestige, and income

9. Identifying with the profession individually and as a group through a national association

10. Seeing the profession as a lifelong occupation

Gratz and Boulton (1996) described the dynamic process of moving from an occupation to a profession by using Erikson's eight stages. For example, a profession in its infancy gains trust by the "provision of adequate resources, adequate preparation, and a body of appropriate knowledge" (p. 74), and during its mature years, generativity of a profession is marked by the "impetus for developing new professional leadership, fostering new ideas, and expanding the field's body of knowledge" (p. 77).

Early childhood care and education has many barriers that keep the field from being recognized as a profession. B. Caldwell (1990) stated that the early childhood education field suffers from a lack of conceptual clarity and standard terminology. She identified five issues critical to the professional identity of early childhood care and education: to determine (a) "just what we do" (p. 3), (b) "what we cannot (or should not) do" (p. 3), (c) "how we should do that which we do" (p. 4), (d) "where we should do what we do" (p. 4), and (e) "how we communicate what we do" (p. 5). Bredekamp (1992) articulated the following barriers:

1. The field has a diverse system of regulation. With 50 teacher licensure/certification programs and 50 state child care licensing codes as well as other regulations, professional preparation is difficult to regulate.

2. Preparation programs at various institutions differ.

3. Early childhood is not a viable career option for many because of the low compensation.

4. A dilemma exists between being exclusive (keeping out unqualified persons) and being inclusive (ensuring persons access to the field although they come from diverse backgrounds).

Professionals

Professions have **professionals** who practice or conform to the technical and ethical standards of the profession. When a field is not totally recognized as a profession, determining who is included (and also excluded) as a professional is difficult. G. Morgan (1995) stated that we are comfortable using *professional* as an adjective (e.g., professional preparation, professional organization) but find it difficult to use as a noun. G. Morgan defined an **early childhood professional** as "anyone who is working and learning with young children and/or their parents and who is on a professional path toward deeper commitment and further learning" (pp. 24–25). She clarified her definition by saying that the definition is appropriate only if the field meets these and other "only ifs" (a term used by Morgan): (the field) is free from bias, welcomes diversity, and attracts generalists; uses a broad knowledge base that meets the needs of all practitioners; involves lifelong and challenging learning suited to the work of the practitioner; and views parents as colleagues. Similarly, the NAEYC stated that the early childhood field includes anyone engaged in services to young children and that the early childhood profession includes anyone who has acquired some professional knowledge and is on a professional development path (NAEYC, 1994a). Morgan(2000b) thinks the terms *professions* and *professional* are being associated with the terms *"dedicated, committed, expert, businesslike"* (p. 141).

Professionalism

For a profession to render services, **professionalism** is required. In early childhood care and education, professionalism involves the use of professional knowledge and skills to meet the needs of children and families and collaborate with community agencies and other professional groups. More specifically, professionalism involves knowledge and skills that are goal oriented and intended to achieve specific outcomes, adhere to a high standard of performance, and require informed judgment to apply effectively (Katz, 1984a). In an attempt to overcome the barriers to professionalism in early childhood care and education, two avenues have been especially pursued: professional development and the adoption of a code of ethics.

Professionalism and Professional Development. The NAEYC believes that the main route to professionalism is to develop an articulated professional development system. The NAEYC formalized its quest for professionalization of the field by launching the National Institute for Early Childhood Professional Development in 1991. A career lattice was used to symbolize the roles and settings within the profession and the preparation required for persons working in each given role or setting (J. Johnson & McCracken, 1994). Certainly all professionals believe in professional development and a commitment to the field. However, not all professionals agree with the ideas associated with career ladders and lattices as discussed in chapter 4. Professionalism is also seen as one of the outcomes of early childhood preparation programs at the associate, baccalaureate, and advanced levels and as one of the outcomes for the professional preparation of special educators (NAEYC, 1996a). Furthermore, the Child Development Associate credential's sixth goal is "to maintain a commitment to professionalism" (Council for Early Childhood Professional Recognition, 1997, p. 3).

Quality in-service activities also promote professionalism. P. Bloom, Sheerer, and Britz (1991) described an individual's professional orientation as a commitment to the field of early childhood education and as a desire to grow and change. They designed an assessment tool to measure an individual's professional orientation (see P. Bloom, Sheerer, & Britz, pp. 242–243). This tool can be used in the hiring process and for ascertaining professional growth after hiring by comparing the baseline score (at the point of hiring) with increases in scores.

Professionalism and a Code of Ethics.   A **code of ethics,** a statement of professional conduct, is another sign of a mature profession. Practitioners share a code of ethics highlighting proper relations and responsibilities to each other and to clients or others outside the profession. Codes of ethics are simply collectively agreed upon guidelines for professionals to use in their decision making and actions with others when ethical issues are involved. Because these documents often do not hold a legal status, individuals who fail to conform rarely face legal or professional sanctions. Thus, in some professions codes of ethics are being replaced by customer-protection measures (G. Morgan 2000b).

Ethical literacy is critical for the professional. This literacy involves identifying ethical issues (i.e., knowing the difference between ethical and other types of judgments), carrying out ethical decision making by applying certain skills and strategies to ethical dilemmas, and engaging in ethical conduct (Nash, 1996).

The issue of early childhood care and education professional ethics was raised with the NAEYC members. The 1985 survey was funded by the NAEYC and the Wallace Alexander Gerbode Foundation. Feeney and Kipnis (1985) stated that the survey showed that early childhood educators were in "ethical pain." Ninety-three percent of all respondents (and 100% of specialists) agreed or strongly agreed that attention to ethical issues and the development of a code of ethics should be an important priority in the field. Data also showed that relationships with parents and with staff and administrators are the areas of greatest concern among early childhood educators. The major ethical problems reported were unprofessional behavior, information management, child abuse and neglect, and referrals to outside agencies (Feeney & Sysko, 1986). The *Code of Ethical Conduct and Statement of Commitment* was adopted in 1989 (Feeney & Kipnis, 1989) and revised in 1992 (Feeney & Kipnis, 1992) and again in 1997 (Feeney & Kipnis, 1998). The adopted code of ethics sets forth professional re-sponsibilities in four areas of professional relationships: children, families, colleagues, and community and society. A proposed addendum to the code concerning ethics and the early childhood teacher educator was proposed by Freeman, Feeney, and Moravcik (2003). The Ethics Commission decided that the code should be "encouraged" rather than "enforced" at this time, should be incorporated into the ongoing projects of the association, and should be reviewed at regular intervals (Feeney, 1990).

Skill development is involved in learning to translate a code of ethics into professional action (Freeman & Brown, 1996; Jacob-Timm & Hartshorne, 1998). Brophy-Herb, Kostelnick, and Stein (2001) proposed a model for teaching about ethics using the NAEYC code. Many professional materials are available (Feeney & Freeman, 1999; Feeney, Freeman, & Moravick, 2000).

ENGAGING IN INFORMED ADVOCACY

Advocacy is supporting, speaking for, and taking action on causes for children and their families and for the profession. *The Code of Ethical Conduct and Statement of Commitment* includes advocacy as part of professionalism when it states: "Because the larger society has a measure of responsibility for the welfare and protection of children, and because of our specialized expertise in child development, we acknowledge our obligation to serve as a voice for children everywhere" (Feeney & Kipnis, 1998, p. 6).

Advocacy may be classified in several ways:

1. **Case advocacy** refers to a situation in which a particular child or family is not receiving services or benefits for which it is eligible. The advocate takes the necessary steps to right the situation. Sometimes case advocacy is also called *personal advocacy.*

2. **Class advocacy** involves more than an isolated incident; rather, it is advocacy on behalf

of a group—migrants, people with disabilities, or minority groups. Class advocacy is needed because decisions far removed from the daily lives of young children and their families have profound effects on them. These decisions may be made by a local school board or corporation or by a state or federal agency. Class advocacy can be subdivided as follows:

a. **Public policy advocacy** involves influencing public policies and practices. These advocates challenge those who receive public funds and who develop laws, regulation, and policies for the use of these funds.

b. **Private-sector advocacy** involves private-sector policies and practices. These advocates challenge business leaders who implement policies affecting families' well-being (e.g., family leave policies; employer-supported child care) or who invest in goods and services for children.

Advocacy may be viewed as taking an immediate action (e.g., lobbying on behalf of specific legislation or a particular regulation, building a coalition around a specific focus) or as setting goals for later initiatives (e.g., networks publicizing needs, demonstrating the cost-effectiveness of specific programs, contributing to political action campaigns, and voting for candidates concerned about children).

Advocacy for children and their families has had a long history. The federal government recognized the importance of advocacy with the establishment of the Children's Bureau within the U.S. Department of Health and Human Services' Administration for Children and Families and with the establishment of a Center for Child Advocacy within the Office of Child Development. The private sector has been involved in advocacy, too; for example, the Center for the Study of Public Policies for Young Children, a part of the High/Scope Educational Research Foundation, was founded by the Carnegie Corporation of New York. Many professional organizations have a long history of advocacy efforts, such as the CWLA, the National PTA, the CDF, the NAEYC, the National Association for Child Care Resource and Referral Agencies, and the Child Care Action Campaign (see appendix 5). Today, not only are advocacy efforts increasing, but also training for public policy and advocacy is on the rise. Advocacy is a vital component of professional preparation (NAEYC, 2001). Workshop training and materials on advocacy are provided by various professional associations.

Eliminating Problems in Advocacy

Advocacy involves getting the right connection between the advocate and the policy maker. Sometimes connections are not made because of shortcomings within the profession and a lack of training for the roles involved in advocacy.

One shortcoming of the profession seems to be a focus on conflicting ideologies within the field. In some cases, conflicting ideologies have prevented a united effort on behalf of children and their families (Thornburg, 2001). Furthermore, inconsistent and confusing terminology, a reflection of inconsistent ideologies, causes problems in describing our profession and its components (Hyson, 2001); thus, policy makers and practitioners have a difficult time communicating.

Early childhood care and education professionals must move away from an apolitical stance (Silin, 1988). Being politically aware produces many benefits, such as informing the government about needs and knowing the issues that are emerging. The United States is the only major industrialized nation without a specific child care policy. According to Goffin (1988), certain societal assumptions have hindered our responsiveness to young children and their families. We must be politically smart (i.e., know the political climate) and embed our issues within a bigger context. For example, Head Start and other publicly funded intervention programs of the 1960s were embedded in the War on Poverty.

Kagan (2000a) stated that we need to present a clear vision. She pointed out that we often begin programs without assessing their impact on existing services and that we often approach policy makers without all the specifics.

Networking with other professionals increases support for the profession (Levine, 1992). Change more often occurs when a position is supported by several professional groups rather than one group (Ellison & Barbour, 1992).

Many professionals shy away from advocacy because they see it as a role for gifted leaders. Certainly, gifted leaders are needed, but each individual concerned about young children and their families may assume one or several roles in influencing public policy. A. Robinson and Stark (2002) described several roles in advocacy, such as advisors, researchers, contributors, and friends.

Becoming an Effective Advocate

Advocacy requires the highest level of leadership. Blank (1997) described the following leadership characteristics:

1. Having a long-term plan
2. Reaching beyond the early childhood care and education community
3. Finding opportunities to move the issue forward
4. Making use of supportive data
5. Developing new advocacy approaches
6. Deciding on the priorities of many worthy issues
7. "Hanging tough" but knowing when to compromise
8. Supporting new leaders

Muenchow (1997) added the following requirements to effective advocacy: (a) knowing the governmental process including budgeting, (b) matching the argument with the audience,

and (c) choosing the right messenger and making the message personal (e.g., parents as storytellers of needs). A. Robinson and Stark (2002) stated that advocates need to know how to use and prepare materials for advocacy. Position statements can be used in preparing for legislative testimony and for developing a **briefing paper** (a paper that describes one problem, proposes desired policy, and gives an example of how the policy works in another location). Other major materials that are frequently prepared are **key facts** (a one- or two-sided page listing important facts) and **action alerts** (which include requests for immediate action on an issue, a statement of why the action is needed, and a detailed description of what action is needed).

BECOMING INVOLVED IN RESEARCH

Often early childhood professionals see themselves concerned with practice rather than with theory and research (Almy, 1988). This raises a question about whether the early childhood field meets one of the criteria for professionalism (Silin, 1988). Although advances in education lag behind those in other professions in which research occupies a position of major importance (e.g., medicine), research is now recognized as a major way to effect improvements in education. Without research being considered vital to all factors influencing the profession, practitioners are less likely to influence others (Almy, 1988). Research contributes to the impetus to make needed changes or to reaffirm past decisions. Research can influence the design of social policy; for example, research on Head Start changed public policy. Research findings give credibility to issues (Goffin & Lombardi, 1988). Research can influence practical program actions, staff development content, and parent education and family support. In short, research that is program based can serve as a program audit because of its ecological validity.

Teachers as Researchers: Historical Perspective

Spodek (1988) believes that all teachers are researchers because they continually process information gathered as they work. As a result, they construct implicit theories on which to base future action. Spodek's point is well supported in the history of early childhood care and education.

Teacher research has a long history. Observation was the method used prior to the beginnings of scientific child study. Comenius advocated the use of observation techniques to learn about children and to improve teaching strategies. The naturalistic observations of Rousseau were designed to study children's learning processes. Montessori determined the children's "sensitive periods" for learning specific concepts by using structured observations (Mills, 2000). In the 1900s, scientific child study and progressive educational philosophy were combined in the work of Lucy Sprague Mitchell, who founded the Bureau of Education Experiments, which supported both naturalistic and experimental studies. The research of Caroline Pratt and Harriet Johnson extended the work of Mitchell (Zeichner & Noffke, 2001).

As controlled scientific research became well established, distance between researcher and practitioner occurred because researchers wanted to establish their field as more "pure" science untainted by any practical considerations. For decades, research was limited to experimental studies that were considered scientifically sound and thus valid. Eventually, practitioners began to reject experimental research as irrelevant to their needs and as "unreadable." Some researchers even began to note that research had lost its social problem-solving relevancy (Sears, 1975).

Again, the boundary lines between researcher and practitioner were blurring. In addition to the call for relevancy, other factors promoted the role of teacher-researcher. **Action research,** research that explores practical questions within one's own world of work, came into prominence in the 1940s and 1950s. The growth of qualitative methodologies (e.g., ethnography, narrative inquiry, biography, descriptive studies, case studies, historical research) grew with the concerns about the relevance of experimental methods for solving all problems. Teacher research, which came into the foreground in the 1980s (Cochran-Smith & Lytle, 1999), drew upon action research models and qualitative methodologies. The impetus for teacher research came about as a result of many educators who were interested in social constructivism (Vygotsky, 1978); in reflective, inquiry-based practices (Schön, 1983); and in the Reggio Emilia approach in which teachers view themselves as learners (Fu, Stremmel, & Hill, 2002).

Teachers as Researchers: Current Trends

The early childhood profession needs to foster a culture in which teacher research is valued. Many teachers and even directors of programs are unaware of the relationship between teacher research and professional development. Teachers need to evaluate the impact of different ecological settings on children's development and learning; for example, D. Phillips (1987) said that research literature on child care was essentially urban although 25% of young children attend programs in rural settings (Mathews, Thornburg, Espinosa, & Ispa, 2000). Through teacher research, teachers create local knowledge and thus offer better services (V. Kelly, 1996).

Some teachers prefer to study their own classrooms (Cochran-Smith & Lytle, 1999) and thus regard research as everyday practice (Paley, 1981). Other teachers collaborate in their research with program colleagues (Hankins, 1998) and with university researchers (Charlesworth & DeBoer, 2000; Stremmel & Hill, 1999). Collaborative teacher research is also becoming a component of some teacher preparation programs (Cooney, Buchanan, & Parkinson, 2001).

HELPING OTHERS FIND A PLACE IN THE PROFESSION

Helping others find a place in the profession of early childhood care and education is a major leadership responsibility. This is certainly a form of advocacy because others are encouraged to contribute. Early childhood educators can help others find a place in the profession by doing the following:

1. Providing places for student teachers, interns, and others in their programs.

2. Writing and verbally consulting with others on careers in early childhood care and education.

3. Sharing skills and knowledge with others who work with young children. Mentoring, as discussed in chapter 4, is one of the major ways of helping others find a place in the profession. Mentoring can be done for any role in the profession and helps both the mentor and the protégé.

4. Encouraging others to continue their education through independent study, conferences, short courses, formal degrees, and participation in professional organizations and setting an example by continuing their own education.

5. Striving for vital partnerships outside of the local program. Partnerships with businesses, philanthropic groups, and social service agencies involve others in a shared vision and common goals for the benefit of all. With the contributions of others, the profession grows and improves for the benefit of all young children and their families.

TRENDS AND ISSUES

Although the field of early childhood care and education has had a history of more than 150 years and many individuals have made lasting contributions, the expansion of the field and the changing social structure of society call for even greater insight and commitment. Many issues have been examined, from a broad perspective in chapter 1 to close-up views in chapters 2 through 10. Once again, it seems fitting to look at the broad issues. Kagan (1991a) called for three linked strategies in "seeking excellence" in this field:

1. **Move from "programs" to "systems."** Professionals have had a rich history with many different roots, and the early childhood profession has come under various auspices. From the early childhood profession's many program models, professionals have learned the elements and principles that work. Most of these are now part of the standards written by various professional associations. As Greenman (1988) said, professionals want programs in which every child can "spend a childhood" (p. 15). Professionals now need a commitment to institutionalize these standards more widely. Yet, local programs can be unique in meeting the special needs and desires of the families they serve.

2. **Move from a particularistic to a universal vision.** The diverse nature of our field has led to a lack of connections among programs, to confusion for policy makers, and consequently to fragmented and inefficient services. Kagan and Neuman (1997a) called for *conceptual leadership*. Such leadership is similar to what Nanus (1992) referred to as *visionary leadership*. Conceptual leaders think in the long term and in creative ways. They recognize the need for collaboration in addressing current and projected challenges. Collaboration is not new to early childhood programs but is even more needed today (Kagan, 1991b; Kagan & Rivera, 1991). Kagan and Neuman (1997a) see conceptual leadership as broader than visionary leadership because conceptual leadership focuses beyond a "single program, funding stream, or service" (p. 61), notes changes needed within the broader context of society, and attempts to cultivate links beyond the field. Clifford (1997) also affirmed the need to

include others from many disciplines—child development, education, psychology, medicine, public health, social work, and anthropology.

3. **Move from short- to long-term commitments.** We need to move from thinking about early childhood programs serving limited segments of our society or fulfilling short-term needs to seeing the field as a permanent part of our social fabric. Perreault (1991) said that society (e.g., the media, government, religious and civic groups, professional associations, employers) are early childhood programs' "new extended family."

The hard work of making early childhood programs better must continue. Over the years, we have seen many sectors of society committed to various programs. Now, we must contribute to the profession by coming together on behalf of our children and their families.

SUMMARY

Recent years have seen many calls for professionalism in early childhood education. Professionalism involves the use of professional knowledge and skills in maintaining, extending, and improving services to children and their families. Professionalism is marked by the development of professional skills and knowledge and by a willingness to abide by a code of ethics.

Families and children are dependent on professionals who know their needs and who can make their needs visible to decision makers. If we as early childhood educators fail to raise our collective voice on behalf of children and their families, the problems faced by children and their families will never be solved and our commitment will be broken. Thus, advocacy is the way we actualize our professional responsibility.

The knowledge base of our profession is created through research. Researchers in psychology and education and teachers in the field need to be working on more joint projects. Researchers need to be aware of the many concerns

of daily practice, and teachers need to use the eye of the researcher as they practice.

Early childhood educators need to confirm their professionalism by helping others become involved. Encouragement and assistance are needed in helping others develop a sense of identity within the profession. We need more of the dauntless men and women who carry the banner of early care and education at every level of involvement.

The long and diverse history of early childhood care and education has filled pages with significant ideas and with the impressive accomplishments of both individuals and supportive associations; agencies; foundations; and religious, civic, and corporate groups. Professionals need to take another look at the entire field to plan the course of action. Diversity has enriched the field with ideas but also has led to problems of incoherence. At least three negative repercussions are seen as a result of this diversity. First, some ideas have stood the test of time and have worked across program settings. Yet, some programs fail to incorporate these ideas, which, as set forth in various standards, need to be embraced by the entire field. Second, early childhood care and education has some competing programs. These programs sustain incoherence. Collaboration at the national, state, and local levels is needed to give coherence to the field. Third, for young children and their families to really profit from the various efforts, a central vision and a sustained effort must be manifested.

Professionalism is dynamic. Early childhood education will continue to change in positive ways as all of us who call ourselves professionals become involved in promoting professionalization, engaging in informed advocacy, becoming involved in research, and helping others find a place in the profession. And, this profession needs administrators who take the leadership role in seizing opportunities to make a difference in the lives of young children and their families.

We have long realized that early childhood programs are a microcosm of our world. Out of the disquieting and challenging beginning of our new century, we have been energized once again. Our vision for a well-educated and peaceful citizenry and for leadership in the world's marketplace must begin with good choices for children and their families. We must act now. Change is necessary. Some changes may involve improvement in the local early childhood program, but other changes require much broader action. As professionals we need to create plans of action and networks of people that will allow us to reach our shared vision of quality services that meet the needs of all our young children and their families, provide a "good place to work" for all our professionals, and invite a supportive community.

FOR FURTHER READING

Bisplinghoff, B. S., & Allen, J. (Eds.). (1998). *Engaging teachers: Creating teaching and researching relationships*. Portsmouth, NH: Heinemann.

Bredekamp, S., & Willer, S. (1993). Professionalizing the field of early childhood education: Pros and cons. *Young Children, 48*(3), 82–84.

Clyde, M., & Rodd, J. (1989). Professional ethics. There's more to it than meets the eye. *Early Child Development and Care, 53,* 1–112.

Feeney, S., & Freeman, N. K. (1999). *Ethics and the early childhood educator: Using the NAEYC Code*. Washington, DC: National Association for the Education of Young Children.

Feeney, S., Freeman, N. K., & Moravcik, E. (2000). *Teaching the NAEYC Code of Ethical Conduct: Activity sourcebook*. Washington, DC: National Association for the Education of Young Children.

Fennimore, B. S. (1989). *Child advocacy for early childhood educators*. New York: Teachers College Press.

Freeman, N. K., & Brown, M. H. (1996). Ethics instruction for preservice teachers. How are we doing in ECE? The public's and our profession's growing concern with ethics. *Journal of Early Childhood Teacher Education, 17*(2), 5–18.

Goffin, S. G., & Lombardi, J. (1988). *Speaking out: Early childhood advocacy*. Washington, DC: National Association for the Education of Young Children.

Helm, J. H., Beneke, S., & Steinheimer, K. (1998). *Windows on learning: Documenting young children's work*. New York: Teachers College Press.

Hubbard, R. S., & Power, B. (1993). *The art of classroom inquiry: A handbook for teacher-researchers*. Portsmouth, NH: Heinemann.

Hubbard, R. S., & Power, B. (1999). *Living the questions: A guide for teacher-researchers*. York, ME: Stenhouse.

National Association for the Education of Young Children. (1995). *A call to action on behalf of children and families*. Washington, DC: Author.

Robinson, A., & Stark, D. R. (2002). *Advocates in action: Making a difference for young children*. Washington, DC: National Association for the Education of Young Children.

Spodek, B., Saracho, O. N., & Peters, D. L. (Eds.). (1988). *Professionalism and the early childhood practitioner*. New York: Teachers College Press.

TO REFLECT

1. Bowman (1995) pointed out that at professional conferences, sessions discussing public policy topics have the fewest participants whereas sessions featuring "Music for Monday Mornings" are filled to capacity. What do you think this says about our profession? How could this situation be changed?

2. What are some topics that you, as a prospective or practicing administrator or teacher, would like to see addressed in teacher research?

3. A class in administration is discussing collaboration. One student commented, "We always talk about all we can accomplish through collaboration, but doesn't collaboration come with a price tag?" What are the price tags attached to collaboration?

Appendix 1
Resources for Program Planning

INFANTS AND TODDLERS

Balaban, N. (1992). The role of the child care professional in caring for infants, toddlers, and their families. *Young Children, 47*(5), 66–71.

Bergen, D., Reid, R., & Torelli, L. (2001). *Educating and caring for very young children: The infant/toddler curriculum.* New York: Teachers College Press.

Bredekamp, S., & Copple, C. (Eds.). (1997). Part 3, Developmentally appropriate practice for infants and toddlers. In *Developmentally appropriate practice in early childhood programs* (Rev. ed., pp. 55–94). Washington, DC: National Association for the Education of Young Children.

Carnegie Task Force on Meeting the Needs of Young Children. (1994). *Starting points: Meeting the needs of our youngest children.* New York: Carnegie Corporation.

Cawlfield, M. E. (1992). Velcro time: The language connection. *Young Children, 47*(4), 26–30.

Couchenour, D. (1993). *Bright ideas: Learning all day.* Little Rock, AR: Southern Early Childhood Association.

Daniel, J. E. (1993). Infants to toddlers: Qualities of effective transitions. *Young Children, 48*(6), 16–21.

Dodge, D. T., Dombro, A. L., & Koralek, D. G. (1992). *Caring for infants and toddlers* (Vols. 1 and 2). Washington, DC: Teaching Strategies.

Eddowes, E. A. (1993). *Bright ideas: Handmade toys.* Little Rock, AR: Southern Early Childhood Association.

Edwards, C. P., & Raikes, H. (2002). Extending the dance: Relationship-based approaches to infant/toddler care and education. *Young Children, 57*(4), 10–17.

Gandini, L., & Edwards, C. P. (Eds.). (2001). *Bambini: The Italian approach to infant/toddler care.* New York: Teachers College Press.

Garner, B. P. (1993). *Bright ideas: The physical environment for infants and toddlers.* Little Rock, AR: Southern Early Childhood Association.

Godwin, A., & Schrag, L. (1988). *Setting up for infant care: Guidelines for centers and family day care homes.* Washington, DC: National Association for the Education of Young Children.

Gonzalez-Mena, J. (1992). Taking a culturally sensitive approach to infant-toddler programs. *Young Children, 47*(2), 4–9.

Gonzalez-Mena, J., & Eyer, D. (1997). *Infants, toddlers, and caregivers* (5th ed.). Mountain View, CA: Mayfield.

Greenberg, P. (1987). Ideas that work with young children: What is curriculum for infants in family day care (or elsewhere)? *Young Children, 42*(5), 58–62.

Greenberg, P. (1991). *Character development: Encouraging self-esteem and self-discipline in infants, toddlers, and two-year-olds.* Washington, DC: National Association for the Education of Young Children.

Greenman, J., & Stonehouse, A. (1996). *Prime times: A handbook for excellence in infant and toddler programs.* St. Paul: Redleaf.

Harms, T., Cryer, D., & Clifford, R. M. (2003). *Infant/Toddler Environment Rating Scale* (Rev. ed.). New York: Teachers College Press.

Hodge, S. (1993). *Bright ideas: Special needs.* Little Rock, AR: Southern Early Childhood Association.

Honig, A. S. (1993). Mental health for babies: What do theory and research teach us? *Young Children, 48*(3), 69–76.

Honig, A. S. (1995). Singing with infants and toddlers. *Young Children, 50*(5), 72–78.

Honig, A. S. (2000). The Eriksonian approach: Infant/toddler education. In J. Roopnarine & J. Johnson (Eds.), *Approaches to early childhood education* (3rd ed., pp. 97–121). Upper Saddle River, NJ: Merrill/Prentice Hall.

Honig, A. S. (2002). *Secure relationships: Nurturing infant/toddler attachments in early care settings.* Washington, DC: National Association for the Education of Young Children.

Hughes, F. P., Elicker, J., & Veen, L. C. (1995). A program of play for infants and their caregivers. *Young Children, 50*(2), 52–58.

Kovach, B. A., & Da Ros, D. A. (1998). Respectful, individual, and responsive caregiving for infants. *Young Children, 53*(3), 61–64.

Kupetz, B. N., & Green, E. J. (1997). Sharing books with infants and toddlers: Facing the challenges. *Young Children, 52*(2), 22–27.

Lally, J. R. (1995). The impact of child care policies and practices on infant/toddler identity formation. *Young Children, 51*(1), 59–67.

Lally, J. R., Griffin, A., Fenichel, E., Segal, M. M., Szanton, E. S., & Weissbourd, B. (1995). *Caring for infants and toddlers in groups: Developmentally appropriate practice.* Washington, DC: ZERO TO THREE/The National Center for Infants, Toddlers, and Families.

Meyerhoff, M. K. (1994). Of baseball and babies: Are you unconsciously discouraging father involvement in infant care? *Young Children, 49*(4), 17–19.

Post, J., & Hohmann, M. (2000). *Tender care and early learning.* Ypsilanti, MI: High/Scope Educational Research Foundation.

Raikes, H. (1996). A secure base for babies: Applying attachment concepts to the infant care setting. *Young Children, 51*(5), 59–67.

Reinsberg, J. (1995). Reflections on quality infant care. *Young Children, 50*(6), 23–25.

Ross, H. W. (1992). Integrating infants with disabilities? Can "ordinary" caregivers do it? *Young Children, 47*(3), 65–71.

Steinberg, M., Williams, S., & DaRos, D. (1992). Caregivers' corner. Toilet learning takes time. *Young Children, 48*(1), 56.

Stonehouse, A. (Ed.). (1991). *Trusting toddlers: Planning for one- to three-year-olds in child care centers.* St. Paul, MN: Toys 'n Things Press.

Surbeck, E., & Kelley, M. F. (Eds.). (1990). *Personalizing care with infants, toddlers, and families.* Olney, MD: Association for Childhood Education International.

Vaughn, E. (1993). *Bright ideas: Books for babies.* Little Rock, AR: Southern Early Childhood Association.

YOUNG CHILDREN: DIRECT-INSTRUCTION VIEW

Alberto, P. A., & Troutman, A. C. (1990). *Applied behavior analysis for teachers.* Upper Saddle River, NJ: Merrill/Prentice Hall.

Bereiter, C. (1990). Aspects of an educational theory. *Review of an Educational Research, 60,* 603–624.

Carnine, D., Carnine, L., Karp, J., & Weisberg, P. (1988). Kindergarten for economically disadvantaged children: The direct instruction component. In C. Warger (Ed.), *A resource guide to public school early childhood programs* (pp. 73–98). Alexandria, VA: Association for Supervision and Curriculum Development.

Gersten, R., & George, N. (1990). Teaching reading and mathematics to at-risk students in kindergarten: What we have learned from field research. In C. Seefeldt (Ed.), *Continuing issues in early childhood education* (pp. 245–259). Upper Saddle River, NJ: Merrill/Prentice Hall.

Iran-Nejad, A., McKeachie, W. J., & Berliner, D. C. (1990). Toward a unified approach to learning as a multi source phenomenon [Special issue]. *Review of Educational Research, 60*(4).

Neisworth, J. T., & Buggey, T. J. (2000). Behavioral analysis and principles in early childhood education. In J. L. Roopnarine & J. E. Johnson (Eds.), *Approaches to early childhood education* (3rd ed., pp. 123–148). Upper Saddle River, NJ: Merrill/Prentice Hall.

Success for All. //www.successforall.net/curriculum/sfa.htm>

Watkins, K. P., & Durant, L. (1992). *Complete early childhood behavior management guide.* West Nyack, NY: Center for Applied Research in Education.

Wittrock, M. C., & Lumsdaine, A. A. (1997). Instructional psychology. In M. R. Rosenzweig & I. W. Porter (Eds.), *Annual Review of Psychology* (Vol. 28, pp. 417–459). Palo Alto, CA: Annual Reviews.

YOUNG CHILDREN: PIAGET-BASED VIEW

Bredekamp, S., & Rosegrant, T. (Eds.). (1992). *Reaching potentials: Appropriate curriculum and assessment for young children* (Vol. 1). Washington, DC: National Association for the Education of Young Children.

Bredekamp, S., & Rosegrant, T. (Eds.). (1995). *Reaching potentials: Transforming early childhood curriculum and assessment* (Vol. 2). Washington, DC: National Association for the Education of Young Children.

Brooks, J. G., & Brooks, M. G. (1993). *In search of understanding: The case for constructivist classrooms.* Alexandria, VA: Association for Supervision and Curriculum Development.

Burchfield, D. W. (1996). Teaching *all* children: Four developmentally appropriate curricular and instructional strategies in primary-grade classrooms. *Young Children, 52*(1), 4–10.

DeVries, R., & Kohlberg, L. (1987). *Programs of early education: The constructivist view.* New York: Longman.

DeVries, R., & Kohlberg, L. (1990). *Constructivist early education: Overview and comparison with other programs.* Washington, DC: National Association for the Education of Young Children.

DeVries, R., Zan, B., Hildebrandt, C., Edmiaston, R., & Sales, C. (2002). *Developing constructivist early childhood curriculum: Practical principles and activities.* New York: Teachers College Press.

Fosnot, C. T. (1996). *Constructivism: Theory, perspectives, and practice.* New York: Teachers College Press.

Fowlkes, M. A. (1991). Gifts from childhood's godmother: Patty Smith Hill. In J. D. Quisenberry, E. A. Eddowes, & S. L. Robinson (Eds.), *Readings from Childhood Education* (Vol. 2, pp. 11–16). Olney, MD: Association for Childhood Education International.

Greenberg, P. (1990). Ideas that work with young children. Why not academic preschool? (Part 1). *Young Children, 45*(2), 70–80.

Greenberg, P. (1992). Why not academic preschool? (Part 2). Autocracy or democracy in the classroom? *Young Children, 47*(3), 54–64.

Gronlund, G. (1995). Bringing the DAP message to kindergarten and primary teachers. *Young Children, 50*(5), 4–13.

Hendrick, J. A. (1992). When does it all begin? Teaching the principles of democracy in the early years. *Young Children, 47*(3), 51–53.

Hohmann, C., & Buckleitner, W. (1992). *High/Scope K–3 curriculum series: Learning environment.* Ypsilanti, MI: High/Scope Press.

Hohmann, M., & Weikart, D. P. (1995). *Educating young children.* Ypsilanti, MI: High/Scope Educational Research Foundation.

Kamii, C. (Ed.). (1990). *Achievement testing in the early grades: The games grown-ups play.* Washington, DC: National Association for the Education of Young Children.

Kamii, C., & DeVries, R. (1980). *Group games in early education: Implications of Piaget's theory.* Washington, DC: National Association for the Education of Young Children.

Katz, L. G., & Chard, S. (2000). *Engaging children's minds: The project approach (Rev. ed.).* Norwood, NJ: Ablex.

Prawat, R. S. (1992). Teachers' beliefs about teaching and learning: A constructivist perspective. *American Journal of Education, 3,* 354–395.

Wasserman, S. (1990). *Serious players in the primary classroom.* New York: Teachers College Press.

Weikart, D. P., & Schweinhart, L. (2000). The High/Scope curriculum for early childhood care and education. In J. L. Roopnarine & J. E. Johnson (Eds.), *Approaches to early childhood education* (3rd ed., pp. 277–293). Upper Saddle River, NJ: Merrill/Prentice Hall.

Williams, K. C. (1997). "What do you wonder?" Involving children in curriculum planning. *Young Children, 49*(6), 78–81.

YOUNG CHILDREN: DEVELOPMENTAL-INTERACTION VIEW

Biber, B. (1977). A developmental-interaction approach. Bank Street College of Education. In M. C. Day & R. K. Parker (Eds.), *The preschool in action: Exploring early childhood programs* (2nd ed., pp. 421–460). Boston: Allyn & Bacon.

Biber, B. (1981). The evolution of the developmental-interaction view. In E. K. Shapiro & E. Weber (Eds.), *Cognitive and affective growth: Developmental interaction* (pp. 9–30). Hillsdale, NJ: Erlbaum.

Biber, B. (1984). *Early education and psychological development.* New Haven, CT: Yale University Press.

Biber, B., Shapiro, E., & Wickens, D. (1977). *Promoting cognitive growth: A developmental interaction point of view* (2nd ed.). Washington, DC: National Association for the Education of Young Children.

Cuffaro, H. K., Nager, N., Shapiro, E. K. (2000). The developmental-interaction approach at Bank Street College of Education. In J. L. Roopnarine & J. E. Johnson (Eds.), *Approaches to early childhood education* (3rd ed., pp. 263–276). Upper Saddle River, NJ: Merrill/Prentice Hall.

Gilkeson, E. C., Smithberg, L. M., Bowman, G. W., & Rhine, W. R. (1981). Bank Street model: A developmental-interaction approach. In W. R. Rhine (Ed.), *Making schools more effective: New directions from Follow Through* (pp. 249–288). New York: Academic Press.

Mitchell, A., & David, J. (Eds.). (1992). *Explorations with young children: A curriculum guide from the Bank Street College of Education*. Beltsville, MD: Gryphon.

Nager, N., & Shapiro, E. K. (Eds.). (2000). *Revisiting a progressive pedagogy: The developmental-interaction approach*. Albany: State University of New York Press.

Shapiro, E. K. (1991). *Teacher: Being and becoming*. New York: Bank Street College of Education.

Shapiro, E. K., & Weber, E. (Eds.). (1981). *Cognitive and affective growth: Developmental interaction*. Hillsdale, NJ: Erlbaum.

YOUNG CHILDREN: MONTESSORI

American Montessori Society. (1996). *American Montessori Society position papers*. New York: Author.

Chatlin-McNichols, J. (1992). *The Montessori controversy*. Albany, NY: Delmar.

Hainstock, E. G. (1997). *The essential Montessori: An introduction to the woman, the writings, the method, and the movement*. New York: Plume.

Humphryes, J. (1998). The developmental appropriateness of high-quality Montessori programs. *Young Children, 53*(4), 4–16.

Kramer, R. (1988). *Maria Montessori: A biography*. Reading, MA: Addison-Wesley.

Loeffler, M. H. (Ed.). (1992). *Montessori in contemporary American culture*. Portsmouth, NH: Heinemann.

Montessori, M. (1964). *The Montessori method* (A. E. George, Trans.). New York: Schocken.

Montessori, M. (1965). *Spontaneous activity in education* (F. Simmonds, Trans.). New York: Schocken.

Montessori, M. (1964). *Dr. Montessori's own handbook*. Cambridge, MA: Robert Bentley.

Torrence, M. (2000). Montessori education today. In J. L. Roopnarine & J. E. Johnson (Eds.), *Approaches to early childhood education* (3rd ed., pp. 191–220). Upper Saddle River, NJ: Merrill/Prentice Hall.

YOUNG CHILDREN: ECOLOGICAL-BASED VIEW

Armstrong, T. (1993). *Seven kinds of smart: Identifying and developing your many intelligences*. New York: Penguin.

Berk, L. E., & Winsler, A. (1995). *Scaffolding children's learning: Vygotsky and early childhood education*. Washington, DC: National Association for the Education of Young Children.

Bodrova, E., & Leong, D. J. (1996). *Tools of the mind: The Vygotskian approach to early childhood education*. Upper Saddle River, NJ: Merrill/Prentice Hall.

Coles, R. (2000). *The Erik Erikson reader*. New York: Norton.

Edwards, C., Gandini, L., & Forman, G. (Eds.). (1993). *The hundred languages of children: The Reggio Emilia approach to early childhood education*. Norwood, NJ: Ablex.

Forman, E. A., Minick, M., & Stone, C. A. (Eds.). (1993). *Context for learning: Sociocultural dynamics in children's development*. New York: Oxford University Press.

Gandini, L. (1993). Fundamentals of the Reggio Emilia approach to early childhood education. *Young Children, 49*(1), 4–8.

Hendrick, J. (Ed.). (1997). *First steps toward teaching the Reggio way*. Upper Saddle River, NJ: Merrill/Prentice Hall.

Malaguzzi, L. (1993). For an education based on relationships. *Young Children, 49*(1), 9–12.

Reggio Children & Project Zero. (2001). *Making learning visible: Children as individual and group learners*. Reggio Emilia, Italy, & Cambridge, MA: Reggio Children and Harvard Graduate School of Education.

Vygotsky, L. (1967). Play and its role in the mental development of the child. *Soviet Psychology, 12,* 62–76.

FAMILY CHILD CARE

Baker, A. C. (1992). A puzzle, a picnic, and a vision: Family day care at its best. *Young Children, 47*(5), 36–38.

Baker, A. C., & Manfredi/Pettit, L. (1998). *Circle of love: Relationships between parents, providers and children in family child care*. St. Paul, MN: Redleaf.

DeBord, K. (1993). A little respect and eight more hours in the day: Family child care providers have special needs. *Young Children, 48*(4), 21–26.

Dodge, D. T., & Colker, L. J. (1991). *The creative curriculum for family child care*. Washington, DC: Teaching Strategies.

Galinsky, E., Howes, C., Kontos, S., & Shinn, M. (1994). *The study of children in family child care and relative care: Highlights of findings*. New York: Families and Work Institute.

Gonzalez-Mena, J. (1991). *Tips and tidbits: A book for family day care providers.* Washington, DC: National Association for the Education of Young Children.

Harms, T., & Clifford, R. (1989). *Family Day Care Rating Scale (FDCRS).* New York: Teachers College Press.

Koralek, D. G., Colker, L. J., & Dodge, D. T. (1993). *Caring for children in family child care.* Washington, DC: Teaching Strategies.

Modigliani, K., & Bromer, J. (1998). *Quality standards for WAFCC accreditation.* Boston: Wheelock College Family Child Care Project.

Modigliani, K., Bromer, J., & Lutton, A. (1998). *Training resources for family child care accreditation.* Boston: Wheelock College Family Child Care Project.

Osborn, H. (1994). *Room for loving, room for learning: Finding the space you need in your family child care home.* St. Paul, MN: Redleaf.

SCHOOL-AGE CHILD CARE

Albrecht, K., & Plantz, M. (1993). *Developmentally appropriate practice in school-age child care programs* (2nd ed.). Dubuque, IA: Kendall/Hunt.

Blakley, B., Blau, R., Brady, E. H., Streibert, C., Zavitkovsky, A., & Zavitkovsky, D. (1989). *Activities for school-age child care: Playing and learning.* Washington, DC: National Association for the Education of Young Children.

Bumgarner, M. A. (1999). *Working with school-age children.* Mountain View, CA: Mayfield.

Click, P. (1998). *Caring for school-age children.* Albany, NY: Delmar.

Harms, T., Jacobs, E. V., & White, D. R. (1996). *School-age care environment rating scale.* New York: Teachers College Press.

Koralek, D., Newman, R., & Colker, L. (1995). *Caring for school-age children.* Washington, DC: Teaching Strategies.

Musson, S. (1994). *School-age care: Theory and practice.* Don Mills, Ontario, Canada: Addison-Wesley.

National Institute on Out-of-School Time. (1998). *Working together for quality care after school.* Boston: Author.

Newman, R. L. (1993). *Trainer's guide, keys to quality in school-age child care.* Rockville, MD: Montgomery County (MD) Child Care Division.

O'Connor, S. (1995). *ASQ: Assessing school-age child care quality.* Wellesley, MA: School-Age Child Care Project.

Roman, J. (Ed.). (1998). *The NSACA standards for quality school-age care.* Boston: National School-Age Care Alliance.

Seligson, M. A. (Ed.). (1993). *School-age child care: An action manual for the 90s and beyond.* Westpoint, CT: Auburn House.

Seppanen, P., Love, J., deVries, D., Bernstein, L., Seligson, M., Marx, F., & Kicker, E. (1993). *National study of before- and after-school programs.* Portsmouth, NH: RMC Research.

Sisson, L. (1995). *Pilot standards for school-age child care.* Washington, DC: National School-Age Care Alliance.

MULTICULTURAL/ANTIBIAS UNDERSTANDINGS

Anderson, M. P. (1996). Frequently asked questions about NAEYC's linguistic and cultural diversity position paper. *Young Children, 51*(2), 13–16.

Ballenger, C. (1999). *Teaching other people's children: Literacy and learning in a bilingual classroom.* New York: Teachers College Press.

Banks, J. A., & Banks, C. A. M. (Eds.). (1995). *Handbook of research on multicultural education.* New York: Macmillan.

Beaty, J. (1997). *Building bridges with multicultural picture books.* Upper Saddle River, NJ: Merrill/Prentice Hall.

Berns, R. (1997). *Child, family, school, community* (4th ed.). New York: Harcourt Brace.

Bromer, J. (1999). Cultural variations in child care: Values and actions. *Young Children, 54*(6), 72–78.

Byrnes, D. A., & Kiger, G. (Eds.). (1996). *Common bonds: Anti-bias teaching in a diverse society* (2nd ed.). Olney, MD: Association for Childhood Education International.

Carlsson-Paige, N., & Levin, D. E. (1992). Making peace in violent times: A constructivist approach to conflict resolution. *Young Children, 48*(1), 4–13.

Cary, S. (1997). *Second language learners.* York, ME: Stenhouse.

Chang, H. N-L., Muckelroy, A., & Pulido-Tobiassen, D. (1996). *Looking in, looking out: Redefining child care and early education in a diverse society.* San Francisco: California Tomorrow.

De Gaetano, Y., Williams, L. R., & Volk, D. (1998). *Kaleidoscope: A multicultural approach for the primary school classroom.* Upper Saddle River, NJ: Merrill/Prentice Hall.

Delpit, L. (1995). *Other people's children: Cultural conflict in the classroom.* New York: New Press.

deMelendez, W. R., & Ostertag, V. (1997). *Teaching young children in multicultural classrooms—Issues, concepts, and strategies.* Albany, NY: Delmar.

Derman-Sparks, L. (Ed.). (1991). *Anti-bias curriculum: Tools for empowering young children.* Washington, DC: National Association for the Education of Young Children.

Derman-Sparks, L. (1999). Markers of multicultural/antibias education. *Young Children, 54*(5), 43.

Gallas, K. (1998). *Sometimes I can be anything: Power, gender, and identity.* New York: Teachers College Press.

Gonzalez-Mena, J. (1992). Taking a culturally sensitive approach in infant-toddler programs. *Young Children, 47*(2), 4–9.

Gonzalez-Mena, J. (1997). *Multicultural issues in child care.* Mountain View, CA: Mayfield.

Gonzalez-Mena, J. (1998). *The child in the family and the community.* Upper Saddle River, NJ: Merrill/Prentice Hall.

Hale, J. (1994). *Unbank the fire: Visions for the education of young children.* Baltimore: Johns Hopkins University Press.

Hale-Benson, J. E. (1992). *Black children: Their roots, culture, and learning styles* (Rev. ed.). Baltimore: Johns Hopkins University Press.

Harkness, S., & Super, C. (Eds.). (1996). *Parents' cultural belief systems: Their origins, expressions, and consequences.* New York: Guilford.

Hendrick, J. (1992). Where does it all begin? Teaching the principles of democracy in the early years. *Young Children, 47*(3), 51–53.

Kendall, F. E. (1996). *Diversity in the classroom: New approaches to the education of young children* (2nd ed.). New York: Teachers College Press.

Lee, F. Y. (1995). Asian parents as partners. *Young Children, 50*(3), 4–8.

Little Soldier, L. M. (1992a). Building optimum learning environments for Navajo students. *Childhood Education, 68,* 145–148.

Little Soldier, L. M. (1992b). Working with Native American children. *Young Children, 47*(6), 15–21.

Lynch, E. W., & Hanson, M. J. (1998). *Developing cross-cultural competence: A guide for working with young children and their families.* Baltimore: Brookes.

Mallory, B. L., & New, R. S. (Eds.). (1994). *Diversity and developmentally appropriate practices: Challenges for early childhood education.* New York: Teachers College Press.

McCracken, J. B. (1992). *Teacher's guide to learning activities: Grades K–2.* Washington, DC: Americans All.

McCracken, J. B. (1993). *Valuing diversity: The primary years.* Washington, DC: National Association for the Education of Young Children.

National Association for the Education of Young Children. (1995). *NAEYC Position Statement. Responding to linguistic and cultural diversity—Recommendations for effective early childhood education.* Washington, DC: Author.

Neugebauer, B. (Ed.). (1992). *Alike and different: Exploring our humanity with young children* (Rev. ed.). Washington, DC: National Association for the Education of Young Children.

Ramsey, P. (1998). *Teaching and learning in a diverse world* (2nd ed.). New York: Teachers College Press.

Rigg, P., Kazemek, F. E., & Hudelson, S. (1993). Children's books about the elderly. *Rethinking Schools, 7*(3), 25.

Thompson, B. J. (1993). *Words can hurt you: Beginning a program of anti-bias education.* Menlo Park, CA: Addison-Wesley.

Wardle, F. (1992). *Biracial identity: An ecological development model.* Denver: Center for the Study of Biracial Children.

Washington, V., Johnson, V., & McCracken, J. B. (1995). *Grassroots success! Preparing schools and families for each other.* Washington, DC: National Association for the Education of Young Children.

Whitney, T. (1999). *Kids like us: Using persona dolls in the classroom.* St. Paul, MN: Redleaf.

INCLUSION OF CHILDREN WITH SPECIAL NEEDS

Allen, K. E. (1992). *The exceptional child: Mainstreaming in early childhood education* (2nd ed.). Albany, NY: Delmar.

Blenk, K., & Fine, D. L. (1995). *Making school inclusion work: A guide to everyday practices.* Cambridge, MA: Brookline Books.

Bowe, E. (2000). *Birth to five: Early childhood special education* (2nd ed.). Albany, NY: Delmar.

Bricker, D. (1995). The challenge of inclusion. *Journal of Early Intervention, 19,* 179–194.

Bricker, D., & Pretti-Frontezak, K. (Eds.). (1996). *Assessment, Evaluation, and Programming System*

(AEPS) measurement for three to six years: Vol. 3. Baltimore: Brookes.

Bricker, D., & Waddell, M. (Eds.). (1996). *Assessment, Evaluation, and Programming System (AEPS) curriculum for three to six years: Vol. 4.* Baltimore: Brookes.

Brown, M. H., & Conroy, M. A. (Eds.). (1997). *Inclusion of preschool children with developmental delays in early childhood programs.* Little Rock, AR: Southern Early Childhood Association.

Chandler, P. A. (1994). *A place for me: Including children with special needs in early care and education settings.* Washington, DC: National Association for the Education of Young Children.

Cook, R. E., Tessier, A., & Klein, M. D. (2000). *Adapting early childhood curricula for children with special needs* (5th ed.). Upper Saddle River, NJ: Merrill/Prentice Hall.

Davis, M. D., Kilgo, J. L., & Gamel-McCormick, M. (1998). *Young children with special needs: A developmentally appropriate approach.* Boston: Allyn & Bacon.

Gargiulo, R., Kilgo, J. L., & Graves, S. (1999). *Young children with special needs: An introduction to early childhood special education.* Albany, NY: Delmar.

Gould, P., & Sullivan, J. (1999). *The inclusive early childhood classroom: Easy ways to adapt learning centers for all children.* Beltsville, MD: Gryphon.

Honig, A. S. (1997). Creating integrated environments for young children with special needs. *Early Childhood Education Journal, 25*(2), 93–100.

Hoskins, B. (1995). *Developing inclusive schools: A guide.* Reston, VA: Council for Exceptional Children.

Miller, R. (1996). *The developmentally appropriate inclusive classroom in early education.* Albany, NY: Delmar.

O'Brien, M. (1997). *Inclusive child care for infants and toddlers: Meeting individual and special needs.* Baltimore, MD: Brookes.

Russell-Fox, J. (1997). Together is better: Specific tips on how to include children with various types of disabilities. *Young Children, 52*(4), 81–83.

Safford, P. L. (Ed.). (with Spodek, B., & Saracho, O. N.). (1994). *Early childhood special education.* New York: Teachers College Press.

Spodek, B., & Saracho, O. N. (1994). *Dealing with individual differences in the early childhood classroom.* New York: Longman.

Tertell, E. A., Klein, S. M., & Jewett, J. L. (Eds.). (1998). *When teachers reflect: Journeys toward effective, inclusive practice.* Washington, DC: National Association for the Education of Young Children.

Villa, R. A., & Thousand, J. T. (Eds.). (1995). *Creating an inclusive school.* Alexandria, VA: Association for Supervision and Curriculum Development.

Walker, B., Hafenstein, N. L., & Crow-Enslow, L. (1999). Meeting the needs of gifted learners in the early childhood classroom. *Young Children, 54*(1), 32–36.

Winter, S. M. (1999). *The early childhood inclusion model: A program for all children.* Olney, MD: Association for Childhood Education International.

Wolery, M., & Bredekamp, S. (1994). Developmentally appropriate practices and young children with disabilities; Contextual issues in the discussion. *Journal of Early Intervention, 18,* 331–341.

Wolery, M., & Wilbers, J. S. (Eds.). (1994). *Including children with special needs in early childhood programs.* Washington, DC: National Association for the Education of Young Children.

Appendix 2
State Licensing and Certification Agencies

State	State Department Responsible for Licensing	State Department Responsible for Certification
Alabama	Department of Human Resources Child Day Care Partnership www.dhr.state.al.us/fsd/child_care.asp	Department of Education www.alsde.edu/html/home.asp
Alaska	Division of Family and Youth Services www.eed.state.ak.us/EarlyDev/licensing.htm	Department of Education and Early Development www.eed.state.ak.us/
Arizona	Department of Health Services www.hs.state.az.us/als/childcare/index.htm	Department of Education www.ade.state.az.us/
Arkansas	Department of Human Services Division of Child Care and Early Childhood Education www.state.ar.us/childcare/provinfo.html	Department of Education, General Education Division www.arkedu.state.ar.us/
California	Department of Social Services Community Care Licensing Division http://ccld.ca.gov/	Department of Education www.cde.ca.gov/
Colorado	Department of Human Services Division of Child Care www.cdhs.state.co.us/childcare/licensing.htm	Department of Education www.cde.state.co.us/
Connecticut	Department of Public Health Child Day Care Licensing www.dph.state.ct.us/BRS/day_care/day _care.htm	Department of Education www.state.ct.us/sde/
Delaware	Department of Services for Children, Youth and Families Office of Child Care Licensing http://www.state.de.us/kids/occlhome.htm	Department of Education www.doe.state.de.us/
District of Columbia	Licensing Regulation Administration Human Services Facility Division www.daycare.com/districtofcolumbia/	District of Columbia Public Schools www.k12.dc.us/dcps/home.html

State	State Department Responsible for Licensing	State Department Responsible for Certification
Florida	Department of Children and Families Child Care Services www5.myflorida.com/cf_web/myflorida2/ healthhuman/childcare/licensing.html	Department of Education www.firn.edu/doe/index.html
Georgia	Department of Human Resources Office of Regulatory Services, Child Care Licensing Section www2.state.ga.us/Departments/DHR/ORS/ orsccl.htm	Department of Education www.doe.k12.ga.us/index.asp
Hawaii	Department of Human Services Benefit, Employment & Support Services Division www.state.hi.us/dhs/	Department of Education www.k12.hi.us
Idaho	Department of Health & Welfare Child Care Licensing Office www2.state.id.us/dhw/ecic/CC/Child_Ca.htm	Department of Education www.sde.state.id.us/Dept/
Illinois	Department of Children & Family Services Bureau of Licensure & Certification www.state.il.us/agency/dhs/childcnp.html	State Board of Education www.isbe.net/
Indiana	Family & Social Services Administration Division of Family and Children www.carefinderindiana.org/	Department of Education www.doe.state.in.us/
Iowa	Department of Human Services Division of Behavioral Development & Protective Services www.dhs.state.ia.us/policyanalysis/ RulesPages/RulesChap.htm #Licensing 7.20Standards	Department of Education www.state.ia.us/educate/
Kansas	Department of Health and Environment Child Care Licensing & Registration www.kdhe.state.ks.us/bcclr/index.html	Department of Education www.ksde.org/
Kentucky	Cabinet for Health Services Division of Licensing & Regulation www.lrc.state.ky.us/kar/922/002/090.htm	Department of Education www.kentuckyschools.org/
Louisiana	Department of Social Services Bureau of Licensing www.dss.state.la.us/offos/html/licensing.html	Department of Education www.doe.state.la.us/DOE/asps/home.asp
Maine	Department of Human Services Office of Child Care and Head Start www.state.me.us/dhs/cclicensing.htm	Department of Education www.state.me.us/education/homepage.htm

State	State Department Responsible for Licensing	State Department Responsible for Certification
Maryland	Department of Human Resources Child Care Administration www.dhr.sailorsite.net/cca/	Department of Education www.msde.state.md.us/
Massachusetts	Office of Child Care Services www.qualitychildcare.org/licensing.html'	Educational Improvement Group www.doe.mass.edu/
Michigan	Department of Consumer & Industry Services Division of Child Day Care Licensing www.cis.state.mi.us/brs/cdc/home.htm	Department of Education www.mi.gov/mde/
Minnesota	Department of Human Services Division of Licensing www.dhs.state.mn.us/Licensing	Department of Children, Families, and Learning www.cfl.state.mn.us/
Mississippi	Department of Health Division of Child Care www.msdh.state.ms.us/documents.childcare .regs.pdf	State Department of Education www.mde.k12.ms.us/
Missouri	Department of Health Bureau of Child Care, Safety and Licensure www.health.state.mo.us/LicensingAnd Certification/welcome.html	Department of Elementary and Secondary Education www.dese.state.mo.us
Montana	Department of Public Health and Human Services Quality Assurance Division www.dphhs.state.mt.us/about_us/divisions/ quality_assurance/quality_assurance.htm	Office of Public Instruction www.opi.state.mt.us/
Nebraska	Department of Health and Human Services Child Care www.hhs.state.ne.us/crl/childcare.htm	Department of Education www.nde.state.ne.us/
Nevada	Department of Human Resources Division of Child and Family Services, Bureau of Child Care Licensing www.leg.state.nv.us/NAC/NAC-432A.html	State Department of Education www.nde.state.nv.us/
New Hampshire	Department of Health and Human Services Office of Program Suport, Bureau of Child Care Licensing www.dhhs.state.nh.us/DHHS/BCCL/	Department of Education www.ed.state.nh.us/
New Jersey	Division of Youth and Family Services Bureau of Licensing www.state.nj.us/humanservices/dyfs/ licensing.html	Department of Education www.state.nj.us/education/

State	State Department Responsible for Licensing	State Department Responsible for Certification
New Mexico	Child Services Unit/Licensing www.daycare.com/newmexico/	State Department of Education www.sde.state.nm.us/
New York	State Department of Family Assistance Office of Children and Family Services www.ocfs.state.ny.us/main/becs/starting.htm	Education Department www.nysed.gov/
North Carolina	Division of Child Development Regulatory Services Section www.dhhs.state.nc.us/dcd/provider.htm	Department of Education www.ncpublicschools.org/
North Dakota	Department of Human Services Early Childhood Services www.lnotes.state.nd.us/dhs/dhsweb.nsf	Department of Public Instruction www.dpi.state.nd.us/
Ohio	Department of Job & Family Services Bureau of Child Care and Development www.state.oh.us/odjfs/cdc/	Department of Education www.ode.state.oh.us/
Oklahoma	Department of Human Services Office of Child Care www.okdhs.org/childcare	State Department of Education www.sde.state.ok.us/
Oregon	Employment Department Child Care Division www.findit.emp.state.or.us/childcare/ rules.cfm	Department of Education www.ode.state.or.us/
Pennsylvania	Department of Public Welfare, Bureau of Child Day Care Office of Children, Youth & Families www.dpw.state.pa.us/ocyf/childcarewks/ ccwregccp.asp	Department of Education www.pde.state.pa.us/pde_internet/site/ default.asp
Rhode Island	Department of Children, Youth, and Families Day Care Licensing Unit www.dcyf.state.ri.us/licensing.htm	Department of Elementary and Secondary Education www.ridoe.net/
South Corolina	Department of Social Services Division of Child Day Care Licensing and Regulatory Services www.state.sc.us/dss/cdclrs/	Department of Education www.myscschools.com/
South Dakota	Department of Social Services Child Care Services www.state.sd.us/social/CCS/Licensing/ infolic.htm	Department of Education and Cultural Affairs www.state.sd.us/deca
Tennessee	Department of Human Services Child Care Services Unit www.state.tn.us/humanserv/childcare.htm	State Department of Education www.state.tn.us/education/

State	State Department Responsible for Licensing	State Department Responsible for Certification
Texas	Department of Protective and Regulatory Services Child Care Licensing www.tdprs.state.tx.us/Child_Care/	Education Agency www.tea.state.tx.us/
Utah	Department of Health Bureau of Licensing, Child Care Unit www.health.state.ut.us/hsi/hfl/index.html	State Office of Education www.usoe.k12.ut.us/
Vermont	Department of Social Rehabilitation Services Child Care Services Division, Child Care Licensing Unit www.state.vt.us/srs/childcare/licensing/license.htm	Department of Education www.state.vt.us/educ/
Virginia	Department of Social Services Division of Licensing Programs www.dss.state.va.us/division/license/	Department of Education www.pen.k12.va.us/go/VDOE/
Washington	Department of Social and Health Services Division of Child Care and Early Learning www.dshs.wa.gov/esa/dccel/licensingfield.shtml	Office of Superintendent of Public Instruction www.k12.wa.us/
West Virginia	Department of Health and Human Resources Day Care Licensing www.wvdhhr.org/oss/childcare/licensing.htm	Department of Education www.wvde.state.wv.us/
Wisconsin	Department of Children & Family Services Bureau of Regulation and Licensing www.dhfs.state.wi.us/rl_dcfs/index.htm	Department of Public Instruction www.dpi.state.wi.us/
Wyoming	Department of Family Services Division of Juvenile Services http://dfsweb.state.wy.us/childcare.html	Department of Education www.k12.wy.us/

Appendix 3
Competencies of Early Care and Education Program Administrators

This list of director competencies was adapted from a list I prepared based on work by Joe Perrault and Nancy Travis at Save the Children, refined through class discussion and assignments by administrators from across the country who participate in administrators' courses at Wheelock College. The following competencies should be possessed by administrators:

1. The ability to plan and implement a developmentally appropriate care and education program for children and families.

A competent director has

- The ability to hire competent staff to work with children and contribute to their further development in a staff development plan that includes frequent feedback sessions between director and children.

- Knowledge of current research findings in child and human development theory and their applicability to children's programs. This includes knowledge of brain development.

- Knowledge of caring concepts, including their history and applicable theory, in relation to other child development findings.

- Familiarity with best practices in programming for children.

- Focus on the child in the family.

- Understanding of the potential of observation as a tool in programming, and support for observation and documentation as an important staff function.

- Ability to inspire and stimulate staff to continuous improvement of the program with attention to:
  —Pacing for a long day
  —Transitions
  —Family culture and values
  —Family-friendly service
  —Presentation skills and communicating to parents
  —Display of child work to give meaning to the activities of the program
  —Anti-bias curriculum
  —Developmentally appropriate practice for all children

For work with families, directors need competence in all the above, plus

- Helping relationships.

- Family development, parent development, education, leadership development, and interprofessional perspectives.

- Skills in feedback and communication.

- Empathy with parent perspectives.

- Skills to support family culture and language; ability to negotiate across differences.

- Respect for centrality of the parent role in a child's life.

- Ability to see the child care program as a support for parent's lives (family centric) rather than exclusively focusing on the parent as part of a supportive environment for the early care and education program (center centric).

2. The ability to develop and maintain an effective organization.

A competent director must

- Understand the legal form of the organization, its philosophical base, its history, and its goals.
- Be able to sense and respond to environmental influences and to stakeholders, both external and internal.
- Understand and comply with all applicable rules and regulations.
- Develop a management philosophy that includes a clear mission statement and clear objectives based on the organization's values and the needs expressed by parents in the community.
- Develop and implement strategies for management that build teamwork and participation of staff; make effective use of time and other resources; engage in short-term problem solving and long-term planning.
- Work with and contribute to board development in organizations that have boards; develop advisory groups where applicable.
- Be able to evaluate the program and all its components and use this evaluation to change and improve the program.
- Know basic strategic planning processes.

3. The ability to plan and implement administrative systems that effectively carry out the program's mission, goals, and objectives.

A competent director is ultimately responsible for

- Systems for implementing curriculum, addressing all aspects of development for each child appropriate to their individual age, culture, and level of development.
- Regular communication with parents that respects their values and culture; involves them

appropriately in the life of the program; supports their lives, including their home language; and focuses on contributing to the parent–child dyad and improving the quality of life for families.

- Nutrition and food service management.
- Recruitment and enrollment of children, as well as attention to separation issues for children and parents.
- Social services and health care, appropriate to the needs of the parent group.
- Organization of tasks and decision-making teamwork throughout the organization.
- Systems for maintaining all aspects of the physical facility in a safe and healthy condition, as well as in a creative design that contributes to learning and teaching.
- Knowledge of basic total quality management concepts.

4. The ability to administer effectively a program of personnel management and staff development.

In the organization as a whole, a competent director must effectively

- Give and receive feedback.
- Gather needed information through regular communication with all staff and parents.
- Facilitate the development of community among staff, among parents, among the board or advisory groups, and among children.
- Maintain personal stability and confidence, self-awareness, desire for growth, and the ability to change.
- Set the stage for recruiting, accepting, and retaining a diverse group of staff members.

For staff development and support, a competent director must

- Observe objectively and give positive and negative feedback in a way that helps individuals to change.

- Motivate and challenge people and set a high standard.
- Communicate clear expectations for performance and ensure that goals and objectives are met.
- Possess effective training skills and knowledge of training methods.
- Have the skills needed, including interviewing skills, to hire the right person.
- Supervise performance over time, with follow through, so that poor performance leads to termination and good performance is recognized.
- Have knowledge of different supervisory styles and methods that can meet individual needs of supervisees and be appropriate to classroom staff as well as the cook, maintenance staff, office staff, and other nonclassroom personnel.
- Model appropriate behavior.
- Understand different cultural styles of interacting, leading, and participating.

5. The ability to foster good community relations and to influence child care policy that affects the program.

A competent director must

- Have knowledge of community services and functions, including knowledge of:
  —Child care resource and referral organizations and what they offer parents and providers
  —Ending fees, charged and service options, and how to network to form professional collaborative relationships with other program administrators
  —Health services, social services, and other vendors and providers of functions needed by the program and the parents using them
  —Community-based organizations such as religious institutions that have influence on families' lives
  —Child care policies and changes that are made in them, including regulatory policies, funding policies, and governmental structure
  —Legislative processes and how to participate in them
  —Media and other ways to develop public support
- Use this knowledge to build networks and coalitions as needed.
- Have effective skills in communication, including:
  —Public speaking
  —Writing letters
  —Writing proposals, marketing plans, and business plans
  —Communicating in languages other than English
  —Giving media interviews and maintaining media contacts
  —Supervising or producing brochures, flyers, parent handbooks, and other materials
  —Maintaining regular communication with other advocates
  —Maintaining a commitment to educate the community on issues affecting young children and their programs on a regular basis

6. The ability to maintain and develop the physical facility.

A competent director must have the knowledge and skills to

- Establish procedures to monitor and correct in order to maintain compliance with all applicable codes—fire, safety, health, sanitation, building, and zoning.
- Maintain all equipment to ensure safe working condition and have knowledge of procedures for maintenance and repair.
- Establish and maintain safe security practices and equipment at all times.
- Ensure appropriate room arrangement/ space design and support the design and

redesign of effective space, based on knowledge of environmental psychology and early childhood education.

7. The legal knowledge necessary for effective management.

The competent director must be able to work with legal counsel and will have general personal knowledge in the following areas

- Applicable regulatory standards and concepts, including the rights of licensees
- Custody issues that affect child care
- Confidentiality and child welfare laws that affect child care
- Labor laws that affect child care
- Antidiscrimination laws that affect child care and employee rights
- Working knowledge of liability issues
- Health rules
- Basics of contracts that affect the center

8. The ability to apply financial management tools.

The competent director will assume responsibility for financial management and will have the ability to direct the accountant or other financial staff on how

to present figures on income, expenditures, enrollment, and other information in ways that inform decision making. This includes the ability and knowledge needed to

- Mobilize needed resources, including the use of fund-raising, marketing, unrelated business income, and governmental grants or third-party purchase-of-service agreements.
- Maintain accurate and complete financial expenditure records.
- Use financial tools in planning:
  —Effective budget planning and monitoring
    Establishing a staffing pattern for each room
    Setting an annual budget and projections
    Conducting deviation analysis
    Conducting functional cost analysis
  —Cash-flow projection
  —Break-even analysis
- Identify federal, state, and local funding sources, both public and private.
- Understand basic marketing concepts.
- Develop and implement fee policies that fit the needs of the organization.
- Develop a compensation structure that rewards retention and increased knowledge and skills of staff.

Note: The above competencies are needed by directors of centers who serve as executives, fully responsible for program operation. If the income side of the budget is someone else's responsibility, as is usually the case in public school–based programs or Head Start, the director may not need the full range of competencies. Directors of small programs and group child care home licensees need the competencies at a more generalist level than directors of large programs.

Reprinted by permission of the publisher from Culkin, M. L., *Managing Quality in Young Children's Programs: The Leader's Role,* (New York: Teachers College Press, © 2000 by Teachers College, Columbia University. All rights reserved.) pp. 53–57.

Appendix 4
Accreditation Criteria Examples

ACCREDITATION BY THE NATIONAL ACADEMY OF EARLY CHILDHOOD PROGRAMS*

Each component (i.e., interactions among staff and children; curriculum; relationships among teachers and families; staff qualifications and professional development; administration; staffing; physical environment; health and safety; nutrition and food service; and evaluation) begins with a goal statement. For example, the goal statement for the component physical environment is:

Goal: The indoor and outdoor physical environment fosters optimal growth and development through opportunities for exploration and learning.

The goal statement is followed by the rationale. For example:

Rationale: The physical environment affects the behavior and development of the people, both children and adults, who live and work in it. The quality of the physical space and materials provided affects the level of involvement of the children and the quality of interaction between adults and children. The amount, arrangement, and use of space, both indoors and outdoors, are to be evaluated.

*Source: National Association for the Education of Young Children. (1998). *Accreditation criteria and procedures of the National Association for the Education of Young Children.* Washington, DC: Author. Reprinted with permission from the National Association for the Education of Young Children.
Please Note: A review and revision process is now taking place.

The criteria for the component follow. These criteria indicate whether a goal is being achieved. For example:

1. G-1. The indoor and outdoor environments are safe, clean, attractive, and spacious. There is enough usable space indoors so children are not crowded. There is a *minimum* of 35 square feet of usable playroom floor space indoors per child and a *minimum* of 75 square feet of play space outdoors per child. Program staff have access to the designated space in sufficient time to prepare the environment before children arrive.

2. G-2. Activity areas are defined clearly by spatial arrangement. Space is arranged so that children can work individually, together in small groups, or in a large group. Space is arranged to provide clear pathways for children to move from one area to another and to minimize distractions.

3. G-3. The space for children (3 years and older) is arranged to facilitate a variety of small group and/or individual activities including block building, sociodramatic play, art, music, science, math, manipulatives, and quiet book reading and writing. Other activities such as sand/water play and woodworking are also available on occasion. Carpeted space as well as hard surfaces such as wood floors and ample crawling/ toddling areas are provided for infants and young toddlers. Sturdy furniture is provided so nonwalkers can pull themselves up or balance themselves while walking. School-age children are provided separate space arranged to facilitate a variety of age-appropriate activities and permit sustained work on projects.

4. G-4. Age-appropriate materials and equipment of sufficient quantity, variety, and durability are readily accessible to children and arranged on low, open shelves to promote independent use by children.

Materials are rotated and adapted to maintain children's interest.

5. G-5. Individual spaces for children to store their personal belongings are provided.

6. G-6. Private areas are available indoors and outdoors for children to have solitude.

7. G-7. The environment includes soft elements such as rugs, cushions, or rocking chairs.

8. G-8. Sound-absorbing materials are used to cut down on excessive noise.

9. G-9. Outdoor areas include a variety of surfaces such as soil, sand, grass, hills, flat sections, and hard areas for wheel toys. The outdoor area includes shade; open space; digging space; and a variety of equipment for riding, climbing, balancing, and individual play. The outdoor area is protected by fences or by natural barriers from access to streets or other dangers.

10. G-10. The work environment for staff, including classrooms and staff rooms, is comfortable, well-organized, and in good repair. The environment includes a place for adults to take a break or work away from children, an adult-sized bathroom, a secure place for staff to store their personal belongings, and an administrative area that is separated from the children's areas for planning or preparing materials.

Finally, each criterion has interpretive statements. For example G-7 above, the interpretive statements are:

Softness can be provided in many ways—cozy furniture such as rockers and pillows; carpeting; grass outdoors; adults who cuddle children on their laps; and soft materials such as play dough, water, sand, and finger paint.

GUIDELINES FOR PREPARATION OF EARLY CHILDHOOD PROFESSIONALS

For current guidelines consult: National Association for the Education of Young Children. (1998). *Guidelines for preparation of early childhood professionals*. Washington, DC: Author.

Please note that a review and revision process of these standards is taking place. See: National Association for the Education of Young Children. (2001). *NAEYC guidelines revision. NAEYC standards for early childhood professional preparation*. Washington, DC: Author.

Appendix 5
Professional Organizations of Concern to Early Childhood Educators

Alliance for Early Childhood Finance
www.earlychildhoodfinance.org

American Academy of Pediatrics
www.aap.org

American Montessori Society
www.amshq.org

Association Montessori International/USA
www.montessori-ami.org

The Center for the Child Care Workforce
www.ccw.org

The Center for Early Childhood Leadership
www.nl.edu/cecl

Child Care Action Campaign
www.childcareaction.org

Child Care Law Center
www.childcarelaw.org

Child Welfare League of America
www.cwla.org

Children's Defense Fund
www.childrensdefense.org

Council of Chief State School Officers
www.ccsso.org

Council for Exceptional Children
www.cec.sped.org

Council for Professional Recognition
www.cdacouncil.org

Division for Early Childhood of the Council for Exceptional Children
www.dec-sped.org

Early Head Start National Resource Center
www.ehsnrc.org/

Ecumenical Child Care Network
www.eccn.org

Families and Work Institute
www.familiesandwork.org

Food and Nutrition Information Center
www.nal.usda.gov/fnic

Foundation for Child Development
www.ffcd.org

High/Scope Educational Research Foundation
www.highscope.org

International Reading Association
www.ira.org

National Association for Bilingual Education
www.nabe.org

National Association for Child Care Resource and Referral Agencies
www.naccrra.org

National Association of Early Childhood Specialists in State Departments of Education
http://ericps.crc.uiuc.edu/naecs

National Association of Early Childhood Teacher Educators
www.naecte.org

National Association for the Education of Young Children
www.naeyc.org

National Association for Family Child Care
www.nafcc.org

National Association for Sick Child Daycare
www.nascd.com

National Association of State Boards of Education
www.nasbe.org

National Association of State Directors of Special Education
www.nasdse.org

National Black Child Development Institute
www.nbcdi.org

National Center for Children in Poverty
http://cpmcnet.columbia.edu/dept/nccp

National Child Care Information Center
www.nccic.org

National Coalition for Campus Children's Centers
www.campuschildren.org

National Head Start Association
www.nhsa.org

The National Institute for Early Education Research
http://nieer.org

National Latino Children's Institute
www.nlci.org

National PTA
www.pta.org

National School Age Care Alliance
www.nsaca.org

National Women's Law Center
www.nwlc.org/

Society for Research in Child Development
www.srcd.org

Southern Early Childhood Association
www.seca50.org

The Urban Institute
www.urban.org

Wheelock College Institute for Leadership and Career Initiatives (formerly Center for Career Development in Early Care and Education)
http://institute.wheelock.edu

Zero to Three: National Center for Infants, Toddlers, and Families
www.zerotothree.org

Appendix 6
Suppliers of Materials and Equipment for Early Childhood Programs

SUPPLIERS OF CHILDREN'S FURNITURE AND LEARNING MATERIALS

abc School Supply, Inc.
www.abcschoolsupply.com

Accu-Cut Systems
www.accucut.com

Activa Products
www.activa-products.com

The Angeles Group
www.angeles-group.com

Becker School Supplies
www.shopbecker.com

Beckley Cardy
www.beckleycardy.com

Binney & Smith
www.binney-smith.com

Child Forms
www.childforms.com

Child Safe Products
www.childsafeproducts.com

Childcraft Education Corporation
www.childcrafteducation.com

Children's Factory
http://busy-kids.com

Community Playthings
www.communityplaythings.com

Constructive Playthings
www.constructplay.com

Custom Playground Designs
www.customplayground.com

Dick Blick Art Materials
www.dickblick.com

Discovery Toys, Inc.
www.discoverytoysinc.com

Environments, Inc.
www.eichild.com

ETA/Cuisenaire
www.etacuisenaire.com

Flagship Carpets (Educational Division)
www.Flagshipcarpets.com

GameTime
www.gametime.com

Groundscape Technologies
www.groundscapetech.com

Insect Lore Products
www.insectlore.com

Jonti-Craft, Inc.
www.jonti-craft.com

Kimbo Educational
www.kimboed.com

Kompan (Unique Playgrounds)
www.Kompan.com

Lakeshore Learning Materials
www.lakeshorelearning.com

Landscape Structures, Inc.
www.playlsi.com

Learning Resources, Inc.
www.learningresources.com

Lego Dacta
www.pitsco-legodacta.com

Music for Little People
www.mflp.com

Nienhuis Montessori
www.nienhuis.com

Puppet Partners
www.puppetpartners.com

Rhythm Band Instruments, Inc.
www.rhythmband.com

Safeplay Systems
www.safeplayturf.com

Texwood Furniture
www.texwood.com

Tout About Toys, Inc.
www.toutabouttoys.com

Tree Blocks
www.treeblocks.com

PUBLISHERS OF CHILDREN'S SOFTWARE

Berkley Systems, Inc.
www.berksys.com

Big Top Productions
www.bigtop.com

Broderbund Software, Inc.
www.broderbund.com

Bytes of Learning, Inc.
www.bytesoflearning.com

Claris Corporation
www.claris.com

Compu-Teach, Inc.
www.compu-teach.com

Corel Corporation
www.corel.com

Creative Wonders
www.creativewonders.com

Davidson & Associates, Inc.
www.davidson.com

The Discovery Channel
www.discovery.com

Disney Interactive, Inc.
www.disney.com

Don Johnston, Inc.
www.donjohnston.com

Edmark Corporation
www.edmark.com

Educational Productions
www.edpro.com

Expert Software, Inc.
www.expertsoftware.com

Fractal Corporation
www.fractal.com

Graphix Zone
www.gzone.com

Humongous Entertainment
www.humongous.com

IBM Multimedia Studio
www.ibm.com

Knowledge Adventure
www.knowledgeadventure.com

The Learning Company
www.learningco.com

Maxis
www.maxis.com

MECC
www.mecc.com

Merit Software
www.meritsoftware.com

Micrografx, Inc.
www.micrografx.com

Micrograms Software
www.micrograms.com

Microsoft Corporation
www.microsoft.com

Mindscape, Inc.
www.mindscape.com

Mobius Corporation
www.mobius.com

Modern Media Ventures, Inc.
www.gustown.com/Info/mmv.html

National Geographic Soft
www.nationalgeographic.com

Optimum Resource, Inc.
www.stickybear.com

Queue, Inc.
www.queueinc.com

Sanctuary Woods Multimedia
www.sanctuarywoods.com

Scholastic New Media
www.scholastic.com

Sierra On-Line
www.sierra.com

Society for Visual Education Media
www.svemedia.com

Soleil Software, Inc.
www.soleil.com

Sunburst Communications
www.sunburst.com

Terrapin Software, Inc.
www.terrapinlogo.com

Tom Snyder Productions
www.tomsnyder.com

Viacom New Media
www.viacom.com

Virgin Sound and Vision
www.vsv.com

William K. Bradford Publishing
www.wkbradford.com

BUSINESS MANAGEMENT SOFTWARE

Child Care Office Pro
www.childcareoffice.com

Daycare Software (Pinnacle Software Systems)
www.daycaresoft.com

EZ Care 2 (SofterWare)
www.softerware.com/ezcare2/

KidKeeper
www.kidkeeper.com

Kindersoft (Showcase Computer System Product)

www.kindersoft.co.uk

Orgamation Technologies

www.orgamation.com

ProCare Software (Professional Solutions)

www.procaresoft.com

SoftCare

www.soft-care.com

SELECTING CHILDREN'S BOOKS

See lists provided in early childhood texts, in which books are often categorized by type of book and by age appropriateness. Following are two examples of texts that offer good lists of children's books:

Morrow, L. M. (1993). *Literacy development in the early years* (2nd ed., pp. 336–361). Boston: Allyn & Bacon.

Schickedanz, J. A. (1999). *Much more than the ABCs.* Washington, DC: National Association for the Education of Young Children.

In addition to these types of listings, consider books that have won, or been runners-up for, awards such as the following:

The ALA Notable Children's Books List

Boston Globe—Horn Book Award

Caldecott Medal

Appendix 7
Financial Assistance

FEDERAL ASSISTANCE

Major Programs

- Corporation for National & Community Service
  (Website not listed)

94.011	Foster Grandparent Program

- Department of Agriculture
  www.usda.gov/

10.553	School Breakfast Program
10.555	National School Lunch Program
10.556	Special Milk Program for Children
10.557	Special Supplemental Nutrition Program for Women, Infants, and Children
10.558	Child and Adult Care Food Program
10.559	Summer Food Service Program for Children
10.564	Nutrition Education and Training Program

- Department of Education
  www.ed.gov/

84.010	Title I Grants to Local Educational Agencies
84.011	Migrant Education—State Grant Program
84.027	Special Education—Grants to States
84.173	Special Education—Preschool Grants
84.181	Special Education—Grants for Infants and Families with Disabilities
84.196	Education for Homeless Children and Youth
84.206	Javits Gifted and Talented Students Education Grant Program
84.213	Even Start—State Educational Agencies
84.214	Even Start—Migrant Education
84.215	Fund for the Improvement of Education
84.257	National Institute for Literacy
84.258	Even Start—Indian Tribes and Tribal Organizations
84.286	Ready to Change
84.287	Twenty-First Century Community Learning Centers
84.288	Bilingual Education—Program Development and Implementation Grants
84.289	Bilingual Education—Program Enhancement Grants
84.290	Bilingual Education—Comprehensive School Grants
84.291	Bilingual Education—Systemwide Improvement Grants

84.292	Bilingual Education—Research Programs
84.295	Ready-to-Learn Television
84.303	Technology Innovation Challenge Grants
84.307	National Institute on Early Childhood Development and Education
84.310	Parental Assistance Centers
84.314	Even Start—Statewide Family Literacy Program
84.318	Technology Literacy Challenge Fund Grants
84.323	Special Education—State Program Improvement Grants for Children with Disabilities
84.324	Special Education—Research and Innovation to Improve Services and Results for Children with Disabilities
84.325	Special Education—Personnel Preparation to Improve Services and Results for Children with Disabilities
84.326	Special Education—Technical Assistance and Dissemination to Improve Services and Results for Children with Disabilities
84.327	Special Education—Technology and Media Services for Individuals with Disabilities
84.328	Special Education—Parent Information Center
84.329	Special Education—Studies and Evaluations
84.335	Child Care Access Means Parents in School
84.338	Reading Excellence
84.340	Class Size Reduction
84.342	Preparing Tomorrow's Teachers to Use Technology

84.349	Early Childhood Educator Professional Development
84.350	Transition to Teaching
84.355	Child Care Provider Loan Forgiveness Demonstration
84.357	Reading First State Grants
84.359	Early Reading First
84.363	School Leadership

- Department of Health and Human Services
  www.hhs.gov/

93.558	Temporary Assistance for Needy Families
93.575	Child Care and Development Block Grant
93.577	Early Learning Fund
93.596	Child Care Mandatory and Matching Funds of the Child Care and Development Fund
93.600	Head Start
93.630	Developmental Disabilities Basic Support and Advocacy Grants
93.926	Healthy Start Initiative
93.994	Maternal and Child Health Services Block Grant to the States

- Department of the Interior
  Bureau of Indian Affairs
  www.doi.gov/bureau-indian-affairs.html

15.042	Indian School Equalization Program
15.043	Indian Child and Family Education
15.130	Indian Education—Assistance to Schools
15.144	Indian Child Welfare Act—Title II Grants

The Catalog of Federal Domestic Assistance provides comprehensive information on each program including information contacts. All or parts of the catalog are available online at <www.cfda.gov/>.

Additional Help in Locating Federal Assistance

ED Grants (Department of Education's grants)
www.ed.gov/pubs/KnowAbtGrants/

The Federal Register
www.access.gpo.gov/
(Choose National Archives and Records Administration's Office.)

GrantsNet (Department of Health and Human Services' grants)
www.hhs.gov/grantsnet

The Women's Bureau for Entrepreneurial Training (U.S. Small Business Administration)
www.sba.gov/womeninbusiness/wnet.html

FOUNDATION SUPPORT

The Chronicle of Philanthropy
http://philanthropy.com/

The Foundation Center
http://fdncenter.org

The Grantsmanship Center Magazine
www.tgci.com/publications/magazine.htm

J.C. Downing Foundation's *Basic Principles for Grant Seekers*
www.jcdowning.org/resources/generalguide.htm

The Taft Group
www.galegroup.com/servlet/BrowsePublisherServlet?region=9&imprint=000 &id=828

COMMUNITY RESOURCES

Child Care Aware (Locates local CCR&R agency.)
www.childcareaware.org

Local Initiatives Support Consortium
www.lisnet.org

Also contact professional organizations listed in appendix 5.

Appendix 8
Handbook for Families and Volunteers

Hubbards Independent School District
Kindergarten–Primary School

CONTENTS

1. OUR SCHOOL

It's going to be 4 months before I can start kindergarten. I went to see my school today so I can find out about kindergarten. That way I'll be ready to go in September.

My school is in a big building. I've never seen so many toys, books, and records. And, they even have hamsters and lots of other animals—almost like a zoo!

My teacher's name is _____.
I asked her lots of questions and found out all about kindergarten. My school is a kinder-garten–primary school. The kids will be 5, 6, 7, and 8 years old. My teacher said there will be plenty of things for all of us to do. At first I'll have easy things to do. Then as I learn, I'll get harder things to do. My teacher said that most children go to school here 4 years, but a few go 3 years and a few stay 5 years. It's called a "continuous progress" approach. I don't understand what that means, but you will hear about it in the Spring Orientation meeting tomorrow.

2. ENTRANCE REQUIREMENTS

Age

Little children can't go to kindergarten. I'm big now. I'm 5! This was printed in our newspaper:

A child may attend kindergarten if he or she is 5 years old on or before September 15.

Birth Certificate
Our state requires that children have a legal birth certificate to enter school. I have to bring it when I register. If you do not have it, you will need to write to

The Bureau of Vital Statistics
State Capitol Building

_____
(Capital City)

_____
(State)

_____
(ZIP Code)

The charge is $ _____.

Emergency Information Form

You always give me lots of good food, put me to bed early, and let me play outside. I'm very careful because skinned knees hurt. My teacher will take care of me while I'm at school and will need an "emergency information form" in case I get sick or hurt. It's in the back of this book. I'll get your pen and you can give my teacher the information.

Health History

Physical Examination

Immunizations

Dental Examination

My teacher says that I must be healthy and strong in kindergarten. You will have to call my doctor and dentist soon because they're so busy. They have to write on all the other forms in the back of this handbook. Will I need to get a pen for the doctor and the dentist? I'll bring one, just in case.

3. REGISTRATION, SUPPLIES, AND CLOTHING

Registration

I am assigned to the school in the school attendance area in which I live. You found out where my class was by calling the elementary school director's office. About 2 weeks before school starts, our town's newspaper will tell all about the school attendance areas and when to register.

The newspaper will also tell you about bus routes and the times the bus will pick me up and bring me back home if I am to ride the bus.

Supplies

My teacher gave me a list of supplies. Here is a copy.

> One box of large washable crayons.
> One 20 in. × 48 in. plastic mat stitched crosswise in several sections.
> One terry cloth apron with Velcro fasteners.

These supplies are sold in our two discount stores.

Clothing

With so many children and with so much for each of us to do in kindergarten, the teacher says these are good qualities for school clothes:

1. Labeled for identification
2. Easy to handle (large buttons and buttonholes, underwear convenient for toileting, boots the child can put on and remove, loops on coats and sweaters for hanging)
3. Washable
4. Sturdy
5. Not too tight
6. Shoes that are comfortable for play

4. ATTENDANCE, SESSION TIMES, AND EARLY DISMISSAL

Attendance

Our school has attendance regulations. My teacher says it is important that I go to school every day so I'll get to do all the fun things with my friends.

Session Times

Our kindergarten starts at _____ and closes at _____. I should arrive at school no more than 10 minutes before school starts. If you take me to school in the car, we should drive in the circular driveway, and I should enter the school at the side door. I should never leave our car at the curb by the street. You can pick me up at the same place right after school.

Early Dismissal

My teacher says that I'm not to leave early unless there is an emergency. These are the rules families have to follow:

1. Only the principal can dismiss a student.
2. A student cannot be excused by a telephone call without verification of the telephone call.
3. A student can be dismissed only to a parent or a person properly identified.

5. LUNCH AND MILK

I want to eat lunch and drink milk with the other children. Here's a note that tells all about it.

A hot lunch will be served in the cafeteria every day. It costs _____ cents a day, or you may pay $ _____ a week. Checks may be made payable to _____. If your child wishes to bring his or her lunch, milk will cost _____ cents a day. Those who wish to inquire whether their children qualify for free or reduced-cost lunches may secure forms in the central office.

When sending money to school, place it in an envelope and write the child's name and the teacher's name on the envelope.

6. A CHILD STAYS HOME

When Ill

I'm supposed to stay home if I'm sick. Here is a list of reasons:

Blood in stools
Diarrhea (negative stool cultures required for some illnesses)
Difficult breathing
Fever accompanied by behavior changes or symptoms of an illness until the child receives a professional evaluation
Inexplicable irritability or persistent crying
Lethargy (more than usual tiredness)
Mouth sores with drooling
Persistent abdominal pain
Rash with fever or behavior change
Uncontrolled coughing
Unspecified respiratory tract illness
Vomiting (two or more times in 24 hours)
Wheezing

Certain Diseases

Chicken pox (until lesions have dried)
Haemophilus influenza, type b (HIb) infection
Head lice (from end of school day until after first treatment)
Hepatitis A (until one week after onset)

Herpes simplex (sores and drooling)
Impetigo (until 24 hours after treatment begins)
Measles (until 6 days after rash appears)
Meningitis
Mumps (until 9 days after swelling)
Pertussis (until 14 days after laboratory confirmed onset)
Purulent conjunctivitis (until 24 hours after treatment begins)
Rubella (until 6 days after rash appears)
Scabies (until treatment is completed)
Shingles (if sores have not crusted)
Streptococcal pharyngitis (until 24 hours after treatment begins) or other streptococcal infections
Tuberculosis

During Family Emergency

I may stay home if there is a death or serious illness in our family.

During Extremely Inclement Weather

Mom and Dad, you must decide if the weather is too bad for me to go to school. Sometimes there will be no school during bad weather. Local radio and TV stations carry school closing announcements are WKID, WKDG-TV, and WBUG-TV.

Take a Note

I'm supposed to take a note when I come back to school telling my teacher why I've been absent. If I've been to the doctor, I must get a note signed by the doctor before I return to school.

7. EVERYDAY EXPERIENCES

When I visited the kindergarten at my school, I saw children doing many things in the building and outdoors. Some of the children were singing in the music room, some boys were feeding the hamsters, a girl was walking on a balance beam, and a big boy was reading a story to a little boy. My teacher said that in the kindergarten–primary school we do all those things and much more, like counting, painting, working with clay, reading books, learning about ourselves and people near and far, and visiting places in our town. We even eat together at lunch and have a snack in the morning and afternoon.

8. SPECIAL EXPERIENCES

Field Trips

When our class plans a field trip, the school asks our parent (guardian) whether we can go. The teacher will send a note to you each time we go on such a trip, and you will have to sign it.

Parties and Treats

Birthdays are a lot of fun. When it is my birthday, I can share some treats with my class. My teacher will give you a list of all the rules about birthday treats. Even grown-ups have rules!

We will have five other celebrations. My teacher will send a note to you.

At our school we do not exchange gifts on any holiday. We just say, "Happy Holidays!" We can make cards. My teacher will send you a list of names.

Taking Things to School

Sometimes I can take a book, a game, a picture, or an object from nature and souvenirs from trips. You can help me choose what to take so that I don't take fragile, valuable (i.e., expensive family treasure), sharp-edged objects, or toy guns, knives, etc.

9. HOW FAMILIES CAN HELP

Guess what? My teacher at school says that all the children's families are teachers, too! There are lots of teachers. Here is a letter from my schoolteacher.

Dear Family Member,

As a family member, you have been responsible for the early teaching of your child. Although he/she is now old enough for school, you will still be the most important teacher in your child's life. Here are some ways you can help your child in school.

1. Attend individual and group conferences as often as you can.
2. Read and answer all notes from the school.
3. Give special help to your child by promoting good health and safety habits.

> Praising your child for things done well.
> Talking about everyday experiences.
> Planning family activities.
> Reading stories.
> Watching children's television shows with your child.
> Providing materials for cutting, drawing, writing, and building.
> Helping your child start a collection, such as leaves or rocks.
> Teaching your child to take care of toileting needs, to dress (outdoor clothing), and to put away toys.

10. YOUR CHILD'S PROGRESS

Our school doesn't send home report cards, but you can find out how I'm doing in school. My teacher will get together with you several times this year, and you will talk about how I'm doing and see my portfolio.

You can talk with my teacher anytime, and you can see me in school, too. My school will also have some special meetings for you. I have a list of the meetings the teacher planned. There's a blank space by each one. You can record the time when you get a note or telephone call from my teacher.

Get-acquainted conference (approximately 2 weeks after the beginning of school)

_____

Fall individual conference (November)

_____

Spring individual conference (April)

_____

11. FAMILY MEMBER'S CHECKLIST

Here's a "Family Member's Checklist" to make sure everything is done.

Have you read this handbook? _____

Does your child have a legal birth certificate? _____

Have you completed and signed the emergency information form? _____

Have you completed and signed the health history form? _____

Has your physician completed and signed the physical examination form? _____

Has your physician completed and signed the immunization record form? _____

Has your dentist signed the dental report form? _____

Do you know the date of registration? _____

Have you obtained the school supplies? _____

Are all outdoor clothes labeled? _____

Does your child have the right type of school clothes? _____

Are you following the suggestions given in the section "How Families Can Help"? _____

List any questions you would like to discuss with the staff. _____

12. FORMS

Remember those forms* that are part of the entrance requirements? Here they are, and you will have to take them when I go to school the first day.

EMERGENCY INFORMATION

Child's name _____
Home address _____ Phone number _____
Father's name _____
Place of business _____ Phone number _____

---

*Forms from the state or funding agency should be used if provided.

Mother's name _____
Place of business _____ Phone number _____
Give name of another person to be called in case of emergency if parent or guardian cannot be reached:
Name _____ Phone number _____
Address _____ Relationship _____
Physician to be called in case of emergency
1st choice _____ Phone number _____
2nd choice _____ Phone number _____
Name of hospital to be used in emergency
1st choice _____
2nd choice _____
Other comments _____
_____
_____
Date _____ Signed _____
(Parent or guardian)

HEALTH HISTORY

Child's name _____
General evaluation of family's health _____
_____
Family deaths (causes) _____
_____

Child's illnesses. If your child has had any of these diseases, please state the age at which he or she had them.

_____ measles
_____ mumps
_____ whooping cough
_____ poliomyelitis
_____ rheumatic fever
_____ scarlet fever
_____ diphtheria
_____ serious accident
_____ smallpox
_____ diabetes
_____ heart disease
_____ meningitis
_____ epilepsy
_____ chicken pox
_____ pneumonia
_____ asthma, hay fever

Has your child ever had tests for tuberculosis?
_____

Skin test? _____ Date _____
Chest X ray? _____ Date _____

Please check any of the following that you have noted recently:

_____ frequent sore throat
_____ persistent cough
_____ frequent headaches
_____ poor vision
_____ dizziness
_____ frequent styes
_____ dental defects
_____ speech difficulty
_____ tires easily
_____ shortness of breath
_____ frequent nosebleed
_____ allergy
_____ frequent urination
_____ fainting spells
_____ abdominal pain
_____ loss of appetite
_____ hard of hearing
_____ four or more colds per year

Describe your child socially and emotionally.
_____
_____
_____

Are there any matters that you would like to discuss with the school staff?_____
_____

Date _____ Signed _____
(Parent or guardian)

PHYSICAL EXAMINATION

Child's name _____
Comment on any significant findings:
Length/height in./cm _____ %ile _____
Weight lb/kg _____ %ile _____
Head circumference in./cm _____ %ile _____
Blood pressure (age 3 and older) _____/_____
Eyes: Right _____ Left _____ Squint _____
Ears: Right _____ Left _____ Discharge _____
Nose _____ Throat _____

Glands _____ Tonsils _____
Cardiorespiratory _____
Abdomen _____
Genitalia/breasts _____
Extremities/joints/back/chest _____
Hernia _____
Nutrition _____
Posture _____
Neurological/developmental _____
Screenings (if indicated)
   Lead _____
   Anemia _____
   Urinalysis _____
   Hearing _____
   Vision _____
T.B. test
Tine _____ Reaction _____ Pos. _____ Date _____
Mantoux _____ Neg._____ Date _____
Chest X ray _____ Results _____ Date _____
Does the school program need to be adjusted for this child?
_____
_____
_____

Date _____ Signed _____
M.D. or D.O.

IMMUNIZATION RECORD

Child's name _____

Immunization	Date
DTap/DTP/Td	_____
Poliomyelitis	_____
HIB	_____
HEP B	_____
MMR	_____
Varicella	_____
Pneumocaccal	_____
Other	_____

Date _____ Signed _____
M.D. or D.O.

DENTAL REPORT

Child's name _____
Cavities _____ Gums _____

Malocclusion _____
Please explain any abnormal findings or deformities _____
_____

Please indicate care given
Prophylaxis _____ Cavities filled _____
Extractions _____ Orthodontics _____
What additional care do you plan for this child?
_____
_____
Date _____ Signed _____
                        D.D.S.

MEDICATION PERMISSION FORM

Medications for children can be administered only when requested by the prescribing physician. Each container shall be childproof and carry the name of the medication, the name of the person for whom it was prescribed, the name of the prescribing physician, and the physician's instructions. Each child's medication shall be stored in its original container. This is in compliance with state and federal laws.

Child's Name _____
Prescription name and number _____
Pharmacy name _____
Physician's name _____ Phone _____
Description of medication (e.g., white liquid, red capsules)
_____
Illness/condition _____
Dosage _____ Time(s) of day to be given _____
Precautions _____
Date prescribed _____
Date to be discontinued _____

_____   _____
Signature of physician   Date

_____   _____
Signature of parent (guardian)   Date

Note: Because of space limitations, sections of the Handbook for Families and Volunteers are indicated by numbers and headings. In making your school's handbook, arrange materials attractively on each page. A short paragraph can be centered, and drawings, and so forth, can be added.

References

Abbott, C. F., & Gold, S. (1991). Conferring with parents when you're concerned that their child needs special services. *Young Children, 46*(4), 10–14.

Abbott-Shim, M. S. (1990). In-service training: A means to quality care. *Young Children, 45*(2), 14–18.

Adams, G., & Poersch, N. O. (1997). Who cares? State commitment to child care and early education. *Young Children, 52*(4), 66–69.

Adams, G., Schulman, K., & Ebb, N. (1998). *Locked doors: States struggling to meet the needs of low-income working families.* Washington, DC: Children's Defense Fund.

Adams, G. S. (1965). *Measurement and evaluation in education, psychology, and guidance.* New York: Holt, Rinehart & Winston.

Adams, P. K., & Taylor, M. K. (1985). *A learning center approach to infant education.* Columbus, GA: Columbus College, School of Education. (ERIC Document Reproduction Service No. ED253315)

Aday, R. H., Evans, E., McDuffie, W., & Sims, C. R. (1996). Changing children's attitudes about the elderly: The longitudinal effects of an intergenerational partners program. *Journal of Research in Childhood Education, 10*(2), 143–151.

Alexander, K. L., & Entwisle, D. R. (1988). Achievement in the first two years of school: Pattern and processes. *Monographs for the Society of Research in Child Development, 53*(2, Serial No. 218).

Allan, L. L. (1997). Do you resent and stonewall parents—Matthew's line. *Young Children, 52*(4), 72–74.

Allen, M., Brown, P., & Finlay, B. (1992). *Helping children by strengthening families.* Washington, DC: Children's Defense Fund.

Allison, J. (1999). A tribute to a great scholar and colleague. *Childhood Education, 75,* 260–263.

Almy, M. (1975). *The early childhood educator at work.* New York: McGraw-Hill.

Almy, M. (1988). The early childhood educator revisited. In B. Spodek, O. N. Saracho, & D. L. Peters (Eds.), *Professionalism and the early childhood practitioner* (pp. 48–55). New York: Teachers College Press.

Alvarado, C., Burnley, L., Derman-Sparks, L., Hoffman, E., Jiménez, L. I., Labyzon, J., Ramsey, P., Unten, A., Wallace, B., & Yasui, B. (1999). *In our own way: How anti-bias work shapes our lives.* St. Paul, MN: Redleaf.

American Academy of Pediatrics, American Public Health Association, & National Resource Center for Health and Safety in Child Care. (2002). *Caring for our children* (2nd ed.). Elk Grove Village, IL: American Academy of Pediatrics.

American Society for Testing and Materials. (1999). *Standard consumer safety performance specification for playground equipment for public use* (Document #F1487–98). West Conshohocken, PA: Author.

Anderson, C., Nagle, R., Roberts, W., & Smith, J. (1981). Attachment to substitute caregivers as a function of center quality and caregiver involvement. *Child Development, 52,* 53–61.

Anderson, J. (1947). The theory of early childhood education. In N. B. Henry (Ed.), *The forty-sixth yearbook of the National Society for the Study of Education, Part II* (pp. 70–100). Chicago: University of Chicago Press.

Andreasen, A. R. (1995). *Marketing social change: Changing behavior to promote health, social development, and the environment.* San Francisco: Jossey-Bass.

Anthony, M. A. (1998). Stages of director development. *Child Care Information Exchange, 123,* 81–83.

Arin-Krump, J. (1981). *Adult development: Implications for staff development.* Manchester, MA: Adult Development and Learning.

Arizona Center for Educational Research and Development. (1983). Tucson Early Education Model (TEEM). Tucson, AZ: Author.

Aronson, S. S. (1991). *Health and safety in child care.* New York: HarperCollins.

Aronson, S. S. (1993). Tree climbing and care of sand play areas. *Child Care Information Exchange, 90,* 79–80.

Aronson, S. S. (Ed.). (2002). *Healthy young children: A manual for programs.* Wahington, DC: National Association for the Education of Young Children.

Ashton-Warner, S. (1963). *Teacher.* New York: Simon & Schuster.

Association for Childhood Education International. (1986). *When parents of kindergartners ask "why."* Olney, MD: Author.

Association for Childhood Education International. (1997). Preparation of early childhood teachers: ACEI position paper. *Childhood Education, 73,* 164–165.

Association for Supervision and Curriculum Development. (1988). *A resource guide to public school early childhood programs.* Alexandria, VA: Author.

Atkinson, A. M. (1987). Fathers' participation and evaluation of family day care. *Family Relations, 36*(2), 146–151.

Austin, J. S. (2000). When a child discloses sexual abuse: Immediate and appropriate teacher responses. *Childhood Education, 77,* 2–5.

Ayers, W. (1992). Disturbances from the field: Recovering the voice of the early childhood teacher. In S. Kessler & B. B. Swadener (Eds.), *Reconceptualizing the early childhood curriculum: Beginning the dialogue* (pp. 256–266). New York: Teachers College Press.

Azer, S. L., & Hanrahan, C. (1998). *Early care and career development initiatives in 1998.* Boston: Wheelock College, Center for Career Development in Early Care and Education.

Bailey, D. B., Jr., Burchinal, M., & McWilliam, R. A. (1993). Age of peers and early childhood development. *Child Development, 64,* 848–862.

Baker, K. R. (1968). Extending the indoors outside. In S. Sunderlin & N. Gray (Eds.), *Housing for early childhood education* (pp. 59–70). Olney, MD: Association for Childhood Education International.

Balaban, N. (1992). The role of the child care professional in caring for infants, toddlers, and their families. *Young Children, 47*(5), 66–71.

Bandura, A. (1977). *Social learning theory.* Upper Saddle River, NJ: Prentice Hall.

Bandura, A. (1982). Self-efficacy mechanisms in human agency. *American Psychologists, 37,* 122–147.

Bar-Or, O. (2000). Juvenile obesity, physical activity, and lifestyle changes. *The Physician and Sports Medicine, 28*(11), 51–58.

Barbett, S., & Korb, R. A. (1999). *Current funds, revenues, and expenditures of degree-granting institutions: Fiscal Year 1996.* Washington, DC: U.S. Department of Education, Office of Educational Research and Improvement.

Barbour, N. H., & Seefeldt, C. (1993). *Developmental continuity: Across preschool and primary grades.* Olney, MD: Association for Childhood Education International.

Barker, L., Wahlers, K., Watson, K., & Kibler, R. (1987). *Groups in process.* Upper Saddle River, NJ: Prentice Hall.

Barker, R. G. (1951). *One boy's day.* New York: Harper.

Barnett v. Fairfax County School Board, 927 F. 2d 146 (4th Cir. 1991), *cert. denied,* 112 S. Ct., 175 (1991).

Barnett, W. S. (1986). Methodological issues in economic evaluation of early intervention programs. *Early Childhood Research Quarterly, 1,* 249–268.

Barnett, W. S. (1993a). Benefit-cost analysis of preschool education: Findings from a 25-year follow-up. *American Journal of Orthopsychiatry, 63,* 500–508.

Barnett, W. S. (1993b). New wine in old bottles: Increasing coherence in early childhood care and education policy. *Early Childhood Research Quarterly, 8,* 519–558.

Barnett, W. S. (1995). Long-term effects of early childhood programs on cognitive and school outcomes. *Future of Children, 5*(3), 25–50.

Barnett, W. S. (2000). Economics of early childhood intervention. In J. P. Shonkoff & S. J. Meisels (Eds.), *Handbook of early childhood intervention* (2nd ed., pp. 589–612). New York: Cambridge University Press.

Barnett, W. S., & Escobar, C. M. (1990). Economic costs and benefits of early intervention. In S. J. Meisels & J. P. Shonkoff (Eds.), *Handbook of early childhood intervention* (pp. 560–582). New York: Cambridge University Press.

Barnett, W. S., Frede, E. C., Mobasher, H., & Mohr, P. (1987). The efficacy of public preschool programs and the relationship of program quality to program efficacy. *Educational Evaluation and Policy Analysis, 10*(1), 37–39.

Baruch, D. (1939). *Parents and children go to school.* Chicago: Scott, Foresman.

Beaty, J. J. (1996). *Preschool appropriate practices* (2nd ed.). Orlando, FL: Harcourt, Brace.

Beaty, J. J. (2002). *Observing development of the young child* (5th ed.). Upper Saddle River, NJ: Merrill/Prentice Hall.

Behrmann, M. M., & Lahm, E. A. (1994). Computer applications in early childhood special education. In J. L. Wright & D. D. Shade (Eds.), *Young children: Active learners in a technological age* (pp. 105–120). Washington, DC: National Association for the Education of Young Children.

Belle, D. (1997). Varieties of self-care: A qualitative look at children's experiences in the after-school hours. *Merrill-Palmer Quarterly, 43,* 478–496.

Bellis, M. (1997). *Looping and its implications for North Hanover Township Public Schools.* Research report. North Hanover Township, NJ: North Hanover Township Public Schools.

Bellm, D., Breuning, G. S., Lombardi, J., & Whitebook, M. (1992). On the horizon: New policy initiatives to enhance child care staff compensation. *Young Children, 47*(5), 39–42.

Bellm, D., Burton, A., Shukla, R., & Whitebook, M. (1997). *Making work pay in the child care industry: Promising practices for improving compensation.* Washington, DC: Center for the Child Care Workforce.

Bellm, D., Whitebook, M., & Hnatiuk, P. (1997). *The early childhood mentoring curriculum: A handbook for mentors.* Washington, DC: Center for the Child Care Workforce.

Bender, J. (1978). Large hollow blocks: Relationship of quantity to block building behaviors. *Young Children, 33*(6), 17–23.

Bentzen, W. (2000). *Seeing young children: A guide to observing and recording behaviors.* Albany, NY: Delmar.

Bereiter, C. (1990). Aspects of educational learning theory. *Review of Educational Research, 60,* 603–624.

Bereiter, C., & Englemann, S. (1966). *Teaching disadvantaged children in the preschool.* Upper Saddle River, NJ: Prentice Hall.

Bergan, J. R., & Field, J. K. (1993). Developmental assessment: New directions. *Young Children, 48*(5), 41–47.

Bergen, D. (1993/94). Authentic performance assessments. *Childhood Education, 70,* 99, 102.

Bergen, D. (1994). Teaching strategies: Developing the art and science of team teaching. *Childhood Education, 70,* 300–301.

Bergen, D., & Coscia, J. (2001). *Brain research and childhood education: Implications for educators.* Olney, MD: Association for Childhood Education International.

Bergen, D., Reid, R., & Torelli, L. (2001). *Educating and caring for very young children. The infant/toddler curriculum.* New York: Teachers College Press.

Berger, E. (2000). *Parents as partners in education: The school and home working together* (5th ed.). Upper Saddle River, NJ: Merrill/Prentice Hall.

Berk, L. E., & Winsler, A. (1995). *Scaffolding children's learning: Vygotsky and early childhood education.* Washington, DC: National Association for the Education of Young Children.

Bermudez, A., & Marquez, J. (1996). An examination of a four-way collaborative to increase parental involvement in the schools. *The Journal of Educational Issues of Language Minority Students, 16,* 1–16.

Berrueta-Clement, J., Schweinhart, L., Barnett, W., Epstein, A., & Weikart, D. (1984). Changed lives: The effects of the Perry Preschool Program on youths through age 19. *Monographs of the High/Scope Educational Research Foundation* (No. 8). Ypsilanti, MI: High/Scope Press.

Berry, P. (1993). Young children's use of fixed playground equipment. *International Play Journal, 1,* 115–131.

Betz, C. (1994). Beyond time-out: Tips from a teacher. *Young Children, 49*(3), 10–14.

Bhattacharya, J., & Currie, J. (2001). Youths and nutrition risk: Malnourished or misnourished? In J. Gruber (Ed.), *Risky behavior among youths: An economic analysis* (pp. 483–521). Chicago: University of Chicago Press.

Biber, B. (1984). *Early education and psychological development.* New Haven, CT: Yale University Press.

Bijou, S. W. (1976). *Child development: The basic stages of early childhood.* Upper Saddle River, NJ: Prentice Hall.

Bingham, A. A. (1995). *Exploring the multi-age classroom.* York, ME: Stenhouse.

Birch, L. L., Johnson, S. L., & Fisher, J. A. (1995). Children's eating: The development of food acceptance patterns. *Young Children, 50*(2), 71–78.

Blank, H. K. (1997). Advocacy leadership. In S. L. Kagan & B. T. Bowman (Eds.), *Leadership in early care and education* (pp. 39–45). Washington, DC: National Association for the Education of Young Children.

Blank, H. K., & Adams, G. (1997). *State departments in child care and early education, 1997.* Washington, DC: Children's Defense Fund.

Blau, D. M., & Hagy, A. P. (1998). The demand for quality in child care. *Journal of Political Economy, 106,* 104–146.

Bloch, M. N. (1991). Critical science and the history of child development's influence on early education research. *Early Education and Development, 2,* 95–108.

Bloom, B. S. (1964*). Stability and change in human characteristics.* New York: Wiley.

Bloom, P. J. (1989). *The Illinois directors' study: A report to the Illinois Department of Children and Family Services.* Evanston, IL: National College of Education, Early Childhood Professional Development Project.

Bloom, P. J. (1995a). Building a sense of community: A broader view. *Child Care Information Exchange, 101,* 47–50.

Bloom, P. J. (1995b). Shared decision making: The centerpiece of participatory management. *Young Children, 50*(4), 55–60.

Bloom, P. J. (1996). The quality of work life in early childhood programs: Does accreditation make a difference? In S. Bredekamp & B. A. Willer (Eds.), *NAEYC accreditation: A decade of learning and the years ahead* (pp. 13–24). Washington, DC: National Association for the Education of Young Children.

Bloom, P. J. (1997a). Decision-making influences: Who has it? Who wants it? *Child Care Information Exchange, 114,* 7–14.

Bloom, P. J. (1997b). *A great place to work: Improving conditions for staff in young children's programs* (Rev. ed.). Washington, DC: National Association for the Education of Young Children.

Bloom, P. J. (1997c). Navigating the rapids: Directors reflect on their careers and professional development. *Young Children, 52*(7), 32–38.

Bloom, P. J. (2000a). *Circle of influence: Implementing shared decision making and participative management.* Lake Forest, IL: New Horizons.

Bloom, P. J. (2000b). Images from the field: How directors view their organizations, their roles, and their jobs. In M. L. Culkin (Ed.), *Managing quality*

in young children's programs: The leader's role (pp. 59–77). New York: Teachers College Press.

Bloom, P. J. (2000c). *Workshop essentials: Planning and presenting dynamic workshops.* Lake Forest, IL: New Horizons.

Bloom, P. J., Sheerer, M., & Britz, J. (1991). *Blueprint for action: Achieving center-based change through staff development.* Mt. Rainer, MD: Gryphon.

Bodrova, E., & Leong, D. J. (1996). *Tools of the mind: The Vygotskian approach to early childhood education.* Upper Saddle River, NJ: Merrill/Prentice Hall.

Bontá P., & Silverman, B. (1993). Making learning entertaining. In N. Estes & M. Thomas (Eds.), *Rethinking the roles of technology in education* (pp. 1150–1152). Cambridge: Massachusetts Institute of Technology.

Boocock, S. S., Barnett, W. S., & Frede, E. (2001). Long-term outcomes of early childhood programs in other nations: Lessons for America. *Young Children, 56*(5), 43–50.

Booth, C. L., & Kelly, J. F. (1999). Child care and employment in relation to infants' disabilities and risk factors. *American Journal on Mental Retardation, 104,* 117–130.

Boutte, G. S., Keepler, D. L., Tyler, V. S., & Terry, B. Z. (1992). Effective techniques for involving "difficult" parents. *Young Children, 47*(3), 19–22.

Bouverat, R. W., & Galen, H. L. (Eds.). (1994). *The Child Development Associate national program: The early years and pioneers.* Washington, DC: Council for Early Childhood Professional Recognition.

Bove, C. (1999). *L'inserimento del banbino al nido.* (Welcome the child into infant care): Perspectives from Italy. *Young Children, 54*(2), 32–34.

Bowman, B. T. (1986). Birthday thoughts. *Young Children, 41*(2), 3–8.

Bowman, B. T. (1989). Self-reflection as an element of professionalism. *Teachers College Record, 90,* 444–451.

Bowman, B. T. (1990). Child care: Challenges for the '90's. *Dimensions, 18*(4), 27, 29–31.

Bowman, B. T. (1992). Reaching potentials of minority children through developmentally and culturally appropriate programs. In S. Bredekamp & T. Rosegrant (Eds.), *Reaching potentials: Appropriate curriculum and assessment for young children* (Vol. 1, pp. 128–136). Washington, DC: National Association for the Education of Young Children.

Bowman, B. T. (1995). The professional development challenge: Supporting young children and families. *Young Children, 51*(1), 30–34.

Boyd, B. J., & Schneider, N. I. (1997). Perceptions of the work environment and burnout in Canadian child care providers. *Journal of Research in Childhood Education, 11,* 171–180.

Bradburn, E. (1989). *Margaret McMillan: Portrait of a pioneer.* London: Routledge.

Brand, S. (1996). Making parent involvement a reality: Helping teachers develop partnerships with parents. *Young Children, 51*(2), 76–81.

Brandon, R. N., Kagan, S. L., & Joesch, J. M. (2000). *Design choices: Universal financing for early care and education.* Seattle: University of Washington.

Brandon, R. N., & Wilson, T. (1999). *Exploring an investment approach to financing quality early care and education for working families.* Seattle: University of Washington, Human Services Policy Center.

Brandt, R. (1996). On a new direction for teacher evaluation: A conversation with Tom McGreal. *Educational Leadership, 53*(6), 30–33.

Bransford, J. D., Brown, A. L., & Cocking, R. R. (Eds.). (1999). *How people learn: Brain, mind, experience, and school.* Washington, DC: National Academy Press.

Bredekamp, S. (Ed.). (1987). *Developmentally appropriate practice in early childhood programs serving children from birth through age 8* (Exp. ed.). Washington, DC: National Association for the Education of Young Children.

Bredekamp, S. (1990). *Regulating child care quality: Evidence from NAEYC's accreditation system.* Washington, DC: National Association for the Education of Young Children.

Bredekamp, S. (1992). The early childhood profession coming together. *Young Children, 47*(6), 36–39.

Bredekamp, S. (2000). Issues and barriers in the credentialing process. In M. L. Culkin (Ed.), *Managing quality in young children's programs: The leader's role* (pp. 170–184). New York: Teachers College Press.

Bredekamp, S., & Copple, C. (Eds.). (1997). *Developmentally appropriate practice in early childhood programs: Revised.* Washington, DC: National Association for the Education of Young Children.

Bredekamp, S., & Rosegrant, T. (Eds.). (1992). *Reaching potentials: Appropriate curriculum and assessment for young children* (Vol. 1). Washington, DC: National Association for the Education of Young Children.

Bredekamp, S., & Rosegrant, T. (1995a). Reaching potentials through national standards: Panacea or pipe dream? In S. Bredekamp & T. Rosegrant (Eds.), *Reaching potentials: Transforming early childhood curriculum and assessment* (Vol. 2, pp. 5–14). Washington, DC: National Association for the Education of Young Children.

Bredekamp, S., & Rosegrant, T. (1995b). Transforming curriculum organization. In S. Bredekamp & T. Rosegrant (Eds.), *Reaching potentials: Transforming early childhood curriculum and assessment* (Vol. 2, pp. 167–176). Washington, DC: National Association for the Education of Young Children.

Bredekamp, S., & Willer, S. (1992). Of ladders and lattices, cores and cones: Conceptualizing an early childhood professional development system. *Young Children, 47*(3), 47–50.

Brennan, P., Mednick, S., & Kandal, E. (1991). Congenital determinants of violence and property offending. In D. J. Pepler & K. H. Rubin (Eds.), *The development and treatment of childhood aggression* (pp. 87–90). Hillsdale, NJ: Erlbaum.

Bricker, D. D., Peck, C. A., & Odom, S. L. (1993). Integration: Campaign for the new century. In C. A. Peck, S. L. Odom, and D. D. Bricker (Eds.), *Integrating young children with disabilities into community programs: Ecological perspectives on research and implementation* (pp. 271–276). Baltimore: Brookes.

Briggs v. Board of Education of Connecticut, 882 F. 2d 688 (2d Cir. 1989).

Brody, G. H., & Flor, D. L. (1997). Maternal psychological functioning, family processes, and child adjustment in rural, single-parent, African-American families. *Developmental Psychology, 33,* 1000–1011.

Bromer, J. (1999). Cultural variations in child care: Values and actions. *Young Children, 54*(6), 72–78.

Bronfenbrenner, U. (1979). *The ecology of human development: Experiments by nature and design.* Cambridge, MA: Harvard University Press.

Bronfenbrenner, U. (1986). Ecology of the family as a context for human development: Research perspectives. *Developmental Psychology, 22,* 723–742.

Bronfenbrenner, U. (1989). Ecological systems theory. In R. Vasta (Ed.), *Six theories of child development: Revised formulations and current issues. Annals of child development: A research annual* (Vol. 6, pp. 187–249). Greenwich, CT: JAI.

Bronfenbrenner, U., & Morris, P. A. (1998). The ecology of developmental process. In W. Damon (Series Ed.) & R. M. Lerner (Vol. Ed.), *Handbook of child psychology: Vol. 1. Theoretical models of human development* (pp. 993–1028). New York: Wiley.

Bronson, M. B. (1994). The usefulness of an observational measure of young children's social and mastery behaviors in early childhood classrooms. *Early Childhood Research Quarterly, 9,* 19–45.

Brooks-Gunn, J., & Duncan, G. J. (1997). The effects of poverty on children and youth. *Future of Children, 7*(2), 55–71.

Brophy-Herb, H. E., Kostelnik, M. J., & Stein, L. C. (2001). A developmental approach to teaching about ethics using the NAEYC Code of Ethical Conduct. *Young Children, 56*(1), 80–84.

Brown, N. H., & Manning, J. P. (2000). Core knowledge for directors. In M. L. Culkin (Ed.), *Managing quality in young children's programs: The leader's role* (pp. 78–96). New York: Teachers College Press.

Brown, W. H., Horn, E. M., Heiser, J. G., & Odom, S. L. (1996). Project BLEND: An inclusive model of early childhood intervention services. *Journal of Early Intervention, 20,* 364–375.

Brown-DuPaul, J., Keyes, T., & Segatti, L. (2001). Using documentation panels to communicate with families. *Childhood Education, 77,* 209–213.

Bruder, M. B., Klosowski, S., & Daguio, C. (1991). A review of personnel standards for Part H of P.L. 99–457. *Journal of Early Intervention, 16,* 173–180.

Bruer, J. T. (1999). *The myth of the first three years: A new understanding of early brain development and lifelong learning.* New York: Free Press.

Bryant, D. M., Burchinal, M., Lau, L. B., & Sparling, J. J. (1994). Family and classroom correlates of Head Start children's developmental outcomes. *Early Childhood Research Quarterly, 9,* 289–309.

Bryant, D. M., Clifford, R. M., & Peisner, E. S. (1991). Best practices for beginners: Developmental appropriateness in kindergarten. *American Educational Research Journal, 28,* 783–803.

Burchinal, M. R., Roberts, J. E., Nabors, L. A., & Bryant, D. M. (1996). Quality of center child care and infant cognitive and language development. *Child Development, 67,* 606–620.

Burden, P. R. (1987). *Establishing career ladders.* Springfield, IL: Charles C. Thomas.

Burghardt, J., & Devaney, B. (1993). *The School Nutrition Dietary Assessment Study: Summary of findings.* Washington, DC: U.S. Department of Agriculture.

Burke, D. L. (1996). Multi-year teacher/student relationships are a long-overdue arrangement. *Phi Delta Kappan 77,* 360–361.

Burnette, J. (1998). *Reducing the disproportionate representation of minority students in special education* (ERIC/OSEP Digest #E566). Reston, VA: ERIC Clearinghouse on Disabilities and Gifted Education. (ERIC Document Reproduction Service No. ED417501)

Burns, M. S., Delclos, V. R., Vye, N. J., & Sloan, K. (1992). Changes in cognitive strategies in dynamic assessment. *International Journal of Dynamic Assessment and Instruction, 2,* 45–54.

Burts, D. C., & Buchanan, T. K. (1998). Preparing teachers in developmentally appropriate ways to teach in developmentally appropriate classrooms. In C. Seefeldt & A. Galper (Eds.), *Continuing issues in early childhood education* (2nd ed., pp. 129–158). Upper Saddle River, NJ: Merrill/Prentice Hall.

Burts, D. C., Hart, C. H., Charlesworth, R., DeWolf, D. M., Ray, J., Manuel, K., & Fleege, P. O. (1993). Developmental appropriateness of kindergarten programs and academic outcomes in first grade. *Journal of Research in Childhood Education, 8*(1), 23–31.

Burts, D. C., Hart, C. H., Charlesworth, R., Fleege, P., Mosley, J., & Thomasson, R. H. (1992). Observed activities and stress behaviors of children in developmentally appropriate and inappropriate classrooms. *Early Childhood Research Quarterly, 7,* 297–318.

Burts, D. C., Hart, C. H., Charlesworth, R., & Kirk, L. (1990). A comparison of frequencies of stress behaviors observed in kindergarten children in classrooms with developmentally appropriate and developmentally inappropriate instructional practices. *Early Childhood Research Quarterly, 5,* 407–423.

Bushell, D., Jr. (1973). The behavior analysis classroom. In B. Spodek (Ed.), *Early childhood education* (pp. 163–175). Englewood Cliffs, NJ: Prentice Hall.

Buysee, V., Wesley, P. W., & Keyes, L. (1998). Implementing early childhood inclusion: Barrier and support factors. *Early Childhood Research Quarterly, 13,* 169–184.

Byrnes, M. (1990). The regular education initiative debate: A view from the field. *Exceptional Children, 56,* 345–349.

Cadden, V. (1994, March). The state of the states. *Working Mother,* pp. 31–38.

Caldwell, B. M. (1968). The fourth dimension in early childhood education. In R. D. Hess & R. M. Baer (Eds.), *Early education: Current theory, research, and action* (pp. 71–81). Chicago: Aldine.

Caldwell, B. M. (1977). Child development and social policy. In M. Scott & S. Grimmett (Eds.), *Current issues in child development* (pp. 61–87). Washington, DC: National Association for the Education of Young Children.

Caldwell, B. M. (1985). What is quality child care? In B. M. Caldwell & A. Hillard (Eds.), *What is quality child care?* (pp. 1–16). Washington, DC: National Association for the Education of Young Children.

Caldwell, B. M. (1990). "Educare": New professional identity. *Dimensions, 18*(4), 3–6.

Caldwell, B. M. (1991). Continuity in the early years: Transitions between grades and systems. In S. L. Kagan (Ed.), *The care and education of America's young children: Obstacles and opportunities* (pp. 69–90). Chicago: University of Chicago Press.

Caldwell, T. H., Sirvis, B., Todaro, A., & Accouloumre, D. S. (1991). *Special health care in the school.* Reston, VA: Council for Exceptional Children.

Campbell, C. J., & Ramey, C. T. (1994). Effects of early intervention on intellectual and academic achievement. A follow-up study of children from low-income families. *Child Development, 65,* 684–698.

Campbell, N. D., Applebaum, J. C., Martinson, K., & Martin, E. (2000). *Be all that we can be: Lessons from the military for improving our nation's child care system.* Washington, DC: National Women's Law Center.

Capizzano, J., Adams, G., & Sonenstein, F. (2000). *Child care arrangements for children under five: Variation across states. New federalism: National survey of America's families, Series B (No. B-7).* Washington, DC: The Urban Institute.

Caples, S. E. (1996). Some guidelines for preschool design. *Young Children, 51*(4), 14–21.

Cardelle-Elawar, M., & Wetzel, K. (1995). Students and computers as partners in developing students'

problem-solving skills. *Journal of Research on Computing in Education, 27,* 378–401.

Carlisle, A. (2001). Using multiple intelligences theory to assess early childhood curricula. *Young Children, 56*(6), 77–83.

Carlson, H. L., & Stenmalm-Sjoblom, L. (1989). A cross-cultural study of parents' perceptions of early childhood programs. *Early Childhood Research Quarterly, 4,* 505–522.

Carlsson-Paige, N., & Levin, D. E. (1985). *Helping young children understand peace, war, and the nuclear threat.* Washington, DC: National Association for the Education of Young Children.

Carnegie Corporation of New York. (1994). Starting points: Executive summary of the report of the Carnegie Corporation of New York Task Force on Meeting the Needs of Young Children. *Young Children, 49*(5), 58–61.

Carnegie Corporation of New York. (1996). *Years of promise: A comprehensive learning strategy for America's children.* New York: Author.

Carnegie Forum on Education and the Economy. (1986). *A nation prepared: Teachers for the 21st century.* New York: Carnegie Corporation of New York.

Carnegie Task Force on Meeting the Needs of Young Children. (1994). *Starting points: Meeting the needs of our youngest children.* New York: Carnegie Corporation of New York.

Carter, M. (1992). Honoring diversity: Problems and possibilities for staff and organization. In B. Neugebauer (Ed.), *Alike and different: Exploring our humanity with children* (Rev. ed., pp. 70–81). Washington, DC: National Association for the Education of Young Children.

Carter, M. (1993). Developing a cultural disposition in teachers. *Child Care Information Exchange, 90,* 52–55.

Carter, M., & Curtis, D. (1998). *The visionary director: A handbook for dreaming, organizing, and improvising in your center.* St. Paul, MN: Redleaf.

Caruso, J. J. (1991). Supervisors in early childhood programs: An emerging profile. *Young Children, 46*(6), 20–26.

Caruso, J. J., & Fawcett, M. T. (1999). *Supervision in early childhood education: A developmental perspective* (2nd ed.). New York: Teachers College Press.

Casper, L. M. (1995). *What does it cost to mind our preschoolers?* Current Population Reports (U.S.

Bureau of the Census publications No. 70–52). Washington, DC: U.S. Government Printing Office.

Cassidy, D. J., Buell, M. J., Pugh-Hoese, S., & Russell, S. (1995). The effect of education on child care teachers' beliefs and classroom quality: Year one evaluation of the TEACH Early Childhood Associate Degree Scholarship Program. *Early Childhood Research Quarterly, 10,* 171–183.

Cataldo, C. Z. (1982). Very early childhood education for infants and toddlers. *Childhood Education, 58,* 149–154.

Caughy, M. D., DiPietro, J., & Strobino, M. (1994). Day-care participation as a protective factor in the cognitive development of low-income children. *Child Development, 65,* 457–471.

Cauthen, N., Knitzer, J., & Ripple, C. (2000). *Map and track: State initiatives for young children and families.* New York: National Center for Children in Poverty.

Cavallaro, C. C., Haney, M., & Cabello, B. (1993). Developmentally appropriate strategies for promoting full participation in early childhood settings. *Topics in Early Childhood Special Education, 13,* 293–307.

Center for Career Development in Early Care and Education at Wheelock College. (2000). *The power of mentoring.* Boston: Wheelock College, Institute for Leadership and Career Initiatives.

Center for the Child Care Workforce. (1998). *Current data on child care salaries and benefits in the United States.* Washington, DC: Author.

Center for the Child Care Workforce. (2000). *Current data on child care salaries and benefits in the United States.* Washington, DC: Author.

Center for the Child Care Workforce & Human Services Policy Center. (2002). *Estimating the size and components of the U.S. child care workforce and caregiving population. Key findings from the Child Care Workforce estimate* (Preliminary report). Washington, DC, and Seattle, WA: Authors.

Chaille, C., & Britain, L. (1997). *The young child as scientist: A constructivist approach to early childhood science education.* New York: Longman.

Chandler, P. A. (1994). *A place for me: Including children with special needs in early care and education settings.* Washington, DC: National Association for the Education of Young Children.

Char, C., & Forman, G. E. (1994). Interactive technology and the young child: A look to the future. In J. L. Wright & D. D. Shade (Eds.), *Young children: Active learners in a technological age* (pp. 167–177). Washington, DC: National Association for the Education of Young Children.

Charlesworth, R. (1998). Developmentally appropriate practice is for everyone. *Childhood Education, 74,* 274–282.

Charlesworth, R., & DeBoer, B. B. (2000). An early childhood teacher moves from DIP to DAP: Self-study as a useful research method for teacher researcher and university professor collaboration. *Journal of Early Childhood Teacher Education, 21*(2), 149–154.

Charlesworth, R., Hart, C. H., Burts, D. C., & DeWolf, M. (1993). The LSU studies: Building a research base for developmentally appropriate practice. In S. Reifel (Ed.), *Advances in early education and day care: Perspectives in developmentally appropriate practice* (Vol. 5, pp. 3–28). Greenwich, CT: JAI.

Charlesworth, R., Hart, C. H., Burts, D. C., Thomasson, R. H., Mosley, J., & Fleege, P. O. (1993). Measuring the developmental appropriateness of kindergarten teachers' beliefs and practices. *Early Childhood Research Quarterly, 8,* 255–276.

Chattin-McNichols, J. (1992). *The Montessori controversy.* Albany, NY: Delmar.

Cherlin, A. (1999). Going to extremes: Family structure, children's well-being, and social science. *Demography, 36,* 421–428.

The Child Mental Health Foundations and Agencies Network. (2000). *A good beginning: Sending America's children to school with the social and emotional competence they need to succeed.* Bethesada, MD: The National Institute of Mental Health, Office of Communications and Public Liaison.

Child Welfare League of America. (1945). *Day-care: A partnership of three professions.* Washington, DC: Author.

Child Welfare League of America. (1960). *Standards for day-care service.* New York: Author.

Children's Defense Fund. (2001). *The state of America's children: Yearbook 2001.* Washington, DC: Author.

The Children's Foundation. (2001). *2001 family child care licensing study.* Washington, DC: Author.

The Children's Foundation. (2002). *2002 child care center licensing study.* Washington, DC: Author.

Chipman, M. (1997). Valuing cultural diversity in the early years: Social imperatives and pedagogical insights. In J. P. Isenberg & M. R. Jalongo (Eds.), *Major trends and issues in early childhood education* (pp. 43–55). New York: Teachers College Press.

Cicchetti, D., & Toth, S. L. (2000). Child maltreatment in the early years of life. In J. D. Osofsky & H. E. Fitzgerald (Eds.), *WAIMH handbook of infant mental health, Vol. 4: Infant mental health in groups at high risk* (pp. 255–294). New York: Wiley.

Cinnamond, J., & Zimpher, N. (1990). Reflectivity as a function of community. In R. Clift, W. Houston, & M. Pugach (Eds.), *Encouraging reflective practice in education* (pp. 57–72). New York: Teachers College Press.

Clark, C. M., & Peterson, P. L. (1986). Teachers' thought processes. In M. C. Wittrock (Ed.), *Handbook of research on teaching* (3rd ed., pp. 255–296). New York: Macmillan.

Clarke-Stewart, K. A. (1988). Evolving issues in early education: A personal perspective. *Early Childhood Research Quarterly, 3,* 139–149.

Clarke-Stewart, A., & Gruber, C. (1984). Day care forms and features. In R. C. Ainslie (Ed.), *Quality variations in day care* (pp. 35–62). New York: Praeger.

Class, N. E. (1968). *Licensing of child care facilities by state welfare departments.* Washington, DC: U.S. Department of Health, Education & Welfare, Children's Bureau.

Class, N. E. (1972). *Basic issues in day care licensing.* Washington, DC: U.S. Department of Health, Education & Welfare, Office of Education.

Clements, D. H. (1994). The uniqueness of the computer as a learning tool: Insights from research and practice. In J. L. Wright & D. D. Shade (Eds.), *Young children: Active learners in a technological age* (pp. 31–50). Washington, DC: National Association for the Education of Young Children.

Clements, D. H., & Nastasi, B. K. (1992). Computers and early childhood education. In M. Gettinger, S. N. Elliott, & T. R. Kratochwill (Eds.), *Preschool and early childhood treatment directions* (pp. 187–246). Hillsdale, NJ: Erlbaum.

Clements, D. H., & Nastasi, B. K. (1993). Electronic media and early childhood education. In B. Spodek (Ed.), *Handbook of research on the education of young children* (pp. 251–275). New York: Macmillan.

Clements, D. H., Sarama, J., & DiBiase, A.-M. (Eds.). (2003). *Engaging young children in mathematics: Findings of the 2000 National Conference on Standards for Preschool and Kindergarten Mathematics Education.* Mahwah, NJ: Erlbaum.

Clewett, A. S. (1988). Guidance and discipline: Teaching young children appropriate behavior. *Young Children, 43*(4), 25–36.

Clifford, R. M. (1997). Partnerships with other professionals. *Young Children, 52*(5), 2–3.

Clyde K. and Sheila K. v. Puyallup School District, No. 93–35572, F. 3d (9th Cir. 1994).

Clyde, M., & Rodd, J. (1989). Professional ethics: There's more to it than meets the eye. *Early Child Development and Care, 53,* 1–12.

Cochran-Smith, M., & Lytle, S. L. (1999). The teacher research movement: A decade later. *Educational Researcher, 28*(7), 15–25.

Cohen, D. H., Stern, V., & Balaban, N. (1997). *Observing and recording the behavior of young children* (4th ed.). New York: Teachers College Press.

Cohen, D. K., & Spillane, J. P. (1993). Policy and practice: The relations between governance and instruction. In S. Fuhrman (Ed.), *Designing coherent educational policy* (pp. 35–95). San Francisco: Jossey-Bass.

Cole, M. (1998). *Cultural psychology: A once and future discipline.* Cambridge, MA: Belknap Press.

Cole, M., & Cole, S. R. (1993). *The development of children* (2nd ed). New York: Oxford University Press.

Coleman, M. (1997). Families and schools: In search of common ground. *Young Children, 52*(5), 14–21.

Coleman, M., & Churchill, S. (1997). Challenge to family involvement. *Childhood Education, 73,* 144–148.

Coleman, M., & Wallinga, C. (2000a). Connecting families and classrooms using family involvement webs. *Childhood Education, 76,* 209–214.

Coleman, M., & Wallinga, C. (2000b). Teacher training in family involvement: An interpersonal approach. *Childhood Education, 76,* 76–81.

Collins, J. E., & Porras, J. I. (1994). *Built to last: Successful habits of visionary companies.* New York: Harper Business.

Collins, R. C. (1993). Head Start: Steps toward a two-generation program strategy. *Young Children, 48*(2), 25–33, 72–73.

Comer, J. P. (1988). *Maggie's American dream: The life and times of a black family.* New York: Penguin.

Comer, J. P., & Haynes, N. M. (1991). Parent involvement in schools: An ecological approach. *The Elementary School Journal, 91,* 271–278.

Committee for Economic Development, Research, and Policy. (1987). *Children in need: Investment strategies for the educationally disadvantaged, Executive summary.* New York: Author.

Committee for Economic Development, Research, and Policy. (1991). *The unfinished agenda: A new vision for child development and education.* New York: Author.

Committee for Economic Development, Research, and Policy. (1993). *Why child care matters: Preparing young children for a more productive America.* New York: Author.

Consumer Product Safety Commission. (1999). *Safety hazards in child care settings.* Washington, DC: Author.

Cook, J. T., & Martin, K. S. (1995). *Differences in nutrient adequacy among poor and non-poor children.* Boston: Tufts University, Center on Hunger, Poverty, and Nutrition Policy.

Cooney, M. H., Buchanan, M., & Parkinson, D. (2001). Teachers as researchers: Classroom inquiry initiatives at undergraduate and graduate levels in early childhood education. *Journal of Early Childhood Teacher Education, 22*(3), 151–159.

Copeland, M. L. (1996). Code blue! Establishing a child care emergency plan. *Child Care Information Exchange, 107,* 19.

Cosgrove, M. S. (1991). Cooking in the classroom: The doorway to nutrition. *Young Children, 46*(3), 43–46.

Cost, Quality, and Child Outcomes Study Team. (1995). *Cost, quality, and child outcomes in child care centers, Public report* (2nd ed.). Denver: University of Colorado at Denver, Economics Department.

Council of Chief State School Officers. (1995). *Moving toward accountability for results: A look at ten states' efforts.* Washington, DC: Author.

Council of Chief State School Officers. (1999). *Early childhood and family education: New realities, new opportunities. A Council Policy Statement.* Washington, DC: Author.

Council for Early Childhood Professional Recognition. (1996). *The Child Development Associate system and competency standards: Pre-school caregivers in center-based programs.* Washington, DC: Author.

Council for Early Childhood Professional Recognition. (1997). *The Child Development Associate national credentialling program.* Washington, DC: Author.

Council for Professional Recognition. (2000). *National directory of early childhood teacher preparation institutions* (4th ed.). Washington, DC: Author.

Cowan, P. A., Powell, D. R., & Cowan, C. P. (1998). Parenting interventions: A family systems perspective. In W. Damon, I. E. Sigel, & K. A. Renninger (Eds.), *Handbook of child psychology, Vol. 4: Child psychology in practice* (5th ed., pp. 3–72). New York: Wiley.

Cryer, D., & Phillipsen, L. (1997). Quality details: A close-up look at child care program strengths and weaknesses. *Young Children, 52*(5), 51–60.

Cuffaro, H. (1995). *Experimenting with the world: John Dewey and the early childhood classroom.* New York: Teachers College Press.

Culkin, M. L. (2000). Children's program administrators and the advancement of an administrative credential. In M. L. Culkin (Ed.), *Managing quality in young children's programs: The leader's role* (pp. 1–19). New York: Teachers College Press.

Cunningham, B. (1994). Portraying fathers and other men in the curriculum. *Young Children, 49*(6), 4–13.

Cunningham, B., & Watson, L. W. (2002). Recruiting male teachers. *Young Children, 57*(6), 10–15.

Dahl, K. (1998). Why cooking in the classroom? *Young Children, 53*(1), 81–83.

Dahlberg, G., & Asen, G. (1994). Evaluation and regulation: A question of empowerment. In P. Moss & A. Pence (Eds.), *Valuing quality in early childhood services* (pp. 157–171). New York: Teachers College Press.

Daniel, J. (1996). Family-centered work and child care. *Young Children, 51*(6), 2.

Danielson, C., & Abrutyn, L. (1997). *An introduction to using portfolios in the classroom.* Alexandria, VA: Association for Supervision and Curriculum Development.

Darling-Hammond, L. (1998). Teachers and teaching: Testing policy hypotheses from a National Commission report. *Educational Researcher, 27*(1), 5–16.

Darling-Hammond, L., & Falk, B. (1997). Using standards and assessments to support student learning. *Phi Delta Kappan, 79,* 190–199.

Darling-Hammond, L., Wise, A. E., & Klein, S. P. (1999). *A license to teach: Raising standards for teaching.* San Francisco: Jossey-Bass.

Davies, D. (1991). Schools reaching out: Family, school, and community partnerships for student success. *Phi Delta Kappan, 72,* 376–382.

Davis, M. D. (1932). *Nursery schools: Their development and current practices in the United States* (Bulletin No. 9). Washington, DC: Office of Education.

Davis, M. D. (1964). How NANE began. *Young Children, 20,* 106–109.

Day, D. E. (1983). *Early childhood education: A human ecological approach.* Glenview, IL: Scott, Foresman.

Day, M. C. (1977). A comparative analysis of center-based preschool programs. In M. C. Day & R. K. Parker (Eds.), *The preschool in action* (2nd ed., pp. 461–487). Needham Heights, MA: Allyn & Bacon.

Day, M. C., & Parker, R. K. (1977). *The preschool in action* (2nd ed.). Needham Heights, MA: Allyn & Bacon.

DeBord, K., Hestenes, L. L., Moore, R. C., Cosco, N., & McGinnis, J. R. (2002). Paying attention to the outdoor environment is as important as preparing the indoor environment. *Young Children, 57*(3), 32–35.

DeBord, K., & Regueros-de-Atiles, J. (1991). *Teacher perceptions of mixed-age groupings of children.* Research report. (ERIC Document Reproduction Service No. ED360047)

Decker, C. A., & Decker, J. R. (2001). *Planning and administering early childhood programs* (7th ed.). Upper Saddle River, NJ: Merrill/Prentice Hall.

Delgado-Gaitin, C. (1991). Involving parents in the schools: A process of empowerment. *American Journal of Education, 100*(1), 20–46.

Dempsey, J. D., & Frost, J. L. (1993). Play environments in early childhood education. In B. Spodek (Ed.), *Handbook of research on the education of young children* (pp. 306–321). New York: Macmillan.

Dempsey, J. D., Strickland, E., & Frost, J. L. (1993). What's going on out here? An evaluation tool for your playground. *Child Care Information Exchange, 91,* 41–44.

Denning, R., & Smith, P. (1997). Cooperative learning and technology. *Journal of Computers in Mathematics and Science Teaching, 16,* 177–200.

Derman-Sparks, L. (1992). Reaching potentials through antibias, multicultural curriculum. In S. Bredekamp & T. Rosegrant (Eds.), *Reaching potentials: Appropriate curriculum and assessment for young children* (Vol. 1, pp. 114–127). Washington, DC: National Association for the Education of Young Children.

Derman-Sparks, L., & A.B.C. Task Force. (1989). *Anti-Bias Curriculum: Tools for empowering young children.* Washington, DC: National Association for the Education of Young Children.

Derman-Sparks, L., & Ramsey, P. G. (1992). Multicultural education reaffirmed. *Young Children, 47*(2), 10–11.

Derman-Sparks, L., & Ramsey, P. G. (2000). A framework for culturally relevant, multicultural, and antibias education in the 21st century. In J. Roopnarine & J. Johnson (Eds.), *Approaches to early childhood education* (3rd ed., pp. 379–404). Upper Saddle River, NJ: Merrill/Prentice Hall.

DeVries, R., Haney, J. P., & Zan, B. (1991). Sociomoral atmosphere in direct-instruction, eclectic, and constructivist kindergartens: A study of teachers' enacted interpersonal understanding. *Early Childhood Research Quarterly, 6,* 449–471.

DeVries, R., & Kohlberg, L. (1987). *Constructivist early education: Overview and comparison with other programs.* Washington, DC: National Association for the Education of Young Children.

DeVries, R., Reese-Learned, H., & Morgan, P. (1991). Socio-moral development in direct-instruction, eclectic, and constructivist kindergartens: A study of children's enacted interpersonal understanding. *Early Childhood Research Quarterly, 6,* 473–517.

Dewey, J. (1897). My pedagogic creed. *School Journal, 54,* 77–80.

Dewey, J. (1916). *Democracy and education: An introduction to the philosophy of education.* New York: Macmillan.

Dewey, J. (1964). The relation of theory to practice in education. In R. Archambault (Ed.), *John Dewey on education: Selected writings* (pp. 313–338). New York: Random House.

Diffily, D., & Morrison, K. (Eds.). (1997). *Family-friendly communication for early childhood programs.* Washington, DC: National Association for the Education of Young Children.

Dillon, S. (1994, April 7). Special education soaks up New York's school resources. *The New York Times,* p. 16.

Dinkmeyer, D., & McKay, G. (1976). *Systematic training for effective parenting.* Circle Pines, MN: American Guidance Service.

Division of Early Childhood of the Council for Exceptional Children. (2001). *Position statement on interventions for challenging behavior.* Denver, CO: Author. (Available online <http://www.dec-sped.org/positions/chalbeha.hmtl>)

Division for Early Childhood Task Force on Recommended Practices. (1993). *DEC recommended practices: Indicators of quality in programs for infants and young children with special needs and their families.* Reston, VA: Council for Exceptional Children.

Dixon, R. A., & Lerner, R. M. (1992). A history of systems in developmental psychology. In M. H. Bornstein & M. E. Lamb (Eds.), *Developmental psychology: An advanced textbook* (3rd ed., pp. 3–59). Hillsdale, NJ: Erlbaum.

Dixon, S. (1990). Talking to the child's physician: Thoughts for the child-care provider. *Young Children, 45*(3), 36–37.

Dodd, E. L., & Brock, D. R. (1994). Building partnerships with families through home-learning activities. *Dimensions of Early Childhood, 22*(2), 37–39, 46.

Dodge, D. T., Colker, L. J., & Heroman, C. (2002). *The creative curriculum for preschool* (4th ed.). Washington, DC: Teaching Strategies.

Dodge, D. T., Dombro, A. L., & Koralek, D. G. (1991). *Caring for infants and toddlers, Vol. 1.* Washington, DC: Teaching Strategies.

Dodge, D. T., Jablon, J., & Bickart, T. S. (1994). *Constructing curriculum for the primary grades.* Washington, DC: Teaching Strategies.

Doherty, K. W. (2002). Early learning. Quality counts 2002: Building blocks for success. *Education Week, 21*(17), 54–56.

Dokecki, P., Hargrove, E., & Sandler, H. (1983). An overview of the Parent-Child Development Center social experiment. In R. Haskins & D. Adams (Eds.), *Parent education and public policy* (pp. 80–111). Norwood, NJ: Ablex.

Donovan, E. (1987). *Preschool to public school: A teacher's guide to successful transition for children with special needs.* Syracuse, NY: Jowonio School.

Dooling, M. V., & Ulione, M. S. (2000). Health consultation in child care: A partnership that works. *Young Children, 55*(2), 23–26.

Dopyera, J. E., & Lay-Dopyera, M. (1990). Evaluation and science in early childhood education: Some critical issues. In C. Seefeldt (Ed.), *Continuing issues in early childhood education* (pp. 285–299). New York: Merrill/Macmillan.

Downs, R. B. (1978). *Friedrich Froebel.* Boston: Twayne.

Drake, M. M. (1992). Menu evaluation, nutrient intake of young children, and nutrition knowledge of menu planners in child care centers in Missouri. *Journal of Nutrition Education, 24,* 145–148.

Drucker, P. (1990). *Managing the nonprofit organization: Principles and practices.* New York: HarperCollins.

Duff, R. E., Brown, M. H., & Van Scoy, I. J. (1995). Reflection and self-evaluation: Keys to professional development. *Young Children, 50*(4), 81–88.

Duncan, G. J., Yeung, W. J., Brooks-Gunn, J., & Smith, J. R. (1998). How much does childhood poverty affect the life chances of children? *American Sociological Review, 63,* 406–423.

Dunn, L., Beach, S. A., & Kontos, S. (1994). Quality of the literacy environment in day care and children's development. *Journal of Research in Childhood Education, 9,* 24–34.

Dunn, L., & Kontos, S. (1997). What have we learned about developmentally appropriate practice? *Young Children, 52*(5), 4–13.

Durkin, D. (1987). A classroom observation study of reading instruction in kindergarten. *Early Childhood Research Quarterly, 2,* 275–300.

Early Childhood Education Linkage System. (2002). *Model child care health policies* (4th ed.). Rosemont, PA: Author. (Available through NAEYC)

Early Childhood and Literacy Development Committee of the International Reading Association. (1986). Literacy development and pre-first grade: A joint statement of concerns about present practices in pre-first grade reading instruction and recommendations for improvement. *Young Children, 41*(4), 10–13.

Edkin, K., & Lein, L. (1997). *Making ends meet: How single mothers survive welfare and low wage work.* New York: Sage.

Edmiaston, R., Dolezal, V., Doolittle, S., Erickson, C., & Merritt, S. (2000). Developing individualized education programs for children in inclusive settings: A developmentally appropriate framework. *Young Children, 55*(4), 36–41.

Education Week. (2000, January). *Special Report. Quality counts 2000: Who should teach?* Washington, DC: Editorial Projects in Education, Inc.

Edwards, C. P. (1998). Partner, nurturer, and guide: The role of the teacher. In C. Edwards, L. Gandini, & G. Forman (Eds.), *The hundred languages of children: The Reggio approach—advanced reflections* (2nd ed., pp. 179–198). Greenwich, CT: Ablex.

Edwards, C. P., Gandini, L., & Forman, G. (Eds.). (1998). *The hundred languages of children: The Reggio approach—advanced reflections* (2nd ed.). Greenwich, CT: Ablex.

Edwards, P. A., & Young, L. S. Y. (1992). Beyond parents: Family, community, and school involvement. *Phi Delta Kappan, 74,* 72, 74, 76, 78, 80.

Egan, K. (1983). *Education and psychology: Plato, Piaget, and scientific psychology.* New York: Teachers College Press.

Einbinder, S. D., & Bond, J. T. (1992). *Five million children: 1992 update.* New York: National Center for Children in Poverty.

Elicker, J. (2002). Viewpoint. More men in early childhood education? Why? *Young Children, 57*(6), 50–54.

Elicker, J., & Fortner-Wood, C. (1995). Adult-child relationships in early childhood programs. *Young Children, 51*(1), 69–78.

Elicker, J., & Mathur, S. (1997). What do they do all day? Comprehensive evaluation of a full-day kindergarten. *Early Childhood Research Quarterly, 12,* 459–480.

Elicker, J., Noppe, I. C., Noppe, L. D., & Fortner-Wood, C. (1997). The parent-caregiver relationship scale: Rounding out the relationship system in infant child care. *Early Education and Development, 8,* 83–100.

Eliot, A. (1978). America's first nursery school. In J. Hymes (Ed.), *Living history interviews* (pp. 7–26). Carmel, CA: Hacienda.

Elkind, D. (1983). Montessori education: Abiding contributions and contemporary challenges. *Young Children, 38*(2), 3–10.

Elkind, D. (1986). Formal education and early childhood education: An essential difference. *Phi Delta Kappan, 67,* 631–636.

Elkind, D. (1988). The resistance to developmentally appropriate practice with young children: The real issue. In C. Warger (Ed.), *A resource guide to public school early childhood programs* (pp. 53–62). Alexandria, VA: Association for Supervision and Curriculum Development.

Elkind, D. (1989). Developmentally appropriate practice. Philosophical and practical implications. *Phi Delta Kappan, 71,* 113–117.

Elkind, D. (1994). *Ties that stress. The new family imbalance.* Cambridge, MA: Harvard University Press.

Elkind, D. (1998). Computers for infants and young children. *Child Care Information Exchange, 123,* 44–46.

Ellison, C., & Barbour, N. (1992). Changing child care systems through collaborative efforts: Challenges for the 1990s. *Child and Youth Care Forum, 21,* 299–316.

Endsley, R. C., Minish, P. A., & Zhou, Q. (1993). Parent involvement and quality day care in proprietary centers. *Journal of Research in Childhood Education, 7*(3), 53–61.

Epstein, A. S. (1993). Training for quality: Improving early childhood programs through Systematic Inservice Training. *Monographs of the High/Scope Educational Foundation, No. 9.* Ypsilanti, MI: High/Scope Press.

Epstein, A. S. (1999). Pathways to quality in Head Start, public school, and private nonprofit early childhood programs. *Journal of Research in Childhood Education, 13*(2), 101–119.

Epstein, J. L. (1991). Paths to partnerships: What we can learn from federal, state, district, and school initiatives. *Phi Delta Kappan, 72,* 344–349.

Epstein, J. L. (1995). School/family/community partnerships. *Phi Delta Kappan, 76,* 701–712.

Epstein, J. L. (2001). *School, family, and community partnerships: Preparing educators and improving schools.* Boulder, CO: Westview.

Epstein, J. L., & Sanders, M. (1998). What we learn from international studies of school-family-community partnerships. *Childhood Education, 74,* 392–394.

Erikson, E. H. (1950). *Childhood and society.* New York: Norton.

Erikson, E. H. (1951). *A healthy personality for every child: A digest of the fact-finding report to the Mid-Century White House Conference on Children and Youth.* Raleigh, NC: Health Publications Institute.

Esbenstein, S. (1987). *An outdoor classroom.* Ypsilanti, MI: High/Scope Press.

Espinosa, L. (1992). The process of change: The Redwood City story. In S. Bredekamp & T. Rosegrant (Eds.), *Reaching potentials: Appropriate curriculum and assessment for young children* (Vol. 1, pp. 159–166). Washington, DC: National Association for the Education of Young Children.

Essa, E. L., Favre, K., Thweatt, G., & Waugh, S. (1999). Continuity of care for infants and toddlers. *Early Child Development and Care, 148,* 11–19.

Ewen, D., & Goldstein, A. (1996). *Report on the states using Child Care and Development Block Grant Quality Improvement Funds.* Prepared for the Child Care Bureau, Administration on Children, Youth, and Families, U. S. Department of Health and Human Services. Washington, DC: U.S. Government Printing Office.

Fagan, J. (1994). Mother and father involvement in day care centers serving infants and young toddlers. *Early Child Development and Care, 103,* 95–101.

Fagan, J. (1996). Principles for developing male involvement programs in early childhood settings: A personal experience. *Young Children, 51*(4), 64–71.

Fallon, B. J. (Ed.). (1973). *40 innovative programs in early childhood education.* Belmont, CA: Fearon.

Family Resource Coalition. (1993). *Family support programs and family literacy.* Chicago: Author.

Fantini, M. (1970). *Community control and the urban school.* New York: Praeger.

Fashola, O. S., & Slavin, R. E. (1998). Schoolwide reform models: What works? *Phi Delta Kappan, 79,* 370–379.

Federal Interagency Forum on Child and Family Statistics. (2002). *America's children: Key national indicators of well-being 2002.* Washington, DC: U.S. Government Printing Press.

Fedor v. Mauwehu Council of Boy Scouts, 143 A.2d 466 (Conn. 1958).

Feeney, S. (1990). Update on the NAEYC Code of Ethical Conduct. *Young Children, 45*(4), 20–21.

Feeney, S., & Christensen, D. (1979). *Who am I in the lives of children?* New York: Merrill/Macmillan.

Feeney, S., & Freeman, N. K. (1999). *Ethics and the early childhood educator: Using the NAEYC Code.* Washington, DC: National Association for the Education of Young Children.

Feeney, S., Freeman, N. K., & Moravick, E. (2000). *Teaching the NAEYC Code of Ethical Conduct: Activity sourcebook.* Washington, DC: National Association for the Education of Young Children.

Feeney, S., & Kipnis, K. (1985). Public policy report: Professional ethics in early childhood education. *Young Children, 40*(3), 54–58.

Feeney, S., & Kipnis, K. (1989). The National Association for the Education of Young Children Code of Ethical Conduct and Statement of Commitment. *Young Children, 45*(1), 24–29.

Feeney, S., & Kipnis, K. (1992). *Code of Ethical Conduct and Statement of Commitment.* Washington, DC: National Association for the Education of Young Children.

Feeney, S., & Kipnis, K. (1998). *Code of Ethical Conduct and Statement of Commitment.* Washington, DC: National Association for the Education of Young Children.

Feeney, S., & Sysko, L. (1986). Professional ethics in early childhood education: Survey results. *Young Children, 42*(1), 15–20.

Fein, G., & Schwartz, P. M. (1982). Developmental theories in early education. In B. Spodek (Ed.), *Handbook of research in early childhood education* (pp. 82–104). New York: Free Press.

Ferguson, D. L. (1995). The real challenge of inclusion: Confessions of a "rabid inclusionist." *Phi Delta Kappan, 77,* 281–287.

Ferguson, R. F. (1998). Can schools narrow the black-white test score gap? In C. Jencks & M. Phillips (Eds.), *The black-white test score gap* (pp. 318–374). Washington, DC: The Brookings Institute.

Fewell, R. R. (1986). Child care and the handicapped child. In N. Gunzenhauser & B. M. Caldwell (Eds.), *Group care for young children* (pp. 35–46). Skillman, NJ: Johnson & Johnson.

Fewell, R. R., & Vadasky, P. F. (1987). Measurement issues in studies of efficacy. *Topics in Early Childhood Special Education, 7,* 885–896.

Fils, D. (2002). A relationship with a purpose: Accreditation facilitation projects and early childhood programs. *Young Children, 57*(4), 36–38.

Fischer, J. L., & Eheart, B. K. (1991). Family day care: A theoretical basis for improving quality. *Early Childhood Research Quarterly, 6,* 549–563.

Foote, R. A. (1990). *Finding childcare in metropolitan Atlanta 1990.* Atlanta: Save the Children/Child Care Support Center.

For Your Information. (2002). Child passenger safety. *Young Children, 57*(4), 49.

Forest, I. (1927). *Preschool education: A historical and critical study.* New York: Macmillan.

Forman, E. A., Minick, N., & Stone, C. A. (Eds.). (1993). *Contexts for learning: Sociocultural dynamics in children's development.* New York: Oxford University Press.

Forman, G. E., & Fosnot, C. T. (1982). The use of Piaget's constructivism in early childhood education programs. In B. Spodek (Ed.), *Handbook of research in early childhood education* (pp. 185–211). New York: Free Press.

Forman, G. E., & Fyfe, B. (1998). Negotiated learning through design, documentation, and discourse. In C. Edwards, L. Gandini, & G. Forman (Eds.), *The hundred voices of children: The Reggio approach—advanced reflections* (2nd ed., pp. 239–260). Greenwich, CT: Ablex.

Fosnot, C. T. (1989). *Inquiring teachers, inquiring learners: A constructivist approach for teaching.* New York: Teachers College Press.

Fowell, N., & Lawton, J. (1992). An alternative view of appropriate practice in early childhood education. *Early Childhood Research Quarterly, 7,* 53–73.

Fox-Barnett, M., & Meyer, T. (1992). The teacher's playing at my house this week. *Young Children, 47*(2), 45–50.

Frank, L. K. (1937). The fundamental needs of the child. *Mental Hygiene, 22,* 353–379.

Frede, E. C. (1998). Preschool program quality in programs for children in poverty. In W. S. Barnett & S. S. Boocock (Eds.), *Early care and education of children in poverty: Promises, programs, and long-term outcomes* (pp. 77–98). Buffalo: State University of New York Press.

Frede, E., & Barnett, W. S. (1992). Developmentally appropriate public school preschool: A study of implementation of the High/Scope curriculum and its effects on disadvantaged children's skills at first grade. *Early Childhood Research Quarterly, 7,* 483–499.

Freeman, N. K., & Brown, M. H. (1996). Ethics instruction for preservice teachers: How are we doing in ECE? The public's and our profession's growing concern with ethics. *Journal of Early Childhood Teacher Education, 17*(2), 5–18.

Freeman, N. K., & Brown, M. H. (2000). Evaluating the child care director: The collaborative professional assessment process. *Young Children, 55*(5), 20–28.

Freeman, N. K., Feeney, S., & Moravcik, E. (2003). Ethics and the early childhood teacher educator: A proposed addendum to the NAEYC Code of Ethical Conduct. *Young Children, 58*(3), 82–86.

Friedman, S. L., & Haywood, H. C. (Eds.). (1994). *Developmental follow-up: Concepts, domains, and methods.* San Diego: Academic Press.

Fromberg, D. P. (2002). *Play and meaning in early childhood education.* Boston: Allyn & Bacon.

Frost, J. L. (1992a). *Play and playscapes.* Albany, NY: Delmar.

Frost, J. L. (1992b). Reflections on research and practice in outdoor play environments. *Dimensions of Early Childhood, 20*(4), 6–10, 40.

Frost, J. L., & Klein, B. (1983). *Children's play and playgrounds.* Austin, TX: Playscapes International.

Frost, J. L., & Wortham, S. C. (1988). The evolution of American playgrounds. *Young Children, 43*(5), 19–28.

Frost, J. L., Wortham, S. C., & Reifel, S. (2001). *Play and child development.* Upper Saddle River, NJ: Merrill/Prentice Hall.

Fu, V. R., Stremmel, A. J., & Hill, L. T. (2002). *Teaching and learning: Collaborative exploration of the Reggio Emilia approach.* Upper Saddle River, NJ: Merrill/Prentice Hall.

Fuchs, D., & Fuchs, L. S. (1994). Inclusive schools movement and the radicalization of special education reform. *Exceptional Children, 60,* 294–300.

Fuchs, D., & Fuchs, L. S. (1995). Sometimes separate is better. *Educational Leadership, 52*(4), 22–26.

Fuchs, D., & Fuchs, L. S. (1998). Inclusion versus full inclusion. *Childhood Education, 74,* 309–316.

Fuhr, J. E. (with Barclay, K. H.). (1998). The importance of appropriate nutrition and nutrition education. *Young Children, 53*(1), 74–80.

Gabbard, C. (2000). Physical education. Should it be part of the core curriculum? *Principal, 79*(3), 29–31.

Gage, J., & Workman, S. (1994). Creating family support systems: In Head Start and beyond. *Young Children, 50*(1), 74–77.

Galinsky, E. (1987). *The six stages of parenthood.* Reading, MA: Addison-Wesley.

Galinsky, E. (1988). Parents and teacher-caregivers: Sources of tension, sources of support. *Young Children, 43*(3), 4–12.

Galinsky, E. (1989). Update on employer-supported child care. *Young Children, 44*(6), 2, 75–77.

Galinsky, E. (1990). Why are some parent/teacher partnerships clouded with difficulties? *Young Children, 45*(5), 2–3, 38–39.

Galinsky, E., Bond, J. T., & Friedman, D. E. (1993). *The changing workforce: Highlights of the national study.* New York: Families and Work Institute.

Galinsky, E., & Friedman, D. E. (1993). *Education before school: Investing in quality child care.* New York: Committee for Economic Development.

Galinsky, E., Howes, C., Kontos, S., & Shinn, M. (1994). The study of children in family child care and relative care: Key findings and policy recommendations. *Young Children, 50*(1), 58–61.

Galinsky, E., Shubilla, L., Willer, B., Levine, J., & Daniel, J. (1994). State and community planning for early childhood systems. *Young Children, 49*(2), 54–57.

Galinsky, E., & Weissbourd, B. (1992). Family-centered child care. In B. Spodek & O. N. Saracho (Eds.), *Yearbook in early childhood education: Vol. 3. Issues in child care* (pp. 47–65). New York: Teachers College Press.

Galley, M. (2002). State policies on kindergarten are all over the map. Quality counts 2002: Building blocks for success. *Education Week, 21*(17), 45.

Gandini, L. (1993). Fundamentals of the Reggio Emilia approach to early childhood education. *Young Children, 49*(1), 4–8.

Gandini, L. (1998). Education and caring spaces. In C. Edwards, L. Gandini, & G. Forman (Eds.), *The hundred languages of children: The Reggio approach—advanced reflections* (2nd ed., pp. 161–178). Greenwich, CT: Ablex.

Gannett, E. (1990). *City initiatives in school-age child care* (Action Research Paper No. 1). Wellesley, MA: School-Age Child Care Project.

Garbarino, J., & Abramowitz, R. H. (1992). *Children and families in the social environment* (2nd ed.). New York: Aldine.

Garbarino, J., & Ganzel, B. (2000). The human ecology of early risk. In J. P. Shonkoff & S. J. Meisels (Eds.), *Handbook of early childhood intervention* (2nd ed., pp. 76–93). New York: Cambridge University Press.

García Coll, C., & Magnuson, K. (2000). Cultural differences as sources of developmental vulnerabilities and resources. In J. P. Shonkoff & S. J. Meisels (Eds.), *Handbook of early childhood intervention* (2nd ed., pp. 94–114). New York: Cambridge University Press.

Gardner, H. (1983). *Frames of mind: Theory of multiple intelligences.* New York: Basic Books.

Gardner, H. (1993). *Multiple intelligences: The theory in practice.* New York: Basic/HarperCollins.

Gardner, H. (1998). Foreword: Complementary perspectives on Reggio Emilia. In C. Edwards, L. Gandini, & G. Forman (Eds.), *The hundred languages of children: The Reggio approach—advanced reflections* (2nd ed., pp. xv–xviii). Greenwich, CT: Ablex.

Gardner, H. (1999). *The disciplined mind: What all students should understand.* New York: Simon & Schuster.

Gargiulo, R. (1985). *Working with parents of exceptional children.* Boston: Houghton Mifflin.

Gartrell, D. J. (1995). Misbehavior or mistaken behavior? *Young Children, 50*(5), 27–34.

Gartrell, D. J. (1998). *A guidance approach for the encouraging classroom.* Albany, NY: Delmar.

Gartrell, D. J. (2000). *What the kids said today.* St. Paul, MN: Redleaf.

Gershon, N. B., & Moon, R. Y. (1997). Infant sleep positions in licensed child care centers. *Pediatrics, 100*(1), 75–77.

Gesell, A. (1931). Maturation and patterning of behavior. In C. Murchinson (Ed.), *A handbook of child psychology* (pp. 209–235). Worchester, MA: Clark University Press.

Giangreco, M., Dennis, R., Coninger, C., Edelman, S., & Schattman, R. (1993). "I've counted Jon": Transformational experiences of teachers educating students with disabilities. *Exceptional Children, 59,* 359–372.

Ginsburg, H. P. (1997). *Entering the child's mind: The clinical interview in psychological research and practice.* New York: Cambridge University Press.

Ginsburg, H. P., Jacobs, S. F., & Lopez, L. S. (1993). Assessing mathematical thinking and learning potential. In R. B. Davis & C. S. Maher (Eds.), *Schools, mathematics, and the world of reality* (pp. 237–262). Boston: Allyn & Bacon.

Glascott, K. (1994). A problem of theory for early childhood professionals. *Childhood Education, 70,* 131–132.

Glickman, C. D., Gordon, S. P., & Ross-Gordon, J. M. (1998). *Supervision of instruction: A developmental approach* (4th ed.). Boston: Allyn & Bacon.

Goal I Technical Planning Group. (1993, December). *Reconsidering children's early development and learn-*

ing: Toward shared beliefs and vocabulary. Washington, DC: National Education Goals Panel.

Godwin, A., & Schrag, L. (1996). *Setting up for infant/toddler care: Guidelines for centers and family child care homes* (Rev. ed.). Washington, DC: National Association for the Education of Young Children.

Goffin, S. G. (1988). Public policy report. Putting our advocacy efforts into a new context. *Young Children, 43*(3), 52–56.

Goffin, S. G. (1989). Developing a research agenda for early childhood education. What can be learned from the research on teaching? *Early Childhood Research Quarterly, 4*, 187–204.

Goffin, S. G. (2002). What's next for the Project to Reinvent NAEYC Accreditation? *Young Children, 57*(1), 57–58.

Goffin, S. G., & Lombardi, J. (1988). *Speaking out: Early childhood advocacy.* Washington, DC: National Association for the Education of Young Children.

Goffin, S. G., & Stegelin, D. A. (1992). *Changing kindergartens: Four success stories.* Washington, DC: National Association for the Education of Young Children.

Goffin, S. G., & Wilson, C. S. (2001). *Curriculum models and early childhood education: Appraising the relationship* (2nd ed). Upper Saddle River, NJ: Merrill/Prentice Hall.

Gomby, D., Culross, R., & Behrman, R. (1999). Home visiting: Recent program evaluations—Analysis and recommendations. *Future of Children, 9*(1), 4–26.

Goncu, A. (Ed.). (1999). *Children's engagement in the world: Sociocultural perspectives.* London: Cambridge University Press.

Gonzalez-Mena, J. (2002). *The child in the family and community* (3rd ed.). Upper Saddle River, NJ: Merrill/Prentice Hall.

Good, L. A. (1993). Kindergarten report cards: The new look. *Principal, 72*(5), 22–24.

Goodlad, J. I., Klein, M. F., & Novotney, J. M. (1973). *Early schooling in the United States.* New York: McGraw-Hill.

Goodman, I. F., & Brady, J. P. (1988). *The challenges of coordination: Head Start's relationship to state-funded preschool initiatives.* Newton, MA: Educational Development Center.

Goodnow, J. J. (1996). Acceptable ignorance, negotiable disagreement: Alternative views of learning. In D. R. Olson & N. Torrance (Eds.), *The handbook of education and human development: New models of learning, teaching, and schooling* (pp. 355–367). Oxford, UK: Blackwell.

Goodwin, A. L. (1997). *Assessing for equity and inclusion: Embracing all our children.* New York: Routledge.

Gordon, I. J. (1969). *Early child stimulation through parent education* (Final report to the Children's Bureau, U.S. Department of Health, Education & Welfare). Gainesville, FL: Institute for Development of Human Resources.

Gordon, J. (2000). How our field participates in undermining quality in child care. *Young Children, 55*(6), 31–34.

Gordon, T. (1970). *Parent effectiveness training.* New York: Peter H. Wyden.

Gormley, W. T., Jr. (1991). State regulations and the availability of child-care services. *Journal of Policy Analysis and Management, 10*(1), 78–95.

Gormley, W. T., Jr. (1995). *Everybody's children: Child care as a public problem.* Washington, DC: The Brookings Institution.

Gormley, W. T., Jr. (1997). Regulatory enforcement: Accommodations and conflict in four states. *Public Administration Review, 57*, 285–293.

Grant, C., & Sleeter, C. (1989). *Turning on learning: Five approaches for multicultural teaching plans for race, class, gender, and disability.* New York: Merrill/Macmillan.

Grant, J., Johnson, B., & Richardson, I. (1996). *The looping handbook.* Peterborough, NH: Crystal Springs.

Gratz, R. R., & Boulton, P. J. (1995). Pregnant staff and parental leave: Policies and procedures. *Young Children, 50*(5), 79–83.

Gratz, R. R., & Boulton, P. J. (1996). Erikson and early childhood educators: Looking at ourselves and our profession developmentally. *Young Children, 51*(5), 74–78.

Gray, S. W., & Klaus, R. A. (1970). The early training project: A seventh year report. *Child Development, 41*, 909–924.

Gray, S. W., Ramsey, B., & Klaus, R. (1982). *From 3 to 20: The Early Training Project.* Baltimore, MD: The University Park Press.

Greathouse, B., Moyer, J. E., & Rhodes-Offutt, E. (1992). Increasing K–3 teachers' joy in teaching. *Young Children, 47*(3), 44–46.

Greenberg, P. (1987). Lucy Sprague Mitchell: A major missing link between early childhood education in the 1980s and progressive education in the 1890s–1930s. *Young Children, 42*(5), 70–84.

Greenberg, P. (1989). Parents as partners in young children's development and education: A new American fad? Why does it matter? *Young Children, 44*(4), 61–75.

Greenberg, P. (1990). Before the beginning: A participant's view. *Young Children, 45*(6), 41–52.

Greenberg, P. (1992). Why not academic preschool? Part 2: Autocracy or democracy in the classroom? *Young Children, 47*(3), 54–64.

Greenman, J. T. (1988). *Caring spaces, learning places: Children's environments that work.* Redmond, WA: Exchange Press.

Greenman, J. T. (2001). *What happened to the world? Helping children cope in turbulent times.* South Watertown, MA: Bright Horizons Family Solutions.

Greenman, J. T., & Johnson, N. (1993). *Child care center management.* Minneapolis: Greater Minneapolis Day Care Association.

Greenman, J. T., & Stonehouse, A. (1996). *Prime times: A handbook for excellence in infant and toddler programs.* St. Paul, MN: Redleaf.

Greenspan, S. I., & Weider, S. (1998). *The child with special needs: Encouraging intellectual and emotional growth.* Reading, MA: Perseus Books.

Greer v. Rome City School District, 950 F.2d 688 (11th Cir. 1991), *opinion withdrawn by,* 956 F.2d 1025 (11th Cir. 1992), *opinion reinstated in part by,* 967 F.2d 470 (11th Cir. 1992).

Griffin, G. A. (Ed.). (1999). *The education of teachers: Ninety-eighth yearbook of the National Society for the Study of Education.* Chicago: University of Chicago Press.

Gronlund, G. (1998). Portfolios as an assessment tool: Is collection of work enough? *Young Children, 53*(3), 4–10.

The Growing Up in Poverty Project, University of California at Berkeley and Yale University. (2000). *Remember the children: Mothers balancing work and child care under welfare reform. Wave 1 findings—California, Connecticut, Florida.* Berkeley: University of California, Graduate School of Education/PACE (Policy Analysis for California Education).

Grubb, W. N. (1991). Choosing wisely for children: Policy options for children. In S. L. Kagan (Ed.), *The care and education of America's young children: Obstacles and opportunities* (pp. 214–236). Chicago: University of Chicago Press.

Guddemi, M., & Eriksen, H. (1992). Designing outdoor learning environments for and with children. *Dimensions of Early Childhood, 20*(4), 15–24, 40.

Gundling, R., & Hyson, M. (2002). National Board Certification. The next professional step? *Young Children, 57*(5), 60–61.

Guralnick, M. J. (1988). Efficacy research in early childhood intervention programs. In S. L. Odom & M. B. Karnes (Eds.), *Early intervention for infants and children with handicaps: An empirical base* (pp. 75–88). Baltimore: Brookes.

Guralnick, M. J. (1989). Recent developments in early intervention efficacy research: Implications for family involvement in P.L. 99–457. *Topics in Early Childhood Special Education, 9*(3), 1–17.

Guralnick, M. J. (1990). Social competence and early intervention. *Journal of Early Intervention, 14*(1), 3–14.

Haight, W. L., & Miller, P. J. (1993). *Pretending at home: Early development in a socialcultural context.* Albany: State University of New York Press.

Haith, M. M. (1972). *Day care and intervention programs for infants.* Atlanta: Avatar Press.

Hale, J. E. (1994). *Unbank the fire: Vision for the education of African American children.* Baltimore: Johns Hopkins University Press.

Hale-Benson, J. (1982). *Black children: Their roots, culture, and learning styles.* Baltimore: Johns Hopkins University Press.

Hale-Benson, J. (1986). *Visions for children: African American Early Childhood Education Program.* (ERIC Document Reproduction Service No. ED303269)

Hall, E. T. (1977). *Beyond culture.* Garden City, NY: Anchor Press/Doubleday.

Hall, G. S. (1897). *The story of a sand-pile.* New York: E. L. Kellogg.

Halpern, R. (1992). Issues of program design and implementation. In M. Larner, R. Halpern, & D. Harkavy (Eds.), *Fair Start for children: Lessons learned from seven demonstration projects* (pp. 179–197). New Haven, CT: Yale University Press.

Hanhan, S. F. (2003). Parent-teacher communication: Who's talking? In G. Olsen & M. L. Fuller (Eds.),

Home-school relations: Working successfully with parents and families (2nd ed., pp. 111–133). Boston: Allyn & Bacon.

Hankins, K. H. (1998). Cacophony to symphony: Memoirs in teacher research. *Harvard Educational Review, 68,* 80–95.

Hanson, M. J., & Lovett, D. (1992). Personnel preparation for early interventionist: A cross disciplinary survey. *Journal of Early Intervention, 16,* 123–135.

Hanson, M. J., & Lynch, E. W. (1989). *Early intervention: Implementing child and family services for infants and toddlers who are at risk or disabled.* Austin, TX: PRO-ED.

Harms, T. O. (1992). Designing settings to support high-quality care. In B. Spodek & O. N. Saracho (Eds.), *Yearbook in early childhood education: Vol. 3. Issues in child care* (pp. 169–186). New York: Teachers College Press.

Harms, T. O., & Clifford, R. M. (1989). *The Family Day Care Rating Scale.* New York: Teachers College Press.

Harms, T. O., & Clifford, R. M., & Cryer, D. (1998). *Early Childhood Environment Rating Scale—Revised.* New York: Teachers College Press.

Harms, T. O., & Cryer, D. (1978). Parent newsletter: A new format. *Young Children, 33*(5), 28–32.

Harms, T. O., Cryer, D., & Clifford, R. M. (2003). *Infant/Toddler Environment Rating Scale—Revised.* New York: Teachers College Press.

Harms, T. O., Jacobs, E. V., & White, D. R. (1995). *School-Age Care Environment Rating Scale.* New York: Teachers College Press.

Hart, C. H., & Burts, D. C., & Charlesworth, R. (Eds.). (1997). *Integrated curriculum and developmentally appropriate practice—Birth to age eight.* Albany: State University of New York Press.

Hart, C. H., Burts, D. C., Durland, M. A., Charlesworth, R., DeWolf, M., & Fleege, P. O. (1998). Stress behaviors and activity type participation of preschoolers in more or less developmentally appropriate classrooms: SES and sex differences. *Journal of Research in Childhood Education, 12*(2), 176–196.

Hartle, L., & Johnson, J. E. (1993). Historical and contemporary influences of outdoor play environments. In C. H. Hart (Ed.), *Children on playgrounds* (pp. 14–42). Albany: State University of New York Press.

Hartley, R. E., Frank, L., & Goldenson, R. M. (1957). *The complete book of children's play.* New York: Crowell.

Haseloff, W. (1990). The efficacy of the parent-teacher partnership of the 1990s. *Early Child Development and Care, 58,* 51–55.

Haskell, E. M. (Ed.). (1896). *Child observations: First series. Imitation and allied activities.* Boston: Heath.

Haskins, R. (1989). Beyond metaphors: The efficacy of early childhood education. *American Psychologist, 44,* 247–282.

Hatch, J. A. (2002). Accountability shovedown: Resisting the standards movement in early education. *Phi Delta Kappan, 83,* 457–462.

Hatch, J. A., & Freeman, E. B. (1988a). Kindergarten philosophies and practices: Perspectives of teachers, principals, and supervisors. *Early Childhood Research Quarterly, 3,* 151–166.

Hatch, J. A., & Freeman, E. B. (1988b). Who's pushing whom? Stress and kindergarten. *Phi Delta Kappan, 70,* 145–147.

Haugland, S. W. (1992). Effects of computer software on preschool children's developmental gains. *Journal of Computing in Childhood Education, 3*(1), 15–30.

Haugland, S. W. (1999). What role should technology play in young children's learning? *Young Children, 54*(6), 26–31.

Haugland, S. W., & Shade, D. D. (1994a). Early childhood computer software. *Journal of Computing in Childhood Education, 5*(1), 83–92.

Haugland, S. W., & Shade, D. D. (1994b). Software evaluation for young children. In J. L. Wright & D. D. Shade (Eds.), *Young children: Active learners in a technological age* (pp. 63–76). Washington, DC: National Association for the Education of Young Children.

Haugland, S. W., & Wright, J. L. (1997). *Young children and technology: A world of discovery.* Boston: Allyn & Bacon.

Haupt, J. H., Larsen, J. M., Robinson, C. C., & Hart, C. H. (1995). The impact of DAP inservice training on the beliefs and practices of kindergarten teachers. *Journal of Early Childhood Teacher Education, 16*(2), 12–18.

Hauser-Cram, P. (1990). Designing meaningful evaluations of early childhood services. In S. Meisels & J. Shonkoff (Eds.), *Handbook of early childhood intervention* (pp. 583–602). New York: Cambridge University Press.

Hayden, J. (1996). *Management of early childhood services: An Australian perspective.* Wadsworth Falls, NSW: Social Science Press.

Hayes, C. D., Palmer, J. L., & Zaslow, M. (1990). *Who cares for America's children: Child care policy for the 1990s.* Washington, DC: National Academy Press.

Head Start Bureau. (1991). *Parent and Child Center (PCC) Program fact sheet.* Washington, DC: Author.

Head Start Bureau. (2001). Head Start child outcomes framework. *Head Start Bulletin,* no. 70. Washington, DC: U.S. Department of Health and Human Services, Administrator for Children and Families. (Available online: <http://www.headstartinfo.org/pdf/im00_18a.pdf>)

Healthy Child Care America. (1996). Healthy child care America: A blueprint for action. *Young Children, 51*(5), 57–58.

Healy, J. M. (1998). *Failure to connect: How computers affect our child's minds—For better and worse.* New York: Simon & Schuster.

Hebbeler, K. (1995). *Shortages in professions working with young children with disabilities and their families.* Chapel Hill, NC: National Early Childhood Technical Assistance System.

Heck, R. H., Larsen, T.J., & Marcoulides, G. A., (1990). Instructional leadership and school achievement: Validation of a causal model. *Educational Administration Quarterly, 26*(2), 94–125.

Helburn, S. W. (Ed.). (1995). *Cost, quality, and child outcomes in child care centers.* Technical report. Denver: University of Colorado at Denver, Department of Economics, Center for Research in Economics and Social Policy.

Helburn, S. W., & Culkin, M. L. (1995a). *Cost, quality, and child outcomes in child care centers: Executive summary.* Denver: University of Colorado at Denver.

Helburn, S. W., & Culkin, M. L. (1995b). Costs, quality, and child outcomes in child care centers: Key findings and recommendations. *Young Children, 50*(4), 40–44.

Hellison, D. R., & Cutforth, N. J. (1997). Extended day programs for urban children and youth: From theory to practice. In H. J. Walberg, O. Reyes, & R. P. Weissberg (Eds.), *Children and youth: Interdisciplinary perspectives* (pp. 223–249). Thousand Oaks, CA: Sage.

Helm, J. H., Beneke, S., & Steinheimer, K. (1998). *Windows on learning: Documenting young children's work.* New York: Teachers College Press.

Helm, J. H., & Katz, L. G. (2001). *Young investigators: The project approach in the early years.* New York: Teachers College Press.

Helping young children in frightening times. (2001). *Young Children, 56*(6), 6–7.

Hemmeter, M. L., & Grisham-Brown, J. (1997). Developing children's language skills in inclusive early childhood classrooms. *Dimensions of Early Childhood, 25*(3), 6–13.

Hemmeter, M. L., Maxwell, K. L., Ault, M. J., & Schuster, J. W. (2001). *Assessment of practices in early elementary classrooms.* New York: Teachers College Press.

Hendrick, J. (1992). Where does it all begin? Teaching the principles of democracy in the early years. *Young Children, 47*(3), 51–53.

Hennig, M., & Jardin, A. (1976). *The managerial woman.* New York: Pocket Books.

Henniger, M. L. (1993). Enriching the outdoor play experience. *Childhood Education, 70,* 87–90.

Henniger, M. L. (1994). Planning for outdoor play. *Young Children, 49*(4), 10–15.

Henry, M. (2000). Open doors, open minds: Working with families and community. In N. J. Yelland (Ed.), *Promoting meaningful learning: Innovations in educating early childhood professionals* (pp. 105–116). Washington, DC: National Association for the Education of Young Children.

Herman, J. L., & Winters, L. (1994). Portfolio research: A slim collection. *Educational Leadership, 52,* 48–55.

Herr, J., Johnson, R. D., & Zimmerman, K. (1993). Benefits of accreditation: A study of directors' perceptions. *Young Children, 48*(4), 32–35.

Hess, R., & McGarvey, L. (1987). School-relevant effects of educational uses of microcomputers in kindergarten classrooms and homes. *Journal of Educational Computing Research, 3,* 269–287.

Hewes, D. W. (2000). Looking back: How the role of the director has been understood, studied, and utilized in ECE programs, policy, and practice. In M. L. Culkin (Ed.), *Managing quality in young children's programs: The leader's role* (pp. 23–39). New York: Teachers College Press.

Hiebert, E. H., & Adams, C. S. (1987). Fathers' and mothers' perceptions of their preschool children's emergent literacy. *Journal of Experimental Child Psychology, 44,* 25–37.

High/Scope Educational Research Foundation. (1992). *High/Scope Child Observation Record*. Ypsilanti, MI: High/Scope Press.

High/Scope Educational Research Foundation. (1998). *High/Scope Program Quality Assessment*. Ypsilanti, MI: High/Scope Press.

Hilliard, A. G., III. (1991). Equity, access, and segregation. In S. L. Kagan (Ed.), *The care and education of America's young children: Obstacles and opportunities* (pp. 199–213). Chicago: University of Chicago Press.

Hill-Scott, K. (2000). Leadership in child development programs: Prospects for the future. In M. L. Culkin (Ed.), *Managing quality in young children's programs* (pp. 203–220). New York: Teachers College Press.

Hills, T. W. (1987). Children in the fast lane: Implications for early childhood policy and practice. *Early Childhood Research Quarterly, 2,* 265–273.

Hilton, A., & Liberty, K. (1992). The challenge of ensuring educational gains for students with severe disabilities who are placed in more integrated settings. *Education and Training in Mental Retardation, 27,* 167–175.

Hirsch, E. S. (Ed.). (1996). *The block book* (3rd ed.). Washington, DC: National Association for the Education of Young Children.

Hirsch-Pasek, K. (1991). Pressure or challenge in preschool? How academic environments affect children. In L. Rescorla, M. C. Hyson, & K. Hirsch-Pasek (Eds.), *New directions in child development. Academic instruction in early childhood: Challenge or pressure?* (No. 53, pp. 39–46). San Francisco: Jossey-Bass.

Hirsch-Pasek, K., Hyson, M. C., & Rescorla, L. (1990). Academic environments in preschool: Do they pressure or challenge young children? *Early Education and Development, 1,* 401–423.

Hitz, M. C., & Wright, D. (1988). Kindergarten issues: A practitioners' survey. *Principal, 67*(5), 28–30.

Hitz, R., & Driscoll, A. (1988). Praise or encouragement? *Young Children, 43*(5), 6–13.

Hitz, R., & Richter, S. (1993). School readiness: A flawed concept. *Principal, 72*(5), 10–12.

Hofferth, S. L., Brayfield, A., Deich, S., & Holcomb, P. (1991). *National child care survey 1990: A National Association for the Education of Young Children study.* Washington, DC: The Urban Institute.

Hofferth, S. L., & Chaplin, D. D. (1998). *State regulations: Effects on cost, quality, availability, and use of child care programs* (Working paper). Washington, DC: The Urban Institute.

Hoffman, E. (2002). *Changing channels.* St. Paul, MN: Redleaf.

Hohmann, C., & Buchleitner, W. (1992). *Learning environment.* Ypsilanti, MI: High/Scope Press.

Hohmann, M., & Weikart, D. P. (1995). *Educating young children: Active learning practices for preschool and child care programs.* Ypsilanti, MI: High/Scope Press.

Holmes, M. C. (1937). The kindergarten in American pioneer period. *Childhood Education, 13,* 269–273.

Honig, A. S. (1993). Mental health for babies: What do theory and research teach us? *Young Children, 48*(3), 69–76.

Honig, A. S. (1995). Singing with infants and toddlers. *Young Children, 50*(5), 72–78.

Honig, A. S. (1996). Early childhood education: Training for the future. *Early Childhood Development and Care, 121,* 135–145.

Honig, A. S. (2002). *Secure relationships: Nurturing infant/toddler attachment in early care settings.* Washington, DC: National Association for the Education of Young Children.

Honig, A. S., & Brill, S. (1970). *A comparative analysis of the Piagetian development of twelve-month-old disadvantaged infants in an enrichment center with others not in such a center.* Syracuse, NY: Syracuse University Children's Center.

Hoover-Dempsey, K. V., Bassler, O. C., & Brissie, J. S. (1987). Parent involvement: Contributions of teacher efficacy, school socioeconomic status, and other school characteristics. *American Educational Research Journal, 24,* 417–435.

Hoover-Dempsey, K. V., & Sandler, H. M. (1997). Why do parents become involved in their children's education? *Review of Educational Research, 67,* 3–42.

Horowitz, F. D., & O'Brien, M. (1989). In the interest of the nation: A reflective essay on the state of our knowledge and the challenges before us. *American Psychologist, 44,* 441–445.

Howe, M. B. (2000). Improving child care and promoting accreditation: The military model. *Young Children, 55*(5), 61–63.

Howell, N. M. (1999). Cooking up a learning community with corn, beans, and rice. *Young Children, 54*(5), 36–38.

Howells, R. F. (1993). A new approach to school-age child care. *Principal, 72,* 29.

Howes, C. (1983). Caregiver behavior in center and family day care. *Journal of Applied Developmental Psychology, 4,* 99–107.

Howes, C. (1992). Child outcomes of child care programs. In B. Spodek & O. N. Saracho (Eds.), *Yearbook in early childhood education: Vol. 3. Issues in child care* (pp. 31–46). New York: Teachers College Press.

Howes, C. (1997). Children's experiences in center-based child care as a function of teacher background and adult-child ratio. *Merrill-Palmer Quarterly, 43,* 404–425.

Howes, C. (2000). Social-emotional classroom climate in child care, child-teacher relationships, and children's second grade peer relations. *Social Development, 9,* 191–205.

Howes, C., & Galinsky, E. (1996). Accreditation of Johnson & Johnson's child development center. In S. Bredekamp & B. A. Willer (Eds.), *NAEYC accreditation: A decade of learning and the years ahead* (pp. 47–60). Washington, DC: National Association for the Education of Young Children.

Howes, C., & Hamilton, C. E. (1992). Children's relationships with caregivers: Mothers and child care teachers. *Child Development, 63,* 867–878.

Howes, C., & Hamilton, C. E. (1993). Child care for young children. In B. Spodek (Ed.), *Handbook of research on the education of young children* (pp. 325–335). New York: Macmillan.

Howes, C., & Norris, D. (1997). Adding two school age children: Does it change quality in family child care? *Early Childhood Research Quarterly, 12,* 327–342.

Howes, C., Phillips, D., & Whitebook, M. (1992). Thresholds of quality: Implications for the social development of children in center–based child care. *Child Development, 63,* 449–460.

Howes, C., Smith, E., & Galinsky, E. (1998). *The Florida Child Care Quality Improvement Study: 1996 Report.* New York: Families and Work Institute.

Howes, C., & Stewart, P. (1987). Child's play with adults, toys, and peers: An examination of family and child care influences. *Developmental Psychology, 23,* 423–430.

Hoy, W., & Miskel, C. (1987). *Educational administration.* New York: Random House.

Humphryes, J. (1998). The developmental appropriateness of high-quality Montessori programs. *Young Children, 53*(4), 4–16.

Hunt, J. M. (1961). *Intelligence and experience.* New York: Ronald.

Hunt, J. M. (1968). Revisiting Montessori. In J. L. Frost (Ed.), *Early childhood education rediscovered: Readings* (pp. 102–127). New York: Holt, Rinehart & Winston.

Hunt, P., & Goetz, L. (1997). Research on inclusive educational programs, practices, and outcomes for students with severe disabilities. *Journal of Special Education, 31,* 3–29.

Hurst, B., Wilson, C., & Cramer, G. (1998). Professional teaching portfolios: Tools for reflection, growth, and advancement. *Phi Delta Kappan, 79,* 578–582.

Hyman, I. (1997). *The case against spanking.* San Francisco: Jossey-Bass.

Hymes, J. L., Jr. (1944). The Kaiser answer: Child service centers. *Progressive Education, 21,* 222–223, 245–246.

Hyson, M. (2001). Reclaiming our words. *Young Children, 56*(3), 53–54.

Hyson, M. (2002). Preparing tomorrow's teachers. NAEYC announces new standards. *Young Children, 57*(2), 78–79.

Hyson, M. C. (1994). *The emotional development of young children: Building an emotion-centered curriculum.* New York: Teachers College Press.

Hyson, M. C., Hirsch-Pasek, K., & Rescorla, L. (1990). The classroom practices inventory: An observation instrument based on NAEYC's guidelines for developmentally appropriate practices for 4- and 5-year-old children. *Early Childhood Research Quarterly, 5,* 475–494.

Inoway-Ronnie, E. (1998). High/Scope in Head Start programs serving Southeast Asian immigrant and refugee children and their families: Lessons from an ethnographic study. In J. Ellsworth & L. J. Ames (Eds.), *Critical perspectives on Project Head Start: Revisioning the hope and challenge* (pp. 167–199). Albany: State University of New York Press.

International Reading Association & National Association for the Education of Young Children. (2000). Joint position statement. In S. B. Neuman, C. Copple, & S. Bredekamp, *Learning to read and write* (pp. 1–26). Washington, DC: National Association for the Education of Young Children. (Available online: <www.naeyc.org/resources/position_statements/psreadO.htm>)

Irvine, D. J. (1982, April). *Evaluation of the New York State Experimental Prekindergarten Program.* Paper presented at the annual meeting of the American Educational Research Association, New York.

Irving, K., & Tennent, L. (1998). *Observing and analysing young children's behavior* (CD-ROM). Sydney, Australia: Prentice Hall.

Irwin, D. M., & Bushnell, M. M. (1980). *Observational strategies for child study.* New York: Holt, Rinehart, and Winston.

Isaacs, S. (1930). *Intellectual growth in young children.* London: Routledge & Kegan Paul.

Isaacs, S. (1933). *Social development in young children.* London: Routledge & Kegan Paul.

Isbell, R. (1995). *The complete learning center book.* Beltsville, MD: Gryphon.

Isbell, R., & Exelby, B. (2001). *Early learning environments that work.* Beltsville, MD: Gryphon.

Isenberg, J. P. (1999). *The state of the art in early childhood professional preparation.* Washington, DC: National Institute on Early Childhood Development and Education.

Isenberg, J. P., & Jalongo, M. R. (2000). *Creative expression and play in early childhood* (3rd ed.). Upper Saddle River, NJ: Merrill/Prentice Hall.

Isenberg, J. P., & Quisenberry, N. (2002). A position paper of the Association for Childhood Education International. Play: Essential for all children. *Childhood Education, 79,* 33–39.

Jacob-Timm, S., & Hartshorne, T. S. (1998). *Ethics and law for school psychologists.* New York: Wiley.

Jacobs, F. (1988). The five-tiered approach to evaluation: Context and implementation. In H. B. Weiss & F. H. Jacobs (Eds.), *Evaluating family programs* (pp. 37–68). New York: Aldine DeGruyter.

Jacobs, N. L. (1992). Unhappy endings. *Young Children, 47*(3), 23–27.

Jacobson, L. (2002). Defining quality. Quality counts 2002: Building blocks for success. *Education Week, 21*(17), 24–28, 30–31.

Javernick, E. (1988). Johnny's not jumping: Can we help obese children? *Young Children, 43*(2), 18–23.

Jenkins, L., Speltz, M., & Odom, S. (1985). Integrating normal and handicapped preschoolers: Effects on child development and social interaction. *Exceptional Children, 52,* 7–18.

Jensen, B. J., & Bullard, J. A. (2002). The mud center: Recapturing childhood. *Young Children, 57*(3), 16–19.

Jersild, A. T. (1946). *Child development and the curriculum.* New York: Teachers College Press.

Jipson, J. (1991). Developmentally appropriate practice: Culture, curriculum, connections. *Early Education and Development, 2,* 120–136.

Johnson, H. M. (1924). *A nursery school experiment.* New York: Bureau of Educational Experiments.

Johnson, J., & McCracken, J. B. (Eds.). (1994). *The early childhood career lattice: Perspectives on professional development.* Washington, DC: National Association for the Education of Young Children.

Johnson, J. E., Christie, J. F., & Yawkey, T. D. (1987). *Play and early childhood development.* Glenview, IL: Scott, Foresman.

Johnson, L. C. (1987). The developmental implications of home environments. In C. S. Weinstein & T. G. David (Eds.), *Spaces for children: The built environment and child development* (pp. 139–173). New York: Plenum.

Johnston, L., & Mermin, J. (1994). Easing children's entry to school: Home visits help. *Young Children, 49*(5), 62–68.

Johnston, W. B., & Packer, A. H. (1987). *Workforce 2000: Work and workers for the 21st century.* Indianapolis: Hudson Institute.

Joint Committee on Teacher Planning for Students with Disabilities. (1995). *Planning for academic diversity in America's classrooms: Windows on reality, research, change, and practice.* Lawrence: University of Kansas Center for Research on Learning.

Jones, B., Valdez, G., Norakowski, J., & Rasmussen, C. (1994). *Designing learning and technology for educational reform.* Oakbrook, IL: North Central Regional Educational Laboratory.

Jones, E. (1986). *Teaching adults: An active learning approach.* Washington, DC: National Association for the Education of Young Children.

Jones, E. (1994). Breaking the ice: Confronting status differences among professionals. In J. Johnson & J. B. McCracken (Eds.), *The early childhood career lattice: Perspectives on professional development* (pp. 27–30). Washington, DC: National Association for the Education of Young Children.

Jones, E., & Nimmo, J. (1994). *Emergent curriculum.* Washington, DC: National Association for the Education of Young Children.

Jones, E., & Nimmo, J. (1999). Collaboration, conflict, and change: Thoughts on education as provocation. *Young Children, 54*(1), 5–10.

Jones, E., & Prescott, E. (1978). *Dimensions of teaching-learning environments II: Focus on day care.* Pasadena, CA: Pacific Oaks College.

Jordan, K. F., Lyons, T. S., & McDonough, J. T. (1992). *Funding and financing for programs to serve K–3 at-risk children: A research review.* Washington, DC: National Education Association.

Jorde-Bloom, P. (1992a). Looking inside: Helping teachers assess their beliefs and values. *Child Care Information Exchange, 88,* 11–13.

Jorde-Bloom, P. (1992b). Staffing issues in child care. In B. Spodek & O. N. Saracho (Eds.), *Yearbook in early childhood education: Vol. 3. Issues in child care* (pp. 143–168). New York: Teachers College Press.

Jorde-Bloom, P. (1995). Shared decision making: The centerpiece of participatory management. *Young Children, 50*(4), 55–60.

Jorde-Bloom, P. (1997). Leadership: Defining the elusive. *Leadership Quest, 1*(1), 12–15.

Jorde-Bloom, P., & Sheerer, M. (1991, June). *The effect of Head Start leadership training on program quality.* Paper presented at the Society for Research in Child Development, National Working Conference on Child and Family Research, Arlington, VA.

Jorde-Bloom, P., & Sheerer, M. (1992). The effects of leadership training on child care program quality. *Early Childhood Research Quarterly, 7,* 579–594.

Kagan, S. L. (1988). Current reforms in early-childhood education: Are we addressing the issues? *Young Children, 43*(2), 27–32.

Kagan, S. L. (1989). Early care and education: Beyond the schoolhouse doors. *Phi Delta Kappan, 71,* 107–112.

Kagan, S. L. (1991a). Excellence in early childhood education: Defining characteristics and next decade strategies. In S. L. Kagan (Ed.), *The care and education of America's young children: Obstacles and opportunities* (pp. 237–258). Chicago: University of Chicago Press.

Kagan, S. L. (1991b). *United we stand: Collaboration in child care and early education services.* New York: Teachers College Press.

Kagan, S. L. (1992). Readiness past, present, and future: Shaping the agenda. *Young Children, 48*(1), 48–53.

Kagan, S. L. (1994a). Families with children: Who is responsible? *Childhood Education, 71,* 4–8.

Kagan, S. L. (1994b). Leadership: Rethinking it—Making it happen. *Young Children, 49*(5), 50–54.

Kagan, S. L. (2000a). Financing the field: From mistakes to high stakes. *Young Children, 55*(3), 4–5.

Kagan, S. L. (2000b). Making assessment count . . . What matters? *Young Children, 55*(2), 4.

Kagan, S. L. (2000c). What's in a name? *Young Children, 55*(4), 4.

Kagan, S. L., & Bowman, B. T. (1997). Leadership in early care and education: Issues and challenges. In S. L. Kagan & B. T. Bowman (Eds.), *Leadership in early care and education* (pp. 3–8). Washington, DC: National Association for the Education of Young Children.

Kagan, S. L., Brandon, R. N., Ripple, C. H., Maher, E. J., & Joesch, J. M. (2002). Supporting quality in early childhood care and education: Addressing compensation and infrastructure. *Young Children, 57*(3), 58–65.

Kagan, S. L., & Cohen, N. E. (1997). *Not by chance: Creating an early care and education system for America's children. Full report, the Quality 2000 Initiative.* New Haven, CT: Bush Center in Child Development and Social Policy.

Kagan, S. L., & Garcia, E. E. (Eds.). (1991). Educating linguistically and culturally diverse preschoolers [Special issue]. *Early Childhood Research Quarterly, 6*(3).

Kagan, S. L., & Neuman, M. J. (1997a). Conceptual leadership. In S. L. Kagan & B. T. Bowman (Eds.), *Leadership in early care and education* (pp. 59–64). Washington, DC: National Association for the Education of Young Children.

Kagan, S. L., & Neuman, M. J. (1997b). Highlights of the Quality 2000 initiative: Not by chance. *Young Children, 52*(6), 54–62.

Kagan, S. L., & Newton, J. W. (1989). Public policy report. For-profit and nonprofit child care: Similarities and differences. *Young Children, 45*(1), 4–10.

Kagan, S. L., Powell, D. R., Weissbourd, B., & Zigler, E. F. (Eds.). (1987). *America's family support programs.* New Haven, CT: Yale University Press.

Kagan, S. L., & Rivera, A. M. (1991). Collaboration in early care and education: What can and should we expect? *Young Children, 47*(1), 51–56.

Kagan, S. L., Rivera, A. M., Brigham, N., & Rosenblum, S. (1992). *Collaboration: Cornerstones of an early childhood system.* New Haven, CT: Yale University, Bush Center in Child Development and Social Policy.

Kagan, S. L., Rosenkoetter, S., & Cohen, N. E. (Eds.). (1997). *Considering child-based outcomes for young children: Definitions, desirability, feasibility, and next steps.* New Haven, CT: Yale University, Bush Center in Child Development and Social Policy.

Kahn, A., & Kamerman, S. (1987). *Child care: Facing the hard choices.* Dover, MA: Auburn House.

Kahn, E. D. (1989). *Past caring: A history of U.S. preschool care and education for the poor, 1820–1965.* New York: Columbia University, School of Public Health, National Center for Children in Poverty.

Kamii, C. (Ed.). (1990). *Achievement testing in the early grades: The games grown-ups play.* Washington, DC: National Association for the Education of Young Children.

Kamii, C., & Peper, R. (1969). *A Piagetian method of evaluating preschool children's development in classification.* Washington, DC: U.S. Office of Education, Bureau of Elementary and Secondary Education. (ERIC Document Reproduction Service No. ED039013)

Kaplan, P. (1998). *The human odyssey.* Pacific Grove, CA: Brooks & Cole.

Karnes, M. B., Shwedel, A. M., & Williams, M. B. (1983). A comparison of five approaches for educating young children from low-income homes. In Consortium for Longitudinal Studies, *As the twig is bent: Lasting effects of preschool programs* (pp. 133–169). Hillsdale, NJ: Erlbaum.

Karoly, L. A., Greenwood, P. W., Everingham, S. S., Houbé, J., Kilburn, M. R., Rydell, C. P., Sanders, M., & Chiesa, J. (1998). *Investing in our children: What we know and don't know about the costs and benefits of early childhood interventions.* Santa Monica, CA: Rand.

Karp, R., Martin, R., Sewell, T., Manni, J., & Heller, A. (1992). Growth and academic achievement in inner-city kindergarten children. *Clinical Pediatrics, 31,* 336–340.

Karweit, N. (1993). Effective preschool and kindergarten programs for children at risk. In B. Spodek (Ed.), *Handbook of research on the education of young children* (pp. 91–104). New York: Macmillan.

Katz, L. G. (1984a). The professional early childhood teacher. *Young Children, 39*(5), 3–11.

Katz, L. G. (1984b). The professional preschool teacher. In L. G. Katz (Ed.), *More talks with teachers* (pp. 27–42). Urbana, IL: ERIC Clearinghouse on Elementary and Early Childhood Education.

Katz, L. G. (1991a). Pedagogical issues in early childhood education. In S. L. Kagan (Ed.), *The care and education of America's young children: Obstacles and opportunities* (pp. 50–68). Chicago: University of Chicago Press.

Katz, L. G. (1991b). *Readiness: Children and schools.* Urbana, IL: ERIC Clearinghouse on Elementary and Early Childhood Education. (ERIC Document Reproduction Service No. ED330495)

Katz, L. G. (1995a). A developmental approach to the education of young children: Basic principles. *International School Journal, 14*(2), 49–60.

Katz, L. G., (1995b). *Talks with teachers of young children: A collection.* Norwood, NJ: Ablex.

Katz, L. G. (1999). *Multiple perspectives on the quality of programs for young children.* Hong Kong: Keynote address at the International Conference of the World Organization for Early Childhood Education, March 20–21, 1999. (ERIC Document Reproduction Service No. ED428868)

Katz, L. G., & Chard, S. C. (2000). *Engaging children's minds: The project approach* (2nd ed.). Norwood, NJ: Ablex.

Katz, L. G., Evangelou, D., & Hartman, J. A. (1990). *The case for mixed-age grouping in early education.* Washington, DC: National Association for the Education of Young Children.

Katz, L. G., & McClellan, D. E. (1997). *Fostering children's social competence: The teacher's role.* Washington, DC: National Association for the Education of Young Children.

Katz, L. G., & Raths, J. D. (1986). Dispositions as goals for teacher education. *Teaching and Teacher Education, 1,* 301–307.

Kelley, R. (1991). *The power of followership: How to create leaders who people want to follow and followers who lead themselves.* New York: Doubleday.

Kelly, J. F., & Booth, C. L. (1999). Child care for infants with special needs: Issues and applications. *Infants and Young Children, 12,* 26–33.

Kelly, V. (1996). Action research and the early years of education. *Early Years, 17*(1), 41–46.

Kennedy, D. (1991). The young child's experience of space and child care center design: A practical meditation. *Children's Environments Quarterly, 8*(1), 37–48.

Kennedy, E., & Davis, C. (1998). U.S. Department of Agriculture School Breakfast Program. *American Journal of Clinical Nutrition, 67,* 798S–803S.

Kerr, V. (1973). One step forward—two steps back: Child care's long American history. In P. Roby (Ed.), *Child care: Who cares?* (pp. 157–171). New York: Basic Books.

Kessler, S. A. (1991a). Alternative perspectives on early childhood education. *Early Childhood Research Quarterly, 6,* 183–197.

Kessler, S. A. (1991b). Early childhood education as development: Critique of the metaphor. *Early Education and Development, 2,* 137–152.

Kessler, S. A., & Swadener, B. B. (Eds.). (1994). *Reconceptualizing the early childhood curriculum: Beginning the dialogue.* New York: Teachers College Press.

Kessler-Harris, A. (1982). *Out of work: A history of wage earning women in the United States.* New York: Oxford University Press.

Kielar, J. (1999). An antidote to the noisy nineties. *Young Children, 54*(5), 28–29.

Kilpatrick, W. H. (1918). The project method. *Teachers College Record, 19,* 319–335.

King, E. W., Chipman, M., & Cruz-Jansen, M. (1994). *Educating young children in a diverse society.* Boston: Allyn & Bacon.

Kirst, M. (1991). Improving children's services: Overcoming barriers, creating new opportunities. *Phi Delta Kappan, 72,* 615–618.

Kisker, E. E., Hofferth, S. L., Phillips, D. A., & Farquhar, E. (1991). *A profile of child care settings: Early education and child care in 1990.* Washington, DC: U.S. Department of Education.

Klefstad, J. (1995). Cooking in the kindergarten. *Young Children, 50*(6), 32–33.

Kliebard, H. M. (1986). *The struggle for the American curriculum 1893–1958.* New York: Routledge.

Knapp, M. S. (1995a). How shall we study comprehensive, collaborative services for children and families? *Educational Researcher, 24*(4), 5–16.

Knapp, M. S. (Ed.). (1995b). *Teaching for meaning in high-poverty classrooms.* New York: Teachers College Press.

Knitzer, J., & Page, S. (1998). *Map and track: State initiatives for young children and families.* New York: Columbia University, National Center for Children in Poverty.

Knudsen-Lindauer, S., & Harris, K. (1989). Priorities for kindergarten curricula: Views of parents and teachers. *Journal of Research on Childhood Education, 4*(1), 51–61.

Kohlberg, L., & Mayer, R. (1972). Development as the aim of education. *Harvard Educational Review, 42,* 449–496.

Kohn, A. (2000). *The case against standardized testing: Raising the scores, running the schools.* Portsmouth, NH: Heinemann.

Kohn, A. (2001a). Fighting the tests: Turning frustration into action. *Young Children, 56*(2), 19–24.

Kohn, A. (2001b). Five reasons to stop saying "Good Job!" *Young Children, 56*(5), 24–28.

Kontos, S. (1984). Congruence of parenting and early childhood perceptions of parenting. *Parenting Studies, 1*(1), 5–10.

Kontos, S., & Dunn, L. (1989). Attitudes of caregivers, maternal experiences with day care, and children's development. *Journal of Applied Developmental Psychology, 10,* 37–51.

Kontos, S., & File, N. (1992). Conditions of employment, job satisfaction, and job commitment among early intervention personnel. *Journal of Early Intervention, 16,* 155–165.

Kontos, S., Howes, C., & Galinsky, E. (1997). Does training make a difference to quality in family child care? *Early Childhood Research Quarterly, 12,* 351–372.

Kontos, S., Howes, C., Shinn, M., & Galinsky, E. (1995). *Quality in family child care and relative care.* New York: Teachers College Press.

Kontos, S., Machida, S., Griffin, S., & Read, M. (1992). Training and professionalism in family day care. In D. L. Peters & A. R. Pence (Eds.), *Family day care: Current research for informed public policy* (pp. 188–208). New York: Teachers College Press.

Kontos, S., & Stremmel, A. (1988). Caregivers' perceptions of working conditions in a child care environment. *Early Childhood Research Quarterly, 3,* 77–91.

Kontos, S., & Wells, W. (1986). Attitudes of caregivers and the day care experiences of families. *Early Childhood Research Quarterly, 1,* 47–67.

Koralek, D. G., Colker, L. J., & Dodge, D. T. (1995). *The what, why, and how of high-quality early childhood education: A guide for on-site supervision* (Rev. ed.). Washington, DC: National Association for the Education of Young Children.

Korenman, S., Miller, J. E., & Sjaastad, J. E. (1995). Long-term poverty and child development in the United States. National Longitudinal Survey of Youth. *Children and Youth Service's Review, 17,* 127–155.

Kostelnik, M. J. (1992). Myths associated with developmentally appropriate programs. *Young Children, 47*(4), 17–23.

Kraft, S., & Snell, M. (1980). Parent-teacher conflict: Coping with parental stress. *Pointer, 24,* 29–37.

Kramer, R. (1988). *Maria Montessori: A biography.* Reading, MA: Addison-Wesley.

Kremer-Hazon, L., & Ben-Peretz, M. (1996). Becoming a teacher: The transition from teacher's college to classroom life. *International Review of Education, 32*(4), 413–422.

Kromhout, O. M., & Butzin, S. M. (1993). Integrating computers into the elementary school curriculum: An evaluation of nine Project CHILD model schools. *Journal of Research on Computing in Education, 26*(1), 55–69.

Krueger, A. (1999). Experimental estimates of education production functions. *Quarterly Journal of Economics, 114,* 497–532.

Kuball, Y. E. (1999). A case for developmental continuity in a bilingual K-2 setting. *Young Children, 54*(3), 74–79.

Kuhn, A. (1947). *The mother's role in childhood education: New England concepts, 1830–1860.* New Haven, CT: Yale University Press.

Laird, R. D., Pettit, G. S., Dodge, K. A., & Bates, J. E. (1998). The social ecology of school-age child care. *Journal of Applied Developmental Psychology, 19,* 341–360.

Lally, J. R. (1995). The impact of child care policies and practices on infant/toddler identity formation. *Young Children, 51*(1), 58–67.

Lally, J. R., Griffin, A., Fenichel, E., Segal, M. M., Szanton, E. S., & Weissbourd, B. (1995). *Caring for infants and toddlers in groups: Developmentally appropriate practice.* Arlington, VA: Zero to Three.

Lally, J. R., Lerner, C., & Lurie-Hurvitz, E. (2001). National survey reveals gaps in the public's and parents' knowledge about early childhood development. *Young Children, 56*(2), 49–53.

Lally, J. R., Mangione, P. L., & Honig, A. S. (1987). *The Syracuse University Family Development Research Program: Long-range impact of early intervention on low-income children and their families.* San Francisco: Center for Child and Family Studies, Far West Laboratory for Educational Research and Development.

Lally, J. R., Provence, S., Szanton, E., & Weissbourd, B. (1986). Developmentally appropriate care for children from birth to age 3. In S. Bredekamp (Ed.), *Developmentally appropriate practice in early childhood programs serving children from birth through age 8* (Exp. ed., pp. 17–33). Washington, DC: National Association for the Education of Young Children.

Lamb, M. E. (1998). Non-parental child care: Context, quality, correlates. In W. Damon, I. E. Sigel, & K. A. Renninger (Eds.), *Handbook of child psychology: Vol. 4. Child psychology in practice* (5th ed., pp. 73–134). New York: Wiley.

Lambert, D. J., Dellman-Jenkins, M., & Fruit, D. (1990). Planning for contact between the generations: An effective approach. *Gerontologist, 30,* 553–556.

Langhorst, B. H. (1989). *Assessment in early childhood: A consumer's guide.* Portland, OR: Northwest Regional Educational Laboratory.

Larner, M. (1996). Parents' perspectives on quality in early care and education. In S. Kagan & N. Cohen (Eds.), *Reinventing early care and education: A vision for quality systems* (pp. 21–42). San Francisco: Jossey-Bass.

Larner, M., & Mitchell, A. (1992). Meeting the child care needs of low-income families. *Child and Youth Care Forum, 21,* 317–334.

Larsen, J. M., & Robinson, C. (1989). Later effects of preschool on low-risk children. *Early Childhood Research Quarterly, 4,* 133–144.

Latimer, D. J. (1994). Involving grandparents and other older adults in the preschool classroom. *Dimensions of Early Childhood, 22*(2), 26–30.

Laufer, R. S., & Wolfe, M. (1977). Privacy as a concept and a social issue: A multidimensional developmental theory. *Journal of Social Issues, 33*(3), 22–42.

Lavatelli, C. S. (1970). *Piaget's theory applied to an early childhood curriculum.* Boston: American Science and Engineering.

Lawler, E. E., Mohrman, S. A., & Ledford, G. E., Jr. (1992). *Employee involvement and total quality management.* San Francisco: Jossey-Bass.

Leavitt, R. L. (1987). *Invisible boundaries: An interpretive study of parent-provider relationship.* Chicago:

Spencer Foundation. (ERIC Document Reproduction Service No. ED299035)

Leithead, M. (1996). Happy hammering . . . A hammering activity center with built-in success. *Young Children, 51*(3), 12.

Lemerise, T. (1993). Piaget, Vygotsky, and Logo. *Computing Teacher, 20*(4), 24–28.

Levenstein, P. (1970). Cognitive growth in preschoolers through verbal interaction with mothers. *American Journal of Orthopsychiatry, 40,* 426–432.

Levenstein, P. (1987). The mother-child program. In M. C. Day & R. K. Parker (Eds.), *The preschool in action* (pp. 27–49). Needham Heights, MA: Allyn & Bacon.

Levin, R. A. (1991). The debate over schooling: Influences of Dewey and Thorndike. *Childhood Education, 68,* 71–75.

Levine, M. (1992). Observations on the early childhood profession. *Young Children, 47*(2), 50–51.

Levine-Coley, R. (1998). Children's socialization experiences and functioning in single-mother households: The importance of fathers and other men. *Child Development, 69,* 219–230.

Lewis, A. C. (1997). Washington seen . . . *The Education Digest, 63*(2), 73–74.

Lewis, M. L. (2000). The cultural context of infant mental health: The development niche of infant-caregiver relationships. In C. H. Zeanah (Ed.), *Handbook of infant mental health* (2nd ed., pp. 91–107). New York: The Guilford Press.

Likert, R. (1967). *The human organization.* New York: McGraw-Hill.

Lipsky, D. K., & Gartner, A. (1991). Restructuring for quality. In J. W. Lloyd, A. C. Repp, & N. N. Singh (Eds.), *The regular education initiative: Alternative perspectives on concepts, issues, and models* (pp. 43–56). Sycamore, IL: Sycamore.

Litwak, E., & Meyer, H. (1974). *School, family, and neighborhood: The theory and practice of school-community relations.* New York: Teachers College Press.

Loewy, M. (1998). Suggestions for working with fat children in schools. *Professional School Counseling, 1*(4), 18–23.

Lombardi, J. (1999). Viewpoint. Child care is education . . . and more. *Young Children, 54*(1), 48.

Love, J. M., Logue, M. E., Trudeau, J. V., & Thayer, K. (1992). *Transitions to kindergarten in American schools: Final report of the National Transition Study.*

Washington, DC: U.S. Department of Education, Office of Policy and Planning.

Lowman, L. H., & Ruhmann, L. H. (1998). Simply sensational spaces: A multi-"s" approach to toddler environments. *Young Children, 53*(3), 11–17.

Lozoff, B., Jimenez, E., Hagen, J., Mollen, E., & Wolf, A. W. (2000). Poorer behavior and developmental outcome more than 10 years after treatment for iron deficiency in infancy. *Pediatrics, 105*(4), E51.

Lozoff, B., Klein, N. K., Nelson, E. C., McClish, D. K., Manuel, M., & Chacon, M. E. (1998). Behavior of infants with iron-deficiency anemia. *Child Development, 69*(1), 24–36.

Lubeck, S. (1989). Four-year-olds and public schooling? Framing the question. *Theory and Practice, 28*(1), 3–10.

Lubeck, S. (1994). The politics of developmentally appropriate practice: Exploring issue of culture, class, and curriculum. In B. L. Mallory & R. S. New (Eds.), *Diversity and developmentally appropriate practices* (pp. 17–43). New York: Teachers College Press.

Lubeck, S. (1998). Is developmentally appropriate practice for everyone? *Childhood Education, 74,* 283–292.

Ludlow, B. L., & Berkeley, T. R. (1994). Expanding the perceptions of developmentally appropriate practice. In B. L. Mallory & R. S. New (Eds.), *Diversity and developmentally appropriate practices* (pp. 107–118). New York: Teachers College Press.

Lukaszewski, T. E. (1996). New accounting requirements for non-profits. *Child Care Information Exchange, 111,* 35–38.

Lynch, E. W., & Hanson, M. J. (Eds.). (1998). *Developing cross-cultural competence: A guide for working with children and their families* (2nd ed.). Baltimore: Brookes.

Lynn, L. (1997). Family involvement in schools: It makes a big difference, but remains rare. *The Harvard Education Letter, 13*(5), 3–5.

Maccoby, E. E., & Zellner, M. (1970). *Experiments in primary education: Aspects of Project Follow-Through.* New York: Harcourt Brace Jovanovich.

Malaguzzi, L. (1993). History, ideas, and basic philosophy. In C. Edwards, L. Gandini, & G. Forman (Eds.), *The hundred languages of children: The Reggio Emilia approach to early childhood education* (pp. 41–89). Norwood, NJ: Ablex.

Mallory, B. L. (1998). Educating young children with developmental differences: Principles of inclusive practices. In C. Seefeldt & A. Galper (Eds.), *Continuing issues in early childhood education* (2nd ed., pp. 213–237). Upper Saddle River, NJ: Merrill/Prentice Hall.

Mallory, B. L., & New, R. S. (1994). *Diversity and developmentally appropriate practice.* New York: Teachers College Press.

Mallory, N. J., & Goldsmith, N. A. (1990). Head Start works! Two Head Start veterans share their views. *Young Children, 45*(6), 36–39.

Maloney, J. (1995). A call for options. *Educational Leadership, 52,* 25.

Mancke, J. B. (1972). Liability of school districts for the negligent acts of their employees. *Journal of Law and Education, 1,* 109–127.

Mangione, P. L., & Maniates, H. (1993). Training teachers to implement developmentally appropriate practice. In S. Reifel (Ed.), *Advances in early education and day care. Vol. 5, Perspectives in developmentally appropriate practice* (pp. 145–166). Greenwich, CT: JAI.

Manning, D., & Schindler, P. J. (1997). Communicating with parents when their children have difficulties. *Young Children, 52*(5), 27–33.

Marcon, R. A. (1992). Differential effects of three preschool models on inner-city 4-year-olds. *Early Childhood Research Quarterly, 7,* 517–530.

Marcon, R. A. (1993). Socioemotional versus academic emphasis: Impact on kindergarteners development and achievement. *Early Child Development and Care, 96,* 81–91.

Marcon, R. A. (1994a). Doing the right thing for children: Linking research and policy reform in the District of Columbia Public Schools. *Young Children, 50*(1), 8–11.

Marcon, R. A. (1994b). *Early learning and early identification follow-up study: Transition from the early to the later childhood grades. 1990–93.* Washington, DC: District of Columbia Public Schools, Center for Systemic Change.

Marion, M. (1999). *Guidance of young children.* Upper Saddle River, NJ: Merrill/Prentice Hall.

Marked kindergarten progress in the Northwest. (1925). *Childhood Education, 1,* 303–305.

Marotz, L. R., Cross, M. Z., & Rush, J. M. (1997). *Health, safety, and nutrition for young children.* Albany, NY: Delmar.

Marshall, H. H. (1995). Beyond "I like the way . . ." *Young Children, 50*(2), 26–28.

Martin, S. (1998). *Take a look: Observation and portfolio assessment in early childhood.* Reading, MA: Addison-Wesley.

Marx, F., & Seligson, M. (1988). *The public school early-childhood study: The state survey.* New York: Bank Street College.

Mathews, M. C., Thornburg, K. R., Espinosa, L., & Ispa, J. (2000). Project REACH: Training rural child care providers. *Young Children, 55*(3), 82–87.

May, D., & Vinovskis, M. (1977). A ray of millennial light: Early education and social reform in the infant school movement in Massachusetts. In T. Harevian (Ed.), *Family and kin in urban communities* (pp. 62–69). New York: New Viewpoints.

McCarthy, J. (1988). *State certification of early childhood teachers: An analysis of the 50 states and the District of Columbia.* Washington, DC: National Association for the Education of Young Children.

McCartney, K., Scarr, S., Phillips, D. A., & Grajek, S. (1985). Day care as intervention: Comparisons of varying quality programs. *Journal of Applied Developmental Psychology, 6,* 247–260.

McCormick, L., & Feeney, S. (1995). Modifying and expanding activities for children with disabilities. *Young Children, 50*(4), 10–17.

McCuskey, D. (1940). *Bronson Alcott, teacher.* New York: Macmillan.

McGinnis, J. R. (2002). Enriching the outdoor environment. *Young Children, 57*(3), 28–30.

McKey, R., Condelli, L., Ganson, H., Barrett, B., McConkey, C., & Plantz, M. (1985). *The impact of Head Start on children, families, and communities* (DHHS Publication No. OHDS 85–31193). Washington, DC: Government Printing Office.

McMillan, M. (1919). *The nursery school.* London: J. M. Dent.

Mead, M. (1970). *Culture and commitment: A study of the generation gap.* Garden City, NY: Natural History Press/Doubleday.

Meek, A. (1998). America's teachers. *Educational Leadership, 55*(5), 12–17.

Meisels, S. J. (1985). The efficacy of early intervention: Why are we still asking these questions? *Topics in Early Childhood Special Education, 5,* 1–12.

Meisels, S. J. (1992). Doing harm by doing good: Iatrogenic effects of early childhood enrollment and promotion policies. *Early Childhood Research Quarterly, 7,* 155–175.

Meisels, S. J. (2000). On the side of the child: Personal reflections on testing, teaching, and early childhood education. *Young Children, 55*(6), 16–19.

Meisels, S. J., & Atkins-Burnett, S. (1994). *Developmental Screening in Early Childhood: A Guide* (4th ed.). Washington, DC: National Association for the Education of Young Children.

Meisels, S. J., & Atkins-Burnett, S. (2000). The elements of early childhood assessment. In J. P. Shonkoff & S. J. Meisels (Eds.), *Handbook of early childhood intervention* (2nd ed., pp. 231–257). New York: Cambridge University Press.

Meisels, S., Dichtelmiller, M., Jablon, J., Dorfman, A., & Marsden, D. (1997). *Work sampling in the classroom: A teacher's manual. The Work Sampling System.* Ann Arbor, MI: Rebus.

Meisels, S. J., Dorfman, A., & Steele, D. (1995). Equity and excellence in group-administered and performance-based assessments. In M. T. Nettles & A. L. Nettles (Eds.), *Equity in educational assessment and testing* (pp. 196–211). Boston: Kluwer Academic Publishers.

Meisels, S. J., Jablon, J. R., Marsden, D. B., Dichtelmiller, M. L., Dorfman, A. B., & Steele, D. M. (1994). *An overview: The Work Sampling System.* Ann Arbor, MI: Rebus.

Meisels, S. J., & Shonkoff, J. P. (2000). Early childhood intervention. In J. P. Shonkoff & S. J. Meisels (Eds.), *Handbook of early childhood intervention* (2nd ed., pp. 3–34). New York: Cambridge University Press.

Meisels, S. J., & Wasik, B. A. (1990). Who should be served? Identifying children in need of early intervention services. In S. J. Meisels & J. P. Shonkoff (Eds.), *Handbook of early childhood intervention* (pp. 605–632). New York: Cambridge University Press.

Melmed, M. (1997). Parents speak: Zero to Three's findings on parents' view of early childhood development. *Young Children, 52*(5), 46–49.

Meltz, B. F. (1990, December 4). A little privacy: Children need a space to call their own. *Tallahassee Democrat,* p. D1.

Mikkelsen, E. J. (1997). Responding to allegations of sexual abuse in child care and early childhood education programs. *Young Children, 52*(3), 47–51.

Miller, B. M., O'Connor, S., & Sirignono, S. W. (1995). Out of school time: A study of children in three low-income neighborhoods. *Child Welfare, 74,* 1249–1280.

Miller, L. B., & Bizzell, L. P. (1983). Long-term effects of four preschool programs: Sixth, seventh, and eighth grades. *Child Development, 54,* 727–741.

Miller, L. B., Bugbee, M. R., & Hyberton, D. W. (1985). Dimensions of preschool: The effects of individual experience. In I. E. Sigel (Ed.), *Advances in applied developmental psychology* (Vol. 1, pp. 25–90). Norwood, NJ: Ablex.

Miller, L. B., & Dyer, J. L. (1975). Four preschool programs: Their dimensions and effects. *Monographs of the Society for Research in Child Development, 40*(5–6, Serial No. 162).

Miller, L. G., & Albrecht, K. M. (2000). *Innovations: The comprehensive infant curriculum.* Beltsville, MD: Gryphon.

Miller, P. J., & Goodnow, J. J. (1995). Cultural practices: Toward an integration of culture and development. *New Directions for Child Development, 67,* 5–16.

Miller, P. S., & Stayton, V. D. (1998). Blended interdisciplinary teacher preparation in early education and intervention: A national study. *Topics in Early Childhood Special Education, 18*(1), 49–58.

Miller, P. S., & Stayton, V. D. (1999). Higher education culture—A fit or misfit with reform in teacher education? *Journal of Teacher Education, 50,* 290–302.

Mills, G. (2000). *Action research: A guide for the teacher researcher.* Upper Saddle River, NJ: Merrill/Prentice Hall.

Minuchin, S. (1984). *Family kaleidoscope.* Cambridge, MA: Harvard University Press.

Missiuna, C., & Samuels, M. (1989). Dynamic assessment: Review and critique. *Special Services in the Schools, 5*(1/2), 1–22.

Mitchell, A. (1988). *The Public School Early Childhood Study: The district survey.* New York: Bank Street College Press.

Mitchell, A. (1996). Licensing: Lessons from other occupations. In S. L. Kagan & N. E. Cohen (Eds.), *Reinventing early care and education: A vision for a quality system* (pp. 101–123). San Francisco: Jossey-Bass.

Mitchell, A. (2000). The case for credentialing directors now and considerations for the future. In M. L. Culkin (Ed.), *Managing quality in young chil-*

dren's programs: The leader's role (pp. 152–169). New York: Teachers College Press.

Mitchell, A., Cooperstein, E., & Larner, M. (1992). *Child care choices, consumer education, and low-income families.* New York: Columbia University, School of Public Health.

Mitchell, A., & David, J. (Eds.). (1992). *Explorations with young children: A curriculum guide for the Bank Street College of Education.* Mt. Rainer, MD: Gryphon.

Mitchell, A., & Morgan, G. G. (2001). *New perspectives on compensation strategies.* Boston: Wheelock College, Institute for Leadership and Career Initiatives.

Mitchell, A., Stoney, L., & Dichter, H. (1997). *Financing child care in the United States: An illustrative catalog of current strategies.* Philadelphia: Ewing Marion Kauffman Foundation and the Pew Charitable Trusts.

Mitchell, A. L. (1993). Shouldn't preschool people advocate for better elementary schools, too? *Young Children, 48*(5), 58–62.

Mitchell, A. W., Seligson, M., & Marx, F. (1989). *Early childhood programs and the public schools: Between promise and practice.* Dover, MA: Auburn House.

Mocan, H. N., Burchinal, M., Morris, J. R., & Helburn, S. W. (1995). Models of quality in early childhood care and education. In S. W. Helburn (Ed.), *Cost, quality, and child outcomes in child care centers: Technical report* (pp. 287–295). Denver: University of Colorado at Denver.

Modigliani, K. (1990). *Assessing the quality of family child care: A comparison of five instruments.* Boston: Wheelock College, Family Child Care Project.

Montessori, M. (1966). *The secret of childhood* (M. J. Costelloe, S. J., Trans.). New York: Ballantine. (Original work published 1936)

Moon, J., & Schulman, L. (1995). *Finding the connections: Linking assessment, instruction, and curriculum in elementary mathematics.* Portsmouth, NH: Heinemann.

Moore, E. K. (1997). Race, class, and education. In S. L. Kagan & B. T. Bowman (Eds.), *Leadership in early care and education* (pp. 69–74). Washington, DC: National Association for the Education of Young Children.

Moore, L., & Brown, D. L. (1996). The mixed-age approach: A public school perspective. *Dimensions of Early Childhood, 24*(2), 4–10.

Moore, R. C. (1993). *Plants for play: A plant selection guide for children's outdoor environments.* Berkeley, CA: MIG Communications.

Morgan, B., & Gibson, R. K. (1991). Nutritional and environmental interactions in brain development. In R. K. Gibson & A. C. Petersen (Eds.), *Brain maturation and cognitive development: Comparative cross-cultural perspectives* (pp. 91–106). New York: Aldine De Gruyter.

Morgan, E. L. (1989). Talking with parents when concerns come up. *Young Children, 44*(2), 52–56.

Morgan, G. G. (1985). Programs for young children in public schools? Only if . . . *Young Children, 40*(4), 54.

Morgan, G. G. (1986). Gaps and excesses in the regulation of child care: Report of a panel. *Review of Infectious Diseases, 8,* 634–643.

Morgan, G. G. (1994). A new century/A new system for professional development. In J. Johnson & J. B. McCracken (Eds.), *The early childhood career lattice: Perspectives on professional development* (pp. 39–46). Washington, DC: National Association for the Education of Young Children.

Morgan, G. G. (1995). *Is professional a noun?* Boston: Wheelock College, Institute for Leadership and Career Initiatives.

Morgan, G. G. (1996). Licensing and accreditation: How much quality is "quality"? In S. Bredekamp & B. A. Wilier (Eds.), *NAEYC accreditation: A decade of learning and the years ahead* (pp. 129–138). Washington, DC: National Association for the Education of Young Children.

Morgan, G. G. (1997). *Taking the lead: Director credentialing information packet.* Boston: Wheelock College, Center for Career Development in Early Care and Education.

Morgan, G. G. (1999). *The bottom line for children's programs: What you need to know to manage the money.* Watertown, MA: Steam Press.

Morgan, G. G. (2000a). The director as a key to quality. In M. L. Culkin (Ed.), *Managing quality in young children's programs: The leader's role* (pp. 40–58). New York: Teachers College Press.

Morgan, G. G. (2000b). A profession for the 21st century. In M. L. Culkin (Ed.), *Managing quality in young children's programs: The leader's role* (pp. 133–151). New York: Teachers College Press.

Morgan, G. G., Azer, S. L., Costley, J. B., Genser, A., Goodman, I. F., Lombardi, J., & McGimsey, B. (1993). *Making a career of it: The state of states report on career development in early care and education.* Boston: Wheelock College, Center for Career Development in Early Care and Education.

Morgan, G. G., Curry, N., Endsley, R. C., Bradford, M. R., & Rashid, H. M. (1985). *Quality in early childhood programs: Four perspectives* (High/Scope Early Childhood Policy Papers, No. 3). Ypsilanti, MI: High/Scope Educational Research Foundation. (ERIC Document Reproduction Service No. ED264944)

Morrison, A. M. (1992). *The new leaders: Guidelines on leadership diversity in America.* San Francisco: Jossey-Bass.

Morrow, L. M., Strickland, D. S., & Woo, D. G. (1998). *Literacy instruction in half- and whole-day kindergarten.* Newark, DE: International Reading Association.

Mosteller, F. (1995). The Tennessee study of class size in the early school grades. *Future of Children, 5,* 113–127.

Muenchow, S. (1997). Commentary. In S. L. Kagan & B. T. Bowman (Eds.), *Leadership in early care and education* (pp. 46–47). Washington, DC: National Association for the Education of Young Children.

Murphy, D. M. (1997). Parent and teacher plan for the child. *Young Children, 52*(4), 32–36.

Murray, C. G. (2000). Learning about children's social and emotional needs at snack time—Nourishing the body, mind, and spirit of each child. *Young Children, 55*(2), 43–52.

NAEYC Business. (1988). Antidiscrimination policy. *Young Children, 44*(1), 38.

NAEYC Policy Brief. (2001). Financing the early childhood education system. *Young Children, 56*(4), 54–57.

Nahikian-Nelms, M. L., Syler, G., & Mogharrehan, C. N. (1994). Pilot assessment of nutrition practices in a university child care program. *Journal of Nutrition Education, 26*(5), 238–240.

Nanus, B. (1992). *Visionary leadership.* San Francisco: Jossey-Bass.

Nash, R. J. (1996). *"Real world" ethics: Frameworks for educators and human services professionals.* New York: Teachers College Press.

Nastasi, B. K., & Clements, D. H. (1994). Effectance motivation, perceived scholastic competence, and higher-order thinking in two cooperative computer environments. *Journal of Educational Computing Research, 10,* 241–267.

National Association of Early Childhood Specialists in State Departments of Education. (1987). *Unacceptable trends in kindergarten entry and placement: A position statement of the NAECS/SDE.* Lincoln, NE: Author.

National Association for the Education of Young Children. (1984). NAEYC position statement on nomenclature, salaries, benefits, and the status of the early childhood profession. *Young Children, 40*(1), 52–55.

National Association for the Education of Young Children. (1987). NAEYC position statement on quality, compensation, and affordability in early childhood programs. *Young Children, 43*(1), 31.

National Association for the Education of Young Children. (1988). Early childhood teacher education. Traditions and trends: An executive summary of colloquium proceedings. *Young Children, 44*(1), 53–57.

National Association for the Education of Young Children. (1990). NAEYC position statement on school readiness. *Young Children, 46*(1), 21–23.

National Association for the Education of Young Children. (1991). *Early childhood teacher education guidelines.* Washington, DC: Author.

National Association for the Education of Young Children. (1993). Washington update. The United Nations Convention on the Rights of the Young Child. *Young Children, 48*(6), 65.

National Association for the Education of Young Children. (1994a). NAEYC position statement: A conceptual framework for early childhood professional development. *Young Children, 49*(3), 68–77.

National Association for the Education of Young Children. (1994b). *Principles to link by: Integrated service systems that are community-based and school-linked.* Washington, DC: Author.

National Association for the Education of Young Children. (1995a). NAEYC position statement on quality, compensation, and affordability. *Young Children, 51*(1), 39–41.

National Association for the Education of Young Children. (1995b). *National Association for the Education of Young Children position statement: Responding to linguistic and cultural diversity: Recommendations for effective early childhood education.* Washington, DC: Author.

National Association for the Education of Young Children. (1996a). *Guidelines for preparation of early childhood professionals.* Washington, DC: Author.

National Association for the Education of Young Children. (1996b). NAEYC position statement: Technology and young children—ages three through eight. *Young Children, 51*(6), 11–16.

National Association for the Education of Young Children. (1996c). *What are the benefits of high-quality early childhood programs?* (Brochure). Washington, DC: Author.

National Association for the Education of Young Children. (1997a). NAEYC position statement. Developmentally appropriate practice in early childhood programs serving children from birth through age 8. In S. Bredekamp & C. Copple (Eds.), *Developmentally appropriate practice in early childhood programs* (Rev. ed., pp. 3–30). Washington, DC: Author.

National Association for the Education of Young Children. (1997b). NAEYC position statement on the prevention of child abuse in early childhood programs and the responsibilities of early childhood professionals to prevent child abuse. *Young Children, 52*(3), 42–46.

National Association for the Education of Young Children. (1998a). *Accreditation criteria and procedures of the National Association for the Education of Young Children.* Washington, DC: Author.

National Association for the Education of Young Children. (1998b). NAEYC position statement on licensing and public regulation of early childhood programs. *Young Children, 53*(1), 43–50.

National Association for the Education of Young Children. (2001). *NAEYC guidelines revision. NAEYC standards for early childhood professional preparation.* Washington, DC: Author.

National Association for the Education of Young Children & the National Association of Early Childhood Specialists in State Departments of Education. (1991). Guidelines for appropriate curriculum content and assessment in programs serving children ages 3 through 8: A position statement. *Young Children, 46*(3), 21–38.

National Association for the Education of Young Children & National Association of Early Childhood Specialists in State Departments of Education. (2002). *A joint position statement. Early learning standards: Creating the conditions for success.* Washington, DC & Alexandria, VA: Authors. (Available online: <www.naeyc.org/resources/position_statements/creating/conditions.asp>)

National Association of Elementary School Principals. (1990). *Standards for quality programs for young children.* Alexandria, VA: Author.

National Association of Elementary School Principals. (1996). *Principal profile.* Alexandria, VA: Author.

National Association for Sick Child Daycare. (2000). *About NASCD.* Retrieved May 13, 2002, from <http://www.nascd.com/contact.htm>

National Association of State Boards of Education. (1988). *Right from the start: A report of the NASBE Task Force on Early Childhood Education.* Alexandria, VA: Author.

National Black Child Development Institute. (1987). *Safeguards: Guidelines for establishing programs for 4-year-olds in the public schools.* Washington, DC: Author.

National Black Child Development Institute. (1993). *Paths to African American leadership positions in early childhood education: Constraints and opportunities.* Washington, DC: Author.

National Center on Child Abuse and Neglect. (1997). *Child maltreatment 1995: Reports from the states to the National Center on Child Abuse and Neglect.* Washington, DC: U.S. Department of Health and Human Services.

National Center for Education Statistics. (1996). *Early childhood education program participation for infants, toddlers, and preschoolers.* Washington, DC: U.S. Department of Education.

National Center for Education Statistics. (1997). *The condition of education 1997.* Washington, DC: U.S. Department of Education.

National Center for Education Statistics. (1999). *Digest of education statistics, 1998.* Washington, DC: U.S. Department of Education.

National Center for Education Statistics. (2000). *America's kindergartners: Findings from the Early Childhood Longitudinal Study, Kindergarten Class of 1998–99, Fall 1998.* Washington, DC: U.S. Department of Education. (Available online: <http://nces.ed.gov/pubs2001/2001023.pdf>)

National Center for Education Statistics. (2001). *Digest of Educational Statistics. Table 68. Teachers in public and private elementary schools, by selected characteristics: 1993–1994.* Washington, DC: U.S. Department of Education.

National Commission on Excellence in Education. (1983). *A nation at risk: The imperative for educational reform.* Washington, DC: Author.

National Commission on Excellence in Education. (1984). *Nation at risk: The full account.* Washington, DC: Author.

National Council of Teachers of Mathematics. (1991). *Professional standards for teaching mathematics.* Reston, VA: Author.

National Council of Teachers of Mathematics. (2000). *Principles and standards for school mathematics.* Reston, VA: Author. (Available online: <http://standards.nctm.org/document/index.htm>)

National Council of Teachers of Mathematics & National Association for the Education of Young Children. (2002). *Early childhood mathematics: Promoting good beginnings.* Washington, DC: National Association for the Education of Young Children. (Available online: <www.naeyc.org/resources/position_statements/psmath.htm>)

National PTA. (2000). *Building successful partnerships: A guide for developing parent and family involvement programs.* Indianapolis: National Educational Service.

National Research Council. (1997). *Educating one and all: Students with disabilities and standards-based reform.* Washington, DC: National Academy Press.

National Research Council. (1999a). *High stakes testing for tracking, promotion, and graduation.* Washington, DC: National Academy Press.

National Research Council. (1999b). *How people learn: Brain, mind, experience, and school.* Washington, DC: National Academy Press.

National Research Council. (1999c). *Starting out right: A guide to promoting children's reading success.* Washington, DC: National Academy Press.

National Research Council. (2001). *Eager to learn: Educating our preschoolers.* Washington, DC: National Academy Press.

National Research Council and Institute of Medicine. (1998). *From generation to generation: The health and well-being of children in immigrant families.* Washington, DC: National Academy Press.

National Research Council and Institute of Medicine. (2000). *Early childhood intervention: Views from the field. Report of a workshop.* Washington, DC: National Academy Press.

National Society for the Study of Education. (1929). *Twenty-eighth yearbook of the National Society for the Study of Education: Preschool and parental education.* Bloomington, IL: Public School Publishing.

National Task Force on School Readiness. (1991). *Caring communities: Supporting young children and families.* Alexandria, VA: National Association of State Boards of Education.

Needle, R. H. (1980). Teacher stress: Sources and consequences. *Journal of School Health, 50,* 96–99.

Neill, S. R. St. J., & Denham, E. J. M. (1982). The effects of preschool building design. *Educational Research, 24*(2), 107–111.

Neilsen, L. E., & Finkelstein, J. M. (1993). A new approach to parent conferences. *Teaching K-8, 24*(1), 90–92.

Nelson, M. K. (1990). *Negotiated care: The experience of family day care providers.* Philadelphia: Temple University Press.

Neugebauer, R. (1993a). Employer interest in child care growing and diversifying. *Child Care Information Exchange, 94,* 66–72.

Neugebauer, R. (1993b). State-of-the-art thinking on parent fee policies. *Child Care Information Exchange, 94,* 4–12.

Neugebauer, R. (1993c). Status report #1 on school-age child care. *Child Care Information Exchange, 89,* 11–15.

Neugebauer, R. (1993d). Status report on children's programs on campus. *Child Care Information Exchange, 90,* 70.

Neugebauer, R. (2000). What is management ability? In M. L. Culkin (Ed.), *Managing quality in young children's programs: The leader's role* (pp. 97–111). New York: Teachers College Press.

Neuman, S. B., Copple, C., & Bredekamp, S. (2000). *Learning to read and write: Developmentally appropriate practices for young children.* Washington, DC: National Association for the Education of Young Children.

Neuman, S. B., Hagedorn, T., Celano, D., & Daly, P. (1995). Toward a collaborative approach to parent involvement in early education: A study of teenage mothers in an African-American community. *American Educational Research Journal, 32,* 801–824.

Newberger, J. J. (1997). New brain development research—A wonderful window of opportunity to build public support for early childhood education. *Young Children, 52*(4), 4–9.

Newman, M., Rutter, R. A., & Smith, M. S. (1989). Organizational factors that affect school sense of efficacy, community, and expectations. *Sociology of Education, 62,* 221–238.

Newman, S. B., Vander Ven, K., & Ward, C. R. (1992). *Guidelines for the productive employment of older adults in child care.* Pittsburgh, PA: Generations Together.

NICHD Early Child Care Research Network. (1996). Characteristics of infant care: Factors contributing to positive caregiving. *Early Childhood Research Quarterly, 11,* 269–306.

NICHD Early Child Care Research Network. (1997a). Child care in the first year of life. *Merrill-Palmer Quarterly, 43,* 340–360.

NICHD Early Child Care Research Network. (1997b). Poverty and patterns of child care. In J. Brooks-Gunn & G. J. Duncan (Eds.), *Consequences of growing up poor* (pp. 100–131). New York: Sage.

NICHD Early Child Care Research Network. (1998a). Early child care and self-control, compliance, and problem behavior at twenty-four and thirty-six months. *Child Development, 69,* 1145–1170.

NICHD Early Child Care Research Network. (1998b). Relations between family predictors and child outcomes: Are they weaker for children in child care? *Developmental Psychology, 34,* 1119–1128.

NICHD Early Child Care Research Network. (1999). Child care and mother-child interaction in the first three years of life. *Developmental Psychology, 35,* 1399–1413.

NICHD Early Child Care Research Network. (2000). The relation of child care to cognitive and language development. *Child Development, 71,* 958–978.

Nicholson, S., & Shipstead, S. G. (2002). *Through the looking glass: Observations in the early childhood classroom* (3rd ed.). Upper Saddle River, NJ: Merrill/Prentice Hall.

Nilsen, B. A. (2000). *Week by week: Plans for observing and recording young children.* Albany, NY: Delmar.

Nimnicht, G. P., & Brown, E. (1972). The toy library: Parents and teachers learning with toys. *Young Children, 28,* 110–117.

Noddings, N. (1992). *The challenge to care in schools: An alternative approach to education.* New York: Teachers College Press.

Nokes, C., van den Bosch, C., & Bundy, D. (1998). *The effects of iron deficiency and anemia on mental health and motor performance, educational achievement, and behavior in children.* Washington, DC: International Nutritional Anemia Consulting Group.

Novick, R. (1998). The comfort corner: Fostering resiliency and emotional intelligence. *Childhood Education, 74,* 200–204.

Nunez, R. (1996). *The new poverty: Homeless families in America.* New York: Insight Books/Plenum Publishing.

Nuttall, E. V., Romero, I., & Kalesnik, J. (Eds.). (1999). *Assessing and screening preschoolers: Psychological and educational dimensions* (2nd ed.). Boston: Allyn & Bacon.

Oakes, P. B., & Caruso, D. A. (1990). Kindergarten teachers' use of developmentally appropriate practices and attitudes about authority. *Early Education and Development, 1,* 445–457.

Oberti v. Board of Education of the Borough of Clementon School District, 995 F. 2d 1204 (3d Cir. 1993).

O'Brien, L. M. (1993). Teacher values and classroom culture: Teaching and learning in a rural Appalachian Head Start program. *Early Education and Development, 4,* 5–19.

Odland, J. (1995). Children's rights and the future. *Childhood Education, 71,* 224–B.

Odom, S. L., & Diamond, K. E. (1998). Inclusion of young children with special needs in early childhood education: The research base. *Early Childhood Research Quarterly, 13,* 3–25.

Odom, S. L., & McEvoy, M. A. (1988). Integration of young children with handicaps and normally developing children. In S. L. Odom & M. B. Karnes (Eds.), *Early intervention for infants and children with handicaps: An empirical base* (pp. 241–267). Baltimore: Brookes.

Odom, S. L., Wolery, R. A., Lieber, J., & Horn, E. (2002). In S. L. Odom (Ed.), *Widening the circle: Including children with disabilities in preschool programs* (pp. 120–136). New York: Teachers College Press.

Odoy, H. A. D., & Foster, S. H. (1997). Creating play crates for the outdoor classroom. *Young Children, 52*(6), 12–16.

Oettinger, K. B. (1964). *It's your Children's Bureau* (Rev. ed.). (Children's Bureau Publication #357). Washington, DC: Children's Bureau.

Ogden, C. (1998). *Third national health and nutrition examination survey.* Atlanta: Centers for Disease Control.

O'Hanlon, W. H., & Weiner-Davis, M. (1989). *In search of solutions.* New York: Norton.

Olds, A. R. (1998). Places of beauty. In D. Bergen (Ed.), *Reading from play as a medium for learning and development* (pp. 123–127). Olney, MD: Association for Childhood Education International.

Olds, A. R. (1999). *The child care design guide: Day care centers that honor the spirit of place.* New York: McGraw-Hill.

Olds, A. R. (2001). *Child care design guide.* New York: McGraw-Hill.

Olds, D. L., Henderson, C. R., Jr., Kitzman, H., Eckenrode, J. J., Cole, R. E., & Tatelbaum, R. C. (1999). Prenatal and infancy home visitation by nurses: Recent findings. *Future of Children, 5*(3), 51–75.

Olds, D. L., & Kitzman, H. (1993). Review of research on home visiting for pregnant women and parents of young children. *Future of Children, 3*(3), 53–92.

Olenick, M. (1986). *The relationship between day-care quality and selected social policy variables.* Unpublished doctoral dissertation, University of California, Los Angeles.

Olmstead, P. P., & Lockhart, S. (1995). Do parents and teachers agree? What should young children be learning? *High/Scope Resource, 14*(1), 7–9.

Olsen, G. (1993). The exit interview: A tool for program improvement. *Child Care Information Exchange, 92,* 71–75.

Olson, L. (2002). Starting early. Quality counts 2002: Building blocks for success. *Education Week, 21*(17), 10–12, 14, 16, 18–22.

Osin, L., & Lesgold, A. (1996, Winter). A proposal for the re-engineering of the educational system. In F. B. Murray, & J. Raths (Eds.), *Review of education research* (pp. 621–656). Washington, DC: American Educational Research Association.

Osmon, F. (1971). *Patterns for designing children's centers.* New York: Educational Facilities Laboratories.

Packard Foundation. (1995). *The future of children. Long-term outcomes of early childhood programs.* Los Altos, CA: Center for the Future of Children, Author.

Packard Foundation. (1996). *Financing child care: The future of children.* Los Altos, CA: Author.

Paley, V. G. (1981). *Wally's stories.* Cambridge, MA: Harvard University Press.

Pallas, A. M., Natriello, G., & McDill, E. L. (1989). The changing nature of the disadvantaged population: Current dimensions and future trends. *Educational Researcher, 18,* 16–22.

Palloway, E. A., & Patton, J. R. (1997). *Strategies for teaching learners with special needs* (6th ed.). Upper Saddle River, NJ: Merrill/Prentice Hall.

Palmer, L. A. (1916). *Play life in the first eight years.* New York: Guinn.

Papert, S. (1993). *The children's machine: Rethinking school in the age of the computer.* New York: Basic.

Parker, S., & Temple, A. (1925). *Unified kindergarten and first-grade teaching.* New York: Guinn.

PDK and the recruitment of men and minorities: Report available. (1998-99). *News, Notes, and Quotes, 43*(2), 10.

Peabody, E. (1835). *Record of a school: Exemplifying the general principles of spiritual culture.* Boston: James Munroe.

Peck, C. A., Furman, G. C., & Helmstetter, E. (1993). Parent and teacher perceptions of outcomes for nonhandicapped children enrolled in integrated early childhood programs: A statewide study. *Journal of Early Intervention, 16,* 15–63.

Pederson, J. (1985). The adventure playground of Denmark. In J. L. Frost & S. Sunderlin (Eds.), *When children play* (pp. 201–208). Olney, MD: Association for Childhood Education International.

Peel, J., & McCary, C. E. (1997). Visioning the "little red schoolhouse" for the 21st century. *Phi Delta Kappan, 78,* 698–705.

Peet, S. H., Powell, D. R., & O'Donnel, B. K. (1997) Mother-teacher congruence in perceptions of the child's competence and school engagement: Links to academic achievement. *Journal of Applied Developmental Psychology, 18,* 373–393.

Peisner-Feinberg, E. S., & Burchinal, M. R. (1997). Relations between preschool children's child-care experiences and concurrent development: The Cost, Quality, and Outcomes Study. *Merrill-Palmer Quarterly, 43*(3), 451–477.

Pellegrini, A. D., & Smith, P. K. (1998). Physical activity play: The nature and functions of a neglected aspect of play. *Child Development, 69,* 577–598.

Pena, D. (2000). Parent involvement: Influencing factors and implications. *Journal of Educational Research, 94,* 42–54.

Pence, A. R. (1986). Infant schools in North America, 1825–1840. In S. Kilmer (Ed.), *Advances in early education and day care* (Vol. 4, pp. 1–25). Greenwich, CT: JAI.

Perreault, J. (1991). Society as extended family: Giving a childhood to every child. *Dimensions, 19*(4), 3–8, 31.

Perry, P. (2001). Sick kids. *American Way, 4,* 64–65.

Peth-Pierce, R. (2001). *A good beginning: Sending America's children to school with the social and emotional competence they need to succeed.* Monograph based on two papers commissioned by the Child Mental Health Foundations and Agencies Network (FAN). Chapel Hill: University of North Carolina.

Pettit, G. S., Laird, R. D., Bates, J. E., & Dodge, K. A. (1997). Patterns of after-school care in middle childhood: Risk factors and developmental outcomes. *Merrill-Palmer Quarterly, 43,* 515–538.

Phillips, C. B. (1994a). The challenge of training and credentialing early childhood educators. *Phi Delta Kappan, 76,* 214–217.

Phillips, C. B. (1994b). The movement of African-American children through sociocultural contexts: A case of conflict resolution. In B. L. Mallory & R. S. New (Eds.), *Diversity and developmentally appropriate practices: Challenges for early childhood education* (pp. 137–154). New York: Teachers College Press.

Phillips, D. A. (Ed.). (1987). *Quality child care: What does research tell us?* Washington, DC: National Association for the Education of Young Children.

Phillips, D. A. (1991). Daycare for young children in the United States. In E. C. Melhuish & P. Moss (Eds.), *Daycare for young children: International perspectives* (pp. 161–184). London: Tavistock/Routledge.

Phillips, D. A., & Crowell, N. A. (Eds.). (1994). *Cultural diversity in early education: Results of a workshop.* Washington, DC: National Academy Press.

Phillips, D. A., Howes, C., & Whitebook, M. (1992). The social policy context of child care: Effects on quality. *American Journal of Community Psychology, 20*(1), 25–51.

Phillips, D. A., Lande, J., & Goldberg, M. (1990). A state of child care regulation: A comparative analysis. *Early Childhood Research Quarterly, 5,* 151–179.

Phillips, D. A., McCartney, K., & Scarr, S. (1987). Child care quality and children's social development. *Developmental Psychology, 23,* 537–543.

Phillipsen, L., Burchinal, M., Howes, C., & Cryer, D. (1997). The predictor of process quality from structural features of child care. *Early Childhood Research Quarterly, 12,* 281–303.

Piaget, J. (1952). *The origins of intelligence in children.* New York: Norton.

Piaget, J. (1959). *Language and thought of the child* (3rd ed.). London: Routledge & Kegan Paul.

Pines, A., & Maslach, C. (1980). Combating staff burnout in a day care center: A case study. *Child Care Quarterly, 9,* 6–9.

Pipes, P. L., & Glass, R. P. (1989). Nutrition and feeding of children with developmental delay and related problems. In P. L. Pipes (Ed.), *Nutrition in infancy and childhood* (4th ed., pp. 361–386). St. Louis, MO: Mosby.

Piscitelli, B. (2000). Practicing what we preach: Active learning in the development of early childhood professionals. In N. J. Yelland (Ed.), *Promoting meaningful learning: Innovations in educating early childhood professionals* (pp. 37–46). Washington, DC: National Association for the Education of Young Children.

Plomin, R. (1997). *Behavioral genetics.* New York: Freeman.

Poest, C. A., Williams, J. R., Witt, D. D., & Atwood, M. E. (1990). Challenge me to move: Large muscle development in young children. *Young Children, 45*(5), 4–10.

Pogrow, S. (1996, September 25). On scripting the classroom. *Education Week,* pp. 20, 52.

Pond-Smith, D., Richarz, S. H., & Gonzalez, N. (1992). A survey of food service operations in child care centers in Washington State. *Journal of the American Dietetic Association, 92,* 483–484.

Pope, S., & Stremmel, A. (1992). Organizational climate and job satisfaction among child care teachers. *Child and Youth Care Forum, 21*(1), 39–52.

Poster, M., & Neugebauer, R. (1998). How experienced directors have developed their skills. *Child Care Information Exchange, 121,* 90–93.

Powell, D. R. (1987a). Comparing preschool curricula and practices: The state of research. In S. L. Kagan & E. F. Zigler (Eds.), *Early schooling: The national debate* (pp. 190–211). New Haven, CT: Yale University Press.

Powell, D. R. (1987b). Day care as a family support system. In S. L. Kagan, D. R. Powell, B. Weissbourd, & E. F. Zigler (Eds.), *America's family support programs: Perspectives and prospects* (pp. 115–132). New Haven, CT: Yale University Press.

Powell, D. R. (1987c). Methodological and conceptual issues in research. In S. L. Kagan, D. R. Powell, B. Weissbourd, & E. F. Zigler (Eds.), *America's family support system* (pp. 311–328). New Haven, CT: Yale University Press.

Powell, D. R. (1989). *Families and early childhood programs*. Washington, DC: National Association for the Education of Young Children.

Powell, D. R. (1990). Home visiting in the early years: Policy and program design decisions. *Young Children, 45*(6), 65–73.

Powell, D. R. (1991). How schools support families: Critical policy tensions. *Elementary School Journal, 91,* 307–319.

Powell, D. R. (1994). Parents, pluralism, and the NAEYC statement on developmentally appropriate practice. In B. C. Mallory & R. S. New (Eds.), *Diversity and developmentally appropriate practices* (pp. 166–182). New York: Teachers College Press.

Powell, D. R. (1998). Research in Review: Reweaving parents into the fabric of early childhood programs. *Young Children, 53*(5), 60–67.

Powell, D. R., & Diamond, K. E. (1995). Approaches to parent-teacher relationships in U.S. early childhood programs during the twentieth century. *Journal of Education, 177,* 71–94.

Powell, D. R., & Sigel, I. E. (1991). Searches for validity in evaluating young children and early childhood programs. In B. Spodek & O. N. Saracho (Eds.), *Yearbook in early childhood education: Vol. 2. Issues in early childhood curriculum* (pp. 190–212). New York: Teachers College Press.

Powell, I., Eisenberg, D. R., Moy, L., & Vogel, J. (1994). Costs and characteristics of high-quality early childhood education programs. *Child and Youth Care Forum, 23,* 103–118.

Pratt, C. (1948). *I learn from children.* New York: Simon & Schuster.

Prescott, E. (1984). The physical setting of day-care. In J. T. Greenman & R. W. Fuqua (Eds.), *Making day care better* (pp. 44–65). New York: Teachers College Press.

Prescott, E. (1987). The environment as organizer of intent in child-care. In C. S. Weinstein & T. G. David (Eds.), *Spaces for children: The built environment and child development* (pp. 73–86). New York: Plenum.

Prescott, E., Jones, E., & Kritchevsky, S. (1972). *Day care as a child-rearing environment* (Vol. 2). Washington, DC: National Association for the Education of Young Children.

Presser, H. B., & Cox, A. G. (1997). The work schedules of low-educated American women and welfare reform. *Monthly Labor Review, 120,* 25–34.

Quality, compensation, and affordability. The updated staffing study: A valuable resource for advocates. (1998). *Young Children, 53*(5), 42–43.

Queralt, M., & Witte, A. D. (1998). Influences on neighborhood supply of child care in Massachusetts. *Social Service Review, 17,* 17–47.

Raab, M., & Dunst, D. J. (1997). Early childhood program assessment scales and family support practices. In S. Reifel (Series Ed.) & C. J. Dunst & M. Wolery (Vol. Eds.), *Advances in early education and day care: Vol 8. Family policy and practice in early education and child care programs* (pp. 105–131). Greenwich, CT: JAI.

Rabitti, G. (1994). An integrated art approach in preschool. In L. G. Katz & B. Cesarone (Eds.), *Reflections on the Reggio Emilia approach* (pp. 51–67). Urbana, IL: ERIC Clearinghouse on Elementary and Early Childhood Education.

Raikes, H. (1996). A secure base for babies: Applying attachment concepts to the infant care setting. *Young Children, 51*(5), 59–67.

Rambusch, N. M. (1962). *Learning how to learn: An American approach to Montessori.* Baltimore: Helicon.

Ramey, C. T., Bryant, D. M., & Suarez, T. M. (1985). Preschool compensatory education and the modifiability of intelligence: A critical review. In D. Ditterman (Ed.), *Current topics in human intelligence* (pp. 247–296). Norwood, NJ: Ablex.

Ramey, C. T., & Ramey, S. L. (1998). Early intervention and early experience. *American Psychologist, 58,* 109–120.

Ramey, C. T., Ramey, S. L., Gaines, K. R., & Blair, C. (1995). Two-generation early intervention programs: A child development perspective. In S. Smith (Ed.), *Two-generation programs for families in poverty: A new intervention strategy. Advances in Applied Developmental Psychology* (Vol. 9, pp. 199–228). Norwood, NJ: Ablex.

Rand, M. K. (2000). *Giving it some thought: Cases for early childhood practice.* Washington, DC: National Association for the Education of Young Children.

Raver, C. (2002). Emotions matter: Making the case for the role of young children's emotional development for early school readiness. *SRCD Social Policy Report, 16*(3). Ann Arbor, MI: Society for Research in Child Development.

Read, K. H. (1976). *The nursery school: Human relationships and learning* (6th ed.). Philadelphia: Saunders.

Reisner, E. H. (1930). *The evolution of the common school.* New York: Macmillan.

Rescorla, L. (1991). Parent and teacher attitudes about early academics. In L. Rescorla, M. C. Hyson, & S. K. Hirsch-Pasek (Eds.), *Academic instruction in early childhood: Challenge or pressure?* (pp. 13–19). San Francisco: Jossey-Bass.

Reynolds, A. J. (1994). Effects of preschool plus follow-on intervention for children at risk. *Developmental Psychology, 30*, 787–804.

Rhodes, L., & Nathenson-Mejia, S. (1992). Anecdotal records: A powerful tool for organizing literacy assessment. *Reading Teacher, 45*, 502–509.

Ripple, R. E., & Rockcastle, V. E. (Eds.). (1964). *Piaget rediscovered: A report of the Conference on Cognitive Studies and Curriculum Development.* Ithaca, NY: Cornell University, School of Education.

Rivkin, M. S. (1995). *The great outdoors: Restoring children's right to play outside.* Washington, DC: National Association for the Education of Young Children.

Robinson, A., & Stark, D. R. (2002). *Advocates in action: Making a difference for young children.* Washington, DC: National Association for the Education of Young Children.

Robinson, S. L. (1993/94). Out of the mouths of experts. *Childhood Education, 70*, 84–86.

Robinson, S. L. (1997). The grading ritual: Unreliable and unsuitable—But unalterable? *Young Children, 52*(5), 86–87.

Robinson, S. L., & Lyon, C. (1994). Early childhood offerings in 1992: Will we be ready for 2000? *Phi Delta Kappan, 75*, 775–778.

Robles de Melendez, W., & Ostertag, V. (1997). *Teaching young children in multicultural classrooms.* Albany, NY: Delmar.

Rodd, J. (1998). *Leadership in early childhood: The pathway to professionalism* (2nd ed.). New York: Teachers College Press.

Rofrano, F. (2002). "I care for you": A reflection on caring as infant curriculum. *Young Children, 57*(1), 49–51.

Rogoff, B. (1990). *Apprenticeship in thinking: Cognitive development in social context.* New York: Oxford University Press.

Rogoff, B., & Chavajay, P. (1995). What's become of research on the cutural basis of cognitive development? *American Psychologist, 50*, 859–877.

Rohacek, M. H., & Russell, S. D. (1998). Public policy report. Child care subsidy yields returns. *Young Children, 53*(2), 68–71.

Rose, D. F., & Smith, B. J. (1993). Preschool mainstreaming: Attitude barriers and strategies for addressing them. *Young Children, 48*(4), 59–62.

Rosegrant, T., & Bredekamp, S. (1992). Planning and implementing transformational curriculum. In S. Bredekamp & T. Rosegrant (Eds.), *Reaching potentials: Appropriate curriculum and assessment for young children* (Vol. 1, pp. 66–73). Washington, DC: National Association for the Education of Young Children.

Rosenholtz, S. J., Bassler, D., & Hoover-Dempsey, K. (1986). Organizational conditions of teacher learning. *Teaching and Teacher Education, 2*(2), 91–104.

Roskos, K. A., & Neuman, S. B. (1994). Of scribbles, schemas, and storybooks: Using literacy albums to document young children's literacy growth. *Young Children, 49*(2), 78–85.

Runyan, C., Gray, D., Kotch, J., & Kreuter, M. (1991). Analysis of U.S. child care safety regulations. *American Journal of Public Health, 81*, 981–985.

Rusakoff, D. (2000, July 6). A cost squeeze in child care: Families wonder where the aid is. *The Washington Post*, pp. A1, A8.

Rusher, A. S., McGrevin, C. Z., & Lambiotte, J. G. (1992). Belief systems of early childhood teachers and their principals regarding early childhood education. *Early Childhood Research Quarterly, 7*, 277–296.

Rushton, S., & Larkin, L. (2001). Shaping the learning environment: Connecting brain research to developmentally appropriate practices. *Early Childhood Education Journal, 29*(1), 25–33.

Russell-Fox, J. (1997). Together is better: Specific tips on how to include children with various types of disabilities. *Young Children, 52*(4) 81–83.

Rutter, M. (2000). Resilience reconsidered: Conceptual considerations, empirical findings, and policy implications. In J. P. Shonkoff & S. J. Meisels (Eds.), *Handbook of early childhood intervention* (2nd ed., pp. 651–682). New York: Cambridge University Press.

Ryan, M. P. (1975). *Womanhood in America: From Colonial times to the present.* New York: New Viewpoints.

Sallis, J., McKenzie, T., Kolody, B., Lewis, M., Marshall, S., & Rosengard, P. (1999). Effects of health-related physical education on academic achievement: Project Spark. *Research Quarterly in Exercise and Sport, 70*(2), 127–134.

Salovey, P., & Sluyter, D. (Eds.). (1997). *Emotional development and emotional intelligence: Educational implications.* New York: Basic.

Sameroff, A. J., & Fiese, B. H. (2000). Transactional regulation: The development ecology of early intervention. In J. P. Shonkoff & S. J. Meisels (Eds.), *Handbook of early childhood intervention* (2nd ed., pp. 135–159). New York: Cambridge University Press.

Sandall, S., McLean, M. E., & Smith, B. J. (2000). *DEC recommended practices in early intervention/early childhood special education.* Longmont, CO: Sopris West.

Sandham, J. L. (2002). Adequate financing. Quality counts 2002: Building blocks for success. *Education Week, 21*(17), 43–46.

Santrock, J. (2003). *Children* (7th ed.). Boston: McGraw-Hill.

Sapon-Shevin, M. (1996). Full inclusion as disclosing tablet: Revealing the flaws in our present system. *Theory Into Practice, 35,* 35–41.

Saracho, O. N., & Spodek, B. (1983). *Understanding the multicultural experience in childhood education.* Washington, DC: National Association for the Education of Young Children.

Sargent, P. (2001). *Real men or real teachers? Contradictions in the lives of men elementary school teachers.* Harriman, TN: Men's Studies Press.

Sargent, P. (2002). Under the glass: Conversations with men in early childhood education. *Young Children, 57*(6), 22–30.

Schapiro, D., & Hellen, B. (1998). *Montessori community resource.* Minneapolis, MN: Jola.

Schein, E. H. (1993). How can organizations learn faster? The challenge of entering the green room. *Sloan Management Review, 34*(2), 85–92.

Schiller, P., & Dyke, P. C. (2001). *The pratical guide to quality child care.* Beltsville, MD: Gryphon.

Schneider, A. M. (1991). *Mentoring women and minorities into positions of educational leadership: Gender differ-*

ences and implications for mentoring. Houston, TX: Paper presented at the Annual Conference of the National Council of States on Inservice Education, Nov. 21–26, 1991. (ERIC Document Reproduction Service No. ED344843)

Schön, D. (1983). *The reflective practitioner.* New York: Basic Books.

Schorr, L. B. (1994). The case for shifting to results-based accountability. In N. Young, S. Gardner, L. Coley, L. Schorr, & C. Bruner (Eds.), *Making a difference: Moving to outcome-based accountability for comprehensive service reforms* (pp. 13–28). Falls Church, VA: National Center for Service Integration.

Schorr, L. B. (1997). *Common purpose: Strengthening families and neighborhoods to rebuild America.* New York: Doubleday.

Schreiber, M. E. (1996). Lighting alternatives: Considerations for child care centers. *Young Children, 51*(4), 11–13.

Schulman, K., & Adams, G. (1998). *The high cost of child care puts quality care out of reach for many families.* Washington, DC: Children's Defense Fund.

Schulman, K., & Blank, H. (2002). State child care assistance policies. *Young Children, 57*(1), 66–69.

Schulman, K., Blank, H., & Ewen, D. (2001). *A fragile foundation: State child care assistance policies.* Washington, DC: Children's Defense Fund.

Schulz, J. (1987). *Parents and professionals in special education.* Boston: Houghton Mifflin.

Schweinhart, L. J., Barnes, H. V., & Weikart, D. P. (1993). The High/Scope Perry preschool study through age 27. *Monographs of the High/Scope Educational Research Foundation.* Ypsilanti, MI: High/Scope Press.

Schweinhart, L. J., Barnes, H. V., & Weikart, D. P. (with Barnett, W. S., & Epstein, A. S.). (1993). *Significant benefits: The High/Scope Perry Preschool Study through age 27,* High/Scope Educational Research Foundtion Monograph, no. 10. Ypsilanti, MI: High/Scope Press.

Schweinhart, L. J., Koshel, J. J., & Bridgmann, A. (1987). Policy options for preschool programs. *Phi Delta Kappan, 68,* 524–530.

Schweinhart, L. J., & Weikart, D. (1985). Evidence that good early childhood programs work. *Phi Delta Kappan, 66,* 545–555.

Schweinhart, L. J., & Weikart, D. P. (1997a). The High/Scope preschool curriculum comparison study through age 23. *Early Childhood Research Quarterly, 12,* 117–143.

Schweinhart, L. J., & Weikart, D. P. (1997b). *Lasting differences: The High/Scope preschool curriculum comparison study through age 23.* Ypsilanti, MI: High/Scope Foundation.

Sciarra, D. J., & Dorsey, A. G. (1998). *Developing and administering child care centers* (4th ed.). Albany, NY: Delmar.

Scott, D. M. (2002). Restructuring of Academy improves service to programs seeking accreditation. *Young Children, 57*(2), 73–74.

Scott, L. C. (1983). Injury in the classroom: Are teachers liable? *Young Children, 38*(6), 10–18.

Scribner, S. (1985). Vygotsky's uses of history. In J. V. Wertsch (Ed.), *Culture, communication, and cognition* (pp. 119–145). Cambridge, England: Cambridge University Press.

Sears, R. R. (1975). Your ancients revisited: A history of child development. In E. M. Hetherington (Ed.), *Review of child development research* (Vol. 5, pp. 1–75). Chicago: University of Chicago Press.

Seefeldt, C. (2002). *Creating rooms of wonder.* Beltsville, MD: Gryphon.

Seefeldt, C., & Barbour, N. (1988). "They said I had to . . ." Working with mandates. *Young Children, 43*(4), 4–8.

Seefeldt, C., & Warman, B. (1990). *Young and old together.* Washington, DC: National Association for the Education of Young Children.

Seligson, M. (1986). Child care for the school-age child. *Phi Delta Kappan, 67,* 637–640.

Seligson, M. (2001). School-age child care today. *Young Children, 56*(1), 90–94.

Shade, D. D. (1996). Software evaluation. *Young Children, 51*(6), 17–21.

Shakeshaft, C. (1989). *Women in educational administration.* Newbury Park, CA: Sage.

Shane, P. G. (1996). *What about America's homeless children?* Thousand Oaks, CA: Sage.

Shapiro, E. K., & Biber, B. (1972). The education of young children: A developmental interaction approach. *Teachers College Record, 74,* 55–79.

Shapiro, E. K., & Nager, N. (2000). The developmental-interaction approach to education: Retrospect and prospect. In N. Nager & E. K. Shapiro (Eds.),

Revisiting a progressive pedagogy: The developmental-interaction approach (pp. 11–46). Albany, NY: State University of New York Press.

Shearer, M., & Shearer, D. (1972). The Portage Project: A model for early childhood education. *Exceptional Children, 36,* 210–217.

Shepard, L. A. (1991). The influence of standardized tests on the early childhood curriculum, teachers, and children. In B. Spodek & O. N. Saracho (Eds.), *Yearbook in early childhood education: Vol. 2. Issues in early childhood curriculum* (pp. 166–189). New York: Teachers College Press.

Shepard, L. A. (1994). The challenges of assessing young children appropriately. *Phi Delta Kappan, 76,* 206–212.

Shepard, L. A., Kagan, S. L., & Wurtz, E. (1998a). Goal One Early Childhood Assessments Resource Group recommendations. *Young Children, 53*(3), 52–54.

Shepard, L. A., Kagan, S. L., & Wurtz, E. (Eds.). (1998b). *Principles and recommendations for early childhood assessments.* Washington, D.C: National Education Goals Panel.

Shepard, L. A., & Smith, M. L. (1988). Escalating academic demand in kindergarten: Counterproductive policies. *Elementary School Journal, 89,* 135–147.

Shepard, O. (1937). *Pedlar's progress: The life of Bronson Alcott.* Boston: Little, Brown.

Shirah, S., Hewitt, T. W., & McNair, R. H. (1993). Preservice training fosters retention: The case for vocational training. *Young Children, 48*(4), 27–31.

Shoemaker, C. J. (2000). *Leadership and management of programs for young children* (2nd ed.). Upper Saddle River, NJ: Merrill/Prentice Hall.

Shonkoff, J. P., & Phillips, D. A. (Eds.). (2000). *From neurons to neighborhoods: The science of early childhood development.* Washington, DC: National Academy Press.

Shore, R. (1997). *Rethinking the brain: New insights into early development.* New York: Families and Work Institute.

Shores, E. F., & Grace, C. (1998). *The portfolio book: A step-by-step guide for teachers.* Beltsville, MD: Gryphon.

Shriver, M. D., & Kramer J. J. (1993). Parents in an early childhood special education program: A descriptive analysis of parent demographics and level of involvement. *Psychology in the Schools, 30,* 255–263.

Sigel, I. E. (1990). Psychoeducational intervention: Future directions. *Merrill-Palmer Quarterly, 36,* 159–172.

Sigel, I. E., Secrist, A., & Forman, G. (1973). Psychoeducational intervention beginning at age two: Reflections and outcomes. In J. Stanley (Ed.), *Compensatory education for children, ages two to eight* (pp. 25–62). Baltimore: Johns Hopkins Press.

Silin, J. G. (1988). Becoming knowledgeable professionals. In B. Spodek, O. N. Saracho, & D. L. Peters (Eds.), *Professionalism and the early childhood practitioner* (pp. 117–134). New York: Teachers College Press.

Silin, J. G. (1995). *Sex, death, and the education of children: Our passion for ignorance in the age of AIDS.* New York: Teachers College Press.

Simeonsson, R. J., & Bailey, D. B. (1990). Family dimensions in early intervention. In S. J. Meisels & J. P. Shonkoff (Eds.), *Handbook of early childhood intervention* (pp. 428–444). New York: Cambridge University Press.

Simmons, B., & Brewer, J. (1985). When parents of kindergartners ask "Why?" *Childhood Education, 61,* 177–184.

Simmons, B. J., Stalsworth, K., & Wentzel, H. (1999). Television violence and its effects on young children. *Early Childhood Education Journal, 26*(3), 149–153.

Simons, J. A., & Simons, F. A. (1986). Montessori and regular preschools: A comparison. In L. G. Katz & K. Steiner (Eds.), *Current topics in early childhood education* (Vol. 6, pp. 195–223). Norwood, NJ: Ablex.

Skeen, P., Garner, A. P., & Cartwright, S. (1984). *Woodworking for young children.* Washington, DC: National Association for the Education of Young Children.

Skinner, B. F. (1938). *The behavior of organisms: An experimental analysis.* Upper Saddle River, NJ: Prentice Hall.

Skinner, B. F. (1953). *Science and human behavior.* New York: Macmillan.

Slaby, R. G., Roedell, W. C., Arezzo, D., & Hendrix, K. (1995). *Early violence prevention: Tools for teachers of young children.* Washington, DC: National Association for the Education of Young Children.

Slavin, R. E., & Madden, N. A. (Eds.). (2001). *Success for All: Research and reform in elementary education.* Mahwah, NJ: Erlbaum.

Slavin, R. E., Madden, N. A., Dolan, L., & Wasik, B. A. (1996). *Every child/every school: Success for All.* Thousand Oaks, CA: Corwin Press.

Slikker, W., & Chang, L. (1998). *Handbook of developmental neurotoxicology.* San Diego, CA: Academic Press.

Small, M. (1998). *Our babies, ourselves: How biology and culture shape the way we parent.* New York: Anchor Books.

Smith, A. (1992). Early childhood educare: Seeking a theoretical framework in Vygotsky's work. *International Journal of Early Years Learning, 1*(1), 47–61.

Smith, B. S. (1997). Communication as a curriculum guide: Moving beyond ideology to democracy in education. *Childhood Education, 73,* 232–233.

Smith, C. J., Hendricks, C. M., & Bennett, B. S. (1997). *Growing, growing strong.* St. Paul, MN: Redleaf.

Smith, J. R., Brooks-Gunn, J., & Klebanov, P. K. (1997). Consequences of living in poverty for young children's cognitive and verbal ability and early school achievement. In G. J. Duncan & J. Brooks-Gunn (Eds.), *Consequences of growing up poor* (pp. 132–189). New York: Sage.

Smith, K. (2000). *Who's minding the kids? Child care arrangements: Fall 1995. Current Population Reports, P70–70.* Washington, DC: U.S. Census Bureau.

Smith, M. S. (1975). Evaluation findings in Head Start Planned Variation. In A. Rivlin & P. M. Timpane (Eds.), *Planned Variation in education* (pp. 101–112). Washington, DC: The Brookings Institution.

Smith, S. (Ed.). (1995). Two-generation programs for families in poverty: A new intervention strategy. *Advances in Applied Psychology, 9.* Norwood, NJ: Ablex.

Smith, T. B., & Newman, S. (1993). Older adults in early childhood programs: Why and how. *Young Children, 48*(3), 32–35.

Smith, T. E. C., & Dowdy, C. A. (1998). Educating young children with disabilities using responsible inclusion. *Childhood Education, 74,* 317–320.

Smylie, M. (1992). Teacher participation in school decision making: Assessing willingness to participate. *Educational Evaluation and Policy Analysis, 14*(1), 53–67.

Snider, M. H., & Fu, V. R. (1990). The effects of specialized education and job experience on early childhood teachers' knowledge of developmentally appropriate practice. *Early Childhood Research Quarterly, 5,* 68–78.

Snow, C. E., Burns, S., & Griffin, P. (Eds.). (1998). *Preventing reading difficulties in young children.* Washington, DC: National Academy Press.

Snow, C. W., Teleki, J. K., & Reguero-de-Atiles, J. T. (1996). Child care center licensing standards in the United States: 1981 to 1995. *Young Children, 51*(6), 36–41.

Snyder, A. (1972). *Dauntless women in childhood education 1865–1931.* Olney, MD: Association for Childhood Education International.

Sommerville, C. J. (1982). *The rise and fall of childhood.* Beverly Hills, CA: Sage.

Sosna, D. (2000). More about woodworking with young children. *Young Children, 55*(2), 38–39.

Spaggiari, S. (1998). The community-teacher partnership in the governance of the schools: An interview with Lella Gandini. In C. Edwards, L. Gandini, & G. Forman (Eds.), *The hundred languages of children: The Reggio approach—advanced reflections* (2nd ed., pp. 99–112). Greenwich, CT: Ablex.

Spicer, S. (2002). States try to specify what young children should learn. Quality counts 2002: Building blocks for success. *Education Week, 21*(17), 24–28, 30–31.

Spitzer, S., Cupp, R., & Parke, R. D. (1992). School entrance age, social acceptance, and self-perceptions in kindergarten and 1st grade. *Early Childhood Research Quarterly, 10,* 433–450.

Spodek, B. (1973a). Curriculum models in early childhood education. In B. Spodek (Ed.), *Early childhood education* (pp. 27–34). Upper Saddle River, NJ: Prentice Hall.

Spodek, B. (1973b). *Early childhood education.* Upper Saddle River, NJ: Prentice Hall.

Spodek, B. (1987). Thought processes underlying preschool teachers' classroom decisions. *Early Child Care and Development, 28,* 197–208.

Spodek, B. (1988). Implicit theories of early childhood teachers: Foundations for professional behavior. In B. Spodek, O. N. Saracho, & D. L. Peters (Eds.), *Professionalism and the early childhood practitioner* (pp. 161–172). New York: Teachers College Press.

Spodek, B. (1991a). Early childhood curriculum and cultural definitions of knowledge. In B. Spodek & O. N. Saracho (Eds.), *Yearbook in early childhood education: Vol. 2. Issues in early education* (pp. 1–20). New York: Teachers College Press.

Spodek, B. (1991b). Early childhood teacher training. Linking theory and practice. In S. L. Kagan (Ed.), *The care and education of America's young children: Obstacles and opportunities* (pp. 110–130). Chicago: University of Chicago Press.

Spodek, B. (1996). The professional development of early childhood teachers. *Early Child Development and Care, 115,* 115–124.

Spodek, B., & Brown, P. C. (1993). Curriculum alternatives in early childhood education: A historical analysis. In B. Spodek (Ed.), *Handbook of research on the education of young children* (pp. 91–104). New York: Macmillan.

Spodek, B., & Saracho, O. N. (1992). Child care: A look to the future. In B. Spodek & O. N. Saracho (Eds.), *Yearbook in early childhood education: Vol. 3. Issues in child care* (pp. 187–197). New York: Teachers College Press.

Staff self-evaluation form. (1992). *Child Care Information Exchange, 87,* 19–20.

Stainback, S., & Stainback, W. (1992). *Curriculum considerations in inclusive classrooms: Facilitating learning for all students.* Baltimore: Brookes.

Stamp, L. N., & Groves, M. M. (1994). Strengthening the ethic of care: Planning and supporting family involvement. *Dimensions of Early Childhood, 22*(2), 5–9.

Stanford, B. H., & Yamamoto, K. (Eds.). (2001). *Children and stress: Understanding and helping.* Olney, MD: Association for Childhood Education International.

Steedman, C. (1990). *Childhood, culture, and class in Britain: Margaret McMillan, 1860–1931.* London: Virago Press.

Stephens, K. (1991). *Confronting your bottom line: Financial guide for child care centers.* Redmond, WA: Exchange Press.

Stevenson, D. L., & Baker, D. P. (1987). The family-school relation and the child's school performance. *Child Development, 58,* 1348–1357.

Stevenson, H. W., Chen, C., & Uttal, D. H. (1990). Beliefs and achievement: A study of Black, White, and Hispanic children. *Child Development, 61,* 508–523.

Stewart, I. S. (1982). The real world of teaching two-year-old children. *Young Children, 37*(5), 3–13.

Stiggins, R. (1991). *Facing the challenge of the new era of assessment.* Portland, OR: Northwest Evaluation Association.

Stipek, D., & Byler, P. (1997). Early childhood education teachers: Do they practice what they preach? *Early Childhood Research Quarterly, 12,* 305–325.

Stipek, D., Daniels, D. H., Galluzzo, D., & Milburn, S. (1992). Characterizing early childhood education programs for poor and middle-class children. *Early Childhood Research Quarterly, 7,* 1–19.

Stipek, D., Feiler, R., Daniels, D. H., & Milburn, S. (1995). Effects of different instructional approaches on young children's achievement and motivation. *Child Development, 66,* 209–223.

Stipek, D., Milburn, S., Clements, D., & Daniels, D. H. (1992). Parents' beliefs about appropriate education for young children. *Journal of Applied Developmental Psychology, 13,* 293–310.

Stipek, D., Rosenblatt, L., & DiRocco, L. (1994). Making parents your allies. *Young Children, 49*(3), 4–9.

Stone, C. (1995). School/community collaboration: Comparing three initiatives. *Phi Delta Kappan, 76,* 794–800.

Stone, D. (2000). *Why we need a care movement. The Nation.* New York: The Nation Company.

Stoneham, L. (2001). Diabetes on a rampage. *Texas Medicine, 97*(11), 42–48.

Stonehouse, A., & Woodrow, C. (1992). Professional issues: A perspective on their place in pre-service education for early childhood. *Early Child Development and Care, 78,* 207–223.

Stoney, L. (1999). Looking into new mirrors: Lessons for early childhood finance and system building. *Young Children, 54*(3), 54–57.

Stoney, L., & Greenberg, M. (1996). The financing of child care: Current and emerging trends. Special issue on financing child care. *Future of Children, 6*(2), 83–102.

Stork, S., & Engel, S. (1999). So, what is constructivist teaching? A rubric for teacher evaluation. *Dimensions of Early Childhood, 27*(1), 20–27.

Stott, E., & Bowman, B. (1996). Child development knowledge: A slippery base for practice. *Early Childhood Research Quarterly, 11,* 169–183.

Strain, P., Hoyson, M., & Jamieson, B. (1985). Normally developing preschoolers as intervention agents for autistic-like children: Effects on class deportment and social interaction. *Journal of the Division for Early Childhood, 9,* 105–115.

Stremmel, A. J., & Hill, L. T. (1999). Towards multicultural understanding: A reflective journey. In V. R. Fu & A. J. Stremmel (Eds.), *Affirming diversity through democratic conversations* (pp. 141–155). Upper Saddle River, NJ: Merrill Prentice Hall.

Strickland, C. E. (1969). Transcendentalist father: The child-rearing practices of Bronson Alcott. *Perspectives in American History, 3,* 5–73.

Strickland, C. E. (1982). Paths not taken: Seminal models of early childhood education in Jacksonian America. In B. Spodek (Ed.), *Handbook of research in early childhood education* (pp. 321–340). New York: Free Press.

Strupp, B. J., & Levitsky, D. A. (1995). Enduring cognitive effects of early maturation: A theoretical reappraisal. *Journal of Nutrition, 125,* 2221S–2232S.

Study releases new findings on quality child care. (1997). *Young Children, 52*(4), 75.

Sturmey, P., & Crisp, A. G. (1986). Portage guide to early education: A review of research. *Education Psychology, 6,* 139–157.

Sullivan, A. K., & Strang, H. R. (2002/03). Bibliotherapy in the classrooms: Using literature to promote the development of emotional intelligence. *Childhood Education, 79,* 74–80.

Surbeck, E. (1998). Challenges of preparing to work in collaborative early childhood settings. *Early Childhood Education Journal, 26*(1), 53–55.

Surr, J. (1992). Early childhood programs and the Americans With Disabilities Act (ADA). *Young Children, 47*(2), 18–21.

Sussman, C. (1998). Out of the basement: Discovering the value of child care facilities. *Young Children, 53*(1), 10–17.

Swadener, B. B., & Kessler, S. (1991a). Introduction to the special issue. *Early Education and Development, 2*(2), 85–94.

Swadener, B. B., & Kessler, S. (Eds.). (1991b). Reconceptualizing early childhood education [Special issue]. *Early Education and Development, 2*(2).

Swadener, S. (1995). Nutrition education for preschool children. *Journal of Nutrition Education, 27,* 291–297.

Swick, K. (1987). Teacher reports on parental efficacy/involvement relationships. *Instructional Psychology, 14,* 125–132.

Swick, K., Van Scoy, I., & Boutte, G. (1994). Multicultural learning through family involvement. *Dimensions of Early Childhood, 22*(4), 17–21.

Sykes, M. (1994). Creating a climate for change in a major urban school system. *Young Children, 50*(1), 4–7.

Taking the Lead Initiative. (1999a). *The many faces of leadership*. Boston: Wheelock College, Center for Career Development in Early Care and Education, Taking the Lead Initiative.

Taking the Lead Initiative. (1999b). *An overview of director credentialing initiatives: State credentials (as of May, 1998)*. Boston: Wheelock College, Center for Career Development in Early Care and Education, Taking the Lead Initiative.

Taking the Lead Initiative. (2000). *The power of mentoring*. Boston: Wheelock College, Center for Career Development in Early Care and Education, Taking the Lead Initiative.

Talbot, J., & Frost, J. L. (1989). Magical playscapes. *Childhood Education, 66,* 11–19.

Talley, K. (1997). National accreditation: Why do some programs stall in self-study? *Young Children, 52*(3), 31–37.

Taylor, B. J. (1999). *A child goes forth: A curriculum guide for preschool children*. Upper Saddle River: Merrill/Prentice Hall.

Taylor, K. W. (1981). *Parent and children learn together: Parent cooperative nursery schools*. New York: Teachers College Press.

Teal, W., Hiebart, E., & Chittenden, E. (1987). Assessing young children's literacy development. *Reading Teacher, 40,* 772–776.

Tertell, E. A., Klein, S. M., & Jewett, J. L. (Eds.). (1998). *When teachers reflect: Journeys toward effective, inclusive practice*. Washington, DC: National Association for the Education of Young Children.

Theilheimer, R. (1993). Something for everyone: Benefits of mixed-age grouping for children, parents, and teachers. *Young Children, 48*(5), 82–87.

Thoman, E. (1987). *Born dancing: How intuitive parents understand their baby's unspoken language*. New York: Harper & Row.

Thompson, D. S. (1984). *The professionalism of early childhood educators and administrators: Problems and prospects* [Opinion paper]. (ERIC Document Reproduction Service No. ED256468)

Thompson, P. W. (1992). Notations, conventions, and constraints: Contributions to effective use of concrete materials in elementary mathematics. *Journal of Research in Mathematics Education, 23,* 123–147.

Thompson, R. A. (1997). Early sociopersonality development. In W. Damon (Series Ed.) & N. Eisenberg (Vol. Ed.), *Handbook of child psychology: Vol. 3: Social, emotional, and personality development* (5th ed., pp. 25–104). New York: Wiley.

Thompson, R. A., & Wyatt, J. M. (1999). Current research on child maltreatment: Implications for educators. *Educational Psychology Review, 11,* 173–201.

Thornburg, K. R. (2001). How can we be better advocates? *Young Children, 56*(4), 4–5.

Thouvenelle, S., & Bewick, C. J. (2003). *Completing the computer puzzle: A guide for early childhood educators*. Boston: Allyn & Bacon.

Tilbury, D. (1994). The critical learning years for environmental education. In R. A. Wilson (Ed.), *Environmental education at the early childhood level* (pp. 11–13). Washington, DC: North American Association for Environmental Education.

Title V. Section 522a, U.S. Code 1976 Edition: Containing the general and permanent laws of the U.S., in force on January 3, 1977 (Vol. 1). (1977). Washington, DC: U.S. Government Printing Office.

Todd, C. M., Albrecht, K. M., & Coleman, M. (1990). School-age child care: A continuum of options. *Journal of Home Economics, 82*(1), 46–52.

Torelli, L., & Durrett, C. (1998). *Landscapes for learning: Designing group care environments for infants, toddlers, and two-year-olds*. Berkeley, CA: Spaces for Children.

Townley, K., Thornburg, K., & Crompton, D. (1991). Burnout in teachers of young children. *Early Education and Development, 2,* 198–204.

Travis, N., & Perreault, J. (1983). *A history of family child care*. Atlanta: Save the Children Foundation.

Trawick-Smith, J., & Lambert, L. (1995). The unique challenges of the family child care provider: Implications for professional development. *Young Children, 50*(3), 25–32.

Troen, S. K. (1975). *The public and the schools: Shaping the St. Louis system 1838–1920*. Columbia: University of Missouri Press.

Udell, T., Peters, J., & Templemann, T. P. (1998). From philosophy to practice in inclusive early childhood programs. In K. M. Paciorek & J. H. Munro (Eds.), *Early Childhood Education 99/00* (20th ed., pp. 95–99). Guilford, CT: Dushkin/McGraw-Hill.

U.S. Bureau of the Census. (1992). *Elderly in the United States*. 1990 Census of Population and Housing Series CPH-L-74. Washington, DC: U.S. Department of Commerce.

U.S. Bureau of the Census. (1997). *Who's minding our preschoolers?* Washington, DC: U.S. Department of Commerce.

U.S. Bureau of the Census. (2001). *Americans with disabilities. Household Economic Studies, 1997, Table 5, Current Population Reports* (pp. 70–73). Washington, DC: U.S. Department of Commerce.

U.S. Bureau of Labor Statistics. (1996). *Occupational employment statistics (OES) program survey.* Washington, DC: U.S. Department of Labor.

U.S. Bureau of Labor Statistics. (1998). *Occupational projections and training data.* Washington, DC: U.S. Department of Labor.

U.S. Bureau of Labor Statistics. (1999, March). *Marital and family characteristics of the labor force: Current population survey.* Washington, DC: U.S. Department of Labor.

U.S. Congress, Office of Technology Assessment. (1995). *Risks to students in school.* Washington, DC: U.S. Government Printing Office.

U.S. Consumer Product Safety Commission. (1997). *Handbook for public playground safety* (Document #325). Washington, DC: Author.

U.S. Department of Agriculture. (2000). *Food Guide Pyramid for Young Children—A daily guide for 2- to 6-year-olds.* Washington, DC: U.S. Department of Agriculture Center for Nutrition Policy & Promotion. (Available online: <www.usda.gov/cnpp/KidsPyra>)

U.S. Department of Education. (1991). *America 2000: An education strategy.* Washington, DC: Author.

U.S. Department of Education. (1994). *Strong families, strong schools: Building community partnerships for learning.* Washington, DC: Author.

U.S. Department of Education. (1999). *To assure the free appropriate education of all children with disabilities: Twenty-first annual report to Congress on the implementation of the Individuals with Disabilities Education Act.* Washington, DC: Author.

U.S. Department of Education. (2001). *Twenty-third annual report to Congress on the implementation of the Individuals with Disabilities Education Act.* Washington, DC: Author.

U.S. Department of Health, Education & Welfare. (1972). *Guides for day care licensing.* Washington, DC: Author.

U.S. Department of Health and Human Services. (1999). *Access to child care for low-income working families.* Washington, DC: Author.

U.S. Department of Health and Human Services. (2002, April 19). *Year 2000 child abuse and neglect findings released.* (Retrieved May 29, 2002, from <http://www.acf.dhhs.gov/news/press/2002/abuse.html>)

U.S. Department of Labor, Women's Bureau. (1995). *Care around the clock: Developing child care resources before and after 5.* Washington, DC: Author.

U.S. General Accounting Office. (1995). *Early childhood centers: Services to prepare children for school often limited,* GA01HEHS-95-21. Washington, DC: Author.

U.S. General Accounting Office. (1999). *Child care: How do military and civilian center costs compare?* Washington, DC: U.S. Government Printing Office.

U.S. General Accounting Office. (2000). *Child care state efforts to enforce safety and health requirements,* GAO/HEHS-OO-28. Washington, DC: Author.

Vance, E., & Weaver, P. J. (2002). *Class meetings: Young children solving problems together.* Washington, DC: National Association for the Education of Young Children.

Vandell, D. L., & Su, H. (1999). Child care and school-age children. *Young Children, 54*(1), 62–71.

Vandell, D. L., & Wolfe, B. (2000). *Child care quality: Does it matter and does it need to be improved?* Washington, DC: Department of Health and Human Services.

Vander Ven, K. (1988). Pathways to professional effectiveness for early childhood educators. In B. Spodek, O. N. Saracho, & D. L. Peters (Eds.), *Professionalism and the early childhood practitioner* (pp. 137–160). New York: Teachers College Press.

Vandewalker, N. C. (1925). Facts of interest about kindergarten laws. *Childhood Education, 1,* 323–325.

Vaughn, E. (1990). Everything under the sun: Outside learning center activities. *Dimensions, 18*(4), 20–22.

Veenman, S. (1995). Cognitive and non-cognitive effects of multigrade and multi-age classes: A best-evidence synthesis. *Review of Educational Research, 65,* 319–381.

Vergeront, J. (1987). *Places and spaces for preschool and primary: Indoors.* Washington, DC: National Association for the Education of Young Children.

Vergeront, J. (1988). *Places and spaces for preschool and primary: Outdoors.* Washington, DC: National Association for the Education of Young Children.

Verstegen, D. A. (1994). The new wave of school finance litigation. *Phi Delta Kappan, 76,* 243–250.

Vollmer, H. W., & Mills, D. L. (1966). *Professionalization.* Englewood Cliffs, NJ: Prentice Hall.

Vygotsky, L. S. (1978). *Mind in society* (M. Cole, S. Schribner, V. John-Steiner, & E. Souberman, Trans.). Cambridge, MA: Harvard University Press.

Wagenblast v. Odessa School Dist., 758 P. 2d 968 (Wash. 1988).

Wallach, F., & Afthinos, I. D. (1990). *An analysis of the state codes for licensed day care centers focused on playgrounds and supervision.* New York: Total Recreation Management Services.

Wallach, F., & Edelstein, S. (1991). *Analysis of state regulations for elementary schools focused on playgrounds and supervision.* New York: Total Recreation Management Services.

Wallach, L. B. (2001). Volunteers in Head Start: How to strengthen your program. *Young Children, 56*(5), 37–40.

Walsh, D. J. (1989). Changes in kindergarten: Why here? Why now? *Early Childhood Research Quarterly, 4,* 377–391.

Walsh, D. J. (1991). Extending the discourse on developmental appropriateness: A developmental perspective. *Early Education and Development, 2,* 109–119.

Walsh, D. J., Smith, M. E., Alexander, M., & Ellwein, M. C. (1993). The curriculum as mysterious and constraining: Teachers' negotiations of the first year of a pilot programme for at-risk 4-year-olds. *Journal of Curriculum Studies, 25,* 317–332.

Wardle, F. (1990). Bunny ears and cupcakes for all: Are parties developmentally appropriate? *Child Care Information Exchange, 74,* 39–42.

Wardle, F. (1999). In praise of developmentally appropriate practice. *Young Children, 54*(6), 4–12.

Wardle, F. (2001). View point. Supporting multiracial and multiethnic children and their families. *Young Children, 56*(6), 38–39.

Warfield, M. E., & Hauser-Cram, P. (1996). Child care needs, arrangement, and satisfaction of mothers of children with developmental disabilities. *Mental Retardation, 34,* 294–302.

Warman, B. (1998). Trends in state accreditation policies. *Young Children, 53*(5), 52–55.

Warner, L., & Craycraft, K. (1991). *Learning in centers: Kids communicating.* Carthage, IL: Good Apple.

Warrick, J., & Helling, M. K. (1997). Meeting basic needs: Health and safety practices in feeding and diapering infants. *Early Childhood Education Journal, 24*(3), 195–199.

Washington Update. (2001). A balancing act—surpluses, tax cuts, and investments: Can we have all three? *Young Children, 56*(2), 75.

Washington, V., & Andrews, J. D. (Eds.). (1998). *Children of 2010.* Washington, DC: National Association for the Education of Young Children.

Wasserman, R., Dameron, D., Brozicevic, M., & Aronson, R. (1989). Injury hazards in home day care. *Journal of Pediatrics, 114,* 591–593.

Weber, E. (1969). *The kindergarten: Its encounter with educational thought in America.* New York: Teachers College Press.

Weber, E. (1970). *Early childhood education: Perspectives on change.* Worthington, OH: Charles A. Jones.

Weikart, D. P. (1981). Effects of different curricula in early childhood intervention. *Educational Evaluation and Policy Analysis, 3,* 25–35.

Weikart, D. P. (1983). A longitudinal view of preschool research effort. In M. Perlmutter (Ed.), *Development and policy concerning children with special needs. The Minnesota Symposia on Child Psychology* (Vol. 16, pp. 175–196). Hillsdale, NJ: Erlbaum.

Weikart, D. P. (1989). Hard choices in early childhood care and education: A view to the future. *Young Children, 44*(3), 25–30.

Weikart, D. P. (1995). Early childhood education. In J. H. Block, S. T. Everson, & T. R. Guskey (Eds.), *School improvement programs: A handbook for educational leaders* (pp. 289–312). New York: Scholastic Leadership Policy Research.

Weikart, D. P., Rogers, L., Adcock, C., & McClelland, D. (1971). *The Cognitively-Oriented Curriculum: A framework for preschool teachers.* Urbana: University of Illinois.

Weikart, D. P., & Schweinhart, L. J. (1991). Disadvantaged children and curriculum effects. In L. Rescorla, M. C. Hyson, & K. Hirsch-Pasek (Eds.), *Academic instruction in early childhood: Challenge or pressure?* (pp. 57–64). San Francisco: Jossey-Bass.

Weikart, D. P., & Schweinhart, L. P. (1992). High/Scope Preschool Program outcomes. In J. McCord & R. E. Tremblay (Eds.), *Preventing antisocial behavior: Intervention from birth through adolescence* (pp. 67–86). New York: Guilford.

Weiss, H. B. (1993). Home visits. Necessary but not sufficient. *Future of Children, 3*(3), 112–128.

Weissbourd, B. (1983). The family support movement: Greater than the sum of its parts. *Zero to Three, 4,* 8–10.

Werner, E. (2000). Protective factors and resilence. In J. P. Shonkoff & S. J. Meisels (Eds.), *Handbook of early childhood intervention* (2nd ed., pp. 115–132). New York: Cambridge University Press.

Wesley, P. W. (2002). Early intervention consultants in the classroom: Simple steps for building strong collaboration. *Young Children, 57*(4), 30–35.

West, J., Hausken, E., Chandler, K. A., & Collins, M. (1991). *Experiences in child care and early childhood programs of first and second graders prior to entering first grade: Findings from the 1991 National Household Study. Statistics in brief.* Washington, DC: National Center for Education Statistics.

West, J., Wright, D., & Hausken, E. (1995). *Child care and early education program participation of infants, toddlers, and preschoolers. Statistics in brief.* Washington, DC: National Center for Education Statistics.

West, S., & Cox, A. (2001). *Sand and water play: Simple, creative activities for young children.* Beltsville, MD: Gryphon.

Westinghouse Learning Corporation. (1969). *The impact of Head Start: An evaluation of the effects of Head Start on children's cognitive and affective development.* Athens: Ohio University, Westinghouse Learning Corporation. (ERIC Document Reproduction Service No. ED036321)

White, B. (1988). *Educating infants and toddlers.* Lexington, MA: Lexington Books.

White, K. R., Taylor, M.J., & Moss, V. D. (1992). Does research support claims about the benefits of involving parents in early intervention programs? *Review of Educational Research, 62,* 91–125.

White, S., & Buka, S. (1987). Early education: Programs, traditions, and policies. In *Review of research in education* (Vol. 14, pp. 43–91). Washington, DC: American Educational Research Association.

White, S., & Coleman, M. (2000). *Early childhood education: Contexts for learning.* Upper Saddle River, NJ: Merrill/Prentice Hall.

Whitebook, M. (2002). *Working for worthy wages. The child care compensation movement, 1970–2001.* New York: Foundation for Child Development.

Whitebook, M., & Bellm, D. (1999a). *An action guide for child care center teachers and directors.* Washington, DC: Center for the Child Care Workforce.

Whitebook, M., & Bellm, D. (1999b). *Taking on turnover: An action guide for child care teachers and directors.* Washington, DC: Center for the Child Care Workforce.

Whitebook, M., & Eichberg, A. (2002). Finding a better way: Defining policies to improve child care workforce compensation. *Young Children, 57*(3), 66–72.

Whitebook, M., Hnatiuk, P., & Bellm, D. (1994). *Mentoring in early care and education: Refining an emerging career path.* Washington, DC: Center for the Child Care Workforce.

Whitebook, M., Howes, C., & Phillips, D. A. (1990). *Who cares? Child care teachers and the quality of care in America* (Final Report of the National Child Care Staffing Study). Oakland, CA: Child Care Employee Project.

Whitebook, M., Howes, C., & Phillips, D. A. (1998). *Who cares? Child care teachers and the quality of child care in America: Final report, National Child Care Staffing Study.* Washington, DC: Center for the Child Care Workforce.

Whitebook, M., Howes, C., Phillips, D. A., & Pemberton, C. (1991). Who cares? Child care teachers and the quality of child care in America. In K. M. Paciorek & J. H. Munro (Eds.), *Annual editions, Early childhood education 91/92* (pp. 20–24). Guilford, CT: Dushkin/McGraw Hill.

Whitebook, M., Phillips, D., & Howes, C. (1993). *National Child Care Staffing Study revisited: Four years in the life of center-based child care.* Oakland, CA: Child Care Employee Project.

Whitebook, M., Sakai, L., & Howes, C. (1997). *NAEYC accreditation as a strategy for improving child care quality: Executive summary.* Washington, DC: Center for the Child Care Workforce.

Wien, C. A. (1996). Time, work, and developmentally appropriate practice. *Early Childhood Research Quarterly, 11,* 377–403.

Wien, C. A., & Kirby-Smith, S. (1998). Untiming the curriculum: A case study of removing clocks from the program. *Young Children, 53*(5), 8–13.

Willer, B. (1990). Estimating the full cost of quality. In B. Willer (Ed.), *Reaching the full cost of quality in early childhood programs* (pp. 1–8). Washington, DC: National Association for the Education of Young Children.

Willer, B. (1992). An overview of the demand and supply of child care in 1990. *Young Children, 47*(2), 19–22.

Willer, B. (Ed.). (1994). A conceptual framework for early childhood professional development: NAEYC position statement, adopted November 1993. In J. Johnson & J. B. McCracken (Eds.), *The early childhood career lattice: Perspectives on professional development* (pp. 4–21). Washington, DC: National Association for the Education of Young Chilldren.

Willer, B., & Bredekamp, S. (1990). Public policy report. Redefining readiness: An essential requisite for educational reform. *Young Children, 45*(5), 22–24.

Williams, C. L. (1992). The glass escalator: Hidden advantages for men in the "female" professions. *Social Problems, 39,* 253–267.

Williams, K. C. (1997). "What do you wonder?" Involving children in curriculum planning. *Young Children, 52*(6), 78–81.

Wilson, R. A., Kilmer, S. J., & Knauerhase, V. (1996). Developing an environmental outdoor play space. *Young Children, 51*(6), 56–61.

Winter, S. M., Bell, M. J., & Dempsey, J. D. (1994). Creating play environments for children with special needs. *Childhood Education, 71,* 28–32.

Wipple, G. M. (Ed.). (1929). Preschool and parental education. In National Society for the Study of Education, *Twenty-eighth Yearbook: Part I. Organization and development* (pp. 1–463). Bloomington, IL: Public School Publishing.

Wolery, M., Huffman, K., Holcombe, A., Martin, C., Brookfield, J., Schroeder, C., & Venn, M. (1994). Preschool mainstreaming: Perceptions of barriers and benefits by faculty in general early childhood education. *Teacher Education and Special Education, 17*(1), 1–9.

Wolery, M., Strain, P. S., & Bailey, D. B., Jr. (1992). Reaching potentials of children with special needs. In S. Bredekamp & T. Rosegrant (Eds.), *Reaching potentials: Appropriate curriculum and assessment for young children* (Vol. 1, pp. 92–111). Washington, DC: National Association for the Education of Young Children.

Wolfe, J., & Brandt, R. (1998). What we know from brain research. *Educational Leadership, 56*(3), 8–14.

Wood, C. (1994). Responsive teaching: Creating partnerships for systemic change. *Young Children, 50*(1), 21–28.

Wood, D. J., Bruner, J., & Ross, G. (1976). The role of tutoring in problem solving. *Journal of Child Psychology and Psychiatry, 17,* 89–100.

Woodcock, L. P. (1941). *Life and ways of the two-year-old.* New York: E. P. Dutton.

Woody, T. (1934). Historical sketch of activism. In G. M. Wipple (Ed.), *National Society for the Study of Education, Thirty-third yearbook* (Part II, pp. 9–44). Bloomington, IL: Public School Publishing.

Workman, S. H., & Gage, J. A. (1997). Family-school partnerships: A family strengths approach. *Young Children, 52*(4), 10–14.

Wortham, S. C., & Wortham, M. R. (1992). Nurturing infant and toddler play outside: Three cells of possibility. *Dimensions of Early Childhood, 20*(4), 25–27.

Wright, H. A. (1960). Observational child study. In P. H. Mussen (Ed.), *Handbook of research methods in child development* (pp. 71–139). New York: Wiley.

Yarosz, D. J., & Barnett, W. S. (2001). *Early care and education program participation 1991–1999.* New Brunswick, NJ: Rutgers University, Center for Early Education Research.

Yawkey, T. D. (1987). Project P.I.A.G.E.T.: A holistic approach to early childhood education. In J. Roopnarine & J. Johnson (Eds.), *Approaches to early childhood education* (pp. 197–212). New York: Merrill/Macmillan.

Yell, M., & Shriner, J. (1997). The IDEA amendments of 1997: Implications for special and general education teachers, administrators, and teacher trainers. *Focus on Exceptional Children, 30*(1), 2–19.

Yoshikawa, H. (1995). Long-term effects of early childhood programs on social outcomes and delinquency. *Future of Children, 5*(3), 51–75.

Young, K. T. (1990). American conceptions of infant development from 1955 to 1984: What experts are telling parents. *Child Development, 61,* 17–28.

Zaslow, M. (1991). Variation in child care quality and its implications for children. *Journal of Social Issues, 47*(2), 125–139.

Zeichner, K. M., & Noffke, S. E. (2001). Practitioner research. In V. Richardson (Ed.), *Handbook of research on teaching* (4th ed., pp. 298–330). Washington, DC: American Educational Research Association.

Zellman, G. L., & Johansen, A. S. (1998). *The implementation of the Military Child Care Act of 1989*. Santa Monica, CA: RAND.

Zigler, E. F. (1989). Addressing the nation's child care crisis: The school of the twenty-first century. *American Journal of Orthopsychiatry, 59,* 484–491.

Zill, N., Collins, M., West, J., & Hausken, E. G. (1995). Appropriate kindergarten: A look at preschoolers in the United States. *Young Children, 51*(1), 35–38.

Zimiles, H. (1986). The social context of early childhood in an era of expanding preschool education. In B. Spodek (Ed.), *Today's kindergarten: Exploring the knowledge base, expanding the curriculum* (pp. 1–14). New York: Teachers College Press.

Zinzeleta, E., & Little, N. K. (1997). How do parents really choose early childhood programs? *Young Children, 52*(7), 8–11.

Zonder, A. (1997). Quality, compensation, and affordability. Six things directors can do to improve staff compensation and quality. *Young Children, 52*(2), 46.

Author Index

Subject Index